Russian Studies, Political Science, and the Philosophy of Technology

Russian Studies, Political Science, and the Philosophy of Technology

Russian Studies, Political Science, and the Philosophy of Technology

Edited by
Guoli Liu and Joanna Drzewieniecki

LEXINGTON BOOKS
Lanham • Boulder • New York • London

Published by Lexington Books
An imprint of The Rowman & Littlefield Publishing Group, Inc.
4501 Forbes Boulevard, Suite 200, Lanham, Maryland 20706
www.rowman.com

86-90 Paul Street, London EC2A 4NE

British Library Cataloguing in Publication Information Available

Library of Congress Cataloging-in-Publication Data Available

ISBN 9781666906356 (cloth) | ISBN 9781666906363 (epub)

I am lucky enough to have known Fred Fleron for more than six decades. We first met during his time as a graduate student of mine at Brown, in 1959. In the years since, Fred and I have stayed in touch, and I am proud to consider him a lifelong friend. If I were to enumerate Fred's many qualities, I would respond with the words loyal, hardworking, steadfast, and a good storyteller. Each and every one of these traits makes Fred the special person he is—while also contributing to his remarkable academic persona. In addition, Fred's industry and curiosity have shaped him into a scholar of preeminent caliber, while his research and published works bring enlightenment to all who are fortunate enough to have read them.

Lea Williams
Brown University

Contents

List of Figures

List of Tables

Figure 0.1 Professor Frederic J. Fleron, Jr. *Source*: Photo by Frederic J. Fleron, Jr.

Foreword

Frederic J. Fleron, Jr.

Editors' note: In the months before his passing in June 2021 Professor Fleron was busy working on two book manuscripts but he also found time to put down some of his thoughts for this foreword. His first concern was to express his gratitude to all those who had influenced his intellectual development and those with whom he had worked on various projects. He also felt privileged to have known, studied under, and/or collaborated with outstanding scholars and public intellectuals. Due to his untimely passing, Fleron did not get around to putting into words his thanks to those who made this Festschrift possible, but both the editors and the contributors to this volume are well aware that he was thrilled to be honored in this way. Here are some of Frederic Fleron's thoughts as he looked back on his career:

During the summers of my undergraduate years, I was fortunate to live less than 20 miles from Cambridge, Massachusetts, and that enabled me to take courses at Harvard University from several distinguished scholars: Samuel Beer, Louis Hartz, Hans Morgenthau, and Henry Kissinger. Hans Kohn was not teaching a summer course at the time, but he was in residence in Cambridge with an office at Harvard, and he was very generous with his time for students. By the summer following my junior year, I had already read all of his famous books on nationalism, and we had many a pleasant conversation on the subject.

I spent the following summer (1959) in Madison, Wisconsin, where I audited a course on U.S. foreign policy taught by William Appleman Williams at the University of Wisconsin. At the time, he was quite popular both on and off campus for his famous book *The Tragedy of American Diplomacy.* This experience and having attended courses by such distinguished exponents of realpolitik and the realist school of international relations (Morgenthau and

Kissinger) stood me in good stead when I taught courses on American foreign policy both early and late in my teaching career.

After receiving my PhD from Indiana University under the tutelage of some excellent professors, I then met and/or worked with various distinguished scholars, policy makers, and diplomats on various projects: Robert C. Tucker, Alexander Dallin, Fred I. Greenstein, Harold D. Lasswell, Frederick C. Barghoorn, Jerry F. Hough, Zbigniew K. Brzezinski, McGeorge Bundy, Ambassador Llewelyn Thompson, John Hazard, Jan F. Triska, Gordon Skilling, Carl Beck, Timothy Colton, Robert (Bill) V. Daniels, members of the Academies of Sciences and government ministers in the USSR, Poland, Hungary, and Czechoslovakia. In 1973, I attended the Praxis Summer School at Korčula, Yugoslavia, chaired by Rudi Supek and attended by leading Marxist scholars from around the world. It was there that I met Mihailo Markovic and Gajo Petrovic, among others.

Among my friends from the Budapest School were Mihály Vajda, Ágnes Heller, Ferenc Fehér, György Márkus, and Maria Márkus, all of them students or colleagues of György Lukács. We would get together for dinner and "forty drops" at the residence of Mihály and Judith Vajda near the top of Gul Baba whenever I was in Budapest. We would do the same in Buffalo, New York occasionally. Friends and acquaintances from the Telos Group included Paul Piccone, Bart Grahl, Lee Smith, Raya Dunayevskaya (personal secretary to Leon Trotsky until the 1939 Molotov-Ribbentrop Pact), Andrew Arato, Jean Cohen, Susan Buck-Morss, Russell Jacoby, Paul Breines, and Carl Boggs.

Public intellectuals with whom I had occasion to engage in repartee include Elizabeth Hardwick, Max Black, May Brodbeck, David Montgomery, Leon Botstein, Steven B. Sample, and Stephen Jay Gould.

A great story accompanies my two meetings with the distinguished Harvard sociologist, Pitirim Sorokin. I first met him when I was in 8th or 9th grade in junior high school. My dear mother decided it was time for me to start acquiring some culture, so she took me to a lecture by Sorokin at Wellesley College. He talked mainly about his experiences of escaping from Russia in the summer of 1917 during the "July Days" when the Bolsheviks were attempting to overthrow the Provisional Government headed by Alexander Kerensky. Sorokin was Kerensky's personal secretary at the time. After arriving in the United States, Sorokin pursued his studies at Harvard University, where he got his PhD and went on to be Chair of Harvard's Department of Sociology. After he retired from Harvard, Sorokin and his wife toured the world spending a semester or so teaching at or visiting universities across the globe. In spring 1965, they visited an old friend, Melvin DeFleur, at the University of Kentucky in Lexington on the very day I arrived in Lexington for a job interview at UK. DeFleur had been one of my professors at Indiana University and subsequently joined the UK faculty.

Upon arriving in Lexington, I phoned DeFleur to see if we could get together. He invited me and my wife to dinner with Sorokin and his wife the following evening. That evening I told Sorokin about attending his lecture at Wellesley College, that years before I had bought and read his book *Leaves from a Russian Diary*, and that he was the inspiration behind my pursuit of a doctorate in Russian/Soviet studies. During the course of the evening, our host asked Sorokin if he had ever drank Kentucky moonshine. Sorokin replied in the negative, whereupon our host produced a gallon jug of moonshine which was passed around the table until we had consumed much, if not all, of it. What a memorable evening it was.

I wish to express my appreciation and respect to a number of scholars, teachers, and compatriots who I greatly respected and who contributed to the formation of my thinking and weltanschauung: Erwin L. Levine, Gene L. Mason, Robert Sharlet, D. Bruce Hutchinson, K. Roald Bergethon, William T. (Ted) Bluhm, Joel Feinberg, Edward J. Brown, Allen McConnell, Whitney T. Perkins, Harriet Tippet, Joseph F. (Jeff) Levy, Nicolas Spulber, John Wilson Lewis, Ezra Vogel, Charles Tilly, Robert George, Sinclair Armstrong, Kenneth Vanlandingham, Laurie Rhodebeck, Byrum Carter, Darrell P. Hammer, Bernard S. Morris, Nicolas Spulber, Mendel Sachs, Otto van Copenhagen, Kurt Müller-Vollmer, Kurt Mayer, David and Jane Manwaring, Alex and Joanne Prisley, Roger Vaughan, Alfred B. Smiley, Robert Pyper, Charles Knowles, Peter Blakeley, Zenovia (Zena) Zacher-Parry, S. Sydney Ulmer, Michael Parenti, Wendell Berry, William Kunstler, Gatewood Galbraith, Edward Pritchard, Robert Spalding, Rita Mae Kelly, Raymond Tanter, Benjamin R. Barber, James MacGregor Burns, Harry Eckstein, Zbigniew K. Brzezinski, Seweryn Bialer, Ambassador Llewelyn Thompson, Albrecht Wellmer, Pitirim Sorokin, Raya Dunayevskaya, Stephen Jay Gould, Albert Cohen, Sheldon Stryker, Melvin DeFleur, Paul Diesing, John Dings, Gary Hoskin, Gordon B. Turner, Richard V. Burks, John P. Hardt, Dan N, Jacobs, William A. Welch, M. George Zaninovich, Donald Carlisle, Theodore H. von Laue, Merle Fainsod, Kenneth Jowitt, Alfred G. Meyer, Barry Farrell, and Rennselaer W. Lee III.

My profound gratitude and special appreciation go to Kim Kerns, Julian Fleron, Ingeri Nel Eaton, Lou Jean Fleron, Lea Williams, Munroe Eagles, Claude Welch, Frank Zagare, William Dunn, Andrew Feenberg, William Leiss, Carl Mitcham, Alexander Motyl, John S. Nelson, Jarosław Piekałkiewicz, Blair Ruble, William Reisinger, Erik P. Hoffmann, W. Bowdoin Davis, John Thorpe, John Lane, Vaughan Blankenship, Frank Marini, Peter Linebaugh, Herbert Reid, Ernest Yanarella, Randy Ihara, Jerry Gaines, Robert Siegler, Richard N. Rosecrance, Warren F. Ilchman, Alvin Magid, Ed Strainchamps, Fred See, Ed Dudley, Clyde (Kip) Herreid, Lowell Dittmer, Charles Schlacks, Jr., Richard Farkas, and James Kuhlman.

Last but not least, my academic career has been enriched by all the students who studied with me; some are among the contributors to this collection. It is a joy to follow their successful professional growth and development. I am confident that the future of Russian studies and political inquiry is bright. The journey ahead is long, but the future is highly promising.

Acknowledgments

We wish to express our profound gratitude and appreciation to Professor Frederic J. Fleron, Jr. It is his innovative scholarship, passionate teaching, mentorship, and genuine friendship that brought together the authors of the articles in this collection. We all celebrate Fleron's outstanding scholarship and distinctive contributions to political science in the areas of Soviet and Russian studies, philosophy of technology, and the logic of comparative political inquiry. We hope that this volume will inspire readers to build on the contributions to scholarship made by Fleron as well as the authors whose articles appear here.

We are deeply grateful to all the authors of the articles in this collection. Work on this project began in 2019. In spring 2020, the Covid-19 pandemic arrived and changed all our lives. Our authors faced multiple challenges in their professional and personal lives. Still, they all remained committed to this project and submitted their articles by the deadline. The Sixteen chapters included here represent original scholarly contributions or serious reflections on the topics of interest to Frederic Fleron and they expand our understanding of these critical issues. One chapter is a reprint and two are reworked versions of previous publications. The authors are all distinguished scholars—some collaborated with Fleron starting in the 1960s, others worked closely with him since the 1970s, and still others studied with him between the 1970s and the early 2000s. The content of this volume reflects the fruitful integration of diverse theoretical and methodological approaches long advocated by Fleron.

The editors as well as many of the contributors to this volume owe a profound debt to the Department of Political Science at the State University of New York at Buffalo (UB). Fleron taught at UB during most of his career together with some of the professors whose studies appear here and many of the rest of the contributors did their graduate studies at UB. All of us benefitted greatly from the wonderful teaching and/or collegiality of professors Fleron, Claude Welch, Frank Zagare, Gary Hoskin, and Munroe Eagles, among many other dedicated faculty members. The Political Science Graduate Program provided students with an excellent environment for learning, research, and professional growth and development. Program alumni who contributed to this collection include Seymen Atasoy, Russell Bova, Vesna Danilovic, Joanna Drzewieniecki, David Foley, Farida Jalalzai, Guoli Liu, Lisa Parshall, and Nathaniel Richmond.

When preparing this book, we received wise guidance and strong support from professors Munroe Eagles (University at Buffalo), Claude Welch (SUNY Distinguished Service Professor Emeritus), and Erik P. Hoffmann (Professor Emeritus, University at Albany). We are also grateful to Professor Lea Williams (Professor Emeritus of History, Brown University) who provided the epigraph for this volume. Lea Williams was Frederic Fleron's teacher and mentor when he was a MA student at Brown. Fleron's wife Kimberly A. Kerns provided strong encouragement and shared her insights into her husband's academic work.

Guoli Liu expresses his heartfelt thanks to coeditor Joanna Drzewieniecki for her thoughtfulness, diligence, and superb skills. Joanna's great efforts significantly enhanced the quality of this book. Guoli is also grateful to his colleagues at the College of Charleston for providing an excellent environment for teaching and research and he extends special thanks to John Creed, Chris Day, Claire Curtis, Brian Fisher, Lynne Ford, France Hollis, Gibbs Knotts, Mark Long, Jordan Ragusa, and Kendra Stewart for their support. Joanna Drzewieniecki thanks her Scottish colleague Kenneth Hermse, with whom she translates and copy edits the academic journal of the Universidad del Pacífico (Lima, Peru) *Apuntes*, for always keeping her on her editing toes, and Guoli Liu for bringing her into this project.

Finally, we are grateful to Eric Kuntzman and Jasper Mislak, our editors at Lexington Books, for their guidance, professionalism, and great skill in moving this manuscript forward to publication.

Guoli Liu and Joanna Drzewieniecki

Introduction

Guoli Liu and Joanna Drzewieniecki

This volume was prepared by the colleagues and former students of Professor Frederic J. Fleron, Jr. (1938–2021) to celebrate his outstanding scholarship in the field of political science as well as his excellent teaching and mentoring skills that influenced generations of students. The collection includes chapters by leading academics who have been inspired by Fleron's distinctive contributions to the following areas of political science and Russian studies: first, Fleron adapted the concept of co-optation from political science to the study of the leadership of the Soviet Union; second, he successfully applied Harry Eckstein's congruence theory to the comparative study of democratization in post-Soviet countries; and third, Fleron created mediation theory in the field of philosophy of technology.

Fleron specialized in Soviet and Russian studies and the sociopolitical impact of technology. His research and theoretical contributions to these fields are internationally recognized. From the beginning of his career, he was an advocate for the full integration of Soviet and Russian studies into political science, where a focus on Sovietology had led to the estrangement of this subfield. He brought Philip Selznick's theory of co-optation into the study of the Soviet leadership with revealing results. He pioneered the application of Harry Eckstein's congruence theory of authority patterns in state-society relations to the analysis of post-Soviet politics in Russia. Just as importantly, Fleron developed the mediation theory of the technology-culture-society nexus, which has broad theoretical and empirical implications for the study of technology and society as well as technology transfer.

Frederic Fleron began his university studies at Brown University where he received a Bachelor's degree in political science in 1959 and a Master's degree in 1961 and then went on to Indiana University where he was awarded a doctorate in Government in 1969. His first academic position was at the University of Kentucky (1965–1970), but he spent the majority of his academic career at the State University of New York at Buffalo (1970–2003), becoming Professor Emeritus of Political Science and University Research Scholar upon his retirement. His desire to engage with students remained strong however, and he served as an adjunct professor at Westfield State University in Massachusetts between 2008 and 2018.

Fleron authored seven books on Russian foreign and domestic policy and technology transfer and was preparing two more for publication at the time of his death in June 2021. He also contributed numerous book chapters and articles to academic journals and participated in various capacities in diverse academic conferences. In addition, he took part in a variety of other academic projects and collaborations and served as a consultant for various institutions, including among others the U.S. Congress, the State Department, and the BBC.

Both inside and outside the classroom, Fleron excelled as a teacher, mentor, colleague, and not coincidentally as a friend. Both his undergraduate and graduate classes enjoyed high enrollment and generations of students are grateful for his mentoring outside the classroom. Sometimes this mentoring continued after students graduated and some students became life-long friends. Similarly, he kept in touch with academic colleagues around the country throughout his life and kept up warm friendships with many. His former University at Buffalo colleague, Munroe Eagles noted in an online tribute shortly after Fleron's passing: "Fred was one of the warmest and most giving individuals I've ever known. A gracious host, he loved to share the good things in life with good friends—and there were many of the latter." Most people who knew Fleron would agree.

Finally, he also found time throughout his life for political and social activism. In just one example of the latter, which illustrates the heartfelt convictions that guided these activities, he and his wife Kim—a certified massage therapist—headed to New York City immediately after 9/11 and both provided help to first responders for a number of weeks.

This introduction is divided into five sections. The first four explore Fleron's accomplishments during his academic career and the many people who influenced his intellectual development and professional life. We are grateful that Fleron was able to share his perceptions of the latter with us during the early stages of this project. The first section explores the intellectual influences that helped shaped Fleron's academic career and pursuits. The second examines his major scholarly contributions and achievements while the third presents his accomplishments as a teacher and mentor as well as an academic leader. The fourth section reviews his activities related to international technology transfer which included participation in real-life negotiations. The final section provides introductions to each of the studies included in this volume.

MAJOR INTELLECTUAL INFLUENCES

Below, we provide an overview of the most important intellectual influences on Fleron's development as a scholar and teacher, as he described them to us. These include professors whose classes he attended, colleagues at various universities, and students with whom he studied as well as students that he himself taught. Some of the names included here will be recognized by all readers while others are less well-known, but all contributed to making Fleron the excellent scholar and academic that he was.

Fleron's interest in Russia and the USSR was first kindled by a speech by Pitrim Sorokin (former personal secretary to Alexander Kerensky, head of the Provisional Government in Russia during 1917) at Wellesley College, which he attended as a junior high school student. When he went on to study at Brown University in the second half of the 1950s, Fleron had an opportunity to explore this interest but just as importantly, he benefited from the many fine professors he encountered there, including his mentor Lea Williams, and professors Edward J. Brown, Joel Feinberg, Whitney T. Perkins, Robert George, Sinclair Armstrong, Kurt Müller-Vollmer, Allen McConnell, and Kurt Mayer. Another formative experience at Brown were the four year-long, inter-disciplinary Identification and Criticism of Ideas Program seminars he attended, and William T. Bluhm's year-long seminar on the growth of the modern state. Such interdisciplinary approaches would be a recurring theme in Fleron's endeavors in academia.

When he was a sophomore, Fleron had the good luck of meeting three fellow students who became scholars of renown: Warren Ilchman (UC Berkeley), Richard N. Rosecrance (Cornell and UCLA), and Erwin L. Levine (Skidmore College). All three had a profound influence on his intellectual development, kindling his interest in all things political.

Returning home for summer vacations in the Boston area, Fleron took summer courses at Harvard University taught by leading American political scientists, including Samuel Beer, Louis Hartz, Hans Kohn, Hans Morgenthau, and Henry Kissinger. These courses expanded his knowledge and sharpened his analytical skills.

After earning his MA in political science at Brown, Fleron entered the PhD program in Government at Indiana University where he studied with many outstanding teachers and scholars, including Robert C. Tucker, Milton Hobbs, Darrell P. Hammer, Byrum Carter, Albert Cohen, Sheldon Stryker, Melvin

DeFleur, and Nicolas Spulber. Tucker's lectures and a reading course during his first semester of doctoral study at Indiana University opened new vistas on Soviet politics for the budding scholar. Fleron's PhD dissertation focused on Soviet elites. He recounts that Harold Lasswell helped him resolve a logjam in this study when Fleron drove him to the Cincinnati airport after Lasswell's colloquium at the University of Kentucky in Lexington. Lasswell, of course, was one of the most innovative social scientists of his generation.

During his doctoral studies, Fleron formed close bonds with several fellow graduate students including Lou Jean Brown, Erik P. Hoffmann, Rita Mae Kelly, Ray Tanter, Jeff Levy, Robert Sharlet, Jeff Sharlet, and Jarosław Piekałkiewicz. He kept in touch for the rest of his life with Erik P. Hoffmann and Robert Sharlet, and renewed his friendship with Jarek Piekałkiewicz in the last years of his life.

Fleron's first full-time teaching job was in the Political Science Department of the University of Kentucky (1965–1970). He credits several colleagues and students there for significantly influencing his intellectual and professional development, including professors Alvin Magid, Frank Marini, Gene Mason, Ernest Yanarella, Herb Reid, and Gatewood Galbraith, and students Randall Ihara, Jerry Gaines, and Phil Patton.

In 1969, Carl Beck, a renowned expert on comparative communism brought Fleron into the University of Pittsburgh Research Group on Communist Elites. This led to their 1973 coauthored book *Comparative Communist Political Leadership* along with Milton Lodge, Derek Waller, William A. Welsh, and George Zaninovich.

Meanwhile, Fleron's former Indiana University professor Robert C. Tucker moved to Princeton University in 1962. In 1970, he invited Fleron to join the American Council of Learned Societies Planning Group on Comparative Communist Studies. Other members of the Planning Group during his tenure (1970–1975) included Donald L.M. Blackmer (M.I.T.), John W. Lewis (Stanford), Richard Burks (Wayne State), Nicolas Spulber (Indiana), and Mark Field (Boston University).

Fleron moved to the Department of Political Science at the State University of New York (SUNY) at Buffalo in 1970. During his first few years there, he worked closely with the group that published the influential New Left journal, *Telos*, including Paul Piccone, Andrew Feenberg, and William Leiss. He also joined the study group on Marxism and Critical Theory that included professors Paul Diesing, George Iggers, Zenovia Sochor-Perry, Lee Smith, Bart Grahl, and others.

In late 1980s and early 1990s, Fleron played a leading role in the formation of a new Undergraduate College and its curriculum, as will be discussed below. The University at Buffalo General Education Program (1986–1993) was an interdisciplinary effort that included representatives of a variety of disciplines ranging from engineering to the social sciences, and the natural sciences to the humanities.[1] Fleron noted that interaction with all these participants taught him much about their disciplines and undoubtedly they also learned a good deal from him.

Fleron continually maintained and established ties with scholars working at various universities. For example, he was an Associate of the Harriman Institute on Russian, Eurasian and East European Studies at Columbia University from 1992 to 1995. He particularly appreciated the intellectual input of Alexander Motyl, Giovanni Sartori, and Dick Howard.

Perhaps Fleron's greatest collaboration cum learning experience was working with Harry Eckstein (along with Erik P. Hoffmann and William Reisinger) on the important book they coauthored: *Can Democracy Take Root in Post-Soviet Russia? Exploration in State-Society Relations*. The genesis of this collaboration occurred when fellow University at Buffalo professor Munroe Eagles recommended Fleron get in touch with Eckstein after they read his book *Regarding Politics* in an informal faculty study group. Visits to Eckstein at the University of California, Irvine followed and eventually led to the coauthored book.

Other scholars who Fleron credits with providing friendship and scholarly camaraderie over the years include Zbigniew K. Brzezinski (Director of Columbia University's Research Institute on Communist Affairs and President Carter's National Security Advisor), Marshall Shulman (Director of the Russian Institute at Columbia University), and John N. Hazard (Columbia University School of Law).

Back at the University at Buffalo, Fleron gave credit to the following professors in the Department of Political Science who nurtured him over the years: Vaughn Blankenship, John Lane, Munroe Eagles, Chris Holoman, Gary Hoskin, Bill Mishler, Bob Stern, Claude Welch, Laurie Rhodebeck, Don Rosenthal, Franco Mattei, and Frank Zagare.

In addition to fellow professors, Fleron always recognized the stimulation he received from the many students (both graduate and undergraduate) who populated his courses since the 1960s.

Finally, and most importantly, we would be remiss if we did not mention that Fleron also credited his family not only for their love but also for their role in his development as a human being and an intellectual. His core family included his mother and father, his ex wife Lou Jean, his two wonderful children Julian and Ingeri, and his spouse Kimberly. Through life experiences and intellectual discussions with them on a variety of topics (inter alia, politics, philosophy, labor relations, mathematics, chaos theory, philosophy of science, teaching methods, and biological science), he came to better appreciate and understand the wonders and mysteries of this world.

SCHOLARLY CONTRIBUTIONS AND MAJOR INTELLECTUAL ACHIEVEMENTS

As a political scientist specialized in Soviet, post-Soviet, and postcommunist studies, Fleron excelled at the elaboration and application of theory to developments in his areas of specialization. In addition, during the beginning years of his career he became interested in the discussions around science and technology in the early days of the Soviet Union. This inspired him to develop a subspecialty in the diffusion and transfer of technology which stretched beyond the boundaries of area studies. Below is a brief synopsis of Fleron's contributions in his areas of specialization.

1. 1967–1968. Brought political socialization studies to Appalachia through the study "The Malevolent Leader: Political Socialization in an American Sub-Culture" (Fleron, Jaros, and Hirsch 1968).
2. 1967–1973. Pioneered the integration of Communist Studies into the social sciences (Fleron 1968, Fleron 1969a, Fleron 1969b, and Fleron 1972).
3. 1969–1973. Applied Selznick's theory of co-optation to the study of Soviet political leadership (Fleron 1969c, Fleron 1969d, Fleron and Kelly 1970, Fleron 1970, Fleron and Kelly 1971, and Beck, Fleron, Lodge, Waller, Welsh, and Zaninovich 1973).
4. 1971, 1991. Co-edited major textbooks on Soviet foreign policy (Fleron and Hoffmann 1971 and an expanded edition in 1980: Fleron, Hoffmann, and Laird 1991).
5. 1973–1977. Applied cultural diffusion theory to the study of technology transfer from capitalist to communist states (Fleron 1975, Fleron 1977a, Fleron 1977b, and Fleron 1977c).
6. 1974–1980. Developed the mediation theory of the technology-culture-society nexus (Fleron 1975, Fleron 1977a, Fleron 1977b, and Fleron 1977c).
7. 1991–1998. Promoted the integration of post-Sovietology into political science and comparative politics (Fleron and Hoffmann 1991, Fleron 1993, Fleron and Hoffmann 1993, Fleron 1996a, Fleron 1996b, Fleron, Ahl, and Lane 1998, Fleron, Hahn, and Reisinger 1997).
8. 1995–1998. Pioneered the application of Eckstein's congruence theory of authority patterns in state-society relations to the analysis of post-Soviet politics in Russia (Eckstein, Fleron, Hoffmann, and Reisinger 1998).
9. 2007–2021. Developed a social science philosophy of technology in response to the two major existing paradigms: the engineering philosophy of technology and the humanities philosophy of technology. This constituted a systematic exploration of his mediation theory of technology,

which he first developed in the mid-1970s, by examining the linkages between the technical and social division of labor, the theft of knowledge, and the disqualification of human experience through abstraction.

10. 2014–2016. Pioneered the application of Robert Merton's middle-range approach for integrating theory and empirical research to a linkage between Russian studies and comparative politics (Fleron 2017).

In addition to the outstanding contributions summarized above, Fleron participated in more than two dozen professional conferences during his professional career as well as more than 50 colloquia, symposia, and research conferences at such prestigious universities as Harvard, Yale, Princeton, Stanford, Columbia, Michigan, Johns Hopkins, Glasgow (Scotland), Toronto, Ottawa, McMaster, as well as the Kennan Institute for Advanced Russian Studies at the Woodrow Wilson International Center for Scholars in Washington, DC.

Testimony to the breadth of his contributions to the discipline of political science is the fact that Frederic Fleron received multiple citations in the 1975 *Handbook of Political Science*, ed. Fred I. Greenstein and Nelson Polsby, including the volumes on *Micropolitical Theory* (vol. 2), *Macropolitical Theory* (vol. 3), and *Policies and Policymaking* (vol. 6). More than 25 years later, he was cited twice in the 2002 edition of *Political Science: The State of the Discipline* published by the American Political Science Association. Fleron features prominently in David Engerman's authoritative history of Soviet studies (Engerman 2009, 255, 331).

OUTSTANDING TEACHER AND ACADEMIC LEADER

Frederic J. Fleron was an outstanding teacher, mentor, and academic leader. His teaching had a deep and long-lasting impact on his many students at Brown University (1960–1961), Indiana University (1963–1965, 1967), the University of Kentucky (1965–1970), the State University of New York at Buffalo (1970–2003), and Westfield State University (2008–2018). Generations of students testify that Fleron was one of the most passionate, dedicated, skillful, and impactful teachers they had ever encountered. His undergraduate classes and graduate seminars were always meticulously prepared, fully engaged, very thoughtful, and effectively delivered. Even decades after taking Fleron's classes, many students still vividly remember the key concepts and critical theories that they learned and other valuable lessons that continue to sustain their intellectual growth and real-life endeavors. John Nelson writes in this collection (chapter 13):

> Frederic J. Fleron is the first political scientist to make me aware of the historical development of political science as a discipline—by including me in his

explorations of attempts to study Russian politics in times of Soviet secrecy and American behavioralism: what a privilege, and what a treat!

During a distinguished teaching career in higher education that spanned more than five decades, Fleron taught two dozen different courses on a wide range of subjects on the undergraduate and graduate levels. His undergraduate courses included American National Government; Issues in Contemporary Politics; Political Leadership; Politics and Society; Politics of Technology; Science and Technology Policy; Soviet Foreign Policy; Politics of the USSR; East European Politics; Russian Politics & Foreign Policy; Comparative Bureaucracy; Political Change; International Organization; Comparative Communist Political Systems; The Iraq War; American Public Policy; American Foreign Policy; and Politics, Technology, and the Environment. Fleron's graduate seminars included Introduction to Political Inquiry; Comparative Politics; Politics of the USSR; Building Democracies; Soviet Foreign Policy; Political Change; Political Movements and Ideologies; Politics of Post-Soviet Russia; Political Leadership and Elites; Comparative Bureaucracy; Politics of Technology and Culture; Public Policy Analysis; and Research Frontiers of Comparative Politics.

Fleron's personal philosophy of teaching and learning at the college level was based on the identification and evaluation of ideas, not on indoctrination or inculcation of one particular point of view. For him, educating was not cloning. He strongly believed that we should teach skills as well as content, but above all we should encourage and empower students to think for themselves. Although faculty should present their views, they should do so only when accompanied by the reasoning and evidence behind their interpretations and by open-minded comparison with other perspectives and conclusions.

Fleron consistently encouraged critical thinking, and he taught contending perspectives on key issues. He often encouraged colleagues to "Teach the issues! Teach the conflict!" He was convinced that this was how students learned best. They should be exposed to clashing ideas and viewpoints, and then asked to identify the strengths and weaknesses in each position before developing their own stance. In this way, students learn how to think critically and insightfully, and they formulate and corroborate their own positions clearly and persuasively.

One example of this approach is the way that Fleron conducted his graduate seminar on the philosophy of social science, titled Introduction to Political Inquiry. The first third of the course reviewed the basic principles of logical positivism/empiricism. The remainder of the course criticized logical positivism and presented issues from the perspectives of realism, antirealist empiricism, constructivism, phenomenology, language analysis, ethno-methodology, and hermeneutics. Students particularly enjoyed discovering Fleron's views regarding the strengths and weaknesses of each perspective.

Professor Fleron's preferred method of teaching political science at the undergraduate level was to supplement important readings with well-crafted lectures, documentary films, and discussions with students both inside and outside the classroom. In his view, weaving these several formats together with imagination and creativity can provide students with a multifaceted approach to learning that addresses different learning styles (verbal, aural, and visual), generates student interest, makes learning enjoyable, stimulates intellectual development, and encourages a high level of achievement. During his half century of university teaching, Fleron taught a wide range of students: traditional undergraduates, non-traditional night school students, a mix of traditional and non-traditional summer school students, and graduate students. In later years, he added online courses to his repertoire. All in all, he developed a comprehensive and comprehensible mix of formats to effectively serve these very different student audiences. And his students at all levels responded very favorably to his approach.

A major challenge for college teachers is to encourage and empower students to become proactive learners who are willing and able to discuss and write about the subjects at hand. In his teaching, Fleron skillfully utilized both lectures and classroom discussions to unpack and clarify central concepts and ideas in assigned readings and videos and to help students compare and appraise the perspectives of various authors. He helped students view exams and papers as opportunities to develop their analytical skills, express their viewpoints, and to receive frank but constructive feedback from the instructor. Testing and writing, then, were not to be dreaded, but rather seen as opportunities to express new-found knowledge.

At the beginning of each semester, Fleron presented students with a syllabus that outlined topics and assignments that were due at various points throughout the semester. He thoughtfully provided students with two helpful lists. The first was a list of no more than a dozen essay questions that engaged the key issues covered by the course. The second was a list of IDs (written definitions of key concepts, people, and events, and their significance) that they would encounter in the course materials. The items on both lists were arranged in the order in which they would be presented and served as road maps for the course. These would then appear on exams, and one of the essay questions would serve as the student's term paper topic. This approach tended to demystify the learning experience and put students more at ease from the outset.

In addition, Professor Fleron invited students to consult with him during office hours to seek his evaluation of their initial outlines of one or two long essay questions and a few IDs. When exams were returned to students in class, he would spend part of the class going over each question, and students with excellent answers were invited to read them to the class. This approach effectively demonstrated that students could produce the goods and that there are various kinds of valued goods. Most students responded quite favorably to these teaching techniques.

In smaller, seminar-type settings for both freshman and graduate students, Fleron utilized some additional techniques. While he relied principally on discussion and the Socratic method, he sometimes also delivered well-prepared lectures. In addition, he might ask a particular student to be prepared at the next class meeting to critique a particular reading or to compare the perspectives of two or more authors on a particular point. This was quite useful in enabling students to become more active participants in classroom discussions.

Professor Fleron supervised a dozen PhD dissertations (three of which were published as books) and served on more than another 30 dissertation committees. He was a wonderful mentor who masterfully guided the growth of his graduate students at each stage of their intellectual development. He also offered great advice to his PhD students and younger colleagues on teaching, research, and professional development. Even decades after they completed the degree programs, many former students continued to seek his academic advice.

During the 33 years that Fleron was on the faculty of the University at Buffalo, he held various positions related to ensuring robust undergraduate and graduate programs in political science as well as the university-wide undergraduate General Education Program. In the Department of Political Science, he served as Director of Undergraduate Studies (1977–1981), Director of Graduate Studies (1991–2001), and Director of Graduate Admissions (for 15 years between 1980 and 2001). In these capacities, he carried out analyses of course registration patterns and developed new enrollment strategies. During his tenure as Director of Graduate Admissions, both the quality and quantity of graduate students enrolled in the program increased significantly. Almost every year, one or two incoming graduate students received Presidential Fellowships. Not every department at the University at Buffalo could match this record over more than a dozen years.

Curriculum development was one of Fleron's major interests and responsibilities in all his administrative capacities. As Director of Undergraduate Studies, he introduced several curriculum reforms in the undergraduate program. For example, he created several interdisciplinary sophomore level courses for non-majors intended to increase student enrollments in political science courses, including Politics & Literature; Political Economy; Political Sociology; Political Psychology, and so on. He taught Politics & Technology and Politics & Society himself several times over the years. These courses provided non-majors with a variety of political science courses in which they would not have to compete for grades with majors in the discipline. The plan worked. The courses attracted scores of students each year and are still in the UB political science undergraduate curriculum 30 years later.

As Director of Graduate Studies, Fleron undertook several curricular innovations in the graduate program. In particular, he introduced a required first-year seminar on the philosophy of social science: Introduction to Political Inquiry. Teaching this seminar rotated among three senior professors and Fleron taught it a dozen times. In addition, he introduced several other new courses into the graduate curriculum: Politics of Technology & Culture; Political Culture; Building Democracies; Politics in the USSR; Politics in Post-Soviet Russia; and Comparative Bureaucracy.

Fleron worked with colleagues to develop the Core Course Requirement for the PhD program which included four courses: Introduction to Political Inquiry, Research Methods, Basic Statistics, and Graduate Social Statistics. In addition, all students were required to take four of the five Field Core Courses: Political Philosophy, Comparative Politics, International Politics, American Politics, and Public Policy. These core courses also served the function of Common Experience Courses—courses in which all students had to enroll, thereby giving them a common frame of reference and basis for interaction.

Fleron participated with particular interest and enthusiasm in the wholesale revision of the University at Buffalo's General Education (GenEd) Program in the late 1980s and early 1990s. He came to this program with already well-defined ideas about what general education should consist of and the relationship between acquiring general and specialized knowledge. He believed that specialized knowledge was best provided through academic disciplines or, in some cases, through interdisciplinary majors. When it came to general knowledge, Fleron was convinced that a general knowledge program should at least assure that students (1) obtain and can demonstrate and utilize a variety of basic skills (reading, writing, dialogue, and mathematics) at an appropriate level and (2) are presented with a core curriculum that includes courses in world civilization, physical and biological science, humanities and the arts, and the social and behavioral sciences. In Fleron's opinion, the best way to achieve these two goals is through Common Experience Courses which give students a level learning field by requiring them all to engage the same intellectual issues and challenges in the same courses.

Fleron participated in the major reform of the undergraduate curriculum both as an administrator charged with designing, implementing, and supervising curricular innovations and as an instructor in some of the new courses. As one of three dozen or so senior faculty (Senior Members) of the Undergraduate College (UGC), which would become the institutional home for the new GenEd Program, he actively participated in the many long discussions and debates that preceded the actual design of the new program.

Furthermore, as Associate Vice Provost for Undergraduate Education in 1988–1990, Fred had primary responsibility for designing and supervising a pilot program for the World Civilization dimension of GenEd. He was also responsible for coordinating the work of the various subcommittees of the Curriculum Committee and presenting proposals for curricular revision to both the Faculty Senate and the higher administration (Provost and President) for discussion and approval. During this process he developed considerable experience in program planning, feasibility studies, project management, financial projections for new programs, office management, and liaison to various academic departments and administrative support personnel. It is very impressive that he performed these duties for three years while carrying a full teaching load at the same time.

In general, as a member of the university community in Buffalo, Fleron worked successfully with administrators and support staff at all levels, from university presidents and provosts to deans, and from department chairs to office staff. As a result, he served as an experienced resource for department and division administrators. He fully appreciated the important roles played by administrative staff and support personnel in assisting and managing academic departments. As always, he treated everyone with respect, no matter their position.

INTERNATIONAL TECHNOLOGY TRANSFER

In addition to Fleron's more theoretical interest in the philosophy of technology he was also interested in international technology transfer and its effects on societies. In one outstanding effort, Fleron organized, convened, and chaired an international conference on Technology and Communist Culture sponsored by the Planning Group on Comparative Communist Studies of the American Council of Learned Societies in 1975. The conference was made possible by a grant from the Carnegie Corporation and was held at the Rockefeller Foundation Study and Conference Center in Lake Como, Italy. Fleron went on to edit and contribute to the conference proceedings: *Technology and Communist Culture: The Socio-Cultural Impact of Technology Transfer under Socialism* (Fleron 1977a). He also published a report on the conference in the quarterly *Technology and Culture* (Fleron 1977c).

During 1978 and 1979, Fleron served as a member of the East–West Technology Transfer Advisory Panel, Office of Technology Assessment of the United States Congress, chaired by McGeorge Bundy (who served as

National Security Advisor to presidents John F. Kennedy and Lyndon B. Johnson from 1961 to 1966). While a member of this congressional advisory panel, Fleron organized several research projects, colloquia, and workshops at professional conferences. Several of these projects resulted in the publication of books and special issues of journals.

In the course of his research and activities on technology transfer, Fleron had the opportunity to engage in discussions regarding the theory and practice of international technology transfer with government officials and research scholars from a number of international and national institutions in the USSR, Poland, Hungary, and Czechoslovakia, as well as United Nations bodies. All these conversations informed his study of themes related to technology. For example, Fleron engaged in discussions with a variety of Soviet officials involved in East–West technology transfer in government ministries, researchers at the USSR Academy of Sciences, and members of the Institute for US and Canadian Studies. In Poland, he held extensive meetings over the course of several years concerning international technology transfer with government officials and members of the Polish Academy of Sciences. He had similar discussions about international technology transfer with government officials and members of the Academies of Science of both Hungary and Czechoslovakia.

KamaZ and Gemcor

In the mid-1970s Fleron had the opportunity to participate in an important venture in technology transfer between the United States and the Soviet Union, which had three different dimensions: technical, economic, and political. The technical dimension involved transfer of technology from an American firm to a Soviet firm. The economic dimension consisted of a two-way foreign trade deal that would deliver steel alloy plate to a Soviet firm in exchange for Soviet crude oil sent to an American refinery. The political dimension centered on a sister-city relationship between a U.S. city and a Soviet city. To understand the interaction among these three dimensions, a little background is in order.

In the late 1960s, the Soviet Union decided to build a huge truck plant in the village of Naberezhnye Chelny on the banks of the Kama River, halfway between Moscow and the Ural Mountains. This truck plant—named the Kama River Industrial Project (KamaZ) was designed to produce 150,000 triple axle diesel trucks per year plus 250,000 diesel engines—a capacity greater than all North American truck plants combined. Their goal was to turn out one 8-to-11-ton truck every 90 seconds. KamaZ is so enormous that its floor plan is literally the size of the Bronx (40 square miles), one of the five boroughs of New York City.

The world wondered what the Soviets were going to do with 150,000 triple axle trucks per year. In 1979, the answer became apparent: KamaZ was producing the trucks and gun carriages that the Red Army used to transport troops and materiel when they invaded Afghanistan. KamaZ was a firm that benefited significantly from technology transfer but this invasion was a clear reminder that technology transfer could have both positive and negative consequences.

KamaZ was the beneficiary of extensive transfers of technology from literally dozens of countries to the USSR during the 1970s. Judging from the location of the donor countries' flags in front of the main administration building at KamaZ, Japan was the largest donor country. The United States played a lesser role.

One U.S. donor company was the General Electro-Mechanical Corporation (Gemcor) located in Buffalo, New York. Thomas Speller Sr., the President of Gemcor, had developed a new process of holding large steel beams together by cold-squeezed rivets with a precision and tolerance such that the joints were fuel-tight under high pressure. The advantage of cold-squeezed rivets was that they were not heated to high temperatures and thus did not have their temper and tensile strength compromised. As a result, Gemcor got contracts from Boeing and McDonnell Douglas to construct semi-automated assembly lines to employ Speller's cold-squeezed riveting process in the assembly of frames for Boeing 747 and DC-10 aircraft.

The Soviets got wind of Speller's process and Gemcor's contracts with Boeing and McDonnell Douglas. As a result, as part of their search for international partners to provide technology for KamaZ, they sent Soviet engineers to Buffalo in the mid-1970s to hammer out a trade agreement that included two interesting elements. First, the Soviets agreed to pay cash on the barrel head in USD for Gemcor's semi-automated assembly line FOB Port of New York. Second, Gemcor agreed to allow the Soviets to have a team of Soviet engineers (plus a political officer, of course) in residence at the Gemcor factory in North Buffalo.

Fleron was both a keen observer of and direct participant in this experiment in technology transfer that partnered a capitalist donor enterprise and a Communist recipient enterprise. It was a case of serendipity since at the time he was the director of an international research project on the sociocultural impact of capitalist technology transfer on socialist countries. He ended up spending numerous hours discussing the details of the KamaZ–Gemcor collaboration with both the Soviet and American engineers.

During his discussions with the Soviet engineers at Gemcor, it became clear that these engineers were experiencing some difficulties with their collaborators in some countries. Fleron spent many hours with them discussing quality control problems. One of their most pressing problems concerned their contract with Great Britain to produce steel alloy for the KamaZ stamping division for the doors, roofs, and hoods of their trucks. As Fleron tells it, the Soviets claimed that the British tried to cheat them by reducing the amount of aluminum in the alloy so that when the steel plates were cold stamped on the door, roof, and hood molds they cracked and crumbled beyond use. As a result, the Soviets were looking for an alternative source of steel plates for their stamping division. Fleron suggested that they talk to people at the Ford Motor Company's Stamping Plant in Woodlawn, just south of Buffalo, and at Bethlehem Steel in Lackawanna, NY. However, in the end and due to U.S. domestic political factors, the technology transfer and local cooperation projects between Buffalo and Naberezhnye Chelny were not fully materialized.

Fleron's participation in this multifaceted venture provided him with valuable insights into many aspects of international cooperation (and non-cooperation) in technology transfer. He noted that one can learn from both successful and unsuccessful experiences. The political and foreign trade dimensions of this particular venture did not succeed for internal political reasons on the U.S. side, perhaps to the detriment of the Buffalo area economy. But the technology transfer dimension was a great success for both partners.

ABOUT THIS COLLECTION

This book is divided into three parts: part I (chapters 1–8) focuses on Russian and post-Soviet studies; part II (chapters 9–11) explores the philosophy of technology; and part III (chapters 12–19) examines the logic of political inquiry and comparative politics. Each part of the volume addresses one of the three areas in which Professor Fleron made an outstanding contribution to the advancement of knowledge and scholarly exploration.

Russian and Post-Soviet Studies

Blair Ruble (chapter 1) presents an interesting case study of the city of Yekaterinburg, Russia, which highlights the regional dimensions of political systems. His study is inspired by what he refers to as "Fleron's 1969 paradigm-shattering volume *Communist Studies and the Social Sciences*." In that volume, Paul Shoup argues that studies of subnational entities could bridge the then existing divide between Soviet studies and interdisciplinary trends in social sciences. Ruble provides us with just such a study that contributes to the comparative studies of cities not just in Russia but around the world. The study is distinctive and especially important because in addition to a sociopolitical summary of the history of the city, Ruble provides a detailed examination of elements of the social and cultural life in Yekaterinburg at the end of the Communist era and afterward, including crime and gangs, rock music, and the literary life of the city as well as some of the interactions of these phenomenon with political actors.

Frederic Fleron played a significant role, both before and after the Soviet Union ended, in strengthening the links between scholars analyzing Soviet/post-Soviet politics and the comparative politics subfield. In this vein, William Reisinger and Marina Zaloznaya (chapter 2) examine Russian democratic values from both comparative and longitudinal perspectives using data from nationally representative political values surveys conducted in Russia in six different years from 1990 to 2015, with comparisons to Ukraine, Lithuania, and Georgia. Their study contributes to our understanding of the usefulness of commonly used measures of democratic values and whether they capture enduring orientations. The authors suggest that further investigations of democratic values in Russia and elsewhere can benefit by revisiting the points Fleron raised about the first wave of studies on this issue.

Russell Bova (chapter 3) provides a thoughtful essay, or a "think-piece," as he calls it, using as a starting point the 30th anniversary of the fall of the Soviet Union. This event initially inspired enormous optimism among observers and scholars. In addition, it advanced—but not entirely assured—the integration of Russian studies into comparative politics, something Fleron had long argued for. Bova notes that this integration, at its most successful, should be a two-way street and global theory building must incorporate Russia and the other postcommunist countries. He points out three areas where such analysis can currently be particularly fruitful. First, while the fall of the Soviet Union generated great enthusiasm about democracy, today democracy is under attack in many countries, a phenomenon that needs to be analyzed globally. Second, Bova notes that political culture has frequently been "both used and abused" as an explanatory variable for understanding democratization. He provides evidence that culture—but not only culture—does matter. Finally, he uses the Russian case to demonstrate that institutions also matter, alluding to the Fleron's co-edited book on congruence theory, which noted the reciprocal relationship between political culture and the institutional choices made during attempts to establish democratic systems. As a whole, this chapter is intended to provide food for thought and inspiration for additional research and debate.

In chapter 4, Nathaniel Richmond, who has spent 45 years studying Russia, starts from the premise that "to understand Russia, it is necessary to think like a Russian." After a brief explanation of how Russians think, Richmond goes on to provide a set of keys that he thinks are essential to understanding Russia's political past and future. These include (1) since the revolution, the least expected among the elite has usually emerged as the new leader; (2) in the absence of free, fair, and meaningful elections, new leaders always attempt to justify and legitimize their rule by repudiating the prior leader's policies and by trying to enhance Russia's global role; (3) the "good old days" for Russians was during the USSR, especially in the post–World War II and post-Stalin eras, but that does not mean they want to recreate the USSR today; the "bad old days" was the decade following the USSR's collapse, and any repetition of that era is to be avoided. Finally drawing on his suggestive discussion of these "keys," Richmond goes on to describe Russian politics, the economy, society, and foreign policy under Putin.

In chapter 5, Alexander Motyl—in a revised version of an article originally published in *Foreign Policy*—examines Russia´s foreign policy interests today and provides recommendations of how other countries should deal with Russia. Arguing against the currently popular notion that Russia has had, and always will have immutable national interests, Motyl nevertheless contends that current Russian foreign policy cannot be understood without understanding its historical emergence and evolution. After a brief synopsis of changing Russian interests from the fourteenth century to the consolidation of the USSR, Motyl goes on to review changing Russian interests in the wake of the collapse of the Soviet Union and under Putin. A separate section reviews Russia's recent actions and perceptions of Ukraine and Crimean issues. The chapter ends with detailed advice on how the West and neighboring countries should deal with Putin's imperial ambitions.

In chapter 6, Jarosław Piekałkiewicz and Joanna Drzewieniecki provide a first-hand account of Piekałkiewicz's participation in the Polish Underground's 1944 Warsaw Uprising. After the war, Piekałkiewicz immigrated to the United States and studied in the PhD Program at Indiana University with Fleron. This chapter is included here at Fleron's special request. It provides an unusually honest account of the participation of a brave 18-year-old in the 63-day ultimately unsuccessful uprising staged by the second largest anti-Nazi resistance movement during World War II (after Tito's Yugoslavian partisans). All the action described takes place in an approximately three block area. The account stands out not only because it is probably the last such first-hand participant account to be published but also because it neither embellishes nor idealizes. It does not gloss over the fear that fighters experience and the death and destruction they witness. Finally, it provides a realistic description of urban guerrilla warfare with which most of the readers of this collection will likely be unfamiliar.

In chapter 7, Timothy K. Blauvelt, Christofer Berglund, and Jesse Driscoll use social methodology to study identity formation in the republic of Georgia, implementing Frederic Fleron's long advocated goal of applying social methodology to the study of Soviet and post-Soviet states. The authors' interest lies in discovering the attitudes of Georgian citizens towards the ethnolinguistic groups living in the country, which include—in addition to ethnic

Georgians—Russians, Armenians, and Azeris. To carry out their study, the authors revised the design of the "matched-guise" experiment which has long been in use but has some serious methodological flaws. They then applied their design to a large-scale field test in Georgia with encouraging preliminary results which are presented in this chapter. They conclude that their design makes the match-guise experiment a cutting-edge method of eliciting respondents' attitudes towards ethno-linguistic groups thus contributing to the research on identity formation.

One of the key things learned by those of us who studied the Soviet Union and Russia with Frederic Fleron was the ongoing importance of the relationship between the central government and subnational entities in defining the politics of this nation throughout its history. In chapter 8, David Foley examines these relationships, how they have been adjusted over time, and what these adjustments mean for the possible consolidation of democracy in Russia in the future. He argues that Russian federal governance is based on strong personal-vertical relationships. Delving into the mechanisms of power, he notes that over the years since the fall of the Soviet Union, the power of governments of the republics has weakened for the most part but local powerbrokers do play an important role as is particularly evident in the case of cities. Foley analyzes the asymmetries of the federal system and how Putin's policies have increased them. He refers to what he calls a "pseudo ethno-federation" that has been created and examines how the districting structure reinforces and exacerbates ethno-national plurality while maintaining a weak civil society. This rich study also analyzes the faults in the party system which has been adjusted by the current government and how Putin has benefited from this as well as from the lack of ideologies.

Philosophy of Technology

In chapter 9, Andrew Feenberg proposes a critical theory of technology which supplements the Critical Theory of the Frankfurt School. He starts out by noting that technology has been depoliticizing many aspects of social life and that the normative dimension of politics seems to be disappearing. Still, there are signs that technology is beginning to return to the public sphere as evidenced, for example, by environmental movements. Further democratization of technology requires a deeper understanding of how it affects society. Feenberg provides an insightful critique of previous philosophical approaches to technology with special attention to thinkers such as Foucault, Marcuse, Marx, and the members of the Frankfort School. He then proposes the addition of the notions of "formal bias" and "substantive bias" to the critical theory of technology. Understanding these biases may provide one of the keys to the democratization of technology.

In chapter 10, William Leiss engages with the concept of environmental domination, with reference to a recent article on the subject by Sharon R. Krause. After reviewing some of the problematic aspects of Krause's approach, Leiss proposes substituting the somewhat different concept of "eco-dominion." The basis of the idea of eco-dominion is that humanity's right over nature is limited to its right of use of living animals for sustenance, as articulated in the first chapter of the Book of Genesis. This text has had a powerful influence over the centuries and encourages us to focus on the fate of wild and domesticated animals when we seek to formulate an appropriate ethical response to humanity's relations with non-human nature. This task is particularly urgent today as global population growth poses an extinction threat to other species. Leiss concludes by suggesting that the narrower concept of eco-dominion is a better fit for describing the human relation to non-human nature than the more expansive concept of environmental domination; however, he adds that neither concept appears to be sufficiently robust to confront the looming ecological crisis.

In a special contribution, Carl Mitcham (chapter 11) critically examines the interactions of engineering, technology, and ethics through the lens of his own academic career. As he describes each stage of this career, we not only learn about his interests, accomplishments but also about the many debates related to various aspects of the philosophy of technology and engineering ethics that took place over time. Mitcham also recounts his experiences in teaching and curriculum development. For example, when Science, Technology, and Society (STS) programs became popular, he became deeply involved with STS teaching, collaborating on textbooks, and engaging in the sometimes lively debates that this approach generated; in the process, he became a leader in the field. Still his greatest love is engineering ethics and he argues that it is much more than professionalism: it is expanded critical reflection on the manifold and manifest transformations that engineering introduces into our lifeworld.

Logic of Political Inquiry and Comparative Politics

William N. Dunn (chapter 12) provides a probing, in-depth analysis of what he calls the "lost legacy of the policy sciences." After briefly reviewing the broad sweep of the applied social and behavioral sciences in the nineteenth century, Dunn centers his analysis on the period from 1932 to 1942, when the policy sciences were founded at the University of Chicago and Yale. He provides a fresh, detailed theoretical analysis of the work of the policy scholars of the time, with particular emphasis on Harold Lasswell. Dunn analyzes what concepts such as pragmatism, the maximization postulate, and "decisional functionalism" meant to the theoreticians of the time. He also explains why the University of Chicago played such a crucial role in policy studies until Robert Maynard Hutchins became president. Dunn finishes by outlining the options for future research programs building on this lost legacy.

John S. Nelson (chapter 13) traces how political science developed from a classical discipline to a modern one, continually emerging and re-emerging, as it revolved around behavioral reinventions nearly every generation. In the last decades of the twentieth century, many new "approaches" have been proposed, including, for example, cybernetics, political psychology, political dynamics, and political socialization: none has disappeared and some have formed subfields of their own, usually for a fairly short time. Still not one of these approaches has come close to permeating the modern discipline of political science as have liberal institutionalism, transactionalism, behavioralism, and rationalism. Nelson argues that comparative political inquiries and some branches of international studies entered the current century turning toward "thick" encounters with cultural institutions by contrast with the "thin" generalizations available from statistical analysis of most national and international data. He anticipates that the two innovations most likely to reconfigure political science as a discipline are informatics and cultural studies (in non-Marxian forms). Nelson goes on to conclude that the discipline's late twentieth-century interest in democratization and the rediscovery of civil society combine with renewed interest in political communication to move the discipline from liberal representations to cultural representations but notes that—as always—we cannot know what the future might hold.

In chapter 14, Munroe Eagles and Seymen Atasoy explore the prospects for democracy in Turkey by examining the sentiments of the country's electorate since 2002 through an analysis of the Turkish results from the World Values Survey (2007, 2012, and 2017). The years since 2002 have been dominated by former Prime Minister and now President Recep Tayyip Erdoğan and his Justice and Development Party (AKP). The authors review changing approval among the Turkish public in this period for the institutions crucial for democracy such as the parliament, the judicial system, political parties, and the press. They also discuss the three broad and distinctive rationales for being willing to cast a ballot for the AKP: those relating to social capital endowments; the religiosity of respondents; evaluations of the performance of AKP governments; and the political values and attitudes of respondents. After presenting the results of their empirical study which suggest, among other things, that many Turks embrace democracy while simultaneously holding attitudes that appear at least on the surface to be inherently anti-democratic, Eagles and Atasoy conclude with an analysis of the current challenges facing this NATO member and emergent economic and regional power.

In chapter 15, Frank Zagare draws a sharp contrast between classical deterrence theory and perfect deterrence theory. He argues that perfect deterrence theory is a completely general theory of conflict initiation, escalation, and resolution. It is designed to be applicable across time and space. Indeed, its empirical domain is not restricted to contentious nuclear relationships. Rather, its analytic framework can be used to understand the full range of situations wherein at least one actor's goal is to preserve the existing distribution of value. Unlike classical deterrence theory, perfect deterrence theory is logically consistent and in accord with the empirical record. In perfect deterrence theory, a capable threat is a necessary condition for deterrence success. But it is not sufficient, as it is in classical deterrence theory. Threat credibility plays an important role in the operation of both direct and extended deterrence relationships, but it is neither necessary nor sufficient for deterrence to prevail; under certain conditions, the presence of a credible threat may actually precipitate a deterrence failure. In perfect deterrence theory the cost of conflict and status quo evaluations are also important strategic variables in so far as their values determine the characteristics of the players' threats. Perfect deterrence theory is consistent with a policy of minimum deterrence, it recommends a conditionally cooperative diplomatic approach to resolve disputes, opposes even the selective proliferation of nuclear and other weapons of mass destruction, and supports arms control agreements and other limitations on redundant military expenditures. This chapter further develops the theory of perfect deterrence (Zagare and Kilgour 2000).

Inspired by Frederic Fleron's advocacy for methodological rigor, Vesna Danilovic (chapter 16) employs a mixed research design that combines qualitative and quantitative methods to analyze the behavior of France, Russia, Turkey, and Britain in the period leading up to the Crimean War of 1853–1856. She notes that there is general agreement that this was a war that all states involved preferred to avoid and did not want to fight. The question is then, why did they fight? Danilovic triangulates theoretical, qualitative-historical, and quantitative analysis to address this question. After providing a case study of the war, she employs quantitative empirical analysis to show how different bargaining strategies can be critical to the outbreak of war, focusing on the issue of how the choice of particular bargaining tactics can lead rational actors to war despite their ex ante preferences for peace. Reviewing the approaches of previous waves of deterrence theorists, Danilovic makes her own contribution to the study of why wars take place.

In chapter 17, Farida Jalalzai focuses on women heads of state and government, a cohort that has been relatively little studied. She provides an overview of the state of the literature and highlights opportunities that women leaders have to empower women within society. She finds that in the gender and politics literature, quantitative models coexist with rich qualitative studies, and increasingly, a combination of both approaches. Jalalzai devotes a section of her chapter to the conditions that have been found to facilitate women's rise to power in countries around the world. She then goes on to assess the potential benefits that women executives offer women as a group including "empowerment as policy makers" and "empowerment and symbols," noting successes and obstacles, as well as the need for more research. Finally, she contends that an emphasis on women's ability to empower women through their roles as policy makers, selectors, and symbols, offers an alternative but complementary way to assess the effects of women executives.

When Frederic Fleron passed away in June 2021, he was working on two major book projects. One of these was a collaboration with Lisa Parshall entitled *The Logic of Political Inquiry*, a subject that reflects on the issues at the very heart of Fleron's academic career as an educator and a scholar. In chapter 18, Parshall provides some key points from their manuscript that address two of the most important issues it raises. The first, broadly stated, is the importance of familiarizing political scientists with the philosophy of science. This goes to heart of how knowledge is produced in our discipline. As the authors point out, the lingering divide between logical positivism/empiricism (LP/E) and post-LP/E logics of inquiry misses the point that there is no such thing as a single, holistic approach to social inquiry that would allow an answer to every worthy inquiry. The research approach taken will limit the kinds of questions to be asked and how, or whether, one can answer them. Without some knowledge of the basic issues and controversies in contemporary philosophy of science, this myopia will be perpetuated by each successive generation of political scientists. And it is this myopia that the authors intend to contribute to curing through their work. The second, related topic discussed in this chapter is the problem of incommensurability. For Fleron and Parshall this was the central problématique of their study: whether or not the assumptions, methodology, and logic of inquiry of positivism and post-positivism are commensurable or incommensurable, whether their ontologies and epistemologies could be transcended or at least reconciled.

In "The Compleat Academic: Frederic Fleron's Academic Troika," Claude E. Welch (chapter 19) recounts Fleron's accomplishments as a productive scholar, outstanding teacher, and heavily involved university citizen. Welch demonstrates that Fleron excelled in all three of these broad responsibilities. He became respected for the quality of his instruction, whether in high-enrollment undergraduate classes, small graduate seminars, or guided independent study with individual students. He published widely and extensively, sharing the fruits of his research with others. Confronting drastic changes in "Sovietology," and recognizing the significance of technological advances on political systems, Fleron expanded the purview of his publications and teaching. Finally, Fleron gave generously of his time, during his 33 years at the University at Buffalo. His extensive service touched hundreds, most notably via the Undergraduate College. His service invariably proved innovative, exciting, and well-adapted to issues undergraduates in particular confront in their own careers.

This volume is a celebration of the outstanding scholarship exemplified by Fleron's pathbreaking works, and a call to engage in a truly creative and persistent search for truth through theoretical inquiry, area studies, and policy debates. The differing assumptions, approaches, and conclusions of the authors whose studies are gathered here attest to the diversity of theoretical perspectives and methodological approaches in comparative political inquiry, Russian and postcommunist studies, the philosophy of technology, and the dynamic interactions of technological innovation and sociopolitical change.

Fleron was a world-renowned scholar in political science and area studies. His theoretical innovations and methodological rigor will continue to inspire many generations of scholars and students to further explore many complex and challenging issues. It is exciting to see so many puzzles being successfully solved on the never-ending journey of scholarship. Political scientists, area specialists, policy advisers, and students can profit from reading the chapters contained here.

NOTES

1. Fleron found the contributions of the following particularly helpful and interesting: university president Steve Sample (Engineering), Vice Provost John Thorpe (Mathematics), Tom Headrick (Law), John Dings (English), Fred See (English), Charlie Keil (Center for the Americas), Ed Dudley (Modern Languages and Literature), Barbara Bono (English), Ed Strainchamps (Music), Jim Bono (History), Liz Kennedy (Women's Studies), Clyde Herreid (Biology), Orville Murphy (History), Denny Malone (Engineering), and Mendel Sachs (Physics),

REFERENCES

Beck, Carl, Frederic J. Fleron, Jr., Milton Lodge, Derek Waller, William Welsh, and George Zaninovich. 1973. *Comparative Communist Political Leadership*. New York: David McKay.

Eckstein, Harry, Frederic J. Fleron, Erik P. Hoffmann, William M. Reisinger, Richard Ahl, R. Russell, Philip G. Roeder, Barnett R. Rubin, Jack Snyder, and Neil Robinson. 1998. *Can Democracy Take Root in Post-Soviet Russia? Explorations in State-Society Relations*. Lanham, MD: Rowman & Littlefield.

Engerman, David C. 2009. *Know Your Enemy: The Rise and Fall of America's Soviet Experts*. Oxford: Oxford University Press.

Fleron, Frederic J., Jr. 1968. "Soviet Area Studies and the Social Sciences: Some Methodological Problems of Communist Studies." *Soviet Studies (Glasgow)* 19, no. 3: 313–339.

———. 1969a. *Communist Studies and the Social Sciences: Essays on Methodology and Empirical Theory*. Chicago: Rand McNally.

———. 1969b. "Research Strategies for the Study of Communist Systems." *Canadian Slavic Studies* 30, no. 3: 544–552.

———. 1969c. "Toward a Reconceptualization of Political Change in the Soviet Union: The Political Leadership System." *Comparative Politics* 1, no. 2: 228–244.

———. 1969d. "Cooptation as a Mechanism of Adaptation to Change: The Soviet Political Leadership System." *Polity* 2, no. 2: 176–201.

———. 1970. "Representation of Career Types in the Soviet Political Leadership." In *Political Leadership in Eastern Europe and the Soviet Union*, edited by R. Barry Farrell, 108–139. Chicago: Aldine.

———. 1972. "Concept Formation in Comparative Communist Studies." *Politikka (Helsinki)* 13, no. 2: 22–44.

———. 1975. "Technology and Communist Culture: Some Comparative Dimensions of Cultural Diffusion." In *Comparative Socialist Systems: Essays on Politics and Economics*, edited by Carmelo Mesa-Lago and Carl Beck, 186–200. Pittsburgh: University of Pittsburgh Center for International Studies.

———, ed. 1977a. *Technology and Communist Culture: The Socio-Cultural Impact of Technology Transfer Under Socialism*. New York: Praeger.

———. 1977b. "The Western Connection: Technical Rationality and Soviet Politics." *Soviet Union* 4, no. 1: 58–84.

———. 1977c. "Conference Report, 'Technology and Communist Culture: Bellagio, Italy, August 22–28, 1975'." *Technology and Culture* 18, no. 4: 659–665.

———. 1993. "Whither Post-Sovietology? Comparative Politics and Lessons for the Present." *The Harriman Institute Forum* 6: 3–13.

———. 1996a. "Post-Soviet Political Culture in Russia: An Assessment of Recent Empirical Investigations." *Europe-Asia Studies (Glasgow)* 48, no. 2: 225–260.

———. 1996b. "The Logic of Inquiry in Post-Soviet Studies: Art or Science?" *Communist and Post-Communist Studies* 29, no. 3: 245–274.

———. 2017. *Russian Studies & Comparative Politics: Views From Metatheory & Middle-Range Theory*. Lanham, MD: Lexington Books.

Fleron, Frederic J., Jr., Dean Jaros, and Herbert Hirsch. 1968. "The Malevolent Leader: Political Socialization in an American Sub-Culture." *The American Political Science Review* 62, no. 2: 564–575.

Fleron, Frederic J., Jr., and Erik P. Hoffmann, eds. 1971. *The Conduct of Soviet Foreign Policy*. Chicago: Aldine-Atherton.

Fleron, Frederic J., Jr., and Erik Hoffmann. 1991. "Sovietology and Perestroika: Methodology and Lessons From the Past." *The Harriman Institute Forum* 5, no. 1: 1–12.

Fleron, Frederic J., Jr., and Erik P. Hoffmann, eds. 1993. *Post-Communist Studies and Political Science: Methodology and Empirical Theory in Sovietology*. Boulder: Westview Press.

Fleron, Frederic J., Jr., Erik P. Hoffmann, and Robbin F. Laird, eds. 2017 (1991). *Soviet Foreign Policy: Classic and Contemporary Issues*. New York: Routledge. (Also Published as *Classic Issues in Soviet Foreign Policy and Contemporary Issues in Soviet Foreign Policy: From Brezhnev to Gorbachev*. New York: A. de Gruyter, 1991).

Fleron, Frederic J., Jr., Jeffrey Hahn, and William M. Reisinger. 1997. "Public Opinion Surveys and Political Culture in Post-Soviet Russia." *Proceedings of a Kennan Institute Seminar, Occasional Paper* #266. Washington, DC: Kennan Institute for Advanced Russian Studies, Woodrow Wilson International Center for Scholars.

Fleron, Frederic J., Jr., Richard Ahl, and Finbarr Lane. 1998. "Where Now in the Study of Russian Political Parties?" *Journal of Communist Studies and Transition Politics (Glasgow)* 14, nos. 1–2: 224–252.

Fleron, Frederic J., Jr., and Rita M. Kelly. 1970. "Personality, Behavior, and Communist Ideology." *Soviet Studies (Glasgow)* 21, no. 3: 297–313.

Fleron, Frederic J., Jr., and Rita M. Kelly. 1971. "Motivation, Methodology and Communist Ideology." In *The Behavioral Revolution and Communist Studies: Applications of Behaviorally Oriented Political Research on the Soviet Union and Eastern Europe*, edited by Roger E. Kanet. New York: Free Press.

Piekałkiewicz, Jarosław. 2020. *Dance With Death: A Holistic View of Saving Polish Jews During the Holocaust*. Lanham: Hamilton Books.

Polsby, Nelson W., and Fred I. Greenstein. 1975. *Handbook of Political Science*. Reading: Addison-Wesley.

Zagare, Frank C., and Kilgour Marc D. 2000. *Perfect Deterrence*. New York: Cambridge University Press.

I

RUSSIAN AND POST-SOVIET STUDIES

Chapter 1

Highlighting Regional Dimensions of Political Systems

The Case of Yekaterinburg in Russia

Blair A. Ruble

In his contribution to Frederic Fleron's 1969 paradigm shattering volume *Communist Studies and the Social Sciences*, Paul Shoup wrote,

> Replicative studies, for example, may make valuable contributions to comparative work and never compare nations as such. There is also a place in the comparative approach for the study of different periods in one nation's development (so-called vertical comparisons) and the analysis of regional differences within one country if they have as part of their purpose, the study of similarities and differences among political systems. (Shoup 1969, 67)

Shoup's passage was one of many throughout Fleron's compendium that fired the imaginations of students in graduate courses across North America. For some, the important task of comparing Soviet and Communist political systems with their counterparts elsewhere could be advanced by case studies of local governance, which immediately conjured up multiple appropriate comparisons.

Two decades would pass before Gorbachevian perestroika and glasnost made meaningful on the ground field research possible in cities and regions across the Soviet Union. The vision of regional and city case studies never died. By the late 1980s, Villanova University political science professor Jeffrey W. Hahn was able to piece together support from the Carnegie Corporation of New York, The Juridical Faculty at Moscow State University, and the Institute of Legislation and Comparative Law of the Government of the Russian Federation to launch the first comprehensive study of a Russian provincial city; the Soviet "Middletown" of Yaroslavl. Between 1990 and

1995 Hahn, American research team members Timothy Colton, Jerry Hough, and Blair Ruble were joined by several Russian and American graduate students in working with Russian partners Georgi. Barabashev, Mikhail N. Marchekno, Alex Gasparishvili, Sergei Glavatskii, Sergei Tumanov (Moscow State University), Vesvolod Vasiliev, Lev Okunov (Institute of Legislation and Comparative Law), Lev Kruglikov (Yaroslavl State University), and Tatiana Rumiantseva (Yaroslavl Center for Public Opinion and Sociological Research) in conducting research on political life, economic and social transformation as the city moved through its initial post-Soviet transition. Among the many U.S. graduate students conducting field research under the auspices of the project were Jo Andrews, Henry Hale, Lolly Jewitt, Susan Lehmann, Beth Mitchnick, and Katherine Stoner-Weiss. These efforts resulted in a small bookcase of monographs, dissertations, collected volumes, journal articles, and conference papers building off Shoup's proposal to create a base for meaningful transnational comparative research at the regional and city level (Hahn 2001).

Numerous other studies followed examining political life in such disparate Russian post-Soviet cities and regions as Komi, Nizhni Novgorod, and Vladivostok. These efforts in one way or another trace their way back to Fleron's call for the integration of the study of communist systems, regional studies, and comparative politics. Shoup's observations sparked the thought among many that cities were ripe for comparisons. The changes wrought by Gorbachev made such research possible.

Studies of Russian and post-Soviet cities and regions built up throughout the 1990s, transforming how scholars approached the political systems emerging from the former Soviet Union. Indeed, a new conventional wisdom took shape counseling against viewing Russia from the top down. A vibrant field of Russian local government and politics consolidated just in time for Vladimir Putin to launch a new wave of centralization. Nonetheless, the accumulation of case studies demonstrated that even Putin's seeming invincibility shields meaningful local politics below. The brief profile of Yekaterinburg to follow provides a small illustration of the texture and depth that is added to research on Russia by following up on the proposal by Shoup and Fleron for more comparative study of Communist political systems.

THE CASE OF YEKATERINBURG

Yekaterinburg, which would become Russia's fourth largest city at the beginning of the twenty-first century, was established in 1723, late in the reign of Peter I ("the Great"), just on the Asian side of the Ural Mountains, somewhat more than 900 miles east of Moscow. The city was named after

Saint Catherine, to honor Tsar Peter's wife, Ekaterina. It drew settlers from across the Russian Empire, growing slowly and achieving the status of a town only in 1796 (Starikov, Zavgel'skaia, Tokmenninova, and Cherniak 2008). It eventually emerged as a major mining and manufacturing center, prospering from the exploitation of the rich mineral deposits throughout the Urals region, and enriching great industrial dynasties in the process (Bavil'skii 1996). The arrival of the Trans-Siberian Railroad in the late nineteenth century further secured Yekaterinburg's status as one of Russia's most important industrial centers (Ames 1947, 67).

The city, in fact, was unusual for Imperial Russia in that it was an industrial headquarters city rather than an administrative center (Perm served as the region's provincial capital for much of the period) (Antropova 2004). As Urals Federal University professors Sergei Kropotov and Maria Litovskaya have argued, the city's "uniqueness" lies in the fact that "it was one of the first specifically created industrial cities in the world" (Kropotov and Litovskaya 2010, 43). Yekaterinburg quickly attracted a diverse population of workers and specialists, including a significant Jewish population at a time when the empire's Jews were largely prohibited from moving beyond the Pale of Settlement in the lands annexed following the final partition of Poland in the late eighteenth century (Deutsch 2011).

Local mine and factory owners were less concerned with the details of such imperial policies than they were with using engineering knowledge to make their businesses profitable. As the political analyst Leon Aron has noted, Yekaterinburg's "industrialists and merchants became well known for their wealth, curiosity, and civic-mindedness. They were indefatigable travelers, collectors of nature's curiosities, and connoisseurs of the arts. They founded museums, theaters, and libraries" (Aron 2000, 12). Consequently, they employed people who could do the job, no matter how much they were discriminated against elsewhere.

Jews, following the extension of the military draft to men who were not Orthodox Christians in 1827, and others came to the region to serve their 25-year compulsory military service and frequently never returned home (Antropova 2004). Many political exiles and released prisoners similarly sought out the region's cities after having served their Siberian sentences. The city was a place where smart outsiders could thrive. Even today, residents often claim that they judge someone only by how hard he or she works.

Yekaterinburg became the sort of melting pot of empire that promotes unrefined interethnic, interconfessional, interprofessional, and interclass propinquity. The city long has been a place where diversity has been converted into an asset. On one hand, numerous arrivals to the Urals region maintained their religious institutions and schools. According to the 1897 census, for example, between 85% and 97% of Jews in the four Urals provinces (guberniia) spoke Yiddish at home. On the other hand, residents from various backgrounds worked alongside people different from themselves in jobs ranging from the most menial to the professions (Antropova 2004).

This pattern was true for many religious and national groups, promoting a sort of rough-and-ready tolerance and mixing of cultures. As a result, some of the worst pathologies of Imperial Russian ethnic relations largely bypassed the city and region. For example, the only pogroms to take place in the city before 1917 were those provoked by police agents of the Ministry of Internal Affairs on orders from their Saint Petersburg superiors in October 1905. Attacks throughout the entire Urals region remained tame by Russian standards, though still sadly tragic four Jews were killed in Ufa, and one Jew and one Russian perished in Yekaterinburg at the time. Only slightly higher death tolls occurred in Vyatka and Chelyabinsk (Antropova 2004). Without question, local Black Hundreds, Bundist socialists, revolutionary socialists, Zionists, and Islamic Revivalists were active in the years leading up to the outbreak of World War I; yet they never gained the traction of their brethren in other regions around the empire (Antropova 2004).

Many factors promoted a frontier-like sensibility of live and let live, among them being the fact that Yekaterinburg was not as large as it was economically important. People, no matter how different, were not complete strangers to one another. Moreover, the city's intellectual achievements, though often considerable, were of a practical rather than ideological bent. Saint Petersburg, by contrast, has arguably spawned or imported every major Russian ideological movement for the past 300 years, from Peter the Great's imperial, absolutist modernization idea to today's postmodernist hyperrealism.

In Yekaterinburg, the best and brightest throughout the Urals region focused their attention on how to get things done. Intellectual, ideological, political, artistic, and even architectural fashions arrived somewhat later there than in the cosmopolitan artistic centers of European Russia; and when they arrived, they often became more grounded in the realities of everyday life (Bukharkina 2000; and Beliaev 2005).

The practicality of intellectual life in the Urals is reflected in the region's primary prerevolutionary scientific honor, an annual award established by Imperial chamberlain Pavel Nikolaevich Demidov in 1831. The awards promoted the work in physics, chemistry, geology, biology, astronomy, and the earth sciences before being suspended in 1866 in accordance with the original bequest a quarter century after Demidov's death. Reconstituted in 1993, the contemporary incarnation of the Demidov Prize more often recognizes work in the humanities and social sciences (Ponizovkin 1996).

Yekaterinburg was constantly at the center of many events that shaped Russia's destiny. The city was the focal point of intense fighting during the Russian Civil War, and after the Bolshevik Revolution, the basement of one of the city's merchant houses—Ipatiev House—became the scene of the bloody execution of Russia's royal family—Tsar Nicholas, his wife Alexandra, his four daughters, and his son and trusted aides—on July 17, 1918 (Service 1997, 107).

Half-dozen years later, in 1924, the city was renamed for Yakov Sverdlov, the Bolshevik who gave the final order for their execution (Harris 1999, 102). This moniker would remain until the collapse of the Soviet Union in 1991 (though the surrounding province, or oblast, has retained the Sverdlovsk name). Boris Yeltsin, then the Sverdlovsk regional party first secretary, dispatched wrecking crews in the middle of an autumn 1977 night to tear the house down on orders from then–KGB chairman Iurii Andropov (Aron 2000, 112–114).

During the Soviet period, Stalin's Great Leap Forward, beginning with the inauguration of the First Five-Year Plan in 1928, stimulated further growth (Kropotov and Litovskaya 2010, 45–46). The city became home to numerous heavy industrial plants, including the largest machinery plant in a "European economy," the giant Uralmash works (Davies 1994, 135–57; Krzhivitskaia, Molchanova, Fedorova, and Shcherbenok 2010a, 92–201). The city exploded, with tens of thousands of new residents streaming in to fill the factories that were springing up all around (Luk'ianin, 2008). Moreover, Uralmash, which opened on July 15, 1933, was not just a factory (Kropotov and Litovskaya 2010, 51–54). The project also included a gigantic new "socialist city" (sotsgorod) for more than 100,000 workers and their families that had been built according to the principles of "disurbanization," which called for massive decentralized housing—with commercial blocks covering between 6 and 10 hectares, on which housing surrounded by tree-lined allées opened onto green areas, with sports, education, and cultural facilities carefully spaced and mixed together with stores and worker kitchens (fabrika kukhnia) (Rastorguev, Tokmeninova, and Fol'pert, 2011).

In many ways, the new industrial city became revolution-inspired Sverdlovsk, while the city's imperial historic center evolved into an appendage (one that would eventually be connected to the industrial city by a single subway line that opened in the 1990s). This distinction between the older and newer cities underscored a central cleavage within Soviet society between the industrial proletariat and the urban intelligentsia. For the intelligentsia, the Uralmash neighborhood and its residents were only "semicivilized."

The new socialist city that grew up around Uralmash is but part of the story of the city's Stalinist reinvention (Luk'ianin, 2008). The entire town was being rebuilt, as German, Polish, and Moscow architects, representing the latest avant-garde styles, designed one of the most impressive concentrations of modernist Constructivist and Bauhausian buildings—about 140 structures—to be found anywhere (Luk'ianin 2008; Rastorguev 2011; Freedman 2013). Major cultural institutions sprang up, and were housed, at times, in buildings of the latest Constructivist style (Krzhivitskaia, Molchanova, Fedorova, and Shcherbenok 2010b, 101–3). Although the local opera house had opened in 1912 and featured opera and ballet companies dating back many decades before, the city's musical comedy theater was only founded years later, in 1932—as were its puppet theater, also founded in 1932; the local conservatory, in 1934; various literary museums, throughout the 1920s and 1930s; and its renowned folk chorus, in 1943 (Gilyova 2010; Turbanov 2010; Demidova 2011; Luk'ianin 1996; Aron 2000, 106–8). Consequently, the city's growth as a vibrant cultural center paralleled its rise as an industrial giant. Beyond the performing arts, these institutions encouraged local youth to embrace cultural pursuits through their connections to the region's vast factories and industrial enterprises that had grown up at the same time (Luk'ianin 2002).

Sverdlovsk escaped German occupation during World War II, becoming a major evacuation destination for important factories and educational and cultural institutions from cities further west, including Moscow and Leningrad. Today's modern and efficient international airport at Kol'tsovo initially served as a landing strip for Lend Lease flights from the United States, beginning in December 1943 (Gladkova 2000, 11). All sorts of other facilities, together with their operating specialists, remained after the war, creating a powerful urban center dominating a vast region astride the Soviet Union's geographic center (Harris 1999, 32–36). They were joined by exiled notables, including the World War II hero Marshal Konstantin Zhukov, together with engineers and mathematicians, artists and lawyers, and writers and musicians who had fallen prey to Stalin's last purges against Jewish "cosmopolitans" (Aron 2000, 13). Several of contemporary Yekaterinburg's cultural luminaries, such as the popular poet-playwright-actor Vladimir Balashov, trace their familial connections to the city during this era (Luk'ianin, 2002). Others, such as the local literary lion Valentin Lukyanin, arrived somewhat later to study and work in local industry (Luk'ianin 2008).

The postwar city had grown to become home to slightly more than one million people. Cold War Sverdlovsk was a focal point for Soviet military industrial production, which drew on both the city's many factories and its numerous research facilities. Uralmash produced the famous T34 tank and its Cold War successors, together with critical aviation and rocketry components, as well as the giant heavy machinery that propelled the Soviet industrial machine for decades.

DYNAMISM AND STAGNATION

The consequences of such concentration of military-industrial-research capacity in the city proved to be both positive and negative. In 1979, a local research site specializing in biological warfare accidentally released anthrax into the atmosphere, leading to one of the worst biological contaminations of a civilian population in history (Guillemin 2002). Moreover, Soviet-era Sverdlovsk's important role in defense research and development as well as industrial production prompted the authorities to limit access to the city, which meant that foreigners and unapproved Soviet citizens were banned from crossing its boundaries.

On a more positive note, the city's overall significance for the Soviet defense effort amplified the region's political status and power (Aron 2000, 52–105). Local political leaders developed their own distinctive style with roots in the region's past. As Yeltsin's biographer, Leon Aron, writes, "Yekaterinburg's unique history, demography, and industry contributed to the emergence of what might be called the Ural school of Communist Party leadership. As a rule, the Ural Party bosses were competent, tough, independent, strong, seemingly incorruptible, even austere, and direct" (Aron 2000, 14).

By the mid-1980s, the incoming Communist Party general secretary, Mikhail Gorbachev, was raiding the local elites for effective administrators. He brought Sverdlovsk's Communist Party regional first secretary, Yeltsin, to Moscow to tear apart the capital's entrenched local party elite. Gorbachev similarly summoned Uralmash's director, Nikolai Ryzhkov, to the Kremlin, where he became the general secretary's longest-serving prime minister (holding the office from 1985 until 1991) (Aron 2000, 48–128).

As home to the sorts of pragmatic intellectuals needed to produce giant machinery and weapons of mass destruction, the city likewise generated a vibrant theatrical and musical life. Sverdlovsk remained innovative, even during the years that became known as the "Brezhnev Era of Stagnation [Zastoi]." Because it was closed to the outside world, and therefore out of the Soviet mainstream, the local scene enjoyed many more degrees of freedom of expression than larger, more open cities that were closer to the Soviet heartland (Luk'ianin 2008). This vitality was especially visible in popular music.

Brezhnev era Sverdlovsk emerged as one of the Soviet Union's most creative centers for rock 'n' roll music, rivaled only by Leningrad (now Saint Petersburg). Its distinctive "Urals Rock" movement (led by such bands as Urfin Dzhyus, Chaif, Nautilus Pompilius, Nastya, Trek, Agata Kristi, and Smyslovye Galliustinatsii) transformed late Soviet and post-independence Russian popular music.

Beyond rock, nonconformist artists such as Evgeny Malakhin, known as "Bukashkin" (a small insect), sustained a vibrant underground art scene that was known as far away as Moscow, Saint Petersburg, and Odessa. The city's homegrown literary journal, *Ural'skii sledopyt* (Ural Pathfinder), established itself as the Soviet Union's leading outlet without peer for science fiction. And the region's more traditional, "thick" literary journal, *Ural*, remained one of the leading outlets for creative writing outside the political and cultural capitals of Moscow and Leningrad.

Given the Soviet policy of establishing a full range of cultural and educational institutions in cities with more than one million residents, Yekaterinburg simultaneously offered a complete range of official theaters, covering all major genres of dance; opera; philharmonic, choral, and chamber music; drama; musical comedy and operettas; children's theater; and the circus arts. All these institutions were supported by the local Communist Party's leadership, though not without interference and controversy (Aron 2000, 106–8). These state-supported cultural institutions steadfastly sustained high-quality companies for ballet, opera, musical comedy, modern dance, puppet, and dramatic theater. Later, more independent ventures, such as Natalia Baganova's internationally recognized Provincial Dance Company, would readily find audiences that had been nurtured by the larger local companies (Freedman 2013).

The city's dynamism could, however, take other, less savory forms. Multigenerational criminal gangs, which would win the city the dubious title of post–Soviet Russia's "crime capital" during the 1990s, in fact were created and thrived during the Brezhnev era. The same advantages of geography that allowed the city to link east and west also attracted criminal groups, which easily penetrated its tough local working-class culture while attracting into their bands former convicts released from camps to the east (Handelman1995, 73–92, 234–37, 332–47). The very attributes which made cities a center of pragmatic diversity reemerged once the straitjacket of Soviet centralism loosened. As they did, Yekaterinburg became a relevant case for comparison with industrial cities worldwide.

MANAGING MIGRATION

Local elites leveraged the region's political connections during the Yeltsin presidency to attract international attention (there currently are over a dozen consulates in the city) as well as foreign investment. In 2010, prior to the imposition of Western economic sanctions follow Russia's annexation of Crimea four years later, *Forbes* magazine described Yekaterinburg as among the best sustainable business climates within the Russian Federation. As elsewhere in Russia, Yekaterinburg needed to attract migrants from around the country and beyond if it is to benefit from sustained economic growth. Unlike many other Russian cities, the political leaders of Yekaterinburg set out to do so. The city, in fact, became a major destination for transnational seasonal and permanent migrants.

While still a predominantly Russian city, Yekateriburg experienced increasingly active migration networks with Tajikistan, and the surrounding Sverdlovskaia region (oblast). Local Tadjik leaders claimed, for example, that between 150,000 and 200,000 Tajiks had fled to the city and region since the end of the Tajik Civil War in 1997 (Mirzoyev 2010). Tajiks were the largest—but not the only—immigrant community that had come to the city in recent years. Significant Uzbek, Chinese, and Kyrgyz communities could be found as well.

Goodwill in and of itself has not proven sufficient ground for the promotion of diversity and tolerance. Local officials believed that the first hurdle to ensure that migrants are properly treated is to have them officially registered, thereby making them less vulnerable to harassment by the police and more able to switch jobs and residences. Accordingly, the region's commissioner on human rights, nongovernmental agencies in the region, and several consulates actively assisted immigrants to properly file all the necessary documentation for legal residence in the Russian Federation (Merzliakovo 2010; and Orozbaev 2010). In 2007 city officials approached a new nongovernmental organization called Urals' Home (Ural'skii dom) to develop an integrated "migration bridge" that would provide support structures for migrants from Kyrgyzystan (Drobina 2009; Artemova 2010).

At a time when many Russian cities were losing population, Yekaterinburg slowly grew, in no small measure due to the arrival of migrants from neighboring Central Asian countries. The city showed signs of becoming increasingly attractive to skilled workers. By the time of the 2010 census, the city's population stabilized at 1,350,100 residents. The relative proportion of professionals and medical personnel within the Yekaterinburg Kyrgyz community increased as local officials regularized the migrant experience. Some of those professionals, as well as their colleagues from other migrant communities, found work teaching in the city's numerous secondary schools and institutions of higher education.

UNCONTROLLED CARTELS

As noted above, Brezhenev era Sverdlovsk had a reputation as one of the most criminally violent in the entire Soviet Union (Finckenauer and Voronin, 2001, 3–16). The same factors that enriched its economic and cultural life also made it a natural center for vice. The city was sufficiently far from Moscow to be beyond its direct control yet close enough to remain within reach and close enough to the Siberian prisons to become a magnet for newly released prisoners (Ruble 1999). It stood astride major transportation routes connecting narcotics-growing fields to the south and east and drug markets to the west, with a vast population of factory workers and their families who were beginning to feel the first indications of a national economic collapse that would shut down their factories. Everything about the city promoted the emergence of vast, disciplined, aggressive, and malevolent bands of armed criminals, hangers-on, and wannabes (Voronin 1998).

As the Soviet industrial economy collapsed in the late 1980s and early 1990s, criminal cartels moved in to lay claim to the region's vast mineral wealth; to seize and dismantle the vast factories that could only be used as scrap; to sell off light and heavy weaponry from military bases that were no longer under any form of discernible control; to traffic in desperate human beings trying to find some way to survive; to push drugs, and to launder their profits; and to extort more (Voronin 1998). The larger "mafiyas," such as Tsentral'nye (which grew up around the Central Market), the Afgantsy (made up of Afghan war veterans), the Siniye (a gang of former prisoners), and the Azerbaizhantsy (consisting of criminals from the former Soviet republic branched out into many areas (Voronin 1998, 7–8). Other gangs, which were often rooted in specific enterprises (such as the powerful and massive Uralmash gang, and the less potent Miko-Invest and Sakirtan cartels) tended to specialize in their operations (Voronin 1998).

The transition taking place in the criminal world paralleled the larger transformations in the Soviet and post-Soviet economy. The Centrals (Tsentral'nye) dominated the city during the late Soviet period as they exerted control over an energetic black-market trade in goods and services that initially was based at the central market and spread out from there. With the decline of the Uralmash plant, a group of former professional sportsmen, their friends, and relatives from the neighborhoods surrounding the factory began to seize the assets of the once-gigantic plant. Their gang, which coalesced by 1991, entered turf battles with the older Centrals, unleashing a brutal and massive gang war between the two groups following the June 16, 1991 assassination of the Uralmash boss Grigorii Tsyganov. Explosions, shootings, and murders became a daily occurrence from 1992 until 1994, with Yekaterinburg becoming known as the most criminal-plagued city in Russia.

The Uralmash gang emerged victorious by late 1994, forcing the Centrals out of much of their original territory. Uralmash operatives allegedly expanded their horizons, reputedly laying claim to various local, regional, and national political positions. Having become increasingly secure, Uralmash began to go "legit," reportedly taking over legal real estate, hotels, industrial, financial, and construction businesses in Russia and abroad in Europe and the United States.

Gang control of the city hardly disappeared, even as tactics evolved from less-licit to more-licit activities. By the late 1990s, an estimated 60% of all enterprises in Yekaterinburg were controlled by criminal organizations, while between 70% and 80% of private and privatized firms and commercial banks were said to pay protection money to criminal groups, corrupt officials, and racketeers (Voronin 1998, 8).

More generally, numerous successful gangs expanded their drug, arms, and nuclear materials trading worldwide through outposts in Cyprus, India, the United States, Poland, Germany, and China (Voronin 1998, 6–7). Many still busied themselves by victimizing residents. In November 1997, a quarter of all city residents claimed to have themselves been victims of crime (Voronin 1998, 12). This mayhem would come under official control slowly during the late 1990s and early 2000s, as local, regional, and national political leaders began to persistently impose coherence on the Russian state.

By the time Vladimir Putin became Russian president, the Uralmash gang had become well situated to avoid a direct confrontation with the more centralized Russian state, in large measure because it had already left its more overtly criminal activities behind. But its underlying network of criminal power undoubtedly remained in place (Bloomfield 2008). Foot soldiers were easily recruited in a city where tens of thousands of young factory workers could not find a job. Mafiya bands, some associated with the Centrals, others associated with Uralmash, and others not associated at all, including at least 76 organized and countless more unorganized groups, fought over turf, leading to an especially pernicious outburst of widespread urban violence, death, and havoc (Voronin 1998, 7).

As younger and younger gang members fell in this onslaught, a local culture grew up promoting opulent funeral services, in which the deceased gangsters were laid to rest under ever more ornate tombstones (Hutchinson 1997). Two competing cemeteries on the opposite sides of Yekaterinburg filled up with the extravagant graves of criminals who had been rubbed out by other criminals. The 1994 tombstone of Central boss Mikhail Kuchin, for example, is a 10-foot-high malachite monument encrusted with precious stones, with Kuchin's carved visage holding the keys to his beloved Mercedes-Benz and wearing a designer suit over an unbuttoned shirt displaying an Orthodox Christian cross (Matich 1998).

At least one local gangster, Evgenii Monakh, turned his attention to writing detective stories. The son of a well-placed family that included a teacher of philosophy in a Communist Party school, he turned to a life of crime, and in 1994 he began to write about his experiences with vibrant, colorful style. Two years later, he was dead, the victim of the sort of story he himself celebrated as an author (Bonet 1996). His last story, "Smiling before Death," appeared in a special double issue of *Ural*, bringing local literary and criminal life full circle (Monakh 1996).

A world in spectacular meltdown places human vice on prominent display and forces survivors to find meaning wherever they can. Where is human dignity to be found in a world so full of violence and degradation? Does it matter? Are there limits to unbridled cynicism? What does it mean to be human? How can one show the human being at his or her absolute most perverse and still find honor? Such themes, not surprisingly, came to dominate local literature and dramaturgy in Yekaterinburg. They provided the fodder for the creative impulses that could be supported by the institutional foundations provided by journals and theaters, enriched by a distinctive urban "soul" fervently being expressed in pop music and culture.

As was the case everywhere across Russia, after the demise of the Soviet Union, local leaders in Yekaterinburg were left on their own to confront the terrible dislocations of post-Soviet deindustrialization. They tried with varying degrees of success to parlay connections with their former colleagues in Moscow to open the city and its economy to the world at large, to sustain a population hovering above one million souls. Two decades later, the city's continued vitality demonstrates these local leaders' general success.

AN UNOFFICIAL CULTURAL "SECOND FRONT"

Such pragmatism toward diversity found expression in the city's distinctive cultural policies during the Brezhnev years. As the harshest elements of the Stalinist police state began to recede following the Great Leader's death in 1953, a distinctive Soviet youth culture at odds with official ideology began to emerge. The first Soviet rock 'n' roll bands appeared in Estonia and Latvia, and eventually in Moscow and Leningrad, during the early 1960s. The new music took off by mid-decade with the arrival of the Beatles over shortwave radios and, eventually, contraband cassette tape recordings (Troitsky 1998, 22–29). By the 1970s, Soviet rock bands had found their own worldview.

The genre swept the country, with homegrown groups such as Mashina Vremini (Time Machine), Akvarium (Aquarium), and Zvuki Mu (the Sounds of Mu) grabbing large followings in the Urals region. Their popularity forced the Communist Party and state bureaucrats lording over official culture to sponsor their own, tamer equivalents and to elevate politically neutral disco music and dancing to the level of a cultural icon (Troitsky 1998, 30–50).

A quasi-underground Soviet rock scene thrived in the dark shadows of official institutions, such as those attached to Sverdlovsk's massive factories, including restaurants and workers' clubs, palaces of culture, and on festival stages often controlled by Young Communist League (Komsomol), trade union, and factory officials. Rock music and video salons became a meaningful source of income for official institutions as well as for their officers (Ramet, 1994). Some speculate that these revenues became the basis for the primitive accumulation of capital during the Gorbachev years, eventually enabling officials to move into the privatization of metals, coal, natural gas, and oil as the Soviet Union collapsed (Zhuk 2010).

Ever more portable recording technologies allowed musicians to spread their sound across the entire Soviet Union so that, by the 1980s, a robust, complex, and varied rock music culture had taken root, ranging from ubiquitous disco groups to punk and everything in between (Troitsky 1998, 50–96). Soviet rock survived a round of repression unleashed in 1984 by disgruntled cultural overlords who had taken advantage of the rapid turnover of Communist Party general secretaries following Brezhnev's death in late 1982.

Yekaterinburg's rock scene remained distinctive in important ways. By the early 1980s, talented and creative bands emerged in the city, which combined a pop sound with sharp critiques of social problems. Vyacheslav Butusov's Nautilius Pampilius in the 1980s and the Samoilov brothers' Agata Kristi in the 1990s brought together the gloomy longings of a "lost generation" with songs of love and social protest. The group Chaif (from the local slang word for "pleasure," derived from the Russian word for tea), perhaps the longest-running group, dating back to the 1980s and continuing on stage for a third of a century and more, proudly declared its connection to its native city, both in song and in charitable activities (Troitsky 1988; Stites 1992).

These bands, and others like them, were the creations of the "technical intelligentsia" that dominated the city. Some band members were trained architects; others were conservatory graduates. For instance, Yulia Chicherina (a descendant of Lenin's and Stalin's commissar of foreign affairs, Georgii Chicherin) spent her childhood years as a serious music student and later formed the popular band named Chicherina that continues to perform around Russia today.

Bands like hers combined philosophical thought, social criticism, musical sophistication, and a drive for a rollicking good time to create songs that distinguished the "Urals Rock" sound from other Russian rock styles. Collectively, their music reflected the preoccupation of youth with an urban culture and intellectual sensibility who seek to integrate a sharp critical perspective while not shying away from the ugly realities of life. They have helped to define their city's special sense of self, which the local writer Valentin Lukyanov has identified as its distinctive "soul" (Luk'ianin 2008).

THE "PROVINCIAL" WRITTEN WORD

The local pragmatic approach to cultural policy evident in music extended to the written word. Struggling to gain control over an entrenched Communist Party elite, the rising leader Nikita Khrushchev undertook the first of what would become an unending, three-and-a-half-decade stream of failed reforms that sought to make the Soviet economy more efficient while breaking the stranglehold of the party's elite (nomenklatura) over the country. In January 1957, Khrushchev announced that he would reorganize the country's economic system by separating agricultural and industrial bureaucracies into parallel sets of regional economic councils (sovnarkhozy), which simultaneously would merge several political regions into larger transregional units. Despite subsequent refinements, the new system created more chaos than efficiency, helping to lead to the October 1964 internal Communist Party coup that removed Khrushchev from office. As one of the designated sovnarkhoz seats, Yekaterinburg was poised to receive recognition normally reserved for the capitals of the various union republics (e.g., to use their post–Soviet Union names, Kyiv in Ukraine, Almaty in Kazakhstan, Tbilisi in Georgia, and Bishkek in Kyrgyzstan). Literary journals were among the accoutrements of status.

During the days of the USSR, the preponderance of literary publications in the Russian Federation had been based in Moscow and Leningrad, with new regional journals being launched in Vladivostok at the end of World War II, and in Arkhangelsk to the far north in 1965 (Luk'ianin 2008). As a result, "provincial" writers had little opportunity to publish their works independently from the official overlords in Moscow. Some regional journals from the early Soviet era such as Sverdlovsk's *Shturn* and *Ural'skii sledopyt* held on until Stalin centralized cultural institutions during the mid-1930s. And some annual literary almanacs such as Sverdlovsk's *Ural'skii sovremennik*, which would continue to be published for 37 years, sprang up around the country to fill this gap. But none of these publications attained the reverence preserved in Russian literary circles for the sacred "thick" journal the name evoking its serious literary intent as well as its physical heft; which, since the late nineteenth century, has been the preferred outlet for Russian creative writing (Luk'ianin 2008).

Moscow's and Leningrad's prestigious thick journals such as *Novyi Mir*, *Znayia*, and *Druzhba narodov* led the literary explosion of publishing once-banned works that would become known as "the Thaw." Seeing an opportune moment, Sverdlovsk's and its region's writers moved quickly to replicate the success of the central journals at a regional level, using the city's new status as a sovnarkhoz center to leverage support from regional party and state authorities.

Thus, in 1957 Vadim Ocheretin and other writers relaunched *Ural'skii Sledopyt*, a journal that had managed to run for nine issues in 1935 before succumbing to Communist Party censorship. Ocheretin and his successor Soviet-era editors (Vladimir Shustov, Ivan Akulov, and the two-decade-serving Stanislav Meshavkin) firmly established the reborn journal as the premier outlet for science fiction writing in the Soviet Union, gaining international recognition for their efforts. By publishing homegrown Soviet authors as well as translations of international writers, *Ural'skii Sledopyt* developed a cult following that reached far beyond the Urals region. The journal's Aelita Festival became the Soviet Union's premier event showcasing science fiction, bringing the genre's most talented writers to Yekaterinburg each year. They simultaneously used the journal as a platform to promote a discussion of environmental concerns, both within the region and nationally throughout the Soviet Union, while focusing on regional literary history from time to time.

In addition, the Regional Communist Party Committee (Obkom) designated Ocheretin as the editor of a second, broad-based thick literary journal, *Ural*, which was intended to showcase regional writers and themes. Given that it was managed by the local division of the official Writers' Union and was overseen by party officials, *Ural* focused on promoting a regional identity among local writers (Orlov 2002).

After a number of political interventions by the party, including reprimands and dismissals of early editors, the journal firmly secured its stature as a leading regional literary journal once Valentin Lukyanin assumed its editorship in 1980. Lukyanin set out to promote the works of young authors; expand *Ural*'s focus to include plays as well as short stories, novels, and poems; and reach out to a wider community through discussion clubs and other events (Artiushina 2007). He, too, would prompt political controversy.

In 1982, Lukyanin serially published Konstantin Lagunov's novel Bronzovyi dog (The Bronze Mastiff) in *Ural*'s August, September, and October issues (Aron 2000, 118–20). The journal included almost documentary reportage tied together by fictionalized narratives, offering a "portrayal of the true face of the oil barons" of the West Siberian petroleum belt in the neighboring Tyumen Region. In his chronicle of shocking transgressions against "communist morality," many of Lagunov's characterizations presaged the behavior of post-Soviet Russian oil oligarchs.

Tyumen party and state officials immediately expressed their outrage with the regional party first secretary, Georgii Bogomyakov, probably telephoning his Sverdlovsk counterpart Yeltsin about the matter. Meanwhile, the journal's readership skyrocketed, and letters of support started pouring in from around the country.

The Lagunov Affair had hardly simmered down when Lukyanin proposed publishing Nikokai Nikonov's story (povest') "Starikova gora" (The Old

Man's Mountain) in the journal's January 1983 issue. Set in the fictional village of Makarovka, Nikonov's tale exposed the social pathologies and degradations of Soviet rural life a half century after collectivization, ending with the line "The land was waiting for its owner" (Aron 2000, 119–23; Nikonov, 1990). Given the brutality of collectivization in the region (the infamously legendary pioneer (scout) Pavlik Morozov, who condemned his father by denouncing him to the authorities, lived in the region's Gerasimovka village) Nikonov was poking at an even rawer nerve than Lagunov had.

Uncertain censors turned the galley proofs of the January 1983 *Ural* issue over to the Regional Party Committee, which deleted approximately one-sixth of the text. Once published, *Ural* became the object of an array of attacks by the Communist Party and KGB. Eventually, in May 1983, Lukyanin was summoned to a meeting of the committee's Executive Bureau, where he was excoriated by First Secretary Yeltsin and other members of his team for four and a half hours. After a public admission of serious shortcomings, Lukyanin held onto his editorial position, while Lagunov and Nikonov avoided official sanctions. And copies of the January 1983 issue of *Ural* remained hidden away in most regional libraries despite a Communist Party order that they be destroyed.

Ural exerted a primal force of gravity, around which the region's literary life could grow and flourish. It published articles focusing on local and regional history as well as traditions, cultural life, and peculiarities, thus giving definition to a distinctive regional identity (Kiseleva 1996). Its very existence provided an outlet for the range of the region's various authors of competing styles and temperaments from across Siberia, both young and old (Slobozhaninova 2008).

Lukyanin's catholic embrace of a regional literary vision reflected the pragmatic tolerance that so marked the region and proved to be especially important for promoting local writers during the height of the Brezhnev era (Leiderman 2000). Consequently, as with rock music, nonconformist artists, local novelists, short story writers, poets, literary and theatrical critics, and playwrights maintained their distinctive voices. These efforts gained additional outside support from many prominent writers from throughout the Urals and beyond, such as Lev Davydychev in Perm, Evgenii Ananyev in Tyumen, and Viktor Astafyev in Krasnoyarsk (Leiderman 2000).

Ural became such a beloved institution that, in the late 1990s, when its existence was in question due to the various economic and other uncertainties of post-Soviet life, prominent local authors stepped in to breathe new life into the journal. The internationally renowned Yekaterinburg playwright and dramatist Nikolai Kolyada took over the journal's editorial offices in July 1999, at a time when its official subscription numbers had dropped to a mere 300, and when there were no more manuscripts in the queue to be published. He parlayed his connections to attract new writers, linking the journal to theater festivals and generally making *Ural* essential reading for anyone interested in the New Russian Writing movement. A decade later, he passed the journal along to the worthy hands of his protégé, the internationally renowned local playwright Oleg Bogaev, who is expanding the journal's readership on the Internet (Kolyada 2008).

WORDS ON STAGE AS WELL AS ON THE PAGE

Kolyada during this time became a center of gravity around which much of the new drama world of Yekaterinburg revolved. In December 2001, he founded his own company, the Kolyada Theatre, which initially performed at Pushkin House in a historic Yekaterinburg neighborhood. In 2004, the company moved to its own small stage in a nineteenth-century mansion, where it performed a contemporary repertoire for adults and children's plays for younger audiences. But trouble loomed, with the company being displaced after a fire, only regaining cramped temporary quarters after raucous protests, hunger strikes by Kolyada himself, and the eventual intervention of Sverdlovsk governor Alexander Misharin in November 2010.

Though operating with almost no state funding, Kolyada kept his company together at times by asking its members to bring in any items that they no longer needed at home, and by drawing on the considerable international interest in his work to secure support for his actors and protégés. Following the announcement of a new 2012 tour in France, one of his lead actors evidently exclaimed, "What, Paris again?" Plans for a newly constructed permanent home for the company were announced in March 2011 (Kolyada 2011).

Kolyada soon attracted controversy. Unlike many among the Russian intelligentsia, he publicly and enthusiastically embraced the 2012 candidacy of Prime Minister Vladimir Putin for a return term as Russian president. Appearing on the popular local talk TV show *Enin*, Kolyada explained that he believed "we cannot find a better leader. I will vote for him that is my opinion and my right. All others on offer seem absolutely unworthy to assume such a position" (Freedman 2012). The move brought Kolyada a wave of outrage and approbation from many former supporters, combined with charges that he had sold out to those in power to secure his new theater. This anger threatened to undermine many of Kolyada's other projects, such as local festivals. In the end, Kolyada was able to secure his new theater (though the challenges of the Covid-19 pandemic in 2020 brought the company perilously close to shutting down).

The local theater scene proved more vibrant than the political controversies swirling around Kolyada might imply. Beyond Kolyada himself, several

Yekaterinburg playwrights have contributed to the transformation of writing for the Russian stage. At least four among them—Vassily Sigarev, Oleg Bogayev, and the Presnyakov brothers, Vladimir and Oleg—have become international sensations on their own terms. These leading playwrights—as well as lesser authors emerging from Kolyada's nest—wrote and directed plays about troops returning from Chechnya, haunting encounters by soldiers with their past, living spirits and dying souls, the tragedy of terrorism (e.g., plays about the 2004 attack on a school in the Caucasus town of Beslan), and harsh depictions of corruption, infidelity, alcoholism, drug abuse, the indignities of age, and social inequality (Freedman 2012; Arkhipov 2004). The theater thus became a forum for stimulating discussion around some of the city's—and nation's—most troubling issues.

BACK TO THE FUTURE

Shoup's proposal that subnational political entities might help bridge the divide between Soviet Studies of the time and social science disciplinary trends might easily have been passed over had Fleron's volume not become a highly valued addition to the curricula of courses on Soviet politics. The suggestion, however, spoke to students at the time because it set up a way forward for meaningful integration of Soviet Studies and political science. As the example of Yekaterinburg reveals, meaningful comparisons which add to both the study of the post-Soviet realm and to political science empirical research and theory become possible once researchers ask different questions. Fleron's commitment to tilting the frame for posing research queries helped make such exciting research possible.

REFERENCES

Ames, Edward. 1947. "A Century of Russian Railroad Construction: 1837–1938." *American Slavic and East European Review* 6, nos. 3–4: 57–74.

Antropova, Irina. 2004. "Iz istorii evreev Urala." *Ural*, no. 11. http:/uraljournal.ru/archive

Arkhipov, Aleksandr. 2004. "Dembel'skii poezd: P'esa v odnom deist'vii." *Ural*, no. 5.

Aron, Leon. 2000. *Yeltsin: A Revolutionary Life.* London: HarperCollins.

Artemova, Irina. 2010. "Patent dlia migranta." *Ural'skii rabochii*, December 21.

Artiushina, Valentina. 2007. "Dva resiatiletiia v *Ural* sovetskogo perioda." *Ural*, no. 8.

Bartov, Arkadii. 2005. "Mif Sankt-Peterburga: Etalon giperreal'nosti i kul'tura vtorichnosti." *Ural*, no. 8.

Bavil'skii, Dmitrii. 1996. "Demidovskii vremennik." *Ural*, no. 2.

Beliaev, Sergei. 2005. "Vecher budetlian: Nemuzykal'nie sametko o muzykal'nom zale." *Ural*, no. 11.

Bloomfield, Adrian. 2008. "Russian Mafia Killings Threaten Putin Legacy." *Telegraph (London)*, February 22.

Bonet, Pilar. 1996. "Evgenii Monakh prevratil svoi kriminal'nyi opyt' v pisatel'skuiu zolotuiu zhilu." *Ural*, nos. 11–12.

Bukharkina, Ol'ga. 2000. "Vdol' po ulitse po glavnoi." *Ural*, no. 12.

Davies, R. W. 1994. "Industry Under Central Planning, 1929–1941." In *The Economic Transformation of the Soviet Union, 1913–1945*, edited by R. W. Davies, Mark Harrison, and S. C. Wheatcroft, 135–157. New York: Cambridge University Press.

Demidova, Sofia. 2011. "Deistvo v Sverdlovske." *Ural*, no. 6.

Deutsch, Nathaniel. 2011. *The Jewish Dark Continent: Life and Death in the Russian Pale of Settlement*. Cambridge: Harvard University Press.

Drobina, Izol'da. 2009. "Gastarbaitery domoi ne toropiatsia." *Ural'skii rabochii*, January 23.

Finckenauer, James O., and Yuri A. Voronin. 2001. *The Threat of Russian Organized Crime*, 3–16. Washington: National Institute of Justice of US Department of Justice.

Fleron, Frederic J., Jr. 1969a. *Communist Studies and the Social Sciences: Essays on Methodology and Empirical Theory*. Chicago: Rand McNally & Co.

Fleron, Frederic J., Jr. 1969b. "Toward a Reconceptualization of Political Change in the Soviet Union: The Political Leadership System." In *Communist Studies and the Social Sciences*, edited by Frederick J. Fleron, Jr., 222–243. Chicago: Rand McNally & Co.

Freedman, John. 2012. "A Playwright for Putin." *Moscow Times*, January 24.

Freedman, John. 2013a. "Russia's 'Third Cultural Center,' Yekaterinburg." *Moscow Times*, May 26, 2013.

Freedman, John. 2013b. "Yekaterinburg, the Capital of Constructivism." *Moscow Times*, June 22, 2013.

FSGS. 2010. *Vserossiiskaia perepis' naseleniia 2009 goda. Goroda s chislennost'iu postoiannogo naseleniia 1 mil.Chelovek i bolee.Tablitsa 17, 80–88, at 80*. Moscow: Federal'nais sluzhba gosudarstvennoi statistiki.

Gilyova, Raisa. 2010. "Boites' snobizma: Otbiraite istinno prekrasnoe." *Ural*, no. 12.

Gladkova, Inna. 2000. "Belyi dom iz krasnogo kirpicha." *Ural*, no. 11.

Guillemin, Jeanne. 2002. "The 1979 Anthrax Epidemic in the USSR: Applied Science and Political Controversy." *Proceedings of the American Philosophical Society* 146, no. 1: 18–36.

Hahn, Jeffrey H., ed. 2001. *Regional Russia in Transition: Studies From Yaroslavl'*. Baltimore: The Johns Hopkins and Woodrow Wilson Center Presses.

Handelman, Stephen. 1995. *Comrade Criminal: Russia's New Mafiya*. New Haven: Yale University Press.

Harris, James R. 1999. *The Great Urals: Regionalism and the Evolution of the Soviet Union*. Ithaca: Cornell University Press.

Hutchinson, Samuel. 1997. "Whacked But Not Forgotten." *New York Times Magazine*, April 13.

Kiseleva, E. 1996. "Strannyi gorod." *Ural*, no. 4.

Kolyada, Nikolai. 2008. "Zhurnalu *Ural:* 50 Let." *Ural*, no. 1.

Kolyada, Nikolai. 2011. "Vse eto nachinalos' s nulia, s nulia, s nulia." *Novaia gazeta*, November 28.

Kropotov, Sergei, and Maria Litovskaya. 2010. "Urban Space and Production of a Dream." In *First Ural Industrial Biennial of Contemporary Art 9.09–10.10.2010: Special Projects*, edited by Alisa Prudnikova, 43–57. Yekaterinburg: National Center for Contemporary Art.

Krzhivitskaia, Helena, Galina Molchanova, Ksenia Fedorova, and Andrey Shcherbenok. 2010a. "The Ural Heavy Engineering Plant (UZTM, Uralmashzavod)." In *First Ural Industrial Biennial of Contemporary Arts*, edited byAlisa Prudnikova, 91–100. Yekaterinburg: National Center for Contemporary Art.

Krzhivitskaia, Helena, Galina Molchanova, Ksenia Fedorova, and Andrey Shcherbenok. 2010b. "Center of Culture 'Ordzhinikidzevskiy'." In *First Ural Industrial Biennial of Contemporary Art 9.09–10.10.2010: Special Projects*, edited by Alisa Prudnikova, 101–103. Yekaterinburg: National Center for Contemporary Art.

Leiderman, Naum. 2000. "Blagodaria i vopreki: Provintsial'nyi zhurnal v gody zastoiia." *Ural*, no. 11.

Luk'ianin, Valentin. 1996. "Zhizn' posle zhizni (o 'donnykh ottozhenniakh' uralskoi literatury)." *Ural*, no. 4.

Luk'ianin, Valentin. 2002. "Smotrie chashche v nebo, gospoda." *Ural*, no. 10.

Luk'ianin, Valentin. 2008. "Gorod i dusha: Chelovek stroit gorod—gorod stroit cheloveka." *Ural*, no. 8.

Matich, Olga. 1998. "Whacked But Not Forgotten': Burying the Mob." Paper Delivered at Conference on Russia at the End of the Twentieth Century: Culture and Its Horizons in Politics and Society, Stanford University, Stanford, CA.

Merzliakovo, Tatiana. 2010. Commissioner on Human Rights in the Sverlovsk Region. Interview With Blair A. Ruble. Yekaterinburg, Russia, June 8.

Mirzoyev, Farukh. 2010. Board of the Regional Non-Governmental Institution "Solomon–Tajik Cultural Community." Interview With Blair A. Ruble. Yekaterinburg, Russia, June 8.

Monakh, Evgenii. 1996. "Ulibnis' pered smert'iu: Povest." *Ural*, nos. 11–12.

Nikonov, Nikolai. 1990. *Povesti*. Sverdlovsk: Sredne-Ural'skoe Izdatel'stvo.

Orlov, Naum. 2002. "V teatre moei pamiaty . . . Ustnye passkazy, sapisannye Dmitriem Bavil'skim." *Ural*, no. 3.

Orozbaev, Turfali. 2020. Consul General of the Kyrgyz Republic in Yekaterinburg. Interview With Blair A. Ruble. Yekaterinburg, Russia, June 9.

Ponizovkin, Andrei. 1996. "Sobitie: Laureaty demidovskoi premii." *Ural*, no. 2.

Prudnikova, Alisa, ed. 2010. *First Ural Industrial Biennial of Contemporary Art 9.09–10.10.2010: Special Projects*. Yekaterinburg: National Center for Contemporary Art.

Ramet, Sabrina. 1994. *Rocking the State: Rock Music and Politics in Eastern Europe and Russia.* Boulder: Westview Press.

Rastorguev, Andrei. 2011. "Nasledie eksperimenta: Iz istorii arkhitekturnogo avangarda na Urale." *Ural*, no. 8.

Rastorguev, Andrei, Liudmilla Tokmeninova, and Astrid Fol'pert. 2011. "Nasledie eksperimenta: Iz istorii arkhitekturnogo avangarda na Uralem." *Ural*, no. 6.

Rosan, Chrstina, Blair A. Ruble, and Joseph S. Tulchin, eds. 1999. *Urbanization, Population, Environment, and Security: A Report of the Comparative Urban Studies Project.* Washington: Woodrow Wilson International Center for Scholars.

Ruble, Blair A. 1999. "Institutional Weakness, Organized Crime and the International Arms Trade." In *Urbanization, Population, Environment, and Security: A Report of the Comparative Urban Studies Project*, edited by Christina Rosan, Blair A. Ruble, and Joseph S., 6–7. Washington: Woodrow Wilson International Center for Scholars.

Service, Robert. 1997. *A History of Twentieth-Century Russia.* Cambridge: Harvard University Press.

Shoup, Paul. 1969. "Comparing Communist Nations: Prospects for an Empirical Approach." In *Communist Studies and the Social Sciences: Essays on Methodology and Empirical Theory*, edited by Frederic J. Fleron, Jr., 6493. Chicago: Rand McNally & Co.

Slobozhaninova, Lidia. 2008. "Ural': Yavlenia obshchenatsional'noe." *Ural*, no. 1.

Starikov, A. A., V. E. Zavgel'skaia, L. I. Tokmenninova, and V. Cherniak. 2008. *Yekaterinburg: Istoriia goroda v arkhitekture.* Ekaterinburg: Sokrat.

Stites, Richard. 1992. *Russian Popular Culture: Entertainment and Society Since 1900.* New York: Cambridge University Press.

Troitsky, Artemy. 1988. *Back in the USSR: The True Story of Rock in Russia.* London: Faber & Faber.

Turbanov, Igor. 2010. "Ekaterinburg: Piat' blikov." *Ural*, no. 4.

Voronin, Yuriy. 1998. *Organized Crime: Its Influence on International Security and Urban Community Life in the Industrial Cities of the Urals, Comparative Urban Studies Occasional Paper 17.* Washington: Woodrow Wilson International Center for Scholars.

Yekaterinburg City Official Website. 2010. https://www.ekburg.ru (accessed July 15, 2021).

Zhuk, Sergei I. 2010. *Rock and Roll in the Rocket City: The West, Identity, and Ideology in Soviet Dnepropetrovsk, 1960 1985.* Washington: Woodrow Wilson Center Press and Johns Hopkins University Press.

Chapter 2

The Democratic Promise of the Putin Generation?

Cultural Legacies, Generational Cohorts, and Democratic Values in Russia

William M. Reisinger and Marina Zaloznaya

Democracy is in decline or under attack globally at present (V-Dem Institute 2020), including in long-established democracies.[1] The time is right for renewed study of democratic values.[2] The "democratic values" literature, inspired by Lipset (1960), Eckstein (1961 [1992]) and Almond and Verba (1963), now includes over six decades of comparative empirical research on public views about democracy. The key intuition of this literature is that, because democracies are regimes in which "the people rule," views held by the public broadly must be an important factor in understanding where and how democracy operates (see the discussion in Thomassen 2007). This focus on public values has its critics, including those who question the public's role at all and those who stress that values must lead to collective action for outcomes to be affected (for reviews of the literature, see Welzel 2009, Jepsen 2011, Malone 2011, Moeller and Skaaning 2013). Nevertheless, large-scale survey results conducted in dozens of countries over four-plus decades make a convincing case that the prevalence in a society of people holding democracy-supporting values influences democratization and democratic functioning worldwide (for a recent study, see Claassen 2020).

Naturally, assessing the importance of democratic values requires analyzing them in autocracies as well as in democracies. Russia is a valuable site for examining public democratic values for several reasons. A populous and powerful state, Russia is perhaps the most consequential personalist autocracy today. Understanding the support basis for its current regime is vital for policy reasons as well as for contributing to theory building. Also, the Russian public may now be poised to play a bigger role than for some time.

Questions about Russia without Vladimir Putin in charge are being discussed widely. The 2020 constitutional amendments were meant to postpone such questions but have not. Nor have 2021's drastic crackdowns on opposition made clear how the regime will secure public support going forward.

Those studying Russian democratic values in the Putin era can build on a rich literature of investigations from the Soviet period and the 1990s. The Harvard Interview Project in the early 1950s (Bauer, Inkeles, and Kluckholm 1956, Inkeles and Bauer 1959) and the Soviet Interview Project in the late 1970s and early 1980s (Millar 1987) interviewed former Soviet citizens who were then living outside the USSR to analyze citizens' views of Soviet politics, economics and society, including differences by gender, education, age, and other social categories. Nonetheless, Western scholars were excited when Soviet reforms in the late 1980s created opportunities to gather data using representative surveys and other interview techniques. The Soviet Union and, later, its successor states served as laboratories to test theories of political change. By the early 1990s, several different research teams were collaborating with in-country specialists to conduct surveys tackling, inter alia, democratic values (e.g., Miller, Reisinger, and Hesli 1990–1991, Shiller, Boycko, and Korobov 1991, Dobson and Grant 1992, Finifter and Mickiewicz 1992, Gibson, Duch, and Tedin 1992, Miller, Reisinger, and Hesli 1993, Gibson and Duch 1994, Reisinger et al. 1994; surveys of the literature include Wyman 1994, Fleron and Ahl 1998 [2017]). Frederic Fleron, who had played a significant role in bridging Soviet studies and comparative politics, contributed to this wave of survey-based investigations by helping scholars maintain clarity about the concept of political culture and the challenges of using it to analyze democratic change.

Attention to democratic values in Russia and other post-Soviet countries waned from the mid-1990s on, even though survey research as a whole in these countries continued to be strong. Russia's return to authoritarian rule lessened scholars' interest in the debates connected to the democratic values literature. The analyses that were done in the 2000s (e.g., Colton and McFaul 2002, Hale 2011) were, in a sense, downplaying the role of democratic values: they stressed that the Russian public should not be blamed for the autocratic regime. We argue, though, that scholars have strong reasons to study democratic values in Russia now just as they did three decades ago.

We examine Russian democratic values from both comparative and longitudinal perspectives using data from nationally representative surveys of the mass public's political values conducted in 1990, 1991, 1992, 1995, 1997, and 2015 in Russia, with comparisons to Ukraine, Lithuania, and Georgia. Like other recent studies (Boycko and Shiller 2016, Gaber et al. 2019, Pyle 2021), we take advantage of the ability to compare democratic values at the end of the Soviet regime with the public's values during the current regime.

Doing this is particularly valuable for Russia because an increasing share of the population has no adult memory of the Soviet period or even of the 1990s. They have only known Putin as the country's leader and been ruled by a particular form of autocracy. If they have developed distinctive outlooks and expectations, the regime will need to take those into account.

Our analyses of trends in Russia contribute to the broader comparative literature on democratic values by addressing whether commonly used measures capture enduring orientations, as theorists posit. We find that it depends on which dimensions of democratic values are being investigated. We examine seven questions reflecting widely used dimensions and find that only some show over-time stability as expected. Those that ask directly about democracy or its key institutions show the most volatility from survey to survey, suggesting they are tapping institutional trust or support more than democratic values.

In addition, we tackle two longstanding debates in the comparative literature. First, do people form their political values as youths and then largely retain those values thereafter, creating political generations that can be observed? Second, do good economic and social conditions cause people to adopt the values of the existing regime and its institutions—a prosperous democracy spurring democratic values but a prosperous autocracy creating distrust of democracy—or do such conditions give rise to democratic values even in an autocracy (Inglehart 2018)? We find that Russians' support for democratic values varies by which dimension a question captures. For many of the seven questions we examine, the level of support is low in comparative terms, though support is satisfactorily high for having competitive elections and the right to oppose government policies. Moreover, responses from 2015 are not, as might have been expected, lower than those in the 1990s. We show that this is to some extent caused by higher support for democratic values among the generation that came of age while Putin has been in power, suggesting that his authoritarian regime's success at creating economic growth and political stability may not be cementing ever stronger public support but instead creating a desire for a more liberal politics.

WHAT ARE DEMOCRATIC VALUES?

In line with Fleron's (1968 [2017]) influential discussion of concept formation and definitions, it is important to review what we mean by democratic values. Which kind of political outlooks, once they have become widespread in a society, help promote democratization and resist democratic decay? Scholars of democratic values have answered this in quite a few ways, and it is worth clarifying these ways.

First, not all the outlooks seen as supporting democracy are "values," strictly speaking. Values are beliefs involving value judgments: x is better than y. Most of the beliefs studied in the democratic values literature are, in fact, values: a person values competitive elections or not, for example. They need not all be, however. For instance, interpersonal, or societal, trust is commonly treated as a democratic value. This is the belief that most people, including those outside one's family and friends, can (or cannot) be trusted. Democracy benefits from a high level of interpersonal trust because it facilitates cooperation and acceptance of the other side's electoral victories (Almond and Verba 1963, Putnam 1993, Brehm and Rahn 1997, Newton 2001, Inglehart and Welzel 2005, Tang 2005). Interpersonal trust is an evaluative judgment about one's society rather than a value in the strict sense.

A second distinction concerns judgments about democracy as a regime type[3] versus evaluations of democracy's procedures and norms. Logically, we should expect that, when many people want their country to be governed, democratically democratic institutions and practices will gain better prospects. Those who value democracy as their political regime are more likely to defend it and play positive roles in it. Major comparative survey projects have therefore included questions asking how much the respondents value democracy for their country. The most recent wave of World Values Surveys, for example, includes a question asking whether a democratic political system is a very good, fairly good, fairly bad, or very bad way of governing the country and another asking, "How important is it for you to live in a country that is governed democratically?" (Haerpfer et al. 2020).

Despite the logic of assessing a country's level of democratic values with such questions, doing so has drawbacks. The primary one is that the term democracy has become widely, almost universally, accepted as a positive description of a political system (Inglehart 2003, Schedler and Sarsfield 2007). This pattern partly results from the term's ideological ascendancy in the twentieth century, especially during the third wave of democratization from the 1970s to the end of 1990s. More recently, autocratic regimes have become skilled at convincing their citizens that their system is democratic (von Soest and Grauvogel 2015, Hu 2018). Therefore, while overt support for democracy may be a necessary democratic value, it cannot by itself explain cross-national patterns of transitions to democracy or democratic stability.

Most research into democratic values therefore goes beyond overt support for democratic governance to assess people's commitment to the core principles and norms on which democracy rests (Norris 2017a, 24). For example, democracy requires limits on how the political majority uses its (temporary) control of state institutions. The public will accept such limits more readily when they have tolerance toward out-groups or minorities (Sullivan, Piereson, and Marcus 1982, Sullivan et al. 1985, Gibson 1998, Stenner 2005, Gibson

2007) and when they value protecting individuals' rights and freedoms from state power (Gibson and Duch 1993, Inglehart and Welzel 2005). In addition, democracy requires that elites and citizens follow its procedures even when they dislike the outcome. Thus, democratic values should include support for those procedures, especially free-and-fair competitive elections. A society's level of democratic values has also been examined by measuring values that signal a willingness to abandon democracy in tough times, such as a desire for order (Gibson 1997) and the preference for rule by a "strong leader" who may need to disregard democratic procedures (Inglehart 2003). Research into the distributions of these values makes sense: they are logically connected to the functioning of democracy, they avoid the downside of asking directly about support for democracy, and they tend to produce more variance within and among countries. Yet, as we show below, they may nonetheless have distinct properties that must be accounted for.

Another distinction is whether democratic values are orientations or attitudes. The early work in the democratic values literature assumed that scholars were exploring what Eckstein (1988, 790) labels "orientations": general and enduring outlooks. Attitudes, in contrast, are shorter-term responses to external stimuli which "derive from and express" orientations (ibid.; for a more extended discussion of this and related distinctions, see Fleron 1996 [2017], 182-194). Current events should have a small impact on people's political orientations even as they alter the attitudes people express. In principle, comparative theories about democratic values should rest on cross-national patterns of relatively enduring orientations rather than situational attitudes.[4] As an example, what if an interviewee expressed support for selecting leaders through competitive elections but that viewpoint was primarily the result of her favored party having won the most recent election? Some years later, if chosen again to be surveyed, she would respond in the negative following her party's defeat. Her responses would reflect changeable attitudes rather than a basic orientation toward a key procedure of democratic governance. They would not help analysts understand who values democracy per se. To put it another way, the object of public support (legitimacy) being investigated would not be the regime, using Easton's (1965, 286-288) well known typology, but the authorities. The study of democratic values would then be, in effect, a subset of the large literature on political or institutional support and trust (Zmerli and van der Meer 2017, Uslaner 2018).

Keeping democratic values research distinct is important, though. Democracy requires the existence of opposition to those holding power (Warren 2017) while maintaining support for the democratic system among even those whose preferred party or candidate loses elections (Anderson et al. 2005). However, it should not be an axiom that the questions commonly used in the democratic values literature are indeed tapping people's enduring orientations. As we show below, this depends on what we ask people about democracy.

Finally, assuming democratic values are relatively enduring over a person's lifetime, do they primarily exhibit continuity or generational change? Political-culture approaches have tended to stress elements of continuity: the role that family, churches, schools, and other institutions play in passing down values from one generation to another (Eckstein 1988, Fuchs 2007). Because of these factors, each country or other large social group will have its own distinctive pattern of values, which will change only slowly. Yet, without denying the sources of continuity, it is possible to place greater emphasis on how each generation differs from its predecessors. Because people form their core political orientations as teens or young adults, what is going on in the country will tend to affect all those of the right age in similar ways, including the political values they adopt. Those values can then be traced among that generation even as they grow older. Numerous studies have shown that generations, or cohorts, are important in public opinion (see the review in Neundorf and Smets 2017). The most notable comparative example has been Inglehart's (1977, 2018) argument that conditions of material security during the formative years shape one's political outlooks, including democratic values. Numerous scholars of Soviet politics found evidence of noteworthy generational cohorts (see the discussion in Bahry 1987, 71-73). Data from interviews with émigrés in the Harvard Project of the 1950s and the Soviet Interview Project of the 1980s, as well as interviews with Soviet citizens in 1990 all reveal cohort differences in political values and engagement (Bahry 1987, 1993). Sorting out the elements of continuity and generational change is thus important when studying democratic values.

HOW WE MEASURE DEMOCRATIC VALUES

Our data come from a total of six representative opinion surveys conducted in 1990, 1991, 1992, 1995, 1997, and 2015. Those in the 1990s were conducted in Russia, Ukraine, and Lithuania. The 2015 survey was conducted in Russia, Ukraine, and Georgia. University of Iowa researchers designed the surveys and questionnaires, in consultation with in-country firms which carried out the surveys. All the surveys involved face-to-face interviews in the respondents' homes.

We analyze seven measures of democratic values. They are representative of the measures most often employed in the literature, as discussed above, with the exception of a measure of tolerance. All are coded so that higher values indicate greater support for the democratic value.

1) The variable "best system" is a dummy variable created from a question asking respondents to choose between the Soviet system prior to perestroika, the current political system, and Western-style democracy. Those who selected the latter receive a score of one. Respondents who chose one of the first two options or did not answer the questions are scored as zero.
2) The variable we label "democracy > strong leadership" has responses on a 4-point scale to the statement: "Our country needs strong leadership more than democracy." Scores of 1–4 correspond to fully agree, agree, disagree, and fully disagree.
3) For the 1991–1997 surveys, the variable "party competition needed" contains responses to the statement: "Competition among many political parties will make the political system stronger." In 2015, we used a slightly different wording: "Our political system is stronger when candidates from more than one party have a realistic chance to win an election." In all years, scores of 1–4 correspond to fully disagree, disagree, agree, and fully agree.
4) The variable "public has right to oppose/protest" uses the same 4-point scale for responses to "Any individual or organization has the right to organize opposition or resistance to any governmental initiative."
5) The variable "freedom even if disorder" has agreement/disagreement with the statement "It is better to live in an orderly society than to allow people so much freedom they become disruptive." Scores of 1–4 correspond to fully agree, agree, disagree, and fully disagree.
6) The variable "protect rights of accused" uses the same scale for reactions to "It is very important to stop crime, even if it means violating the rights of the accused."
7) The variable "interpersonal trust" comes from the standard question used to tap this dimension: "Speaking generally, do you think that most people can be trusted or one needs to be careful in dealings with other people?" Those who indicate most people can be trusted receive scores of one, others receive scores of zero.

RUSSIANS' SUPPORT FOR DEMOCRATIC VALUES

Table 2.1 provides indicators of the central tendency in our seven measures of democratic values (proportions for the dichotomous variables and averages for the others) from five surveys conducted in Russia. Each measure was asked in 2015 and at least one of the four surveys from the 1990s. Under each score from the 1990s, we show how that year's average compares to 2015, as a proportion of the scale being used. The bigger the gap between the years, the higher this number.

Table 2.1 Averages of Democratic Values Questions by Year of Survey, Russia

	1991	*1992*	*1995*	*1997*	*2015*
Best system				21.1%	10.1%
Difference from 2015 as % of the scale (0–1)				11.1%	
Democracy > strong leadership			1.81	1.52	1.84
As % of the scale (1–4)			0.8%	10.5%	
Party competition needed	2.87	2.76	2.45	2.39	3.00
As % of the scale (1–4)	4.5%	7.8%	18.2%	20.3%	
Public has right to oppose/ protest		2.78	2.89	2.98	2.84
As % of the scale (1–4)		2.2%	1.4%	4.7%	
Freedom even if disorder	1.96	1.96	1.77	1.54	1.72
As % of the scale (1–4)	8.1%	8.0%	1.6%	6.2%	
Protect rights of accused	2.24	2.14	2.22	2.17	2.10
As % of the scale (1–4)	4.7%	1.1%	4.0%	2.2%	
Interpersonal trust	26.9%	32.7%			31.3%
As % of the scale (0–1)	4.4%	1.4%			

Sources: Miller, Reisinger and Hesli 2000; Reisinger, Claypool and Zaloznaya 2015.

We find that support among Russians for some democratic values is notably low, both in the 1990s and in 2015. Those selecting Western democracy as their preferred political system are only one-fifth of the population in 1997 and go down to one-tenth in 2015. For the questions with 1–4 scales, the midpoint is 2.5, and the averages for democracy over strong leadership, for freedom over order, and for protecting the rights of the accused are all below the midpoint. Those expressing interpersonal trust remain below a third of the population between 1991 and 2015. For two of the measures, though, Russians in the aggregate land well above the midpoint in support for key democratic features: multiparty electoral competition and the public's right to express opposition to the authorities.

Two things are noteworthy in this pattern of low and high support levels. First, the two questions where democratic values are solid are those concerning the public's own ability to participate in politics: to vote for a party of their choosing and to engage in protests. A strong level of support for multiparty elections has remained a feature of Russian public opinion since such elections were initiated in the late 1980s (Finifter and Mickiewicz 1992, Gibson, Duch, and Tedin 1992, Colton and McFaul 2002, Hale 2011). Similarly, maintaining opposition rights has been found to be well supported in Russia in other surveys (Hale 2011). Second, these two questions do not counterpose the democratic element to some other attractive thing. They do not ask the respondent to consider trade-offs. The questions where the average score falls on the nondemocratic side of the scale (below 2.5) are ones that couch the democratic value as a trade-off: with strong leadership, social order, or reducing crime. They deliberately make choosing the democratic option more difficult. As we show below, the averages from Ukraine and Lithuania on these questions also fall below the midpoint. Russians should be understood not as rejecting democracy, freedom and rights but as willing to trade them off.

COMPARISONS WITH POST-SOVIET NEIGHBORS

How do Russian levels of acceptance of democratic values compare with those in Ukraine and Lithuania, surveyed in the same 1990s surveys, and Ukraine and Georgia, surveyed also in 2015? One might expect these countries' values to be quite similar to Russia's because of the shared experience as components of a single state, the Soviet Union, with a distinctive ideology, economy, and Party regime. Many scholars have offered explanations for why living under Leninist-style communism would leave a strong legacy (e.g., Jowitt 1992, Tucker 1992), and recent studies confirm that the publics of postcommunist countries share similar tendencies in their outlooks which reflect the experiences of communist rule (Pop-Eleches and Tucker 2017). On the other hand, well before the end of the Soviet Union, it was clear that different nationality groups retained many distinct cultural elements. Many insightful students of Russian politics and history have pointed out pre-communist Russian cultural features that remained important during and after Soviet times (Berlin 1957, White 1979, Keenan 1986, Tucker 1992, McDaniel 1996). It is therefore of interest to counterpose Russians' support for democratic values to that of their neighbors and former fellow citizens.

Table 2.2 shows the same measures of central tendency as in table 2.1 but for all the countries for each year available. In addition, it provides the results of t-tests of the difference in means between Russia and each of the other countries. Where a t-test is statistically significant, an arrow next to it indicates the direction of that country's average compared to Russia's. For most of the measures and most years, each of the four countries shows a distinctive profile. The strength of each country's general political and economic connections to Western Europe matches the most common rank ordering, with Georgia and Lithuania having higher scores than Ukraine, which is closer to but higher than Russia. One exception is that Georgians in 2015 show less support than Russians for democracy over strong leadership and for freedom even if disorder. The extremely low level of interpersonal trust in Georgia is also noteworthy.

Commitment to protecting the rights of the accused in Russia is not notably high, its values being below the midpoint as shown in table 2.1. It

Table 2.2 Democratic Values in Four Postcommunist Countries, 1990–2015 (T-Tests between Russia and Indicated Country)

	Years	*Russia*		*Ukraine*		*Georgia*		*Lithuania*
Best system	1997	21.2%	<	28.5%			<	50.2%
(proportion selecting democracy)				(4.40**)				(13.37**)
	2015	10.1%	<	43.8%	<	38.5%		
				(25.00**)		(20.46**)		
Democracy > strong leadership	1995	1.81	<	1.97			<	2.13
				(5.28**)				(7.49**)
	1997	1.52	<	1.62			<	2.10
				(3.12**)				(14.74**)
	2015	1.84		1.85	>	1.66		
				(0.23)		(-5.08**)		
Party competition needed	1991	2.87	<	3.14			<	2.99
				(6.31**)				(2.28*)
	1992	2.76	<	2.89				2.71
				(3.16**)				(-1.18)
	1995	2.45		2.46				2.49
				(0.15)				(0.89)
	1997	2.39		2.42				2.47
				(0.57)				(1.37)
	2015	3.00		2.99	<	3.23		
				(-0.40)		(6.84**)		
Public has right to oppose/protest	1992	2.78	<	2.92			<	3.01
				(3.76**)				(5.21**)
	1995	2.89		2.78				2.90
				(-3.53**)				(0.28)
	1997	2.98	<	3.19				2.98
				(5.19**)				(0.02)
	2015	2.84	<	3.24	<	3.49		
				(13.56**)		(20.33**)		

Freedom even if disorder	1991	1.96		1.97 (-1.83)			<	2.26 (14.41**)
	1992	1.96		1.99 (0.79)			>	1.82 (-2.93**)
	1995	1.77	<	1.88 (4.18**)				1.80 (0.88)
	1997	1.54		1.49 (-1.44)			<	1.70 (4.26**)
	2015	1.72		1.72 (-0.09)	>	1.47 (-8.09**)		
Protect rights of accused even if more crime	1991	2.24		2.19 (-1.03)			>	1.86 (-7.00**)
	1992	2.14	>	1.94 (-4.29**)			>	1.79 (-6.28**)
	1995	2.22		2.19 (-1.04)			>	1.73 (-11.80**)
	1997	2.17	>	2.06 (-2.66**)			>	1.83 (-6.97**)
	2015	2.10		2.14 (1.17)	<	2.40 (7.41**)		
Interpersonal trust	1991	26.9%	>	22.8% (-2.27*)			>	14.0% (-6.32**)
	1992	32.7%	>	20.9% (-6.02**)				29.1% (-1.48)
	2015	31.3%	<	34.9% (2.22*)	>	5.6% (-17.81**)		

Sources: Miller, Reisinger and Hesli 2000; Reisinger, Claypool and Zaloznaya 2015.

is interesting, therefore, that its average exceeds that of both Ukraine and Lithuania in each survey in the 1990s. By 2015, Ukraine's level is a bit higher with Georgia's more clearly exceeding Russia's and Ukraine's, though also being below the midpoint of the scale. Lithuania, despite its 50% support for Western-style democracy in 1997, has scores below the midpoints for other values, such as democracy over strong leadership, freedom even if disorder, and protecting rights of the accused. The same applies to Georgia in 2015. So, Russia is not alone exhibiting modest levels of democratic values. It is, however, for many of the measures, distinct for having the lowest levels.

ORIENTATIONS OR ATTITUDES?

We turn now to the question of whether the outlooks studied by scholars of democratic values should be considered stable orientations or more malleable attitudes. We return to the data on Russia in table 2.1. If democratic values are stable orientations, we should expect to find support for these hypotheses:

H1a: The mean scores for a country will change only modestly from the earliest survey year to 2015.

H1b: Variations in a country's mean scores from year to year will be small and not easily explainable with reference to the country's political situation at the time of the survey.

For most of the questions, we do see stability in the average responses, considering that each survey interviewed different samples. Note that most of the gaps between the 1990s surveys and the 2015 results in table 2.1 are under 10% of the scale. The right to oppose, freedom even if disorder, protecting rights of the accused, and interpersonal trust all have similar average scores over a quarter century of data collection. They seem to be capturing enduring political orientations and thus support for H1a. Concerning H1b, it is hard to think of how the Russian political contexts at the time of the surveys would account for the relatively small variation among them.

The first three measures in the table, however, show more variability, in ways that can be attributed to the changing political context. The question about the best system refers to "Western democracy," and by the time of the 2015 survey, anti-Western feelings were high, and the regime had been systematically critiquing the West as hostile to Russia. It would be indeed surprising if support had not fallen. The question about democracy versus strong leadership produces very similar responses in 1995 and 2015 but takes a dip in 1997. Is there something about the Russian political context to explain this? Yes—1997 was when, arguably, President Boris Yeltsin's leadership was at its nadir. He had had a heart attack in 1996 and would have another in late 1997. The functioning of the federal state was poor on multiple fronts, and his approval ratings were sliding (Treisman 2011). The need for strong leadership was surely on most Russians' minds. In 2015, by contrast, Russians' support for Putin was high, making the need for strong leadership seem less pressing and allowing more Russians to signal their support for democracy. The question about multiparty competition takes a dip in the 1995 and 1997 surveys, years when Russia's ballots held dozens of "couch parties."[5] (Forty-three party lists were on the 1995 ballot for election to the lower house of Russia's parliament. Another 30 ran in one of the single-member-district races countrywide.) Most Russians found the proliferation of parties, slogans, and images to be confusing and frustrating. By 2015, however, the party system had been managed, permitting a more limited number of choices, and support for multiparty elections was back to even higher than in the early 1990s.

WHAT ROLE FOR GENERATIONAL CHANGE?

When we find that the level of support for democratic value shifts across our surveys, particularly from the 1990s to 2015, we may be able to attribute the shift to some aspect of the country's political or economic context, affecting the entire public in a more or less uniform fashion—for instance, the change from the weak national leadership of the late 1990s to the perceived strength of Putin's leadership in 2015. Alternatively, however, shifts in values could reflect generational changes that do not stem from citizens' reactions to their immediate contexts at the time of the surveys. If that is the case, changing attitudes are due to older generations exiting the population and new ones entering. We therefore hypothesize the following:

H2a: Democratic values will show distinctive generational means.
H2b: Generational distinctions will be similar across survey years.
H2c: Political and economic conditions during respondents' formative periods will be more influential in shaping their values than conditions at the time of the survey.

Concerning the nature of the generational effects, we propose two additional, rival hypotheses. The first comes from what might be called "civics" expectations, that youth will be taught to value the kind of political system in operation or promoted by political leaders during their formative years. As noted, this includes expectations that living in an authoritarian regime will be a factor in decreasing support for democratic values. The second hypothesis comes from Inglehart's work and emphasizes material security rather than the type of political system.

H3a: Generations that came of age during periods of comparative liberalization will have higher average democratic values, ceteris paribus, than others.
H3b: Generations that came of age during periods of relative stability and security will have higher democratic values than others.

The boundaries of political generations can be set in different ways. Given the topic of democratic values and the countries we examine, we will follow other studies of Russian outlooks (Rose and Carnaghan 1995, Hendley 2017) by distinguishing those who came of age under different Soviet, then Russian leaderships. We use age 15 as the target age for when a person's core political views have been formed (Rose and Carnaghan 1995, 34). The earliest generation in our surveys includes people born through 1920 and who therefore came of age in the early Soviet period, prior to high Stalinism. The next generation are those born between 1921 and 1939, who came of age during the Terror and the rest of Stalin's life. Those born between 1940 and 1950 came of age under Khrushchev and those between 1951 and 1969 under Brezhnev or his short-term successors. The Gorbachev generation was born between 1970 and 1976, the Yeltsin generation between 1977 and 1987, and the Putin generation from 1988 on.[6] Given Soviet and post-Soviet Russian history, the generations who came of age when national political conditions were most to least liberal are: Yeltsin, Gorbachev, Khrushchev, Putin, early Soviet, and Stalin. The Brezhnev and Putin periods provided the most material security relative to the others.

Table 2.3 takes data from all the available years for each of our seven measures of democratic values and breaks down the proportions or averages by political generation. Note that the generations variable is not the same as age at the time of the survey. Of course, the two things are correlated: those in the early Soviet generation are quite old in all the surveys. Yet those in the Gorbachev generation, as an example, can range in age from 20 to 45 years old at the time we interviewed them, depending on which survey they participated in.

For six of the measures, the generational differences are statistically significant, as shown by the f-test statistics at the bottom of those columns. For five of the measures, the f-test is large and significant at .000, indicating that one or more of the generations' averages are clearly different from others. Support for the right to oppose governmental policy does show variation, but it is weaker. (Note that support for this value is above the midpoint among every generation.) The one measure that shows no statistically significant generational variation is the (low) level of interpersonal trust. Setting aside

Table 2.3 Generational Differences in Average Democratic Values, Russia, All Surveys

Generation	*Range of Birth Years*	*Best System 1997–2015*	*Democ. > Str. Ldrshp. 1995–2015*	*Party Competition 1990–2015*	*Right to Oppose 1992–2015*	*Freedom 1990–2015*	*Rights of Accused 1991–2015*	*Interpers. Trust 1990–92 and 2015*
Early Soviet	–1920	8.6%	1.58	2.44	2.72	1.54	1.82	31.7%
Stalin	1921–1939	9.8%	1.53	2.61	2.81	1.66	1.99	30.0%
Khrushchev	1940–1950	10.3%	1.66	2.77	2.88	1.86	2.17	31.1%
Brezhnev and interregnum	1951–1969	16.9%	1.75	2.78	2.90	1.93	2.29	27.9%
Gorbachev	1970–1976	24.7%	1.83	2.72	2.87	1.92	2.26	28.8%
Yeltsin	1977–1987	12.7%	1.89	2.96	2.93	1.72	2.09	33.9%
Putin	1988–	17.9%	1.94	3.00	2.88	1.83	2.13	29.7%
F-test:		10.70**	22.55**	18.17**	2.74*	30.24**	26.44**	1.36

Note: * < .5; ** < .01.
Sources: Miller, Reisinger and Hesli 2000; Reisinger, Claypool and Zaloznaya 2015.

the right to oppose and trust measures, which vary insubstantially, how the others differ across generations deserves attention.

Notice first the measures in the second and third columns: valuing democracy over strong leadership and multiparty competition. As seen in table 2.1, their average values dipped in the late 1990s before returning higher levels in 2015, and this fit with two sources of public frustration during the former period: poor national leadership and a proliferation of minor parties. While acknowledging such period effects, it is noteworthy that scores on these two measures get consistently higher as one goes from the older to the more recent political generations. For example, the Khrushchev-generation's average is higher than the previous two, while the Brezhnev generation's average exceeds that. Those of the Putin generation, who were socialized an era of relative prosperity and stability under an authoritarian regime, nonetheless have the highest average scores on these two views of democracy.

Three other measures—democracy as the best system, freedom even if disorder, and protecting the rights of the accused—do not rise monotonically. Each, though, shows a notable decline among those in the Yeltsin generation, who came of age in from 1992 to 2002, compared to the levels among the Gorbachev, Brezhnev, and Khrushchev generations. They then rebound among the Putin-generation respondents, who came of age after 2002. The 1990s were a period of terrible economic suffering and insecurity in Russia, which affected Russian society in numerous ways (Gaber et al. 2019, Sharafutdinova 2019, Pyle 2021). Under Putin, though, economic growth resumed and public concern about crime and disorder receded. This pattern supports hypothesis 3b, suggesting that national conditions of material insecurity will strongly affect those coming of age under them.

These generational differences are not an artifact of combining the surveys from the 1990s and 2015. It remains almost entirely the same when using only data from the 2015 survey. Table 2.4 shows the same results as in table 2.3 except using the 2015 data only. (That survey includes no one from the early Soviet generation.) With fewer cases, the f-test statistics are smaller for several of the variables. Multiparty competition loses its cross-generational significance, with those from earlier generations showing more support for this institution than they did in the 1990s. Perhaps familiarity by 2015 with regular elections (albeit non-competitive ones) accounts for this. Interpersonal trust, which varied little across the generations when including all the surveys, shows significant variation when using only the 2015 data, primarily because Stalin-generation respondents indicate a much higher level of trust than those in the other generations. With these exceptions, the cross-generational patterns shown in table 2.3 are replicated here.

Table 2.4 Generational Differences in Average Democratic Values, Russia, 2015 Survey Only

Generation	*Range of Birth Years*	*Best System*	*Democ. > Str. Ldrshp.*	*Party Competition*	*Right to Oppose*	*Freedom*	*Rights of Accused*	*Interpers. Trust*
Stalin	1921-39	3.0%	1.38	3.10	2.76	1.41	1.77	45.5%
Khrushchev	1940-50	1.8%	1.63	2.88	2.74	1.63	2.12	33.8%
Brezhnev and interregnum	1951-69	8.5%	1.80	3.03	2.85	1.69	2.15	28.9%
Gorbachev	1970-76	11.7%	1.93	3.00	2.75	1.84	2.04	27.6%
Yeltsin	1977-87	9.4%	1.90	2.99	2.90	1.70	2.07	33.9%
Putin	1988-	17.9%	1.94	3.00	2.88	1.83	2.13	30.0%
F-test:		8.94**	8.11**	1.04	1.74	5.05**	0.91	2.28*

Note: * < .5; ** < .01.
Sources: Miller, Reisinger and Hesli 2000; Reisinger, Claypool and Zaloznaya 2015.

DISCUSSION

Across the several questions we asked about democratic values in Russia, the answers depended on which of the measures was being used. Theorists, in generating their expectations about the outlooks that are labeled democratic values, must therefore pay close attention to the nature of the value and to the phrasing of the question. Questions evoking democracy as a regime or its key institutions will elicit answers that change in light of the political situation, especially depending on what balancing phrase the question has. Both describing democracy as Western and posing freedom as a rival to strong leadership contribute to Russians expressing low support for democracy as a regime. These or similar questions may not do well in testing theories about how a public's commitment to being governed democratically shapes actual democratization or democratic functioning. They may be picking up on attitudes shaped by the near-term performance of the political system (Evans and Whitefield 1995, Rose, Mishler, and Munro 2011, Singer 2018). At the same time, several dimensions of democratic values do exhibit the stability we should find if those questions are tapping political orientations that can guide theorizing about the link between values and political outcomes. The most stable values in the Russian case concern citizen rights rather than leaders or institutions. It is perhaps surprising that the one measure on which most Russians support the democratic viewpoint is the right to oppose the government, given their strong disapproval of disorder and chaos. This finding does accord, however, with the fact that protests have remained frequent in Russia even as Putin has reduced political freedoms (Robertson 2013, Dmitriev 2015, Gabowitsch 2016, Lankina and Skovoroda 2017), and some scholars argue that rebelliousness is a persistent theme in Russian culture (Figes 2002, 134–135).

The biggest difference in Russia's political conditions at the time of our surveys occurs between 1997 and 2015. In 2015, Putin had been in power for 15 years and had firm autocratic control over Russian politics for at least a decade. Russia's experience of relative liberalization and competitive elections lasted a shorter period, roughly from 1989 to 2002. Moreover, Russians' standard of living for most of the liberalized period was terrible, while stability and economic growth marked most of the Putin period. If democratic values are, indeed, learned by living under democratic institutions and, hence, do not take root when successful autocratic institutions operate (Muller and Seligson 1994, Rohrschneider 1999, Salinas and Booth 2011), then Russia's 2015 levels of support for democratic values would be lower than those in the 1990s. Yet our data confound that expectation. With the exception of the question about the best governance system, in response to which support for Western democracy did decline substantially from 1997 to 2015, the averages in 2015 are no different from or higher than those in the earlier surveys.

What, then, explains the stability of or increase in democratic values over this period? No doubt a variety of factors are at work. We have shown that generational change is likely one of those factors. What we call the Putin generation has experienced higher material security during their formative years, and they hold more democratic values than earlier generations. For several of the measures, we find a clear impact on values of the economic and social privations of the 1990s among those who came of age under Yeltsin. Pyle (2021) has shown that those who suffered economically from 1989 to 1994 were less likely to support democracy in the mid-2000s. Similarly, Gaber et al. (2019) find strong effects of suffering during the 1990s on later attitudes, creating what they call a "critical juncture." They study a civic culture index that includes some democratic values and find that it declines steadily from 1990 to 2010. Our results correspond in part to these findings but indicate the need to pull apart generational differences in understanding over-time change.

In several ways, our data from Russia and the other post-Soviet countries challenge the expectations of the original political cultural theories from which the democratic values literature arose. Questions touching on different elements of democratic institutions or norms may be different types of mentalities and thus have different roles in theory. A country's central tendency on a democratic value must be considered an amalgamation of the views of different subsections of society, such as generations. Our findings, in other words, suggest that, as Fleron (2017) has advocated, the democratic values literature can benefit by stressing middle-range theory.

Finally, what does it mean for Russia that its citizens' democratic values have not declined and are stronger among the currently younger generation? It may mean little, of course. Russia's authoritarian regime has a great deal of strength, and the levels of support for democratic values are not so high as to suggest any near-term crisis. On the other hand, Russia's regime is not one that can ignore the public's values. Its leaders have worked hard throughout the Putin era to create strong public support. That support remains critical even after the 2020 constitutional amendments which strengthened the Kremlin's hand in many ways but did not lessen the looming question of what holds the regime together after Putin. If Russians' attachment to the current regime's authoritarianism is declining, even slowly, that could pose an increasing challenge to the regime.

CONCLUSION

We have used data from coordinated surveys conducted across 25 years to examine Russians' support for democratic values and to contrast them with other post-Soviet countries. By comparing public outlooks right as the Soviet Union was ending with those existing in Putin's 15th year in power, we have revisited several issues in the democratic values literature. We show that some of the measures of democratic values most widely used in the comparative literature fluctuate over time in response to the political context, making them not as pertinent to studying support for the regime type of democracy as is generally assumed. We found support, in the case of Russia at least, for neo-modernization theories of public values such as Inglehart's, which argue that material insecurity and distress during a person's formative years lead people away from the values needed to support democracy while better economic times and other forms of security allow people to accept democratic values. This shows up in the contrast between those in the Yeltsin generation and those in the Brezhnev and Putin generations.

The end of communism in Eastern Europe and then in the Soviet Union led several teams of researchers to test propositions drawn from the democratic values literature in the newly independent countries. The predominant question, naturally, was to what extent public views were compatible with the establishment of viable democracies, which all the countries at that time were seeking, or at least pledging to seek. For a variety of reasons, answering this question was highly complicated. Great care was needed in interpreting the newly available data on public opinion in Russia and other postcommunist societies. Fleron provided invaluable attention to conceptual, theoretical and methodological challenges facing this enterprise. By the end of the decade, the big question had been answered in most cases, and the study of democratic values faded where autocracy was in place, including Russia. This prevented a full working out of many of the challenges (see also the points in Bahry 1999). Current investigations of democratic values both in Russia and elsewhere can benefit by revisiting the points Fleron raised about the first wave of studies.

NOTES

1. The surveys reported on in this chapter were made possible by support from the National Science Foundation, grants numbers SES-9009698, SES-9023974, and SBR-9411643; and from the U.S. Army Research Laboratory and the U.S. Army Research Office under grant number W911NF-14-1-0541. The authors are grateful to Ariana Devereaux for research assistance.

2. See the valuable recent debate about whether the rise of populist leaders and parties is due to declining public support for liberal democracy: Foa and Mounk 2016, Inglehart 2016, Alexander and Welzel 2017, Foa and Mounk 2017b, a, Howe 2017, Norris 2017b, Voeten 2017.

3. A political regime is the set of rules governing who can hold power in a country and what they can do with their power (e.g., Fishman 1990, 428).

4. We assume our respondents are not providing misleading answers to our questions. In assessing studies of democratic values in Russia from the 1980s and 1990s, Fleron (1996 [2017]) raised the issue of Tucker's (1960, 1987) "dual Russia": whether Russians answer survey questions about democratic values as they believe the authorities want them to (Russian authorities were promoting democracy in the early 1990s). This is a Russian variant of sensitivity bias, a common challenge for survey research. Generally, there is little evidence of survey respondents in Russia providing false answers because they are sensitive about discussing politics; to the extent there is such sensitivity, it leads instead to non-responses. This is not to say, however, that cues from political authorities will have no effect. Political messaging from elites is clearly a factor that shapes political attitudes. As we explore below, evidence that the pattern of democratic values has responded to such clues will suggest they are attitudes rather than orientations.

5. Russians developed this satirical term to indicate parties so small that all their members could sit on one couch.

6. Our cut-offs are similar to those used by Rose and Carnaghan (1995) and match those of Hendley (2017) except we break off the early Soviet generation from the Stalin generation.

REFERENCES

Alexander, Amy C., and Christian Welzel. 2017. "The Myth of Deconsolidation: Rising Liberalism and the Populist Reaction." *Journal of Democracy Special Web Exchange*. https://www.journalofdemocracy.org/online-exchange-democratic-deconsolidation/

Almond, Gabriel A., and Sydney Verba. 1963. *The Civic Culture: Political Attitudes and Democracy in Five Nations*. Princeton: Princeton University Press.

Anderson, Christopher J., Andre Blais, Shaun Bowler, Todd Donovan, and Ola Listhaug. 2005. *Losers' Consent: Elections and Democratic Legitimacy*. New York: Oxford University Press.

Bahry, Donna. 1987. "Politics, Generations and Change in the USSR." In *Politics, Work and Daily Life in the USSR: A Survey of Former Soviet Citizens*, edited by James R. Millar, 61–99. New York: Cambridge University Press.

Bahry, Donna. 1993. "Society Transformed? Rethinking the Social Roots of Perestroika." *Slavic Review* 52 (3): 512–554.

Bahry, Donna. 1999. "Comrades into Citizens? Russian Political Culture and Public Support for the Transition." *Slavic Review* 58 (4): 841–853.

Bauer, Raymond A., Alex Inkeles, and Clyde Kluckholm. 1956. *How the Soviet System Works: Cultural, Psychological, and Social Themes*. Cambridge, MA: Harvard University Press.

Berlin, Isaiah. 1957. "The Silence in Russian Culture." *Foreign Affairs* 36 (1): 1–24.

Boycko, Maxim, and Robert J. Shiller. 2016. "Popular Attitudes Toward Markets and Democracy: Russia and United States Compared 25 Years Later." *The American Economic Review* 106 (5): 224–229.

Brehm, John, and Wendy Rahn. 1997. "Individual-Level Evidence for the Causes and Consequences of Social Capital." *American Journal of Political Science* 41 (3): 999.

Claassen, Christopher. 2020. "Does Public Support Help Democracy Survive?" *American Journal of Political Science* 64 (1): 118–134.

Colton, Timothy J., and Michael McFaul. 2002. "Are Russians Undemocratic?" *Post-Soviet Affairs* 18 (2): 91–121.

Dmitriev, Mikhail. 2015. "Lost in Transition? The Geography of Protests and Attitude Change in Russia." *Europe-Asia Studies* 67 (2): 224–243.

Dobson, Richard B., and Steven A. Grant. 1992. "Public Opinion and the Transformation of the Soviet Union." *International Journal of Public Opinion Research* 4 (4): 302–320.

Easton, David. 1965. *A Systems Analysis of Political Life*. New York: Wiley.

Eckstein, Harry. 1961 [1992]. "A Theory of Stable Democracy." In *Regarding Politics: Essays on Political Theory, Stability, and Change*, 179–226. Berkeley, CA: University of California Press.

Eckstein, Harry. 1988. "A Culturalist Theory of Political Change." *American Political Science Review* 82 (3): 789–804.

Evans, Geoffrey, and Stephen Whitefield. 1995. "The Politics and Economics of Democratic Commitment: Support for Democracy in Transition Societies." *British Journal of Political Science* 25 (4): 485–514.

Figes, Orlando. 2002. *Natasha's Dance: A Cultural History of Russia*. New York: Metropolitan Books.

Finifter, Ada W., and Ellen Mickiewicz. 1992. "Redefining the Political System of the USSR: Mass Support for Political Change." *American Political Science Review* 86 (4): 857–874.

Fishman, Robert M. 1990. "Rethinking State and Regime: Southern Europe's Transition to Democracy." *World Politics* XLII (3): 422–440.

Fleron, Frederic J. 1968 [2017]. "The Logic of Inquiry in Sovietology: Soviet Area Studies and the Social Sciences." In *Russian Studies and Comparative Politics: Views From Metatheory and Middle-Range Theory*, edited by Frederic J. Fleron, 169–208. Lanham, MD: Lexington Books.

Fleron, Frederic J. 1996 [2017]. "Political Culture in Post-Soviet Russia: Recent Empirical Investigations." In *Russian Studies and Comparative Politics: Views From Metatheory and Middle-Range Theory*, edited by Frederic J. Fleron, 169–208. Lanham, MD: Lexington Books.

Fleron, Frederic J. 2017. *Russian Studies and Comparative Politics: Views From Metatheory and Middle-Range Theory*. Lanham, MD: Lexington Books.

Fleron, Frederic J., Jr., and Richard Ahl. 1998 [2017]. "Does the Public Matter for Democratization in Russia?: What We Have Learned From 'Third Wave' Transitions and Public Opinion Surveys." In *Russian Studies and Comparative*

Politics: Views From Metatheory and Middle-Range Theory, edited by Frederic J. Fleron, Jr., 209–247. Lanham, MD: Lexington Books.

Foa, Roberto Stefan, and Yascha Mounk. 2016. "The Danger of Deconsolidation: The Democratic Disconnect." *Journal of Democracy* 27 (3): 5–17.

Foa, Roberto Stefan, and Yascha Mounk. 2017a. "The End of the Consolidation Paradigm—A Response to Our Critics." *Journal of Democracy Special Web Exchange*. https://www.journalofdemocracy.org/online-exchange-democratic-deconsolidation/

Foa, Roberto Stefan, and Yascha Mounk. 2017b. "The Signs of Deconsolidation." *Journal of Democracy* 28 (1): 5–15.

Fuchs, Dieter. 2007. "The Political Culture Paradigm." In *The Oxford Handbook of Political Behavior*, edited by Russell J. Dalton and Hans-Dieter Klingemann, 161–184. New York: Oxford University Press.

Gaber, Elena, Leonid Polishchuk, Kharis Sokolov, and Denis Stukal. 2019. "Chronicles of a Democracy Postponed: Cultural Legacy of the Russian Transition." *Economics of Transition* 27 (1): 99–137.

Gabowitsch, Mischa. 2016. *Protest in Putin's Russia*. New York: Polity.

Gibson, James L. 1997. "The Struggle Between Order and Liberty in Contemporary Russian Political Culture." *Australian Journal of Political Science* 32 (2): 271–290.

Gibson, James L. 1998. "Putting Up With Fellow Russians: An Analysis of Political Tolerance in the Fledgling Russian Democracy." *Political Research Quarterly* 51 (1): 37–68.

Gibson, James L. 2007. "Political Intolerance in the Context of Democratic Theory." In *The Oxford Handbook of Political Behavior*, edited by Russell J. Dalton and Hans-Dieter Klingemann, 323–341. New York: Oxford University Press.

Gibson, James L., and Raymond M. Duch. 1993. "Support for Rights in Western Europe and the Soviet Union: An Analysis of the Beliefs of Mass Publics." In *Democratization in Eastern and Western Europe*, edited by Frederick D. Weil, Jeffrey Huffman, and Mary Gautier, 241–263. Greenwich, CT: JAI Press.

Gibson, James L., and Raymond M. Duch. 1994. "Postmaterialism and the Emerging Soviet Democracy." *Political Research Quarterly* 47 (1): 5–39.

Gibson, James L., Raymond M. Duch, and Kent L. Tedin. 1992. "Democratic Values and the Transformation of the Soviet Union." *Journal of Politics* 54 (2): 329–371.

Haerpfer, Christian, Ronald Inglehart, Alejandro Moreno, Christian Welzel, Kseniya Kizilova, Jaime Diez-Medrano, M. Lagos, Pippa Norris, E. Ponarin, and Bi Puranen. 2020. "World Values Survey: Round Seven – Country-Pooled Datafile." Collected (Madrid, Spain & Vienna, Austria: World Values Survey Association), Dataset Available From JD Systems Institute & WVSA Secretariat. http://www.worldvaluessurvey.org/WVSDocumentationWV7.jsp.

Hale, Henry E. 2011. "The Myth of Mass Russian Support for Autocracy: The Public Opinion Foundations of a Hybrid Regime." *Europe-Asia Studies* 63 (8). 1357–1375.

Hendley, Kathryn. 2017. *Everyday Law in Russia*. Ithaca, NY: Cornell University Press.

Howe, Paul. 2017. "Eroding Norms and Democratic Deconsolidation." *Journal of Democracy* 28 (4): 15–29.

Hu, Peng. 2018. "Popular Understanding of Democracy in Contemporary China." *Democratization* 25 (8): 1441–1459.

Inglehart, Ronald. 1977. *The Silent Revolution: Changing Values and Political Styles Among Western Publics*. Princeton: Princeton University Press.

Inglehart, Ronald. 2003. "How Solid is Mass Support for Democracy—And How Can We Measure It?" *PS: Political Science & Politics* 36 (1): 51–57.

Inglehart, Ronald. 2016. "The Danger of Deconsolidation: How Much Should We Worry?" *Journal of Democracy* 27 (3): 18–23.

Inglehart, Ronald. 2018. *Cultural Evolution: People's Motivations Are Changing, and Reshaping the World*. New York: Cambridge University Press.

Inglehart, Ronald, and Christian Welzel. 2005. *Modernization, Cultural Change, and Democracy: The Human Development Sequence*. New York: Cambridge University Press.

Inkeles, Alex, and Raymond Bauer. 1959. *The Soviet Citizen: Daily Life in a Totalitarian Society*. New York: Atheneum.

Jepsen, Eric M. 2011. "Processes of Democratization." In *21st Century Political Science: A Reference Handbook*, edited by John T. Ishiyama and Marijke Breuning. Thousand Oaks, CA: Sage.

Jowitt, Ken. 1992. *New World Disorder: The Leninist Extinction*. Berkeley: University of California Press.

Keenan, Edward L. 1986. "Muscovite Political Folkways." *The Russian Review* 45: 115–184.

Lankina, Tomila, and Rodion Skovoroda. 2017. "Regional Protest and Electoral Fraud: Evidence From Analysis of New Data on Russian Protest." *East European Politics* 33 (2): 253–274.

Lipset, Seymour Martin. 1960. *Political Man: The Social Bases of Politics*. Baltimore: Johns Hopkins University Press.

Malone, Mary Fran T. 2011. "Explaining Democratization." In *Achieving Democracy: Democratization in Theory and Practice*, edited by Mary Fran T. Malone, 61–84. New York: Continuum.

McDaniel, Tim. 1996. *The Agony of the Russian Idea*. Princeton, NJ: Princeton University Press.

Millar, James R., ed. 1987. *Politics, Work and Daily Life in the USSR: A Survey of Former Soviet Citizens*. New York: Cambridge University Press.

Miller, Arthur H., William M. Reisinger, and Vicki L. Hesli. 1990–1991. "Public Support for New Political Institutions in Russia, Ukraine and Lithuania." *Journal of Soviet Nationalities* 1 (4): 82–107.

Miller, Arthur H., William M. Reisinger, and Vicki L. Hesli. 1993. *Public Opinion and Regime Change: The New Politics of Post-Soviet Societies*. Boulder, CO: Westview.

Miller, Arthur H., William M. Reisinger, and Vicki L. Hesli. 2000. "University of Iowa Post-Soviet Citizen Surveys." Collected 1990–1992, 1995, 1997. (Iowa City, IA: University of Iowa), Dataset Available From the Inter-University Consortium for Political and Social Research, Study #9945, 6521 and 6574 [1990–1992 data], the Authors [1995 and 1997 data].

Moeller, Joergen, and Svend-Erik Skaaning. 2013. *Democracy and Democratization in Comparative Perspective: Conceptions, Conjunctures, Causes and Consequences*. New York: Routledge.

Muller, Edward N., and Mitchell A. Seligson. 1994. "Civic Culture and Democracy: The Question of Causal Relationships." *American Political Science Review* 88 (3): 635–652.

Neundorf, Anja, and Kaat Smets. 2017. "Political Socialization and the Making of Citizens." In *Oxford Handbooks Online*, Unpaginated.

Newton, Kenneth. 2001. "Trust, Social Capital, Civil Society, and Democracy." *International Political Science Review* 22 (2): 201–214.

Norris, Pippa. 2017a. "The Conceptual Framework of Political Support." In *Handbook on Political Trust*, edited by Sonja Zmerli and Tom W. G. van der Meer, 19–32. Northampton, MA: Edward Elgar.

Norris, Pippa. 2017b. "Is Western Democracy Backsliding—Assessing the Risks." *Journal of Democracy Special Web Exchange*. https://www.journalofdemocracy.org/online-exchange-democratic-deconsolidation/

Pop-Eleches, Grigore, and Joshua Tucker. 2017. *Communism's Shadow: Historical Legacies and Contemporary Political Attitudes*. Princeton, NJ: Princeton University Press.

Putnam, Robert D. 1993. *Making Democracy Work: Civic Traditions in Modern Italy*. Princeton: Princeton University Press.

Pyle, William. 2021. "Russia's "Impressionable Years": Life Experience During the Exit From Communism and Putin-Era Beliefs." *Post-Soviet Affairs* 37 (1): 1–25.

Reisinger, William M., Arthur H. Miller, Vicki L. Hesli, and Kristen Hill Maher. 1994. "Political Values in Russia, Ukraine and Lithuania: Sources and Implications for Democracy." *British Journal of Political Science* 45 (2): 183–223.

Reisinger, William M., Vicki L. Hesli Claypool, and Marina Zaloznaya. 2015. "Surveys on Political Causes and Consequences of Bureaucratic Corruption in the Post-Soviet Region." Collected June–November 2015. (Iowa City, IA: University of Iowa).

Robertson, Graeme. 2013. "Protesting Putinism." *Problems of Post-Communism* 60 (2): 11–23.

Rohrschneider, Robert. 1999. *Learning Democracy: Democratic and Economic Values in Unified Germany*. New York: Oxford University Press.

Rose, Richard, and Ellen Carnaghan. 1995. "Generational Effects on Attitudes to Communist Regimes: A Comparative Analysis." *Post-Soviet Affairs* 11 (1): 28–56.

Rose, Richard, William Mishler, and Neil Munro. 2011. *Popular Support for an Undemocratic Regime: The Changing Views of Russians*. New York: Cambridge University Press.

Salinas, Eduardo, and John A. Booth. 2011. "Micro-Social and Contextual Sources of Democratic Attitudes in Latin America." *Journal of Politics in Latin America* 3 (1): 29–64.

Schedler, Andreas, and Rodolfo Sarsfield. 2007. "Democrats With Adjectives: Linking Direct and Indirect Measures of Democratic Support." *European Journal of Political Research* 46 (5): 637–659.

Sharafutdinova, Gulnaz. 2019. "Russia's Struggle Over the Meaning of the 1990s and the Keys to Kremlin Power." In *PONARS Policy Memo*. Washington, DC: PONARS Eurasia.

Shiller, Robert J., Maxim Boycko, and Vladimir Korobov. 1991. "Popular Attitudes Toward Free Markets: The Soviet Union and the United States Compared." *American Economics Review* 81 (3): 385–400.

Singer, Matthew. 2018. "Delegating Away Democracy: How Good Representation and Policy Successes Can Undermine Democratic Legitimacy." *Comparative Political Studies* 51 (13): 1754–1788.

Stenner, Karen. 2005. *The Authoritarian Dynamic*. New York: Cambridge University Press.

Sullivan, John L., James Piereson, and George E. Marcus. 1982. *Political Tolerance and American Democracy*. Chicago: University of Chicago Press.

Sullivan, John L., Michael Shamir, Patrick Walsh, and Nigel S. Roberts. 1985. *Political Tolerance in Context: Support for Unpopular Political Minorities in Israel, New Zealand, and the United States*. Boulder, CO: Westview Press.

Tang, Wenfang. 2005. *Public Opinion and Political Change in China*. Stanford, CA: Stanford University Press.

Thomassen, Jacques. 2007. "Democratic Values." In *The Oxford Handbook of Political Behavior*, edited by Russell J. Dalton and Hans-Dieter Klingemann, 418–434. New York: Oxford University Press.

Treisman, Daniel. 2011. "Presidential Popularity in a Hybrid Regime: Russia Under Yeltsin and Putin." *American Journal of Political Science* 55 (3): 590–609.

Tucker, Robert C. 1960. "The Image of Dual Russia." In *The Transformation of Russian Society: Aspects of Social Change Since 1861*, edited by Cyril E. Black, 587–605. Cambridge, MA: Harvard University Press.

Tucker, Robert C. 1987. *Political Culture and Leadership in Soviet Russia*. New York: Norton.

Tucker, Robert C. 1992. "Sovietology and Russian History." *Post-Soviet Affairs* 8 (3): 175–196.

Uslaner, Eric M., ed. 2018. *The Oxford Handbook of Social and Political Trust*. New York: Oxford University Press.

V-Dem Institute. 2020. *Autocratization Surges—Resistance Grows: Democracy Report 2020*. Gothenburg, Sweden.

Voeten, Erik. 2017. "Are People Really Turning Away From Democracy?" *Journal of Democracy Special Web Exchange*. https://www.journalofdemocracy.org/online-exchange-democratic-deconsolidation/

von Soest, Christian, and Julia Grauvogel. 2015. "How Do Non-Democratic Regimes Claim Legitimacy? Comparative Insights From Post-Soviet Countries." In *GIGA Working Papers*. Hamburg: German Institute of Global and Area Studies.

Warren, Mark E. 2017. "What Kinds of Trust Does a Democracy Need? Trust From the Perspective of Democratic Theory." In *Handbook on Political Trust*, edited by Sonja Zmerli and Tom W. G. van der Meer, 33–52. Northampton, MA: Edward Elgar.

Welzel, Christian. 2009. "Theories of Democratization." In *Democratization*, edited by Christian Haerpfer, Patrick Bernhagen, Ronald F. Inglehart, and Christian Welzel, 74–90. New York: Oxford University Press.

White, Stephen. 1979. *Political Culture and Soviet Politics*. London: MacMillan.

Wyman, Matthew. 1994. "Russian Political Culture: Evidence From Public Opinion Surveys." *Journal of Communist Studies and Transition Politics* 10 (1): 25–54.

Zmerli, Sonja and Tom W. G. van der Meer, eds. 2017. *Handbook on Political Trust*. Northampton, MA: Edward Elgar.

Chapter 3

Reflections on Postcommunist Transitions

30 Years After the Soviet Collapse

Russell Bova

In the introduction to his seminal 1969 volume, *Communist Studies and the Social Sciences*, Frederic J. Fleron observed that "communist studies are now entering an important period of transition" (Fleron 1969, 27). Writing in 1969, he could not have anticipated the dramatic changes that would sweep much of the communist world just two decades later. Indeed, his volume was focused more on transition in the study of communist regimes, a transition that that he was both observing and advocating, than it was about transition in the form and functioning, let alone the collapse and replacement, of those regimes themselves.

Yet Fleron's book, in questioning the overwhelming tendency of both political scientists and area specialists to view communist systems and the Soviet Union as sui generis, proved to be prescient with respect to the changes in the communist world that were to come (Fleron 1969, 27–28). After the fall of the Berlin Wall in 1989 and the collapse of the USSR in 1991, some scholars began to make the case for the integration of communist, or now postcommunist studies, into the mainstream of political and social science (Bova 1991). Indeed, the 1990s were marked by a double transition in Russian and communist/postcommunist studies as scholars had to "reconsider both how to define the region and how to study it" (Bova 2000, 127).

2021 marked the thirtieth anniversary of the collapse of the USSR. Such occasions provide an invitation for reflection and stocktaking. This chapter is composed of a series of such reflections on postcommunist transitions and how we have studied them. In the early days after the Soviet collapse, scholars and pundits filled many pages with discussion of expectations, predictions, and, indeed, hopes for how things might play out. How have those expectations and hopes fared and, what, if anything, can we say more definitively now than we could reasonably do in the heady days of the early 1990s?

Note that this chapter is not intended to be comprehensive and is not based on new research. It is, instead, intended to be a think-piece, organized around several, at least loosely interconnected issues in understanding the postcommunist world, reflecting on the changes that both have and have not taken place in our understanding of post-Soviet Russia and postcommunist regimes in general over the past few decades. In particular, the focus is on the unfulfilled or, more optimistically, the incomplete promise of democratization in the postcommunist space with particular attention to the factors that have inhibited successful democratic transition. In briefly addressing those factors, I stake out my own views on what the lessons of three decades have taught us. In some cases, I embrace what has now become the prevailing wisdom; in others, my conclusions will likely be contentious. In all cases, at the very least, the intention is to provide food for thought and, possibly, fuel for additional research and debate.

INTEGRATION OF AREA STUDIES AND SOCIAL SCIENCE

The first lesson to be gleaned from the past 30 years of postcommunism is that the integration of Russian and communist studies with social science, in general, and with the study of comparative politics, in particular, has not only accelerated but also was helpful and long overdue. Early in the postcommunist period, and roughly a quarter century after the publication of *Communist Studies and the Social Sciences*, Fleron himself renewed his earlier call for scholars of what was now the former Soviet Union to "employ more of the theories and methods of social scientists who study political behavior in the West" (Fleron and Hoffman 1993, 375). His observation that for half a century the prevailing view was that "social science and Sovietology had little to offer each other" (Fleron and Hoffmann 1993, 371) was made real to me when, as a graduate student in the 1980s, a highly regarded Sovietologist questioned my decision to pursue a cognate field in Economics. Of what use, the question was put to me, is the study of Western economic theory for a student of the USSR and communism?

By the 1990s, I felt vindicated in my choice. Especially in the realm of economics, the strictly area studies approach to the post-Soviet space was becoming, as one economist who himself was trained and practiced as a Soviet area specialist put it, "dead as a doornail" (Millar 1997, 5–6). Micro- and macro-economic concepts and theory were now being deployed to understand the process of economic transition from the command economy model, and postcommunist regimes sought advice on those transitions from Western economic advisors who made no claim to area, cultural, or linguistic expertise but who, simply and presumably, had knowledge and insight into universal economic laws. The most well-known of these advisors was Harvard economist Jeffrey Sachs who provided economic advice to Poland and Russia following similar stints as advisor to countries in Latin America. And, indeed, if knowledge of universal economic principles was now seen as useful in Russia and Eastern Europe, even more was that the case for China where marketization of the domestic economy and integration into the global economy far outpaced that taking place in Russia.

If the transition from area studies was most evident in the realm of economics, the study of postcommunist politics was not that far behind. Trained in the days of the Soviet collapse and transition, a new cadre of "Young Turks" was working to transform the study of the region armed with the concepts and methodological tools of political science and other social sciences (Shea 1998, A16–18). Russian politics was being integrated into comparative politics first, in the 1990s as part of a broader study of democratic transitions from authoritarianism, and then later, as prospects for successful democratization began to wane, as part of the broader comparative study of "electoral authoritarianism," "competitive authoritarianism," "adaptive authoritarianism," and other concepts and classifications which continued to bridge the gap between the post-Soviet space and the rest of the political universe. Indeed, as early as 1998, one scholar observed that "Sovietology may be on the path to becoming an academic slur" (Shea 1996, A16–18).

There has, of course, been pushback, and, perhaps, no one pushed back harder than the late historian Stephen Cohen. In the late 1990s he urged scholars to "stop apologizing for being Russianists" and to "liberate" Russian studies from "comparative political theories that know little or nothing about Russia" (Cohen 1999, 50). Others adopted a more nuanced approach, suggesting that the issue was less area studies versus comparative politics, but, rather, a debate among comparativists as to whether the cases selected for comparison are, indeed, comparable. For example, in her critique of efforts to graft onto the study of postcommunist transitions the concepts and lessons derived from democratic transitions in the global south, Valerie Bunce argued that that the issue is one central to the study of comparative politics: "Are we comparing apples with apples, apples with oranges (which are at least varieties of fruit) or apples with, say, kangaroos?" (Bunce 1995, 112). Yet, if one assumes the latter, it is worth noting that one ends up more or less in the same place as Stephen Cohen in suggesting that Russia, or postcommunist states in general, are somehow unique and not good candidates for integration into the more general study of comparative democratization or comparative politics.

Lest one conclude that understanding of the uniqueness of Russia or, more broadly, of postcommunist regimes, will be lost in the quest for universal laws of social science, it is important to stress that the integration of social science and Russian studies is not a one-way street. While the initial impetus after the Soviet collapse was to investigate what Western social science could contribute to our understanding of Russia, more recently our understanding of Russia and other postcommunist states has itself been drawn upon to contribute to our understanding of the world beyond Russian borders and to the further development of more general social science concepts and theories. To cite just one prominent example, Steven Levitsky and Daniel Ziblatt in *How Democracies Die* draw lessons from the experience of postcommunist states threatened by democratic backsliding, as well as from the record of other failed democracies or failed democratic transitions, to provide comparative insight into the threat to democracy that they saw in the late twentieth- and early twenty-first-century United States (Levitsky and Ziblatt 2018).

The confrontational tone between the two sides of the area studies vs. social science debate was arguably, to borrow from Lenin, an "infantile disorder" of post-Soviet studies with both sides overstating their case (Bova 2000: 142). Russia, like all countries, is a blend of the unique and the universal, and it is precisely that combination that makes it appropriate to integrate the study of Russia, and other postcommunist regimes, into the study of comparative politics. To the extent that one discovers common patterns of political behavior among cases characterized by historical and cultural difference, it only serves to strengthen the case for the discovery of universal political patterns and relationships. Indeed, as the polemical dust has settled, we should be left with a reasonable consensus that both approaches, area studies and social science, have something to contribute to our understanding of Russia with comparative studies of the post-Soviet space less a replacement for than a complement to the area studies approach.

DEMOCRATIZATION: NEITHER EASY NOR INEVITABLE

To suggest today that democratization is neither easy nor inevitable would seem to be stating the obvious. Yet many have suggested and, in a few cases, continue to suggest just the opposite. The democratic optimists were buoyed, no doubt, by the fall of the Berlin Wall in 1989 and the collapse of the USSR in 1991, both of which came at the tail end of what Samuel Huntington had called the third wave of democratization. Originating in the Iberian Peninsula and southern Europe, that third wave washed up on the shores of virtually all of Latin America and significant parts of Asia and Sub-Saharan Africa before making a belated arrival in the communist world.

It is more than a coincidence that Francis Fukuyama's article and subsequent book on the "end of history," which declared the victory of the democratic idea and the elimination of all of its serious ideological challengers, were published in 1989 and in January 1992, respectively, just as the communist regimes, first in east Europe and then in Russia itself, were imploding. As Fukuyama seemed to recognize, the collapse of communist regimes, though fewer in number than the authoritarian regimes that were giving way to democracy elsewhere in the world, was the defining culmination of the third wave insofar as it was not just more authoritarian regimes that were collapsing but an entire ideological superstructure called communism, then the most serious and coherent challenger to democracy as an idea for how to organize politics.

That said, Fukuyama's "end of history" idea was neither the first nor the last effort to be optimistic about the spread of democracy in the late twentieth century. Long before the political and scholarly events of the late 1980s and early 1990s, many Western social scientists subscribed to one or another version of what is generally called convergence theory. The idea of convergence was not just that polities were likely to become more similar but that they would travel in the direction of Western political institutions and norms. Perhaps the most common form of such convergence theory was "modernization theory." Represented by such influential scholars as Seymour Martin Lipset, modernization theory, stated most simply, posited that economic development would produce societies that were both increasingly stratified and increasingly educated. Such societies would generate a new educated, politically aware middle class eager to expand the scope of public participation in the political process. In turn, authoritarian regimes would either have to reform and open up space for such participation or run the risk of rebellion, instability, and even revolution from below. Either way, the logic of economic development ran counter to the logic of authoritarianism.

The democratic optimism of modernization theory was not confined to political scientists. Political leaders in the West, at least intuitively, seemed to subscribe to it as well. In its 1996 National Security Strategy for the United States, the Clinton administration appeared to be channeling the logic of modernization theory in suggesting that "free market nations with growing economies . . . are more likely to feel secure and to work toward freedom" (National Security Strategy 1996). Indeed, much of the subsequent justification for economic engagement with China in the 1990s and beyond was premised on the assumption that economic growth and development in

China would ultimately facilitate and promote Chinese political liberalization, thereby rendering China less of a security challenge and leading to its internal political transformation. It was a meeting of modernization theory with the theory of the democratic peace: that is, don't worry about China—its economic development will lead to political liberalization which, in turn, would serve to pacify U.S.-Chinese relations.

Well beyond the early 1990s, democratic optimism has persisted. In 1999, John Mueller argued that "democracy . . . should not be terribly difficult to institute or to maintain, that no elaborate prerequisites are necessary," and that it is "not fundamentally fragile" (Mueller 1999, 13). He suggests that "any dimwit can do democracy," and that about the only obstacle, once the democratic idea is embraced, is suppression of democracy by "thugs with guns" (Mueller 1999, 16 and 192). In this respect, Mueller's argument shares a certain affinity with the neo-conservative case for the 2003 war against Iraq in which it was similarly argued that the only thing standing between the Iraqi people and democracy was the thug named Saddam Hussein. Fast forward two decades, and Stephen Pinker carries the baton of democratic optimism well into the early twenty-first century arguing, counter to those who emphasize democratic backsliding and authoritarian resurgence, that "the third wave of democratization is far from over, let alone ebbing" (Pinker 2018, 203).

In fact, democratization, over the past two decades, has revealed itself to be more difficult and less assured than optimists such as Fukuyama, Mueller, and Pinker have assumed. In its Freedom in the World 2021 survey, aptly subtitled "Democracy under Siege," Freedom House notes that, globally, 2020 was the "15th consecutive year of decline in global freedom," and noted further that the number of countries where freedom and democracy were deteriorating in 2020 "outnumbered those with improvements by the largest margin recorded since the negative trend began in 2006" (Repucci and Slipowitz 2021, 1).

In the postcommunist world specifically, 19 of 29 states still, according to Freedom House's methodology, remain non-democracies with the number of those postcommunist states experiencing democratic regression in 2020 far outnumbering those where the trend was positive. Among those regressing were Poland, Hungary, and the Czech Republic—each a 1990s democratic transition success story. As for Russia itself, it has become progressively less democratic in the two decades of Putin's reign, making Russia today less free and democratic than both Yeltsin's Russia and Gorbachev's USSR. In short, the global record, that of the postcommunist world, and certainly that of Russia each, to varying degrees, cast serious doubt on the assertions, noted above, that democracy "should not be terribly difficult to institute or to maintain" and that it is "not fundamentally fragile."

CULTURE MATTERS

As an explanatory variable for understanding democratization, the concept of political culture has frequently been both used and abused. Crudely applied, political culture takes on an essentialist tone with dispositions toward authoritarian versus democratic rule seen as baked into the DNA of entire societies and peoples. At its worst, the concept can be deployed in a manner that exudes ethnic, racial, and religious biases by excluding, a priori, entire groups of people from either an interest in or a capability for democratic rule. The tendency, thus, to want to omit cultural factors from explanations of democratic progress is understandable.

Yet the record in the postcommunist world over the past three decades suggests that to ignore culture completely would be an overreaction. A crude marker of cultural dividing lines is religion. While religion and culture are not completely synonymous, the former is a key component of the latter. Sometimes the connection between religion and political culture can be quite overt, as in the case of some forms of Islamic fundamentalism or as in Poland during the communist era when Catholicism was part of what defined oneself as a Pole. In other cases, the importance of religion is more subtle insofar as it serves as a cultural marker, bringing with it a set of values or a shared historical experience that have at least an indirect political importance. In other words, while there might be values intrinsic to a particular religion that carry political significance, it is also the case, and arguably more often so, that the attributes of political culture that define a particular religious group might simply be the result of shared experiences including a shared experience, in some cases, of religious oppression.

Samuel Huntington, citing William Wallace, argued in his 1991 study of the third wave of democratization that the critical cultural and political dividing line in Europe after the Cold War was precisely along the fault lines dividing the lands of Western Christendom from the lands of Orthodoxy and Islam to their East and South (Huntington 1991, 299–300). Table 3.1 shows that Huntington and Wallace, even at that very early stage in the postcommunist era (indeed the Huntington book was published roughly a year prior to the disintegration of the USSR), were prescient. Among the 27 postcommunist states of Europe and Eurasia in existence in 2001, democratization has tended to be most rapid and durable in countries characterized by geographic and cultural proximity to Western Europe. Roughly only a decade removed from communist totalitarianism, the nine Western Christian countries, geographically and culturally in closest proximity to Western Europe, had made remarkable democratic progress with their average Freedom House score on political rights and civil liberties (on a scale from 2 to 14 with 2 the best on those counts) of 3.22. In comparison the Orthodox countries (including

Table 3.1 Religion and Democracy in Postcommunist States *(Freedom House Scores Range from 2 to14. The Lower the Score, the More Free and Democratic.)*

Western Christian			*Orthodox*			*Muslim*		
Country	*2001*	*2021*	*Country*	*2001*	*2021*	*Country*	*2001*	*2021*
Czech Rep	3	2	Romania	4	4	Albania	9	6
Hungary	3	6	Bulgaria	5	4	Bosnia	9	8
Poland	3	4	Moldova	6	6	Kirgiz Rep	11	12
Slovakia	3	2	Macedonia	7	6	Kazakhstan	11	12
Slovenia	3	2	Ukraine	8	7	Azerbaijan	11	13
Lithuania	3	3	Georgia	8	7	Tajikistan	12	13
Estonia	3	2	Armenia	8	8	Uzbekistan	13	13
Latvia	3	3	Serbia	8	7	Turkmenistan	14	14
Croatia	5	3	Russia	10	13			
			Belarus	12	13			
Average	3.22	3.0		7.6	7.5		11.25	11.38

Sources: Compiled by author from data of Freedom House, *Freedom in the World 2000-2001,* available online at http://www.freedomhouse.org/research/index.htm (July 16, 2001) and "Freedom in the World 2021, Aggregate Country and Subcategory Scores 2003-2021," available as a data download at: https://freedomhouse.org/report/freedom-world/2021/democracy-under-siege/countries-and-regions.

Russia) and the Muslim countries had average scores of 7.6 and 11.25, respectively.

Even more notable has been the persistence of these differences over time. Despite democratic backsliding in Hungary and Poland, by 2021 the Western Christian countries improved to an average of 3.0, the Orthodox countries remained roughly steady at an average score of 7.5, while the Muslim country average deteriorated slightly to 11.38. Indeed, the average change in Freedom House score among these 27 countries over the two decades from 2001to 2021 was only 0.07. That the pattern would be established so quickly with remarkably little variation over time suggests that there is something fundamental shaping democratic prospects in these countries and that it is unlikely that such a consistent pattern is merely a function of localized events, individual leaders, or the political choices that they made.

While religious boundaries among the countries in the postcommunist world do, to this point, clearly coincide with empirical patterns of progress toward democratic government, the casual mechanism at work here requires more study and research. While cultural factors represent one likely hypothesis, other explanations cannot be entirely ruled out. Perhaps the most obvious challenger to a cultural argument might be level of socioeconomic development, and, indeed, an early analysis did find some association between democratization in the postcommunist space and level of economic development. Yet that same study found that the association was not as strong as one might expect and that it was less significant than the statistical association between democracy and religion (Fish 1998, 225–226 and 332–333). More recent articles seem to confirm the salience of the cultural factor, particularly as regards attitudes toward women, as an important factor in explaining lack of democratic development in the Muslim world (Fish 2002; Jakli et al. 2019).

That said, even if culture turns out to be the key explanatory variable of postcommunist democratic progress to date, that does not necessarily imply that further democratic progress in the region is impossible insofar as cultures are neither monolithic nor impervious to change. If they were then democracy could never have emerged in Western Europe itself as it was once a continent ruled by kings and autocrats. Likewise, Catholic Latin America and parts of southern Europe were once believed to be characterized by hierarchical political values antithetic to democracy, yet those were exactly the parts of the world most central to Huntington's third wave of democratization in the 1970s and 1980s. Might it be possible to learn democracy and to absorb democratic values by "doing democracy"? If so, the question, then, is what kinds of political choices might maximize the chances of successful democratization in countries where democratic progress has lagged. One possibility is related to the questions of institutional design that every fledgling democracy must make.

INSTITUTIONS MATTER TOO—THE RUSSIAN CASE

The long-existing conventional wisdom among observers of Russia is that it is a country with a political culture inhospitable to democracy. Rooted in the challenges of governing such a large geographic space, insecure borders, and a history of invasion and conquest, the assumption has long been that Russians value security, order, and strong leaders over freedom, democracy, and constrained leaders. Some have taken issue with that conventional wisdom and have suggested that an alternative, more democratic political subculture coexists, in Russia, alongside the more dominant authoritarian values (Petro 1995). That democratic subculture does indeed rear its head from time to time, as witnessed in the late 1980s and early 1990s. A 1991 Pew survey, for example, found that Russians preferred democratic rule to rule by a leader with a strong hand by 51% to 39% (Pew Research Center 2006).

Yet the evidence is that Russia's "democratic moment" was fleeting and that nondemocratic values remain dominant. By 2005, Pew found that preference for a leader with a strong hand had surged to two-thirds with preference for democratic rule down to about one-quarter (Pew Research Center 2006). A 2015 survey by the Levada Center (2015) found that "stabilization of the country's political and economic situation" was the top priority while only 7% said that the top priority was democracy. Likewise, another set of Levada Center surveys indicate that preference for rule by "a strong hand at all times" rose from 25% in 1989 to 58% by 2018 with another 22%, in 2018, agreeing that "there are situations (like now) when it is necessary to give full power to one person" (Levada Analytical Center 2019, 32). Those findings are consistent with an analysis of the relative prioritization of survival values (i.e., concern with physical and economic security) over self-expression values (i.e., concern with autonomy and independence from central authority) in Russia as compared to other societies. Inglehart and Welzel (2005: 63) found that of 81 countries surveyed (representing 85% of global population) Russia ranked second to last in self-expression values, and they argue that the differences among the countries surveyed could only partly be explainable by socioeconomic factors with cultural differences making an independent contribution to the values differences among the countries surveyed (Inglehart and Welzel 2005: 66).

As pessimistic as both the actual record of Russian democracy and the survey trends noted above might be, it remains an open question as to how much political culture constrains political choices and democratic progress and how much political choices and the record of democratic rule serve to shape and re-shape political culture. In other words, has the backsliding on Russia's record of democratization since the heady days of the early 1990s and has the increasingly apparent rejection of democratic values by Russian citizens as reflected in the survey data been more a result of Russia's return to an unalterable set of cultural values or are they more a result of the record of Russian democratization in practice in the 1990s? And, if the latter, what might have been done differently?

In a 1998 volume on congruence theory coauthored by Frederic J. Fleron Jr., an approach to understanding democratization is offered that can serve to integrate both sides of the equation and the capture the reciprocal relationship between a country's pre-existing political culture and the kinds of institutional choices it makes in attempting to establish a new democratic system. As explained by Harry Eckstein, the originator of the theory, congruence theory is premised on the assumption that the viability of a political system is a function of the extent to which governmental patterns of authority "are congruent with the authority patterns of other units of society" (Eckstein 1998: 4). So, stated most simply, governments in places where, say, societal authority patterns are centralized and hierarchical must reflect those societal patterns just as governments in societies characterized by more egalitarian, less centralized, and more democratic authority patterns must reflect those patterns. Mismatches (incongruence) will negatively affect government performance and effectiveness.

Complicating the situation is that, as Eckstein posits, authority relations in even the most democratic societies are "inherently inconsistent with pure democracy" (1998: 21). Thus, even the most democratic governments must contain "balanced disparities," that is, a mix of democratic and authoritarian elements. What that "balance" will look like, ideally, will vary from country to country according to its unique political culture or societal authority patterns. This is precisely where considerations of institutional design enter into the equation, and there are many ways to proceed insofar as there are multiple options for creating and mixing and matching in the design of a fledgling democracy. Democratic systems can be federal or unitary systems, presidential or parliamentary, utilize proportional representation or single-member districts. And none of these choices is strictly binary as there are variations that can be made on all these themes. Indeed, one would be hard pressed to find any two democratic political systems that are exactly alike across all these dimensions.

A Russian soldier is reported to have once observed to the British ambassador, "Oh yes, we must have a Republic, but we must have a good Tsar at its head" (White 1979: 31). Reading that as a primitive articulation of the balanced disparities that characterize Russian authority relations, and, combined with the conventional take on Russian political culture, the temptation might have been to tip the balanced disparities in Russian institutional design in favor of a democracy that provided wide latitude for a powerful leader. Indeed, the Yeltsin constitution of 1993, with its powerful presidency, might be seen as congruent with this sentiment. However, as the previously cited survey data suggests, the issue is not just a strong leader but economic and political stability and order, and it is precisely in those areas where the fledgling Russian democracy of the 1990s failed to deliver.

The turmoil that characterized Russia in the 1990s was a result of many factors, but it is arguably is at least partly related to failures of institutional design. In particular, as I have suggested in more detail elsewhere (Bova, 1998: 177–200) the literature on presidentialism has long pointed to the counterintuitive conclusion that a strong and independent presidency can be a recipe for a weak and ineffective government insofar as it both leads to competition for authority with legislatures and it fails, given fixed terms of office, to provide quick electoral solutions to the challenge of declining governmental popularity and support. A scholar of Latin America, where presidentialism has traditionally predominated, once noted, "the stronger the president, the weaker the presidential system" (Valenzuela 1995: 97).

Rather than reinforcing elements of a democratic subculture and moving Russian political culture on a more democratic trajectory, the 1990s reinforced the least democratic elements in traditional Russian political culture. Indeed, the political and economic instability that characterized Russia in the 1990s served to discredit Russia's inchoate democratic experiment and provided the political space for the steady, systematic erosion of that experiment during the two decades of Putin's rule. Whether a different approach to Russian constitutional design would have made a difference is unclear, but the choices that were made did not maximize the chances.

ELECTORAL AUTHORITARIANISM AND INSTITUTIONAL TURBULENCE

One of the lessons learned from Putin's systematic dismantling of Russia's democratic experiment is that institutions matter to authoritarian leaders too. Putin's version of Russian authoritarianism is not that of the Russian tsars, of Stalin, or even that of Brezhnev's post Stalinist Russia. Putin's twenty-first-century variation on authoritarianism falls into the category of what has been commonly labeled "electoral authoritarianism."

Electoral authoritarian regimes embrace some of the trappings of democracy insofar as they hold elections that are "minimally pluralistic" and "minimally competitive," but they employ a menu of manipulative devices to manage electoral outcomes "so profoundly and so systematically as to render elections instruments of authoritarian rule rather than instruments of democracy" (Schedler 2006: 3). The manipulative devices employed are varied and range from outright fraud in vote counting to more subtle devices such as making it difficult for opposition parties to register and participate in elections, harassment of opposition groups, and limits on opposition media and on opportunities for assembly (Schedler 2002: 36–50). Still another, often underappreciated, mechanism designed to skew electoral outcomes in the regime's favor is as, Sarah Birch (2011) puts it, a propensity for "fiddling electoral rules." In a truly liberal democracy, the outcomes of elections are, by definition, uncertain, but the rules of the electoral competition, subject to occasional reforms done under strict constitutional guidelines, tend to be relatively stable. However, in an electoral democracy, the regime goal is certainty of outcome, and that often requires the kind of fiddling that Birch references.

The purpose of all this fiddling or turbulence in the rules of the game is partly to keep the opposition off balance, as changing rules make it difficult for a fledgling opposition to develop a consistent political strategy. It is also a way for the regime to strike the elusive balance of using elections to maintain a semblance of legitimacy without losing control of the whole process. Drawing from examples in Southeast Asia, William Case (2006: 95–112) argues that electoral authoritarian regimes frequently confront "choice points in which they must decide whether to recalibrate electoral competitiveness." But that recalibration process is tricky to manage.

> Inevitably, the formula for striking that balance will be elusive. The more effective the regime is in staying ahead of the opposition by manipulating electoral rules in its favor, the more it risks undermining electoral legitimacy and the regime itself. Indeed, sophisticated regime leaders will understand that there are times when a carefully calibrated lightening of the weight of the thumb on the scale is necessary, as a way to defuse post-election protests for example. But those same sophisticated leaders might find other means to compensate. Lift the thumb on one scale (e.g. reduce the number of signatures necessary for registration of new opposition parties) but press down more firmly on another (e.g. tighten up the rules for evaluating the validity of signatures). All told, the net result, once again, is constant fiddling with the rules. (Bova and Moriarty 2014)

Putin has employed this game of electoral turbulence in many areas—including in constant changes to the rules for party registration as well as those that govern regional elections. Perhaps the most important use of this tactic, however, has been in the shifting rules for elections to the state Duma. Here is a brief summary and review of how the Duma electoral system has changed over time in postcommunist Russia.

1993: The original system elected half of the 450 seat Duma via a party list system with a 5% threshold. The other 225 seats were elected from single member, first past the post electoral districts.

2005: A 100% PR system with the threshold increased to 7%.

2009: A more minor change affecting the threshold was adopted. Parties receiving 5–6% of the voted would be allocated one seat; parties receiving 6–7% of the vote would receive two seats. The 100% PR system was, for the time being, retained.

2013: On Putin's recommendation (Oxford Analytica 2012) the Duma approved a return to the original 1993 mixed system of 50% PR and 50% single-member districts. That followed a 2011 decision to return to a 5% threshold. These changes would both be effective in time for the 2016 legislative elections.

So, what explains this constant change in the electoral system? Indeed, the original 1993 rules worked quite well for the regime backed United Russia party in the first Putin-era Duma elections held in 2003. In that election, United Russia won 49.3% of the seats with the second-place Communist party trailing far behind with only 11.6%. But even more to the point, United Russia performed well in the single-member districts capturing 102 of 225 races, not including independent candidates who would align with United Russia. Indeed, no other party captured more than 12 seats in the single-member district races, and the key competitor parties (Communist, Liberal Democrats, Motherland) did significantly better in the party list vote than in the single-member districts (Russia Votes 2015). So why reform a system that seemed to be working well for the Putin regime and its United Russia allies? Why move to a 100% PR system when the single-member districts seemed to be working well for the regime?

There were several important considerations. First, while United Russia only won 37.5% of the party list vote in 2003, it ended up with 120 party list seats as a result of numerous parties not meeting the 5% threshold. Second, the single-member districts produced a significant number of independent candidates winning seats (71 seats in the 2003 election). These independent winners were often local notables with name recognition that negated their need to run as a member of United Russia. Third, even United Russia candidates elected from single-member districts posed a potential loyalty problem for the party as they would be torn between the national party and the local needs of their districts. As Rebecca Smyth (2007: 127) has persuasively argued, in the party list vote all power would be held by the established national parties who could, through the building of party lists, enforce loyalty and party discipline among their members. In short, the move to the 100% party lists system was likely due to an effort to exert greater central control over Duma delegates by effectively eliminating independents and reinforcing national party control over all United Russia members in the Duma. Putin's gamble paid off in the 2007 election with United Russia winning 315 seats (70%) in the new 100% PR system. The three main opposition parties that crossed the threshold collected 135 seats (down by about 20 seats from the combined total of all other parties represented in the 2003 Duma).

But then came the renewed 2013 fiddling with the electoral system and a return to the original 50/50 split between party list and single-member district seats. The explanation is found in the declining performance of United Russia from 2007 to 2111. As compared with 2007, United Russia's party list vote fell from 64.3% and 315 seats in the Duma to 49.42% and only 238 seats (a slim majority of the total 450 seats). Given both the international and domestic context within which the 2011 election occurred, this decline in the fortunes of Russia's regime party was not surprising. The lingering impact of the Great Recession of 2008 combined with the unease created in some quarters by Putin's decision to reclaim the presidency in 2012, following the Medvedev interregnum, were among the factors at work. In fact, the result for United Russia would have likely been even worse but for the electoral manipulation that occurred. But even that manipulation did not produce the desired results for the regime. Hence the 2013 reversal to the mixed system, a reversal that key opposition parties opposed. As the Communist Party noted in response to the change, "United Russia is no longer capable of winning elections according to the current system, so the switch to a mixed system has been proposed" (Winning 2013). Indeed, the change paid off for Putin and United Russia in 2016 as United Russia won 343 (76%) of the 450 Duma seats including 203 of the 225 newly reestablished single-member districts (Kolesnikov 2021).

REVERSE SNOWBALLING AND THE IMPACT OF EXTERNAL EVENTS

Part of what contributed to the third wave of democratization from the 1970s to the 1990s was an international environment conducive to democratic change. As Huntington (1991: 85–106) noted, the behavior and policies of key external actors, combined with the demonstration effects produced by successful democratization in other countries, especially those that were geographically proximate and facing similar types of internal challenges, contributed to democratic snowballing and the diffusion of the idea that democracy was the cure to all kinds of internal ailments. By the time we get to the late 1980s and 1990s, the Western democracies seemed globally ascendant as the internal problems faced by the USSR and Russia combined with the 1992 Maastricht Treaty and the related enthusiasm over the new European Union (EU) added to a world environment when autocracy of all stripes increasingly looked like an historical anachronism.

Fast forward to 2021 and the global context has radically changed in a number of ways that are not favorable to democracy in the world in general and in the postcommunist space in particular. First, the countries most important to supporting and modeling democracy for the rest of the world during the third wave have, more recently, experienced a period of relative decline while some autocratic regimes have experienced a rise in global power and stature. The migration crisis, Brexit, and the early handling of the Covid-19 pandemic have taken much of the shine off the EU experiment. Perhaps even more significantly, it is the change in the relative global positions of the United States and China that is driving this perception of democratic decline and autocracy rising. Some scholars, most notably Michael Beckley (2018), take issue with the view of American decline/China's rise, but the conventional wisdom and, perhaps most importantly, the global perception is that autocratic China is ascendant. For example, a 2021 survey conducted in 11 European countries found 59% agreeing that China will be a stronger power than the United States in 10 years' time (Krastev 2021: 10). Previous surveys suggested that this view was a global one. Indeed, even Americans see China, both today and in 20 years' time, as the world's leading economic power (Gallup 2021). This perception of growing Chinese power relative to the United States is not inconsistent with other surveys that suggest that distrust of China is growing around the world (Silver 2020). In fact, the two trends are arguably related insofar as it is the perception of growing Chinese power that is increasingly being perceived as a threat to the interests of other states.

Second, the American commitment to democracy, both at home and abroad, has come under increasing question in recent years. If the third wave was marked by an increasing U.S. assertiveness in promoting democratic development abroad (Huntington 1991: 91–98), recent years, and especially during the Trump administration, have seen U.S. retrenchment in that area. Trump not only was uninterested in democracy promotion because of the costs involved (a reasonable concern in a general period of scarce U.S. resources already thinly spread) but also because his ideological commitment to the spread of democracy as an intrinsic foreign policy priority was, to say the least, in question. Indeed, Trump seemed to suggest greater affinity for autocratic leaders, not least of whom was Vladimir Putin, than for leaders of democracies. Moreover, the January 6, 2021 assault on the U.S. Capitol, the associated Trump-era challenges to democratic norms, and the polarization and dysfunction characterizing American politics in general all serve to take the luster off U.S. democracy. The Biden administration has been verbally committed to a reversal of the Trump approach on all these counts. But resource constraints combined with uncertainty about the 2024 U.S. presidential election and the future of American democracy pose real limits on the impact of Biden's pro-democracy approach.

Third, the Covid-19 pandemic accelerated the trend toward democratic backsliding in many countries. For example, in March 2020 a "state of danger" was declared in Hungary followed, in June, by the "Health Care Act" which allowed Prime Minister Viktor Orbán to rule by decree without legislative approval or oversight and without an end date established. In addition, these measures allowed Orbán to unilaterally suspend any law and to take other extraordinary measures in response to the pandemic (Freedom House 2021). In November 2020, Belarus partly closed its land borders to foreigners ostensibly to contain the spread of the pandemic, but opposition leaders claimed that Covid-19 was simply the justification for a crackdown on foreign influence that was politically motivated. In June 2021 opposition activists in Russia, including members of Navalny's organization and of the Pussy Riot group were arrested, accused of violating Covid-19 safety rules in promoting a protest that allegedly led to the spread of the disease (*New York Times* 2021). As has been true of the impact of the Covid-19 in general across a wide range of issues—from the future of economic globalization, to political polarization, to the future of work, and to how education is delivered in colleges and universities—the pandemic it is best viewed not so much as a fundamental cause but as an accelerant of changes already bubbling. Depending on how one looks at it, the pandemic has provided either the excuse or the courage to do things that would have faced greater resistance in the pre-pandemic world. The same is true with respect to the future of democracy as the pandemic has served to accelerate trends already in evidence.

TOWARD THE FUTURE

The day when happy revelers were singing atop the crumbling Berlin Wall in 1989 seems a long time ago, and their hopeful and infectious expectations for freedom and democracy seem largely unfulfilled. In fairness, not all democratic hopes and gains have been lost. As in previous waves of democratic change it has been two steps forward, one step back. For all of the current pessimism, much of central Europe (despite some regression) remains a far cry from the situation there in the days of the Warsaw Pact, the Baltic states remain free and independent, and much of the former Soviet bloc remains firmly ensconced in Western institutions, most importantly NATO and the EU. In Moldova, President Maia Sandu's European-oriented, reformist politics provide a counterpoint to the democratic backsliding seen elsewhere in the region, and those who take to the streets in Minsk and Moscow to protest rigged elections remind us that there remains some yearning for the promise of the early 1990s to be achieved.

That said, in 2021, democracy and freedom, in the world at large and in the postcommunist world in particular, seem, on balance, to be on the defensive. No case illustrates that more clearly than that of Russia itself. Russia, of course, has always been the big prize in the postcommunist world, and its fate will strongly influence that of its postcommunist neighbors. As one witnesses the increasing crackdown on the Russian media, as the Putin regime expands the scope of the net with which it entangles the so-called foreign agents, as it becomes increasingly brazen, as in the Navalny case, in the measures it uses against any organized opposition, Russia seems to be moving beyond the democratic façade of electoral authoritarianism in the direction of unvarnished autocracy. The legitimacy once expected to be conveyed by the increasingly hollow rituals of Russian electoral authoritarianism is steadily being replaced by outright repression. Indeed, it is an open question as to how long those electoral rituals will continue to be held, as the costs to the regime as measured, for example, by post-election protests might at some point come to be seen as greater than the cost of cancelled elections and even stricter repression.

REFERENCES

Beckley, Michael. 2018. *Unrivaled: Why America Will Remain the World's Sole Superpower*. Ithaca: Cornell University Press.

Birch, Sarah. 2011. *Electoral Malpractice*. New York: Oxford University Press.

Bova, Russell. 1991. "Political Dynamics of the Post-Communist Transition: A Comparative Perspective." *World Politics* 44, no. 1 (October): 113–138.

Bova, Russell. 1998. "Political Culture, Authority Patterns, and the Architecture of the New Russian Democracy." In *Can Democracy take Root in Post-Soviet Russia?*, edited by Harry Eckstein, Frederic J. Fleron, Jr., Erik P. Hoffman, and William M. Reisinger, 177–200. Lanham, MD: Rowman and Littlefield.

Bova, Russell. 2000. "The Double Transition in Russian Area Studies." *Frontiers* 6, no. 1 (Winter): 127–154.

Bova, Russell, and Caitlin Moriarty. 2014. "Vlad be Nimble: Electoral Turbulence as a Strategy of Regime Maintenance in Russia." Unpublished Manuscript.

Bunce, Valerie. 1995. "Should Transitologists Be Grounded?" *Slavic Review* 54 (1): 111–127. doi: 10.2307/2501122.

Case, William. 2006. "Manipulative Skills: How do Rulers Control the Electoral Arena." In *Electoral Authoritarianism: The Dynamics of Unfree Competition*, edited by Andreas Schedler, 95–112. Boulder: Rienner.

Cohen, Stephen F. 1999. "Russian Studies Without Russia." *Post-Soviet Affairs* 15 (1): 37–55.

Eckstein, Harry. 1998. "Congruence Theory Explained." In *Can Democracy take Root in Post-Soviet Russia?*, edited by Harry Eckstein, Frederic J. Fleron, Jr., Erik P. Hoffman, and William M. Reisinger, 3–34. Lanham, MD: Rowman and Littlefield.

Fish, M. Steven. 1998. "Democratization's Requisites: The Postcommunist Experience." *Post-Soviet Affairs* 14 (3): 212–247.

Fish, M. Steven. 2002. "Islam and Authoritarianism." *World Politics* 55 (1): 4–37.

Fleron Jr., Frederic J. 1969. "Introduction, Soviet Area Studies and the Social Sciences: Some Methodological Problems in Communist Studies." In *Communist Studies and the Social Sciences*, edited by Frederic J. Fleron, Jr., 1–33. Chicago: Rand McNally.

Fleron, Frederic J., Jr., and Erik P. Hoffmann. 1993. "Post-Communist Studies and Political Science: Peaceful Coexistence, Detente, and Entente." In *Post-Communist Studies and Political Science*, edited by Frederic J. Fleron, Jr. and Erik P. Hoffmann, 3–23. Boulder: Westview.

Freedom House. 2021. "Freedom in the World 2021: Hungary." https://freedomhouse.org/country/hungary/freedom-world/2021.

Gallup. 2021. "U.S. Position in the World." https://news.gallup.com/poll/116350/position-world.aspx.

Huntington, Samuel. 1991. *The Third Wave: Democratization in the Late Twentieth Century*. Norman: University of Oklahoma Press.

Inglehart, Ronald, and Christian Welzel. 2005. *Modernization, Cultural Change, and Democracy*. New York: Cambridge University Press.

Jakli, Laura, M. Steven Fish, and Jason Wittenberg. 2019. "A Decade of Democratic Decline and Stagnation." In *Democratization*, edited by Christian W. Haerpfer, Patrick Bernhagen, Christian Welzel, and Ronald F. Inglehart, 267–282. Oxford: Oxford University Press.

Kolesnikov, Andrei, and Boris Makarenko. 2021. "Four Unknowns Ahead of Russia's 2021 Parliamentary Elections." *Carnegie Moscow Center*. https://carnegie.ru/commentary/84722.

Kramer, Andrew. 2021. "In Russia, a Virus Lockdown Targets the Opposition." *New York Times*, June 18, 2021. https://www.nytimes.com/2021/03/19/world/europe/russia-covid-opposition.html.

Krastev, Ivan, and Mark Leonard. 2021. "The Crisis of American Power: How Europeans See Biden's America." *European Council on Foreign Relations*. https://ecfr.eu/wp-content/uploads/The-crisis-of-American-power-How-Europeans-see-Bidens-America.pdf.

Levada Analytical Center. 2015. "Stabilization vs. Democracy." *Levada Center Press Release*. https://www.levada.ru/en/2016/04/05/stabilization-vs-democracy/.

Levada Analytical Center. 2019. *Russian Public Opinion 2018*. Moscow: Levada Center. https://www.levada.ru/cp/wp-content/uploads/2019/07/2018-Eng.pdf.

Levitsky, Steven, and Daniel Ziblatt. 2018. *How Democracies Die*. New York: Crown.

Millar, James R. 1997. "Doom Without Gloom: Area Studies and the Economics Profession." *Newsnet: The Newsletter of the AAASS* 37 (4): 5–6.

Mueller, John. 1999. *Capitalism, Democracy, and Ralph's Pretty Good Grocery*. Princeton: Princeton University Press.

Oxford Analytica Daily Brief. 2012. "Weak Ruling Party Forces Putin into Electoral Reform." December 17, 2012. https://www.oxan.com/display.aspx?ItemID=DB180282.

Petro, Nicolai N. 1995. *The Rebirth of Russian Democracy: An Interpretation of Political Culture*. Cambridge, MA: Harvard University Press.

Pew Research Center. 2006. *Russia's Weakened Democratic Embrace. 2005 Pew Global Attitudes Survey.* Washington, DC: Pew Research Center. https://www.pewresearch.org/global/2006/01/05/russias-weakened-democratic-embrace/.

Pinker, Steven. 2018. *Enlightenment Now: The Case for Reason, Science, Humanism, and Progress*. New York: Viking.

Radio Free Europe/Radio Liberty. 2020. "Belarus Partially Shuts Down Borders Over Covid-19 as Protest Crackdown Continues." November 1, 2020. https://www.rferl.org/a/belarus-partially-shuts-borders-over-covid-19-as-protest-crackdown-continues/30923669.html.

Repucci, Sarah, and Amy Slipowitz. 2021. "Freedom in the World 2021: Democracy Under Siege." *Freedom House*, 1–32. https://freedomhouse.org/sites/default/files/2021-02/FIW2021_World_02252021_FINAL-web-upload.pdf.

Russia Votes. 2015. "Results of Previous Elections to the Russian State Duma." *Center for the Study of Public Policy, University of Strathclyde*. http://www.russiavotes.org/duma/duma_elections_93-03.php.

Schedler, Andreas. 2002a. "The Menu of Manipulation." *Journal of Democracy* 13 (2): 36–50.

Schedler, Andreas. 2002b. "The Nested Game of Democratization by Elections." *International Political Science Review* 23 (1): 103–122.

Schedler, Andreas. 2006. "The Logic of Electoral Authoritarianism." In *Electoral Authoritarianism: The Dynamics of Unfree Competition*, edited by Andreas Schedler, 1–26. Boulder, CO: Rienner.

Shea, Christopher. 1998. "New Faces and New Methodologies Invigorate Russian Studies." *The Chronicle of Higher Education*, February 20, 1998.

Silver, Laura, Kat Devlin, and Christine Huang. 2020. "Unfavorable Views of China Reach Historic Highs in Many Countries." *Pew Research Center*. https://www.pewresearch.org/global/2020/10/06/unfavorable-views-of-china-reach-historic-highs-in-many-countries/.

Smyth, Regina, Anna Lowry, and Brandon Wilkening. 2007. "Engineering Victory: Institutional Reform and Formal Institutions and the Formation of a Hegemonic Party Regime in the Russian Federation." *Post-Soviet Affairs* 23 (2): 118–137.

The White House. 1996. "A National Security Strategy of Engagement and Enlargement." https://history.defense.gov/Portals/70/Documents/nss/nss1996.pdf?ver=4f8riCrLnHIA-H0itYUp6A%3d%3d.

Valenzuela, Arturo. 1995. "Chile: Origins and Consolidation of a Latin American Democracy." In *Politics in Developing Countries: Comparing Experiences With Democracy*, edited by Larry Diamond, Juan J. Linz, and Seymour Martin Lipset, 67–118. Boulder, CO: Rienner.

White, Stephen. 1979. *Political Culture and Soviet Politics.* New York: St. Martin's.

Winning, Alexander. 2013. "Duma Endorses Election Reform in First Reading." *Moscow Times. Johnson's Russia List.* April 17, 2013. http://russialist.org/duma-endorses-election-reform-in-first-reading/.

Chapter 4

Reflections on Russia

A Century (Plus) After the Revolution

Nathaniel I. Richmond

November 2017 marked the 100th anniversary of the Russian Revolution, an event of immense historical importance. The recent centenary of the Revolution is a good opportunity to pause and reflect on Russia's past and present, and to speculate about its future.

THE IMPORTANCE OF THINKING LIKE A RUSSIAN

The most important concept that I have learned in more than 45 years of Russia-watching is that to understand Russia, it is necessary to think like a Russian. This is very difficult, often impossible for Americans, because we have a completely different mindset. If I had to compare the American and Russian mindsets in three key words they would be as follows: Americans are individualistic, optimistic, and superficial. Russians, on the other hand, are collectivist, pessimistic, and deep (deep in the philosophic sense—profound).

These are, of course, generalizations and don't apply to everyone in either country. But in general, it has been my observation that Russians, especially the older generation, are very conservative, very religious, bordering on superstitious, fatalistic, very suspicious of others' motives, and generally, not risk takers.

There is a Russian proverb that captures the importance of not taking risks: "The tallest tree gets cut down first." Thus, don't stick your neck out, don't stand out from the crowd, don't call attention to yourself, or you will put yourself at risk.

They have another saying that I think also illustrates the Russian mindset: "An optimist is an uninformed pessimist." In other words, if you knew what I know, you would be pessimistic also.

So, to understand Russia, we need to try to see their lives, their country, and the world through their eyes. The optimal way to do this, of course, is to live in Russia for an extended period and to interact with a wide variety of Russian society. It also helps to be a consumer of the Russian media, but with independent and opposition voices being silenced, this is not as useful as it once was, for example, during the early post-Soviet decade. Without trying to understand Russia through their own eyes and life experiences, however, we will forever be at a loss to understand why they do the things they do.

UNDERSTANDING RUSSIA'S PAST AND PRESENT: THE KEYS TO UNDERSTANDING RUSSIA'S FUTURE

Russia's Past

When thinking about Russia over the course of the last 100 years four things that stand out to me:

1) Since the Revolution the least expected among the elite has usually emerged as the new leader.
2) In the absence of free, fair, and meaningful elections, new leaders always attempt to justify and legitimize their rule by repudiating the prior leader's policies and by trying to enhance Russia's global role.
3) The "good old days" for Russians was during the USSR, especially in the post–World War II and post-Stalin eras, but that doesn't mean they want to recreate the USSR today.
4) The "bad old days" was the decade following the USSR's collapse, and any repetition of that era is to be avoided.

Since the Revolution the Least Expected among the Elite Has Usually Emerged as the New Leader

Prior to the Revolution, Russia was an absolute monarchy, and there was an order of succession that was hereditary. For about 300 years, from 1613 to 1917, the Romanov Dynasty ruled Russia and the crown (usually) passed from father to son or from brother to brother. With the overthrow of the Provisional Government in November 1917 and the subsequent establishment of a Communist government, Russian leaders paid scant attention to the issue of leadership succession. This was probably due, in part, to their Marxist belief in the "withering away of the state" which would abrogate the need for elites, political succession, and so on.

In *The State and Revolution* Lenin, quoting Engels's *Anti-Dühring*, wrote:

> The interference of the state power in social relations becomes superfluous in one sphere after another, and then ceases of itself. The government of persons is replaced by the administration of things and the direction of the processes of production. The state is not "abolished," it withers away. (Lenin, 1918, 12)

Gravely ill following a series of strokes in the early 1920s, Lenin dictated his "Testament," a candid assessment of Russia's other leaders. Lenin's illness and subsequent death in 1924 began a succession struggle that played out over the course of several years, culminating with Stalin, an uneducated, brooding, paranoid introvert whom the other leaders looked at with contempt, and the least likely among the inner circle of leaders to assume control, consolidating his power by the late 1920s.

About Stalin, Lenin wrote:

> Comrade Stalin, having become Secretary-General, has unlimited authority concentrated in his hands, and I am not sure whether he will always be capable of using that authority with sufficient caution. (Lenin, 1922, Continuation)

Later, Lenin added:

> Stalin is too coarse and this defect, although quite tolerable in our midst and in dealing among us Communists, becomes intolerable in a Secretary-General. That is why I suggest that the comrades think about a way of removing Stalin from that post and appointing another man in his stead who in all other respects differs from Comrade Stalin in having only one advantage, namely, that of being more tolerant, more loyal, more polite, and more considerate to the comrades, less capricious, etc. (Lenin, 1923, Addition)

Stalin accomplished his remarkable assumption of absolute power not because he was a brilliant Marxist theoretician or spellbinding orator—he wasn't. Rather, as the party's General Secretary, he created a list of positions and oversaw appointments to fill those positions, thus creating a cadre beholden to and loyal to him.

The least expected among the Soviet leaders assuming power was repeated following Stalin's death in 1953 with Khrushchev, a flamboyant peasant whom the other leaders considered to be a bombastic clown, consolidating his power a few years later. At first, Khrushchev copied Stalin's tactic of aligning with other leaders to oust the most immediate threat. In Stalin's case, that was Trotsky whom Stalin ousted and later had assassinated. In Khrushchev's case, the immediate threat was Beria who was ousted from the leadership and then quickly executed.

Like Stalin, Khrushchev boldly struck to seize power by discrediting his political opponents. Unlike Stalin, however, Khrushchev began by detailing some of his predecessor's (Stalin's) crimes, human rights abuses, and poor military decision-making during the Great Patriotic War (World War II). He then linked his political opposition to those policies.

Brezhnev, a dull, colorless apparatchik who had been demoted during the last years of Khrushchev's rule, was installed as leader following Khrushchev's overthrow in 1964. Politically, Brezhnev was the opposite of Khrushchev, and was chosen by the other leaders because he was viewed as a non-threat to them. Plodding and cautious, Brezhnev was able to oust challengers and critics alike from the pinnacle of the Soviet leadership. Having done so he consolidated his power by 1971. The hallmark of his governance was his "stability of cadres" bargain that long delayed generational leadership change until Gorbachev began that process soon after he ascended to power in 1985.

Yeltsin, a flamboyant, hot-tempered, outspoken, crusading anti-corruption politician who was purged from Gorbachev's inner circle, managed a remarkable political comeback and succeeded Gorbachev following the collapse of the USSR in 1991. Elected President of the Russian Soviet Federated Socialist Republic (RSFSR) in June 1991 as a critic of Gorbachev's *Perestroika* policy arguing that the policy was too timid, Yeltsin was instrumental in facilitating the collapse of the USSR.

And finally, Putin's becoming Russia's president following Yeltsin's surprise resignation on the last day of 1999 culminated his improbable rise from obscure KGB operative to the pinnacle of Russian power. In each of these examples, the least expected person ultimately assumed power.

In the Absence of Free, Fair, and Meaningful Elections, New Leaders Always Attempt to Justify and Legitimize Their Rule by Repudiating the Prior Leader's Policies and by Trying to Enhance Russia's Global Role

No longer a monarchy, yet absent free, fair, and meaningful elections, Soviet and post-Soviet leaders attempted to legitimize their rule by repudiating the prior leader's policies and by trying to enhance Russia's global role. Hence, despite his claims of continuing Lenin's policies, Stalin's "Socialism in One Country" policy was a sharp reversal of Lenin's commitment to world revolution. Khrushchev's policy of "de-Stalinization" was an abrupt reversal of Stalin's policies and legacy.

Brezhnev implemented "de-Khrushchevization" and "re-Stalininzed" the USSR, albeit on a limited basis. Gorbachev repudiated Brezhnev's policies of "stability" and "mature socialism" condemning Brezhnev's era as one of "stagnation" and instead embraced dynamic change in the form of *perestroika*. Following the collapse of the USSR, Yeltsin deemed Gorbachev too timid and implemented radical political, economic, and social changes for nearly a decade, until Putin assumed power and reversed most of Yeltsin's policies.

Every leader in the post-Tsarist era (except for Andropov and Chernenko who each governed for about a year and thus whose leadership was too brief to fully consider) has successfully staked their claim to leadership based on sharply repudiating, sometimes in action only (Stalin, Brezhnev, Putin), other times by word and deed (Khrushchev, Gorbachev, Yeltsin), their predecessor's policies.

The "Good Old Days" for Russians Was during the USSR, Especially in the Post–World War II and Post-Stalin Eras, but that Doesn't Mean They Want to Recreate the USSR Today

When Russians think about their country's past, their version of "the good old days" is the USSR. Recognizing that not everything was perfect during the Soviet era, they often speak of their country's past in terms of their "mountains of accomplishments" that were achieved at the expense of "mountains of crimes." The "mountains of accomplishments" refers to the rapid industrialization and near-universal education of their society, their improbable defeat of Nazi Germany, and their post–World War II superpower status. But rapid industrialization and their other accomplishments came at a very high cost in terms of human lives: the purges, the collectivization of agriculture and the ensuing famines, the forced paced industrialization, and the military victory of Germany cost in total tens of millions of lives.

At the last census conducted in the USSR in the 1989, the total population was a little less than 300 million. But under normal circumstances, absent war, revolution, collectivization, and so on, their population should have been about 450 million. More than 150 million either met premature deaths or were never born under these circumstances. The political repression that touched nearly every family, the economic mismanagement, and the poor strategy before and during World War II constituted the "mountain of crimes."

President Putin has described the 1991 collapse of the USSR as "the greatest geopolitical tragedy of the Twentieth Century," and a vast majority of Russians probably would agree (Osborn, 2011). But this does not mean that Putin, other leaders, or Russians in general have any appetite to try to forcibly recreate the USSR. At a minimum, they probably want to exercise power in the "Near Abroad," their traditional sphere of interest, including the Baltics, Ukraine, Belarus, and Moldova, the Caucasus, and Central Asia. At most, some leaders would favor a federation of Slavic nations including Russia, Belarus, Ukraine, Kazakhstan, and parts of Moldova and Georgia. This Slavic federation would also exercise influence over Russia's traditional sphere of interest beyond the federation's borders.

The "Bad Old Days" Was the Decade Following the USSR's Collapse, and Any Repetition of that Era Is to Be Avoided

When Russians think of their country's past and "the bad old days," they are referring to the decade following the collapse of the USSR. Yeltsin's attempt at radical economic reform, dubbed "shock therapy" resulted in hyperinflation that wiped out the life savings of many, and impoverished Russia to the point where it depended on the West for foreign aid. This was a blow to Russians not only in terms of their physical standard of living, but also was a psychological blow to Russians who took pride in their country's position as a superpower.

Russia's prominent role on the global stage was one of the sources of legitimacy of Soviet and Russian rulers throughout the twentieth century. Under Yeltsin, Russia was reduced to begging from the West and was humiliated by the expansion of NATO to Russia's former allies and even included some former Soviet republics. Righting the Russian ship of state by reversing many of Yeltsin's policies would become priorities for President Putin and his allies and supporters at the turn of the twenty-first century.

Russia's Present

We can best understand Russia today by considering a few of the most important issues in each of four categories: politics, economics, society, and foreign affairs. Understanding the key elements in each of these categories together give us the big picture, an overarching view of present-day Russia.

Russia's Politics

Politically, Russia is a kleptocracy, a system defined as rule by thieves (Dawisha, 2014). Corruption in Russia is rampant. Russia is not the first nor is it the only kleptocracy; countries rich in natural resources, especially oil, are particularly vulnerable to this problem. Russia is ranked 129/179 on the most recent (2020) Corruption Perception Index (the higher the number, the more corrupt a country is perceived to be). Ironically, Russians joke among themselves that theirs must be the wealthiest country in the world because everyone has been stealing from the state for a 100 years and there is still quite a bit left to take.

Further politically, President Vladimir Putin has no effective political opposition. Many of the leaders of the political opposition have been jailed, exiled, murdered, or are otherwise sufficiently intimidated and are no longer politically active. Putin is not without concerns, however. In 2016 he created a 350,000–400,000 strong national guard under his personal command.

Putin's most outspoken critic Alexei Navalny, a crusading anti-corruption politician, has been jailed briefly on several occasions in the last few years, usually for organizing "unapproved" demonstrations. His "criminal record" thus made him ineligible to run against Putin in the 2018 presidential election. He has also lost his vision in one eye, the result of having acid thrown in his face by assailants. In 2020, Navalny was poisoned. In a coma and near death, he spent five months recovering in a German hospital. Upon recovery, he returned to Russia where he was arrested, tried, and sent to a penal colony (France 24, 2021).

Ultimately, Putin faced seven candidates in the 2018 presidential election. Typical of the opposition was Ksenia Sobchak, the daughter of a former St. Petersburg mayor, the late Anatoly Sobchak, who was Putin's political patron. Ms. Sobchak was a television and movie actress, famous for hosting a TV reality show. She was widely seen as a Kremlin-backed candidate who would provide the illusion of an opposition candidate to give legitimacy to the Putin's 2018 reelection. Part of her election platform was to "never criticize Putin" (Richmond, 2018a).

With his political opposition neutralized and no serious challengers on the ballot, President Putin was reelected in 2018 for another six-year term. According to the Central Election Commission of the Russian Federation (CEC) in their official report of March 23, 2018, 67.5% of registered voters voted, and of those who voted, Putin won 76.69%. The other 7 candidates received between 11.77% and 0.65% (Richmond, 2018b).

Along with Putin's 2018 reelection came speculation as to whether Putin would begin to groom a successor or try to remain in power beyond his constitutionally mandated final term (Kendall-Taylor and Frantz, 2018). That issue was put to rest when the Russians approved by referendum on July 1, 2020, a package of constitutional changes and political reforms that will allow President Putin (at least) two more six-year terms to 2036, at which time Putin will be 83 (BBC News, 2020).

The Russian Economy

Economically, Russia suffers from what was once called the "Dutch Disease." The Russian variant of the "Dutch Disease" refers to the practice of using the income from energy exports to purchase imported products rather than producing those other products themselves (Goldman, 2010). When the market for energy collapsed (as it did in early 2020, the result of a price war with the Saudis), Russia no longer had the resources to import nor did it have domestic manufacturing either, which is still the case today.

The oil and gas industry are the mainstay of the Russian economy and accounts for about 70% of Russia's exports. Russia also exports other raw materials including precious metals and timber products. It also has a well-developed armaments industry and is a leading weapons exporter.

But Russia suffers from a lack of economic diversification, and while it is making efforts to expand its economic bases by trying to develop its own high-tech industries, pharmaceutical industry, and so on, it is hampered by a lack of investment funds. Much, if not most of Russia's privately held capital is held in offshore accounts. According to one 2017 estimate, as much as 60% of Russia's GDP is held in offshore accounts (Dizik, 2017). Government funds that could be used to invest in economic diversity are instead dedicated to military modernization. And a lack of foreign direct investment is due to a combination of Western economic sanctions, high levels of corruption, and weak property rights.

Russian Society

On the societal level Russia experienced a population decline on the order of approximately 500,000 to 750,000 annually for more than a decade following the 1991 collapse of the USSR. Current (2020) estimates of Russia's population vary with the Russian Government indicating their population at 146.7 million (January 2020), the UN estimating their population at 145.9 million (August 2020), and the CIA estimating the number at about 141.7 million (July 2020). Russia had a population of about 149 million at collapse of the USSR in 1991.

The severe population decline was attributed to a very low birth rate combined with a soaring death following the breakup of the USSR. The high death rate in turn was the result of a failing health care system, a high murder rate, and rampant alcoholism all rooted in the bankruptcy of the Russian economy following the collapse of the Soviet Union.

Indicative of Russia's demographic problem was the falling life expectancy rate for Russian males. The life expectancy rate in 1986 was 65 years; by 1994, it had fallen to just under 58. It has since climbed to 67.5 in 2017 and rose further to 72.5 in 2020.

Russia's demographic decline, and subsequent anemic growth, however, will make it difficult to expand Russia's already weak economy (ranked 11th in the world by GDP in 2020, barely ahead of South Korea) and will also put pressure on manpower demands for staffing its military. Both trends will make it increasingly difficult for Russia to maintain its great power status in the long run, thus undermining the government's legitimacy.

Russia's Foreign Policies

In terms of foreign policy, Russia under Putin has played an extremely weak hand masterfully. In the near term, Russia likely will continue to try to undermine the European Union (EU) and the North Atlantic Treaty Organization (NATO) in Europe. Russian propagandists are working actively to intensify political divisions within the United States so that we are preoccupied and inward looking, and to sow discord among our allies. Russia was happy to see the UK vote to leave the EU and works to bolster European populist parties in France, in the Netherlands, in Austria, and in other countries seeking to hold referenda on their respective countries' continued participation in the EU.

In the Baltics, in Moldova, and in Ukraine, Russia will continue to try to exert influence in these areas of special interest on their Western border. Ukraine's affairs continue to be unsettled (as are Georgia's).

And despite none of the many candidates in Ukraine's 2019 presidential election being pro-Russian, Russia interfered in the election in various ways (Polyakova, 2019).

In the Middle East, Russia has played a decisive role in the Syrian Civil War, and they have warming relations with Iran and Turkey. They are also seeking to regain influence in Central Asia. And in East Asia, Russia continues to maintain good relations with China based on common interests. While the Russian government has condemned North Korea's nuclear ambitions, they have significantly boosted trade with Pyongyang.

Russia's Future

Based on Russia's past patterns of behavior the most unexpected leader, probably someone we haven't even heard of yet, will succeed Putin sometime in the next decade. That new leader will both repudiate Putin's kleptocracy, and seek to enhance Russia's global influence, probably by reversing Putin's confrontational relationship with the West.

In conclusion, when thinking about Russia's future, we need to expect the unexpected. No one expected the Russian Revolution(s) of 1917. No one predicted Khrushchev's condemnation of Stalin in a "Secret Speech" to the Soviet leadership followed by the policy of de-Stalinization. Nor was the subsequent overthrow of Khrushchev an expected result. No one predicted an attempted coup against Gorbachev or the subsequent collapse of the USSR. No one expected Russia to default on its loans in 1998, or Yeltsin's sudden resignation the following year. Thus, while some aspects of Russia's policies may be predictable, for example attempts to expand its influence in the "near abroad," other aspects concerning Russia, especially its internal politics, will no doubt come as a complete surprise.

REFERENCES

BBC News. 2020. "Putin Strongly Backed in Controversial Reform Vote." *BBC News*, July 2, 2020. https://www.bbc.com/news/world-europe-53255964.

Dawisha, Karin. 2014. *Putin's Kleptocracy: Who Owns Russia?* New York: Simon & Schuster.

Dizik, Alina. 2017. "Saudi and Russian Residents Have Among the Most Offshore Assets." *Chicago Booth Review*, November 17, 2017. https://review.chicagobooth.edu/economics/2017/article/saudi-and-russian-residents-have-among-most-offshore-assets.

France 24. 2021. Russian Court Orders Opposition Leader Alexei Navalny to Serve More Than Two Years in Prison. *france24.com*, February 2, 2021. https://www.france24.com/en/live-news/20210202-russian-court-sentences-opposition-leader-alexei-navalny-to-3-5-years-in-prison.

Goldman, Marshall. 2010. *Petrostate: Putin, Power, and the New Russia*. Oxford: Oxford University Press.

Kendall-Taylor, Andrea, and Erica Frantz. 2018. "Putin's Succession Conundrum: How Authoritarians Navigate the Challenge." www.foreignaffairs.com, March 21, 2018. https://www.foreignaffairs.com/articles/russian-federation/2018-03-21/putins-succession-conundrum.

Lenin, V. I. 1918. *The State and Revolution: The Marxist Theory of the State and the Tasks of the Proletariat in the Revolution*. Lenin Internet Archive (marxists.org).

Lenin, V. I. 1922. *Letter to the Congress. II. Continuation of the Notes*. Lenin Internet Archive (Marxists.org).

Lenin, V. I. 1923. *Letter to the Congress. Addition to the Above Letter*. Lenin Internet Archive (Marxists.org).

Osborn, Andrew. 2011. "Putin: Collapse of the Soviet Union Was 'Catastrophe of the Century.'" *Independent*, October 6, 2011. https://www.independent.co.uk/news/world/europe/putin-collapse-soviet-union-was-catastrophe-century-521064.html.

Polyakova, Alina. 2019. "Want to Know What's Next in Russian Election Interference? Pay Attention to Ukraine's Elections." www.brookings.edu, March 28, 2019. https://www.brookings.edu/blog/order-from-chaos/2019/03/28/want-to-know-whats-next-in-russian-election-interference-pay-attantion-to-ukraines-elections.

Richmond, Nathan. 2018a. "The Candidate List for Russia's Presidential Election." *Utica College Center for Public Affairs and Election Research*, February 19, 2018. https://www.ucpublicaffairs.com/home/2018/2/18/pmjzzs5olp2uton4ypld8yv5hvxx0e?rq=richmond.

Richmond, Nathan. 2018b. "What to Expect After Putin's Re-election?" *Utica College Center for Public Affairs and Election Research*, April 9, 2018. https://www.ucpublicaffairs.com/home/2018/4/9/what-to-expect-after-putins-re-election-by-nathan-richmond?rq=Richmond.

Chapter 5

Making Sense of Russia's Interests

Alexander J. Motyl

It's become fashionable to argue that Russia has had, and always will have immutable national interests and that President Vladimir Putin is merely the latest in a long line of Russian rulers to pursue them vigorously.[1] The implications for the West are obvious. If Putin's Russia is acting in the manner of all Russian states at all times, then one must accept Russia as it is and always will be—expansionist and authoritarian—and accommodate it as best one can. The alternative, as analysts and policy makers who make this claim argue, is war—and no one wants war.

But what if Putin is not coolly pursuing immutable and objectively definable Russian national interests? What if he is captive to perceptions, ideologies, institutional legacies, and historical developments that structure what does and does not count as a national interest? If Putin's Russia is acting singularly and at variance with previous Russian behaviors, then there is nothing inevitable about today's Russia and a different form of foreign policy behavior is perfectly possible.

As anyone with an appreciation of Russian, or any, history knows, no state can pursue identical interests for the duration of its historical existence, because states and their surroundings are always changing. The Russia of today is not the Muscovy of 600 years ago. The Mongols are not the West. And, despite some superficial similarities, Putin is no Ivan the Terrible. Immutability is a fiction. At the same time, geography and strategy do matter, and no elite can just imagine that they do not. As a result, foreign policy is a function of geopolitics, national interests, perceptions, and ideologies, but also of regime type, personality of the leader, historical timing, context, and many other factors.

Understanding today's Russia—and its foreign policy—requires examining its emergence and evolution historically. Above all, it means viewing contemporary Russia as the heir to the Soviet empire and the product of that empire's collapse. Putin's Russia did not just appear magically out of nowhere. It has roots in the Soviet empire, a highly centralized state in which the Russian core determined the internal and external policies of the non-Russian republics. And Putin's Russia is the product of that empire's sudden collapse in 1991. Putin's foreign policy cannot be understood without taking these two factors into account.

BUT FIRST SOME HISTORY

The historical record is replete with evidence of the mutability of Russia's national interests. Back in the thirteenth century, the precursor of modern Russia, the self-styled Muscovite State, came into existence as a tiny principality competing for power with equally tiny principalities in its immediate neighborhood and striving to throw off the "Mongol yoke." In 1380 Dmitri Donskoi defeated the Mongols at Kulikovo; in 1480, Grand Prince Ivan III ended Moscow's tutelage at the Ugra River; 70 years later, the Muscovites captured Kazan and Astrakhan. At that time, such supposedly immutable Russian interests as Ukraine or the Bosporus concerned no one in Moscow, because Muscovy was too far, too small, and too fixated on the Mongol threat from the east. On the other hand, the conquest of Constantinople by the Ottomans in 1453 did convince some Muscovites to think of themselves in terms of an intrinsically imperial notion, the Third Rome.

Muscovy's subsequent expansion into and conquest of Siberia, a process that lasted some 70 years, from 1581 to 1649, was largely driven by trappers out to make a quick ruble (who were followed by Cossacks and army units), and not by geostrategic consideration of national interests. In the sixteenth century, Ukraine and the Ottomans were not yet on Muscovy's radar, while Lithuania, Poland, and Sweden were. It was only in the second half of the seventeenth century, as a consequence of incessant fighting between Poles, Muscovites, Ottoman Turks, Crimean Tatars, and Ukrainian Cossacks, as a result of Poland's merger with Lithuania in 1569, that Muscovy annexed eastern Ukrainian territories and approached the Black Sea, thereby transforming Ukraine and the Ottomans into a strategic interest.

Peter the Great signally changed the definition of Muscovy's national interests by deciding, after an extended visit to Western Europe, that Muscovy needed to modernize and by heeding the advice of Ukrainian clerics that his empire, now termed Russia, should claim lineage with the medieval Kyivan Rus' state, the core of which was located in today's Ukraine. Neither of these ideological moves was dictated by immutable national interests. Peter could not have traveled to Europe. Ukrainian clerics could not have persuaded him that his empire's legitimacy would be enhanced by misinterpreting history and claiming Rus' as Russia's ancestor. At the same time, it surely made realist sense for Peter to adopt these claims and not others.

Once the Russian Empire came into immediate contact with the Ottomans and their Crimean Tatar allies, tensions between the two great powers were probably inevitable. But post-Petrine Russia's relentless expansion into the Black Sea was as much a function of growing Ottoman weakness and the Russian perception of the Turks as enemies of Christianity as of some inherent geostrategic imperative to control the Bosporus. Weakness, decay, and a sense of *mission civilisatrice* also motivated Russia's expansion into Central Asia and the Caucasus in the nineteenth century, finally producing the empire that collapsed in 1918–1921.

HOW EMPIRES END

Empires end in two ways. Most decay and lose territory over time, with the result that the imperial cores emerge from the wreckage with minimal ideological, economic, military, cultural, and political ties with their former colonies. As a result, cores-turned-independent states rarely embark on campaigns to regain lost territories, for the simple reason that they lost the territories long before the empire completely ended. The Ottomans are a good example. Their loss of territory started with the failed siege of Vienna in 1683 and was almost over by the start of World War I. The core of the empire emerged as Turkey and its primary concern was not to reconquer long-lost imperial territories but to assert its independence and to deal with the Greek and Armenian minorities within its boundaries.

Peter the Great's creation, the Russian Empire, collapsed in 1918–1921 and, as we would expect from the suddenness and comprehensiveness of the imperial breakdown, the ideological, economic, military, cultural, and political ties between Bolshevik Russia and the former colonies were still strong. Unsurprisingly, the Bolsheviks felt impelled to embark on a campaign of re-imperialization that ultimately culminated in the formation of the USSR in 1924. The German Reich also collapsed in 1918, with the result that Adolf Hitler consciously pursued re-imperialization vis-à-vis the Rhineland, Austria, the Sudetenland, and Western Poland in the 1930s.

The Soviet empire collapsed in the years between Mikhail Gorbachev's perestroika and the formal dismantling of the USSR on December 31, 1991. Virtually overnight, 14 independent non-Russian states emerged, but with many of the formerly imperial ties that bound them to the core, Russia, still intact. Most Russians viewed their state and nation as superior, and in possession of a civilizing mission with respect, to the non-Russians. Russian language and culture continued to dominate in the post-Soviet space, in no small measure due to decades of Soviet Russification policy. The USSR's central planning organs had created a single economic space held together by, among other things, energy flows and pipelines that guaranteed non-Russian economic dependence on Russia. Russia inherited a huge army and weapons arsenal, while the non-Russians had to scramble to remake the bits and pieces of the Soviet military they inherited into something resembling independent armies. Non-Russian elites were intertwined with Russian elites, and their loyalties were by no means centered on their own states. Finally, Russians in general and their elites in particular, like German and Bolshevik elites and publics in the 1920s and 1930s, felt humiliated by the loss of empire and were determined to make their countries great again.

Small wonder, given all these imperial connections, that post-Soviet Russia, in both its Yeltsinite and Putinite incarnations, has pursued a policy of re-imperialization. The still-regnant Soviet ideology and political culture provided Russian elites with the justification and rationale for pursuing empire. Military superiority, economic dependence, and the ubiquity of the Russian language provided the means. Under President Boris Yeltsin, re-imperialization was "soft," centering on attempts to promote the Commonwealth of Independent States and defend the supposedly aggrieved Russian and Russian-speaking minorities in the non-Russian states.

But Yeltsin also presided over the economic collapse of post-Soviet Russia; it was on his watch that criminality and corruption flourished. Putin had the good fortune of being in the right time at the right place. When he became prime minister and president in 1998–1999, Russia's economy was finally rebounding and energy prices were about to go through the roof. That enabled him to present himself as a strong man who would save Russia by mobilizing the ideology and culture of Russian greatness, strong arming the non-Russians economically and militarily, and engaging in land grabs in Moldova, Georgia, and Ukraine. Naturally, that Putin was an authoritarian with an exalted sense of self, while Yeltsin was a flawed democrat and a drunk, also made a difference.

IMPLICATIONS FOR THE WEST

Seen in this light, Putin's annexation of the Crimea and the war in eastern Ukraine have nothing to do with NATO's putative expansion into Ukraine. Aside from the fact that NATO had expressed no interest in Ukraine's membership, that the West was suffering from "Ukraine fatigue" and assiduously avoided even hinting at Ukraine's theoretical future membership in the European Union, and that few Ukrainians wanted to join NATO before the war of 2014, the argument that Russia would prevent NATO expansion by seizing Ukraine's easternmost and southernmost territories—those farthest from any possible NATO incursion—makes no geopolitical sense. Ukraine came to matter to Western geopoliticians only after the annexation of Crimea and the war in the Donbas.

Why, Then, Did Putin Invade and Seize Ukrainian Territory?

On the one hand, because he wanted to make Russia great again and was paranoid about NATO and the West; on the other hand, because the Maidan revolution had weakened the Ukrainian state, made it an easy target for expansion, and threatened his dictatorial rule by suggesting that democracy and people power could have positive results. Imperial ideology, bizarre perceptions, Ukraine's weakness, and a sense of vulnerability came together to make an invasion highly likely if not inevitable. In fact, the Russian hold on Ukraine would have been much stronger had Putin not invaded and let his puppet, Viktor Yanukovych, continue in office.

HOW, THEN, SHOULD THE WEST AND RUSSIA'S NEIGHBORS BEST DEAL WITH PUTIN'S IMPERIAL AMBITIONS?

First, not by feeding Russia's imperial megalomania by arguing that Russia's national interests necessarily entail hegemony over its neighbors and that its imperial project is legitimate because it is somehow rooted in an immutable Russian character. There are no immutable Russian national interests or Russian soul and all former imperial states lose their ideological drive in time. The same will happen with Russia, unless misguided Western policy makers encourage it.

Second, not by strengthening the economic, political, and military links between Russia and its former colonies. Those links need not be completely severed—after all, it makes perfect sense for Russians and non-Russians to have close economic relations—but they should not be premised on Russian domination and non-Russian dependence. Most of today's world abjures empire, but even if one believed some form of Russian empire to be a good thing, the key question is whether Putin's Russia could pull off such an ambitious project without destabilizing its neighbors and itself.

The answer to that question is No. Back in 1918, the Russian post-imperial core easily outmatched the newly independent non-Russian states. Re-imperialization took place relatively quickly and easily. Today, Russia, while still a regional great power, lacks the hard power to reestablish an empire. It can capture bits of countries or small countries, such as Estonia and Latvia, but there is no way that Russia could reconquer Kazakhstan,

Uzbekistan, or Ukraine. Nor is it clear that Russia could conquer Belarus. Unfortunately, the attempt to reestablish an empire could destabilize some of Russia's neighbors and Russia itself.

Putin has grandiose geopolitical ambitions—extending all the way to Africa and the Middle East—while his economy is roughly the size of Belgium's. Such imperial overreach cannot be sustained for long. At some point in the not too distant future, his foreign policy commitments will resemble those of Brezhnev's USSR and some form of organized or disorganized withdrawal will become imperative.

No less important, Putin has constructed a quasi-fascist state that is overcentralized, corrupt, incapable of modernization, and good only at repression. Since he's that state's linchpin, his departure will expose its internal weaknesses and make it ripe for assault, whether by ambitious elites or disgruntled masses. Ironically, Putin has become Russia's worst enemy—precisely because he is determined to make Russia into an authoritarian empire—a role it cannot sustain.

With respect to Putin's current imperial obsession, Ukraine, the West has two options that are good for Ukraine, good for itself, and good for the Russian people (though not necessarily for Putin).

First, it can grant Ukraine immediate NATO membership while ceding the Crimea and the eastern Donbas to Russia. Putin will squeal, but if he wants empire, that would be the quid pro quo. Second, the West can continue with the status quo, keep the sanctions in place, support Ukraine economically and militarily, and signal to Russia that the West regards Ukraine as a vital strategic asset.

The first option is short term; the second is long term. Both are premised on Putin's continued pursuit of re-imperialization. Naturally, should Russia disintegrate and become smaller or should Putin's successors be democrats—then the calculations change, just as their views of Russia's interests are likely to change. Until they do, however, the West must accept that post-imperial collapse states like Putin's Russia need time to adjust to the loss of empire and are therefore prone to try to revive their lost imperial glory. There are no quick fixes. Patience, resolve, and a commitment to contain Putin's re-imperialization efforts are the only way to proceed.

NOTE

1. A shortened and revised version of this chapter is published as "Putin May Want to Be an Emperor, but Russia Isn't an Imperial Power," October 28, 2019, https://foreignpolicy.com/2019/10/28/putin-may-want-to-be-an-emperor-but-russia-isnt-an-imperial-power/. Permission is granted by the Publisher of *Foreign Policy*.

Chapter 6

The Polish Underground's 1944 Warsaw Uprising—a Participant's View

Jarosław Piekałkiewicz with Joanna Drzewieniecki

INTRODUCTION

Unlike the other chapters in this collection, this is not an academic piece but rather a first-hand account of a man who participated in the Warsaw Uprising of 1944 as a teenager. It is included here at the express request of this volume's honoree, Frederic Fleron. Piekałkiewicz and Fleron originally became friends when they studied together in the PhD program at the Russian and East European Institute at Indiana University. Over the years, they lost touch but they reconnected when Fleron read the book *Needle in the Bone* by Caryn Mirriam-Goldberg, which describes the personal histories and friendship between Piekałkiewicz and Holocaust survivor Lou Frydman, both University of Kansas professors.

In 2017, when Fleron discovered that Piekałkiewicz had an unpublished manuscript on Polish–Jewish relations during World War II, he immediately asked for a copy and after reading it, got in touch with me to see if I would be willing to be the editor; he later helped with the publishing process. The result was *Dance with Death: A Holistic View of Saving Polish Jews during the Holocaust*, published in 2020. At some point, Piekałkiewicz also sent Fleron an unpolished text in which he described his experiences as a fighter during the Warsaw Uprising. It was originally written for his grandchildren. This first-hand account of a feisty and brave young man must have made a profound impression on Fleron since he asked that it be included in this volume. I was once again brought in to edit and provide historical background.

Jarosław Piekałkiewicz, or "Jarek" as everyone calls him, was born on July 24, 1926, in Poznań to a well-off family. He moved with his family to Warsaw at the age of nine. He told his biographer that at the time he was "a prankster and got into fights" (Mirriam-Goldberg 2013, p. 22). This toughness would soon become an asset. The Germans invaded and occupied Poland in September 1939. The Piekałkiewicz family immediately found themselves in economic difficulties, all the more so as Jarek's father had died in August of that year. Jarek's mother decided to send her teenage son to live with relatives in the small town of Biała Podlaska, east of Warsaw. There he attended a commercial school (the Germans had shut down all other types of education for Poles) and helped with a small family grocery store. He also formed a small resistance group of boys his age. An adult cousin put him in touch with the Polish Underground, which was established shortly after Poland's defeat in 1939, and Jarek and his group joined its military arm, the Home Army (Armia Krajowa in Polish).

Then in the fall of 1943, after barely escaping being taken to Germany for forced labor, Jarek was smuggled back to Warsaw. A few months later, a member of the youth resistance group he founded in Biała Podlaska betrayed them to the Germans. Thirteen members were executed. Had Jarek still been there, he too would have been killed. This was one of many times during the war when luck was on his side. It should be noted that the Underground later assassinated the informer.

Meanwhile in Warsaw, Jarek's mother, who was a lieutenant in the Home Army, arranged for him to join an auxiliary unit of the Warsaw Fire Brigade.[1] Jarek's uniform, including a hat that looked very much like that worn by the Viennese police, allowed him relative ease of movement around the city. Jarek attended an Underground-run clandestine high school at the same time as he recruited friends to the Home Army and created new units, whom he trained in urban warfare.

The Polish Underground was the largest resistance movement in Europe during World War II except for Tito's Partisans in Yugoslavia, with an estimated 300,000 members in its military and civilian branches. The German occupation of Poland was much more brutal than that of European countries to its west. The Nazi's ultimate plans were to ethnically cleanse Poland, starting with Jews (approximately one-third of the world's Jews lived in Poland at the time) and going on to all other residents, some of whom were to remain as a temporary workforce while the educated class was to be eliminated (this "elimination" started at the beginning of the war [Piekałkiewicz 2020, 42]). Polish territory was then to be incorporated into the Third Reich. This goal was not to be achieved. By the summer of 1944, the German armed forces were under attack on all fronts and the Soviet Army was at the gates of Warsaw. This was the moment the Home Army chose to carry out their uprising.[2]

The Poles bravely fought the Germans for 63 days, from August 1 to October 2, 1944. Tragically they only got limited help from the Western

Allies and the Soviet Union, for complex political reasons,[3] and finally had to capitulate. The cost of the Uprising was terrible: an estimated 15,000 Polish fighters were killed and another 15,000 were taken as POWs by the Germans after capitulation. Jarek's mother, Kazimierza Piekałkiewicz, was executed after being captured.[4] Between 150,000 and 200,000 civilians were also killed, many in mass executions. German deaths are estimated at about 17,000.[5] The Germans then deliberately destroyed 35% of the buildings of Warsaw. In total 85% of Warsaw was destroyed in World War II.[6]

When the Uprising started, Jarek was 18 years old and eager to fight. The "prankster" had become an experienced fighter who had already seen much death and witnessed much German brutality. Below he recounts his experiences during the Uprising with realism and honesty. He confesses to fear but we feel that he is fearless. He provides compelling testimony of what happened within an approximately three block square area. As he told me, "I am a typical veteran of heavy fighting. I know only what happened right around me. Often I had to make rapid decisions in seconds to stay alive."[7] Reading this testimony, we understand what he means.[8]

Joanna Drzewieniecki, Lima, Peru, August 2021

THE STORY OF A PARTICIPANT IN THE WARSAW UPRISING

As July 1944 progressed, we all knew the Uprising was coming. The Germans knew it as well. They had already constructed bunkers outside the buildings they occupied. We expected the Soviet Army to be at the gates of Warsaw in a matter of just a few days. The first alert came at the end of July. I called my three Home Army section leaders to my family's apartment at 13 Wspólna St. where I was living. We awaited a telephone call from the company commander. After a few hours of nervous waiting, the alert was called off. Everybody left for home. The next alert came on August 1: the Uprising was going to start during rush hour, at five o'clock in the afternoon. The masses of people heading home from work were to serve as cover for the fighters going to their meeting places. Again, my team and I met at the Wspólna St. apartment.

The shooting had started much earlier when people carrying arms to their meeting places clashed with German patrols. At five o'clock on August 1 the whole of Warsaw exploded with gun fire. Still, my phone was silent and we waited and waited. The fighting went on all around us. Finally, I sent my team leaders to be with their people, telling them to join the nearest Home Army unit. We had no arms. Meanwhile, I kept waiting for a phone call with orders, at least for myself. The hours went by, but the phone remained silent. From the top floor window, I saw three men from the German Air Force with their pistols in their hands, their arms waving as they walked down the empty street. They kept walking toward Three Crosses Square (Plac Trzech Krzyży). To this day I regret not dropping a flowerpot on their heads. I would have been safe from retaliation since the heavy door to the house in which our apartment was located was locked fast and so they couldn't have gotten in. Soon they disappeared.

When night fell, I joined some people who were building barricades using large squares of concrete torn from sidewalks. One man said he just came from nearby Hoża St. and saw a Home Army unit taking over the Blue Police[9] station there. I knew where it was because this was our district police station. I went upstairs to say goodbye to my family and then went out in search of my team. To get there I had to cross Marszałkowska St. and the next artery, Poznańska St. Both were dangerous intersections. They could have been patrolled by Germans. I had on my fire brigade cap, but at night and with fighting everywhere, it wouldn't have kept me safe. I ran through both crossings and I got to the Hoża St. police station without any trouble. I saluted the captain, who I learned later was "Jur"[10] (Jerzy Marcinkowski), former commandant of the Air Force base and now a company commander, and said: "Corporal Andrzej reporting for duty" ("Andrzej" was my code name). He welcomed me and told me to sit along the wall with others who, like me, were separated from their units and did not have any arms.

After a while, somebody came to tell us that the apartments facing the street in the house at 62 Hoża St., where the Bahnschutzpolizei (the German railroad police) lived, had to be checked even though they were probably empty. Right then, "Stec," a cadet officer[11] whose real name was Czesław Deminet, came in from a patrol. He said he would go, but needed a volunteer to go with him. Nobody was eager because we did not have guns, but I jumped up and said "I will go." They gave me a handgun, a WIZ (Polish 9 mm-caliber copy of the American colt pistol, produced in Radom) which had been "liberated" from the Blue Police. In addition, I was given a prewar Polish defense hand grenade. The building was just a few houses over from us. The carriage entrance was open. We ran in and Stec tried the first door on the ground floor. It was locked and he wanted to kick it open. I shouted, "Stop, top floor! Hand grenade!" He understood we had to start from the top, because otherwise somebody could throw down a hand grenade at us. We raced up. It was a tall seven-story building. We were breathless as we got to the top. We tried the first door. It was locked. Stec moved away and was about to run to kick it in but again I stopped him. I explained to him that if there was somebody inside with a gun he would be dead. Then I showed him how to kick in the door while holding on to the frame so as to remain out of sight as much as possible. If somebody shot at us, we would throw a grenade in. This method was slower but safer. It took us some time to kick open all the doors. The building was empty. We went back to report to Jur. He then moved his company's command post to the building, because it was the tallest and most solid structure in this neighborhood. The headquarters was installed on the ground floor (figure 6.1).

Seeing that I had volunteered for a very risky job, Jur figured I was good for special assignments and used me that way for the rest of the Uprising. First, I was given a team[12] to command. We became part of the First Platoon commanded by Lieutenant "Alek." My team was made up of myself (Corporal Andrzej) and five new volunteers, who had just joined the Home Army that night. They were: Orzeł (Tadeusz Olechowski), "Kajtek" (Józef Krzysztowski), "Spłonka" (Andrzej Paszewski)[13] as well as a runner and a nurse, whose names I don't remember. "Orzel" (later called "Michał") was a big fellow who was a shoemaker's apprentice. He was fearless. Kajtek

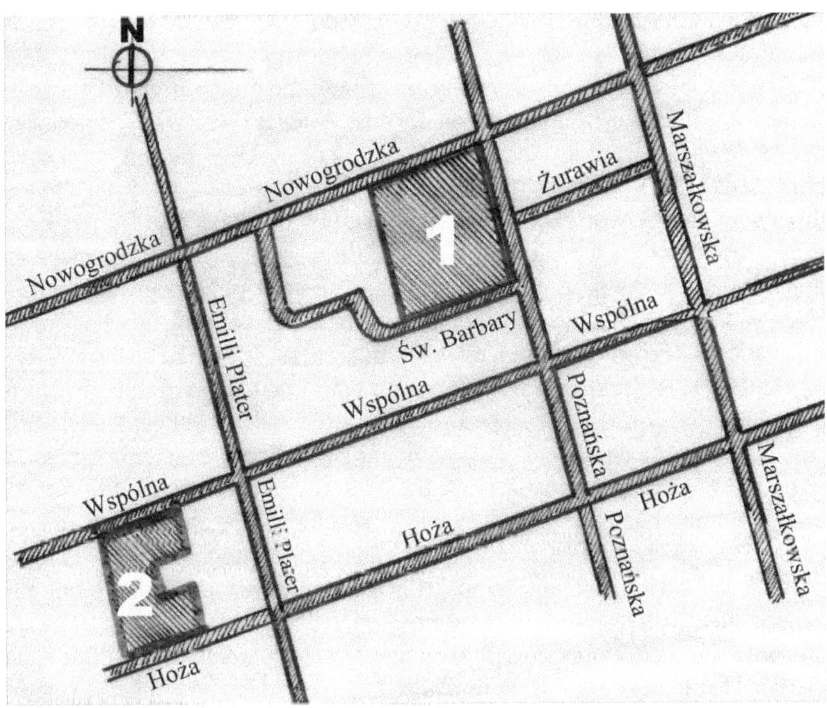

1. Telephone Building (Urząd Telekomunikacyjny i Telegraficzny)

2. Frontleitstelle

Figure 6.1 Area of Operations of the Piekałkiewicz Team, German Strongholds, and Adjacent Streets. Warsaw Uprising 1944. *Source*: Compiled by authors.

was middle class and was always afraid but did what he was ordered to do. I admired his bravery and commitment. Orzeł and Kajtek were about my age. Spłonka was much older, perhaps about 30 and we called him "Grandpa." He was always drunk and pretty useless.

The runner, to whom I gave my fire brigade cap, behaved exactly like a child of Warsaw—very cleverly. Soon after, he disappeared. Was he killed or had he found a more lucrative occupation, or a more exciting unit? The nurse, who did not have a clue about nursing and was not too smart, soon figured out that my unit was too dangerous and hung out with the platoon command. As a matter of fact, that was the best place for her because the other nurses trained her in the rudiments of first aid.

At the beginning I was the only one who was armed with a handgun, the 9 mm WiZ. Eventually, Orzel got a 7.65 or 6.35, a "ladies" handgun. Soon we were both able to get plenty of ammunition for our guns. We also received a French cavalry Berthier rifle. This was a beautiful weapon, but it required special French ammunition and we only had five or six rounds. Only in recent years did I learn that our arms technicians could have remade the rifle for the ammunition we had.

Gradually I was able to get plenty of rounds for my own gun. Orzel also obtained a good deal of ammunition for his. After a time, we received a lot of hand grenades, most produced by the battalion workshop using explosives from German duds, of which there were plenty. This may have been a result of deliberately sloppy work by foreign slave laborers in German factories or by German workers who were too nervous to concentrate because of the incessant allied bombing at the time. We also got a good supply of Molotov cocktails—bottles with paper bandages soaked with something that ignited when mixed with gasoline. The bottles exploded when broken, so we had to be very careful carrying them. We found or were given an empty wooden case that had rope handles and divisions for vodka bottles. We used it to carry our cocktails. Some of the bottles in the case were filled with real vodka, but we never mistook one for the other. Both the grenades and the Molotov cocktails were very useful in street fighting but were no match for the machine guns and mortars that the Germans had in abundance. Not to mention artillery and planes of all kinds.

All in all, our armament seems ridiculously small in number but this was average for a whole company or even for a whole battalion. The Jur Company, which became the 2nd Company of the Zaremba Battalion—later called the Zaremba-Piorun Battalion[14]—had 220 soldiers armed with: 1 heavy machine gun, 1 light machine gun, 25 rifles, 3 hand machine guns, and about 100 pistols (the number of these guns was a little larger because some people had their own private handguns with them). We were also chronically short of ammunition during the Uprising. That's all we had to fight the very well-armed Germans for 63 days.

After joining Jur's Company on the night of August 1, 1944, we were posted the next day to an apartment owned by friends of Stec at the corner of Poznańska and Wspólna streets. From the balcony, we were able to observe the Telecommunications & Telegraph building,[15] which we simply called "Telefony" (Telephone Building). It was occupied by the Germans and located a short block up from us, between Poznańska, Nowogrodzka, and Św. Barbara streets. The building was seven stories high, solidly constructed, and the Germans' had turned it into a strong fortress. There was a bunker outside with a heavy machine gun that commanded the length of Poznańska all the way past Hoża St. I often crossed the street at night and was lucky they did not open fire, as they sometimes did without aiming. During the day it was a death zone. We had to jump across Poznańska from Hoża or even further down Poznańska while it was still dark.

Stec's friends who lived in the apartment where we were posted were a lovely old couple, with a charming eastern Polish accent. The apartment was expensive-looking with rich oriental carpets. We cleaned our boots carefully before proceeding to the room with the balcony with a view of the Telephone Building. The balcony had flower pots that we used for cover. We took 30-minute turns there that morning, while the rest were treated by the couple to an excellent breakfast. That first day was beautiful, sunny, and warm. Suddenly, the German machine gun opened up. I thought that it was firing on us. I ran to the balcony and was assured by the pretty scared guy on duty that they were firing down Poznańska. I looked carefully in that direction and saw the body of a woman lying on the ground but still moving. The German machine gunner kept firing at her, ripping the body to pieces. I was horrified. This was the first dead body I saw during the Uprising. Later I learned she had been running across the street because her children were on the other side. Our people had tried to stop her but she struggled free and ran across. She didn't have a chance. The distance was too short for the Germans to miss. I heard that her children were well taken care of until the end of the Uprising.

At that moment, my superior officer was an old sergeant. I reported what happened to him. For a while our area was quiet again. The rest of Warsaw sounded like a concert with many grand pianos and large drums—constant gunfire and, from time to time, explosions. This "orchestra" was to play this same music for the next two months, with only short intermissions during the nights.

We heard a noise that sounded like a car engine. It got louder and louder. I ran to the balcony and looked out. There was an armored car at the corner of Wspólna and Poznańska. It started firing its cannon. I assumed it was firing at the barricade that connected this side of the street to the block of apartments on the other side of the street, leading all the way to the building opposite the Telephone Building. I could not look out too far because I was afraid of being hit by fire from that building. We were helpless. At the time, we still didn't have those Molotov cocktails to throw at the armored car and our company did not have any nearby positions, besides mine at that corner. After a few shots the armored car turned around and started to leave. In frustration, the old sergeant ran to the balcony and shot at it a few times. It was pretty idiotic, but understandable. After that day, I did not see him on the front lines anymore. With no superior officer with us, I was in command of our team.

That night we were ordered to move to a second floor apartment in a building that was located one door over toward Marszalkowska St. from the corner of Wspólna and Poznańska. It had a balcony facing Wspólna. We were to build a bunker on it, for which we were provided with plenty of sandbags. The local civilians were willing to help. The only problem was that the balcony was under near constant machine gun fire from the Frontleitstelle,[16] which was about a block and half from where we were. The Germans were firing from higher positions and the bullets hit the floor of the balcony, sending sparks into the air. Nobody was willing to try to put in place the heavy sandbags under that much fire. It looked very frightening.

Fortunately, that night was very dark. The Germans must have noticed some movement on the balcony during the day and locked their machine gun on it. I noticed that the bullets always hit exactly the same spot. The Germans would stop after a few rounds and then, after a break, start again. I decided it was my job to get the sandbags into place. I waited for a pause in the firing, took a gulp of vodka, and dropped the first sandbag next to the balcony door. I noticed that the bullets hit a little further. Working fast during each pause in firing, I soon had the first row of sandbags in place. Now I could safely stand and have the bags passed to me. But then they fired at the next row. During each pause I dropped two bags. Then the bullets started hitting the bags. After some serious sweating and some more vodka, I finished the under-fire side of the balcony. Then other people took over. Before dawn, we had the bunker built. The Germans fired furiously at the sandbags, so we put up a second row. "My" bunker survived until the balcony's complete destruction toward the end of the Uprising.

Soon after the night of bunker building, my battalion, named after its commander "Zaremba" (Romuald Radziwiłłowicz[17]) was reorganized. As noted, my team was part of the 2nd Company commanded by Captain Jur. The core of the company was the Home Army Air Force. A number of officers had been in the Polish Air Force before the war. On our berets, in addition to the Polish Eagles, we wore the Air Force "checkerboard." This insignia, which is still used, is a square cloth divided into four smaller squares, alternating red and white (the colors of the Polish flag). Still the majority of the members of my company had nothing to do with the Air Force (when I was a young boy,

I wanted to be a pilot and this was as close as I ever got to being one). Most of those in the company were "lost" from other Home Army units as I was or else recent volunteers. Its 220 members included nurses, sappers, firefighters, and other support staff. The company's front or field of action was Wspólna St. between Poznańska and Emilii Plater. Our "no-man's-land" was the apartment buildings across the street from us on Wspólna St., between our location and the tall Telephone Building, which, as I described above, was fortified and occupied by Germans. They covered Poznańska St. with machine gun fire and the whole area with mortar fire.

As noted above, the armament in the hands of the company was just about as meager as those of my team. Fortunately, later in the Uprising, we had plenty of Molotov cocktails and hand grenades, many homemade and not always reliable. My section found a "home" within the 1st Platoon, stationed at 61 Wspólna St. and commanded by Lieutenant "Alek" (Aleksander Świderski), a prewar fighter pilot. Alek was a very sweet person, not at all what you would expect of a fighter pilot. He treated my team and other younger boys and girls like his children and he warned us not to take too many risks: "Poland will need you in the future," he told us. When there was no fighting, Alek distracted a group of us with funny stories about when he was a pilot. I remember one of these. On one flight, his engine sputtered out and he had to land in a haystack. He had barely enough time to get out before the haystack caught fire. He told us he broke many bones in the landing. He still limped badly when I met him. I have very fond memories of him.

One day early in the Uprising, as we, and seemingly the Germans too, had settled down and everything was quiet—except for that sporadic German machine gun fire along Wspólna and Poznańska—I asked Lieutenant Alek for permission to go and visit my family. He readily agreed and I took off. I had quite a distance to cover. I had to cross two main arteries, Marszałkowska and Krucza streets. Still at that time both were far behind the front lines. Meanwhile the Germans were attacking the outlying districts. The bombings had not yet begun, because nobody knew who controlled what. There were German strongholds, like the one on my front, all over the city.

My family, which lived in a fourth floor apartment on Wspólna, consisted of my maternal grandparents, Jadwiga and Teodor; my uncle, Zdzich and his wife, Masia; and my little sister, Basia. They had plenty of food and water. It was nice to see them safe and well. We did not know where my mother or my aunt Zula[18] were. They were both in the Home Army and were surely participating in the Uprising somewhere in the city. After a good home-cooked meal, I picked up some clean clothes and my leather overcoat and returned to the front. Nothing happened on the way back. Warsaw was full of the sounds of gunfire and explosions, which became the norm until the end of the Uprising. There was always fighting somewhere.

The state of my platoon shocked me. The Germans at the Telephone Building had attacked. They had covered my platoon's positions with a hurricane of submachine gunfire from across the street. The platoon could not respond as they were short of ammunition and did not want to reveal their positions or how weak their defenses were. The fighters could only hide behind the wall of sandbags we had built. The Germans stopped shooting and had seemingly left for lunch. Lieutenant Alek went back into the carriage entrance to warn our nurses not to come out from hiding yet. There was a burst of bullets that nearly completely severed his head from his body. My hero was dead. A German must have shot down from a higher floor, sending his bullets flying over our sand bags.

When I returned, the platoon had been taken over by my buddy with whom I had searched "my" building[19] some nights before: Officer Cadet Stec. The death of Alek taught us a bitter lesson: our fortifications were not sufficient to defend our front. Jur came to inspect the line; Alek had been his friend and the first officer killed in his company. He ordered improvements to the platoon's fortifications. We worked hard all night with the company's sappers and civilian volunteers. We increased our barrier to six sandbags high and three deep and extended it into the street. On top, it was covered with chicken wire to protect against hand grenades. The second floor windows were similarly fortified but had narrow observation and shooting slits. The building's floors were covered with sand as protection against firebombs. The basement and first floor windows were blocked permanently. The sand from the bags placed in the carriage entrance was removed, creating a huge hole that could be bypassed only via the narrow sidewalks on both sides. We called it "The Elephant Trap." On the top floor, the windows were concealed with black covers in accordance with the existing German orders for night blackouts against air raids. Behind them, a squad hid with plenty of hand grenades and Molotov cocktails. At the appropriate time, they bombarded German attackers with them. The whole fortification was our "Sand Castle." It survived the Uprising despite a number of attacks. To those of us who complained of being tired while building up this castle, Stec quoted what General Tadeusz Kosciuszko[20] had said during the construction of West Point: "Better to sweat now than sweat blood later."

My battalion members were all issued the same gray one-piece suits that were perfect for urban warfare and looked very military-like. After building the Sand Castle, we felt like a real and undefeatable army. But in fact, our command knew that it was even too dangerous for us to cross to the other side of Wspólna into the no-man's-land, which was still occupied by civilians. During the day, the Germans at the Telephone Building dominated the space. They forced civilians to clean their building, wash their clothes, and complete various other types of work. The Germans with their superior firepower could overcome our defenses and one or two squads could jump across the street and overrun us.

Only at night, after we got a signal that the Germans had withdrawn from the area, could we send a patrol across and talk to the civilians. Even that was very dangerous. A German ambush with sudden submachine gun fire could easily wipe out our patrol. Also, on the way back, we had to listen for the sound of mortar fire at the Telephone Building. Depending on where you were, you had to move fast, forward or back, to get to shelter on one side or the other of Wspólna. Michał and I went on that dangerous mission a few times. We went step by step with our boots wrapped up in rags in order not to make any noise and often stopping to listen. Fortunately for us, the Germans from the Telephone Building were not as brave and decided that nights were for sleeping. One night when Michał and I were coming back, I heard the popping sound of the mortar being fired. We were in the middle of the street too far from either side. My instincts told me to stop. I shouted "drop" and we both dropped to the pavement. The little bomb exploded just in front of us but caused us no major harm apart from the deafening noise. And a little splinter cracked my glasses, which had been protecting my eyes.

Our Sand Castle must have looked too solid to the Germans, so they decided to destroy it through daily fire from a light machine gun. They rested the gun on a small table placed in a window on the second floor of the building just across the street from us. At night we would find a lot of empty shells just underneath us. Finally, we had enough. One night, our mine squad which was made up of women—who were very capable and very brave—went out protected by our patrol and boobytrapped the table, running a hidden wire across the street to our position. The next morning, when the Germans started their daily game: "boom" and they were gone. That taught them a lesson. Still, we expected there could be some kind of revenge—perhaps they would use civilians as human shields in their future attacks, as they had done in other places.

After this incident, our front returned to the daily routine of trench warfare, with Germans occasionally firing their heavy machine gun from the Frontleitstelle down Wspólna and from the Telephone Building down Poznańska. Our sappers made our defenses stronger through a number of measures. They dug a tunnel under Poznańska beneath the existing barricade, which made the crossing safe even from mortar fire. They also made openings from our second floor apartments to the adjoining buildings and then to others, creating an easy passageway along the whole Wspólna front and also connecting the building with the company command on Hoża St. A factory in our district had some kind of engine that was turned into an electric generator which provided power to pump water through the pipes in our area. It also provided power for our telephone system that connected all units of Jur

Company. With the underground civilian government in charge of our civilian population, we were like a little republic, but with a military dictatorship.

As "all was quiet on the western front," I asked again for permission to visit my family. It was granted by Stec, with the provision that I should return no later than that night. When I returned as ordered, the place was in total chaos. In my absence, the command had decided to move the entire civilian population from the no-man's-land across the street to our side. Few people were informed of this decision in advance to protect against possible spies. It had to be done in complete secrecy. That was why Stec did not know about it when he gave me my pass. With the Germans commanding machine guns and mortar fire, there could have been a terrible massacre if they had discovered what we were doing. Happily for us, the Germans were asleep. With our submachine squad covering them, the whole population was quietly moved to our side, including a person in a wheelchair, I was told.

When I came back, the evacuees were being assigned to houses in our Republic. One young woman cried hysterically, saying that in the panic, she had left one of her children behind. Without hesitation, I asked her where her apartment was and I charged across the street in its direction. As I was running, I heard the sound of heavy boots following me. It was Michał. We found her place without any trouble, but the silly woman had locked the front door. "Trained" by popular Western novels, I took my gun out and shot at the lock a few times. The ricochets whizzed past my ears. "Stop, Stop! You will kill us both!" Michał shouted. Fortunately, the apartment was on the first floor and we could reach the windows. We went to the yard, found the right window and I climbed up onto Michał's shoulders. Again, I took my gun out and holding it by the barrel, I smashed the glass, badly cutting my finger. I got in, went to the front door and let Michał in. We searched the apartment carefully, but it was empty. No sign of a child. We went back. Hell was waiting for me.

Jur came in and told me in no uncertain terms that I had no right to risk my life for nothing and what was more, I had no right to risk the life of one of my subordinates. It was no good telling him that Michał joined me of his own volition, not on my orders. That would have made the situation even worse. Then Jur took me aside: "Now," he said "if you are so brave, go back and set fire to the buildings. But don't tell anybody, ever!" I snuck across the street again, this time alone. The front door of the first apartment I approached was open. I recognized it—it belonged to Mr. Krzyżanowski, the father-in-law of my uncle, Jan Piekałkiewicz. I had visited him there once. He was a wealthy man and the place was richly furnished. I remembered the paintings on the walls. I set fire to the thick, brocaded drapes. I don't remember how. Maybe with some newspapers I found there and matches. Afterward I quickly returned. Somebody else must have set another fire down the street and soon the whole area was burning. This is the first time that I am telling anyone what I did under Jur's orders. In his memoirs, Stec writes that the whole area suddenly burst into flames (Deminet, 1994). He assumed that somebody had left a stove on in a kitchen or something like that. When I met him after the war, I kept my word to Jur and didn't tell him how the fires started. Now both of them are dead. Today, at the corner of Wspólna and Poznańska streets there is a small square where the houses I burned once stood. It has a monument to the Zaremba-Piorun Battalion.[21] I think of it as "my" square.

After the burning of the buildings, patrolling became more difficult. When walking over what was left of them, we had to be careful not to disturb the piles of ruins. Also, our favorite stopping place was gone—the basement of the Poznańska Restaurant. It used to be full of bottles of alcohol and canned goods. Sometimes at night two of us would go "visit" the place: one would stand watch while the other loaded two backpacks full of stuff. During the day, the Germans frequented the restaurant. I still clearly remember the Złota Reneta vodka made by the Baczewski company in the city of Lwów.[22] It was a superb product. (After the war, Mr. Baczewski escaped from Lwów which by then was in Soviet hands and traveled to Vienna where he re-established his company.[23])

One day I was resting in the back room on the second floor of the Sand Castle, when I was awoken by the noise of a large engine and people shouting "Goliath, Goliath." It turned out to be a small tank full of explosives,[24] controlled remotely. The guard from the Sand Castle escaped just in time to the back stairway. The explosion shook the whole house as if there had been an earthquake. The air filled with thick dust. It was hard to breathe, but the house stood firm. Then, following their training, the men who were off duty came running toward us from other positions. The Germans failed to take advantage of the temporary disarray and did not attack.

From then on, we were prepared. When the second Goliath arrived, it was blown up with a heavy grenade, dropped from our "artillery" position on the top floor by Officer Cadet "Inżynier" (Oleg Dydyński). The third Goliath was damaged and turned around by Inżynier and ended up blowing up the gate from which it was sent, destroying the German attack group there. Another lesson for them! They did not try using the Goliaths again. Inżynier was promoted to the rank of lieutenant and decorated with the Virtuti Military Cross (Poland's highest military distinction). Jur, who organized and participated in the defense, was also decorated and promoted to the rank of captain. My friend Stec and Officer Cadet "Skobig" were both promoted to lieutenants. I was scared to death and admired the coolness and self-control of our officers. They were great throughout the whole Uprising.

The Sand Castle was totally destroyed, and the sand from which it was made was spilled all over the place. But we discovered the effectiveness of our artillery. From the ruins across the street, the attacking Germans, with their superior fire power, had trouble reaching our gunners, stationed at the top level of the buildings. In addition, we built a barricade inside the carriage gate, hiding the elephant trap. Soon after, my team (or my whole squad) was transferred to the 2nd Platoon commanded by Lt. Skobig and his deputy Lt. Inżynier. Its location was just below my balcony bunker (Wspólna 57), which was used as an observation post from Wspolna down to the Frontleitstelle. The Germans stopped firing machine guns at my bunker. They must have figured out that I had done such a good job with the sandbags that they couldn't do any damage. They did fire during the day at any movement behind the barricade. They must have positioned their gun on a higher floor and using a scope could see anybody going across.

Without us noticing, September arrived. It got a little cooler which was a great relief, especially with all the fires around us. We had already been fighting the Germans for a whole month. Gradually, the Home Army was losing districts. First, the western part of the city—Wola—and then the Old Town and two outlying districts: Mokotów and Żoliborz. The Germans concentrated their forces for crushing attacks on places of their own choosing. In Wola, they murdered thousands upon thousands of civilians: men, women, children, the sick and wounded in hospitals, residents of old people's homes and orphanages, showing mercy to no one. A dramatic evacuation of residents was organized from the old city and other districts through the sewer canals. Many were drowned or got lost and the weak collapsed into the river of shit. The sewers were a labyrinth. There were examples of fantastic bravery in which guides, many of them young women, went back a few times to direct different groups. Nurses dragged the wounded disregarding their own safety. The canals were witness to an unknown number of heroines.[25]

Soon I experienced the smell of the sewer war myself. I was ordered to report to Jur at company headquarters. A man in work clothes was with him. Jur introduced him as the Canal Master. The man handed me a hand-drawn map. Jur told me that it allegedly showed how to get behind the German lines and told me to go and reconnoiter to see whether this was true, but to be careful not to get into a confrontation with the Germans. He had me take one of my men with me. The Canal Master assured me that most of the time I would be able to walk upright, with the exception of one place, which he showed me on the map. There I would have to crawl. I telephoned Michał to join us. The Master took us to a nearby round metal plate which covered the entrance to the sewer system. He opened it with a special tool. The plate looked heavy. We climbed down a metal ladder. The smell was overwhelming. The canal itself was higher than a tall person standing. In the middle, there was a brown rushing river and on either side, slightly above the flow, were walkways. I looked at the map. We had to turn left. We walked along the path for some time. It was wet and we had to be careful not to fall into the sewage.

After a while we came to a sewer pipe, located on the other side of the flow: it was where the map showed it to be. We were in the right place. Crossing the river to get to it was difficult. Holding onto one another, we made it across, emerging soaked and smelly. The pipe itself was narrow and wet. We had to crawl through it on our hands and knees. We sweated despite being wet. The pipe opened into the comfort of a major canal. We followed the map until we came to an opening that was marked on it. We made it, we thought, we were behind German lines. I told Michał to run if I yelled to him and not to wait for me or try to fight even if I was captured. I climbed the metal ladder up to the opening. I listened carefully. I heard some voices, but they did not sound German. I pushed the heavy plate up. I saw the legs of a pretty woman. She might have been German. I listened again. The voices were definitely Polish. I pushed the plate up even more. People ran up to it and helped me up.

They were Poles, women and men, and they asked me excitedly if I had come from the Starówka (the Old Town, which was overrun by Germans). I shouted to Michał to come on up. We told the people gathered around us the truth. They were disappointed since they badly wanted news about the Old Town. They told us where we were: deep behind Polish lines, in an area relatively untouched by war. We walked back above ground and reported to Jur about our failure to get behind German lines. He told us not to worry, we had done our best. "Go get yourselves cleaned up," he said. Easier said than done since our water was heavily rationed. I do not remember how we did it, if at all. I think I smelled bad for a long time. But in our platoon, we were considered rather heroic. In fact, I had been lucky, as I so often was. Had we been discovered by the Germans, we would have been dead ducks. And we could have got lost, wandering around forever through the sewer canals.

In our area, we had our own internal front facing the Frontleitstelle in one direction and the Telephone Building in the other. I don't remember if we were aware of the hopelessness of our situation. Maybe we were thinking that in the end the Soviets who had already advanced to the outskirts of Warsaw or else the Western Allies would come to our rescue. Now I know that the officers knew our true situation. But at the time, we, the young rank-and-file, enjoyed fighting the Germans greatly, even if it was a fight that might end in death.

We were running out of food to feed our fighters as well as the large civilian population in our Republic. In the northern part of the downtown (Śródmieście) area where we were located, there was a brewery called Haberbush that made beer for the Germans before the Uprising. Now its large supply of grain was in an area under our control. But it was some distance from our Republic and to get there you had to follow a narrow path through the ruins of buildings and through a trench running across the broad Jerozolimska Av., which was often under mortar fire. Our logistics unit was gradually running out of man and woman power, both its own as well as that from the voluntary civilian force. Also, some of our couriers were wounded. We, the front line troops, had to lend a hand. I had the pleasure of doing this once. It was tough carrying a heavy bag of hard grains, and running with it through the trench was murder. I wished I was bigger and stronger, although generally my slim figure was an advantage—I was a smaller target and could run faster. Fortunately, I was not ordered to be the dromedary again. The grain seized was cooked together with its chaff, as the cooks had no way to separate the two. We called it a "spit dish."

One day, Stec asked me to help him move his mother from a third floor apartment to the basement of the building because she was afraid of the bombs. Since there was no space for her whole bed, we carried only the spring frame and the mattress. In her basement there were four big drums containing chemicals. They were ideal for resting the box spring on. In his memoirs, Stec writes, "Only later did I understand that my poor Mama had slept for six weeks on two drums of Yellow Cake [*sic*]—a starting ingredient for nuclear fuel" (Deminet 1994). It was radioactive. Stec's father was a glass maker and used it to color his products. I assume he was hiding the Yellowcake from the Germans. Neither his mother nor I were affected by the radiation.

Otherwise, things were routine, both during the day and at night, as we watched along Wspólna St. from my bunker and controlled the traffic between us and the buildings along Poznańska St. One day I was off duty, resting in our room next to the bunker, when I heard commotion and somebody shouted that Grandpa—Słonka—was wounded. The German machine guns were firing like mad. I ran downstairs. The fool was trying to get over the barricade to safety while bullets were whistling all around him. I dragged him over and into the house. He was bleeding from one leg. Apparently, the drunken idiot had climbed on top of the barricade, shouting that nobody would stop him from walking the streets of "his" Warsaw. The Germans bloody well tried to, but, luckily for him and for me, they were firing from a great distance and their aim was not that good. Our nurses bandaged his leg. It was only a scratch, but he was bleeding badly. Soon the bandage was wet. I decided to take him to the hospital. Michał and I put him on a stretcher and carried him there. It was difficult because to get from our platoon to the hospital—we had to go through many basements. Now we understood the tough job our nurses had, many of them young girls who were much weaker than we were. When we made it to the hospital, we were met by the noise of a party in the next room. Nobody noticed our arrival. We put Grandpa on the table and I went to the room with the party to get some help. There was a good-sized crowd of people, drinking what I thought was champagne. I made a man in a white coat come with me. Looking at Grandpa, he asked what had happened and said his wound was not life-threatening. He told us to wait a few minutes. "But he is bleeding very badly," I shouted. "And you are a doctor?" he replied. "No, but I have a gun," I said, pulling out my gun and pointing it at him. "All right, all right!" He shouted a woman's name and told her to come out. They took the bloody bandages off Grandpa and cleaned the wound, then the doctor decided that stitches were needed. He told the nurse to do it. "What is your name," he asked me in an irritated voice. When I told him, he insisted that I would hear about it. The nurse tried to defuse the situation and told us it was a wedding celebration. She wanted to keep Grandpa at the hospital, but I decided to take him back to our platoon. A few days later, Jur called: "And now you tried to shoot our chief surgeon!" I told him what had happened and he let me off the hook but warned me never to do it again.

Soon after, I was summoned to company headquarters. When I arrived, I found two men I didn't know, both older than me. The officer on duty lined us up. He commanded us to stand at attention when Jur entered. I was first in line. He said: "Andrzej, as of this date you are promoted to the rank of plutonowy (platoon sergeant) and decorated with the Krzyż Walecznych (Cross of Valor)."[26] He gave me a hug. I could not believe my ears. This was something I did not expect. I was only 18. Later I found out that there was only one other platoon sergeant of a similar age in the whole battalion. I was also given the second highest decoration for bravery. I was very proud. There was a little celebration in my platoon and the girls sewed one more bar on my uniform. I had the rank, but in practice that changed nothing. I was still a spare noncommissioned officer with just two soldiers and a drunk under my command.

That decoration was nearly my last. One day not long after, my two men (Grandpa was not able to participate anymore) and I were asleep on a beautiful sunny day. We were resting after night duty. We were exhausted. I did not hear the explosion when it happened. I found myself on the floor and the room was full of dust. It was very difficult to breathe. I did not know what had happened! I smacked myself to get a grip. I saw that the boys were also on the floor. They looked dead. I shook them one by one. None of us were wounded but we just didn't know what had happened. Many years later, a doctor with past military service told me that we had most likely had concussions. I went downstairs and discovered that a heavy caliber shell from the railroad artillery gun had hit the empty space next to our building. This type of gun was called Big Bertha. It was used during WWI to bombard Paris. In our case, it made a hole as deep as a four-story building. It exploded where a building that was destroyed in 1939 had once stood. It was the only empty space between our building and the two other houses on Wspólna in the direction of Marszałkowska St. Were they aiming at our platoon? We didn't know but it was too close for us, and also too close for the liking of the Germans in the nearby Telephone Building. They shot white flares into the air one after another. Too bad we didn't have flares—we could have protected ourselves from German artillery!

It was my night duty to control the traffic that crossed the Wspólna St. barricade. Once, I was standing at the gate to the apartment entrances, with my back against the wall. Opposite me, a very pretty girl about my age was sitting in a chair. I flirted with her. I saw myself as a "big shot" in my uniform, armed with a gun, and holding a rank that was high for my age. I offered her a cigarette, which she declined. I struck a match to light mine. Something slapped my left cheek with a loud noise. The girl cried out in fear. Instinctively, I moved inside the gate. I touched my face. My hand was bloody—a bullet from a sniper had grazed my face. I told the girl I was fine and that she should go across the street and ask for my replacement. Soon, she came back with Michał. He was very concerned, but I told him it was nothing. I went to the platoon and one of the nurses took out tiny pieces of a bullet from my face. She put some iodine on it and with time my face healed without a mark. As usual I was very lucky: half an inch closer and my head would have been gone. The girl was pretty, but not so beautiful as to look at her once and die.

Being the spare platoon sergeant meant I got all kinds of extra jobs. Once I was called to Skobig's office. With him was a young man with a grim look. "Escort this prisoner to the Gendarmerie," Skobig ordered me. He told me how to get there. I told the man to come with me. The trip was difficult. Instead of the route through the second floors, we had to go through the basements, which were full of civilians. At one point my prisoner stood still and refused to go any further. "They will kill me there," he said, nearly crying. I argued with him that he would have a fair trial, and if he were innocent of whatever he was accused of, he would be set free. He still refused to move. I took my gun out and shot a bullet into the space between his legs. The sound the shot made in the basement sounded like it was a bomb. He jumped up and went the rest of the way without giving me any more trouble. I turned him over to the gendarme, who already knew all about him. Sometime later I again had to go to the Gendarmerie, on what business I don't remember. I met the same officer and asked him about the man. "He is buried there," he said, pointing to the yard. I went cold. Was he so guilty as to deserve a death sentence? I was so shocked that I did not ask what his crime was.

There were still a few dedicated Nazis who were hiding among us and communicated with their own forces. Some were Volksdeusche (ethnic Germans[27]) who had lived in Warsaw before the war, spoke excellent Polish, and knew the city well. They collaborated in two ways: by identifying targets for artillery or planes, or by shooting at our military personnel or civilians. I don't know how the former communicated with the German military but they found a way. For example, there was only one well in our area, located at a dairy. Long lines formed to get water. Soon somebody told the Germans about it and they started shooting mortar bombs at the people waiting for water. People were killed and wounded. But we all still needed water! As I mentioned above, our engineers together with Stec adapted a gasoline engine. It was now used to bring up water through the pipes in the basement we occupied on Hoża St. That basement was connected to the whole underground pipe system of our Republic. That way we had safe access to water. It was obviously rationed, but I personally don't remember this being a problem. Perhaps the military got more than the civilians.

The weather seemed to be working in the Germans' favor. It was sunny and hot during the whole 63 days of the Uprising. I don't remember any rain. A more immediate deadly nuisance were the so-called pigeon nests: real or assumed snipers living among us and shooting from top floors of buildings. This caused some casualties and a lot of panic. Once, when I was visiting my family at their home, a local warden came and asked me to check if somebody was shooting from a top floor room in the next building. I went there with him and indeed, it sounded like shots. I got my gun out, kicked the door open, and moved quickly back behind the frame to wait for gunshots. Nothing happened! The room was empty. Looking back on it now, I think the shooters were not "pigeons" but German military snipers who shot with scopes from tall buildings. Just like the one who nearly killed me. But they created a lot of panic and suspicion among the civilians. What seemed like the sounds of gunfire was often only the sound of ricochets. There was constant shooting all over the city.

Next, my two men and I were sent to fortify the building on the corner of Wspólna and Emilii Plater streets. For some reason no position had been established there even though the building was in a strategic location. Across the street, stood the Peter and Paul Church, which was no-man's-land. Kitty-corner from us was an empty area—once an orchard (Ogród Pomologiczny) that during the war had been turned into small private vegetable plots stretching all the way to our hospital—which, unlike the gardens, was in territory defended by our forces. We could see the tasty red tomatoes ripening in forbidden land. To get to them you had to cross the street under machine gun fire from the Frontleitstelle, which probably also covered the gardens. The tomatoes were invitingly red, but so was our blood. Still, our position was relatively safe, if we stayed put. The Germans at the Frontleistelle could only fire along Wspólna and not at us. The rest of the Emilii Plater was defended by another battalion

With the help of the civilians from the building, who were happy we were coming to defend them, we blocked the basement and the first floor windows completely, using whatever material we could find and plenty of sand bags. We dug sandy earth from the yard (every apartment house had a flower or vegetable garden in the courtyard). On the second floor, we built our normal defensive position, with two rows of sand bags and narrow slits for observation and shooting. The top floor was turned into our artillery position with a large supply of hand grenades and Molotov cocktails. We camouflaged the windows with blackout curtains. We worked very hard all night to get the building ready. By morning this fortress had been completed. We were all exhausted, but now the guard shifts had to start. I took the first three-hour turn. With only three of us it was a tough job. We never got real, good sleep. During my first shift, the company telephone crew installed connections to the company exchange and I could report to Jur that the job was done.

For about a week, things were peaceful, apart from the sporadic machine gun fire along Wspólna St. from the Frontleitstelle. It was noisy, but they could not shoot at us because the angle was wrong. One day, using my opera glasses, I saw the hospital on the other side of the gardens being evacuated in a hurry. Some wounded patients were being carried out on stretchers. It was obvious to me that the Germans were advancing on our defenses. I notified Jur. That same day some "big shots" came to take over from me. It was a squad of about 10 men with a light machine gun. Their leader ordered the removal of some of the sandbags and put a table at the window on which they positioned their machine gun. According to the leader, they needed a good line of sight to fire. I tried to argue with him. The light machine gun with magazines was no match for the German one with its ammunition belt. He should have his machine gun in the basement, and only fire when the enemy infantry came close to our position. This would surprise them and create panic. But he knew better. Fools can't be argued with. Fortunately, he did not remove the artillery from the top floor.

My team returned to our previous location. Not long after, I got a call from Jur to go and find out what was going on at the building we had fortified. "I cannot get a straight answer from them," he said. As I approached Emilii Plater St., I heard fire from a heavy machine gun. It stopped by the time I got there. The whole squad was hiding on the staircase. What I had predicted came to pass. One of them was killed and two were wounded. The rest were scared to death. I reported the situation to Jur and went back to my platoon. It was not long before I got another call from Jur to check on them again. This time the situation was much worse. I heard the loud noise of cannon fire. When I got there, they shouted, "Get down, get down!" I hid with them on the stairway. Just in time! The cannon shell went right through the building and exploded in the courtyard. It was a tank using anti-tank ammunition, it shots going through the windows without exploding. I decided that I had seen enough and took off in a hurry.

I reported to Jur on what I saw. I said I thought Germans would soon send infantrymen to attack. They did indeed, using drunk Ukrainians. Jur issued his normal emergency order. My section was on duty, so I did not have to go. I took our rifle, stood up behind our barricade and rested the gun on top of it. I adjusted the sight to the maximum and waited watchfully. When I saw a running man, I fired three times. He fell, but I cannot claim to have killed or wounded him for sure as there was shooting all around as well as grenade blasts. I could not continue firing because we had only five rounds left for the rifle. Our defenders had done a good job and the attackers retreated. For the rest of the Uprising, the Germans did not try to attack that position again. They had other things to worry about.

The Soviets had advanced into Warsaw and were in the Praga neighborhood on the eastern side of the Vistula River, across from our position. The Germans decided to blow up the Poniatowski Bridge. The defense of the left (western) bank of the river became their priority, especially since the Powiśle district there was still in our hands. Crossing the river would not have been difficult for the Soviets given their air superiority and their artillery. During their westward offensive, they had forced a number of rivers; they had the equipment to do it.

Soviet artillery started to fire on the Germans but sometimes hit us since our front lines were very close to one another. At night their unsophisticated, noisy planes were flown by brave pilots over the roofs of buildings, dropping some food, arms, and ammunition for us. The problem was that they did not use parachutes and consequently many goods were damaged. What's more, their ammunition was useless for our Mausers. The planes also dropped small bombs, which occasionally fell on us and not on the Germans. Still, their activity gave us some joy, especially with the Germans under fire and in fear of these nightly visits. The Soviet planes were very difficult for artillery or fighter planes to shoot down since they operated at night. In recent times, I found out that their pilots were women. I feel grateful to them. It was great to hear the noise of their loud engines at night. Somebody was helping us!

One day, on a trial run, Soviet fighter planes flew overhead and kept the German bombers grounded and their artillery silent. It was wonderful! But it only lasted a day. We had that one normal sunny, quiet day. Even the German machine guns on our front were quiet. Perhaps their crews were sunning themselves. I was sitting on a comfortable easy chair in my bunker on the balcony, looking from time to time along Wspólna St. It was boring. I went into the room to light a cigarette. Suddenly, there was the sharp, loud noise of an explosion. I returned to the balcony. There was a smoking hole in the back of the chair where my chest had been just a minute or two before. I had been very lucky once again. The artillery shell, most likely Russian, struck the top of the building just across the street and the shrapnel hit my chair. That time, my smoking habit saved my life.

Not long after I was again on observation duty in my bunker. For some reason I stood up and looked through my binoculars to the very end of Wspólna

St. There was a tank there. It fired and the shell hit our barricade, blowing a big hole in it. I was mesmerized as its gun moved in my direction. It fired again. As the shot went over my head, I dove into the room. The next shot hit the bunker—with a loud explosion, the whole balcony collapsed. This product of my dangerous work, which I was so proud of, was gone. So was the platoon's observation position. The company engineers repaired the barricade that very night but they could not do anything to restore my bunker. Now observation had to be done from behind the barricade under frequent German machine gun fire. This spare platoon sergeant was not to rest for long. I was called downstairs to receive a call from the company commander. "Andrzej," Jur said, "I am sending a squad to occupy the house on Poznańska St., just across from the Germans. Go with them and find out whether from the attic you can see down Św. Barbara St." The well-armed squad was already waiting for me in the platoon command room. Its commander reported to me that they were ready to go. We sprinted across Wspólna St. to the gate where I had nearly been killed by a sniper. The block's civilian leader was there waiting for us. He told us that the Germans never came across from the Telephone Building. They only fired their mortar at the roofs and the inner courtyard. This was the block with two four-story houses bordering Poznańska St. but which only had an entrance from Wspólna. The third house with a Poznañska St. entrance, had been destroyed by German bombing in 1939. There was no entrance to the apartment block that the Germans could have used to mount an attack. The building's civilian leader offered us soup, which the collective cooked for all the inhabitants. He proudly described the way he organized things to keep his people safe. They were too close to the Germans to be bombed by their artillery or planes. He took me upstairs. Unfortunately, from the top floor or the attic you could only see the beginning of Św. Barbara St., not all the way along it. Regardless, with our mission accomplished, we went back across Wspólna. The civilian leader was very disappointed that we were not going to stay to defend his kingdom. I telephoned Jur to report. Feeling sorry for the civilian, I started my report by describing how well the block was organized. "Do not tell me stories," Jur barked into the phone, "Could you see along Św. Barbara or not?" "I could not" I reported. "That's bad," he said and hung up the phone. I learned my lesson. In war people don't have time for stories.

Soon afterward my team was transferred to another unit. I do not remember if this was the 3rd Platoon, or only a squad belonging to some other platoon. It was located at a tall, six- or seven-story building on Wspólna between the crater from the 1939 bombing and the one left by Big Bertha, in the direction of Marszałkowska. Its top floor dominated the whole neighborhood, which is why it was used for observation. Across the street, there were a number of little huts, built on the ruins of the 1939 bombardment, housing all kinds of retail shops. The troops occupying the building were called the "Company of Cowards"; I do not know why. The building was some distance from the front. It also had no underground connection with the rest of our positions and to get to it, one had to run down the street, exposed to possible machine gun fire, hugging the buildings. For that reason, when my team moved there we did so at night, carrying our trove of Molotov cocktails, hand grenades, ammunition, vodka, some food, and our blankets. It was very dark when we got there. Somebody told us where our room was. As we were unloading, we were talking about why we were transferred to the so-called "cowards" unit. Suddenly a voice boomed from the darkness, "So we are the 'cowards' unit?!" This was our new commander. I apologized profusely, noting that it was others in the company who gave them this label, but the damage was done. We had made a bad start with our new unit.

The unit's main duty was to man the observation post on Poznańska. It was located in the building that Jur wanted me to report on. I went with the on-duty squad to familiarize myself with the setup. The post was located on the second floor of the last building before the ruins. It was kitty-corner from the Telephone Building controlled by the Germans. It was so close that from time to time you could hear the Germans shouting. "Observation" here consisted of sitting in an easy chair with your back to the Germans and using the "mirror position"[28] in such a way that you could see the street close to the German building and listen. You had to be quiet so as not to reveal our position. It was a very boring job. If the Germans were to attack along Poznańska St., we were told to light up the place with Molotov cocktails, to provide targets for our machine gun. The men in the unit considered this to be a very dangerous job. To be that close to the Germans could be unnerving, but as long as they did not attack, we were safe where we were. The angle was such that Germans could not shoot at us with their firearms. They could shoot mortars, and they did, but these little bombs landed further along the street, mostly on roofs or courtyards. However, the German artillery (unlike the mortars which are light weapons) was too close to their own position to shoot. Our location was also too close for air raids. I thought it was the safest place in the whole of our front.

I became interested in those huts across the street from us and the shops they contained. Michał and I ran across the street to investigate them. It turned out they were empty. All we found was some kind of helmet, which we decided to use for shooting practice with my pistol. We shot from a short distance away, but could not hit it. That is why I preferred hand grenades. The first shop belonged to a jeweler. Like the others, it was also empty. Sometime after that, the shop was hit by a Soviet artillery shell. The next time we had a free day, we went to examine it. The explosion had blown a big hole in the floor through to the basement. We climbed a few steps down. What we saw was quite a shock. There, on the basement floor, were two or three bricks of pure gold. "What are we going to do with them?" Michał asked. "We better cover them up well for the owner to find after the war," I said. So we did. Soon after, another shell hit the same shop. All we found was a pile of ash. The gold must have melted into it.

It seemed I was going to get some rest in this reserve unit, away from the front (our observation post was not actually on the front). Then I got another call from Jur. I was to guide an officers' patrol through the ruins. "You know them best," he said. I was pleased with this recognition, but I was also tired due to the many night duties. I met the group at about 11:00 p.m. near where the 1st Platoon was located (the former Sand Castle). The patrol consisted of four or five people. Some carried submachine guns. I only knew Stec and Inżynier, the deputy commander of the company. I instructed them briefly about how to walk through the ruins and we covered our boots with rags. I took the lead as we ran across Wspólna. Then we moved slowly, step by step. Eventually we got to Św. Barbara St. The patrol spread out along the street and I got to a carriage gate very close to the bunker. I was tempted to sneak up to it and throw in a hand grenade, but reason prevailed. I was not there to start a fight—that would make it impossible for the officers to do their job. On the ground in the carriage gate I saw an old sack. I laid down on it. The next thing I knew, somebody was pulling my leg. It was Inżynier. He was furious. Apparently, I had fallen asleep. When we got back to platoon headquarters, he told me he was going to have me court martialed. I was ashamed and afraid. But Jur would not have it. I was his boy and he saved me once again.

Later, when I was resting in the building to which I was assigned, I thought I heard a shot from above. I mentioned this to a guy with me. He smiled, "That is only the 'chorąży'" (warrant officer). I had heard stories about him, how he shot into the German bunker in front of the Telephone Building. The bunker had no back wall and there was a slit in the front wall used for shooting and observation. When there were no Germans looking through it, you could see light, but if there were a German there, it went dark. If someone shot, the German got a bullet right in his face. Polish fire through the slit stopped the Germans from shooting their machine gun down Poznańska St. They could not figure out how it was done. And all they would have had to do was hang up a blanket at the back of the bunker to stop any light coming through the slit. From his position, the warrant officer could also see the flat roof of the main railroad station, which was occupied by Germans. Once he shot a German soldier who had gone out on the roof to wash. His buddy, who came to check on him, also got killed. This warrant officer had been the prewar champion in target shooting. He had a target rifle with a scope.

My curiosity was sparked and I went up to see. In the room on the top floor, I found an old man looking through the scope of a Berthier rifle, just like mine. "Sorry to interrupt," I said. He replied, "Not at all. I am getting tired. You could replace me for a while." I was very eager to do so. The gun was mounted on some kind of construction and aimed far down the street. He told me to sit and look through the scope until I saw a truck racing by and then shoot. I sat down in his place and he left. I was very excited but after a while, I started to get tired looking through the scope. Then, a truck appeared! I pulled the trigger. The truck veered off to the right and disappeared from my vision. Did I kill the driver? Were there other enemy casualties? I will never know. I waited some more, but nothing happened. I told the warrant officer about my kill. He thanked me for replacing him. I left feeling great. I learned that the job of the sniper requires a lot of self-control and that somehow you felt removed from your target. The warrant officer always crossed himself after he killed somebody.

Soon after my experience as a sniper, I asked the commander if my team could permanently take over the Poznańska position. He gladly agreed. Now his squad didn't have any front duty. The three of us moved to the position, taking all our junk. Now I was my own boss and the boss of the whole block of apartments, where perhaps a few hundred people lived. They were very happy to have somebody to defend them against the Germans. We were going to do our best, but our duty was only to provide targets for their machine gun fire thus protecting civilians. What else could the three of us do? But I knew that we would defend the block to the death.

First, together with the civilian leader of the residents, I inspected my new "county" of which I was "the Count." The basement was blocked by coal. This was fine to stop people from entering, but it could easily be set on fire. Still, there was no way I could remove the coal. The first floor windows were solidly barricaded by sandbags thanks to the expertise of our sappers. The second floor observation room was at the end of the building on Poznańska, just across from the Germans. Good for observation, but it could be rendered useless by German fire from across the street. The next day I asked our sappers to cut a passage through all the apartments that were already empty, all the way to Wspólna. That way, I had a clear route for retreat. We put our artillery—most of our Molotov cocktails and hand grenades—on the top floor. If the German's attacked, this was to be Kajtek's job. He was to throw the cocktails and grenades blindly, without aiming or revealing himself. This way he should have been safe from the German fire. Michał was to run into the basement and watch out in case the coal caught fire in the attack. The civilian leader had placed some water buckets down there, and together with his fire brigade, they should have been able to control a fire to some extent. But not if the Germans threw in a larger number of hand grenades or used a flamethrower. I was to be in the observation room, with the telephone that connected me to my troops and the company command. I would be reporting to Jur and waiting for his orders. Hopefully, he would send a well-armed squad and other help. If not, I would retreat or die. But what about the civilians?

The people in this apartment building were mostly still living in their homes. Only those whose apartments faced Poznańska had vacated them because of the constant machine gun and mortar fire. They were well organized to do all the necessary tasks to keep the place clean and protect against fire. There was a communal kitchen where the midday soup was cooked from supplies held in common for those who needed it. The three of us also became the beneficiaries of this tasty meal. We divided the 24 hours of our watch into six-hour rotations. That way we were sometimes on duty at night or, worse, during the early morning. The only entertainment was occasional German mortar fire and the nightly visits of the low-flying Soviet planes whose loud engines sounded like tractors. As I said, I admired the bravery of their pilots. The Germans were afraid of the planes and left them alone because they spotted targets for the Soviet artillery and sometimes dropped bombs themselves. Again, they were not always on target and sometimes hit us. To give them their due, it was hard to aim without a spotter adjusting each artillery round. Also, many of our positions were very close to those of the Germans. As for us, we appreciated the nightly, friendly sound. However, I nearly got killed by them twice.

One day, an old lady came to visit us. She told us that a bomb was resting on the top of her bookshelf. I thought she was nuts, but out of politeness, I went to investigate. But there it was, a small Russian bomb perched on top of the bookshelf. It was the size of a large dog. It had come down through the roof and through the apartment's ceiling, but for some reason it did not explode. It looked undamaged, with a kind of trigger stuck to the side. I told the lady that we would remove it, but advised her to move to the basement. I went to get Michał. We drank some vodka to boost our courage, grabbed a blanket, and went to the lady's apartment. The bomb was not very heavy. The two of us placed it on the blanket, carried it downstairs, and ran through the courtyard and the street to the hole made by the Big Bertha. There, we rolled the bomb down into the crater. We watched it bumping around. Then, we both fell flat—suddenly remembering what we were supposed to do! But the bomb did not explode. We two drunken fools were lucky. As I write this, I am wondering why I did not call our sappers to deal with it.

One afternoon, an officer I didn't know came and gave us two high-power flashlights. We were instructed to go on top of the roof when notified, and, upon hearing the sound of a plane engine, to flash the lights. This was the signal to the pilot that he was leaving the area controlled by us. He was not to make any more drops. We were very excited. Michał and I inspected the roof. Its entrance was through a door from the stairway. This led to a narrow platform in the middle of the roof, which sloped in both directions. Fortunately, the platform faced Wspólna St. The platform was too small for both of us, so we decided to sit on the slope facing the courtyard. We could protect ourselves with ropes tied around the chimney and then to our belts. We practiced this a few times. The Germans could not see into the location we chose. We were safe from their rifle fire, but not from their mortars. Our assumption was that they would be afraid to use the roof of their building because of the air raids. Our nightly Soviet visitor kept them in line and they never fired their mortars at night. We waited for a few nights in nervous excitement. Then the phone call came. It was to be that night. We charged to the roof. It seemed to us that we had to wait for ages. Would we hear the plane? Eventually it sounded loud and clear, accompanied by the fire of German artillery. We started flashing our lights. It flew quite low and was one of the most beautiful sights I have seen in my life. We were not alone. The British allies were supporting us. We would win. Then it was gone. Now, a line of colorful balls seemed to be floating in the sky. Then they exploded, raining shrapnel on us. We sped down the stairs. From that nights' drop, my company got two Sten submachine guns with ammunition. It was not much, but beggars could not be choosers. My own team of three got nothing, except for the excitement.

Later, I did get a gift from a "tractor" plane. It was a beautiful warm September night—just the kind of night to take your girlfriend for a romantic walk. I went downstairs and stood in the entrance to the staircase smoking a cigarette. I heard the friendly noise of the plane and then a "shoo" sound and a loud explosion. I was lifted and thrown up the stairs. Afterward, I was bruised and in pain for a week or two and it was a miracle I did not break my back.

The Germans did not leave us in peace. The apartment on Pozanańska St. had a nice balcony. Of course I could not use the balcony, but I opened its door so the warm fresh air could enter and rested after night duty on a comfortable bed placed against a wall. A mortar hit the balcony and sprayed shrapnel up the wall just above my head. That ended my fresh air.

Then one night we were frightened by the many loud German shouts coming from Św. Barbara St. We rushed to our battle stations. I rang Jur and reported on the situation. It sounded to me like preparation for an attack. But it was very unlikely the Germans would attack us across Poznańska under fire from our machine gun; their attack, so I thought, was most likely to be through the ruins. Long after the war, during a commemoration of the Uprising in Warsaw, Stec told me the old machine gun was called "Stutterer" because it often became blocked. But at the time, I did not know that. It seemed that the Germans were ignorant of this as well. After shouting for some time, the Germans went inside their building. It sounded like they were arguing with one another. Kajtek told us he saw about a hundred Germans.

At the time, I asked him why he did not throw a grenade at them. Of course, it was because he was afraid to do so. But later, I was glad he did not. Ours was an observation position and not a battle position. Our job required us to be silent.

Gradually, the Germans were pushing back our front, using their far superior land and air power. We were losing district after district. They themselves were being pressed by the Soviets, who had pushed them out of Praga, on the eastern side of the Vistula River. The Germans blew up Warsaw's bridges, but, as I noted, the Soviet Army had great experience in crossing large rivers. Without much trouble, they sent the Polish troops under their command,[29] to the Powiśle district on the Vistula, still occupied by our forces. But this was only a propaganda stunt to show that they were helping us to their maximum capacity. The Soviets chose not to deploy their artillery or provide air support while the Germans were employing everything they had to quell the Uprising. Our forces—Home Army units and Poles under Soviet Command—were defeated in heavy fighting with heavy losses.

By the end of September, only the city center was still in our hands. The northern area was already under heavy German attack. We, in the south, were to be next. We knew we could not count on any Soviet support. Then, one day, the West spoke again: a massive American flotilla flew over. They dropped a large number of parachutes. At first, we thought they were dropping men. But the drops only contained arms and ammunition. But it was of little help. Since we held only a small part of Warsaw, the wind blew most of the parachutes over to the Germans. This was the only American drop for us that the Soviets allowed, even though they knew damn well we were beyond help if they did not intervene—which they had no intention of doing. All that was left to us was to fight to the death. But the Germans had much bigger enemies to face. The Uprising was consuming a considerable amount of their human and material resources. They had to end it one way or the other. So they decided to be nice. They permitted civilians to leave Warsaw during a brief ceasefire. It was so strange not to hear the sound of fighting.

I took this opportunity to run to my family at 13 Wspólna St. They were gone. They had left a note saying that they were fine and provided an address in Radom where they expected to go. The roof of the building was smoldering. Most likely the whole place would not last much longer. I went searching for anything that could be of use. I found some of my winter underwear, a sweater, warm socks and gloves, and my fire brigade leather coat. There was also some flour. I took a large bed sheet and wrapped these treasures in it. As I was getting ready to leave, somebody shouted "Robbery is punished by death!" There in the corridor was a fire brigade officer pointing a small pistol at me. I hid behind the corner and got out my own large pistol. I pointed it at him and said, "I am not stealing anything. This is my apartment, Tołłoczko" (my mother's maiden name), "I am just taking some of my own things." Then he saw my uniform and apologized. I told him I had been a member of the fire brigade and we parted as friends.

Most of the civilians in the area controlled by my company did not leave during the ceasefire. Because of our high level of organization and the fact we were close to German positions, which made us relatively safe from German artillery and air raids, they must have thought that we could defend them forever. At the time, I probably thought the same thing. Probably we all thought that the Soviets would push the Germans out and liberate us. I do not know whether anyone left my Republic. Because of the mortars and an occasional friendly bomb from our Soviet allies, most of the civilians lived in their basements. I seldom saw any of them, except for the building leader. I do not remember whether the ceasefire lasted or whether it was redeclared after a resumption of fighting.

One day we saw, in our mirror, a German soldier standing on the street below with a white flag. "They must be surrendering!" we joked. I called Jur. He told me to find out what he wanted. Easier said than done. I could not disclose our position to the Germans. I charged like mad down to Wspólna St. I stopped at the corner, pulled myself together and entered Poznańska St. It was a strange picture—an empty street with only the two of us there. As if it were a duel. I walked slowly, deliberately, to where he stood. He saluted me in military fashion. I saluted him back. He asked me if I knew German. I told him that I did. "My major wants to meet your major," he informed me. I told him, "Fine, I will pass on the message." He looked at my beret. "What is that sign?" he pointed at the Air Force insignia. I told him what it was. "So am I," he said, "We are Air Force Signals. You are a sergeant, so am I." He must have known Polish ranks. He pulled a flat bottle of vodka from his pocket, "Let's have a drink!" It was the Baczewski stuff. He handed it to me and I hesitated. "No, it is not poisoned." He had a good swig. Then I had some. I gave him the bottle back. He smiled, saluted and left. I went back to our position and passed on the message to Jur.

Soon after, Jur and two other officers came out. They all were dressed in English-style battle uniform. They looked very smart. The Germans must have been waiting because they came out immediately. There were also three of them. I could not see their ranks. Both groups saluted each other, but when the German major put his hand out to shake Jur's, he refused to reciprocate. We could not hear what they said, but later we were told that Jur refused to shake hands with a member of the army that murdered civilians. But I drank vodka with one of them. The two groups saluted and parted.

Well! The show was over. We were told that our high command signed the capitulation document. The Western Allies recognized us as part of their armed forces. The Germans would honor that. We were going to become their prisoners of war, subject to the Geneva Conventions. Michał and I went to Jur and asked for permission to break through enemy lines. Our chances were minimal, but for me, after so many years of fighting Germans, capitulation now was unacceptable. Jur gave us a direct order to capitulate. There was no discussion. We were very disciplined. We had to obey. We were given a few days to prepare. I got a rucksack from somewhere. I packed some warm clothes. I hung my leather coat on it. I knew I should not make it too heavy because I might have to walk for a long time.

The place fell into disorder. I saw a dead man lying on the street. A fly came out from his nose. The civilians were to leave the city after we were gone, which I felt bad about. They would not have our protection. In fact, the Germans let them go wherever they wanted. Only in some cases did they send young people to work as slave labor in Germany. An old lady came to us with a Great Dane. She was sobbing, "Could you take care of him? I cannot feed him anymore." I assured her not to worry. Soon after she left, I shot him in the head. He died at once. Michał, who was a shoemaker's apprentice, took his skin off. He made an excellent dogmeat soup. With a good cup of vodka, we had our last feast in Warsaw. We got our service pay for 63 days: most of it in German marks, but some also in dollars.[30] We buried our hand grenades for future use and emptied our Molotov cocktail bottles of their deadly contents.

The next day the whole company, with our firearms and backpacks, lined up in front of company headquarters. Grandpa appeared from somewhere, completely drunk. We were told that we had to parade in front of our generals and their German counterparts and then be disarmed. Jur made a short speech thanking us for our service and then went along our line saying goodbye to each of us. When he came to my section he gave me hell for letting Grandpa get so drunk. "How do you expect him to march straight?" he shouted, "Sober him up!" We were allowed some rest before leaving. We found a white towel and a bottle of cherry juice. We rubbed Grandpa's head with the towel and sprinkled some juice on it. It looked just like blood and a bandage. The only trouble were the flies, which were attracted to the juice. We had to chase them away. Once it was time to march away, he had sobered up enough that with our help he could walk relatively straight. And then off we went. My team was ordered to the end of the column. We first passed by the lines of crying civilian spectators, some of whom were pointing at Grandpa and saying how brave he was to be wounded and still marching with his mates. On the other side, past the podium of the generals, there was a huge hole in the ground where we were forced to throw our weapons. Just before being disarmed, a drunk German Gestapo agent appeared, swearing and waving his gun at us. I was ready to get my pistol out, but he was grabbed by German soldiers and dragged away. I threw my dear pistol into the hole. At the time, I did not realize that I was throwing away a symbolic key to my motherland, which would be gone from me forever.

NOTES

1. Jarek's paternal uncle Jan Piekałkiewicz was the head of the whole Polish Underground from August 1942 to February 1943, when he was captured by the Germans, tortured, and executed in June of that year.

2. This was a controversial decision that is still being debated today, especially in Poland.

3. See for example: Cienciala (1994), Davies (2004), and Peszke (2005).

4. Piekałkiewicz says: "She was my idol. The bravest and most honest person I have ever known. All my life I tried to be like her" (Jarosław Piekałkiewicz, email to Joanna Drzewieniecki, August 8, 2021).

5. See http://www.warsawuprising.com/faq.htm

6. Ibid.

7. Jarosław Piekałkiewicz, email to the Joanna Drzewieniecki, August 9, 2021.

8. Readers who would like to know what happened to Jarek after the Uprising and how he ended up in the United States should read Marriam-Goldberg (2013). Further personal testimony of Jarek's experiences in World War II can be found in Piekałkiewicz (2020).

9. The Polish Police was placed under German control when the German occupied Poland. Poles called it the "Blue Police." While this police force was generally pro-Polish and some were members of Polish Underground, there were also a fair number who betrayed Polish gentiles and Jews; see, for example, Piekałkiewicz (2020, 179–181 and elsewhere).

10. All members of the Polish resistance used code names.

11. In the Polish Army, a cadet officer was someone who had finished officer-training school but had yet to finish the one-year internship required for a promotion to the rank of second lieutenant.

12. The names of military units used here follow current usage. The smallest unit is a team (called "fire team" in the United States), followed in increasing size by a squad, a section, a platoon, a company, a battalion and so forth.

13. Piekałkiewicz has a photo of himself and these three men in his possession.

14. This battalion consisted of three companies with a total of ten platoons as well as auxiliary services.

15. Its name in Polish was the Urząd Telekomunikacyjny i Telegraficzny. Its modern building was finished in 1934. It was located at 45 Nowogrodzka St. at the corner of 29–33 Poznańska and 2 Św. Barbara's. The building survived the war. See: http://www.warszawa1939.pl/obiekt/nowogrodzka-45

16. A very large horseshoe-shaped building stretching from Hoża to Wspólna streets with a courtyard on Emilii Plater St. It housed an auto repair shop, a fuel depot, as well as housing for troops shipping out to other fronts.

17. Rotmistrz Radziwiłłowicz was later severely wounded in the "Zaremba-Piorun" action.

18. Kazimiera Piekałkiewicz and Zula (Zofia) Tołłoczko. Zula, Jarek's godmother, survived the war and lived into her 90s.

19. This building was separated from the "front" of Piekałkiewicz's company on Wspólna St. by one building and a street (Poznańska).

20. Tadeusz (Thaddeus) Kościuszko (1746–1817) was a Polish–Lithuanian military engineer, statesman, and military leader who became a hero in both his homelands and the United States, where he not only fought in the Revolutionary War but also designed and oversaw the construction of West Point.

21. See: https://gloshistorii.pl/en/p/memorial-stone-of-the-battalion-zaremba-piorun/ and http://www.polskaniezwykla.pl/web/place/27289,warszawa-skwer-batalionu-ak-zaremba-piorun.html

22. Now Lviv, in Ukraine.

23. This company continues to produce award-winning vodka and other spirits. See: http://baczewski-vodka.pl/en/

24. For information on the German Goliath Tracked Mine see: https://www.historynet.com/goliath-tracked-mine-the-beetle-that-started-the-rov-craze.htm

25. The 1957 film *Kanał* by the renowned director, Andrzej Wajda, vividly describes escapes through the sewers of Warsaw during the Uprising.

26. Jarek Piekałkiewicz finally received his medal 77 years later on his 95th birthday, after documentation of the award was found at Poland's Ministry of Defense. Robert Rusiecki, Polish Consul General in Houston, and Air Force Major Gen. Cezary Wiśniewski from the Polish Embassy in Washington traveled to Piekałkiewicz's Lawrence, Kansas home, to personally deliver his medal on July 24, 2021. See: https://www2.ljworld.com/news/ku/2021/jul/24/retired-ku-professor-receives-medal-for-wwii-heroism-77-years-after-fighting-in-warsaw-uprising/?fbclid=IwAR3Y4rELcG_PfiK692Gv1W1QozP75dLOoU4MzHxDlW8JYjMn2E8IZ3w4Ldg and https://www.carynmirriamgoldberg.com/a-medal-for-bravery-finally-delivered-after-77-years-everyday-magic-day-1005/

27. Volksdeutsche was a Nazi concept and referred to people who had German ancestry but not German citizenship. After occupying Poland in 1939, the Germans set up a central registration office and those who registered as Volksdeutsche received special benefits during the occupation. Of course, not everyone who was of German descent sided with the occupiers. Still, the implementation of the Volksdeutsche concept did create a fifth column in Polish society. See, for example: http://www1.yadvashem.org>odot_pdf

28. A military term indicating the use of a mirror to see what is going on behind you.

29. These troops were from the First Polish Army created by the Soviets, which was made up of Polish soldiers captured when the Soviet Army invaded Poland on September 17, 1939, as well as other Polish recruits and Soviet personnel. It was popularly referred to as Berling's Army (after its commander, Lt. Gen. Zygmunt Berling) and was under the command of the Red Army.

30. Besides Polish zlotys and German marks, several other currencies circulated underground in occupied Poland, including U.S. dollars and British pounds; for example, see Piekałkiewicz (2020, 59).

REFERENCES

Cienciala, Anna M. 1994. "The Diplomatic Background of the Warsaw Uprising of 1944: The Players and the Stakes." *The Polish Review* 39, no. 4: 393–413. http://www.jstor.org/stable/27920650.

Davies, Norman. 2004. *Rising '44. The Battle for Warsaw*. London: Macmillan.

Deminet, Czesław. 1994. *War Stories From Poland.* Albuquerque: TechEditions.

Mirriam-Goldberg, Caryn. 2013. *Needle in the Bone: How a Holocaust Survivor and a Polish Resistance Fighter Beat the Odds and Found Each Other.* Washington, D.C.: Potomac Books. Kindle.

Peszke, Michael Alfred. 2005. Review of *Rising '44: The Battle for Warsaw by Norman Davies. The Polish Review* 50, no. 2: 193–206. http://www.jstor.org/stable/25779535.

Piekałkiewicz, Jarosław. 2020. *Dance With Death: A Holistic View of Saving Polish Jews During the Holocaust.* Lanham: Hamilton Books.

Chapter 7

Matched-Guise Reloaded

Revising a Classic Experiment for Complex Multilingual Settings

Timothy K. Blauvelt, Christofer Berglund, and Jesse Driscoll

Frederic J. Fleron Jr. advocated tirelessly throughout his career for the application of social science methodology to the study of the Soviet Union and other Communist states.[1] This was a controversial stance during the Cold War, in part because at that time the use of empirical field research techniques common to the study of other regions was inconceivable. With the end of the Cold War, the parameters of social science research in the post-Soviet space became rapidly and dramatically redefined: not only was Fleron's earlier insistence on the applicability of social science theorizing to the region clearly vindicated, but the region itself became a major focal point for new research, where earlier theories and techniques were tested and adapted and new ones generated in a number of exciting directions. One classic technique that was brought to bear was the "matched-guise" experiment, which, given its effectiveness in isolating the cognitive mechanism of language status, showed particular utility in examining sensitive issues of identity and interethnic attitudes. Yet while making use of the technique in the complex, multilingual settings of post-Soviet periphery, the authors encountered difficulties with the standard design of the experiment that can complicate its implementation and compromise the interpretation of the results. In this piece we suggest a revised design of the experiment and offer preliminary results from a large-scale field test that demonstrate the feasibility and utility of the new approach in such complex settings.

INTRODUCTION: THE MATCHED-GUISE EXPERIMENT

A great deal of research in recent years has focused on the formation of identity (or of identification, self-understanding, and groupness, see Brubaker and Cooper, 2000) and on the factors that influence individuals' perceptions of themselves and others. Promising experimental research projects have examined the relative roles of visual appearance and accent in subjects' perceptions of others (Rakic, Steffens, and Mummenday, 2010). One experimental approach that has significant potential for researching such issues is the matched-guise experiment, which has been implemented in various contexts for more than 60 years. Yet various scholars have pointed out difficulties with the standard matched-guise design that complicate implementation and compromise interpretation of results, especially in complex, multilingual settings. In this chapter, we suggest a revised design of the experiment that we hold make it a cutting-edge method for eliciting respondents' attitudes toward ethno-linguistic groups that can contribute to the recent research on identity formation while at the same time avoiding the earlier methodological issues. We offer preliminary results from a large-scale field test that demonstrate the feasibility and utility of the new approach in such multilingual settings.

Described by Suzanne Romaine (1995, 289) as "one of the most well-known experimental paradigms used in obtaining evaluations to spoken language," the matched-guise experiment isolates the cognitive mechanism of language status in the mind of study subjects. Devised by Lambert et al. (1960) as a methodology to elicit implicit attitudes that people hold toward others based on speech or identity, the experiment has been applied in a number of different contexts by practitioners of a variety of fields, from social psychology and sociolinguistics to comparative politics.[2] In the traditional experimental design, speakers are recorded reading a text in multiple languages, dialects, or accents. The recorded voices are played for respondents who are asked to give their reactions to the voices on various criteria. The respondents are led to believe that the voices they are evaluating belong to different individuals, but they are in fact hearing the same individuals reading text in different languages, dialects, or accents (i.e., in different "guises"). This allows the experimenters to compare the respondents' reactions to the same speaker in different guises, under controlled circumstances and without the distortions that results from posing direct questions about various ethnic or social groups (i.e., "social desirability bias").

Early matched-guise experiments showed that individuals received more favorable evaluations from all respondents when speaking in forms closer to standard usage. Later experiments revealed a countertrend in that while dialect group members might rate the standard guise more favorably on characteristics related to prestige or respect, they tended to rate their own speech guise more highly on "affective or emotive" characteristics. Carranza and Ryan (1975) used factor analysis to isolate these two categories: solidarity or friendship on the one hand, and prestige or respect on the other. This approach was used to effect by Kathryn Woolard (1989) in her study of bilingualism and ethnic politics in Catalonia and by Laada Bilaniuk (1997, 2005) in her work in Ukraine. The experiment constituted one of the centerpieces of a contemporary classic of comparative politics (and one of the first major comparative research projects to be implemented across several new states of the former USSR)—David Laitin's (1998) *Identity in Formation: The Russian-Speaking Populations in the Near Abroad.*

The matched-guise methodology has been criticized over the years in a number of aspects, including its controlled nature, its abstractedness from authentic social context, the authenticity of voice stimuli and the perception thereof by the respondents, and the problem of intra-rater reliability. All research methodologies have limitations, and many of these criticisms have been answered in a rich literature on the methodology (see the discussion in Garrett, 2010, 75–108; and also Giles and Bourhis, 1976). This chapter will highlight some problems that the authors encountered in implementing the methodology in a complex, multilingual environment, and will propose a revision of the design that offers some solutions (including to some of the issues brought up in earlier criticism) in such settings. The three fundamental problems the authors encountered involve (1) the difficulty of locating the precise language and accent repertoire of the recorded speakers (the sending of linguistic identity cues); (2) the shortcoming of language or accent as a viable cue to the implied identity of the speaker (the receiving of identity cues);[3] and (3) the problem of comparability across speakers.

SENDING IDENTITY CUES: THE LIMITED REPERTOIRE OF THE SPEAKERS

Of the three problems with the experiment in complex linguistic settings, the language repertoire of the recorded speakers poses the lesser challenge. It is always solvable in principle, yet it can create great difficulties in practice, when time and resources are limited. Even in simple versions of the matched-guise test, it can be challenging to find and record speakers with the necessary combinations of abilities. Faced with the near impossibility of finding an ethnic Russian who could speak even passable Kazakh, for example, Laitin (1998, 221f) was forced to use a Kazakh with a Russian-language background as a "stand-in" for one of his "Russian" voices. But when the number of accents, dialects, or languages in any one location where the experiment is implemented expands beyond two, this difficulty inflates exponentially.

The experiments that the authors conducted in Georgia, for instance, involved speakers of Georgian, Russian, Azerbaijani, and Armenian. It proved very difficult to find multiple subjects with the necessary repertoire of all of these languages, including the proper accents in their non-native languages and whose voices sound similar to one another.[4] Ideally, in order to gather fully comparable data from the Armenian and Azerbaijani ethnic enclaves, one would need to find quadrilingual speakers of Russian, Armenian, Azeri, and Georgian from among the multiple ethnic groups. In practice it was exceedingly difficult to find any Georgians capable of reading the assigned text with any measure of fluency in Armenian or Azeri. Despite having time and extensive contacts, the ideal of finding speakers fluent in all of the necessary languages proved impossible. Substitutions were necessary on several fronts.[5] And even if one were to expend one's resources to find such multilingual speakers, the leverage gained in terms of control and comparability necessarily undermines the integrity of the experiment: The more a single speaker's voice repeats, the more difficult it is to convince the respondents that they are listening to different individuals.

RECEIVING IDENTITY CUES: THE LIMITED RECEPTIVENESS OF THE LISTENERS

A more fundamental problem involves one of the key assumptions of the methodology: That the respondents are sufficiently attuned to the language, dialect, or accent in question to link the voice heard to the identity that the experimenters assume. The respondents express their opinions about the voice on the response instrument. When there are a small number of possible variations involved, the overwhelming majority of respondents most likely recognize the linguistic "cues" in the way that accords with the expectations of the researchers. In the experiments done with Anglophones and Francophones in Quebec, for example, it seems likely that most residents in the pool of respondents would be familiar enough with French accents in English and English accents in French in order to make the necessary assumptions about who they think they are listening to.

Our experience collecting voice recordings in multiple languages and accents suggests that this simple situation rarely holds in more complex settings. When piloting our recordings for linguistic informants it became apparent that while some local listeners are finely attuned to accents and intonations, others are not. Choosing the "best" voices—those that the experimenters expect will induce the cognitive response they intend to measure—often became a matter of unplanned consensus rather than of certainty.[6] As the number of languages and accents increases, the assumption that listeners are able to recognize the intended identities of the speakers rapidly becomes tenuous. In multilingual settings respondents will rarely be familiar with all of the languages and—even less so—with all accent varieties of these languages. Since the purpose of the matched-guise experiment is to solicit implicit attitudes that the subject might not even know she possesses, none of these sorts of concerns necessarily compromise the data—but it leaves a great deal of ex post interpretation in the hands of the researchers.

From the example of our project, it seemed that Georgian speakers could usually recognize a Russian accent in Georgian, and Russian speakers a Georgian accent in Russian. But it seemed less reasonable to assume that an ethnic Georgian would have a specific conception of what an Armenian or an Azerbaijani would sound like when speaking in Georgian, let alone be able to differentiate the two. By the same token, given that many Georgian respondents (even those living in the minority enclaves) do not speak Armenian or Azeri, they may not be able to recognize when those languages are being spoken with a Georgian accent at all. And few of the respondents would be able to readily differentiate an Armenian from a Georgian when they are speaking in Russian. Simply to assume that most respondents are able to do these things most of the time and thus read the "cues" to identify the speakers in the manner that the researchers expect seems to be, at minimum, problematic.

THE PROBLEM OF COMPARABILITY ACROSS SPEAKERS

The standard matched-guise experiment is at its strongest when comparisons are drawn between respondents' reactions to the voice of the same individual speaking in different ways. The fact that the respondents are listening to the very same individual means that subtle differences in tone, pitch, or other acoustic variables are controlled for. Variances in the respondents' reaction to the guises can be highly significant. Yet in practice, researchers cannot resist the temptation to compare the voice pairs across different speakers, as some of the most interesting comparisons that the researchers have tried to make (or would like to make) are those that are not simply within the voice pairs of an individual speaker, but across different speakers. Laitin (1998, 238), for instance, studied the persistence of a "colonial mentality" in former Soviet republics, that is, if ethnic minorities attribute greater respect to Russians speaking Russian than to members of their own ethnic group speaking their own native language. This involved subtracting the respect scores of the Russian speaker speaking Russian from the respect scores of the titular speaker speaking the titular language: A comparison between two completely different individuals. Laitin's analysis, like those in previous implementations of the experiment, involved drawing comparisons of the friendship (called solidarity in Woolard's 1989 study), respect (which Woolard calls prestige) and job status scores among and between the titular and non-titular speakers in their various guises, again implicitly contrasting not just the same individuals in different guises, but different speakers in different guises. Such analysis involves drawing comparisons of various aspects between the titular and non-titular speakers in different guises. This approach compares not just the same individuals in different guises, but different speakers in different guises, raising serious questions of validity.

THE INTRODUCTION OF "IDENTITY TAGS"

Our first modification to the design resulted from our experiment with the standard experiment methodology in Georgia during 2010 and was an attempt to investigate the effects of alternate means of "cueing." As we had a large sample in the capital city of Tbilisi, we split the respondent group to test whether specific ethnic "cues" would make a difference in the responses. Half of the respondents (randomly selected) were played voices introduced with "ethnic identity tags" and the other half heard voices without the tags. These "identity tags" were names that are particularly characteristic of ethnic Georgians and ethnic Russians.[7] In analyzing the results of the experiment and comparing the test group with the control group, it became clear that the "tagged" voices enabled the respondents to hone in on the underlying identity of the speaker with a greater degree of precision.[8] The success of this minor alteration to the methodology led us to consider a more fundamental revision of the design that might address the problems of the sending and receiving of cues and of the comparability of results described above.

THE REVISED DESIGN AND ITS BENEFITS

Based on the success of using these cues in the Tbilisi sample, for our next project in Georgia the following year we connected fictitious identity tags to recurring voice recordings. We recorded multiple speakers with similar voice types speaking in their native languages and in standard form, and then created identity tags in the form of fictitious names characteristic for each of the relevant communities.[9]

During the course of the experiment, the respondents were played the recording of the majority language speaker three times in total, identified as the titular persona and then as members of the minority communities who also speak the majority language fluently. Recordings of the minority speakers were also each played twice, and identified both with the persona of their actual group identity and with the majority-speaker persona. Respondents listen to and evaluate the same native-speaker recordings several times, with shifting identity tags, so as to convey the impression that they are listening to the same "personas" speaking different languages fluently. Thus, in contrast to the traditional methodology in which respondents are asked to evaluate different recordings of the same speaker in different guises, in our version the respondents were asked to evaluate the exact same recordings, but with different identity tags associated with them. In table 7.1 we see how this design could look if implemented in a hypothetical Canadian setting, involving both a dominant English group and French and Mohawk minorities.

In a complex multilingual context, we would probably encounter difficulties in finding, say, an Anglophone capable of reading an assigned text in French and Mohawk. This challenge is likely to be acute if the communities rarely interact. Furthermore, even if we could find skilled polyglots, most of our respondents might well be unable to pinpoint the identity of the speaker since they would probably be unfamiliar with the cues provided by her unusual accent. However, following the revised matched-guise design, we could instead opt to record a native speaker of English, French, and Mohawk, each reading the text without any accent. We then generate fictitious yet characteristic identity tags for an Anglophone (Jennifer Smith), a Francophone (Emmanuelle Travert), and for a Mohawk (Aleshanee Silverheels) "persona." Respondents then listen to and evaluate the same native-speaker recordings several times, albeit with shifting identity tags, so as to convey the impression that they are listening to the same "personas" speaking different languages fluently. This enables us to analyze two distinct treatment effects.

In the traditional design one can only isolate the absolute gain or loss incurred by the same speaker as she is recorded once in her native language "guise" and once when speaking in a foreign language with a non-native

Table 7.1 Illustrating the Comparative Logic of the Revised Matched-Guise Design

	English ID Tag	*French ID Tag*	*Mohawk ID Tag*
Native English speaker recording	"Jennifer Smith" speaking English	"Emmanuelle Travert" speaking English	"Aleshanee Silverheels" speaking English
Native French speaker recording	"Jennifer Smith" speaking French	"Emmanuelle Travert" speaking French	
Native Mohawk speaker recording	"Jennifer Smith" speaking Mohawk		"Aleshanee Silverheels" speaking Mohawk

Source: Compiled by authors.

accent. Linguistic integration can still be gauged in the revised design, by making vertical comparisons in table 7.1, juxtaposing the respondents' reactions to the same "persona" as she speaks in different languages. However, we can also analyze the relative gain or loss incurred by bearers of different identity tags, in spite of the fact that they all speak a certain language fluently. This difference emerges when making horizontal comparisons in table 7.1, thereby analyzing whether speakers of a given language are rated differently depending on their "personae." Provided that respondents accept the ID tags, we can therefore isolate the effects of these tags among speakers of the same language as well as the effects of speaking different languages among bearers of the same tag.

The revised design thus solves the three drawbacks of the traditional approach. It deals with the "repertoire" problem by alleviating the need for recruiting polyglots, with the problem of identity "cueing" by clearly evoking the image of the intended societal group through ID tags rather than through ambiguous accents, and with the problem of comparability. Since the respondents are evaluating the same recordings that have been assigned shifting ID tags, entirely valid comparisons across these identities become possible (horizontal comparisons in table 7.1). At the same time, because identical ID tags are attached to multiple speakers, this enables a degree of comparability across these different recordings (vertical comparisons in table 7.1). This endows the revised design with more analytical leverage than the traditional matched-guise approach, which does not offer any valid basis for making comparisons across different speakers.

A further advantage of the revised design is that is avoids biasing the results in favor of "primordial" findings. In the traditional experiment, accents serve as cues to the identity of the speaker. However, when we listen to a speaker's strained speech and pronunciation in a foreign language, we might evaluate him more negatively simply because we find his accent frustrating—and not because he is a foreigner per se (cf. Laitin 1998, 236–243). In our revised approach, this risk of contamination is avoided altogether since the respondents are asked to evaluate recordings only of native speakers. One could therefore use the revised matched-guise design as a litmus test of tolerance among various respondent groups.[10]

POTENTIAL OBJECTIONS

There are two potential objections that might be raised: the first involving comparability and the second the integrity of the experiment in practice. The first of these drawbacks is the inverse of the advantage of increased comparability across identities. Because the speakers of each language are different individuals (again, each speaker is recorded only in his or her native tongue), the comparison within each fictitious "persona" might be held to be weaker than in the standard matched-guise design, where the same speaker is recorded speaking in different languages. Yet, as described above, the consistency of the identity tags allows for comparability across speakers that compensates for the fact that each language recording is done by a different person. As long as the respondents believe that they are listening to the same individual, we can compare their reactions and conclude if a person of a certain name and surname is seen differently when speaking in different languages. Since we did not have a difficult time finding individuals with voices that were similar in a number of aural characteristics (gender, age, voice tone, manner, etc.), we faced few problems in convincing the respondents that they were listening to the same person. The respondents showed no more doubts than during our administration of the traditional matched-guise experiment.

The second objection concerns the integrity of the experiment in practice: preventing the respondents from "seeing through" the experiment and realizing that the voices that they are told are of different people actually belong to the same person and vice versa. As mentioned earlier, this issue is also problematic for the standard matched-guise design when respondents are expected to evaluate the same speaker differently in different guises, and the inevitable repetition of the same speaker can compromise the experiment. This problem is even more acute in our revised design, as the respondents are asked to listen multiple times to the exact same recording of that speaker. Thus the very factor that gives such an advantage in comparability can also increase the possibility that the experiment will fail because the respondents might recognize that the voices are the same, despite the identity tags.[11] This risk can be mitigated against, however, by (1) assuring that the different speakers' voices sound as similar as possible to one another; (2) keeping the identical tracks as far apart from one another as possible on the experiment recording; and (3) utilizing "dummy voices" as buffers in between the pertinent voices on the recording. The latter can be difficult if the experiment involves a larger number of languages, dialects, or accents, as there is a maximum number of voice tracks that respondents can reasonably be expected to deal with.[12] Yet it is not impossible, and it works particularly well in distracting the respondents from noticing the identical voices if some of these "dummy voices" use interesting or unusual foreign languages, regional dialects, or accents. Another tactic for dealing with this recognition problem is to shorten the playtime of the voices as the experiment progresses so that various particularities of the recordings are rendered less noticeable.[13]

There are inherent advantages and disadvantages to both the traditional and our revised matched-guise design. Increasing the comparability of voice recordings still means risks for experimental integrity. However, we maintain that our revised approach fares significantly better than the traditional design in linguistically and ethnically complex communities. Our revised version offers objective solutions to the problems that we have raised with the standard design, while not introducing any new fundamental drawbacks. Furthermore, this analytical leverage is gained through a revised method that is easier to implement in practice than the traditional matched-guise test.

A STEP-WISE ILLUSTRATION OF THE REVISED DESIGN

By way of illustrating our revised design, consider an elaboration of the hypothetical experiment suggested above involving ethno-linguistic groups of English, French, and Mohawk speakers in Canada. A conventional matched-guise design would confront serious challenges in such a complex multilingual setting. In order to examine all interrelationships among the three ethno-linguistic communities, traditional experimenters would need to locate and record three skilled polyglots: (1) one English speaker, who must be able to speak both French and Mohawk with a recognizable English accent; (2) a French speaker, who speaks English and Mohawk with a typical French pronunciation; (3) and a Mohawk speaker, who can speak English and French with an accent characteristic of his original Mohawk community. A voice schedule for this hypothetical project using the traditional design is sketched out below.

Voice 1—Orientation voice
Voice 2—English speaker in Mohawk
Voice 3—Mohawk speaker in French
Voice 4—English speaker in English
Voice 5—French speaker in Mohawk
Voice 6—Mohawk speaker in Mohawk
Voice 7—French speaker in English
Voice 8—English speaker in French
Voice 9—French speaker in French
Voice 10—Mohawk speaker in English

Such a schedule separates recurring languages and speakers as far as possible, and thereby helps preserve the integrity of the experiment and its results. Other arrangements are also feasible, but it is always preferable to strive at assuring as much separation as possible. However, the experimenters might face insurmountable difficulties in finding the three polyglots required by the traditional design.[14] Moreover, even if they did find the necessary polyglots, the researchers may have solid reasons to doubt the ability of their respondents to discern, for instance, when Mohawk is spoken with an English as opposed to a French accent. In this complex multilingual context, the researchers might well benefit from our revised matched-guise experimental design.

In this situation, we suggest that the researchers are better off finding native speakers of English, French, and Mohawk, who share as many aural features with each another as possible. Each individual would then be recorded only once, as she speaks her native language in standard form. In the next step, we need to create identity tags for each of the three communities, and from our earlier discussion we already have the Anglophone "Jennifer Smith," the Francophone "Emmanuelle Travert," and the Mohawk persona "Aleshanee Silverheels."[15] In accordance with table 7.1, the respondents then listen to the English speaker three times, tagged once with all three of the identity tags. The French and Mohawk speakers are heard only twice, the French speaker with the French and English identity tags and the Mohawk speaker with the English and Mohawk tags. In order to prevent the respondents from "seeing through" the experiment we separate recurring recordings and identity tags and add dummy recordings to our voice schedule (table 7.2).

Rows marked in grey contain dummy voices, with the sole purpose of distracting the respondents from discovering that some recordings recur under different identity tags, while some "personas" are voiced by different people. Apart from keeping the identical tracks as far from one another as possible, the experimenters can also reduce the risks that respondents "see through" the experiment by shortening the playtime of the recordings, in order to conceal their particularities. More specifically, according to this voice schedule, the researchers would have to trick the respondents in those five instances that are marked with an asterisk for the matched-guise experiment to work as envisaged. It is therefore pivotal to record native speakers of English, French, and Mohawk that are as similar to one another as possible in their aural characteristics. If the voices all sound confusingly similar, then the respondents will not have any other clues to evaluate the recordings apart from the identity tag and language of the speaker, which thereby should serve as a "convenient cognitive shorthand for rapidly inferring a wide range of information about [the] person [representing a certain ethno-linguistic group]" (Hale 2008, 243).

This revised design removes the need to find speakers who are capable in all the three languages and whose foreign language pronunciation contains telltale signs of her original group. The issue of sending identity cues is resolved since the respondents, even if they rarely interact with other groups and are unable to decipher accents, are likely to recognize the different languages and be able to read the cues provided by names and surnames. Last

Table 7.2 Presentation of Recordings to Respondents and Associated Risks

#	*Identity tag*	*Function*	*Risk?*
1	Sophie Wilson	Orientation voice	No
2	Jennifer Smith	English ID tag; in standard Canadian English	No
3	Arthur Parsons	Dummy; in English with Newfoundland accent	No
4	Aleshanee Silverheels	Mohawk ID tag; in standard Canadian Mohawk	No
5	Patrick Wong	Dummy; in English with Chinese accent	No
6	Emmanuelle Travert	French ID tag; in standard Canadian English	Yes *
7	Michael Erickson	Dummy; in English with Yooper accent	No
8	Jennifer Smith	English ID tag; in standard Mohawk	Yes**
9	Emmanuelle Travert	French ID tag; in standard Canadian French	Yes***
10	Matthew Atwood	Dummy; in English with Ottawa valley twang	No
11	Anne Campbell	Dummy; in English in Cape Breton accent	No
12	Aleshanee Silverheels	Mohawk ID tag; in standard Canadian English	Yes****
13	Jennifer Smith	English ID tag; in standard Canadian French	Yes*****

*Should not realize the recording is identical to #2.
**Should not realize the recording is identical to #4; should think it is similar to #2.
***Should think the recording is similar to #6.
****Should not realize the recording is identical to #2 and #6; should think it is similar to #4.
*****Should not realize the recording is identical to #9; should think it is similar to #2 and #8.
Source: Compiled by authors.

but not least, the revised experiment allows us to study respondents' attitudes to individuals with different identity tags speaking the same language, as well as to the same "persona" speaking different languages. The complete set of conclusions that can be derived from matching respondents' reactions to the recordings in this hypothetical matched-guise experiment is presented in the following matrices (table 7.3).

For each majority-minority dyad, we can investigate respondent attitudes from both sides of the ethnic divide. Taken together, this design offers researchers generous possibilities for investigating ethno-linguistic boundaries in diverse societies (table 7.4).

SOME RESULTS OF THE REVISED DESIGN EXPERIMENT IN GEORGIA

The authors implemented a matched-guise experiment utilizing the revised design in Georgia over several weeks in the winter of 2011. The experiment was conducted in schools and universities in the capital city and in minority-populated regions, with a sample of 2,019 respondents who are primarily native Georgian, Armenian and Azerbaijani speakers (Berglund,

Table 7.3 Deriving Respondent Attitudes toward English-French Interactions

	English Identity Tag	*French Identity Tag*
Native English speaker recording	"Jennifer Smith" speaking English	"Emmanuelle Travert" speaking English
Native French speaker recording	"Jennifer Smith" speaking French	"Emmanuelle Travert" speaking French
English respondents	One of us	One of them posing as one of us
	One of us posing as one of them	One of them
French respondents	One of them	One of us posing as one of them
	One of them posing as one of us	One of us

Source: Compiled by authors.

Table 7.4 Deriving Respondent Attitudes toward English-Mohawk Interactions

	English ID Tag	*Mohawk ID Tag*
Native English speaker recording	"Jennifer Smith" speaking English	"Aleshanee Silverheels" speaking English
Native Mohawk speaker recording	"Jennifer Smith" speaking Mohawk	"Aleshanee Silverheels" speaking Mohawk
English respondents	One of us	One of them posing as one of us
	One of us posing as one of them	One of them
Mohawk respondents	One of them	One of us posing as one of them
	One of them posing as one of us	One of us

Source: Compiled by authors.

2016b).[16] Three voice recordings were used of young women with similar sounding voices, one Georgian, one Armenian and one Azerbaijani, and three "personas" or name-tag identities were created. The respondents were asked to evaluate the voices using a questionnaire instrument that includes 17 personality attributes and also an open "profession" question that was coded according to a 21-point scale of perceived prestige rankings of professions.[17] The voices were interspersed with "dummy" voices, including some with distracting and amusing accents.

During the administration of the experiment respondents did not appear to realize that some voices in fact belong to the same person and vice versa. Analysis of the data suggests that the integrity of the design was maintained.

As a demonstration of this, we will take a closer look at respondents' evaluations of the profession question. Figure 7.1 shows that the Georgian speaker ranks higher among the entire sample of respondents when she is introduced using a Georgian ID tag (in the first column) than when she is presented with a minority ID tag (in the second column). We obtain a similarly suggestive result for the Armenian speaker, who is rated more highly when introduced as an Armenian (in the third column) than when she is introduced as a Georgian who speaks Armenian (the fourth column). Thus, despite the fact that our respondents are listening to the same exact recordings, they assess that the person speaking has a more prestigious profession—and, it can be inferred, greater professional opportunity—when they believe that the speakers are using their titular language. This suggests somewhat limited professional advantages in Georgia for mutual language acquisition among the different ethnic groups. But more importantly for present purposes, it demonstrates that the respondents' perceptions of the voice recordings were clearly affected by the ID cues.

In figure 7.2 we again examine the respondents' reactions to the same recordings with different ID tags, but this time we divide the respondents according to their Georgian language ability. When comparing the first and third columns, we see that respondents with lower proficiency in Georgian

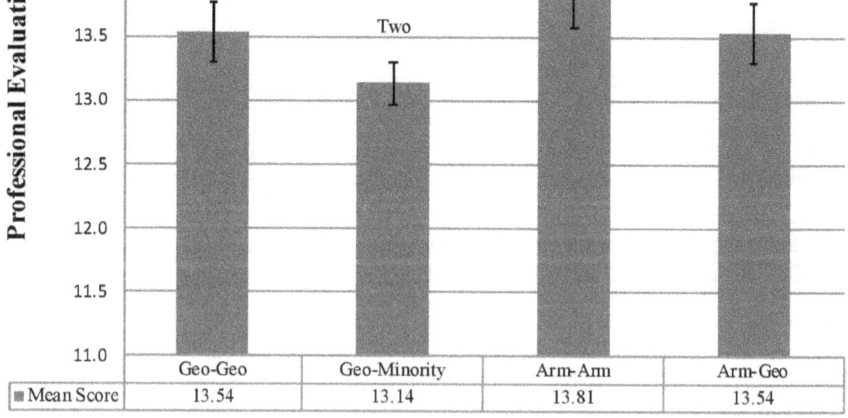

Figure 7.1 Preference for Speakers by Introductions. *Source*: Compiled by authors.

(the category that presumably contains many of the minorities) rate the professional standing of the Georgian-speaking Georgian more highly than respondents with higher proficiency in Georgian (more of whom are presumably ethnic Georgians). When comparing the first two columns, we see that the respondents who know Georgian well think that minorities who speak Georgian have a lower professional standing than ordinary Georgians. By contrast, when comparing the third and fourth columns, it is clear that respondents who do not know Georgian well rank the Georgian speaker equally positively, regardless of whether she is introduced with a Georgian or minority ID tag. Finally, when comparing the second and fourth columns, we learn that Georgian-speaking minorities are considered to have greater professional opportunities by minorities (who speak Georgian poorly) than by Georgians themselves (who speak Georgian well). This indicates that minorities who learn Georgian with the expectation of greater professional opportunities might be in for a disappointment.

These are but small examples drawn from the vast amount of data obtained through the experiment, yet they are sufficient to demonstrate that our revised design produces effective results in practice and that the integrity of the methodology was maintained under real-world conditions.

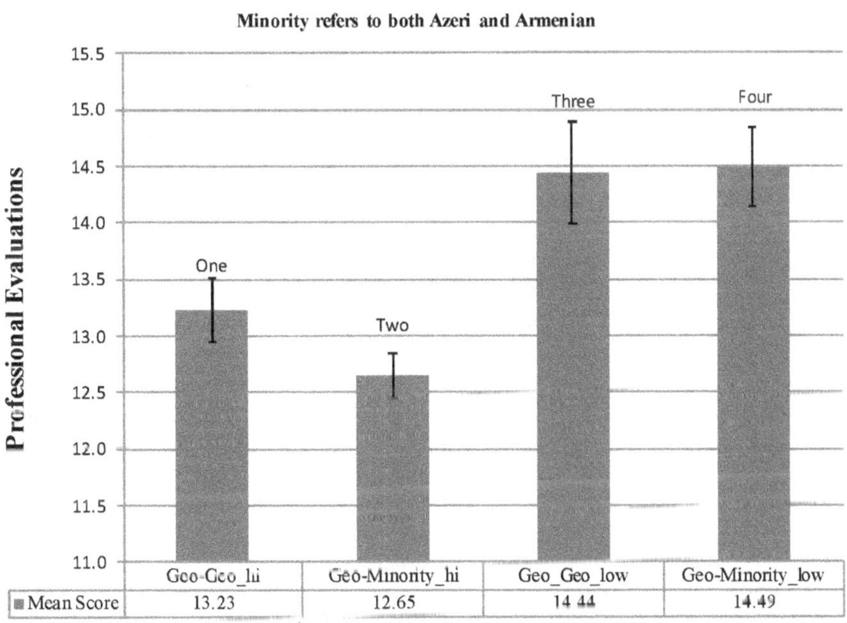

Figure 7.2 Professional Evaluations by Georgian Language Ability. *Source*: Compiled by authors.

CONCLUSION

As field and laboratory experiments gain prestige among social scientists, a number of classic experiments are re-entering the standard vocabulary for scholars and graduate students of a variety of subfields. The purpose of this chapter is to document a number of practical challenges to the implementation of the "matched-guise" experiment and the interpretation of results—challenges that are, at present, solved in an ad-hoc manner by researchers. The revised design procedures described here should produce results that are comparable in most important respects to the data from the classic matched-guise experiment, but with two advantages: (1) it can be replicated at lower cost and (2) the results can be interpreted (and causal processes identified) with less ambiguity, since the design requires pre-committing to the study of particular social boundaries (in the use of identity tags). Despite the heightened risk to experimental integrity that accompanies our design, we found no evidence that respondents "saw through" the deception intrinsic to the experiment. On balance, the revised version of the matched-guise methodology eliminates a number of arbitrary judgment calls which can compromise the validity of the experiment.

NOTES

1. Note on Funding Sources: for the experiment conducted in 2010 partial funding for assistance with field implementation, coding, and data entry was provided by the Caucasus Research Resource Centers (CRRC). Funding for the experiment conducted in 2011 was provided by Sixten Gemzéus stiftelse, The Swedish Foundation for International Cooperation in Research and Higher Education (STINT), Byzantinska resestipendiet, and Borbos Hanssons stipendiefond. The Georgian Foundation for Strategic and International Studies (GFSIS) helped set up meetings with school directors in Tbilisi. None of the aforementioned institutions or funding sources exerted editorial control or influence, and the opinions and conclusions expressed in the chapter are only those of the authors.

2. For a comprehensive recent literature review, see Garrett (2010) and Loureiro-Rodriguez, et al. (2012). Because of its utility in assessing attitudes underlying the issues of ethnicity, nationalism, and accommodation, starting in the 1990s the matched-guise test gained the particular attention of scholars working in the authors' fields of comparative politics and of post-Soviet area studies (especially Woolard, 1989; Laitin, 1998; Bilaniuk, 1997, 2005; Blauvelt 2013; Dragojevic, Berglund and Blauvelt 2015, and Berglund, 2016a, 2020).

3. These first two issues might fall into the categories of the "perception question," the "accent-authenticity question," and the "mimicking-authenticity question" in earlier critiques of the matched-guise test; see Garrett (2010, 77–78).

4. Recordings need to sound similar to one another in order to guard against the effects of intervening variables. Thus, in most versions of the experiment, researchers make sure to use speakers who are all of the same gender and approximate age.

5. As was Laitin (1998), we were forced to make "compromises" such as employing an ethnic Armenian actress from Tbilisi to "play the role" of a Georgian who could also speak Armenian, and using Georgians fluent in Turkish to read the Azeri text. (Turkish and Azeri are from the same language family but are not identical.)

6. This is obviously highly problematic for the validity of the design. In a rural district of Georgia, urban informants from the capital city thought that a voice with a particularly strong district accent sounded like an actor overdoing it, while informants who were actually from the district in question felt that this strongly accented voice was the most authentic! Some form of "crowd-sourcing" may potentially be useful for dealing with this issue.

7. As all the voices in this experiment were female, we used the Georgian women's names Nino, Tamuna, Gvantsa, Sopiko and Salome and the Russian names Olga, Sveta, Tatiana and Lyuda. Although these names are not exclusive to Georgians and Russians, respectively, in Georgia, it is quite rare for them to be interchanged across the ethnic groups, and an indicator of a strong urge toward assimilation.

8. Results are described in more detail in Blauvelt (2013) and Driscoll, Berglund, and Blauvelt (2016). This significance was seen especially among ethnic Armenians who comprise a large proportion of the "Russian-speaking" population of Tbilisi. Armenian respondents reacted more positively to the voices without the ethnic tags, as they probably were more likely to associate these with their own "in-group." When the voices were identified with characteristically Russian names, the Armenian respondents seemed to feel less identification with them. A similar approach was used successfully in Kyrgyzstan by Downey (2015) in consultation with some of the present authors. A modified version of the standard MG experiment also formed the bases of the analysis in Dragojevic, Berglund, and Blauvelt (2018).

9. Names and surnames emerged as the most appropriate cue in the setting of our project. We created a Georgian "persona" with the name "Tamar Maisuradze," an Armenian named "Arpine Sarkisian," and an Azerbaijani named "Afa Mamedova." However, identities might be better conveyed through different types of cues in other cultures.

10. And particularly as a more critical test of tolerance toward integrated but not assimilated others (on the premise that learning a language is integration, whereas adopting a name is assimilation).

11. There is also an inverse risk associated with the fact that the respondents (in their minds) are being asked to assess the same "persona" several times as she speaks in different languages. This might cause the respondents to try to ensure that the "same person" is rated consistently across the languages. Nonetheless, the design is still likely to collect "first impression" reactions, as in the context of the experiment it would be very difficult for the respondents to go back and alter their responses (even in the unlikely event that they are able to keep track of voice numbers and identity tag names).

12. The maximum number of voice tracks that we found viable in practice was 13.

13. The average recording length for a native speaker reading the "Euclidian geometry" text used in recent versions of the experiment (see Woolard 1989; Laitin 1998) is approximately 2 minutes and 20 seconds. In our experience, after the first few voices the respondents start to become restless after about 60 seconds of each voice, and most complete their evaluations within that amount of time.

14. In this situation, in order to conduct the experiment in both French- and Mohawk-speaking communities it would be necessary to record at least two different English speakers, thus reducing the overall comparability of the results.

15. The authors use English Canadian, French Canadian, and Mohawk Canadian names here (generated based on lists of most frequent names in those communities) in this hypothetical project only because they are more likely to be familiar to North American and Western European readers and thus allow the design to be illustrated without the added confusion of the actual Eurasian identities used in the authors' experiments in Georgia. The authors are not specialists in Canada and do not intend to imply that the names suggested here would be appropriate for use in a real experiment.

16. The researchers were careful to avoid conducting the experiment in schools targeted in our 2010 experiments.

17. This scale was elaborated with the help of a focus group organized with the assistance of the Caucasus Research Resource Centers (CRRC)—Georgia.

REFERENCES

Berglund, Christofer. 2016a. "Forward to David the Builder! Georgia's (Re)turn to Language-Centered Nationalism." *Nationalities Papers* 44, no. 4: 522–542.

Berglund, Christofer. 2016b. "Borders and Belonging: Nation-Building in Georgia's Armenian and Azerbaijani Ethno-Regions, 2004–2012." Dissertation, Uppsala University.

Berglund, Christofer. 2020. "Accepting Alien Rule? State-Building Nationalism in Georgia's Azeri Borderland." *Europe-Asia Studies* 72, no. 2: 263–285.

Bilaniuk, Laada. 1997. "Matching Guises and Mapping Language Ideologies in Ukraine." *Texas Linguistic Forum* 37, no. 9: 298–310.

Bilaniuk, Laada. 2005. *Contested Tongues: Language Politics and Cultural Correction in Ukraine*. Ithaca: Cornell University Press.

Blauvelt, Timothy. 2013. "Endurance of the Soviet Imperial Tongue: The Russian Language in Contemporary Georgia." *Central Asian Survey* 32, no. 2: 189–209.

Brubaker, Roger, and Frederick Cooper. 2000. "Beyond 'Identity." *Theory and Society* 29, no. 1: 1–47.

Carranza, Michael A., and Ellen Ryan. 1975. "Evaluative Reactions of Bilingual Anglo and Mexican American Adolescents Towards Speakers of English and Spanish." *International Journal of the Sociology of Language* 6: 83–104.

Downey, Kara. 2015. "Building the Nation, Binding the State: Nationalism, Insecurity, and Ethnic Tolerance in Kyrgyzstan." Dissertation, Stanford University.

Dragojevic, Marko, Christofer Berglund, and Timothy Blauvelt. 2015. "Attitudes Toward Tbilisi- and Mingrelian-Accented Georgian Among Georgian Youth: On the Road to Linguistic Homogenization?" *Journal of Language and Social Psychology* 34, no. 3: 90–101.

Dragojevic, Marko, Christofer Berglund, and Timothy Blauvelt. 2018. "Figuring Out Who's Who: The Role of Social Categorization in the Language Attitudes Process." *Journal of Language and Social Psychology* 37, no. 6: 28–50.

Driscoll, Jesse, Christofer Berglund, and Timothy Blauvelt. 2016. "Language Hierarchies in Georgia: An Experimental Approach." *Caucasus Survey* 4, no. 1: 44–62.

Garrett, Peter. 2010. *Attitudes to Language*. Cambridge: Cambridge University Press.

Giles, Howard, and Richard Y. Bourhis. 1976. "Methodological Issues in Dialect Perception: A Social Psychological Perspective." *Anthropological Linguistics* 18, no. 7: 294–304.

Hale, Henry E. 2008. *The Foundations of Ethnic Politics: Separatism of States and Nations in Eurasia and the World*. Cambridge: Cambridge University Press.

Laitin, David D. 1998. *Identity in Formation: The Russian-Speaking Populations in the Near Abroad*. Ithaca: Cornell University Press.

Lambert, W. R. Hodgson, R. Gardner, and S. Fillenbaum. 1960. "Evaluative Reactions to Spoken Language." *Journal of Abnormal and Social Psychology* 60, no. 1: 44–51.

Loureiro-Rodrigues, V., M. M. Boggess, and A. Goldsmith. 2012. "Language Attitudes in Galicia: Using the Matched-Guise Test Among High School Students." *Journal of Multilingual and Multicultural Development* 34, no. 2: 136–153.

Romaine, Suzanne. 1995. *Bilingualism*, 2nd Edition (Volume 13 of Language in Society). New York: John Wiley & Sons.

Woolard, Kathryn A. 1989. *Double Talk: Bilingualism and the Politics of Ethnicity in Catalonia*. Stanford: Stanford University Press.

Chapter 8

The Future of Janus-Faced Russia and Its Continuing Structural Legacy

David Foley

WHAT NEXT FOR RUSSIAN AUTHORITY PATTERNS?

Most of Russia's struggles with democratic transition and consolidation can be traced to the violations of some very basic guidelines of process and structure that scholars of democratic political change recommend be followed.[1] One of those experts, Eckstein, outlined in specific detail the "successful democracy syndrome," and among the principles included in the recipe for success is the critical point for the successful democracy, namely, that it "has in a more general sense a strong civil society [and that] its basic building blocks are horizontal relationships" (Eckstein, Fleron Jr., Hoffman, and Reisinger 1998, 367). Eckstein concludes his outline by noting that in the end "it is a highly leveled society; and it is not a plural society," suggesting that disparities among the population groups of the state should (and can) be balanced, asymmetry can be anathema to democratic state crafting, and ruling by plurality representation is divisive. It is clear from the analysis presented in this study that the system of Russian federal governance is based on strong personal-vertical relationships, and that not only do the stratifications of the Russian Republic result in a weak civil society, but the districting structure reinforces and exacerbates an ethno-national plurality in Russian mass society. The implementation of a system of vertical authority patterns and segmented regionalism may ensure the state survives in the short term, but the contradictions to democratic consolidation that those same institutionalized and non-institutionalized segmenting asymmetries represent are obstacles to a truly transformative democratizing experience in Russia. The summary conclusion of Gorenburg (Giuliano and Gorenburg 2012) demonstrates how this mix of segmented (asymmetric) regionalism and weak horizontal institutions of legislative power (both at the center and in the regions) as configured was focused on the short-term unity of Russia's political geography and not the long-term unification of all Russians. In Gorenburg's words,

> Despite the weakness at the center and regional decentralization, nationalist separatism did not develop because the entire political institutional environment in the republics had shifted by the end of Russia's first decade. This shift was due to key central state policies that moved the locus of political power within the republics from the legislative to the executive branch, effectively shutting out political opposition, including nationalist groups. (Giuliano and Gorenburg 2012, 185)

The contemporary vertical structures of the Russian center-to-region political management system are a consequence of the elite-led transformation of the complex political geography of the Imperial territories, peoples, and customs by the Tsars of the late nineteenth century, the Bolsheviks, and Soviets of the twentieth century, and the current generation of "treaty-constitutional" reformers that have (temporarily) established a Russian "managed imitation democracy."[2]

THE FOUNDATIONS OF THE PUTIN LEGACY

The mixed electoral system implemented to facilitate both a balance of Duma representation as well as the establishment of a viable political party system has accomplished neither goal. The combination of single-member district (SMD) competition with a party list ballot system has assured that political party victories would result in low-level plurality outcomes, and although a few political parties would survive from one election cycle to the next, the system has also encouraged a plethora of political parties to participate. The consistent policy actions by all three Russian presidential administrations of rule by appointment and decree confounded the consolidation of democracy through active commitments to antidemocratic methods. The net result of the combination of these actions (and inactions) to date has been the reinforcement and consolidation of social segmentations, institutionalized power asymmetries, and vertical power relations quite reminiscent of the Soviet era. Lynch has provided a summary of the Putin state and the foundations of the Putin legacy that begins with the question "What, then, is the essence of 'Putinism'?" This is an important question to answer because who and what Putin represents is in debate, with some analysts arguing that Putin is the all-powerful director of the Kremlin regime and the power vertical represents his personal vertical of power, while others see him as akin to a "prime minister" of a contemporary siloviki. Lynch explains that "it is neither communist nor capitalist, neither totalitarian nor liberal democratic." Instead, Putin has created a distinctive, post-Soviet political amalgam that Russian political scientist Dmitri Trenin has characterized as "unconsolidated authoritarianism" (as opposed to "unconsolidated democracy") and that I term "Potemkin democracy" (Lynch 2011, 81). If Putin is a twenty-first-century Potemkin, the critical question is: Which one? The Potemkin that fooled Catherine II with a prosperous and vibrant pseudo-village or the Potemkin battleship that mutinied and sparked a revolution?

Linz and Stepan (1996) describe in summary form the behavioral, attitudinal, and constitutional benchmarks of democratic consolidation, and conclude that if no significant institutional actors from the social, national, political, or economic regimes of the state "spend significant resources attempting to achieve their objectives by creating a nondemocratic regime," democratic behavior has been consolidated. It would seem that the Russian regime under Putin has done much to block the consolidation of democracy, and in the context of Linz and Stepan's conclusion regarding the consolidation of democratic attitudes when "public opinion holds the belief that democratic procedures and institutions are the most appropriate way to govern collective life in a society such as theirs" it would seem there is little evidence of democratic consolidation even in the shadows of the Russian transition (Linz, and Stepan 1996, 6). The predominance of Putin's Potemkin-like nondemocratic behaviors and attitudes disguised as a "democratic village" will continue to significantly influence policy and process at the two extremes of Russian governance, the federal center and the local regimes. The restrictions and controls placed on the local regimes have moved the dial to a further degree of centralization, as Moses explained, "through reform of local self-government, Putin would consolidate his control over the last remaining vestige of democratic pluralism in Russia, namely the powers still ceded to cities through directly elected and competitive political offices" (Moses 2015, 182).

A final and critical comparative characteristic of what a successful democratization process could have resembled in Russia was described by Rose, Munro, and White who determined "the liberal theory of democracy is demand driven: voters decide what they want, and politicians compete to supply their demands." The Russian experience is a case study of the alternative described by Rose et al. as a "contrast" to the liberal path, "the realist theory [which] is supply driven; the choice of voters is restricted to the parties that elites organize and place on the ballot paper" (Rose, Munro and White 2001, 419). If it can be presumed Russian democracy was initially established with a vision toward the establishment of a system based on the "liberal" model of democracy through the development of a mixed electoral system (PL and SMD) and dual executive branch (President and PM), why in practice did that system consistently spawn multiple parties, an overflow of candidates, consistent patterns of wasted votes and votes "against," and a presidential vertical of power? Have the reforms either proposed or implemented by the Yeltsin and Putin regimes successfully reconfigured the "liberal" system to reflect more closely the characteristics of a "realist" democracy, or was it always planned to be this way?

From the time of the collapse of the Soviet system the process of political change that unfolded in Russia continually resulted in the implementation of thin layers of democratic process and structure over the top of a foundation composed of the system components of a traditional and historical nature that survived from the previous two authoritarian eras. The vertical power patterns of governance and the institutionalized pluralities of the federal system contributed to the confounding of the attempted consolidation of democratic behaviors in such a fashion as to guarantee the system would initially depend on the decree powers of the President to initiate and implement meaningful policy doctrines. Today those decree-like initiatives become ratified legislative outputs of the United Russia (UR) party–dominated federal legislature. The reinforcement of the asymmetries of the federal system not only prevents the development of regionally initiated collective actions but also assures that public attitudes toward meaningful power identifications remain local, parochial, and segregated in their focus. As Golosov notes, "One should note that the institutions of the LRs [local regimes] are entrenched not only due to the complex legacies of the Soviet period but also due to the political consequences of the reforms of the 1990s and 2000s" (Golosov 2004, 37). Democratically founded processes could never be consolidated from the patterns of negotiated relations between the federal regime and the subject regions that emerged from the first months of the establishment of the Russian Federation to reinforce a legacy process of region-to-federal relationships that are first, in a constant state of modification and second, implemented to reinforce loyalty to, and management by, the Kremlin.

Because the Federation Treaty reinforced the Soviet-crafted differentiations among the identifications and relations of the federal government with the subject units based on specific subject unit type characteristics (republic or non-republic, ethnic or non-ethnic), the formalized asymmetry of political relations guaranteed the Republic would be formed as a segmented pseudo ethno-federation.[3] The 1993 (forced) dissolution of the legitimately elected Congress of People's Deputies was done in order to establish a legislature that would be "formally" under Yeltsin's control. The success of Yeltsin's "coup" provided the first post-Soviet stage in the process of consolidating the asymmetrically organized neo-union to be followed by the implementation of an elite-crafted Constitution (barely legitimized by popular ratification)[4] to facilitate the diminishing of the power of the republics and to serve as a legitimizing referendum in support of his elite-enhancing policy initiatives. Yeltsin and his cohorts in the Kremlin may have managed to prevent the dissolution of the Soviet Russian Republic to a confederation of independent republics, but it is evident that Russia is a long way from the consolidation of either a "liberal" or a "realist" form of federal democracy.

FEDERALISM BY CHOICE

Lynn and Novikov described how, in the midst of the early transition process, debates about how the Russian Federation should be structured resulted in the proposal of "three competing federal models which ascribe to three different organizing principles: a territorial principle, a national-territorial principle, and a principle of local self-management" (Lynn and Novikov 1997, 13). In the end the Russian federal state-crafters created a hybrid system that is, by all indications, an amalgam of all three models. The maturation of this mixed system of multiple subject unit types into a form that reflects any one of the three paradigms is confounded by the refusal of the federal regime to allow the development of voluntary groups and associations of subject regions based on complementary unit economic or demographic issues and interests. The state crafting reform policies that have been proposed or have been implemented do more to assure that the final form of the Russian federal state will continue to be a loose mix of all three of the federal models rather than a specifically Russian form closely approximating the most appropriate system territorial-type paradigm.

The hallmark of governance in both the Imperial and the Soviet eras was adopted in stages by both the Yeltsin- and Putin-led regimes as a form of political organization. When the vertical of power relations is combined with the reforms that have been either proposed or instituted since 1999, there emerges a legacy pattern that indicates that it may be the intention of the federal state regime to bypass the regional-intermediate level of governance in favor of the strengthening of a direct vertical of power from the Kremlin to the elites of the locally "self-managed" community. If the Kremlin regime is able to establish a more direct power relationship with localized regimes, it is likely the state will ultimately become a unitary political system that may or may not exhibit the outward appearance of a federation, just as its Soviet predecessor had done. The policy patterns, power relations, and federal structures described in this analysis are directly connected with legacies from the Soviet era and represent the intentional adoption of the Soviet goal of federal centralization and the plurality of social relations in order to achieve a similar goal to that of the Bolsheviks.

THE SILENCES OF ETHNO-FEDERAL ASYMMETRIES

As a case study, Russia not only provides a window on the process of democratic consolidation that demonstrates the impact of legacy on political change, but also demonstrates that legacy alone is an insufficient explanatory variable for the path of transition and consolidation that has been followed by the nascent post-Soviet states. Although legacy is an important aspect of the process of political change, the legacy of Soviet federalism is not unique to Russia, and therefore it cannot stand alone as the explanation for both the general problems associated with post-Soviet transition and the unique problems faced by the Russian political crafters. This analysis has demonstrated that the roots of many of the impediments to the consolidation of a Russian democracy reach through the pre-Soviet, Soviet, and post-Soviet eras of political crafting and political history, yet it would be an erroneous conclusion to place too much emphasis on the legacy of the Soviet era because, as outlined by McFaul's analysis, "the variation among post-communist experiences in the region demonstrates that the shared history of communism was not as consequential as was originally assumed" (McFaul 2002, 265). The legacy of Soviet Communism may be most prevalent and consistent at the mass public levels of post-Soviet societies, and as described by Stoner-Weiss, "the relatively uniform levels of mistrust across regions is a testament to the effectiveness of totalitarianism's atomization of Soviet society" (Stoner-Weiss 1997, 163). It may be a consequence of this atomization that the electorate of the Russian Federation found it an overwhelming task to overcome the lack of ideological leadership in its failure to establish a popular political party system representing a select few nationally identifiable and ideological interests. There is no doubt the political process continues to suffer from "the cumulative effect of decades of participation in elections manipulated on behalf of unpopular and corrupt officials [that] left a legacy of political distrust among many Russians" (White, Pravda and Gitelman 2001, xvi), but it was not this legacy that presented the greatest challenge to democratic consolidation.

The legacy carried over from the Soviet era may be the most difficult to reconcile with any future attempts at the consolidation of a democratic federation; the ethno-territorial core of the federal system. Although this study generally supports the findings of Fish that "ethnically divided societies are regarded as facing myriad obstacles to democratization that are absent in more homogeneous societies" (Fish, 1998, 223), it is the problems associated with the institutionalized districting system that indicate it is likely the consolidation of the ethno-nationally based stratifications into a democratic Republic will likely be the most difficult of legacies to overcome. Opinion polls demonstrate the "homeland" identifications of a significant proportion of the citizens of Russia have a foundation which is consistent with the findings of this analysis; the people identify *en masse* with a national concept of "Russia," but at a personal level they tend to identify with their immediate surrounding community. I find no public opinion polling results indicating significant public identification with the concept of a "Russian Federal Republic" or any significant findings of a unilateral sense of citizenship identification with the intermediate level of federal subject region in which she happens to reside.[5] When questioned on the topic of "popular perceptions of the national homeland and Russian identity" (White 2001, 1–3) at the end of the Yeltsin era the two most frequently selected responses to the question, "When you are talking about the homeland, what do you usually mean?" were "Russia" was the response chosen at a ratio of 34.5% of the respondents, and "city/village of birth and childhood" for 30.9% (White 2001, 1–3). The selection of the Soviet Union as a homeland was the response for only 10.3% of those included in the survey, and when the option "city or village of residence for most of one's life" is merged to provide a total response based on identification with a city or village, the total is 47.2% (White 2001, 1–3). The option provided for identification with the federal subject unit for this sample was the subject republic of residence, and with only 3.6% of the respondents selecting that option, it is evident from these results that the personal identifications of nearly half of the Russians who participated in this poll are divided between the extremes of "Russia" as the homeland at one end, the localized community group perhaps best described as homestead at the other, and the Kremlin-assigned regional designation is thought of as the place they happen to live.

PARTY PARTISANSHIP AND IDEOLOGY IN RUSSIA

This study has important implications pertaining to the obstacles to building a grassroots national political party system and the low plurality outcomes in the election of representatives to a national legislature. There is reason to speculate that the declining turnout numbers in Duma elections, the low-level party plurality outcomes, and the wide spectrum of partisan views which have been represented in the plethora of party platforms point to the low interest in nationalized partisan issues. Future investigation may illuminate further the indications highlighted here suggesting that issues related generally to citizenship, when defined as a shared residence within the internal borders of a subject region of Russia, count for very little. If the normative identifications of the Russian citizens are the nation, language, and traditions at one level and the local community at another more meaningful and personal level, then the reasons for the widespread acceptance of the centralizing national policies that also keep the regional subject unit governments disorganized, weak, and in fear of dissolution by decree become more evident. A Russia that is federally centralized and asymmetric in its structurally defined conditions, including political relations, will remain dependent upon the actions of an authoritarian-like vertical of power rather than the slow grindings of the mechanisms of a democratic process that can never reflect a balance of horizontal power which does not exist. As long as the decree powers of the presidency are justified as a "harsh necessity" by the demands associated with the asymmetry of the ethno-federal system managed by elites with a vested interest in the propagation of the power vertical, the asymmetric characteristics of the system that require the actions of a powerful "superpresident" will continue to be reinforced, and the chances for the consolidation of a federal democracy patterned after any normative model of symmetric relations are unlikely.

The problems related to the establishment of a viable and stable political party system have centered on a key issue: the lack of a national base of sustained partisan political party support that is spread among a select few rival parties. The reforms that have been implemented by the Putin administration do little to address the underlying conditions of why individual candidates have a stronger base of sustained popular support than can be matched by that which the party system produced. Putin's solution to the problem of SMD support of independent candidates was to eliminate the SMD seats in the Duma and then to place party affiliation requirements on all candidates for seats in the lower chamber. Reform of the mixed electoral system was not the solution to the problem of low party identification outcomes nor was the establishment (through decree, legislative regulation, and intimidation) of a "party of power" the way to consolidate ideological interests of popular factions.[6] The party list Duma election process has transitioned through seven election cycles to date, yet the problem for Russia continues to reflect the results demonstrated in the outcome of the 1999 Duma elections when "the number of independents winning single-member seats was almost one and a half times that in 1995, and the vote won by new list parties more than doubled between 1995 and 1999" (Rose, Munro and White 2001, 427).

Panov and Ross observe that "the December 2007 elections radically changed the Russian political landscape" in favor of the PL system. This shift to the PL only election system for 2007 and 2011 signaled a change to what Gel'man (2006, 548) identified as a system of "dominant power politics [where] political competition is low, and the ruling group permits open electoral contests as long as it does not challenge the positions of the dominant actor (who keeps strict control over state resources), while elections are unfair."[7] After the (unusually) high number of activists protested the unfree and unfair elections of 2011, the regime reinstated the mixed PL/SMD system for the 2016 Duma elections and, although the United Russia "party of power" dominated by winning 343 of the 450 Duma seats, a total of 75 political parties participated in some fashion in the election cycle, 20 parties were in direct competition between the PL and SMD ballots (representing an astounding total of 8,500 "candidates" contesting the 450 seats), and yet only 4 parties met the threshold for seat allotment. The temporary suspension of the SMD option may have provided the opportunity for United Russia to consolidate its hold on the Duma faction system as the "party of power," but it did little to solve the problems of divided partisanship and an unconsolidated party system. The lack of reforms in support of political symmetry and democratic process has resulted in the emergence of a system based on a contradiction as described by Gerrits: "The volatility of semi-authoritarian regimes largely follows from their inherently contradictory nature: the combination of authoritarian practices with flawed democratic institutions and procedures. The Russian Federation is no exception" (Gerrits 2010, 46).

REFORM TRAJECTORIES, MANAGED FACTIONALIZATION, AND CONSEQUENCES FOR THE FUTURE

The inherent problem with Russia's mixed electoral system was the creation of an environment in which the four criteria outlined by Rose, Munro, and White to insure the establishment and consolidation of a stable political party system would be violated by design. According to those criteria, the necessary (but not sufficient) conditions for success, met artificially by the consolidation of the powers of the United Russia Party described above, include nationwide party competition, the persistence of the same major parties in competition from one election cycle to the next, the majority of legislature seats consistently won by the major national parties, and that candidates remain loyal to the party after being elected as a Member. The Russian party system as it evolved from the time of Yeltsin's triumph in his head-to-head confrontation with the first (and only) popularly empowered Russian legislature in the summer of 1993 has been demonstrated in this analysis to reflect the consistent policy pattern of the federal regime to continue the legacy of "divide and conquer" when it faced the specter of legitimate political competition. With the power of the executive established by Yeltsin combined with the revisionist Soviet-era "national" policy initiatives of Putin, it should be no surprise the efforts to craft and support a strong national party system were initiated by, and with the support of, a national-central power vertical. Putin's response to the floating party system that saw parties appear and disappear from the PL ballot from one election to the next, and the behavior of the party members in the legislature who shifted allegiance from one party and party faction to the next (with seeming disregard for stated ideological interests) was the establishment of the United Russia Party to satisfy the criteria outlined by Rose, Munro, and White (2001, 425), but under the contradictory conditions of semi-authoritarianism. The critical violation of the fourth criteria was exemplified "between election day and the first meeting of the Duma on 18 January 2000 [when] a total of 147 Duma seats, one third of its membership, changed hands without a single vote being cast."

It was evident by the time Putin came to power that at the grassroots of the party system there was little which bonded the individual voter to a political party. Although it was evident early in the transition that, in general, "Russian politics is thoroughly fractionalized even at the district level" (Moser 1997, 297), the reason for the fractionalization of Russian politics at its foundations has yet to be satisfactorily explained, and the answer to the question of why faction and popular party loyalty are at such low premiums is most likely to be found by the analysis of participation and partisanship closer to "home" at the local-parochial level of Russian civic culture.[8]

By all indications the factionalization of interests in Russia was not an expression of changing political partisanship in the Duma or a manifestation of popular party identifications that shifted for ideological purposes but represent the consequences of the political representation of a divided Russian population into what White and others identified as "five groups of unequal size" (White et. al. 2001, 151). The largest of these five groups represented the 39% of those who were classified in opinion polls as "uncertain" because they had yet to be convinced "that a parliament is desirable or survivable" (White et. al. 2001, 151), but the list also included a relatively balanced quartet of hopeful authoritarians, frustrated authoritarians, confident democrats, and anxious democrats. Hough (1997) described why the Duma factions were initially of a type that interfered with the consolidation of the federal democracy.[9] The Putin regime addressed faction-related issues through the regulatory power of the Kremlin regime or the intimidation power of the United Russia Party in the Duma chamber with the "factionalization" now centered on UR, its "loyal opposition," and the territorial branches that were established due to the election law requirement that parties participating in regional elections must be nationally registered political parties.

As long as the Russian Federal government maintains policies and structural differentiations that reinforce the asymmetric character of (and relations among) the subject units and peoples of the Republic, any unified challenge to the central federal supremacy of authority will continue to be foiled. It has consistently been a concern of the Kremlin regime that reforms in Russia could move in the direction of creating a conducive environment for the establishment of voluntary associations among and between the regional leadership and segments of Russian society, with the result anti-Russian separatist/federalist factions could then "hold together" with dire consequences for the central-federal regime. This fear of separation and autonomy has guided the Putin reform agenda from the early days of his Presidency, from the establishment of the Federal Okrugs and the appointment presidential plenoplatory to his management of the executive branches of the subject regions, his range of election reforms, his reforms through okrug consolidation in the territories, and his new requirements and restrictions on regional political party participation. An important result of these directives, statutes, and constitutional amendments has been the transformation of the one plenary body established for the express purpose of representing the separate interests of the subject regions, The Federation Council, into a chamber populated with agents of Putinism.[10]

It has been hypothesized that in Russia it takes an organized coalition of four unit advocacy types to pose a direct challenge to the integrity of the state to include a catalyst, followers, fence sitters, and integrationists. These four types must combine in such a way that the "catalysts" (expected to be republics) will initiate a challenge to central authority that leads the "followers" (expected to be ethnic okrugs) to action while ensuring that the "fence sitters" (cities and krais) do not find cause to join forces with the "integrationists" (probably oblasts) who desire a federal union, all according to Hanson (1999, 20). Hanson's hypothesis has the test of time in the post-Soviet history that appeared to be headed for more challenges like that of the Chechen Republic, a subject unit that certainly took on the role of "catalyst" as a Republic challenge to the integrity and unity of the federation (and rule from Moscow), but rather than the expected outcome of the catalyst for a challenge to the regime, it seems to have had the opposite effect. With the ethno-national territories showing, by their actions early on, the willingness to sign on to the Federation Treaty, to negotiate bilateral agreements with the Kremlin, or to simply carry on with business as usual (with as much autonomy as they could take), to the most recent Duma election outcomes indicting unusually high turnout levels and overwhelming levels of majority support for Putin's United Russia Party, there is scant evidence the republics will provide anti-Russian secessionist leadership anytime soon.[11]

This analysis provides support for the proposition that liberalization is not a desired goal of the federal reforms that have been proposed or implemented, and if Linz and Stepan (1996, 367) were correct in their conclusion that "liberalization (perestroika and glasnost) but not democratization had severe disintegrative consequences for the USSR," the anti-liberalism of the Putin regime has an explanation. Putin learned from the errors of Gorbachev, his Soviet predecessor, and has not demonstrated any inclination to facilitate any truly liberalizing reforms of the political process or the political party system, nor can we expect any in the foreseeable future. As the Russian President continues to initiate reforms that enhance the decree, appointment, and oversight powers of the federal regime, the mechanisms available to regional political representatives for access to the arenas of policy planning and implementation have become even more limited. The lack of institutionalized procedures for symbiotic region to center interrelations has resulted in an imbalance that has been described by Sakwa (2002, 3) as "particularly acute in Russia [because] the resources available to the various actors in the bargaining process are far from equal, and it is these power asymmetries that shape Russia's distinctive type of federalism and encourage the development of segmented regionalism."

The Imperial era policy of internal colonialism established and institutionalized the practice of a vertical of personal authority and accountability. The particular form of segmented regionalism that now exists in the Russian Republic is a direct result of a policy plan initiated by none other than Joseph Stalin and a vision that was intended to facilitate the formation of a union of people and places that would fulfill a very specific and *ideologically motivated goal*. For the Soviet planner's material considerations were ideologically based and crafted in order to fit a centrally controlled resource, production, and distribution system as well as the relocation of the work force. The social factors that influenced this system formation were focused on the need to maintain divisions among ethno-national groups through regional segmentation and to achieve control by the implementation of a plan of diminishing autonomy for the subsumed traditional political units. The goal that dominated the Soviet strategic vision was the establishment of a command and control state-like political container to provide a structure based on a model of a federal organization when in truth it served to maintain centralized command and control through a political geography structured to facilitate the expansion and containment of additional regions on short notice (such as Sevastopol and the Crimea). Here and elsewhere (Foley 2018), I have outlined the illogic of adopting this system, developed in support of the ideology of centralized command, control, segmentation, and institutionalized heterogeneity, to a free market federal democracy and demonstrated that the consequences to region to center forms and functions of the Russian state is centered in the lack of a progressive application of the historical, material, social, and strategic patterns from the past into the present. Restorationist constructs in contradiction to popular governance and in the absence of a unifying political ideology are crippling to Russian transition, but the problems related to asymmetry and segmented regionalism go deeper still into Russian civic and political culture.

THE REGIONS AS AN ACCUMULATION ALLIANCE

Lapidus provided a most concise and accurate description of "Russia" under Soviet rule and what Russia has become today when she stated, "The USSR could be described as a Russian heartland surrounded, on its northwestern, western and southern peripheries, by non-Russian republics; the 21 ethnically-defined republics of the Russian Federation, by contrast, are more like islands in an ethnically Russian sea" (Lapidus 1999, 75). The issue in Russia today is not the fact that ethno-republics such as Chechnya will find armed rebellion to be their best course of action against their assimilation into the Slavic Republic, but the fact that neither rebellion nor assimilation is possible or feasible for the ethno-regions because they have been purposely segmented out of "Russia." An interesting perspective on this issue of identity was provided by Reisinger and Moraski (2017, 8) who noted "in its electoral culture, the Russian Federation consists of two unequally sized parts: the 'Russian Russia' and the 'Russia of nationalities.'" The Russian state crafters, beginning in 1991, ignored the recommendations of those who proposed a symmetric federal union based on any number of existing and successful paradigms, and chose to form a regionally segmented contractual federal Republic.[12] The "contract" was the Federation Treaty, and it has been previously outlined how much of that contract was contradicted by the Constitution of 1993 (Foley 2018). If the contract was broken and the participants have no recourse to accepting the regional segmentation as most compatible with the confederation like Treaty process, how can the asymmetric union of semi-autonomous regions remain the foundation for a constitutionally based federal system that requires a balance of power and symmetric interrelations between the federal and subfederal regimes?

It has been argued that because Russian rulers for several centuries believed the segmented and asymmetric character of the state-nation required a strong and centralized governing hand, and this legacy could explain why the "predominant view among political scientists [is] that the Russian system is effectively an authoritarian regime," and why so many have concluded that "Russia appears to be ruled by presidential decree" (Remington, Smith, and Haspel 1998, 287). Centralized and authoritarian-like power is not the only important legacy explanation to gain strength regarding the Republic. It has also been demonstrated that the localized power brokers who operated in the ever-present "shadow" political economy reemerged from the Soviet collapse and transition opportunism to influence the Federation formation and consolidation as well.

When Yeltsin declared an end to the legislature in 1993, he sent a message to regional regimes that the Federal Executive Branch of government would never share power in balance with the legislative branch. Rather than pursue the path of rebellion chosen by Chechnya, the remainder of the regional subject units chose to return to the old tried and true (legacy) methods of putting a public face on assimilation and cooperation while pursuing in private the autonomy of action that was successfully achieved under Soviet and Imperial rule through the tradition of "duality." The regional power brokers conceded to the federal government and to the Kremlin, but retained, reformed, and reinforced the powers of localized coalitions. Many of the policies that Putin proposed and implemented are new variations of an old theme, and the local economic and political power brokers learned decades (if not centuries) ago how to operate out of sight of the eyes of the Tsars, the Commissars, and now, the Presidents.

The problem for Russia's future is not so much the fact that these local bosses and entrepreneurs have reemerged in the Republic, but rather the fact of the consequences to any future attempts at democratic consolidation of the type of infrastructure this form of hybrid governance creates. Mitchneck has thoroughly outlined this issue, and he has found a core problem for the future in the fact that the Russian political economy is structured on a foundation of "accumulation alliances." Mitchneck (2001, 364) describes these alliances as a for-profit organization of "public officials as part of an increasingly corrupt group that forms alliances only to extract rent from entrepreneurs." These alliances have been described as

> the major decision makers or repositories of knowledge regarding urban and regional policies and strategies as the backbone of the regional governance environment in Russia. They provided government agents with the ability to achieve goals (and personal ones) not only because they generated access to capital, but also because they increased access to power otherwise outside of the domain of state institutions.[13]

Under Soviet rule, the cities of the regions were established as the centers of economic and political power, and for that reason, the impact of alliances in the regional city centers present an unprecedented challenge to the federal regime. The tension or contradiction between the focus of the government hierarchy on regulation and order while the actual core of economic and political power is beyond their reach is because the Russian political system is organized as a federation but operates in many ways like a hybrid form of the old Soviet segmented and corrupt unitary system.[14]

The paradigms of a federal system consistently demonstrate that the powers of government authority, planning, and enforcement should be devolved through a balanced and congruent pattern of federal-to-regional-to-local regimes and back again, with clear and explicit separations between the powers of the federal regime, the powers of the regional regime, and the powers of the local government. In Russia the power of the middle range, the regional regime, is so weak and ineffectual that it is generally ignored or bypassed by both the local and the federal authorities. This unusual pattern of power relations makes the role of the institutions at the regional level of governance, at best, that of a filter for the processes that are required to maintain the illusion of federalism, democratic order, and a free market. These regional regimes also provide an insulating cover for the activities of the local accumulation alliances centered in the major regional city centers, and it is this relationship that is perhaps most in need of illumination in a future analysis.

I have focused my attentions in this analysis on the method that, according to Gel'Man (1999, 939), had been least used by analysts of Russian political change and transition, "the second dimension of comparative analysis of Russian politics, involving cross regional (i.e., intra-national) comparisons, [that] is still neglected among Western and Russian scholars." I have made little progress in addressing the important issues related to the fact that it has yet to be explained "why nearly identical administrative units of the Soviet empire developed in such different directions over the past 10 years?" (Gel'Man 1999, 942) other than to suggest my concurrence with Makarychev's (2012, 39) conclusion of regional labels as "empty signifiers" of what one can expect of a Russian subject region. In the absence of suitable intra-regional analysis, the transition and consolidation process in Russia has yet to be definitively understood in its proper perspective, thus an effective and logically consistent comparative analysis of the most recent iteration of Russian political change to that of any other former SSR is of limited value.

A REGIONAL SHADOW ALLIANCE?

The citizens of Russia have traditionally identified with the Russian nation as "homeland" when the perspective is an internationally based context of identity, but the local community and the parochial context of a homeland identification it provides in congruence to that of the "nation" appears to be of equally significant importance (or more) to the establishment of a consolidated Russian Federation. To this point, the methods of analysis utilized in the study of Russian political change do not significantly stand apart from studies of other modern regimes that have also experienced a long history of transitional development, and for a case study of Russia to be of particular value to transition studies it is necessary for the characteristics of the state that set it apart from the norm to be the focus of study. It has been established that in Russia power is divided very much along the lines of a personal-vertical of power relations (a relatively common characteristic of authoritarian and authoritarian-like regimes), and as a result the central-federal government (in particular the office of the "superpresident") dominates the crafting of laws, policies, and processes that have been established to maintain the Kremlin's relative advantage in relation to the territorial districts of the Republic. The aspect that seems to be least understood in Russia is the localized power structures and alliances throughout the regions, and how the asymmetric structure of the state facilitates that very traditional clientelist power dynamic. It is at the local-city-village-community core where Russian power politics and the related political economy seem to live and function as an extension of real personal power relations and represent a root indication of the true nature of popular and elite political participation. It is the relationship and patterns between the power brokers in the Kremlin and those who comprise the local power alliances that are most in need of further investigation. Russia is an example of a nation established on the principle that a regionally representative intermediate level of governance is the most suitable means to facilitate the establishment, through component segmentation, of control over the whole of state territory.

A justification for the retention of Russia's asymmetric territorial system was described by Lynn and Novikov who suggested that, in the view of the federation crafters, "the titular nationalities of the republics (and also the okrugs) have a right to their own national territory and one cannot simply ignore or reverse the structures that have been in place for the last seventy years" (Lynn and Novikov 1997, 132). The reforms of the Putin regime since 2003 have directly targeted the ethnically designated Autonomous Okrugs, and the evidence of those reforms suggests little region-centered resistance to the districting reconfigurations that resulted in the loss of first-order region status and direct representation in the Federation Council.

The problems associated with the asymmetric distribution of power represent a spectrum of issues that range from simple problems of inefficiency to significant contradictions of democratic traditions and deeply entrenched inequalities in political, economic, and social relations. A major implication from this study is that the power patterns inherent in federal asymmetry have been incorporated into both the formation and the functioning of the Russian Federal Republic and represent a significant impediment to any future consolidation of a federal democracy. Although it is Putin's vertical of power that manages the "official" Russian state today (as did the Soviet General Secretaries), the localized legacy structures, practices, and regimes of Russia's "longue duree" transformation seem to remain the conduit for political agency and participation now and into the foreseeable future. The question for the future of Russia is the one left unresolved from its past, as Breslauer (2005, 58) points out,

> even if Russia breaks out of its convulsive historical pattern, the question remains: what would a leader such as Putin have to do to institutionalize an alternative that also avoids falling into the "more-normal" pattern of chronic but contained instability found in other middle-income countries?

An additional significant implication of this analysis is the fact the asymmetries of the Russian state system territorially, politically, and economically have resulted in a bifurcation of power centers that are represented by the office of the President in the Kremlin at one extreme, and the alliance members and power brokers of localized interests in the regional cities. The emergence of these two contrasting power poles in Russia has provided evidence and an explanation for the third significant implication of this analysis; the need to better understand the legacy consequences of the federal evisceration policies intended to weaken and capture the relatively "ignored" middle range of regional power in the federal Republic.

The concentration of power and power elites at the subregion/local level is the arena that appears to serve the immediate needs and purposes of the population, and thus what happens to the national political party system before, during, and after a Duma election cycle is of little direct consequence to the average Russian citizen. As long as the asymmetries of the Russian state system retain a value to the patron-client participants in the political and economic "market," they will not be removed or balanced. It would seem it was determined early in the transition process by Russian political entrepreneurs that a segmented and asymmetric Russia is a Russia of opportunity as an oligopoly. The combination of Russian nationalism with the lack of a defining national ideology to justify the acceptance of federal governance, when combined with the lack of real and legitimate authority at the middle range level of regional governance, serves to insulate the power-alliance elites from accountability through law enforcement and from replacement through the electoral "wrath" of an empowered electorate. The hope for the emergence in the future of a substantive Russian federal democracy lies in the investment of true powers into both the federal and the regional legislative and judicial branches of government. The implications of this study suggest the power relations at the local and regional levels must be better understood as a pathway to real reform through a new era of democratic transition instituted in, and evolving from, a bottom-up rather than a continuation of a failed historical pattern of the devolution of personal power by decree and acquiescence from the top-down. Although I argue that the hope for a future Russian democracy lies with the grassroots development of democracy (rather than the support for authority, order, and the social contract) the pitfalls of additional localization of political power was outlined by Turovsky's (2014, 72) observation:

> Under an authoritarian (or hybrid) regime the local electoral victory is a trap for opposition as it increases the level of political instability (not to be confused with the democratic power change), since a local opposition-led regime cannot co-exist with the federal rulers and their loyal supporters on the spot.

LIBERALIZATION WITHOUT DEMOCRACY: THE CENTER MUST HOLD!

The story of post-Soviet Russian transition can be told in three phases. Phase one was initiated by Gorbachev as the main (and tragic) character, who sought to reform the behemoth the Soviet state had become only to fail when he stumbled onto the fact that "glasnost would release the [Russian] nationality genie from the Soviet bottle" (Saivetz 1996, 259). The second phase is a chronicle of the personal initiatives of Yeltsin as a member of the Soviet elite and his undermining of Gorbachev's reforms to his capture of the Russian transition and his "fire sale" of the state to the "reformed" commissars through a particularly Russian form of crony capitalism and corruption. The third phase began with the arrival of the young and dynamic reformer who promised to restore integrity and pride to the Russian nation through a mandate of reforms that promised to honor the social contract the people longed for through a redistribution of the wealth of Russia stolen by the Yeltsin-era oligarchs and the restoration of the structures of order and security through an empowered Russian military, national domestic security force, and local policing regimes.

The Party List elections from 1993 to 1999 represented the "victory" of what I have identified as a "wasted vote" coalition, a coalition of voters based on an "anti-ideology" and popular party anarchy to be replaced by the Putin-era promise of reforms that have culminated in the restoration of the party-centered vertical of power and, in effect, one-party rule. The dependence of the Kremlin on the management of regional Soviets by Moscow appointed commissars has been replicated by the management of regional assemblies required to field candidates from the national parties (resulting in the guarantee of the extension of the reach of the Kremlin United Russia "party of power") and the appointment of candidates to the executive branch of each regional government guarantees loyalty to, and cooperation with, the central regime. The focus of the Putin regime on establishing a deeper reach of federal influence into the regions is a signal of a shift in the nature of the electoral "contest" in Russia from the issues surrounding the triple transition and nation-state stability to the question of who represents the personal interests of the Russian narod. According to Akhremenko and Korgunyuk (2015, 468),

> The change of the dominating electoral cleavage in post-Soviet Russia says a lot about its development direction. In the 1990s, the pro-market modernists versus anti-market traditionalists opposition prevailed in the electoral space, but since 2003 the "authorities versus community" confrontation has pushed the socio-economic disagreements to backstage.[15]

The transformation of the Russian state from an emerging proto-democracy to its current iteration as some variant of hybrid authoritarianism mixed with a procedural semi-democracy has been accomplished through a series of events and initiatives that have emanated from a general desire to counter separatism while avoiding the development of grassroots national-political unity based on an ideologically supported foundation of a free people, a free market, and accountable democratic agency.

If the lessons from the demise of the Imperial system, the capture of the revolution of 1917, the disintegration of the system reforms of the Gorbachev era, and the near collapse of the nascent state under the "shock therapy" of a Yeltsin's kleptocracy (noted for political agency) were to be heeded, the establishment of Putinism can be understood as the "harsh necessity" of the survival of the Center. Just as Stalinism became the force to weld the Soviet Union into a politically viable system, Putinism rescued Russia from its Russianness[16] and established the kind of historical system order that complements the legacy structures of Russia's 100-year transformation.

ETHNONATIONALISM TODAY

An important question often raised about Russia is that of nationalist separatism (e.g., Foley 2018). Is the shadow of secession looming in the ethnic Republics of Russia? In particular, are the insurgencies of the Chechen people likely to spread throughout the Caucasus to Republics adjacent to the external borders of the Russian state? According to the argument of Gorenburg and Giuliano (2012, 85–86)

> despite the weakness at the center and regional decentralization, nationalist separatism did not develop because the entire political institutional environment in the republics had shifted by the end of Russia's first decade. This shift was due to key central state policies that moved the locus of political power within the republics from the legislative to the executive branch, effectively shutting out political opposition, including nationalist groups.

If the central-federalizing policies of the second decade of Russian political transformation resulted in the stabilizing influences regarding ethnonational separatism, what has been the cost? The regionally reported results from the Party List Duma election outcomes shifted in 1999 to indicate the beginnings of the transition of the power of the Kremlin through a selected party organization identified with the strong showing for Unity and continuing with the consolidation of the dominance of the United Russia Party (UR) in every Duma election cycle since 2003. Many analysts concluded the grip of the consolidated coalition of Putin, the Kremlin, and UR left little to offer to an ideologically focused Duma election analysis, but there remains much to be gained from the information provided by the Party List Duma outcomes. The Russian electorate may demonstrate plurality electoral support for Putin's UR party, but the trend since 1993, with the exception of the Duma PL outcomes of 2007, has been a consistent demonstration of a willingness of the electorate to either waste their vote on a distribution of political parties with little chance of gaining Duma seats or by voting for independent non-aligned candidates and, most recently, by a demonstration through amplified results of their restrained approval of the United Russia Party of Power.

Of relevance to this assessment of regional outcomes is the fact the Russian electorate seems to take some satisfaction in exercising their right to the franchise. Turnout numbers for Duma election cycles remained consistent throughout the post-Soviet era with the lowest turnouts of 54% and 55% recorded in 1993 and 2003, respectively, and consistently respectable turnouts at or above 60% recorded in 1995, 1999, 2007, and 2011. An important decline in turnout was reported in the Duma election cycle of 2016 decline to a low of 48% when a remarkable 8,500 candidates were in competition for the 450 available Duma seats in 2016 and 14 parties managed to qualify for the party list ballot. Although the 1999 pro-government Unity party began the trend of pro-Kremlin party victory that has continued with the Putin-backed United Russia in each Duma cycle beginning in 2003, the remarkably resilient "Modified Wasted Vote" (the vote for parties other than the dominant three), votes against all, and the amplified results against UR remain a significant factor to be considered.

Notable from the Duma outcome outlined in this analysis have been the consistent pattern of Oblast anti-regime outcomes and the lack of a meaningful "ethnic" push back on the federal-central reforms of the Yeltsin and Putin administrations. For example, only 16 of 89 subject units and only 5 of 21 Republics negotiated Soglishniias with the Yeltsin regime, and yet 14 of the 21 subject Republics were included on the list of Lowest GRP in the same time period, with none of the poor Republics on the list of Soglishniia. The regional subject district mergers that began in 2003 eliminated 6 first-order subject units and reduced the number of ethnic subject districts (okrugs) from 10 to 4 with no notable backlash in electoral outcomes or in citizen demonstrations. In 1999 when political parties enjoyed the highest levels of plurality support and a Kremlin-backed party (Unity) enjoyed the first victory by Russian PL electoral standards, of the 20 Republics participating in the Duma election cycle, only 3 of 20 supported the Unity party and the MWV plurality was the "winning" outcome in 8 of 20 with the amplified results for Unity at 17 of 20 against. The soon to be decimated Okrug category recorded 9 of 10 party plurality outcomes in support of Unity in 1999, and yet 8/10 Okrug electorates' Wasted Vote outcome was at a 40% margin or greater. The 1999 outcomes for the 50 Oblasts reveal a small majority (28 of 50) providing a party plurality to Unity, but an overwhelming 41 of 50 recorded Wasted Vote outcomes at the highest plurality and the amplified results against Unity dominated all 50 of these non-ethnic Russian electorates.

Although United Russia has been the party plurality victor in each of the Duma cycles from 2003, the results in the Republics and Oblasts have been significant. Beginning in 2003 Chechnya participated in the Duma elections and this break away ethnic Republic gave UR a very suspect victory margin of 80% of the vote, followed in 2007 by the UR margin of 99% and then a 99.5% UR outcome in 2011. This evidence of blatant election tampering seems to be restricted to the Republican subject units as table 8.1 indicates when Republics and Oblasts are compared for the 2003–2011 Duma plurality outcomes. Notable from this comparison is: first, the fact all 21 Republics and all 49 Oblasts supported the UR party at a level of 50% or greater in 2007; and second, the amplified result (AR) outcome divergence. In 2003, AR against UR indicated 11 of the 21 Republics and 46 of the 50 Oblasts had at best a tepid level of support for the Kremlin party to be followed in 2007 by a significant and remarkable pro-Kremlin shift with none of the 21 Republics or (now) 49 Oblasts registering amplified results against UR. The divergence begins in 2003 when 11 of the 21 Republics supported UR at a level of 50% or greater (with only 2 of 50 Oblasts recording support for UR at 50% or greater). In 2007, 12 of the 21 Republics gave UR 70% or greater and 5 of the 21 voted for UR at 90% plus while the Oblast electorate recorded

Table 8.1 Amplified Results and United Russia Comparison Chart

	AR	*UR 50%+*	*UR 70%+*	*UR 90%+*
2003				
Republic	11/21	10/21	3/21	0/21
Oblast	41/50	2/50	0/50	0/50
2007				
Republic	0/21	21/21	12/21	5/21
Oblast	0/49	49/49	0/50	0/49
2011				
Republic	6/21	6/21	9/21	5/21
Oblast	39/48	12/48	0/48	0/48

Source: Compiled by author.

49 of 49 in support of UR at a minimum of 50% to be followed in 2011 with only 11 of 48 at the 50% range and no Oblasts recording UR outcomes in the range of the 70 to 90 percentiles in 2011. The persistence of Kremlin support demonstrated by the Ethnic Republics and in decline in the administratively designated Oblasts suggests a real and measurable difference in the region to center power relationships in the Russian districting system, and it certainly indicates the Republics have been incentivized to provide the electoral appearance of Kremlin support with 70% of the Republics recording UR victories relative to the amplified results outcomes in 2011 (when only 19% of the Oblasts did the same in 2011). In order to discover the nature of the internal pressures in this divergence between administrative and ethically determined subject units a more in-depth study of the local-regional political dynamic is necessary, but a strong inclination of the power dynamic according to Turovsky (2014, 75) is "the main task of the authoritarian dominant party in the Russian regime is to neutralize the opposition by giving it a small share of power for a number of reasons." It is evident that by 2011 the Putin regime had finally established a true Kremlin party of power and the appearance of party faction coalition building, and has demonstrated a procedural willingness to share power in the Duma. Turovsky believes this power sharing occurred because it "helps reduce public criticism of United Russia," but he also points out the dangers of success in that now "United Russia shares with the others responsibility for unpopular policies" (Turovsky 2014, 7). The 10 richest subject units in the Federation include only two ethnic subject units, The Republic of Tatarstan and the Yamel Nenets Autonomous Okrug while in comparison the 10 poorest subject units of the Federation include 9 ethnic subject units, 8 republics, and the Jewish Autonomous Oblast. Table 8.2 represents a simple truth about Russian federalism: the districting scheme may best be described as a new iteration of a prikaz-like system of neocolonial administration with nine ethnic "colonies" representing the only truly non-Russian subject districts of the Republic. The outcomes presented in table 8.2 indicate the transition of these regions from eight of the nine classified as anti-government in 1993 and 1995 (with only one subject Republic providing a split outcome for each of the 93 and 95 cycles) to the trend beginning in 1999 of extraordinary high levels of pro-Kremlin party-of-power support is a suggestion that by 2007 the Putin regime had reestablished a "neo-Imperial" grip of the Kremlin on these non-Russian populations.

In the vast majority of the subject regions reviewed in this analysis, and in contrast to the appearances of PL support for the United Russia party, the continued underlying expressions of political ideological anarchy by the Russian electorate indicate a lack of institutional depth for the Kremlin party of power, and thus United Russia remains an aspirational organization lacking a real depth of popular support, reflecting little in ideological vision

Table 8.2 Ethnic Republics with a Majority Titular Population, N = 9

Republic	Percentage Titular	Results by Party Plurality			UR-Vs-AR		
		1993	*1995*	*1999*	*2003*	*2007*	*2011*
		PL/MWV	PL/MWV	PL/MWV	PL/AR	PL/AR	PL/AR
Chechnya	95% Chechen	----	----	----	80/20	99/0	99/0
Chuvashaia	68% Chuvesh	L22/49	C33/50	C37/34	37/63	62/38	43/57
Ingustia	94% Ingush	C6/87	OH34/59	O89/8	57/43	99/0	91/9
Kabardino-Balkar	57% Kabard 13% Balkar	C21/63	OH/C25/48	O35/20	77/23	96/4	82/18
Kalmykiya	57% Kolmyk	L20/56	OH24/48	U36/26	51/49	73/27	66/34
N. Osetiya	65% Osetiyan	C36/39	C52/32	C43/21	47/53	72/28	68/32
Sakha	50% Yakut	L15/62	C18/61	U27/40	39/61	64/36	49/51
Tartarstan	53% Tatar	L/R22/47	OH29/51	O42/22	59/41	81/19	78/22
Tyva	82% Tuvinian	L10/76	OH28/56	U73/15	67/33	89/11	85/15
Anti-Gov.		8	8	3	3	0	2
Pro-Gov.		0	0	6	6	9	7
Split		1	1	0	0	0	0

Source: Compiled by author.

and dependent on a party structure unlikely to survive long after the end of the Putin phase of Russia's legacy transformation. The Yeltsin phase of the Russian transition may be considered the time when the regime dealt with the ideological question, notable for the struggles to reconcile Russia with the challenge of economic and political liberalization under conditions best described as a contest with the habits of Sovietism. The Putin era has been notable as one of Kremlin power consolidation disguised as ethno-federalism and popular nationalism. The lack of a unifying "Russian" vision for Russia's political, ideological, and economic future is likely to condemn this legacy Republic to the continuation of a long process of transformation from a power centered internal neocolonialism dependent on the enforced stability of the personal power vertical of successive ruling Kremlin regimes to a unified, representative, and politically competitive free market democracy.

NOTES

1. This chapter is a revised version of David Foley, "The Future of Janus-Faced Russia and Its Continuing Structural Legacy," in *The Legacy Structure of Russia's One Hundred Year Transformation*. Lanham: Lexington Books, 2018. Reprinted with permission.

2. For a discussion of "treaty-constitutional" see Kahn (2000, 83); for the explication of "imitation democracies" see Dutkiewicz and Trenin (2011, 112) and for a summary of "managed democracy" see Sakwa (2011, 2).

3. I identify Russia as a pseudo-ethnofederation based on the description of a true ethnofederal union presented by Smith: "Ethnofederal systems accommodate minority interests by creating sub-state jurisdictions (regions, provinces, etc.) dominated by a particular ethnic group and by dividing political sovereignty between a central state and regional jurisdictions" in Forest (2008, 375–87); also see Smith (2008, 378).

4. Notable to the degree of support for the Yeltsin referendum is the relatively low turnout levels in 1993 of less than 55% of the eligible electorate.

5. The exception to this pattern of low levels of regional regime identification are the ethnically related attachments that some population segments express for their namesake region or territory.

6. An added perspective on the emergence of the United Russia Party as "sovietization": "The post-Yeltsin political order has turned back the clock using the 'Party' as a means to institutionalize rule and generate stability" (Referred to the "sovietization thesis" with Putin as the "Party Leader") (Roberts 2012, 3).

7. Also see Panov and Ross 2013, 373.

8. See Reisinger and Moraski (2017, 23) for a detailed and statistically rich study of gubernatorial elections and regional/local variables of (likely) influence.

9. See Hough (1997, 90–92) for full discussion.

10. Today's Russian Federation Council, the upper chamber of the bicameral parliament, effectively represents the federal government in the regions rather than

providing the regions representation in federal policy making (Ross and Turovsky 2013, 59).

11. According to Reisinger and Moraski (2017, 2) "In all cases, the lower the proportion of ethnic Russians in the region, the higher the deference to the Kremlin. Extremely high levels of voting for the Kremlin is associated with extremely high levels of voter turnout at the regional level. We show that levels of deference to the Kremlin that are high enough to suggest elite manipulation begin to be evident in 1995."

12. Contractual federalism is defined in Stoner-Weiss (1999, 88) as "sub-national units entering the federation on a negotiated basis."

13. This describes in Mitchneck's own words the source of his insight. By interviewing at least 12 respondents per region in the regional capital cities of 70 of the 89 subject units (oblasts, krais and republics) (Mitchneck 2001, 364).

14. The acceptance of systemic corruption is clear in the transparency in the costs for obtaining various appointments: an ordinary police official, $50,000 to $100,000; a senior police official in Moscow, $500,000; a judgeship, up to $300,000; a senior official in customs, more than $1 million; a senator in the Federation Council, up to $6 million; and a senior government minister, up to $10 million (Lynch 2011, 89).

15. Note the conclusion of Korgunyuk (2015, 468) "the political space of contemporary Russia is defined by three divisions: (1) socio-economic (social paternalists versus market liberals), (2) authoritarian-democratic and (3) the so-called systemic, which combines features of the first and the second divisions and shows the direction in which the system develops."

16. By Russianness I refer to the atomization of colonialism and as Kaiser suggested, "before Peter the Great, Russia was merely a 'people' (narod); she became a nation (natsiya) thanks to the changes initiated by the reformer" (Kaiser 1994, 38). I would argue that Russianness is represented by that legacy identity as an Imperial natsiya of Russians with colonial ethnics subjugated within the state.

REFERENCES

Axelrod, Robert, and Robert Keohane. 1985. "Achieving Cooperation Under Anarchy." *World Politics* 38, no. 1: 226–254.

Breslauer, George W. 2005. "Regimes of Political Consolidation: The Putin Presidency in Soviet and Post-Soviet Perspective in Leading Russia." In *Putin in Perspective: Essays in Honour of Archie Brown*, edited by Alex Pravda, 37–58. Oxford: Oxford University Press.

Dutkiewicz, Piotr, and Dmitri Trenin. 2011. *Russia: The Challenge of Transformation*. New York: University Press, 2011.

Eckstein, Harry, Frederic J. Fleron, Jr., Erick P. Hoffman, and William M. Reisinger. 1998. *Can Democracy Take Root in Post-Soviet Russia: Explorations in State-Society Relations*. Oxford: Rowman and Littlefield.

Eisenstadt, S. N. 1963. *The Political Systems of Empires*. London: Collier-MacMillan.

Fish, M. Steven. 1998. "Democratization's Requisites: The Postcommunist Experience." *Post-Soviet Affairs* 14, no. 3: 212–247.

Foley, David. 2018. "The Future of Janus-Faced Russia and Its Continuing Structural Legacy." In *The Legacy Structure of Russia's One Hundred Year Transformation.* Lanham, MD: Lexington Books.

Forest, Benjamin. 2008. "The Territorial Politics of Representation." In *The Sage Handbook of Political Geography*, edited by Kevin R. Cox, Murray Low, and Jennifer Robinson, 375–387. Los Angeles: Sage Press.

Gel'man, Vladimir. 1999. "Regime Transition, Uncertainty and Prospects for Democratization: The Politics of Russia's regions in a Comparative Perspective." *Europe-Asia Studies* 51: 939–956.

———. 2006. "From Feckless Pluralism to Dominant Power Politics? The Transformation of Russia's Party System." *Demokratizatsiya* 13: 545–561.

———. 2013. "Cracks in the Wall: Challenges to Electoral Authoritarianism in Russia." *Problems of Post-Communism* 60, no. 2: 3–10.

Gel'man, Vladimir, and Andrey Starodubtsev. 2017. "Political Transitions of Bad Governance in Post-Soviet Eurasia: Towards a Research Agenda." *East European Politics* 2017: 496–515.

Gerrits, Andre W. M. 2010. "Exploring Democracy in the Russian Federation: Political Regime, Public Opinion and International Assistance." *Contemporary Politics* 16, no. 1: 33–48.

Gill, Graeme. 2007. *Politics in Russian Regions*. London: Palgrave.

———. 2015. *Building an Authoritarian Polity: Russia in Posy-Soviet Times.* Cambridge: Cambridge University Press.

Gill, Graeme, and Roderic Pitty. 1997. *Power in the Party*. London: Macmillan.

Giuliano, Elise, and Dmitry Gorenburg. 2012. "The Unexpectedly Underwhelming Role of Ethnicity in Russian Politics, 1991–2011." *Demokratizatsiya* 20, no. 2: 175–188.

Golosov, Grigorii V. 2004. *Political Parties in the Regions of Russia: Democracy Unclaimed.* Boulder: Rienner.

———. "Russia's Regional Legislative Elections, 2003–2007: Authoritarianism Incorporated." *Europe-Asia Studies* 63, no. 3: 397–414.

Greene, Samuel. 2014. *Moscow in Movement: Power and Opposition in Putin's Russia.* Stanford: Stanford University Press.

Hanson, Stephen. "Ideology, Interests, and Identity: Comparing the Soviet and Russian Secession Crisis." In *Center Periphery Conflict in Post-Soviet Russia*, edited by Mikhail A. Alexseev, 15–46. New York: St. Martin's Press.

Hoffman, Erick P. 1998. "Democratic Theories and Authority Patterns in Contemporary Russian Politics." In *Can Democracy Take Root in Post-Soviet Russia: Explorations in State-Society Relations*, edited by Harry Eckstein, Frederic J. Fleron, Jr., Erick P. Hoffman, and William M. Reisinger, 105–150. Oxford: Rowman and Littlefield.

Hough, Jerry F. 1997. *Democratization and Revolution in the USSR 1985–1991.* Washington, D.C.: Brookings Institution Press.

Huntington, Samuel P. 1968. *Political Order in Changing Societies.* New Haven: Yale University Press.

Kahn, Jeff. 2000. "The Parade of Sovereignties: Establishing the Vocabulary of the New Russian Federalism." *Post-Soviet Affairs* 16, no. 1: 58–89.

Kivelson, Valerie A., and Ronald Grigor Suny. 2016. *Russia's Empires*. New York: Oxford University Press.

Korgunyuk, Yury. 2015. "Electoral Cleavage Map of Russia Based on an Analysis of the 2011 State Duma Election and Regional Elections of 2012–2014." *European Politics and Society* 16, no. 4: 467–487.

Kotkin, Stephen. 2016. "Russia's Perpetual Geopolitics: Putin Returns to the Historical Pattern." *Foreign Affairs* 95, no. 3: 2–9.

Lapidus, Gail W. 1999. "Asymmetrical Federalism and State Breakdown in Russia." *Post-Soviet Affairs* 15, no. 1: 74–82.

Linz, Juan J., and Alfred Stepan. 1996. *Problems of Democratic Transition and Consolidation*. Baltimore: Johns Hopkins University Press.

Lipski, A. 2007. "Chego oni boyatsya." *Novaya gazetta* 89: 1–22.

Lynch, Allen C. 2011. *Vladimir Putin and Russian Statecraft*. Washington, D.C.: Potomac Books.

Lynn, Nicholas J., and Alexei V. Novikov. 1997. "Refederalizing Russia: Debates on the Idea of Federalism in Russia." *Publius* 27, no. 2: 127–204.

Makarychev, Andrey. 2012. "Alternative Logics of Russian Regionalism: Critical Theory Perspectives." *Region: Regional Studies of Russia, Eastern Europe, and Central Asia* 1, no. 1: 29–52.

Marsh, Christopher, and James W. Warhola. 2001. "Ethnicity, Ethno-Regionalism, and the Political Geography of Putin's Electoral Support." *Post-Soviet Geography and Economics* 42: 220–233.

McFaul, Michael. 2002. "One Step Forward, Two Steps Back." In *Democracy After Communism*, edited by Larry Diamond and Marc F. Plattner, 112–137. Baltimore: Johns Hopkins University Press.

Mitchneck, Beth. 2001. "The Regional Governance Context in Russia: A General Framework." *Urban Geography* 22: 360–382.

Moser, Robert G. 1997. "The Impact of Parliamentary Electoral Systems in Russia." *Post-Soviet Affairs* 13, no. 3: 284–302.

Moses, Joel C. 2008. "Who Has Led Russia? Russian Regional Political Elites, 1954–2006." *Europe-Asia Studies* 60, no. 1: 33–57.

———. 2015. "Putin and Russian Subnational Politics in 2014." *Demokratizatsiya* 23, no. 2: 181–203.

Oracheva, Oksana. 2007. "Federalism and Defederalization in a Country Transition: The Russian Experience." In *Politics in the Russian Regions*, edited by Graeme Gill, 112–147. London: Palgrave.

Panov, Petr, and Cameron Ross. 2013. "Patterns of Electoral Contestation in Russian Regional Assemblies: Between 'Competitive' and 'Hegemonic' Authoritarianism." *Demokratizatsiya* 21, no. 3: 369–399.

Pravda, Alex. 2005. *Leading Russia—Putin in Perspective: Essays in Honour of Archie Brown*. Oxford: Oxford University Press.

Reisinger, William M., and Bryon Moraski. 2017. *The Regional Roots of Russia's Political Regime*. Ann Arbor: University of Michigan Press.

Remington, Thomas F., Steven S. Smith, and Moshe Haspel. 1998. "Decrees, Laws, and Inter-Branch Relations in the Russian Federation." *Post-Soviet Affairs* 14, no. 4: 287–322.

Reuter, Ora John, and Thomas F. Remington. 2009. "Dominant Party Regimes and the Commitment Problem: The Case of United Russia." *Comparative Political Studies* 42, no. 4: 501–526.

Richter, James, and Kristen Ghodsee. 2009. "The State in Putin's Russia." *Problems of Post-Communism* 56, no. 6: 3–6.

Roberts, Sean P. 2012. *Putin's United Russia Party*. New York: Routledge.

Rose, Richard, Neil Munro, and Stephen White. 2001. "Voting in a Floating Party System: The 1999 Duma Election." *Europe-Asia Studies* 53: 419–443.

Rose, Richard, and William Mishler. 2000. "Comparing Regime Support in Non-Democratic and Democratic Countries." *Democratization* 9, no. 2: 1–20. DOI: 10.1080/714000253.

Ross, Cameron, and Rostislav Turovsky. 2013. "The Representation of Political and Economic Elites in the Russian Federation Council." *Demokratizatsiya* 13, no. 4: 59–88.

Saivetz, Carol R. 1996. "Russia: Problems and Prospects for Democratization." In *Establishing Democracies*, edited by Mary Ellen Fischer, 123–158. Boulder: Westview Press.

Sakwa, Richard. 2002. "Federalism, Sovereignty and Democracy." In *Regional Politics in Russia*, edited by Cameron Ross, 54–93. Manchester: Manchester University Press.

———. 2011. *The Crisis of Russian Democracy: The Dual State, Factionalism and the Medvedev Succession.* Cambridge: Cambridge University Press.

Sharafutdinova, Gulnaz. 2013. "Gestalt Switch in Russian Federalism: The Decline in Regional Power Under Putin." *Comparative Politics* 45, no. 3: 357–376.

Smith, Graham. 1995. *Federalism: The Multiethnic Challenge*. Abington: Routledge. Cited in Forest, 2008, 378.

Stoner-Weiss, Kathryn. 1997. *Local Heroes*. New Jersey: Princeton University Press.

———. 1999. "Central Weakness and Provincial Autonomy: Observations on the Devolution Process in Russia." *Post-Soviet Affairs* 15, no. 1: 87–106.

Turovsky, Rostislav. 2014. "Opposition Parties in Hybrid Regimes: Between Repression and Co-Optation: The Case of Russia's Regions." *Perspectives on European Politics and Society* 15: 68–87.

White, Stephen, Alex Pravda, and Zvi Gitelman. 2001. *Developments in Russian Politics 5.* Durham: Duke University Press.

II

PHILOSOPHY OF TECHNOLOGY

Chapter 9

Critical Theory and Philosophy of Technology

Andrew Feenberg

DEMOCRATIZATION OF TECHNOLOGY

After so many years of debate about nuclear weapons and, more recently, climate change it should be obvious that the future of humanity depends on technology.[1] We are told that the experts have everything in hand, but this is increasingly dubious. On the contrary governments and the experts who advise them seem paralyzed by the challenges they face. Long-term considerations, no matter how well-grounded scientifically, fade before the politics of the moment. And the best laid plans of the experts and their corporate and political masters often go awry.

This chapter is developed from lectures given in Brazil where I noted that while the traffic in São Paulo is an example of what can go wrong, it is also a consequence of *successful* development. I think we can surely do better. But the existing system has momentum and is backed by a dogmatism of quasi-papal proportions. Only significant public movements can divert the process onto new paths. This is precisely the agenda that I address here, and I call it *the democratization of technology.*

The basic principles of democracy are well known. They include voting in multiparty elections, the rights of minorities, and free discussion in the public sphere. Skeptics ask how any of this applies to technology. Can the general public make any sense out of issues involving difficult technical decisions? Who wants to listen to free discussion among incompetents? The answers are obviously "no" and "no one." We should leave technology to experts whose scientific knowledge of nature qualifies them and them alone to design our future.

Indeed, public discussion stops at nature's door. There is no debating mountains or sneezing. The skeptics treat technology as a quasi-natural phenomenon. But this leads straight to technocracy. As technology penetrates ever more deeply into society, it depoliticizes more and more of social life. Issues are removed from the public sphere, where values guide decisions, and transferred to administrations where decisions are made on the basis of facts (and supposed facts.) Values no longer play a role. The normative dimension of politics is in the process of disappearing.

Philosophy calls this attitude toward technology "reification." In accordance with its Latin root, *res*, the word for thing, "reification" means treating a human or social relation as a thing subject to scientific explanation and technical control. The market was the first important instance of reification in this sense. In the nineteenth century it was widely assumed that the market was governed by laws like those of nature. Political interference was strictly excluded. But ever since the Great Depression we have dereified the market through massive government intervention. Economic crises are now treated as political challenges. But, ironically while the market was politicized, the technical sphere was reified and withdrawn from politics. This is the basis of the technocratic ideology which gains tremendous influence after World War II.

Today the reification of technology is frequently under attack. We are familiar with many cases in which the experts bend under public pressure of one sort or another. For example, environmental movements have stimulated innovations responding to new standards. The Internet offers another example of an important technology that is only very loosely controlled by government, business, and experts, and remarkably responsive to public concerns.

The implications of these public interventions are increasingly clear. We are gradually returning technology to the public sphere where it will be subject to normative considerations once again. We need a theory of democracy adapted to this new situation.

The available conceptual framework for understanding such cases is the so-called lay-expert dilemma. Experience with the defects and flaws of technological systems motivates public involvement. Lay people speak out and the experts respond. Out of these interactions between lay and expert improved systems may emerge.

Note that lay actors do not replace experts. Rather, where their relationship is healthy and constructive, they learn from each other, reflecting the *complementarity* of everyday experience and technical rationality. The tension between them is reduced by controversy and dialogue. This is the only way to avoid the catastrophic consequences of technocratic dogmatism revealed after the fall of the Soviet Union. Ordinary people were silenced there for generations, unable to protest obvious abuses of the environment and the human body, with the result that life expectancy is declining and large areas of the country are contaminated by radiation and other poisons.

These considerations on technology have implications for our understanding of the public sphere. What is considered a public issue, suitable for free discussion, has changed over time. Law and war were the most important issues for early democracies and little else qualified as a suitable subject of discussion. But the public sphere expanded throughout the nineteenth century to encompass excluded zones formerly attributed to nature or God. For example, slavery was abolished and marriage and education were removed from religious control and transferred to the secular authorities. Somewhat later at the end of the nineteenth and beginning of the twentieth century governments begin to intervene in the economy removing it from the sphere of nature and placing it in the political sphere. Now we are witnessing a further broadening of the public sphere to incorporate another pseudo-natural domain, technology.

Radical social philosophers responded to this new situation in the 1960s and 1970s. At first they adopted a position I call "left dystopianism," exemplified in the writings of Foucault and Marcuse, the two most prominent social critics in this period. They broke with the essentialism and determinism of earlier notions of technology and introduced a historical perspective with the intent of opening up the future. Their critique of the idea of a singular scientific-technical civilization created a space for thinking about alternative technology and democratic social control.

These left dystopians shared the notion of technology as ideology, as *socially biased.* This is a controversial position that conflicts with the common sense view of technology as neutral. I will be exploring this notion below. Here is a cultural example that can serve as an entry into this way of thinking about technology.

Lauriston Sharpe describes the misadventure of a group of missionaries in the backwoods of Australia in the 1920s. They needed help at the mission and handed out steel axes to the locals as payment for services rendered. But these were aborigines whose economy and culture relied on stone axes made by male members of the community and loaned on occasion to women and children. Stone axes had great symbolic importance in the system of authority, the cosmology, and the trade relations of the tribe. The arrival of freely available steel axes disrupted the culture and left the tribe demoralized and disoriented. Far from being a neutral tool, the stone axe was the bearer of a way of life and, to the surprise of the missionaries, so is a steel axe. What is true of particular tools in cases like this is also true of modern technical systems. The choice between systems determines social worlds.

In the work of Foucault and Marcuse these worlds are political. Technology establishes a new form of domination at the basis of modern life. Foucault argues that the development of new sciences of man in the eighteenth and nineteenth centuries required the imposition of technically rational structures on human beings. Science is not an innocent observer but depends on asymmetrical power relations subordinating the observed object to the observing subject. Criminology, for example, depends on prisons as the technical framework for exposing its objects to systematic observation. Science and technical control go hand in hand.

In Marcuse technology and technical thinking are shown to extend their reach into every aspect of life and thought, eventually blocking transcending critique of social institutions by reducing every discontent to a problem solvable on the terms of the existing system. Consider the example of the demand for "fair wages." This slogan is ambiguous, signifying on the one hand an increase of some sort and on the other hand a utopian demand for fairness. Modern business unionism systematically translates the slogan into a certain percentage while erasing the utopian implication that society could at some point in the future be truly "fair." The injustice of wage labor generally is reduced to a problem solved by minor changes that temporarily defuse class conflict.

The reduction of normative to technical issues, to what sociologists call "operational components," once hit home to me in the most personal way. When I was a student in the 1960s I came across an article quoting secret documents prepared by a committee of university professors, including one of my own. The professors were asked to advise the government on preventing student protest. The problem was literally formulated in terms of the operational components of protest and suggestions for solving it ranged from improving visiting hours in the dorms to reducing the pressure for grades. It never occurred to the committee to suggest ending the war in Vietnam because that was not a politically acceptable variable, an "operational component."

Foucault's and Marcuse's demystification of the apparently rational and necessary course of progress introduced political choice into the technological domain. For these philosophers different technological systems have different implications for human freedom. This view has a certain similarity to the common sense instrumental view of technology, but the emphasis here is on design and system configuration rather than simple use. For example, the instrumentalist does not question the significance of the automobile but simply notes that the driver is free to choose her destination. The critical theorist, by contrast, argues that the automobile is the basis of a particular urban design and other technologies of public transportation offer an alternative. Today we face the live issue of how to configure the Internet, as an advanced form of broadcasting or as the infrastructure of online community. I will return to this question later.

In the 1970s and 1980s technical politics became more and more common, slowly concretizing these themes. Environmentalism has banalized the notion that technology is subject to political control. In the medical field movements for natural childbirth and access to experimental AIDS drugs shattered the illusion of absolute medical authority. Technocracy lost much of its appeal too from the bizarre and ultimately unsuccessful attempt to frame the War in Vietnam as a technical problem that American bombs could solve.

Its decline was accelerated by the emergence of a new paradigm of human relations to technology. The computer and especially the Internet create a space within which human beings interact with and even transform their technologies. This new paradigm replaced the old one based on technical macro-systems such as railroads, telephone networks, and electrical systems, which exclude most human initiative. As technical micro-politics became more common, critical approaches to technology gained increasing plausibility.

Despite their contribution to freeing up the imagination of the future, the early theories of Foucault, Marcuse, and other similar thinkers lacked concreteness. They offered only very general accounts of agency to explain public challenges to technical systems. A lingering dystopian pathos gave their theories widespread popular appeal without actually explaining the new possibilities of action they inspired. It is to correct these methodological weaknesses that I devised the critical theory of technology, the subject of this lecture.

RATIONALITY IN THE CRITICAL THEORY OF TECHNOLOGY

In 1888 Edward Bellamy published *Looking Backward*, the most famous utopian novel of the nineteenth century. In 1932 Aldous Huxley published *Brave New World*, the most famous dystopian novel of the twentieth century. What happened to transform nineteenth-century optimism into twentieth-century pessimism? Why did the nineteenth century foresee utopia and the twentieth century dystopia?

Utopian literature is usually dated from the seventeenth century. In the earliest versions individual and society are perfectly reconciled through a stoic ethos that reduces the competition for scarce resources that causes so much conflict in the real world. In Thomas More's *Utopia* for example the individuals eschew luxury, employing gold for plumbing rather than money. With Marx, utopia is reconceived as a historical potentiality. Reconciliation of individual and society will be possible in the future not through self-abnegation but through the end of scarcity. This Marxian vision is the background to Bellamy's utopia.

Bellamy's hero wakes up after sleeping for more than 100 years in the twentieth century to find that America has become a socialist society. All the institutions are explained to him as rational, that is, both just and efficient.

Adults are enrolled in an industrial army where they enjoy equal pay and are relieved of the most difficult and dangerous work by machines. The hardest jobs are accompanied by a shorter work week so as to recruit workers who value leisure without the need for financial incentives or coercion. The industrial army is commanded by experts of high moral character.

Everyday life and politics are not organized by the army nor are art, literature, science, invention, journalism, and religion. All these activities are pursued freely, without expert control, because they have no scientific basis and hence no use for expert management. Bellamy's utopia is a bipolar society combining collectivism and individualism in ideal proportions. But this is precisely what did *not* happen in the twentieth century when the technical means were actually available to accomplish utopian ends.

Huxley's dystopia is also a rational society, extrapolated from mass manipulation by the emerging broadcast media and Ford's assembly line. His dystopia reconciles individual and society by eliminating individuality. Its rulers argue that all ills stem from the lack of fit between people and the division of labor. Human beings must therefore be reconstructed in mind and body to suit the tasks they are condemned to perform. People become technical objects in this scheme, their genetic heritage a raw material for the production of better adapted models of humanity. The alternative the novel proposes, or rather the dilemma it constructs, distinguishes technological domination from individualistic chaos, the one offering slavery and stability, the other freedom and catastrophe.

Both of these novels concern the radical consequences of total social rationalization. The comparison between them raises the question of the significance of rationality in a dramatic way. In my introductory remarks I emphasized the non-neutrality of technology and the role of values in technical choice. These novels presuppose something very much like that argument. In the one case technical and moral progress are conjoined while in the other technology is bound up indissolubly with domination. But neither of these fictions corresponds exactly with our contemporary situation.

The question the novels do not address is precisely how rationality is combined with values. Each novel posits an essential connection between technical advance and a specific value. This leaves little room for human agency in the technical sphere. But a new politics is emerging that responds to the failures of expertise through democratic interventions by ordinary people with consequences for the design of technologies and technical systems. A new understanding of rationality is needed to respond to the questions raised by this new technical politics.

The need is particularly urgent today since rationality is entangled in the paradox that Huxley identified in his novel. We have discovered that progress in technology, that is to say rationality in its most concrete form, leads not to freedom but to domination. A new elite arises to administer technically mediated institutions and this is not accidental to modernity, an effect of corruption or prejudice, but responds to the requirements of efficiency. Thus the division of modern societies into rulers and ruled is rooted in technological rationality itself. This is the context in which technical politics is lived as resistance to domination.

The fate of medicine is a case in point; it has been transformed from a craft based on the individual labor of doctors and nurses into a vast technical system administered through bureaucratic institutions and increasingly controlled by corporations and governments. As medicine becomes more technically effective, its patients become more and more like things, the objects of technique, and less and less like persons. The demand for more humane procedures put forward in different ways by pregnant women in the 1970s and AIDS patients a decade later restored communicative relations interrupted by the technocratic restructuring of medicine.

To understand such cases, the critique of technology must reverse the notion we inherit from the eighteenth-century Enlightenment according to which rationality is essentially opposed to domination. On this view domination should recede as rationality advances. Thus philosophy claims at least part of the credit for the decline of feudal and religious superstitions and the institution of democracy in America and Europe.

Habermas calls this the "Enlightenment project." It was always questionable, but it seems to have failed disastrously in the last century. The "project" has been challenged historically by two critiques of rationality. On the one hand, a romantic critique of reason itself calls for a retreat from rationality and its entire works. On the other hand, various forms of critical theory attempt to develop a "rational critique of rationality." These two styles of critique imply different politics and it is therefore important to distinguish them clearly.

Romantic resistance to reason as such begins in the late eighteenth century, accompanied by idealization of the past. Rousseau, for example, criticized the division of labor which, he claimed, enslaves modern human beings to a system they cannot control. He contrasted modern men unfavorably with the virtuous peasants of Republican Rome. We have poets, geometers, and physicians, he says, but no citizens, meaning that specialization has deprived the members of society of a vision of the whole and the ability to engage morally with its requirements. Later in the nineteenth century the standardization of products provoked aesthetic dissatisfaction with modernity. Ruskin criticized the disappearance of craft and the debasement of aesthetics in modern society. Modernity is not just unjust but also ugly. Kierkegaard attacked the loss of passion in modern life. Modern man, he charged, is incapable of commitment because he is always reflecting on his situation and calculating his chances. Balzac's antihero Vautrin declaims "J'appartiens à l'opposition qui s'appele la vie." This image of life versus mechanism captures the essence of the romantic critique.

Romantic critique appears to be verified by the twentieth-century catastrophe of reason. Wars, concentration camps, nuclear weapons, and now environmental disaster threaten the Enlightenment project. But this critique of reason does not lead to a constructive politics but rather to withdrawal from the public world. Furthermore, it is difficult to believe that the full content and significance of rationality is exhausted by the division of labor, standardization, accounting, and mechanization. Surely reason has underexploited potentials that can be mobilized in a self-critical approach. This implies a distinction between technical rationality and critical rationality of the sort that is deployed in this lecture.

There are no ready concepts for talking about the paradox of rationality, the fact that the progress of technology has gone hand-in-hand with the progress of domination. That the existing technology favors this development is clear, but it is important to avoid an essentialist critique of technology as such. To understand the paradox without romantic subtexts we need a concept of *social* bias appropriate for the analysis of *rational* systems. This is a departure from the usual concept of bias which is closely associated with prejudice and discrimination. Racial discrimination in hiring is routinely described as biased in this sense.

But bias in a less familiar sense appears in other spheres as well. For example, many everyday objects are adapted to right-handed use. This too could be called a bias but it does not involve prejudice. Rather it is built into the design of the objects themselves. In this it resembles the kind of bias to which technology and other rational systems are susceptible.

In accordance with this distinction, critical theory of technology identifies two types of bias, which I call "substantive" and "formal" bias. The more familiar substantive bias is the object of Enlightenment critique. Eighteenth-century philosophers were confronted with institutions that claimed legitimacy on the basis of stories about the past and religious tradition. Aristocratic privilege was justified by mythic origins such as participation in the crusades. Kings ruled in the name of God. Reason opposed these narrative myths behind religion, monarchy, and feudalism. The Enlightenment judged according to facts and arguments and this judgment was fatal to the *ancien regime*. Much later a similar critique attacked racism and gender bias again in the name of rational ethical principles and scientific knowledge. I call the bias criticized in such cases "substantive" because it is based on pseudo-facts and prejudices. Substantive bias intrudes specific contents that motivate discrimination into domains that ought to be governed by rationality and justice.

Critique of substantive bias seems to imply the purity of reason as such. But things are not so simple. Although rational critique is justified relative to myths and prejudices, it is not without its own form of bias. A brief detour into Marx's critique of the market is useful for understanding this counterintuitive form of bias.

The market appears rational but, strangely, its expansion leads to inequality. This inequality escapes Enlightenment critique because it is not justified by narrative myths but by the exchange of equivalents. In the mid-nineteenth century two styles of critique emerged in response. The French anarchist philosopher Proudhon famously claimed that *property is theft*. He argued that given the outcome, property income cannot be the result of an equal exchange. Various theories of this sort appeared over the years, some arguing that capitalists charge more than goods are worth, others arguing that they pay workers less than their fair share. In either case, capitalism was treated as a fraud rather than as a coherent system. Such arguments usually led to an idealization of peasant small holding.

Marx was a more rigorous thinker. He realized that the critique of the market would have to begin with the fact of equal exchange rather than denying it. The origin of inequality would have to be found in the very rationality of the market. He proved this with an elaborate economic theory that I will not review here. His argument turns on the difference between the amount of wealth required to maintain the worker, which is more or less equivalent to his wages, and what he is capable of producing in the course of the working day, the length of which is set by the capitalist. Since the worker owns and sells his labor power, not the product of his labor, no violation of strict market exchange is involved in setting a workday long enough for the capitalist to make a profit. The injustice of the system is a result of the logic of the market.

With this argument Marx showed that rational systems can be biased by their social context and design and he extended this type of critique to technology as well. Technology too discriminates between rulers and ruled in technologically mediated institutions. This bias does not involve prejudice. A biased technology is still rational in the sense that it links cause and effect in useful patterns. No narrative myths or pseudo-facts obstruct its efficient functioning, and it is certainly free of prejudice. I call this a "formal" bias because it does not violate the formal norms such as control and efficiency under which technology is developed and employed. These norms do not specify a particular substantive goal but are apparently compatible with any goal the technology can be made to serve. However, we observe over and over in history that the pursuit of efficiency and control in fact favors particular social groups and their goals. Technology is not simply a neutral medium in which universal human needs are satisfied, but plays a specific social role in society. As we have seen, this was the case with deskilling through technical innovation.

There are two familiar ways in which rational systems and artifacts are biased. In the first place they require a context for their implementation and that context may have different implications for different individuals or social groups. Consider the case of maps. A map may be a perfect representation of the territory and in that sense highly rational, but it is useless until direction on the map is correlated with direction on the ground. Thus the map does not stand alone but must enter practical reality with a bias in the most neutral sense, an orientation. But a map may also embody a social bias, for example, in the case of early navigation when map-making was a necessary preliminary to the conquest of territory occupied by natives who themselves had no need of maps to get around.

The second way in which rational artifacts are biased is through their design as in the case of right handed tools. Design is shaped by many actors seeking rational solutions to the problems that concern them. Artifacts and systems reflect particular interests through the role of these actors in the design process. This does not make them irrational or inefficient but on the contrary is the way in which they are rational. I employ the concepts of "translation" and "technical code" to understand this apparent paradox.

Technologies are built according to general rules I call "technical codes." These codes lie at the intersection of social demand and natural causality. Social demand is first formulated discursively, in a philosophical or ideological form. Technical codes translate such social discourse into design specifications. The sidewalk ramp is a good example. Until it was introduced, disability was considered a private problem. The interests of the disabled were not represented in the design of sidewalks which obstructed their movements at every crossing. Complaints about this situation were framed in terms of human rights. Once society accepted responsibility for the free movement of the disabled, the design of sidewalks translated the new right. Recognition of this right takes the form of a design specification.

Progress is defined relative to technical codes and not in absolute terms. Unsuccessful alternatives are rejected and forgotten, covered over by a kind of technological unconsciousness which makes it seem as though the chosen path of progress was inevitable and necessary all along. This is what gives rise to the illusion of pure technical rationality. That illusion obscures the imagination of future alternatives by granting existing technology an appearance of universality and necessity it cannot legitimately claim. The role of critical theory of technology is to demystify this appearance in order to open up the future.

THE CONTRIBUTION OF CRITICAL THEORY

In this section I will explain the connection between the critical theory of technology as I have formulated it and the Critical Theory of the Frankfurt School. This focus will take us in two different directions. The first part considers the Frankfurt School's reflections on the paradox of modern rationality, and its failure to resolve that paradox. The second part shows how critical theory of technology supplements the Frankfurt School's critique of technology and helps to address its limitations.

The Frankfurt School was a group of unorthodox Marxist philosophers who founded their Institute for Social Research in Germany shortly before Hitler came to power. Theodor Adorno, Max Horkheimer, and Herbert Marcuse were critical of the Soviet version of communism. They believed that class consciousness had failed to emerge as Marx expected and that the opportunity for proletarian revolution had been missed. They did not despair completely but held out little hope for the future. The problems of modernity, they argued, were rooted in the very nature of rationality. The Frankfurt School focused on technology, as the concrete expression of flawed rationality, free from the illusions of traditional Marxism.

Like Bellamy, Marx believed technology had the potential to liberate humanity. His social analysis leads to faith in the emancipatory effect of a further rationalization process under the control of workers. Later Marxists simplified the argument and concluded that capitalism distorted a pure rationality waiting to emerge under socialism. They believed that progress would solve all the problems with technology.

When Lenin described communism as Soviets plus electricity, he announced a standard modernizing strategy. His government imported and imitated Western technology without much attention to local conditions including the political conditions created by the Soviets, or workers' councils, that ostensibly held power. The result was the importation of operational autonomy along with the equipment, the design of which it had determined. "One-man management" soon became the mantra of Soviet development policy.

We have not seen the emergence of a pure and benign technological rationality under either capitalism or communism, but rather the generalization of technical mediation in the form which capitalism first gave it. Technology reaches medicine, entertainment, sports, and education and frames everyday life and belief. Power follows technology. The enrolment of everyone and everything on the planet in the system has made it possible to spread centralized administration from the factory to society at large. This is a catastrophic reversal of the expectations of the philosophers of the Enlightenment which Marx still hoped to fulfill through socialist revolution.

There are several possible responses to this situation. Traditional Marxists, liberals, and neoliberals hold that modernization must continue until it finally fulfills its promise. The negative consequences so far endured are dismissed as contingent accidents along a path to utopia. Postmodernists despair in enlightenment and give up on reason altogether. The philosophers of the Frankfurt School offered a more complex response, a "dialectic of enlightenment" that recognized the catastrophe of modernity but also the promise of a rational society.

They shifted the emphasis of the Marxist argument from social and economic relations between human beings to the relation of human beings to nature. Adorno and Horkheimer argued that the rational domination of nature leads eventually to the domination of some human beings by other human beings. Every advance of rationality in the struggle with nature is also an advance of domination in society. The Enlightenment project is thus more complex and fraught than it seems.

Horkheimer explained the problem in terms of the split between reason and value. He argued that reason is rooted in the preservation of life but in modern times it is reduced to a pure means, an instrument of power indifferent to life. Horkheimer distinguished accordingly between what he called "objective" and "subjective" reason. Objective reason contains a value within itself. Medicine is an example. It combines rational techniques based on science and experience with a commitment to healing. Until modern times this was the normal form in which reason was deployed in society. But with the emergence of a total civilization of technique reason becomes "subjective" in the sense that it responds to the will rather than to intrinsic purposes of some sort.

Marcuse argued that the success of subjective reason makes possible not only a generous material standard of living but also access to the cultural heritage of the human race, formerly available only to the wealthy. Advancing technology thus proves the obsolescence of class rule just as Marx supposed, but at the same time it provides the means for perpetuating the capitalist system indefinitely through "delivering the goods" and integrating the working class to consumer society. "Technological rationality" thus shatters the dream of Enlightenment. This is a radicalization of Weber's rationalization thesis culminating not in the iron cage of bureaucracy but in an iron cage of technology.

This radical critique does not convince Jürgen Habermas, the most prominent contemporary representative of the Frankfurt School. Habermas introduced communication theory and system theory into Critical Theory and turned it away from the radical critique of modernity toward the reform of the welfare state. He rejects what he considers the anti-modernism of Adorno, Horkheimer, and Marcuse, the first generation of the Frankfurt School. They never explain the critical standard underlying their argument, nor do they propose a concrete reform program. According to Habermas this leaves a gaping normative deficit.

In his 1968 essay on "Technology and Science as Ideology," Habermas addresses Marcuse's version of the Frankfurt School's argument.[2] He claims that Marcuse has two independent critiques of technology. The first critique follows the line taken by Adorno and Horkheimer in viewing technology as intrinsically dominating. This critique has a certain similarity to the romantic critique of rationality discussed earlier although Marcuse develops it in a unique way. The problem is not precisely the substantive bias of rationality condemned by romanticism, but rather the formalistic character of reason itself which has substantive consequences.

This puzzling distinction can be clarified by reference to premodern notions of rationality based on the cultivation of the potentialities of its materials. Traces of such notions persist among some practitioners of technical arts such as architecture and medicine. For Marcuse, the formal neutrality of modern reason, which derives from its mathematical construction of its objects, cancels its connection to potentialities and places it at the disposal of the powerful, ready to serve their subjective values. Frank Lloyd Wright attempted to situate his buildings harmoniously in the landscape, realizing its potential as a site, but the same engineering techniques he employed, freed from any such aesthetic concern, are also available to create steel and glass monstrosities cut off from any relation to nature. Marcuse argues for a social revolution in reason itself, incorporating humane values into its technological applications. Marcuse hoped for the fusion of aesthetic and technical rationality in a new version of objective reason.

Habermas rejects this view which he attributes to a "secret hope" in a communicative relationship to nature. He argues that nature cannot be liberated from the bonds of technology since technology is a generic achievement and not specific to any given society. As such it cannot be transformed by a change in social organization.

Habermas is more sympathetic to Marcuse's second critique. According to this critique the problem with technology is its universalization as a world-view or ideology influencing every aspect of life in modern society. Marcuse writes "When technics becomes the universal form of material production, it circumscribes an entire culture; it projects a historical totality—a 'world.'" This is the Marcusean version of the technocracy thesis according to which experts have taken over and depoliticized public life. Self-expanding technology replaces moral considerations and debate. Habermas finds in this approach a way of separating the critique of technology as such from its use as a legitimating ideology.

Habermas's version of this argument is presented in the course of a critical discussion of Marxism. Where Marx distinguished productive forces and relations of production and identified the tensions between them that motivate class struggle, Habermas argues that class struggle has weakened in intensity as the issues that motivated it have taken on completely new forms. Thus it is necessary to recast the problems Marx addressed at a higher level.

Habermas substitutes his own more general categories, "purposive-rational action" and "communicative interaction," for Marx's forces and relations of production. Purposive-rational action is success- and control-oriented. The technical relation to nature is rational in this sense. It differs from communicative interaction which is based on the norms of ideal speech and aims at mutual understanding rather than technical success. The generic tension between the types of action involved in production and social relations now replaces the original Marxian problematic.

Habermas derives a normative ground from his theory of communication. He claims that we could not communicate without implicitly assuming that our interlocutors speak truly and sincerely. It is only against the background of such assumptions that we can identify deviations from ideal speech such as lying. Institutions based on communicative interaction such as the family and the public sphere thus have an intrinsic normative character.

These distinctions are the basis for a general theory of social organization. On the one hand, every society has an institutional framework based on a system of meanings, practices, and expectations established by communicative interaction. On the other hand, societies have technical subsystems which contain the knowledge, practices, and artifacts that produce the goods required for survival. The balance between the technical and communicative dimensions varies in different forms of society, but the institutional framework was always predominant until modern times.

Habermas distinguishes two stages in the development of modernity in each of which a different technical subsystem intrudes on the institutional framework. In the first phase of bourgeois society the market penetrates everywhere and displaces the institutional framework as the determining instance of social life. So long as the market is interpreted as a quasi-natural phenomenon, it supports bourgeois hegemony. Exchange appears fair since equivalents are traded without coercion. The legitimacy of the ruling interests is established through their identification with the "laws" of the market.

This legitimation fades as governments begin to regulate markets in the twentieth century. In the postwar period technology takes over where the market leaves off in organizing more and more social life. As a result, market legitimation gives way to technological legitimation. The institutional framework is increasingly subordinated to the conditions of economic and technical development. Legitimation now requires the identification of the ruling interests with the efficient functioning of the system. Depoliticization masks continuing domination and justifies a technocratic order. Normative concerns are increasingly evacuated as a dystopian logic takes over.

Habermas's early essay is an attempt to establish a critical but positive relationship to modernity. In the terminology of his later work, he postulates a double rationalization, both technical and communicative. The technical rationalization is of course familiar but Habermas treats progress in freedom, individuality, and democracy as belonging to a parallel communicative rationalization. He does not criticize modernity as such but rather the overemphasis on technical rationalization under capitalism at the expense of communication. Critique should aim at furthering communicative rationalization rather than denouncing technology.

Habermas's later work improved on this theory. He realized that individual action orientations do not a society make. The real problem is coordination among many acting subjects. Habermas distinguished two different types of action coordination characterizing the domains of "lifeworld" and "system" that replace the "institutional framework" and "technical subsystem" of his earlier work. In the new theory coordination is achieved in different ways in each domain, through mutual understanding in the lifeworld and through systems such as the market without the need for much in the way of communicative interaction.

The concept of lifeworld is derived from phenomenology. In Heidegger it is identified with the "world" as a system of meanings implicit in the active relation to things. These meanings are "preconceptual" in the sense that they are prior to and make possible the articulation of meanings in language. Husserl uses the term "lifeworld" to refer to the everyday domain of meanings that underlies scientific conceptualization. Both thinkers draw our attention to meaning as the irreducible medium of experience. Habermas reformulates the concept to emphasize the social context in which meanings are generated and shared.

The lifeworld is essential to the reproduction of the individuals but it is incapable of managing the institutions of a large-scale modern society. For that purpose more impersonal and quasi-mechanical forms of interaction are required and these are made possible by systems of economic exchange and administration. The system concept employed here is derived from the sociology of Talcott Parsons. Parsons developed this concept by generalizing certain features of markets to other social domains. Systems in this sense are self-regulating structures of interaction that enable the achievement of individual goals. They require no collective agreement but only stripped-down and conventional communicative responses such as the typical dialogue involved in making a purchase. Modern society depends on the effectiveness of systems at unburdening the lifeworld of excessively complicated tasks.

Habermas's critique of technocracy can now be reconstructed in terms of these new distinctions. Technocracy is redefined as colonization of the lifeworld by the system. Habermas advocates increased social control of the system by decisions reached freely in the public sphere through communicative acts. But he abstracts completely from technology in this version of his theory. The term does not even appear in the index of his most important book, *The Theory of Communicative Action.* He focuses instead on the welfare state, multiculturalism, and deliberative democracy. He is concerned for example about legal intrusions into the family and ignores such technological intrusions as the medicalization of child birth. But technology is just as important as markets and administrations. It too functions as a system in coordinating action and it too causes many of the most important problems of modern societies. How can a critical theory of modern society omit from its agenda environmentalism, the Internet, economic development in poor countries, and the problem of democratization of technology?

Despite these limitations Habermas's theory is full of important insights some of which I have attempted to incorporate into a new version of critical theory of technology. Perhaps the most important of these insights is his methodological dualism. Habermas recognizes that modern societies operate in two principal worlds, a world of quasi-mechanical institutional interactions and a world structured around meanings and communicative understanding. Each world requires its own method of analysis.

Unfortunately there is an ambiguity in Habermas's application of this dualistic conception. In methodological discussions he tends to argue that the distinction is analytic. This means that system rationality and lifeworld meanings coexist in all social institutions. The weight of the two types of action coordination differs in different institutions, but there is invariably considerable overlap. Sociologists who study organizations verify this approach whenever they show the dependence of formal structures on informal relationships, both of which are necessary to effective functioning. Similarly, economists who study the effects of taxation on incentives for spouses to work illustrate the penetration of system rationality into the family, an institution that is primarily the scene of communicative interaction. Although this interpretation gives a realistic picture of the workings of the various institutions, it makes for problems with the colonization thesis since the system and lifeworld always already interpenetrate each other.

Habermas wavers between this analytic approach and reifying the system and lifeworld as separate spheres. Then institutions are assigned to each sphere and it appears that, for example, the market and state administrations belong to one sphere and the family to another. The colonization thesis makes sense in this context since the colonizer and the colonized are distinct entities. But this is also the context in which the neutrality of the system makes its appearance in Habermas's argument. If the system is external to the lifeworld and its conflicts, then its structure is not controversial, only its reach.

This formulation eliminates the problematic of domination so central to the thinking of the first generation of the Frankfurt school. Social critique is reduced to boundary problems. Apparently, systems are alright in themselves and the only problem is their extent. Of course different groups might have different goals for the system, just as users of tools may have different goals, but goals are external to the self-enclosed instrumental rationality of the system. This leads Habermas to reject radical proposals for changing the internal structure of the system such as self-management. The system is surrendered to capital and the experts.

If Habermas accepts the neutrality thesis, this is because he has no concept of formal bias and hence no conceptual basis for criticizing systems in themselves that does not tip over into romantic rejection. Caught between the neutrality thesis and the "secret hopes" of romantic critique, Habermas is helpless to devise an adequate critical theory of modernity.

To escape these problems, it is necessary to stick rigorously to the idea that "system" and "lifeworld" are a crosscutting analytic distinction throughout all the institutions of modern society. Lifeworld and system are not social spheres but overlapping perspectives on the social world. I therefore propose what I call a double aspect theory of systems according to which they are traversed by the social conditions of their design and configuration. Such a theory can encompass technology along with the markets and administrations analyzed by Habermas.

The logic of this double aspect theory requires careful elaboration. Since system and lifeworld are not separate things, but different aspects of one and the same thing, they cannot interact causally. And yet they are not identical either. Analytically distinguished entities such as these entertain logical relationships of some sort. For example, the Pythagorean theorem explains the relations of the three sides of a right triangle. Similarly, the notion of form explains the relations of the parts of a work of art. The related entities—sides, colors, shapes—cannot exist separately and yet they are distinguishable. We grasp them through special concepts adapted to each case.

Hegel wrote a short essay called "Who Thinks Abstractly" that helps to clarify the relations between aspects in the case that concerns us.[3] His essay reverses the usual understanding of abstract and concrete. It is not the philosopher who thinks abstractly, but the ordinary person who summarizes a complex of relationships in a single trait. Abstraction is thus a synecdoche in which a part stands for the concrete whole. Hegel gives the example of the servant who is treated as merely a servant by a vulgar master, in contrast with the "French noble" who understands that his servant is a person with ideas and purposes just like himself and who relates to him accordingly.

The Habermasian conception of system suggests something similar. Consider market relations. Their communicative simplicity is made possible by abstracting economic exchange from the complex relations that surround it. We enter a store and relate to the clerk exclusively as a clerk, ignoring all other aspects of the clerk's being. This is abstraction in Hegel's sense. In a curious confirmation of Hegel's admiration for France, it is considered proper to first recognize a French clerk as a person with an appropriate greeting. Only then is it polite to relate to the clerk as a clerk.

Systems generally can be considered abstractions from the wider whole of the lifeworld in which they are embedded. What is abstracted is the functional dimension of the lifeworld. Thus a clerk performs an economic function, just as a device performs a technical function. The functional dimension of persons and things is distinguishable but it is not self-subsistent. The clerk cannot be separated from the person who is a clerk, nor the device from the social world in which it serves its function.

An automobile, for example, has a transportation function served by various causal mechanisms, but it is also part of the lifeworld of its owner with significance in terms of beauty, status, social behavior, its impact on urban design, and so on. Of course the abstract idea of the transportation function is useful and the causal mechanisms that serve it can be studied and perfected, but this does not nullify the social meaning of the automobile. In sum, a functional logic operates at the systemic level, abstracted from the meanings that circulate in the lifeworld.

I call this approach instrumentalization theory. In this theory the system level is called the "primary instrumentalization" and the lifeworld level the "secondary instrumentalization." As applied to technology the point of the distinction is to show the relation between two fundamental aspects of every functional artifact: causal structure and social significance.

The primary instrumentalization is an imaginative relationship to technical affordances. A simple example is grasping a stick in order to extend one's reach to a fruit hanging from a high branch. The action depends on causal perceptions and reasoning. All human beings and even some animals are capable of this. Modern technology assembles huge numbers of such affordances in coherent patterns to accomplish goals that go beyond any one individual's needs.

But the logic of such assemblages is not exclusively technical. It is true that it is constrained by causal principles: only an assemblage that "works" succeeds. But there are an infinite number of working combinations available. The secondary instrumentalization determines which ones are realized. At this level the affordances acquire meaning in their social context. This is the lifeworldly significance of the technical; it situates technology in the way of life to which it belongs.

Technological design combines both levels seamlessly and both are necessary. Apart from the simplest technical actions, the construction of a device is always a social act involving the secondary instrumentalization. Invention proceeds from curiosity and technical insight and is usually conditioned by some possible social demand that can be distilled into a notion of function. But unless the demand is sufficiently pressing and general, the invention falls by the wayside regardless of its technical elegance. The history of technology offers some famous examples of causal insights that found no place in the society to which they belonged, for example the steam engine invented by Hero of Alexandria and the wheels used by the Aztecs only in toys. Consider too the example of the zipper. It was invented and reinvented over and over but even when perfected technically it waited long years before anyone would consent to wear it. Determining the meaning of the zipper was just as important as making it zip.

The instrumentalization theory offers a framework within which to analyze the imbrication of the technological system and the lifeworld. The two instrumentalizations refer to different aspects of artifacts and their users, but these are aspects only, not separate spheres able to exist independently of each other. This is crucial. Unlike Habermas's system and lifeworld, here the aspects each reflect the other on its own terms. But the fact that modern societies are able to abstract the functional level of artifacts and to construct technical disciplines on that basis masks their essential social dimension. The abstraction certainly has consequences—it makes modern technology possible—but it does not actually eliminate the social. Recall the example of the sidewalk ramp discussed earlier. The ramp's causal properties are describable in a specification on purely technical terms, but that specification is not purely technical; it represents the rights of the disabled technically. That is its significance in the lifeworld.

Instrumentalization theory draws on some of Habermas's insights to restore the focus on technology and the problem of domination of the first generation of the Frankfurt School without romantic afterthoughts. The theoretical context is different from both, to be sure, but the point of the new formulation is the same, to reconstruct a "rational critique of rationality" in confrontation with technocratic ideology.

The primary instrumentalization specifies those aspects of the technical relation to reality which contain the potential for domination. Functionalizing an object involves more than control; it requires that the object be broken out of its place in its world and stripped of connections with its environment. In the case of human beings the implications are obvious: to return to our example, the clerk is useful only insofar as he does not express his personality too freely from behind the counter. The assembly line worker is in a still tighter straightjacket, forced into a strictly limited role. Natural objects too are "dominated" in some sense where they are denied their own potential for growth and connection.

In their *Dialectic of Enlightenment*, Horkheimer and Adorno appear to condemn instrumental reason as such for harboring these traits. Later qualifications were never elaborated into an alternative theory. Marcuse's argument is more developed. He understands that the potential for domination is not realized as a simple consequence of the deployment of technology, but reflects a specific social context. On his account something like what I have called the primary instrumentalization is value-neutral and hence available to serve in a project of domination. An ambiguity remains regarding whether the critique addresses substantive or formal dimensions of technological rationality.

I have reformulated this theory in a more socially concrete way. In my account, systems acquire a formal bias toward domination through a specific type of secondary instrumentalization which narrows the values they serve to exclude important contexts and consequences. This is what happened in the development of industrial technology under capitalism. But the secondary instrumentalization may also cancel or mitigate the potential for domination by orienting technology toward a broader range of social values. This is the outcome of democratic interventions into technology. Separating these two levels saves the theory from the dilemma of essentialist technophobia or naive acceptance of the neutrality of technology which threatens it in the various formulations of the Frankfurt School. The key concept missing in all these formulations is the notion of formal bias, which makes possible a true critical theory of technology.

NOTES

1. This chapter is based on three lectures delivered in 2010 at the University of Brasilia to a class that included students from several disciplines and a number of rural development specialists associated with the Rede de Tecnologia Social. These lectures opened a course in philosophy of technology which continued after my departure under the leadership of several Brazilian scholars. The program was sponsored by the Fundação Banco do Brasil.

2. Habermas, Jurgen (1970). Technology and Science as Ideology, in *Toward a Rational Society*, J. Shapiro, trans. Boston: Beacon Press.

3. http://www.marxists.org/reference/archive/hegel/works/se/abstract.htm

Chapter 10

Eco-Dominion

William Leiss

This chapter engages with the concept of environmental domination, particularly as that concept is developed in a recent article by Sharon R. Krause. It discusses some of the problematic aspects in that account and proposes to substitute a somewhat different concept, namely, eco-dominion. The idea of eco-dominion is that humanity's right over nature is limited to its right of use of living animals for sustenance, as is articulated in the first chapter of the *Book of Genesis*. The powerful influence of this text across the centuries encourages us to focus on the fate of wild and domesticated animals when we seek to formulate an appropriate ethical response to humanity's relations with non-human nature. At present it is the relentless growth of the global human population which represents an extinction threat to other species. The chapter concludes by suggesting that the narrower concept of eco-dominion presents the issues involved in the human relation to non-human nature more clearly than does the more expansive concept of environmental domination, but also that neither concept appears to be sufficiently robust to confront the looming crisis in this relation.

> And God said, Let us make man in our image, after our likeness: and let them have dominion over the fish of the sea, and over the fowl of the air, and over the cattle, and over all the earth, and over every creeping thing that creepeth upon the earth. . . .
>
> And God blessed them, and God said unto them, Be fruitful, and multiply, and replenish the earth, and subdue it: and have dominion over the fish of the sea, and over the fowl of the air, and over every living thing that moveth upon the earth.
>
> Genesis 1:26, 28 (King James Bible)

INTRODUCTION

A recent contribution on the concept of *environmental domination* defines that concept as "forms of domination that transpire in and through human interactions with more-than-human parts of nature" (Krause 2019, 4). The advantage in this definition is its breadth, since those interactions could encompass everything in nature that is familiar to us, up to and including our solar system. The corresponding limitation is a function of that same breadth: The full scope of such interactions is clearly very large, and one might need a catalog in order to array them for the purpose of properly assessing the concept of environmental domination.[1] In this chapter I follow a quite different path that is markedly narrower in scope. I contrast environmental domination with eco-dominion, where "eco" refers to either *ecological* or *ecosystem*. The term "ecological" commonly refers to relations between living organisms and their environments. "Ecosystem" calls attention to a "community" of living organisms in conjunction with both the biotic and abiotic (nonliving) components of their environment.[2]

In both terms the emphasis is on "living organisms," and that is the key element for my purposes here. I seek to make two main points in what follows. The first is that domination over "more-than-human parts of nature" (to employ Sharon Krause's terminology) is only fully meaningful when the scope of this conception is restricted to the living creatures on the earth, particularly other animals, with which virtually all humans regularly interact on a daily basis. The second is that it is impossible to grasp the *reality* of what is being referred to, in both the terms environmental domination and eco-dominion, unless one consults the scientific accounts dealing with the scale of the human presence on planet earth.

Restricting the scope of the main conception enables us to view modern practices in the context of a very old theme in Western Civilization, namely, the idea of human "dominion" on the earth as presented in the Hebrew Bible's *Book of Genesis*. No other concept of human domination over nature has ever exerted such a powerful influence on human thinking about its relation to nature over the course of millennia—and, arguably, continues to do so, in proportion to the continuing role of Jewish and Christian faith in contemporary society.

There is more. An examination of a few key texts in later Christian dogma shows us that human dominion was by no means considered to be unlimited or absolute. On the contrary, it is shown to have been importantly constrained to what may be called the *right of use*. And right of use, for example, could not possibly be understood, in any sensible calculus, as the right to drive living species to the brink of extinction or beyond. Even when Francis Bacon secularized the religious idea of dominion in the seventeenth century, as we shall see, he did not repeal the limitation; rather, he stated explicitly that the *exercise* of the "right over nature" which mankind possesses (as the gift of God) must be overseen and controlled by both reason and faith. If we were to take this theme down to the present day, we would have in hand a powerful and rational basis for an environmental ethic to guide us into the future.

However, while such an environmental ethic has been well-formulated in recent decades, it has so far failed to confront explicitly the stark reality that humans are driving most terrestrial wild animals to the brink of extinction. Recent scientific studies have shown that the combination of humans and their domesticated animals, especially cattle and pigs, utterly dominate the biomass of the earth, having reduced the populations of wild animals and birds to a miniscule fraction of the total. This fact presents both the concept of environmental domination and that of eco-dominion with a crisis of meaning.

THE CONCEPT OF ENVIRONMENTAL DOMINATION

Sharon Krause writes:

> Environmental domination is a multifaceted phenomenon that includes the political, economic, and cultural forces through which human beings (a) dominate "nature" understood as Earth's more-than-human parts; and (b) are themselves dominated in terms of both (i) the special burdens placed on poor and marginalized people with respect to environmental harms, and (ii) the ways that virtually all of us—even privileged people in the world's most affluent societies—are confined and exploited by forces that degrade the Earth, often in our names and with our participation. (Krause 2019, 2)

To begin our discussion here, it is necessary for us to determine what the concept of environmental domination does and does not mean. The discussion which follows the above quoted passage gives us a clear sense of those "special burdens" borne by the poor, something that has been captured in the idea of environmental justice. However, the last part of the passage is particularly troublesome, because the reference is to all people. And in Krause's full article we never (if I read it correctly) get an adequate sense as to what "the forces that degrade the Earth" actually are. Moreover, we get no better idea about what the all-encompassing term "degrade" means or good examples to illustrate its meaning.

Krause writes (p. 3): "Domination means being in a position of systematic vulnerability to unchecked power and exploitation." I can accept this definition as it applies over the longer course of human political history and persists today as a continuation of practices which originated once larger-scale settled societies were formed in the ancient world. The key developments were the domestication of animals for food and the cultivation of plants in agriculture, taking hold in the Middle East between the years10,000 and 5000 BCE. By the time of the Bronze Age (3000 BCE), the rulers among the Sumerians, Assyrians, and Egyptians were oppressing the poor and exploiting their labor to create warring empires.

Krause then writes (p. 4): "*Environmental* domination refers to forms of domination that transpire in and through human interactions with more-than-human parts of nature"(emphasis in original). But Krause never really tells us what domination over "more-than-human parts of nature" *actually means in terms of various actual parts of nature*—which ought to be named—as well as which of those parts are especially important. Following the sentence just quoted, Krause immediately begins a discussion of "how poor and marginalized people disproportionately bear the brunt of environmental damage" and her text then continues in this vein. In this account environmental domination is just another political instrument for exercising control and exploitation of the underclass. That is undeniably so; but to the extent that this is the case, it has nothing to do with domination over "more-than-human parts of nature."

One needs to know: What is domination over nonhuman nature *per se*? How does it manifest itself? We need some clear criteria for telling us what this form of domination is when we see it. For example, I will have to develop at least one criterion here, in the form of a simple measure for which we have reasonably good data—namely, human population growth on the planet.[3] Some current estimates put the human numbers at around the following levels: 8000 BCE, 5 million; 3000 BCE (Bronze Age), 14 million; 1000 BCE, 50 million; 1 CE, 250 million; 1000 CE, 275 million; 1500 CE, 500 million; and finally reaching 1 billion in 1800 CE. (It stands at 7.7 billion today, showing the huge acceleration in the rate of growth [United States Census Bureau 2021].)

In simplistic terms, humans as a distinct species occupy large areas of the globe which were formerly the exclusive domain of "wild" terrestrial animals and, of course, they also make use of its plant and animal resources for themselves and their domesticated animals. So the criterion for domination being developed here has a specific referent, calling attention to the *displacement* of wild animals by humans since the emergence of the species *Homo sapiens* in Africa between 300,000 and 250,000 years ago (Richter et al. 2017). One can then pick, somewhat arbitrarily, a period at which such displacement became so overwhelming for wild nature that it could reasonably be said that thereafter humans were beginning to dominate the most relevant "more-than-human" part of nature, that is, other terrestrial animals. Perhaps, given the size of the planet's land mass (leaving aside the oceans for now), one might say that this date is 1800 CE.

The year 1800 marks, of course, the beginning of what we know as the Industrial Revolution in Europe. And, I suggest, environmental domination *per se* applies only to the period of industrialism in modern history, on account of the huge dimensions in its impacts on the previously extent natural order. And yet, when we focus *only* or even primarily on the intra-human consequences of domination, as Krause does, are we not compelled to acknowledge that this has been a period of intermittent but steady progress in social relations? For it is precisely during this period that some of the most important aspects of the domination by some humans over others (despotism, bitter poverty and exploitation of the underclass, patriarchy, near-constant warfare) have been powerfully challenged—by thinkers such as Marx and Marcuse, by social democracy, feminism, and other movements—and partially mitigated, admittedly with very different scales of success around the world.

And so, returning to the citation from Krause at the beginning of this section, I suggest that the practices mentioned in b (i) antedate the achievement of any human domination over nature. As to b (ii), it is hard to understand how today's "privileged people" are "confined and exploited" by practices associated with the human domination over nature: What credible evidence is there to support such a claim? Thus I will sum up by arguing here that the ways in which people "are themselves dominated" are entirely independent of the human domination over nature and, strictly speaking, are not relevant to what I have called eco-dominion.[4]

Eco-dominion is now here defined as the ways in which the other wild living species on earth, primarily terrestrial wild plants and animals (excluding microbial life-forms, which are of course fundamentally important to living ecosystems and have major impacts on human life), are being remorselessly pushed to the brink of extinction by the ever-expanding human population.[5] This position in no way disputes the reality of the ongoing oppression by minorities of humans against majorities; it does maintain that the two phenomena are conceptually, historically, and intrinsically different. Domination over nature in the sense just defined is still domination, and Krause's conception—"Domination means being in a position of systematic vulnerability to unchecked power and exploitation"—is accepted here. I also accept Krause's "distinction between domination and perfect control, thus making it possible to understand how human beings can be said to dominate nature even as phenomena such as climate change and superbugs demonstrate the limits of human control." But the form of domination over nature is fundamentally different from what is familiar to us in the ways in which some people come to dominate others over the course of human political history.

THE BIBLICAL CONCEPT OF DOMINION OVER THE EARTH

The powerful language of the *Book of Genesis* is nowhere better illustrated than in the passages used as the epigraph for this chapter (chapter one, verses 26 and 28). Inevitably, this text even made its way into the contemporary controversies over environmental policy: More than 50 years ago the historian Lynn White gave rise to many commentaries on this theme as a result of his widely circulated 1967 article, "The Historical Roots of our Ecological Crisis" (White 1967; see also Williams 1993). Rather than retracing those commentaries, I will pursue just one single line of argument about this key text that is directly relevant to the main theme of this article. That line is the clear emphasis on the *limitation of dominion*, that is, the restriction on its scope to "every living thing that moveth upon the earth." In the concluding section I shall follow this line of argument to the point of basing a modern environmental ethic on it.

In order to pursue this theme one must make use of insights found in the long Christian dogmatic tradition which sought to interpret the meaning of God's gift to humankind of dominion over the earth's living things. First, there is the *Summa Theologica* of Thomas Aquinas, in which Aquinas, referencing Aristotle, is careful to justify the dominion of humans over animals by referring to a hierarchy of reason within God's creation. He then explains the purpose for which dominion over animals was granted:

> So in the state of innocence man had mastership over the animals by commanding them. But of the natural powers and the body itself man is master not by commanding, but by using them. Thus also in a state of innocence man's mastership over plants and inanimate things consisted not in commanding or in changing them, but in making use of them without hindrance. (Aquinas 1981, I: 486ff.; Asselin 1954)

This emphasis on what we might call the "right of use" is further explained in John Calvin's commentary on these passages in the *Book of Genesis* (Calvin, no date):

> *And let them have dominion*: Here he commemorates that part of dignity with which he decreed to honor man, namely, that he should have authority over all living creatures. . . . And hence we infer what was the end for which all things

> were created; namely, that none of the conveniences and necessaries of life might be wanting to men (emphasis in original). In the very order of the creation the paternal solicitude of God for man is conspicuous, because he furnished the world with all things needful, and even with an immense profusion of wealth, before he formed man.

Finally, and most clearly, there is Martin Luther's "Commentary on Genesis":

> What use there was of beasts-of-burden, of fishes and of many other animals in the primitive state of creation and of innocency, is impossible for us clearly to determine, sunk as we are in ignorance of God and of his creatures. . . . Unless therefore these same things were in the same use then, we know not why they should have been created, but because we neither have nor see any other use for all these creatures now. . . . Adam and Eve therefore being thus amply provided with food, needed only to use these creatures to excite their admiration and wonder of God, and to create in them that holiness of pleasure, which we never can know in this state of the corruption of our nature. (Luther 2015)

Do these passages represent an internally imposed limitation, either express or implied, on the scope of dominion in the Biblical tradition? There is the contention that humans are entitled to *use* (for the satisfaction of their own needs) the animal resources that they happen to find in the environment around them. (Their entitlement to use plant resources was taken for granted, because plants do not partake of reason, and thus this use did not require any explicit justification; the same would apply by extension to the use of all other natural substances.)

The key Biblical verse makes an explicit reference to cattle, a domesticated species, and we can assume that all other domesticated animals fall under this license. The other specific references are to fish and birds, that is, wild species; so both domesticated and wild animal species are included without exception. But is it likely that, for example, *the right of use* could be considered to be unlimited? Would it extend as far as the right to render various species of wild animals extinct? This does not appear to be a plausible possibility within Christian dogma. If this limitation were to be acknowledged, then, it would follow that habitation sufficient to support the continued viability of wild animal species known in Biblical times must be preserved; in practice this could mean that humans ought to ensure that large areas of the globe would be set aside for this purpose. And since it is relentless human population growth that most directly threatens the availability of sufficient habitat for maintaining the viability of established populations of wild animals, this rule has implications for the self-imposition of population limits by humankind.

The second limitation has to do with the *intensity* of use. Overfishing and excessive despoliation of waterborne mammals such as whales clearly drives the right of use to the point of absurdity or self-cancellation. Third, there is the matter of the *conditions* of use. Something like factory-farming would appear, again, to drive the argument about the legitimacy of use to the breaking point; since all domesticated animals descend from forebears which were once wild, it seems reasonable to insist that we use these animals (pigs, chickens, cattle, goats, sheep, horses, mules, and others) in their natural state, that is, as free-ranging creatures, with sheltering as needed during nighttime or inclement weather and to discourage predators.

It was Francis Bacon who, writing in the early seventeenth century, appropriated this tradition of religious thought and turned it toward a different cause. For a long time Bacon has been justly celebrated as a champion for a new conception of scientific inquiry which would eventually bring into being the modern sciences of nature. He represented the essence of a new form of inquiry as a kind of intelligent human cunning, whereby natural processes must first be observed and documented closely; then the scientist should seek to replicate the process in the laboratory, always seeking reliable evidence of success through repeatable experiments. This is what Galileo had done, first with his new telescope, with which he discovered the moons of Jupiter. This is what two Dutch scientists had done around the same time, when they dropped two lead balls of different weight from the top of the Nieuwe Kirk in Delft, contradicting what had been believed since the time of Aristotle.

I have explored this general theme elsewhere, where I sought to show that Bacon himself always placed his hopes for an enlarged human mastery of nature in the context of traditional Christian thought—specifically, in the creation story in the *Book of Genesis* (Leiss 1972, 2011). Here I would like to emphasize one key point about Bacon's enterprise which is generally less appreciated and which also has a direct bearing on the preceding discussion. Bacon was wary of offending any prevailing religious sensibilities in his hope to re-frame the human relation to nature and orient it from religion to science. So he worked out a strategy of exposition in which he suggested that humanity's "right over nature" had been lost, due to erroneous ways of thinking dominated by scholastic philosophy, and that it therefore needed to be "recovered." And in this venture, the sciences and religion stand shoulder to shoulder:

> I may hand over to men their fortunes, now their understanding is emancipated and come as it were of age; whence there cannot but follow an improvement in man's estate and an enlargement of his power over nature. For man by the fall fell at the same time from his state of innocency and from his domination over creation. Both of these losses however can even in this life be in some part repaired; the former by religion and faith, the latter by arts and sciences. (Bacon 1960, 284 and 267)

And then he went one step further, by implying that humankind's restored "domination over creation" and "enlargement of [its] power over nature" might be misused; or, in other words, that these newly returned powers had to be *superintended*. He put the point in his usual pithy mode of expression: "Only let the human race recover that right over nature which belongs to it by divine bequest, and let power be given it; the exercise thereof will be governed by sound reason and true religion."[6] No clearer statement has ever been made, at least not until the reaction of some scientists to the success of the atom bomb project in 1945, about the need for independent oversight of the creations of the modern natural sciences made in pursuit of the "exercise" of the human "right over nature" (Byers 2002; Leiss 2008). How "sound reason" might help to realize the need for such oversight will be explored in the concluding section.

THE REALIZATION OF DOMINION IN HUMAN POPULATION INCREASE

As mentioned earlier, the global human population had reached 1 billion by the year 1800. The latest United Nations projection for the size of the human population in the year 2100 is about 11 billion (United Nations 2019). This greatly intensified pressure of the human species on the rest of the world's extent animal and plant species is the direct result of the fecund discoveries and applications in science, technologies, and industrialization made since 1800. Above all the product of one such innovation in particular, namely, the Haber–Bosch process for the synthesis of nitrogen from air, achieved in the early decades of the twentieth century and creating the ammonia used in fertilizer, stands out. There are credible estimates that this single innovation's effect on the food supply is responsible for half of the population increase since the beginning of large-scale production of ammonia (Smil 2001; Erisman et al. 2008).

In effect humans have been engaged in the process of crowding out wild species of animals and plants. The terrible devastation caused by clearing and burning in tropical forests in South America and Southeast Asia is only the most recent in a long series of such transformations of the natural environment. The chemist Paul J. Crutzen first popularized the term "Anthropocene," referring to it as a distinct period—dating from the onset of the Industrial Revolution—during which our species has become so dominant on the planet as to be responsible for a transition to a new geological epoch.[7] The major threats to other life-forms at present, caused by habitat destruction and other factors, involve loss of biodiversity, sharp declines in the population of wild land animals and amphibians, destruction of rainforests and forests, and oceanic acidification.

The sum total of all human impacts on the environment has been called our species' "ecological footprint." Our total demands placed on the store of natural capital (stock of natural resources) can be assessed with respect to the criterion of *sustainability*: Taking both main types of resources, renewable and non-renewable, into account, how likely is it that our current level of demands on resources by the population that exists now, and by further human population increases, can be satisfied from both the planet's regenerative biocapacity and its stock of depleting stores? And for how long into the future? (To be sure, the intensity of average *per capita* demands varies widely across the spectrum of richer and poorer nations.) A consolidated image of our ecological footprint is presented in the idea that at present "1.7 earths" are necessary in order to satisfy total human demands placed on our planet's environmental resources. This means that our present level of demands exceeds the earth's capacity to satisfy them sustainably, that is, indefinitely into the future, and that we are quickly drawing down the accumulated natural capital of the earth—its bioproductivity and stock of non-renewable resources (Mancini et al. 2017). This image also leads to the question as to whether all of these accumulating human impacts may result in what is known as an "ecological collapse," involving a sharp and perhaps sudden reduction in existing biological productivity across the planet as a whole, constraining its carrying capacity for all extant species, including our own.

Recently other scientists have been exploring the concept of "planetary boundaries," a set of nine discrete parameters designed to measure the resilience of the earth's chief biogeophysical systems that sustain human life under present conditions. Their analysis starts with the following observation: "The relatively stable, 11,700-yearlong Holocene epoch is the only state of the ES [Earth System] that we know for certain can support contemporary human societies" (Steffen et al. 2015; see also Lade et al. 2020). Then they ask whether the Holocene earth-system can persist in the face of current human pressures against it, as assessed by measurements in nine dimensions: atmospheric aerosol loading, altered biogeochemical cycles, biosphere integrity, climate change, freshwater use, land-system change, novel entities, ocean acidification, and stratospheric ozone depletion. They regard two of the nine (biosphere integrity and climate change) as "core" or critically important processes. They find that in a total of four of these nine (biogeochemical cycles, biosphere integrity, climate change, and land-system change)—which includes both of the core dimensions—human perturbations may already be pushing the earth-system beyond the boundary zone, the point where it becomes uncertain whether the earth-system that now sustains our species can persist.

THE CRITICAL DIMENSION: BIOMASS

The following definitions of technical terminology are relevant to the discussion in this section: "Anthropomass" is the total physical amount of all humans on earth, "phytomass" is the total amount of living plant matter, and "zoomass" is the total amount of animals. The unit commonly used in making these calculations is "Gt C," which stands for gigatonnes of carbon. Since from the beginning every living things on earth has been a carbon-based life form, this unit provides a convenient comparative measure of the types and totality all life on earth, both past and present. The most careful and complete calculations of the human impact on the earth's biomass have been made by Vaclav Smil who wrote that

> human actions may have thus reduced the biosphere's stock of phytomass by as much as 45 percent during the last two millennia. . . . The global anthropomass surpassed the wild mammalian terrestrial zoomass sometime during the second half of the nineteenth century . . . , by 1900 it was at least 30 percent higher, and . . . by 2000 the zoomass of all wild land mammals was only about a tenth of the global anthropomass. The zoomass of wild vertebrates is now vanishingly small compared to the biomass of domestic animals.[8]

The most recent scientific estimates about the magnitude of the accumulated human impacts on the biosphere, expressed in terms of biomass, are: (1) of all mammals now on earth, 60% are livestock, 36% are humans, and 4% are wild; (2) chickens and other poultry are 70% of all birds, the remaining 30% are wild; (3) since the beginning of human civilization, 83% of wild land mammals and 80% of marine mammals have disappeared (Burgess and Gaines 2018, citing Bar-On et al. 2018). The data is from the most recent scientific calculation in a 2018 journal article published in the *Proceedings of the National Academy of Sciences*; the interested reader should consult Figure 1 in Bar-On et al. 2018, which summarizes the key data in a dramatic graphical format.

The earliest example we have of the human impact on terrestrial wild animals is known as the "megafauna [or quaternary] extinction event," dated roughly from 13,000 to 8000 BCE, that is, through the beginning of the Holocene. Megafauna were large terrestrial land animal species, such as the woolly mammoth, saber-toothed cat, giant hippopotamus, and some hundreds of others, both prey and predators, all of which disappeared from the earth over a relatively short period of time. The causes of the extinction event are thought to be a combination of climate change and human hunting. Much more extreme major events of this type are known from the geological past, especially what are called the five mass extinctions, which were caused by events such as violent and prolonged volcanic eruptions, large asteroid impacts, and sudden climate change. Some scientists contend that a sixth mass extinction is now well under way, and if it is, it will be the first human-caused such event in planetary history. The most conservative estimate of the current species extinction rate in the literature is that "the average rate of vertebrate species loss over the last century is up to 100 times higher than the background rate" (Ceballos et al. 2017; De Vos et al. 2015).

There is a stunning paradox here. From one perspective eco-dominion as defined by the religious tradition—the entitlement to rule over living things—appears to have been wildly successful. From another, we appear to be so thoroughly damaging the Holocene earth-system that has sustained our existence as a species for more than 10,000 years as to call our own future into question. The warnings from scientists in this regard extend across a broad set of causative factors, as listed above, but they are starkest in terms of climate change, including sea-level rise of 10 meters or more if the current trajectory of global greenhouse-gas emissions is not altered (Steffen et al. 2018). On this point Krause (p. 13) commented the following:

> It is worth emphasizing, as Leiss points out, that the domination of nature is not equivalent to full control over it. There is much in nature that we do not control, including many of our own environmental effects, as climate change and superbugs and mass extinctions demonstrate. But domination has never been a matter of perfect control, and it is rarely seamless.

This is potentially misleading with respect to the specific examples chosen. The five major earlier mass extinctions preceded the appearance of *Homo sapiens* on the planet, so they are not relevant; the sixth, however, as noted above, is for the most part (if one accepts the evidence as provided by at least some scientists) human-caused. Existence of superbugs is entirely the result of human mismanagement and misuse of antibiotics we have invented. The climate change some now fear is becoming inevitable is entirely the result of excessive introduction of anthropogenic greenhouse gases into the atmosphere beginning in the late eighteenth century. *Every one of these challenges is potentially under human control.* We have "chosen" not to exercise the self-control which would be necessary to confront and overcome them, although arguably we have adequate means to do so. There are indeed many kinds of natural hazards that are outside our control (earthquakes, hurricanes, and some pathogens, to take a few examples); but even in these cases, we can and do take targeted precautionary and mitigative measures which can substantially reduce the harms they can do, at least in the economically advanced nations.

Anthropogenic climate change, if it is not checked, and so produces significant rises in sea-levels and drastic reductions in the human food supply from extreme heat, will force hundreds of millions, perhaps billions, of people, to flee the territory they now occupy. Many or most of them will not survive this experience. This somber future scenario, should it transpire, could have been avoided, had earlier generations—which possessed knowledge and resources sufficient for the task—decided to take the necessary steps. The scientific scenarios state clearly that these devastating impacts, which are expected to be occurring by year 2100 or sooner, will persist and perhaps intensify *for centuries to come.*[9] Should all of this unfold as predicted, a devastating impact on human population numbers will be the result.

AN ENVIRONMENTAL ETHICS FOR THE PASSING OF ECO-DOMINION

In her conclusions Krause takes the broad conception of environmental domination and asks what changes need to be made in current institutions and practices in order to bring about "a politics of environmental non-domination." Because the conception is so broad, the solutions are correspondingly extensive. They include: decentralizing the economy and restricting the roles of large corporations; introducing checks on the power of states; granting inherent rights to non-human entities, enshrined in constitutional protections, as well as creating many mechanisms of formal representation of their interests in all forms of governance and decision-making; but also new "cultural orientations that refuse the instrumentalization of people and nature and that reject white supremacy, patriarchy, and colonialism." What is implied is that an artful combination of direct (granting of rights) and indirect (combatting colonialism) measures will bring about the desired end-state. All of this together amounts to "a politics of emancipation in the sense that it involves releasing nature and people from unconstrained, exploitative human power."[10]

The number of steps on this agenda is simply far too long, and covers far too diverse a set of requirements, to hold much hope of success in any reasonably foreseeable future. Men and women have been struggling against corporate power since the last quarter of the nineteenth century, and yet it is today more dominant in national economies than it has ever been. White supremacy and colonialism have been and still are central features of the entirety of modern history. Finally, there are few signs at present that state power is diminishing, if one's purview is the world as a whole. Only the idea of constitutional protections for the rights of non-human entities is new, a product of the last 50 years; but whatever the successes that may be counted on this front, they have made no discernable improvements on the treatment of non-human living organisms. To be sure, this whole agenda is worthy of respect from the standpoint of human freedom and dignity. However, all of it (with the sole exception of constitutional protections) could be achieved *without necessarily making any difference at all so far as the human relation to non-human nature is concerned.* Moreover, it seems obvious that this is an ongoing project, centuries-long in the making, and even the most sanguine observer must concede that no point of successful conclusion can yet be glimpsed.

There is another relevant consideration here. Let us suppose that this agenda does actually work across the board. That is, suppose that progress is made against corporate power, oppressive state power, white supremacy, colonialism, and the rest of the mission known as "the politics of environmental non-domination." The conditions of the poor and marginalized populations across the world will be improved—which would be, in and of itself, a very good thing. Human societies in the less economically developed regions, for example, those in Africa and Asia, will be strengthened, in terms of social solidarity, and become more prosperous over time. The end result is likely to be a great expansion, not a diminution, of the human pressure on wild nature, especially its animal species. The problems identified in the concept of environmental domination will worsen in proportion to the success of the political agenda that is supposed to cure them.

For now the relentless expansion of the human population proceeds apace. A tighter focus on the core issue in the human relation to non-human nature is essential. That core issue, I have argued, is our relation to other living things and the ecosystems that sustain them. Nothing else matters much, because "domination" over the rest of the non-human environment is, strictly speaking, meaningless. Our ability to *utilize* the resources of the natural environment as a whole has been immeasurably enlarged via the innovations of science, technology, and industry. But this more adept and cunning (to recall Francis Bacon's formulation) orientation to nature raises, so far as I can see, no fundamental ethical issues, with the sole and important exception that pollution and environmental damages more generally have significant adverse impacts on wildlife as well as humans. Those are the impacts we should focus our attention on.

Earlier it was suggested that eco-dominion, conceived of as the right of use by humans of the other species of animals on the planet (and by extension its plant resources), should not be considered to be an unlimited entitlement. Three propositions limiting this entitlement were advanced. The first is that the right of use cannot plausibly be extended as far as rendering various species of wild animals extinct; it follows that sufficient habitation needed to support the wild animals existent in modern times must be preserved, and in practice this means that humans ought to ensure that large areas of the globe are set aside for this purpose. The second limitation has to do with the intensity of use, a principle that would ban, for example, overfishing and the excessive killing of waterborne mammals such as whales. The third limitation has to do with the conditions of use. Something like factory-farming should not be permitted, for example. Since all domesticated animals are descended from forebears that were once wild, animals should be used in their natural state, that is, as free-ranging creatures. We might refer to these three propositions collectively as an ethic of responsible use.

Taken together, these three propositions both severely restrict the scope of what Francis Bacon calls the human "right over nature" (confining it to the lordship over animals and exempting the planetary environment *per se*) and demand specific changes to the prevailing human modes of action that carry, admittedly, profound and massive implications for human life. For human beings to retreat from entering or exploiting vast tracts of the planetary land surface, and to reduce drastically their appropriation of marine life, say by allowing only near-shore fishing, means a substantial reduction in their consumption of animal protein. Doing away entirely with the daily, lifelong confinement of domestic animals in large enclosures, and stipulating that only small-scale, free-range operations would be permitted, would likewise mean that there would follow radical reductions in the human production and consumption of animal protein. But the inefficiency of producing protein from domesticated animals (which is *20 to 100* times less efficient than sourcing it directly from plant-based foods) is well-known (Gardner et al. 2019; Clark and Tilman 2017). From these changes would follow a drastic lowering of the environmental impacts of human food production and, as an obvious consequence, also would have very large implications for human numbers.

The overall result would turn most or substantially all of humans into vegetarians or vegans, something that has been a choice or necessity for many Hindus for a very long time. It is a lifestyle that ought to be sustainable—in terms of minimizing the ecological footprint of human societies—indefinitely into the future.

So far as our fellow animals are concerned, an orientation that seeks to minimize, rather than maximize, the extinction pressures and adverse living conditions imposed by humans on them will require a rules-based order to codify the new principles of action. Such a scheme was first worked out in detail by Paul Taylor in his book *Respect for Nature* (1986). Taylor developed the "rule of noninterference," stipulating that "with regard to animals and plants living in the wild," we humans should "constantly place constraints on ourselves so as to cause the least possible interference in natural ecosystems and their biota" (Taylor 1986, 309–310). Another elegant construction along these lines is contained in the idea of establishing various types of citizenship for animals laid down by Donaldson and Kymlicka in their well-known 2011 work, *Zoopolis* (also Kymlicka and Donaldson 2014; Edmundson 2015). In this, or in some other more effective way, thc intimate connection between humans, and both wild and domesticated animal species, could become a kind of explicitly "managed" relationship, less spontaneous, perhaps, that an unmanaged one, but likely to be more secure for the weaker partner over the long term. (This does not mean that other forms of nonhuman nature, such as ancient plant cultivars and distinctive ecosystems, could not be granted special status, either legal or otherwise.[11])

But in reality the human pressures on the habitats of wild animals are now, however, reaching a critical stage. Much damage is being inflicted by poaching even within protected reserves, especially in Africa. Many wild animal species require very large ranges in order to flourish in their natural state, but instead the available spaces are shrinking almost everywhere on the globe. An ideal solution would be to design large spaces that would be almost entirely free from human ingress, possibly with limited access allocated to aboriginal peoples; but at present it is impossible to imagine how this might actually happen.[12]

Should humans be able to overcome the looming existential crisis they now face, rooted in the devastating impacts of climate change which are expected to play out over the coming centuries, their numbers would be likely to continue to increase indefinitely. They will then pretty much complete the dominion they exercise over the other living things of the earth, whose territory will be largely reduced to scattered zoos, reserves, and parks.[13] But at some point human numbers may crash, as often happens in animal population dynamics in a process known as "overshoot and collapse" (Cumming and Peterson 2017). This might occur for our own species if our descendants do not succeed in overcoming the climate change crisis, or for some other reason. In either case the survivors may seize the opportunity to jettison their ultimately self-defeating attempt to exert their domination of non-human nature through the immense technological power brought by science and industrialism, and to choose a radically different but likely more sustainable course. Then the end of eco-dominion might be visible in the distance.

NOTES

1. One recurring question about the scope of the issue is whether the concept of domination over nature includes human nature. In other words, is the concept

self-reflexive? Is human nature an eternally unchanging phenomenon, whereas the rest of nature changes unceasingly, as is evident? More particularly, does a sense that it is legitimate for human power to change the *extra-human* environment in fundamental ways include a program to tinker with the *intra-human* biological basis of the human mind? For a good discussion of these themes see Biro (2016).

2. The Latin root of the word "domination" is *dominus*, meaning lord or master, with the connotation of absolute authority. "Dominion," however, has much broader connotations. It is derived from the Middle Latin *dominionem* and the Latin *dominium* and *domus*, with meanings of property, ownership, home, and household, as well as subordinate state or nation (as in the former foreign dominions of the British Empire such as Canada), rule and power.

3. There must be other criteria that are relevant for Krause's concept of environmental domination, since that concept refers to the totality of "more-than-human nature." I am not in a position to speculate on what those criteria might be. My own choice of a key criterion (human population growth) is based on the relation between humans and other living creatures.

4. On pages 11–12 of her article Krause reviews my 1972 book, *The Domination of Nature*, and recapitulates my views on this matter there which I later revised (see chapter 6 in William Leiss, *Under Technology's Thumb*). Specifically, I now believe that all of the aspects of the domination of some people over others which she discusses—environmental justice, elite control disguised by formal democracy, elite control over the industrialized economy, false consciousness ("blind domination"), and others—while they are hugely important in other contexts, are not relevant to what I call eco-dominion.

5. The three "kingdoms of life" are eukaryota (multicellular organisms including fungi, plants, animals, and others), bacteria, and archaea.

6. Ibid., p.119; see the commentary in William Leiss, "Dominion over Nature: The Idols of the Tribe," pages 74–90 in *Under Technology's Thumb*. This conception is important enough to justify providing the language of the Latin original: "Recuperet modo genus humanum jus suum in Naturam, quod ei ex dotatione divina competit; & detur ei copia: usum vero recta Ratio, & sana Religio gubernabit." Francisci Baconis, *Novum Organum Scientiarum* 1612, 127.

7. The term "Anthropocene" has not yet received "official" status as a descriptor of a distinct geological age in the planet's history.

8. Smil (2011, 2012); an earlier estimate is found in Vitousek *et al.* (1997, 494–499). A different type of calculation is made in Schramski et al. (2015).

9. "Continued emission of greenhouse gases will cause further warming and long-lasting changes in all components of the climate system, increasing the likelihood of severe, pervasive and irreversible impacts for people and ecosystems. . . . Many aspects of climate change and associated impacts will continue for centuries, even if anthropogenic emissions of greenhouse gases are stopped. The risks of abrupt or irreversible changes increase as the magnitude of the warming increases" (IPCC 2014, 8).

10. Krause, "Environmental Domination," pages 15–19; see also Jamieson and Di Paola (2016) and Dryzek (2016).

11. See the famous 2010 text by Christopher Stone, *Should Trees Have Standing? Law, Morality, and the Environment*. Krause (2019, 16) writes: "A state that is committed to non-domination of both people and the Earth will include a regime of animal and Earth rights alongside its regime of human rights." For just one recent example see O'Donnell andTalbot-Jones (2018).

12. There are many important concepts and arguments relating to this theme in Donaldson and Kymlicka, *Zoopolis*, chapter 6, "Wild Animal Sovereignty," for example: "Thus, recognition of wild animal sovereignty would bring a halt to the human destruction of wild animal habitat" (p. 205).

13. Many zoos seek to preserve the frozen genetic material of endangered animal species (Roth and Swanson 2018). Norway maintains the Svalbard Global Seed Vault in a remote northern location.

REFERENCES

Aquinas, St. Thomas. 1981. *The Summa Theologica*. First Part, Question 96, "The Mastership Belonging to Man in the State of Innocence" I: 486ff. Chicago: Thomas More Press (Convenient Access: http://www.newadvent.org/summa/1096.htm).

Asselin, D. T. 1954. "The Notion of Dominion in Genesis 1–3." *Catholic Biblical Quarterly* XVI: 277–294.

Bacon, Francis. 1960. *The New Organon*. Indianapolis: Bobbs-Merrill.

Baconis, Francisci. 1612. *Novum Organum Scientiarum*. Venice: Gasparis Girardi. https://archive.org/details/1762novumorganum00baco/page/n4/mode/2up (accessed August 5, 2021).

Bar-On, Y. M., Rob Phillips, and Ron Milo. 2018. "The Biomass Distribution on Earth." *Proceedings of the National Academy of Sciences* 115 (25): 6506–6511 and "Supplementary Information Appendix." https://doi.org/10.1073/pnas.1711842115 (accessed August 5, 2021).

Biro, Andrew. 2016. "Human Nature, Non-human Nature, and Needs." In *The Oxford Handbook of Environmental Political Theory*, edited by T. Gabrielson, C. Hall, J. M. Meyer, and D. Schlosberg. Oxford: Oxford University Press.

Burgess, Matthew G., and Steven D. Gaines. 2018. "The Scale of Life and Its Lessons for Humanity." *Proceedings of the National Academy of Sciences* 115 (25): 6328–6330. https://doi.org/10.1073/pnas.1807019115 (accessed August 5, 2021).

Byers, Nina. 2002. "Physicists and the Decision to Drop the Atomic Bomb." Cornell University, arXiv.org. https://arxiv.org/abs/physics/0210058 (accessed August 5, 2021).

Calvin, John. *Commentary on Genesis—Volume 1, Chapter 1*. Christian Classics Ethereal Library. http://btsfreeccm.org/ pluginfile.php/22760/mod_resource/content/6/Commentary%20Genesis.pdf (accessed August 5, 2021).

Ceballos, G., Paul R. Ehrlich, and Rodolfo Dirzo. 2017. "Biological Annihilation Via the Ongoing Sixth Mass Extinction Signaled by Vertebrate Population Losses and Declines." *Proceedings of the National Academy of Sciences* 114 (10 July):

E6089–E6096. https://doi.org/10.1073/ pnas.1704949114 (accessed August 5, 2021).

Clark, Michael, and David Tilman. 2017. "Comparative Analysis of Environmental Impacts of Agricultural Production Systems, Agricultural Input Efficiency, and Food Choice." *Environmental Research Letters* 12: 064016. https://iopscience.iop.org/article/10.1088/1748-9326/aa6cd5/meta (accessed August 5, 2021).

Cumming, G. S., and G. D. Peterson. 2017. "Unifying Research on Social-Ecological Resilience and Collapse." *Trends in Ecology and Evolution* 32: 695–713.

De Vos, J. M., Lucas N. Joppa, John L. Gittleman, Patrick R. Stephens, and Stuart L. Pimm. 2014. "Estimating the Normal Background Rate of Species Extinction." *Conservation Biology* 29 (2): 452–462. https://doi.org/10.1111/cobi.12380 (accessed August 5, 2021).

Donaldson, Sue, and Will Kymlicka. 2011. *Zoopolis: A Political Theory of Animal Rights*. Oxford: Oxford University Press.

Dryzek, John S. 2016. "Global Environmental Governance." In *The Oxford Handbook of Environmental Political Theory*, edited by T. Gabrielson, C. Hall, J. M. Meyer, and D. Schlosberg. Oxford: Oxford University Press.

Edmundson, William A. 2015. "Do Animals Need Citizenship?" *International Journal of Constitutional Law* 13 (3): 749–765.

Erisman, J., Mark A. Sutton, James Galloway, Zbigniew Klimont, and Wilfried Winiwarter. 2008. "How a Century of Ammonia Synthesis Changed the World." *Nature Geosciences* 1: 636–639. https://doi.org/10.1038/ngeo325 (accessed August 5, 2021).

Gardner, C. C., Jennifer C. Hartle, Rachael D. Garrett, Lisa C. Offringa, and Arlin S. Wasserman. 2019. "Maximizing the Intersection of Human Health and the Health of the Environment With Regard to the Amount and Type of Protein Produced and Consumed in the United States." *Nutrition Reviews* 77 (4): 197–215.

Intergovernmental Panel on Climate Change. 2014. *Climate Change 2014: Synthesis Report.* Geneva, Switzerland: Intergovernmental Panel on Climate Change. https://ar5-syr.ipcc.ch/ipcc/ipcc/resources/pdf/IPCC_SynthesisReport.pdf (accessed August 5, 2021).

Jamieson, D. W., and M. Di Paola. 2016. "Political Theory for the Anthropocene." In *Global Political Theory*, edited by D. Held and P. Maffettone. Cambridge: Polity Press.

Krause, Sharon R. 2019. "Environmental Domination."*Political Theory* 4 (December 2): 1–26. https://doi.org/10.1177/ 0090591719890833 (accessed August 5, 2021).

Kymlicka, Will, and Sue Donaldson. 2014. "Animals and the Frontiers of Citizenship." *Oxford Journal of Legal Studies* 34, no. 2: 201–219. https://doi.org/10.1093/ojls/gqu001 (accessed August 5, 2021).

Lade, S. J., Will Steffen, Wim De Vries, Stephen R. Carpenter, Jonathan F. Donges, Dieter Gerten, Holger Hoff, Tim Newbold, Katherine Richardson, and Johan Rockström. 2020. "Human Impacts on Planetary Boundaries Amplified by Earth System Interactions." *Nature Sustainability* 3: 119–128. https://doi.org/10.1038/s41893-019-0454-4 (accessed August 5, 2021).

Leiss, William. 1972. *The Domination of Nature.* New York: Braziller.

Leiss, William. 1990. *Under Technology's Thumb*. Montreal: McGill-Queen's University Press.

Leiss, William. 2008. *The Priesthood of Science*. Ottawa: University of Ottawa Press.

Leiss, William. 2011. "Modern Science, Enlightenment, and the Domination of Nature: No Exit?" In *Critical Ecologies*, edited by Andrew Biro. Toronto: University of Toronto Press.

Luther, Martin. 2015. *Commentary on Genesis, Volume 1*. Section 16. Project Luther's Commentaries on Genesis. https://www.gutenberg.org/files/48193/48193-h/48193-h.htm#sect16 (accessed August 5, 2021).

Mancini, M. S., Alessandro Galli, Valentina Niccolucci, David Lin, Laurel Hanscom, Mathis Wackernagel, Simone Bastianoni, and Nadia Marchettini. 2017. "Stocks and Flows of Natural Capital: Implications for Ecological Footprint." *Ecological Indicators* 77: 123–128. https://doi.org/10.1016/j.ecolind.2017.01.033 (accessed August 5, 2021).

O'Donnell, E. L., and J. Talbot-Jones. 2018. "Creating Legal Rights for Rivers: Lessons From Australia, New Zealand, and India." *Ecology and Society* 23 (1): 7. https://doi.org/10.5751/ES-09854-230107 (accessed August 5, 2021).

Richter, D., Rainer Grün, Renaud Joannes-Boyau, Teresa E. Steele, Fethi Amani, Mathieu Rué, Paul Fernandes, et al. 2017. "The Age of the Hominin Fossils From Jebel Irhoud, Morocco, and the Origins of the Middle Stone Age."*Nature* 546: 293–296. https://doi.org/:10.1038/nature22335 (accessed August 5, 2021).

Roth, T. L., and W. F. Swanson. 2018. "From Petri Dishes to Politics – A Multi-Pronged Approach is Essential for Saving Endangered Species." *Nature Communications* 9: 2588. https://doi.org/10.1038/s41467-018-04962-7 (accessed August 5, 2021).

Schramski, John R., David K. Gattie, and James H. Brown. "Human Domination of the Biosphere: Rapid Discharge of the Earth-Space Battery Foretells the Future of Humankind." *Proceedings of the National Academy of Sciences* 112 (31): 9511–9517. https://doi.org/10.1073/pnas.1508353112 (accessed August 5, 2021).

Smil, Vaclav. 2001. *Enriching the Earth: Fritz Haber, Carl Bosch and the Transformation of World Food Production*. Cambridge, MA: MIT Press.

Smil, Vaclav. 2011. "Harvesting the Biosphere: The Human Impact." *Population and Development Review* 37 (4): 613–636. https://doi.org/10.1111/j.1728-4457.2011.00450.x (accessed August 5, 2021).

Smil, Vaclav. 2012. *Harvesting the Biosphere*. Cambridge, MA: MIT Press.

Steffen, Will, Johan Rockström, Katherine Richardson, Timothy M. Lenton, Carl Folke, Diana Liverman, Colin P. Summerhayes, et al. 2018. "Trajectories of the Earth System in the Anthropocene." *Proceedings of the National Academy of Sciences* 115 (14 August): 1259825-1–1259825-10 and "Appendix: Supporting Information: Holocene Variability and Anthropocene Rates of Change." https://doi.org/10.1073/ pnas.1810141115 (accessed August 5, 2021).

Steffen, Will, Katherine Richardson, Johan Rockström, Sarah E. Cornell, Ingo Fetzer, Elena M. Bennett, Reinette Biggs, et al. 2015. "Planetary Boundaries: Guiding

Human Development on a Changing Planet." *Science* 347 (6223): 8352–8359. https://doi.org/10.1126/science.1259855 (accessed August 5, 2021).

Stone, Christopher. 2010. *Should Trees Have Standing? Law, Morality, and the Environment*. Oxford: Oxford University Press.

Taylor, Paul W. 1986. *Respect for Nature: A Theory of Environmental Ethics*. Princeton: Princeton University Press.

United Nations, Department of Social and Economic Affairs. 2019. "World Population Prospects 2019." https://population.un.org/wpp/Graphs/Probabilistic/POP/TOT/900 (accessed August 5, 2021)

United States, Bureau of the Census. "Historical Estimates of World Population." https://www.census.gov/data/tables/time-series/demo/international-programs/historical-est-worldpop.html (accessed August 5, 2021).

Vitousek, P., Harold A. Mooney, Jane Lubchenco, and Jerry M. Melillo. 1997. "Human Domination of Earth's Ecosystems." *Science* 227: 494–499.

White, Lynn. 1967. "The Historical Roots of Our Ecological Crisis." *Science* 155: 1203–1207.

Williams, D. T. 1993. "Fill the Earth and Subdue It." *Scriptura* 44: 51–65.

Chapter 11

Engineering Ethics

A Narrative Reflection

Carl Mitcham

PREFACE

It was as a graduate student that I first benefited from Frederic Fleron's knowledge and collegiality, as I was beginning to explore philosophical issues related to technology. He was not my professor; our contact was simply by old fashioned written correspondence. His willingness to take time to share and help educate me about philosophical discussions of technology in the Soviet Union was exceptional and I have always remained personally edified and grateful. Because of this personal connection, I venture to offer this Festschrift an atypical contribution: a critical reflection on one aspect of my intellectual career. Perhaps it can serve as a background or counterpoint to his own. I thank editor Guoli Liu for inviting me to contribute.

My earliest efforts to think philosophically about technology included thinking about engineering, influenced by the fact that my father was a professional mechanical engineering with Otis Elevator Company. In 1852 it was Elasha Otis who invented the fail-safe elevator, a key enabler of skyscraper urbanization and archetype expression of an engineering ethical commitment to safety. My earliest efforts to think about engineering ethics also related this thinking to broader questions of ethics and politics of technology. The itinerary, however, has been circuitous and problematic.

BECOMING PHILOSOPHICAL IN A TECHNO-ENGINEERING AGE

In a 1960 lecture on "Philosophy and the Scientific Image of Man," Wilfrid Sellars began by declaring that "The aim of philosophy, abstractly formulated, is to understand how things in the broadest possible sense of the term hang together in the broadest possible sense of the term." His focus was on how the manifest or common understanding of what it is to be human (free will and all that) can hang together with the scientific understanding (determinism and more).

Sellars exemplified a dominant effort in the mid-twentieth-century American philosophical community that recognized science as the defining feature of modernity. During the same decade, however, I became convinced that it was not science but technology that was more important—indeed, that many changes often attributed to science (from electric lights to airplanes and nuclear energy) were more properly attributed to technology. Scientists often marshaled public support for their research by citing the much more recognizable mirror-image twin of technological product development.

This early interest in taking technology as a philosophical theme at least comparable to science met with limited receptivity in philosophical departments in the different universities (University of Colorado, Western Reserve, Stanford, Brandeis, Fordham) where I bounced around as an undergraduate and then graduate student. But a fellow student at Stanford (Robert Mackey) was sympathetic—and, amazingly enough, a few historians and engineers. Historians of technology and socially conscious engineers were more open to discussion of philosophical issues related to technology than most philosophers. Among historians of technology, Melvin Kranzberg, founding editor of the Society for the History of Technology journal *Technology and Culture*, played a decisive role. One of the most influential engineers was George Bugliarello who in 1973, while Dean of Engineering at the University of Illinois Chicago Circle, invited Mackey and me to participate in the first American conference on the History and Philosophy of Technology. A few years later, Bugliarello, having become President of Brooklyn Polytechnic Institute (later Polytechnic University), recruited me to the faculty there. Once in New York City, I met Professor Stephen Unger, an electrical engineer at Columbia University, who introduced me to the engineering ethics field.

BROOKLYN POLYTECHNIC YEARS

Engineering ethics seemed a convenient entre into philosophy of technology. An early statement of this interpretation, a brief article on "Industrial and Engineering Ethics" (1985), argued that technology was transforming the scope of ethics and stimulating development of various fields of applied ethics; engineering ethics was framed as a case in point. But as a form of professional ethics, engineering ethics remained mostly "internalist" in its concern for professional standards and conduct (such as protecting safety), kickbacks, and whistle blowing. An implication was that such a focus was too narrow.

Through Unger I discovered a debate taking place in the Institute of Electrical and Electronic Engineers (IEEE), the largest professional engineering society in the world, about professional engineering ethics codes and responsibilities, as well as in the Accreditation Board for Engineering and Technology (ABET) about whether engineering ethics should be a required component of engineering programs. When teaching my first course on engineering ethics at Brooklyn Poly in the mid-1980s, I used Unger's *Controlling Technology: Ethics and the Responsible Engineer* (1982) at the basic text—complemented with references to more general arguments by such philosophers as Hans Jonas, Langdon Winner, and Albert Borgmann. The approach was emphasized in a piece contributed to the lay Catholic public affairs magazine *Commonweal*—"Schools for Whistle Blowers: Educating Ethical Engineers" (1987)—which included a lengthy sidebar on "The Ethics of Science and Technology Studies." The following year, at a workshop on "Science, Engineering, and Ethics" organized by the American Association for the Advancement of Science (AAAS), Stephen Cutcliffe and Steve Goldman, two professors in the Lehigh University Science, Technology, and Society (STS) Program, distinguished two approaches to teaching ethics and values in undergraduate STS programs.

> The first is that of engineering ethics. The second includes more general examinations of values and their relationships to technological based choices. (Cutcliffe and Goldman 1988, p. 9)

Subsequently, in a general review of STS course development over the previous two decades, Cutcliffe noted how academics had "approached teaching [STS and ethics] in a variety of ways."

> Closest to the straight engineering ethics approach . . . are those courses that start with an analysis of classical value theories—natural law, utilitarianism, concepts of justice—and then proceed to apply this to specific contemporary problems, again often using a case study method. A typical example is the course taught by Carl Mitcham, of Polytechnic University of New York, entitled "Ethics and Technology," which is distinct from his "Engineering Ethics" course. . . . Mitcham's course focuses, in its final third, on a single problem area that exemplifies the general value concepts introduced—topics have included computer ethics, bioethics, and nuclear weapons. (Cutcliffe 1990, p. 366)

At the AAAS workshop there was general agreement that science, engineering, and ethics courses needed to become

- more interdisciplinary,
- more integrated into the undergraduate curriculum, and
- not too narrowly focused on professional issues alone.

Less acknowledged was any need to engage with the philosophy of technology more generally, that is, to go beyond questions of ethics and social relationships to issues of ontology and epistemology.

FROM SCIENCE, TECHNOLOGY, AND SOCIETY TO SCIENCE AND TECHNOLOGY STUDIES

From the mid-1980s to the mid-1990s was a golden age of Science, Technology, and Society Programs, which initially aspired to function as a new approach to the teaching of what was often called *scientific and technological literacy*. The goal was two-fold: educating science and engineering students to better appreciate the social contexts of their work and non-science majors to better appreciate science and technology as dominant elements in the modern world. Many early STS programs were housed in or closely associated with engineering programs and became loci for ethical and philosophical discussions of engineering.

My own educational engagement with this interdisciplinary field—which included the history, sociology, and philosophy of science and technology—was initially mediated by historian Cutcliffe and philosopher Goldman at Lehigh and then by materials scientist Rustum Roy, a member of the National Academy of Engineering. Roy was another good example of the greater openness to philosophy of technology among engineers than among philosophers.

Two other Penn State STS professors who further opened up this interdisciplinary framework for me and thus influenced some attempts to think engineering ethics as a dimension of technological literacy were William F. Williams, a Visiting Professor of Physics Emeritus from Leeds University in the UK, and Leonard Waks, a Professor of Education. Williams had served as editor-in-chief of the "Science in a Social Context" series of teaching modules published in England. We wound up collaborating on a couple of textbook type reference works in which we infused chapters on ethical issues involved with science, technology, and engineering (Mitcham and Williams 1994; Williams 2000). Waks introduced me to the educational research field and we collaborated on a couple of NSF funded projects to develop more effective introductions to science courses for non-scientists in which we included ethical and policy questions. Together Roy, Williams, and Waks all thought engineering ethics should not be limited to engineers but function within a larger STS context.

As STS flourished, however, it divided into two camps: Those who saw STS primarily as an interdisciplinary contribution to undergraduate general education and those who envisioned a more scholarly, discipline-like program of graduate-level education and research. The first approach centered around the *Bulletin of Science, Technology, and Society* (1981–present) and the National Association for Science, Technology, and Society (from 1983 to early 2000s), both founded by Roy. The second approach re-interpreted the acronym STS as "Science and Technology Studies," privileging social studies of science and technology and a research program often termed "social constructionism." This approach became centered around the journal *Science, Technology, and Human Values* (founded 1975) and the associated Society for the Social Studies of Science (4S).

During my concluding years at Brooklyn Poly and during all ten years at Penn State University the tension between these two approaches was in the background of my teaching and research in engineering ethics. On the one hand, I was critical of the academicization of Science and Technology Studies. I tended to agree with the "social worker thesis" argued by Paul Durbin (1992). Just as social workers have, beyond obligations to behave professionally, further responsibilities to try to change things for the better, so do other professionals such as engineers. On the other, I was attracted by the philosophical challenges of ideas in and arguments among multiple versions of social constructionism.

PENN STATE YEARS

After relocating to Pennsylvania State University in 1989, efforts to deepen engineering ethics continued across a number of fronts. To begin with, my new engineering ethics class shifted from using Unger as its primary text to adoption of Mike Martin and Roland Schinzinger's *Ethics in Engineering* (first edition, 1983; second edition, 1989).

Both the Unger and Martin-Schinzinger textbooks had grown out of the authors' involvement in a "National Project on Philosophy and Engineering Ethics" supported by the National Endowment for the Humanities and based at Rensselaer Polytechnic Institute, 1978–1980 (see Flores 1977). This project funded teams of philosophers and engineers to collaborate in addressing the perceived need for more truly interdisciplinary work. Unger worked with philosopher Tom Rogers, whose influence can be seen in *Controlling Technology*, but who ultimately left philosophy to become a lawyer. Martin was a philosopher at Chapman College (now University); Schinzinger an electrical engineer at the University of California, Irvine. Their book broke new ground in engineering ethics by exploring how the principle of free and informed consent, as developed in human subjects research, might apply to engineering practice. They argued that in many respects engineering involved experimentation on a societal scale. "We believe that the problem of informed consent, which is so vital to the concept of a properly conducted experiment involving human subjects, should be the keystone in the interaction between engineers and the public" (Martin and Schinzinger 1983, p. 60).

The Martin-Schinzinger informed consent thesis, having emerged from an extended collaboration between a philosopher and an engineer, deepened the philosophical character of engineering ethics. What for Unger had been the heart of engineering ethics—that is, engineering professionalism and ethics codes—was taken up into broader questions. While their book continued to place a significant emphasis on engineers, Martin and Schinzinger maintained that "the ethics of engineering is wider in scope than the ethics of engineers" (1983, p. 3). For instance, it introduced epistemological issues of risk assessment—for example, as analyzed in the work of Kristin Shrader-Frechette (1984, 1985)—into the center of engineering ethics. Yet insofar as such philosophical issues were acknowledged, engineering ethics courses became less attractive to engineering programs. They were too philosophical, not practical enough. At least that was my experience when, in the early 1990s, I began teaching engineering ethics at Penn State through the STS Program.

Shortly after arriving at Penn State, having been recruited by Roy as his successor, I was appointed the new director of its STS Program. At the same time the program was shifted from being grouped with a cluster of interdisciplinary programs reporting directly to the Provost and relocated in the College of Engineering. This created new tensions to complicate those already present in the two approaches to STS: the need to meet the needs of engineering students for relevant social science and humanities classes in something like professional education courses versus a desire to engage engineering through broad philosophical questioning.

A second front in my effort to deepen engineering ethics involved criticizing the parochialism of American engineering ethics by exploring engineering ethics codes from the perspective of a wider cultural geography. At the juncture of my transition from Brooklyn Poly to Penn State I received a grant from the National Science Foundation Ethics and Values Studies Program for research on "Engineering Ethics Outside the United States." The goal was to collect and analyze engineering ethics codes of professional engineering societies from as many other countries as possible. The product of this research was a privately published collection of engineering ethics codes and related materials with introductory analysis and supplementary annotated bibliography (Mitcham 1992). A modestly updated version of this collection of codes was subsequently included as an appendix in the *Encyclopedia of Science, Technology, and Ethics* (Mitcham 2005).

An associated outcome of this research called attention to the fact that not all engineering ethics was based on strictly secular ideals. There were religious (especially Christian and Jewish) dimensions especially to technology and ethics.

Still a third front in thinking engineering ethics at Penn State came in the form of a direct challenge from Ivan Illich, a close personal colleague from the 1980s until his death in 2002. Roy, again illustrating an engineer's receptivity to radical social criticism, had brought Illich to Penn State a few years prior to my arrival. From the 1970s Illich had made a frontal intellectual assault on the whole concept of professionalization, which he argued was largely just an ideological subterfuge to defend class power. Trying to come to terms with this criticism destabilized my work in engineering ethics in ways that have continued into the present. Even though I do not completely buy Illich's perspective, I cannot help but see the force of his ideas. Finally, a fourth front at Penn State was an effort to write a textbook on engineering ethics that brought some new issues into the discussion. The result was *Engineer's Toolkit: Engineering Ethics*, coauthored with a colleague in the Penn State Department of Philosophy (Mitcham and Duval 2000) as a not very successful module in a set of modules designed to be mixed as appropriate for general introduction to engineering courses. Looking back now, the most original sections of this volume may have been criticism not just ethical relativism but also absolutism (fanaticism) and an argument for the moral practice of compromise. That slight volume also introduced questions of engineering aesthetics.

COLORADO SCHOOL OF MINES YEARS

In the fall semester 1999 I moved west, from the super-sized, land-grant Penn State multiversity (~50K students) to a much more human-scale and educationally focused Colorado School of Mines (CSM, ~3K students, at that time).

At the 1988 AAAS workshop, a Fund for the Improvement for Post-Secondary Education (FIPSE) representative described some approaches to broadening professional education being supported by this institution. Because of a belief that technical professional "students cannot perform well in their jobs without proper knowledge of culture and society," FIPSE had a funding program called "Professional Education and Liberal Study."

> One example is the Colorado School of Mines, which has assumed that mining engineering is a declining industry in the United States. If they are going to continue to train mining engineers, their engineers and graduates are likely to

> be employed in the third world. And if mining engineers are going to function well in the third world, they need to know about third world cultures, political systems, language, and social processes. They are particularly focused on culture and politics of South American countries at the Colorado School of Mines. (Frankel 1988, p. 91)

This FIPSE grant helped establish a new academic unit named International Studies which, by the time I arrived, had been combined with another service unit into Liberal Arts and International Studies.

Because of the new ABET 2000 criteria (which now included professional ethics education as an accreditation requirement) and a looming ABET assessment exercise in 2001–2002, I was hired with a remit to establish an ethics across the curriculum program. One interpretation of the long difficult effort to establish an EAC program at CSM has been described elsewhere (Mitcham and Engelhardt 2016) and need not be repeated here. The bottom line is that I failed to make the kind of diplomatic alliances with the international political economy program and other campus efforts that might have led to early success. There were numerous missed opportunities. I also never succeeded in creating at CSM a stand-alone engineering ethics course, although I'm less sure this was a serious loss.

More positively, engineering ethics work at CSM involved

- contributions to creation of one of the first humanitarian engineering programs,
- explorations in the ethical dimensions of engineering design,
- arguments for engineering politics and policy as necessary extensions to ethics, and
- efforts to synthesize the ethics of engineering and science.

All of these activities continued to expand and deepen the scope and practice of engineering ethics.

The humanitarian engineering program emerged from teaching a required, first year writing intensive course called Nature and Human Values (Mitcham and Sacks 2001). Some issues related to this broad, alternative approach to engineering ethics are covered in the small volume *Humanitarian Engineering* (Mitcham and Muñoz 2010).

What has been called the empirical turn in the philosophy of technology, strongly associated with the philosophy program at the Delft University of Technology in the Netherlands, began in the early 2000s to highlight the problematics of engineering design. Independently, I began trying to think about engineering design and design in general as a distinctively modern form of human action (see, e.g., Mitcham 1994, 1995, 2001).

Partly though the influence of Robert Frodeman—who, during our collaboration bounced from the U.S. Geological Survey (USGS) to the Center for Science and Technology Policy Research at the University of Colorado, to the Colorado School of Mines, and finally to the University of North Texas—I began to connect engineering ethics with science policy. One of the outcomes of this work is an argument (Mitcham 2009) for engineering ethics to undertake a policy turn.

In conclusion, insofar as science and engineering become technoscience, there is a need to integrate the ethics of science and engineering ethics. This idea was initially enacted by Shrader-Frechette when she invited a contribution on engineering ethics to her book on *Research Ethics* (Shrader-Frechette 1994). Adam Briggle and I tried to take this a step further in *Ethics and Science: An Introduction* (2012).

A CHINESE INFLUENCE

In the mid-2000s another important perspective was added to my engineering ethics work: emerging engagement with Chinese scholars.

Engagement with China goes back to the early 1990s, when Yin Dengxiang, a professor from the Chinese Academy of Social Sciences, came to spend a postdoc semester with STS at Penn State. Shortly after in June 1992 Yin brought Steve Cutcliffe from Lehigh, with whom he had spent another semester, and me to China to give a five-day series of lectures on the STS field. This proved the beginning of a substantial education in Chinese history, culture, and philosophy that has only become more important to me over time.

Chinese scholars have a unique perspective on engineering and engineering ethics from which I continue to learn. Two cases in point: Professor Li Bocong at the University of the Chinese Academy of Sciences and his colleague Professor Wang Nan argue, as if echoing Martin and Schinzinger, that engineering ethics is something different than ethics for engineers. Professor Liu Yongmou, my colleague at Renmin University of China, where I have had a continuing visiting appointment since 2014, has argued for a re-evaluation of the concept of technocracy.

CONCLUSION

Across these different institutional contexts, I have continued to think of engineering ethics as part of the philosophy of technology. As I noted in an exchange with two colleagues in 2013:

> There is a debate . . . with regard to whether philosophy of engineering should be conceived as a sub-discipline of the philosophy of technology or as its own regionalization. Among the general introductions to philosophy of technology, only my *Thinking through Technology: The Path between Engineering and Philosophy* (1994) gives engineering any prominence. Don Ihde's *Philosophy of Technology: An Introduction* (1993), Frederick Ferré's *Philosophy of Technology* (1995), and Val Dusek's *Philosophy of Technology: An Introduction* (2006) all give engineering short shrift. The Olsen, Pedersen, and Hendricks, eds., *A Companion to the Philosophy of Technology* (2009) includes engineering in the titles of only two ("Engineering Science" and "Engineering Ethics") of 98 chapters. (Mitcham and editors 2013, p. vi.)

This atypical focus on engineering, along with a repeated reluctance to accept any narrow version of engineering ethics, is further exemplified in a short perspectives article, "The True Grand Challenge for Engineering: Self-Knowledge" (Mitcham 2014). For me, engineering ethics is much more than professionalism; it is expanded critical reflection of the manifold and manifest transformations that engineering introduces into our lifeworld.

REFERENCES

Cutcliffe, Stephen H. 1990. "The STS Curriculum: What Have We Learned in Twenty Years?" *Science, Technology, & Human Values* 15, no. 3 (Summer): 360–372.

Durbin, Paul T. 1992. *Social Responsibility in Science, Technology, and Medicine*. Bethlehem, PA: Lehigh University Press.

Frankel, Mark S. 1988. *Science, Engineering and Ethics: State-of-the-Art and Future Directions*. Washington, DC: American Association for the Advancement of Science.

Huning, Alois, and Carl Mitcham. 1993. "The Historical and Philosophical Development of Engineering Ethics in Germany." *Technology in Society* 15, no. 4: 427–439.

Martin, Mike W., and Roland Schinzinger. 1989. *Ethics in Engineering*, 2nd edition. New York: McGraw-Hill.

Mitcham, Carl. 1985. "Industrial and Engineering Ethics: Introductory Notes and Annotated Bibliography." *Research in Philosophy and Technology* 8: 251–256.

Mitcham, Carl. 1987a. "Course Syllabus: Engineering Ethics." *Science Technology & Society Curriculum Newsletter* (Lehigh University) nos. 62–63 (November–December): 11.

Mitcham, Carl. 1987b. "Schools for Whistle Blowers: Educating Ethical Engineers." *Commonweal* 114, no. 7 (April 10): 201–205.

Mitcham, Carl. 1992. *Engineering Ethics Throughout the World: Introduction, Documentation, and Bibliography*. University Park, PA: STS Press.

Mitcham, Carl. 1994. "Engineering Design Research and Social Responsibility." In *Research Ethics*, edited by K. S. Shrader-Frechette, 153–168. Totowa, NJ: Rowman & Littlefield.

Mictham, Carl. 1995. "Ethics into Design." In *Discovering Design*, edited by Richard Buchanan and Victor Margolin, 173–189. Chicago: University of Chicago Press.

Mitcham, Carl. 2001. "*Dasein* Versus Design: The Problematics of Turning Making into Thinking." *International Journal of Technology and Design Education* 11: 27–36.

Mitcham, Carl, ed. 2005. *Encyclopedia of Science, Technology, and Ethics*. 4 vols. Farmington, MI: Macmillan Reference.

Mitcham, Carl. 2009. "A Historico–Ethical Perspective on Engineering Education: From Use and Convenience to Policy Engagement." *Engineering Studies* 1, no. 1 (March): 35–53.

Mitcham, Carl, ed. 2013. "Foreword: Prospects in the Philosophy of Engineering: An Exchange Between the Editors and Carl Mitcham." In *Philosophy and Engineering: Reflections on Practice, Principles and Process*, edited by Diane P. Michelfelder, Natasha McCarthy, and David E. Goldberg, v–xi. Dordrecht: Springer.

Mitcham, Carl. 2014. "The True Grand Challenge for Engineering: Self-Knowledge." *Issues in Science and Technology* 31, no. 1 (Fall): 19–22.

Mitcham, Carl, and Arthur Sacks. 2001. "'Nature and Human Values' at the Colorado School of Mines." *Science and Engineering Ethics* 7: 282–293.

Mitcham, Carl, and David Muñoz. 2010. *Humanitarian Engineering*. San Rafael, CA: Morgan and Claypool.

Mitcham, Carl, and Elaine E. Englehardt. 2016. "Ethics Across the Curriculum: Prospects for Broader (and Deeper). Teaching and Learning in Research and Engineering Ethics." *Science and Engineering Ethics*. DOI: 10.1007/s11948-016-9797-7.

Mitcham, Carl, and Shannon Duval. 2000. *Engineer's Toolkit: Engineering Ethics*. Upper Saddle River, NJ: Prentice Hall.

Mitcham, Carl, and William F. Williams, eds. 1994. *Reader's Adviser*. 14th Edition, Vol. 5: *The Best in Science, Technology, and Medicine*. New York: Bowker.

Shrader-Frechette, Kristin. 1984. *Science Policy, Ethics, and Economic Methodology: Some Problems of Technology Assessment and Environmental-Impact Analysis*. Dordrecht: D. Reidel.

Shrader-Frechette, Kristin. 1985. *Risk Analysis and Scientific Method: Methodological and Ethical Problems With Evaluating Societal Hazards*. Dordrecht: D. Reidel.

Shrader-Frechette, Kristin. 1994. *Research Ethics*. Lanham, MD: Rowman and Littlefield.

Unger, Stephen H. 1982. *Controlling Technology: Ethics and the Responsible Engineer*. New York: Holt, Rinehart and Winston.

Williams, William F., ed. 2000. *Encyclopedia of Pseudoscience*. New York: Facts on File.

III

LOGIC OF POLITICAL INQUIRY AND COMPARATIVE POLITICS

Chapter 12

Improving Russian and East European Studies by Building on Pragmatism and the Lost Legacy of the Policy Sciences

William N. Dunn

This chapter proceeds from a consideration of the broad sweep of the applied social and behavioral sciences that began at the outset of the nineteenth century. However, the policy sciences are more than merely applied social sciences; they are founded on the pragmatism of John Dewey and Charles Sanders Peirce, a philosophy of method that eschews the idea that applied science is about the application of theory to practice. Instead, pragmatism is a philosophy of theory and practice, a metatheory of "application" that provides the policy sciences with a distinctly reflective and critical orientation. After documenting the broad sweep of the applied social and behavioral sciences in the nineteenth century, the chapter turns to the years 1932–1943, a period in which the policy sciences were founded at the University of Chicago and Yale University. This period is special because it reveals a lost legacy of persons, theories, and institutions that can provide direction for the future of the policy sciences. This lost legacy is important because it suggests ways to improve theory and research on Russia and Eastern Europe.

HISTORY OF THE APPLIED SOCIAL SCIENCES

One way to think about the future of the policy sciences is to look backward at the historical development of the applied social and behavioral sciences in the nineteenth century, focusing on their empirical content and their policy orientation (Lerner 1951, 1959). However, if we wish to remain true to the policy sciences as they were founded and articulated by Harold Lasswell,

Abraham Kaplan, and Myres McDougal, sweeping historical reviews will be only partially successful, because a necessary feature of success is the *policy orientation*, as defined by Lasswell (1951: 3–15), who argued that products of the social sciences must actually be used by decision-makers faced with policy choices. While there is no doubt that we can learn much in general by studying early survey research conducted by Le Play, or applied social research directed by Booth and Mayhew in England or by DuBois and Addams in the United States, we must distinguish between the applied social sciences and the policy sciences. In this context, wrote Lasswell (1951: 4), the term "policy sciences"

> is not another way of talking about the "social sciences" as a whole, nor of the "social and psychological sciences." Nor are the policy sciences identical with "applied social science" or "applied social and psychological science." [Instead], the policy orientation, as we have seen, stresses but one of many problems which come with the proper scope of the social sciences . . . [the policy sciences must bear on] the policy needs of a given period for *intelligence*. (Emphasis mine)

Hence, the policy sciences are not the same as the applied social sciences, including policy analysis and program evaluation, unless they provide *actionable intelligence*. For this reason, it is doubtful that the policy sciences are equivalent to the *Polizeywissenshaften* in German-speaking countries in the eighteenth century, as Wagner, Weiss, Wittrock, and Wollman (1994/2008) contend. The policy sciences produce knowledge *of* and *in* the policy process (Lasswell 1971: 2–3), a characteristic based on the *unity* of knowledge and action, not their separation into knowledge production and application.

POST–WORLD WAR II DEVELOPMENTS

Another way to contemplate the future of the policy sciences is to build on developments in theory and method following World War II. Here, the usual approach is to point to the development of areas such as cost-effectiveness analysis, operations research, and game theory during and after World War II. We find the rise of nonprofit research organizations such as RAND and the multiplication of professional organizations engaged in the professionalization of policy work, for example, NASPAA, APPAM, ASPA, and NISPAcee. We might also distinguish among methodological and theoretical orientations characteristic of the policy sciences, policy studies, policy research, program evaluation, and microeconomic policy analysis. Under this option we might focus on the rapid growth of policy journals. There are dozens of "core" journals, ranging from the *Journal of Policy Analysis and Management* to the *Journal of Public Administration Research and Theory* to the *Policy Studies Journal*, *Policy Studies Review*, and *Public Policy*. In addition, there are hundreds of "issue area" journals in areas ranging from the environment, energy, health, and welfare to education, housing, national security, and so forth.[1] The difficulty with this approach is that it covers virtually everything, and therefore nothing of specific relevance to the future of the policy sciences. For example, we might identify the number of times core policy authors are mentioned in books and articles since 1930 (see figure 12.1a or map types of policy inquiry in the same period figure 12.1b). Similarly, we can account for the number of times key conceptual frameworks are mentioned (figure 12.1c) as well as well-known books (figure 12.1d).[2]

THE LOST LEGACY, 1932–1943

The 1951 volume by Lerner and Lasswell is frequently and erroneously taken as the point at which the policy sciences were launched. This ignores that the most important aspects of the policy sciences began at the University of Chicago and Yale University some 20 years earlier (see Dunn 2019). The first course titled "Policy Sciences" was offered at Yale Law School by law professor Thurman Arnold and psychologist Edward S. Robinson (Van Doren and Roederer 2012). The term "policy sciences" was also used in a 1943 memorandum by Lasswell titled "Personal Policy Objectives" (Lasswell

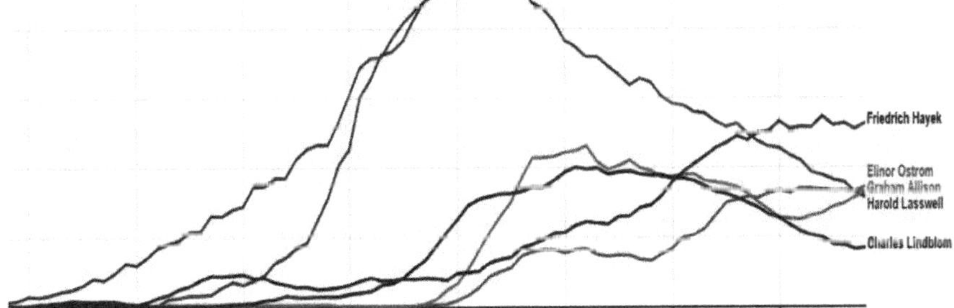

Figure 12.1a Authors. *Source*: Compiled by author.

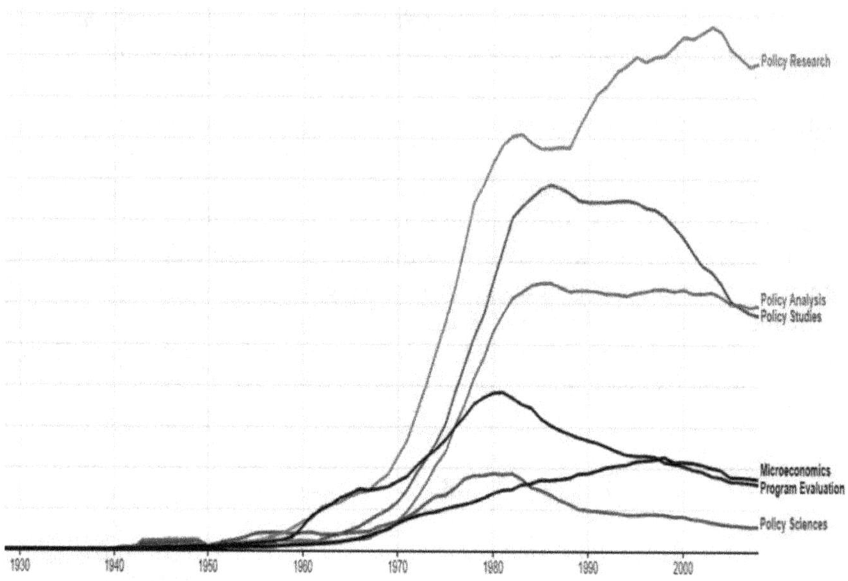

Figure 12.1b Types of Policy Inquiry. *Source*: Compiled by author.

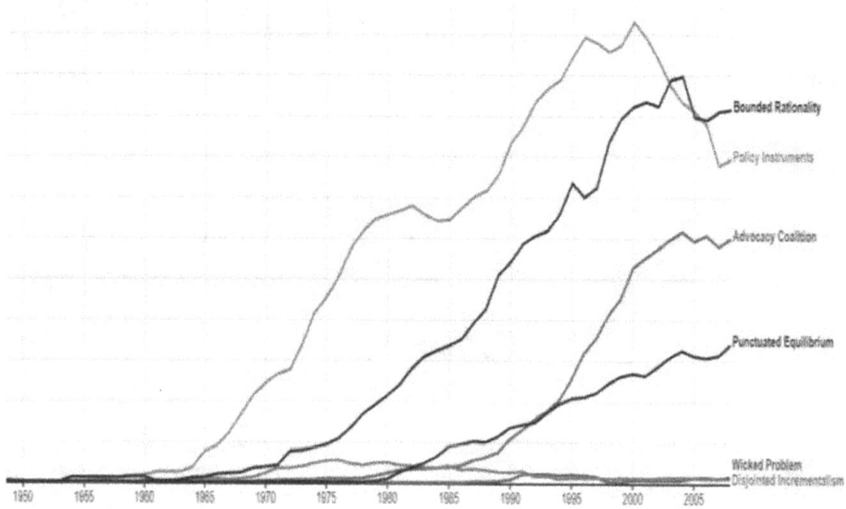

Figure 12.1c Conceptual Frameworks. *Source*: Compiled by author.

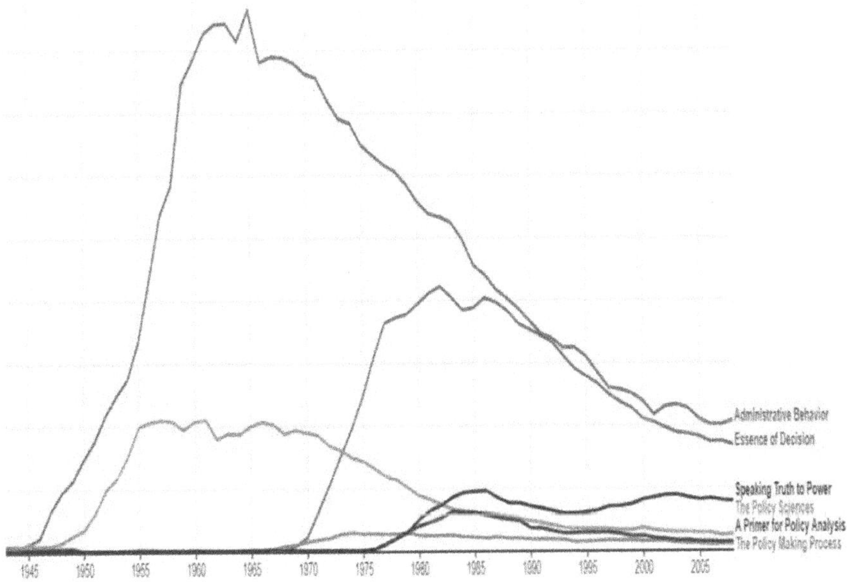

Figure 12.1d Books. *Source*: Compiled by author.

1943). Lasswell had by then joined the law faulty at Yale. Seven years later these initial uses of the term "policy sciences" were followed by the edited volume, *The Policy Sciences* (Lerner and Lasswell 1951), which included only two chapters on the policy sciences, per se, both written by Lasswell.

The aim of the policy sciences, as understood at the time, was to approach government as a science—as a *policy science.* For Arnold (1937: ii), governments should be studied by scientific observation, not "in the light of faiths and symbols." When in 1937 Arnold became Assistant U.S. Attorney General in the Roosevelt Administration, the Yale course in the policy sciences was taken over by Myres S. McDougal, who became Lasswell's lifetime collaborator. Their 30-year collaboration is documented in the 1,588-page *Jurisprudence for a Free Society* (1992), a synthesis of their work in developing the policy sciences. At the same time, Arnold's book, *The Folklore of Capitalism* (1937), thanked Lasswell for his assistance. He was the only social scientist among a group of jurists and law professors who, in contrast to Lasswell, were largely unprepared to study political, social, and economic aspects of law.

By 1938, Arnold, McDougal, and Lasswell were colleagues. Ironically, this was the same year that Lasswell, already a well-established scholar whom Almond (1987) later described as a preeminent twentieth-century social scientist, was denied promotion to a full professorship by University of Chicago President Robert Maynard Hutchins (Bulmer 1984: 204; Dzuback 1991: 173). Lasswell subsequently resigned from Chicago, joining McDougal at Yale Law in 1943, after serving during World War II as Chief of the Experimental Division for the Study of Wartime Communications at the U.S. Library of Congress.[3]

THE CONTEXT OF PRAGMATISM

The principal reason for rejecting these longer views of history is that they represent only part of the legacy of the policy sciences. A full accounting of this legacy discloses that the history of the policy-oriented social sciences includes the philosophy and methodology of pragmatism followed by Harold Lasswell, Abraham Kaplan, and Myres Dougal in the period 1932–1951. Profoundly affected by John Dewey and other pragmatists at the University of Chicago, the policy sciences were never simply "policy-oriented." Rather the policy sciences, as originally conceived, were pragmatic in the specific philosophical sense that they were conveyors of plausibly true or warranted beliefs (knowledge) that are at once value-driven, future-oriented, and continuously adapted and transformed in contexts of practical action. Indeed, the policy sciences, understood as an extension of pragmatism, were a going concern at the University of Chicago and Yale University in this early period (Dunn 2019). Dewey's instrumentalism was already being translated by Lasswell into the idea of continuous decision seminars and his pragmatist mantra: Knowledge must be *of* as well as *in* the decision process. The functionalism of the pragmatists was also translated into a form of teleological explanation that is evident in Lasswell's theory of decision circuits (Lasswell 1956), that is, configurations of multilinear decisions that may be explained in terms of his maximization postulate and base-values of enlightenment, wealth, power, respect, affection, rectitude, and skill. Finally, what Lasswell called the cross-disciplinary manifold was a Chicago prototype of the organization of the policy sciences that he and others advocated after 1951.

Lasswell's relationship with pragmatism has roots in his interaction with pragmatists at the University of Chicago. Ascher and Hirschfelder-Ascher (2004: 7) show how Lasswell's approach to political psychology was affected by Dewey's biologically based functional psychology, despite the fact that Dewey moved to Columbia in 1904. This same pragmatist commitment to theories of functionalism and instrumentalism underlies Lasswell's well-known maxim (1971: 3) that the function of the policy sciences is to create knowledge *of* and *in* the policy making process. Lasswell's policy sciences were a product of various social science "schools" at Chicago, in particular the Chicago School of Pragmatism, which fostered a cohesive network of affiliated colleagues in the social and behavioral sciences.

Regrettably, the relation between pragmatism and the policy sciences has been misunderstood. The policy sciences have been wrongly visualized as the simple application to practical problems of social science theory and methods, for example, the application of microeconomics to problems of choosing alternatives with the smaller opportunity costs, as reflected in lower discount rates for future cost and benefit streams. Properly speaking, however, such applications—which environmental economist Daniel Bromley calls the conventional Paretian approach to pseudo-economic choices (Bromley 2006: 13–14)—are not examples of pragmatism. The error is in assuming that social sciences such as economics and political science are policy sciences, simply because they deal with potentially applicable practical knowledge, as contrasted with traditional social science disciplines, which deal with intellectual knowledge that is valued primarily for its own sake.

Abraham Kaplan, one of the most respected pragmatists of his generation, observes that pragmatism has been widely misunderstood because concepts such as "practice" and "action" have been understood in a restrictive sense. "There is a vulgar pragmatism in which 'action' is opposed to 'contemplation,' 'practice' to 'theory,' and 'expediency' to 'principle'. . . . This vulgar doctrine is almost the direct antithesis of pragmatism, which aims precisely at dissolving all such dualities" (Kaplan 1964: 43–44). In other words, practice is the consummation of theory; theory originates in and guides action. The fusion of the contemplative-theoretical with the practical-contextual are what Lasswell and Kaplan (1950) meant by the term pragmatic. Kaplan (1964: 44) informs us that

> "action" that is relevant to the pragmatic analysis of meaning must be construed in the broadest possible sense, so as to comprise not only the deeds that make up the great world of affairs, by also those that constitute the scientific enterprise. . . . The "usefulness" that pragmatism associates with truth is as much at home in the laboratory and study as in the shop and factory, if not more so.

Therefore, pragmatism is not coextensive with the simple application of theories and methods to practical problems. This is evident in the differences among varieties of pragmatist thought (Menand 2001; Rescher 1995: 710–713; Shields 2004). Whereas Peirce was largely an objectivist, holding that multiple theories mirror in different ways socially constructed beliefs about nature, James was a subjectivist, which partly reflected his skepticism about what he saw as the potentially harmful effects of modern science. For James, beliefs may mirror subjective rather than objective states: Beliefs may make us feel content, secure, or spiritually worthy, apart from objective external conditions. Dewey and colleagues at Chicago, however, were neither objectivists nor subjectivists; they were transactionists. Beliefs fulfill different ends that are realized and adapted through social interaction (Hickman 2009: 143–162). Rucker sums up the differences between the three men:

> Only at the University of Chicago at the turn of the century did there grow up a school of American philosophy. The pragmatism that John Dewey and his colleagues and students collaborated on there had its roots in James and Peirce, but what emerged from their efforts was distinctively their own. . . . Neither James's concern to rescue sentiment from what he saw as the onslaught of science nor Peirce's drive to systematize modern thought represented the main thrust of American culture. The Chicago philosophers shared James's practical orientation, in contrast to Peirce's emphasis on theory . . . as opposed to James's fear that science, too narrowly interpreted, was a threat to human values. The Chicago pragmatists saw both science and values arising from human action, and they proceeded to derive an entire philosophy from the analysis of action. This action-derived philosophy turned out to be a pragmatism different from both Peirce's logic-centered thought and James's psychology-based work. (Rucker 1969: vi)

Dewey and the Chicago School of Pragmatism had a marked influence on philosophy, psychology, sociology, and political science. The worldview of pragmatism, as Bulmer (1984: 29–32) observes, focused on the process of change and adaptation that affects humans as well as physical objects. Activities such as policy implementation and appraisal, for example, generate actions designed to achieve the goal of human dignity and attendant values such as intelligence, power, wealth, and rectitude. "Ends were seen as relative to the circumstances in which action was undertaken" (Bulmer 1984: 29), circumstances that included the seven functionally defined decision processes elaborated by Lasswell (1956b). Values are not fixed or immutable, but contextual and transactional, arising out of the interaction of groups of persons, not individuals working alone. Base-values (means) and scope-values (ends) are in continuous flux. Lasswell later acknowledged his debt to John Dewey and other pragmatists for their approach to public policy (Lasswell 1971: 1).

ABDUCTIVE REASONING AND PUBLIC POLICY

Apart from its basis in functionalist theory, an essential logical feature of pragmatism is abduction, or what C.S. Peirce called the "method of hypothesis." Applied to public policy, abduction is akin to making what Aristotle and others (see von Wright 1971) called practical inference. Table 12.1 shows how a practical inference provides a teleological explanation of an action.[4]

In the first practical inference, 2(a), D may not achieve *a*, and due to the possibility of this exception, the inference cannot be justified by a universal covering law (nomic connection), as would be the case if it were a D-N (deductive-nomological) explanation of the kind favored by many social scientists. Again, in the second practical inference, 2(b), O may not achieve *a* because there is no nomic connection or universal covering law. The first practical inference is a quasi-causal explanation and the second is a quasi-teleological explanation (von Wright 1971: 96–98). The term "quasi," as used here, refers to the absence of a nomic connection such as Alfred Marshall's law of diminishing utility of money, or Avogadro's law of gases.

The two examples of explanation do not conform to the requirements of deductive-nomological (D-N) explanation, which is the favored mode of causal explanation among many positivist social scientists. However, what is important is not whether a form of explanation conforms (or not) to causal explanation in the natural sciences, but whether a form of explanation that is used in the social sciences helps understand why individual and collective actions occur. Conformity to explanations in physics or chemistry is beside the point, because quasi-causal and quasi-teleological explanations enlarge our capacity to understand policy choices.

Daniel Bromley (2006), a gifted interpreter of pragmatism and its applicability to public policy, extends practical reasoning in his theory of volitional pragmatism building on earlier ideas of pragmatists John Dewey and Addison Moore (1910). Bromley shows how abductive reasoning may be used to explain inferences based on practical reasoning (also known as the practical syllogism). Consider the example of a person turning on a light switch: The person

> flips the light switch because he desires that the room be lighted. This desire for a future state (a particular outcome) is the reason for the choice, while the cause is that he flipped the light switch. The flipping of the switch is merely a

Table 12.1 Practical Inference and Teleological Explanation: Individual and Collective Cases

(a)	*(b)*
Decision-maker, D, intends to bring about *p*.	Organization, O, intends to bring about *p*.
D considers that she cannot bring about *p* unless she does *a*.	O considers that it cannot bring about *p* unless it does *a*.
Therefore, D acts to achieve *a*.	Therefore, O acts to achieve *a*.

Source: Compiled by author.

> necessary though quite uninteresting step in the process that starts with reason, entails a causal sequence, and ends with a desired outcome. (Bromley 2006: 7)

The example of the light switch also illustrates Lasswell's "maximization postulate," which states that "living forms are predisposed to complete acts in ways that are perceived to leave the actor better off than if he had completed them differently." The maximization postulate is a form of practical reasoning. The person flips the light switch in order to achieve a future value, a lighted room, which would not have occurred if the switch had not been flipped. Similarly, policy makers may decide to create a future state, an enlightened electorate, in the face of low voter turnout. The value of an enlightened electorate follows a decision to create intelligence by determining the benefits of civic education for voting. The use of intelligence about the causal mechanism linking civic education and voting is a necessary step in the process that begins with the desire for an enlightened electorate, entails the process specified in the causal mechanism, and ends with the desired outcome, an enlightened electorate. It is the future state, an enlightened electorate, which is the reason for the decision, while the causal relation between civic education and voting, established through creating intelligence, is the cause.[5]

Another way to view Lasswell's maximization postulate is to recognize that it involves two kinds of premises: *volitional premises* and *epistemic premises* (Bromley 2006: 14–15; see also Bromley 2008). A *volitional premise* is a proposition concerning an end of action, or what Lasswell and Kaplan (1950) call a goal value such as human dignity. By contrast, an *epistemic premise* refers to a type of knowledge, or what Lasswell called *intelligence.* Knowledge, which we may define as plausibly true belief, provides the ingredients of the causal mechanism that helps realize the volitional premise. Significantly, this conceptualization avoids the concern expressed by Brunner (1991) that the maximization postulate might be misinterpreted as a form of Paretian expected utility, which was not Lasswell's intention. Nor is Paretian expected utility consistent with volitional pragmatism. On the contrary, a pragmatist conception of policy holds that

> new public policy starts with a consideration of particular desired outcomes in the future (the volitional premise). The epistemic premise—of the form, "If Y then X"—connects the desired outcome (Y) with the necessary action (X) to achieve that outcome. . . . the epistemic premise is both a prediction and a prescription. (Bromley 2006: 15)

Abductive reasoning originated with Peirce, who passed the concept down to Dewey and other doctoral students in his classes in logic and scientific method at Johns Hopkins. Although Dewey did not use the concept in his writings, he did discuss abduction without naming it so. In *Logic: The Theory of Inquiry* (1938), he presents a five-step process of inquiry in which the first stage is much like abduction.[6] As Lasswell and Kaplan note (1950: xxv):

> Inquiry has not only a creative role in the formation of policy . . . but also an instrumental role in implementing policy. Thus, the purport of inquiry is not necessarily "theoretical" rather than "practical": both manipulative and contemplative standpoints may be adopted.

They go on to emphasize that inquiry begins with Dewey's *problem situation*, which is identical to the *indeterminate situation* or *surprise* that triggers abduction. Bromley (2006), stressing that abduction is a basic feature of the epistemological theory of pragmatism, sees *volitional pragmatism* as a way for individuals to deploy reasons to justify their decisions.

TELEOLOGICAL EXPLANATION AND CAUSAL MECHANISMS

Volitional pragmatism, a form of what I have called decisional functionalism, supplies a rich and variegated representation of policy making. Although the decision process is temporally ordered, and for this reason meets one of several requirements of a causal mechanism (see Gerring 2010), a theory is needed to explain the operation of the causal mechanism. Although the maximization postulate relates act meanings to subsequent behavior, some argue that this relation is not causal (e.g., Brown 2002). If this were true, Jenkins-Smith and Sabatier (1993) might be correct that Lasswell's decision model is in fact a "heuristic," a means of discovering hypotheses but not of testing and possibly corroborating them. Hence, the "stages heuristic" may not actually permit explanations of how one stage leads to another; it is not a causal model with a clearly defined *explanandum* ("dependent variable") and *explanans* ("independent variable"). In this context, Jann and Wegrich (2007: 57) argue that the "stages heuristic" is inadequate as a theory to explain the policy making process.

In addressing this criticism, it is essential to recognize that Lasswell's *decisional functionalism* affirms that purposeful behaviors and other subjectively meaningful acts provide an explanation of decisions and their effects. For example, the purpose (or function) of policy invocation and application—what we now might call policy implementation—may be said to enable individuals and groups to achieve values of power and skill. As Brown (2002: 290) explains, functionalism is a form of qualitative inquiry, a way to represent and understand act meanings. We understand act meanings when we understand the meaning of acts to participants in the policy making process, as distinguished from understandings derived from our own or someone else's reconstructions of those acts.[7]

For Lasswell, one source of the concept of decision was emerging functionalist theories in biology and the social sciences (McDougal, Lasswell, and Reisman 1967: 258 and note 6), especially the functionalist social and psychological theories of Dewey and other pragmatists (Ascher and Hirschfelder–Ascher 2005). Functionalism explains variations in outcomes of decisions by referring to antecedent purposes, aims, or functions. Although political science and other social science disciplines have preferred deductive-nomological and inductive-statistical models of explanation rather than functional explanations, it is noteworthy that functional models of explanation have recently been productively resurrected in the area of governance and public policy (Peters and Pierre 2016: vii–viii). However, the functional model of decision-making was perhaps destined to be viewed as a mere "heuristic," because traditionally functionalism has been associated with discovering hypotheses through a heuristic process of discovery (the so-called context of discovery), rather than a process of testing hypotheses (the so-called context of justification). Until relatively recently, only the latter has been seen as genuinely theoretical.[8]

However, Lasswell's decisional functionalism may be regarded as a testable theory in the context of justification. To be sure, Brown (2002: 290) contends that functional explanations are not causal, because they are based on

> an understanding of the way in which individuals actually relate to the world from their own standpoint (as best this can be determined) rather than an understanding of their conduct as grasped via conceptual categories imposed on or constraints external to that conduct.

However, as Levison and others have argued, qualitative explanations based on interpretive understanding complement causal explanations based on overt actions and other physical processes (Levison 1966).[9] Act meanings and other processes of practical reasoning, including Lasswell's maximization postulate, may be regarded as quasi-causal because they explain behavior without resorting to a covering law or nomic connection (von Wright 1971: 91–103). Quasi-causal explanations provide explanations in their own right, explanations that complement explanations based on "external" economic and social factors such as income, wealth, and social status. Indeed, functional explanations based on interpretive understanding may complement deductive-nomological (D-N), inductive-statistical, and practical relevance modes of explanation explicated by Wesley Salmon (1984) in his authoritative treatise on scientific explanation. In short, if the central tasks of theory are explanation and prediction, Lasswell's decisional functionalism qualifies as a theory, although explanation and prediction need not be symmetrical. A sound explanation is not necessary for a sound prediction.

Because functional explanations are teleological explanations, they are goal-directed. Although the weight of scholarly opinion has been skeptical of the use of functional explanations in science (Couch 2011), Ernest Nagel, in *The Structure of Science: Problems in the Logic of Scientific Explanation* (1968: 403–405), has argued such explanations can be represented without resort to teleology.

> Consider: The function of A in a system S with organization C is to enable S in environment E to engage in process P.

This statement can be expanded into a causal explanation that is not based on purpose or teleology (Nagel 1968: 403; von Wright 1971: 141–142):

> A system S with organization C in environment E engages in process P.
>
> If S with organization C in environment E does not have A, then S does not engage in process P.

The expansion into a causal explanation can be illustrated with an example from science and technology policy:

> The function of the Office of Technology Assessment (OTA) of the U.S. Congress, which is organized as a bicameral legislature in a democratic environment, is to enable elected members of Congress to engage in legislative processes involving complex issues of science and technology. In democratically elected legislatures, members engage in the legislative process, which is organized in functions that include intelligence, promotion, prescription, invocation, application, termination, and appraisal. If a democratically elected legislature does not have an agency that performs economic and social technology assessments, it will not be able to engage effectively in the legislative process involving complex science and technology issues.[10]

Arguably, this is a kind of deductive-nomological explanation with a lawful regularity, *L*, a set of initial conditions, *C1* and *C2* (the *explanans* and *explanandum*), and the conclusion: *Democratically elected legislatures that do not have an agency that performs technology assessments, or their functional equivalent, will not be able to engage effectively in the legislative process involving complex science and technology issues.* Although the explanation may appear obvious, it is nevertheless a kind of deductive-nomological explanation of the type put forth by Nagel (1968) and Hempel (1965) and seemingly preferred by critics of Lasswell's so-called stages heuristic.

The deductive-nomological (D-N) model is but one type of causal explanation. Lasswell's decisional functionalism also provides explanations, and testable theories and hypotheses, which do not conform to the D-N model. For example, in *A Pre-View of Policy* Sciences (1971: 86–100) Lasswell identifies attributes of information used to evaluate the performance of the circuit of one or more of the seven decisional functions (table 12.1). These attribute variables could form the basis of a "concatenated" or "factor" theory, which Kaplan (1964: 298) contrasts with theories of the deductive or "law" type. One hypothesis is that governments that perform the intelligence function are more likely to achieve the value of enlightenment[11] when the information produced has attributes of dependability, comprehensiveness, selectivity, creativity, and openness (see also McDougal, Lasswell, and Reisman 1972). This and other hypotheses appear just as testable, causally relevant, and falsifiable as do those derived from alternative theoretical frameworks such as the advocacy coalition framework (ACF), which is also a concatenated or factor-type theory, not a deductive-nomological (hierarchical) one.

THE CIRCUITRY OF DECISION-MAKING

Decisions are not policies; but policies are configurations of decisions. Legal realism is a philosophy of law that asserts that in seeking explanations of the development of legislative acts and other policies, the investigator should focus, first, on judicial, legislative, and executive decisions, not on legal principles, doctrines, or rules. "The Realists [capitalization original] successfully demonstrated that, by reference to rules alone, neither scholar nor practitioner could explain why past decisions had been made or how future decisions were likely to be made" (Reisman 1998: 35). Thurman Arnold and Myres McDougal were leading legal realists of their day, and it was legal realism and not pragmatism, per se, which motivated the teaching of the policy sciences in 1932–1933 at Yale. However, legal realists "were much less successful in identifying the tasks the jurist [and other policy makers] should perform and the methods to be deployed" (Falk, Higgins, Reisman, and Weston 1998: 729); hence, the need for social science methodologists such as Lasswell.

In identifying the methods they should deploy in explaining decisions, Lasswell and McDougal (1943), Lasswell and Kaplan (1950/2008), and Lasswell and McDougal (1992) viewed the development of laws and other policies as a process of making authoritative decisions about the achievement of human dignity and values of enlightenment, power, wealth, well-being, affection, respect, rectitude, and skill. To identify the operations required to achieve human dignity and associated values, they identified a broadly iterative process of decision-making with seven functions: intelligence, promotion, prescription, invocation, application, appraisal, and termination (Lasswell and Kaplan 1950; Lasswell 1956b; McDougal and Lasswell 1967). This broadly iterative process is best described as a circuit, not a cycle. Within each of the seven functions are seven sub-functions with the overall configuration resembling a "wheels-within-wheels" structure. In this context, policy scientists and policy makers were seen to develop what Lasswell and McDougal labeled *intelligence*, which was the *sine qua non* of performing each of the remaining six functions. In performing the intelligence function, decision-makers:

- Identify problems in achieving goals
- Chart relevant past decisions
- Analyze factors affecting trends in achieving goals
- Forecast likely future conditions
- Identify and assess likely future decisions
- Clarify values and identify alternative solutions

These procedures, it should be stressed, point toward future decisions, not primarily to present or past ones (see Ascher 1971).

Adaptation and change in decisional functions follow the choice of values, which are contextual "ends-in view," rather than lexical fixed ends that fail to reflect the teleological reason of individuals with the capacity to make genuine choices among alternative values. Base values (Lasswell and Kaplan 1950) are abductive because they "go back to" decisional functions, functions that are instruments for achieving those values. The process of abduction is not deductive, as in rational choice theory, or inductive, as in survey experiments or ethnography, because in policy contexts as in everyday life we regularly deal with indeterminate situations, anomalies, or surprises that Dewey and others have called "problem situations" (Ackoff 1974: 237-39; Rein and White 1977: 262).

The complexity of decisional functions is a consequence of change and adaptation within and across functions, and of the fact that policies are not single decisions, but configurations of decisions. Chester Barnard (1938), who was a key influence on Lasswell and, notably, students at Chicago like Herbert Simon (see Easton 1950), captured the complexity of decisions when he described the decision to relocate a telephone pole from one side of the street to another.[12] Barnard, a successful CEO and classic contributor to public and business administration, suggested that moving the telephone pole

> involves perhaps 10,000 decisions of 100 men located at 15 points, requiring successive analyses of several environments, including social, moral, legal, economic, and physical facts of the environment, and requiring 9,000 redefinitions and refinements of purpose. [However] . . . not more than half-a-dozen decisions will be recalled or deemed worthy of mention. . . . The others will be "taken for granted." (Barnard 1938: 198)

To simplify what appears as an unmanageably huge number of decisions, Lasswell (1956) grouped decisions in seven functions performed by any governmental, private, or nonprofit body; and each of the functions comprises comparable sub-functions *within* functions.[13]

Lasswell's decisional functionalism has other characteristics that have been dismissed or ignored by critics who incorrectly assert that Lasswell's decision model is linear or monocyclical (for a review see Jann and Wegrich 2007). Instead, Lasswell's decision process is best seen as a complex circuit, much as Dewey defined his reflex arc as an organic circuit of stimuli, responses, and purposes. In Lasswell's circuit, the seven major functions proceed forward, backward, laterally, and diagonally, while within each function there are identical sub-functions that also may move forward, backward, laterally, and diagonally. Given that the major functions and sub-functions have *intelligence* at the center of the circuit, where there are more inter-function connections, the entire set of complex decisions form a circuitry of which intelligence is central to other functions (figure 12.2).[14]

Figure 12.2 illustrates Lasswell's description of the decision process (1956b: 96–97), which may be represented as a complex circuit. Overall, the entire arrangement is not linear but multicyclical. "Every agency of government is involved in varying degree with every function; and . . . all the component parts of American society are expected to express themselves at least through the electorate" (Lasswell 1956: 7). When functions are relatively stable in their interactions, they tend to display cyclical fluctuations and "functional interactions occur among (and within) the participants." Using the example of cycles of urban reform and corruption, Lasswell recognizes that

> cycles are rarely if ever "perfect"; they do not re-establish the original state of affairs completely. Political fluctuations are structural as well as cyclical; new patterns of interaction emerge and become relatively stable, and the level of conformity between prescription and conduct may be higher or lower than it was before. (Lasswell 1950b: 97)

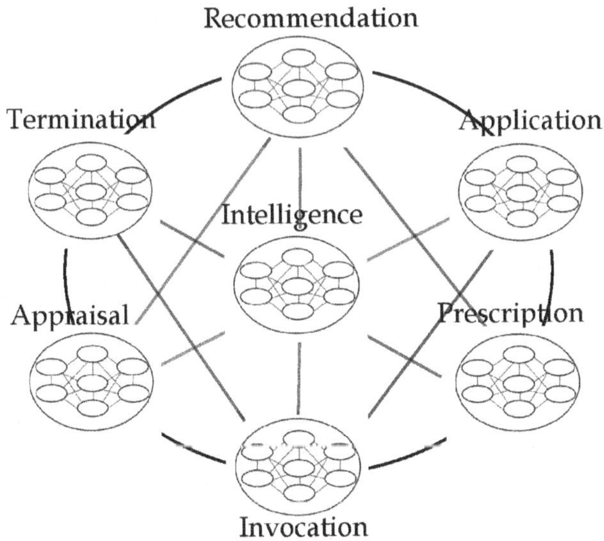

Figure 12.2 The Circuitry of Decision-Making. *Source*: Compiled by author.

THE SOCIAL ORGANIZATION OF THE POLICY SCIENCES

Between 1915 and 1938 philosophy, sociology, and other social sciences flourished, markedly influencing the development of the social sciences in the United States and Western Europe. Lasswell termed the pragmatist institutional network that shaped this achievement the "cross-disciplinary manifold" (Lasswell 1971a). The "manifold" may be visualized as a set of institutional properties including the dates of interaction among Lasswell's teachers, mentors, and colleagues, the focus of their disciplines and their research products, and their status as what Deutsch, Platt, and Senghaas (1970: 373–420) call advances in the social sciences—the rough map of judgments about advancements. Although the social sciences earned an unjustified reputation for unbridled empiricism, Bulmer (1984: Chapter 12) and others (Carey 1975: Ch. 6) provide evidence of a close relationship between pragmatist philosophers and the psychologists, sociologists, and political scientists. In the early period, Dewey was the preponderant influence, while George Herbert Mead, whom Dewey originally brought from Michigan, had the greater impact in the 1920s. The leader of the sociologists, Robert E. Park was a self-conscious pragmatist who developed survey, case study, ethnographic, and life-history methods while studying the working class of Chicago. Park had a significant influence on Lasswell (Bulmer 1984: 125–126), who attended his seminars on research methods and worked as his research assistant. Park as well as the other leading sociologist, Ernest W. Burgess, would today be seen as champions of the application of mixed- or multiple-methods in research on urban problems.

The approach to all the social sciences was multidisciplinary and applied. In the area of public policy, William S. Ogburn, the quantitative sociologist, worked on President Hoover's Commission on Recent Social Trends, as did Merriam, Gosnell, and other political scientists. Lasswell and Leonard B. White were carrying out pioneering studies in political science, while the psychologist L.L. Thurstone was designing methods of attitude measurement that contributed to economic research on expected utility measurement in experimental economics (Hagel and Roth 1995: 5–6). The economist Henry Schultz was laying the foundations of econometrics. Jacob Viner and Frank Knight were developing institutional economics. While there was a general expectation that social science research would contribute the solution to social problems, there was also a focus on democracy and social betterment. This same normative and democratic orientation later appeared in virtually all the works of Lasswell and McDougal in the policy sciences.

Jane Addams and the Hull House Papers are also exemplary of the policy-oriented, reformist, democratic orientation of philosophy and the social sciences in Chicago. The pragmatism of Dewey, James, and Peirce appealed to Addams, and she and Dewey were colleagues, friends, and collaborators. Dewey was a frequent visitor to Hull House before and after leaving Chicago for Columbia. Addams was also close with George Herbert Mead, the pragmatist social psychologist and creator of symbolic interactionism; their influence was mutual. Addams received the Nobel Prize in 1936 and she is credited with founding the American Civil Liberties Union (ACLU). Students at Chicago read Addams's books and, while she would not accept a regular appointment, Addams taught as an adjunct professor.

FINANCIAL AND RESEARCH INFRASTRUCTURE

The financial and research infrastructure, including the erection of new buildings, was characteristic of the cross-disciplinary manifold and the Chicago model (Goodspeed 1916/1972; Storr 1966; see Boyer 2015). The search for outside financial support, for example, from the Carnegie Corporation and the Spelman Rockefeller Memorial Fund, was successful. The Social Science Research Building, which was designed to house the Local Community Research Committee—an interdisciplinary and policy-oriented institution—included a large statistical archive and what then was the most advanced equipment for carrying out statistical analyses (Bulmer 1984: 195–197).

A unique feature of the social science building, at least in the late 1920s, was its deliberate departure from the disciplinary design of the vast majority of social science buildings, which is that of a separate floor, wing, or entire building to house separate disciplines. Instead, the Social Science Research Building mixed faculty from different disciplines, much like a contemporary matrix organization. Ogburn the eminent quantitative sociologist was adjacent to Harold Gosnell, the political scientist who conducted urban surveys; the psychologist L.L. Thurstone and the labs for economic experiments were adjacent to Lasswell; Schultz the economist was next to Herbert Blumer, the qualitative sociologist.

The image of Chicago in these early years is like a cross-disciplinary manifold encased in brick and mortar. Given these material-cum-intellectual innovations, it is tempting to conclude that Chicago's deliberate inter-disciplinarity reflects a philosophically pragmatist design to break down the dualism of disciplines, not by ignoring their disciplinary advantages for developing theory and research, but concurrently by seeking *unity*. As Menand (2001: 324) tells us, unity is the fighting word of pragmatism.

THE DECLINE OF THE CROSS-DISCIPLINARY MANIFOLD

Given the efficacy and robustness of multidisciplinary, policy-oriented social science at Chicago after 1915, the policy sciences, formally proposed between 1932 and 1951 at Yale (McDougal and Lasswell 1943; Lerner and Lasswell 1951), may be regarded as a "second-best" solution to the recovery of the cross-disciplinary manifold at Chicago. The Chicago model (Lasswell 1971b) represented an institutional matrix that was already policy-oriented, multidisciplinary, and contextual, the three characteristics that Lasswell enunciated as defining characteristics of the policy sciences in 1951.

The Chicago School, apart from close connections with the policy sciences, also represented the rise of empirical, policy-oriented empirical research in a new university setting. A distinctive advantage of Chicago was its relatively recent establishment (1898), which provided the university with many fewer traditions and constraints, particularly requirements to teach the classics and general philosophy, subjects in which Chicago did not specialize until the advent of Hutchins's "great books" program. It was comparatively difficult to innovate at old schools such as Harvard, Princeton, and Yale. As Bulmer (1984: Ch. 12), argues, many of the most important conditions for intellectual and institutional creativity were at Chicago.

Between 1915 and 1938, Chicago dominated the policy-oriented social sciences in the United States. The "schools" that made up the university—philosophy, psychology, sociology, political science—and the Chicago School of Pragmatism, the "mega-school" that owed its existence to Dewey, enjoyed the freedom that the older Ivy League universities did not have until the mid-twentieth century. The Chicago schools led a movement away from general social and political theory, political philosophy, and history "toward the firsthand empirical investigation of society by means of personal documents, observations, and interviewing, conducted within an implicit general theoretical framework" (Bulmer 1984: xiii). The community of scholars and cross-fertile institutions of Chicago appear to be rare in the history of the social sciences. The survey of advances in the social sciences between 1900 and 1980 by Deutsch, Markovits, and Platt (1986) profiles 50 major advances in the social sciences,[15] some 36% of which occurred at Chicago between 1910 and 1938. Of the total, five were Lasswell's advances in areas of psychology, communications theory, content analysis, propaganda, and the policy sciences.

By 1938, political science and philosophy were moribund at Chicago (Almond 2004), a situation created by President Hutchins. Under Hutchins, Lasswell and other social scientists got a reputation for conducting "vulgar empiricist research," which was among the reasons that Lasswell and Gosnell were denied promotion to the rank of full professor. Mortimer Adler, reflecting his and Hutchins's preference for philosophical abstraction and normative ethics, replaced the head of philosophy. A journalist from *Fortune* contrasted Hutchins's position with that of Dewey:

> Even those who are willing to admit Hutchins's preoccupation with values, with the oughts of life, are unwilling to grant the final authority to the Aristotelian tradition to define values. They [Dewey and others] insist that no values can be fixed, and [argue] that a valid modern philosophy need not reckon with ideas as they are expressed in the books of ancient and mediaeval times. (Adler 1977: 184)

The unity of theory and practice was realized by means of a *configural* approach that self-consciously combined the contemplative and the practical, rather than keeping them apart in a dualistic relation. Much of this unity was lost with the decline of the political science and philosophy departments. Gabriel Almond, an eminent contributor to fields of political culture and comparative political participation, and one of Lasswell's students at Chicago, also reports that the final blow to political science came from Hutchins (Almond 2004). Parts of what was lost later became the four legs of the policy sciences: problem-oriented inquiry, contextual analysis, multiple qualitative and quantitative methods, and a normative commitment to human dignity and allied social values.

Lasswell's death in 1978 was followed by a handful of commemorative essays as well as critiques of his work. Given Lasswell's preeminence, it is surprising that, in the 20-year period, 1978–1998, there was a relative paucity of references to his books, and then only to about one-third of them, primarily in mainstream political science rather than public policy (Eulau and Zlomke 1999). Only later were there critiques of his work on the policy making process (e.g., Farr, Hacker, and Kazee 2006; Sabatier 1991), as distinct from critiques of his writings on the policy sciences generally (e.g., Tribe 1972). Apart from critics, other policy-oriented political scientists commemorated, defended, or extended Lasswell's work (e.g., Torgerson 1985; Brunner 1991, 1997; DeLeon 1994; Brown 2002; Ascher and Hirschfelder-Ascher 2005). The negligible attention paid to his work on the decision process by mainstream political scientists was no doubt a result of the relative lack of importance of policy studies and policy analysis in political science at that time and today.

However, the main root of misplaced criticism is the lack of understanding that the decision process, along with other aspects of Lasswell's work, are rooted in pragmatism. Because Lasswell's theory of the decision process was based on functional analysis, not on the analysis of stages of activities (although the term "sequence" was regularly used), it is regrettable that it came to be known as the "stages model," "stages heuristic," "stages framework," or "stages metaphor."[16]

THE FUTURE OF THE POLICY SCIENCES

The period 1932–1951 contains a lost legacy of persons, ideas, and institutions that may be used to think about present-day options for the future of the policy sciences. Here, the policy sciences are conceptualized not as a movement (Brunner 1992), but as what sociologists, historians, and philosophers of science variously have called a theory group (Nicholas Mullins), research program (Imre Lakatos), research tradition (Larry Laudan), or disciplinary matrix (Thomas Kuhn). Drawn from the lost legacy of the policy sciences, options for building a future research program include:

- *Distinctive Program Statement.* A program statement should summarize the mission, goals, and objectives of the policy sciences program, clearly stating that the policy sciences are not a form of applied social research. Rather, the policy sciences are an extension of pragmatism and its most basic principle: *The unity of knowledge and action.* The policy sciences are not simply the social and behavioral sciences with a policy orientation. This statement is distinctive because it makes clear that the poor record of the applied social sciences (policy analysis, policy studies, public administration) in establishing curricula that would allow students and faculty to monitor the effects of theories, methods, and substantive findings in the policy making process. Significantly, some of the major works on the history of the policy-oriented social and behavioral sciences (e.g., Wagner, Weiss, Wittrock, and Wollman 1994/2008; Lerner 1959; DeLeon 2006) do not distinguish between policy-oriented social and behavioral sciences and the policy sciences, leading to the conclusion that the social sciences *are* policy sciences. In this context, Lasswell's "policy orientation," which is one of three legs of the policy sciences—the others are contextuality and multidisciplinarity—was defined as social sciences that "have a bearing on the policy needs of a given period for adequate intelligence" (Lasswell 1951: 4). The policy sciences produce knowledge *of* as well as *in* the policy making process (Lasswell 1971: 1–2).

- *Unique Theoretical Orientation.* A central feature of a unique theoretical orientation is the specification of the kinds of knowledge valued in the policy sciences. This distinguishes the policy sciences from other sciences and promises intellectual innovation. The pragmatist theory of knowledge and action that guided Lasswell and others at Chicago and Yale bases explanations on values and subjectively meaningful action. This involves a commitment to teleological explanation as a mode of causal inference (the activity theory of causation). Dewey and other pragmatists, while abandoning the correspondence theory of truth, were fully aware of the logical fallacy of relativism, but opposed the dogmatic uses of the term "truth." Dewey redefined the concept, critically and reflectively, as "warranted assertibility," a concept that has much in common with Jurgen Habermas's "truth-redeeming validity claims" and Stephen Toulmin's "substantial arguments." In this context, pragmatists such as Abraham Kaplan (1968), stressing the pragmatist rejection of dualities such as that of subject and object, uses Dewey's term "objective relativism." The uniqueness of a theoretical orientation such as a policy science grounded in pragmatism appears to have dissipated into multiple clusters of conceptual frameworks, the growth of empirical studies without any particular theoretical identity, and the exponential growth of policy journals.
- *Intellectual Leadership.* The policy sciences are not only an intellectual construct, but a form of social organization as well. Intellectual leaders such as Lasswell and McDougal are needed to communicate the unique theoretical orientation to others, develop new rationales, and assume leadership in research and publishing and practice. However, just as we speak of the "curse of oil," we might also speak of the "curse of preeminence." Lasswell and McDougal, who were preeminent, wrote few coauthored papers, other than those they wrote together. Leadership must be developed

and shared. When even the most productive leaders are not promoted or rewarded by university administrators, entire programs such as that at Chicago have perished.

- *Human Resources Entrepreneurs.* The future of the policy sciences will depend on the placement of students and effective prospecting for research monies to support them. It is not now clear that professors or career services staffs are equipped to place junior members in research, teaching, and training positions. When this function is not performed well, other research programs have not succeeded in maintaining themselves.
- *Knowledge Transaction Specialists.* Knowledge transaction specialists are needed to convert books, articles, and studies into usable knowledge and monitor and evaluate this process. Even a cursory reading of the National Academy of Sciences report, *The Use of Scientific Evidence in Public Policy* (2016) should lead one to the conclusion that public policy schools have failed in this area. Given the pragmatist theoretical orientation of the policy sciences, the policy sciences may be doomed to failure unless knowledge transaction specialists can be cultivated. Apart from their "translational" role, knowledge transaction specialists are needed to arrange and maintain what Lasswell called *continuous decision seminars* involving policy scientists and policy makers.
- *Virtual Research and Training Centers.* Centers that deliberately facilitate communications among different policy science disciplines that specialize in different methods can now be developed online, possibly with results surpassing those at Chicago during Lasswell's time. Centers should have a multidisciplinary commitment that is independent of any one discipline, especially microeconomics. Centers might develop texts, manuals, and other critical syntheses and systematic reviews of methods and research findings.
- *Organization Development Specialists.* The policy sciences are a series of intellectual activities as well as a social organization. Organization development specialists are needed to maintain the cohesiveness and survival of the policy sciences program as a particular kind of social organization. New members must be recruited and trained, awards and honoraria for excellence must be provided, negative sanctions must be available to discipline poor or suboptimal work, financial and human resources must be identified and used to sustain policy science programs, and the performance of functions must be monitored and evaluated and feedback supplied.

These social and intellectual options are likely to contribute to the further adaptation and survival of the policy sciences, while realizing that research programs such as the policy sciences are part of a life-cycle that leads us to expect ascendancy as well as decline or replacement by successors. In the meantime, the lost legacy of the policy sciences can lead us to entertain speculative but historically grounded hypotheses about the future of a program that above all is dedicated to the unity of knowledge and action and the creation of knowledge of and in the policy making process.

NOTES

1. Several decades ago, Michael Marien (1992), who at that time was editor of *Futures Survey*, identified some 400 policy journals.

2. The graphs were constructed using Google Ngram. The Google Ngram Viewer or Google Books Ngram Viewer is an online search engine that charts the frequencies of any set of comma-delimited search strings using a yearly count of n-grams (bigram = two words, trigram = three words) found in sources printed between 1500 and 2008 in Google's text corpora in English, Chinese, French, German, Hebrew, Italian, Russian, or Spanish. Each graph shows the relative frequency of a word(s) out of all words, titles of books, names of authors, concepts in scientific fields, and other sets of words.

3. Harold F. Gosnell, a political scientist who conducted studies of Negro (African American) and machine politics in Chicago, resigned for the same reason in 1942.

4. This is among the main reasons that Lasswell was not a logical positivist (see Ascher and Hirschfelder-Ascher 2005: 7–9).

5. This is the "activity theory of causation" that Cook and Campbell (1979: 25–28) use to explain the nature of causation in field experiments and quasi-experiments.

6. Despite internal conflicts surrounding the definition of pragmatism (e.g., James's pragmatism and Peirce's pragmaticism), Dewey's doctrine of instrumentalism parallels Peirce's pragmatic maxim: "Consider what effects, that might conceivably have practical bearings, we conceive the object of our conception to have. Then, our conception of these effects is the whole of our conception of the object."

7. Colebatch (2002: 125) provides a good example of the logical reconstruction of act meanings of participants in the policy making process when he observes that the "scientific" model of policy making is not so much an accurate theory as an idealistic view of how people think policy should be made.

8. Critics of the distinction no longer see the two contexts as mutually exclusive. They have reformulated the mutually exclusive dichotomy between contexts of discovery and justification, proposed by Hans Reichenbach in 1938.

9. Levison's analysis of Karl Hempel's critique of Max Weber contends that Hempel (1959) overlooked narrative evidence showing that Weber did not reject causality. Weber argued instead that a causal explanation required initial conditions that were based both on external (physical) factors and on subjective ones (interpretive understanding). This is the complementarity thesis, which holds that interpretive and causal explanations are compatible and mutually supportive.

10. The OTA was abolished by act of the U.S. Congress on September 29, 1995 on grounds that its functions could be performed by other agencies. Although the Library

of Congress, the Office of Management and Budget, and the U.S. General Accounting (now Accountability) Office perform technology assessments, they do so without the significant expertise of what was a large specialized staff of 143 employees.

11. Carol Weiss (1979), a major producer of work on knowledge use by policy makers, focused on enlightenment as a consequence of the use of social science knowledge. As editor of the journal (*Science Communication*) in which Sabatier's first paper on the ACF was published, I was particularly concerned that the ACF address Weiss's enlightenment function.

12. Thanks to the late Carol H. Weiss for directing my attention to this passage from Barnard.

13. Visually, this may be represented as a "wheels-within-wheels" structure.

14. The logic and epistemology of functionalism dictates that values explain actions. For this reason, the concept "subsystem" may be confusing if it leaves out the motivating teleological effects of values in shaping acts that are explained by causal mechanisms that are, to use the dualism we find ion the social sciences, "subjective" as well as "objective."

15. I have omitted from the Deutsch et al. list mathematics and political organizing (e.g., Whitehead and Russell, Lenin, Mao-Tse Tung, Mahatma Gandhi).

16. No attempt is made here to distinguish the various meanings of causality. This would unnecessarily lengthen the paper and burden its flow. Useful sources on these questions include Abraham Kaplan (1964), Georg Henrik von Wright (1971), Wesley Salmon (1984), Donald T. Campbell (1989), Guido Imbens and Donald Rubin (2015), and Judea Pearl and Dana Mackenzie (2018).

REFERENCES

Ackoff, R. L. 1974a. "Beyond Problem Solving." *General Systems* XIX: 237–239.

Ackoff, R. L. 1974b. *Redesigning the Future: A Systems Approach to Societal Problems*. New York: John Wiley.

Adelstein, R. 1992. "Charles E. Lindblom. Division II Faculty Publications. Paper 92." http://wesscholar.wesleyan.edu/div2facpubs/92.

Adler, M. J. 1977. *Philosopher at Large: An Intellectual Autobiography*. Chicago: University of Chicago Press.

Almond, G. A. 1987. *Harold Dwight Lasswell, 1902–1978: A Biographical Memoir*. Washington, DC: National Academy Press.

Almond, G. A. 2004. "Who Lost the Chicago School of Political Science?" *Perspectives on Politics* 2, no. 1: 91–93.

Anderson, J. A. 2011. *Public Policymaking: An Introduction*. Boston: Wadsworth.

Ansell, C. K. 2011. *Pragmatist Democracy: Evolutionary Learning as Public Philosophy*. New York: Oxford University Press.

Arnold, T. 1937. *The Folklore of Capitalism*. New Haven: Yale University Press.

Ascher, W. 1978. *Forecasting an Appraisal for Policy-Makers and Planners*. Baltimore: Johns Hopkins University Press.

Ascher, W., and B. Hirschfelder-Ascher. 2004. *Revitalizing Political Psychology: The Legacy of Harold D. Lasswell.* Chicago: Psychology Press.

Auer, M. R. 2007. "The Policy Sciences in Critical Perspective." In *Handbook of Public Administration*, edited by J. Rabin, W. B. Hildreth, G. J. Miller, and J. Rabin, 3rd ed., 541–562. Boca Raton: CRC Press, Taylor & Francis.

Barnard, C. I. 1938. *The Functions of the Executive.* Cambridge, MA: Harvard University Press.

Bower, J. L. 1968. "Chapter 3: Descriptive Decision Theory From the 'Administrative' Viewpoint." In *The Study of Policy Formation*, edited by R. A. Bauer and K. J. Gergen. New York: The Free Press.

Boyer, J. W. 2015. *The University of Chicago: A History.* Chicago: University of Chicago Press.

Braybrooke, D., and C. E. Lindblom. 1963. *A Strategy of Decision: Policy Evaluation as a Social Process.* New York: Free Press of Glencoe.

Brewer, G. D., and P. DeLeon. 1983. *The Foundations of Policy Analysis.* Homewood, IL: Dorsey Press.

Bromley, D. W. 2006. *Sufficient Reason: Volitional Pragmatism and the Meaning of Economic Institutions.* Princeton, NJ: Princeton University Press.

Bromley, D. W. 2008. "Volitional Pragmatism." *Ecological Economics* 68, no. 1: 1–13.

Brown, S. R. 2002. "Structural and Functional Information." *Policy Sciences* 35, no. 3: 285–304.

Brunner, R. D. 1991. "The Policy Movement as a Policy Problem." *Policy Sciences* 24, no. 1: 65–98.

Brunner, R. D. 1997. "Introduction to the Policy Sciences." *Policy Sciences* 30, no. 4: 191–215.

Bulmer, M. 1984. *The Chicago School of Sociology: Institutionalization, Diversity, and the Rise of Sociological Research.* Chicago: University of Chicago Press.

Burgess, E. W. 1916. "The Social Survey: A Field for Constructive Service by Departments of Sociology." *American Journal of Sociology* 21: 492–500.

Campbell, D. T. 1988. *Epistemology and Methodology for Social Science: Collected Papers.* Chicago: University of Chicago Press.

Campbell, D. T., and J. Stanley. 1963. *Experimental and Quasi-Experimental Designs for Research.* Chicago: Rand McNally.

Carey, J. T. 1975. *Sociology & Public Affairs: The Chicago School.* Newbury Park, CA: Sage Publications.

Churchman, C. West. 1967. "Guest Editorial: Wicked problems." *Management Science* B141–B142.

Colebatch, H. K. 2002. *Policy*, 2nd ed. Buckingham, UK: Open University Press.

Collingwood, R. G. 1940. *An Essay on Metaphysics.* Oxford: Clarendon Press.

Cook, T. D., and D. T. Campbell. 1979. *Quasi-Experimentation: Design and Analysis Issues for Field Settings.* Boston: Houghton Mifflin.

Corbacıoğlu, S. 2008. "Invisible University in Public Policy Analysis: Cognitive and Social Networks Among Six Social Scientists." *Review of Public Administration* 2, no. 4: 27–54.

Couch, M. B. 2011. "Causal Role Theories of Functional Explanation." In *Internet Encyclopedia of Philosophy: A Peer Reviewed Academic Resource*, edited by R. A. Bauer and K. J. Gergen. Accessed June 28, 2016. https://philpapers.org/rec/COUCRT.

Coughlin, N. 1973. *Young John Dewey: An Essay in American Intellectual History.* Chicago: University of Chicago Press.

Crick, B. 1959. *The American Science of Politics: Its Origins and Conditions.* Berkeley: University of California Press.

DeLeon, P. 1988. *Advice and Consent: The Development of the Policy Sciences.* New York: Russell Sage Foundation.

DeLeon, P. 1992. "The Democratization of the Policy Sciences." *Public Administration Review* 52, no. 2: 125–129.

DeLeon, P. 1994. "Reinventing the Policy Sciences: Three Steps Back to the Future." *Policy Sciences* 27, no. 1: 77–95.

DeLeon, P. 1999. "The Stages Approach to the Policy Process: What Has it Done? Where Is It Going?" In *Theories of the Policy Process*, 19–32. Boulder: Westview Press.

DeLeon, P. 2008. "The Historical Roots of the Field." In *The Oxford Handbook of Public Policy*, edited by Robert E. Goodin, Michael Moran, and Martin Rein. Oxford: Oxford University Press.

Dery, D. 1984. *Problem Definition in Policy Analysis.* Lawrence, KS: University Press of Kansas.

Deutsch, K., J. Platt, and A. Markovits, eds. 1986. *Advances in Social Science.* Washington, DC: American University Press.

Deutsch, K., John Platt, and Dieter Senghaas. 1971. "Conditions Favoring Major Advances in Social Sciences." *Science* (February): 450–459.

Dewey, J. 1896. "The Reflex Arc Concept in Psychology." *Psychological Review* 3: 357–370.

Dewey, J. [1933]1991. *How We Think.* Amherst: Prometheus.

Dewey, J. [1938]1982. *Logic: The Theory of Inquiry.* New York: Irvington.

Dewey, J., and A. Bentley. 1949. *Knowing and the Known.* Boston: Beacon Press.

Diesing, P. 1992. *How Does Social Science Work? Reflections on Practice.* Pittsburgh: University of Pittsburgh Press.

Dunn, W. N. 1988. "Forethoughts: The Disputed Paternity of Technological Innovation." *Knowledge in Society* 1, no. 2: 3–6.

Dunn, W. N. 2018. *Public Policy Analysis*, 6th ed. New York: Routledge.

Dunn, W. N. 2019. *Pragmatism and the Origins of the Policy Sciences: Rediscovering Lasswell and the Chicago School.* Cambridge: Cambridge University Press.

Dzuback, M. A. 1991. *Robert M. Hutchins: Portrait of an Educator.* Chicago: University of Chicago Press.

Easton, D. 1950. "Harold Lasswell: Policy Scientist for a Democratic Society." *The Journal of Politics* 12, no. 3: 450–477.

Eulau, H., and S. Zlomke. 1999. "Harold Lasswell's Legacy to Mainstream Political Science: A Neglected Agenda." *American Review of Political Science* 2: 75–89.

Falk, R. A., R. Higgins, W. Reisman, and B. Weston. 1998. "Myres Smith McDougal (1906–1998)." *The American Journal of International Law* 92, no. 4: 729–733.

Farr, J., J. S. Hacker, and N. Kazee. 2006. "The Policy Scientist of Democracy: The Discipline of Harold D. Lasswell." *American Political Science Review* 100, no. 4: 579–587.

Fayol, H. [1916]1949. *General and Industrial Management*. London: Pitman.

Garrison, J. 2009. "Dewey's Constructivism: From the Reflex Arc Concept to Social Constructivism." In *John Dewey: Between Pragmatism and Constructivism*, edited by L. Hickman, Stefan Neubert, and Kersten Reich, 84–105. New York: Fordham University Press.

Gerring, J. 2010. "Causal Mechanisms: Yes, But…." *Comparative Political Studies* 43, no. 11: 1499–1526.

Goodspeed, T. W. 1916. *A History of the University of Chicago*. Chicago: University of Chicago Press.

Gulick, L., and L. Urwick, eds. 1937. *Papers on the Science of Administration*. New York: Institute of Public Administration.

Hausman, D. M. 1992. *The Inexact and Separate Science of Economics*. New York: Cambridge University Press.

Hayek, F. 1945. "The Use of Knowledge in Society." *The American Economic Review* 35, no. 4: 519–530.

Hempel, C. G. 1959. "The Logic of Functional Analysis." In *Symposium on Sociological Theory*, edited by L. Gross. Evanston: Harper and Row.

Hempel, C. G. 1965. *Aspects of Scientific Explanation*. New York: Free Press.

Hickman, L. A., Stefan Neubert, and Kersten Reich. 2009. *John Dewey: Between Pragmatism and Constructivism*. New York: Fordham University Press.

Hoppe, R. 1999. "Policy Analysis, Science and Politics: From 'Speaking Truth to Power' to 'Making Sense Together.'" *Science and Public Policy* 26, no. 3: 201–210.

Imbens, G., and D. Rubin. 2015. *Causal Inference for Statistics, Social, and Biomedical Sciences: An Introduction*. Cambridge: Cambridge University Press.

James, W. [1890]1950. *The Principles of Psychology*. London: Dover Press.

James, W. 1907. *Pragmatism, a New Name for Some Old Ways of Thinking: Popular Lectures on Philosophy*. New York: Longman, Green, and Co.

James, W. [1909]1995. *Pragmatism*. Dover Press.

Jann, W., and K. Wegrich. 2007. "Theories of the Policy Cycle." In *Handbook of Public Policy Analysis*, edited by F. Fischer and G. J. Miller, 69–88. New York: Routledge.

Jenkins-Smith, H. C., and P. A. Sabatier. 1993. "The Study of the Public Policy Process." In *Policy Change and Learning: An Advocacy Coalition Approach*, edited by P. A. Sabatier and H. C. Jenkins-Smith. Boulder, CO: Westview Press.

Jones, C. O. 1977. *An Introduction to the Study of Public Policy*, 2nd ed. North Scituate, MA: Duxbury Press.

Kaplan, A. 1964. *The Conduct of Inquiry: Methodology for Behavioral Science*. San Francisco: Chandler Publishing Company.

Karl, B. D. 1975. *Charles E. Merriam and the Study of Politics.* Chicago: University of Chicago Press.

Lasswell, H. D. 1936. *Politics: Who Gets What, When, How.* New York: P. Smith.

Lasswell, H. D. 1938. *Propaganda Technique in the World War.* New York: P. Smith.

Lasswell, H. D. 1941. "The Garrison State." *American Journal of Sociology* 46, no. 4: 455–468.

Lasswell, H. D. 1943. Personal Policy Objectives. *Memorandum*, October 1.

Lasswell, H. D. 1948. "The Structure and Function of Communication in Society." In *The Communication of Ideas*, edited by L. Bryson, 215–228.New York: Institute for Religious and Social Studies.

Lasswell, H. D. 1951. "The Policy Orientation." In *The Policy Sciences: Recent Developments in Scope and Method*, edited by D. Lerner and H. D. Lasswell, 3–15. Palo Alto, CA: Stanford University Press.

Lasswell, H. D. 1956a. *The Decision Process: Seven Categories of Functional Analysis.* Bureau of Governmental Research, College of Business and Public Administration, University of Maryland.

Lasswell, H. D. 1956b. "The Political Science of Science: An Inquiry into the Possible Reconciliation of Mastery and Freedom." *American Political Science Review* 50, no. 4: 961–979.

Lasswell, H. D. 1960. "Technique of Decision Seminars." *Midwest Journal of Political Science* 4, no. 3: 213–236.

Lasswell, H. D. 1965. *World Politics and Personal Insecurity.* New York: Free Press.

Lasswell, H. D. 1971. *A Pre-View of Policy Sciences.* New York: American Elsevier.

Lasswell, H. D., and A. Kaplan. 1950. *Power and Society: A Framework for Political Inquiry.* New Haven: Yale University Press.

Lasswell, H. D., and M. S. McDougal. 1943. "Legal Education and Public Policy: Professional Training in the Public Interest." *The Yale Law Journal* 52, no. 2: 203–295.

Lasswell, H. D., and M. S. McDougal. 1992. *Jurispridence for a Free Society: Studies in Law, Science, and Policy.* New Haven: New Haven Press/Martinus Njihoff Publishers.

Lasswell, H. D., and N. C. Leites. 1965. *Language of Politics: Studies in Quantitative Semantics.* Boston: MIT Press.

Lerner, D., ed. 1959. *The Human Meaning of the Social Sciences.* New York: World Publishing Company

Lerner, D., and H. D. Lasswell, eds. 1951. *The Policy Sciences.* Palo Alto, CA: Stanford University Press.

Levison, A. 1966. "Knowledge and Society." *Inquiry* 9, nos. 1–4: 132–146.

Lindblom, Charles E. 1965. *The Intelligence of Democracy: Decision Making Through Mutual Adjustment.* New York: Free Press.

Lindblom, Charles E. 1991. *Inquiry and Change.* New Haven: Yale University Press.

Lindblom, Charles E., and David K. Cohen. 1979. *Usable Knowledge: Social Science and Social Problem Solving.* New Haven: Yale University Press.

Lynd, R. S. 1939. *Knowledge for What? The Place of Social Science in American Culture.* Princeton: Princeton University Press.

Marien, M. 1992. "The Scope of Policy Studies: Reclaiming Lasswell's Lost Vision." In *Advances in Policy Studies Since 1950*, edited by W. N. Dunn and R. M. Kelly, 449–493. New Brunswick, NJ: Transaction Publishers.

May, J. V., and A. Wildavsky, eds. 1979. *The Policy Cycle*. Beverley Hills, CA: Sage Publications.

McDougal, M. S., H. D. Lasswell, and W. M. Reisman. 1972. "The Intelligence Function and World Public Order." *Temple Law Quarterly* 46: 365.

McDougal, Myres S., Harold D. Lasswell, and W. Michael Reisman. 1967. "The World Constitutive Process of Authoritative Decision." *Journal of Legal Education* 19, no. 3: 253–230.

Menand, L. 1997. *Pragmatism: A Reader*. New York: Vintage.

Menand, L. 2001. *The Metaphysical Club*. New York: Farrar, Straus, and Giroux.

Mitroff, I. I. 1974. *The Subjective Side of Science: A Philosophical Inquiry into the Psychology of the Apollo Moon Scientists*. Amsterdam: Elsevier Scientific.

Moore, A. W. 1910. *Pragmatism an Its Critics*. Chicago: University of Chicago Press.

Mullins, N. C. 1973. *Theories and Theory Groups in Contemporary American Sociology*. New York: Harper and Row.

Nagel, E. 1968. *The Structure of Science: Problems in the Logic of Scientific Explanation*. London: Routledge and Kegan Paul.

Nakamura, R. T. 1987. "The Textbook Policy Process and Implementation Research." *Review of Policy Research* 7, no. 1: 142–154.

National Academy of Sciences. 2009. *The Use of Scientific Evidence in Public Policy*. Washington, DC: National Academies Press.

Parsons, T. 1949. *The Structure of Social Action*. New York: Free Press.

Pearl, J., and D. Mackenzie. 2018. *The Book of Why: The New Science of Cause and Effect*. New York: Wiley.

Peirce, C. S. 1877. "The Fixation of Belief." *Popular Science Monthly* 12 (November 1877).

Peters, B. G., and J. Pierre. 2016. *Comparative Governance: Rediscovering the Functional Dimension of Governing*. Cambridge: Cambridge University Press.

Peters, J. D., and P. Simonson. 2004. *Mass Communication and American Social Thought: Key Texts, 1919–1968*. Washington, DC: Rowman & Littlefield.

Polsby, N. W., R. A. Dentler, and P. A. Smith. 1963. *Politics and Social Life: An Introduction to Political Behavior*. Boston: Houghton Mifflin.

Quade, E. S. 1989. *Analysis for Public Decisions*. New York: North Holland.

Rein, M., and S. White. 1977. "Policy Research: Belief and Doubt." *Policy Analysis* 239–271.

Reisman, W. M. 1998. "Theory About Law: Jurisprudence for a Free Society." *Yale Law Journal* 108: 935–937.

Rescher, N. 1977. *Methodological Pragmatism*. Oxford: Basil Blackwell.

Rescher, N. 1980. *Induction: An Essay on the Justification of Inductive Reasoning*. Pittsburgh: University of Pittsburgh Press.

Rescher, N. 1995. "Pragmatism." In *The Oxford Companion to Philosophy*, edited by T. Honderich, 710–714. Oxford: Oxford University Press.

Rice, S., and H. D. Lasswell, eds. 1931. *Methods in the Social Sciences: A Case Book.* Chicago: University of Chicago Press.

Rorty, R. 1999. "Truth Without Correspondence to Reality." In *Philosophy and Social Hope*, 23–46. Baltimore: Penguin Books.

Rucker, D. 1969. *The Chicago Pragmatists: Dewey, Ames, Angell, Mead, Tufts, Moore*. Minneapolis: University of Minnesota Press.

Sabatier, P. A. 1987. "Knowledge, Policy-Oriented Learning, and Policy Change: An Advocacy Coalition Framework." *Science Communication* 8, no. 4: 649–692.

Sabatier, P. A. 1988. "An Advocacy Coalition Framework of Policy Change and the Role of Policy-Oriented Learning Therein." *Policy Sciences* 21, nos. 2–3: 129–168.

Sabatier, P. A. 1991. "Toward Better Theories of the Policy Process." *PS: Political Science and Politics* 24 (June): 147–156.

Sabatier, P. A., ed. 2006. *Theories of the Policy Process*, 2nd ed. Boulder: Westview Press.

Sabatier, P. A., and C. Weible, eds. 2014. *Theories of the Policy Process*, 3rd ed. Boulder: Westview Press.

Salmon, W. C. 1984. *Scientific Explanation and the Causal Structure of the World.* New Haven: Princeton University Press.

Schickore, J., and F. Steinle, eds. 2006. *Revisiting Discovery and Justification: Historical and Philosophical Perspectives on the Context Distinction*, vol. 14. New York: Springer Science & Business Media.

Shadish, W., T. D. Cook, and D. T. Campbell. 2002. *Experimental and Quasi-Experimental Designs for Generalized Causal Inference.* Chicago: Houghton Mifflin.

Shields, P. 2004. "Classical Pragmatism: Engaging Practitioner Experience." *Administration & Society* 36, no. 3: 351–361.

Shook, J. R., and A. Backe. 2001. *The Chicago School of Functionalism.* 3 vols. Bristol, UK: Thoemmes Press.

Simon, H. A. 1944. "Decision-Making and Administrative Organization." *Public Administration Review* 4, no. 1: 16–30.

Simon, H. A. 1947. *Administrative Behavior: A Study of Decision Making Processes in Administrative Organizations*. New York: Macmillan.

Simon, H. A. 1973. "The Structure of Ill Structured Problems." *Artificial Intelligence* 4, nos. 3–4: 181–201.

Storr, R. J. 1966. *A History of the University of Chicago: Harper's University—The Beginnings*. Chicago: University of Chicago Press.

Tomas, V., ed. 1957. *Charles S. Peirce: Essays in the Philosophy of Science.* New York: Liberal Arts Press.

Torgerson, D. 1985. "Contextual Orientation in Policy Analysis: The Contribution of Harold D. Lasswell." *Policy Sciences* 18, no. 3: 241–261.

Tribe, L. H. 1972. "Policy Science: Analysis or Ideology?" *Philosophy and Public Affairs* 2 (Fall): 66–110.

Van Doren, J., and C. J. Roederer. 2012. "McDougal-Lasswell Policy Science: Death and Transfiguration." *Richmond Journal of Global Law and Business* 11, no. 2: 125–157.

Von Wright, G. H. 1971. *Explanation and Understanding*. Ithaca, NY: Cornell University Press.

Wagner, P., C. H. Weiss, B. Wittrock, and H. Wollman. 2008. *Social Science and Modern States*. Cambridge: Cambridge University Press.

Weimer, D., and A. Vining. 2015. *Policy Analysis: Concepts and Practice*, 5th ed. New York: Routledge.

Yale Law School Legal Scholarship Repository. 1973. New Haven, CN: "Myres S. McDougal."

Chapter 13

Disciplines of Political Learning

How Political Science Arises Repeatedly

John S. Nelson

What if the mind
was never a dutiful scholar?
Call it a lark winging across bright gardens.
An arm. A strobe in a ballroom.
A runner. A sharp stone.
What if the search
was discovered to have no discipline?
Let it be swarms, wider than the fields they devour.
A happening inside halls or answers.
What if a scholar
is not the mind or the search?
Say sign of the times. Say dream antithesis.
Music and the noise that needs it.
No brain. Drain.[1]

Disciplines are communities, institutions, organizations, networks. They have political aspects. Academic disciplines are communities of inquiry and instruction; yet their emergence, consolidation, operation, decline, and displacement are—in important part—political dynamics. As Thomas Kuhn showed, academic disciplines make and unmake themselves through devices as much political as intellectual.[2]

The most developed political studies of academic inquiries include history of science, sociology of scientific knowledge (SSK), and rhetoric of inquiry.[3] That disciplines do not keep ideas and politics separate is a reason for rhetoric of inquiry in particular to tap the republican-rhetorical tradition of politics to interpret and improve inquiries. As an exercise in rhetoric of inquiry, this chapter taps that tradition to analyze the modern discipline of political science, where the political dynamics of modern disciplines are readily apparent.

Modernity by the calendar of political scientists begins with the Renaissance and the Reformation. Continuing to the present, modernity is an enterprise of invention, criticism, and renewal. Modern disciplines of inquiry are such endeavors. They turn modern universities into engines of change such as economies and polities in their powers to remake modern civilizations.[4]

Yet any modern discipline is apt to emerge more than once. Modernization is making anew. If we forget this, it is because any later emergence discredits its predecessor(s) as loose philosophizing without the benefit of true science. Thomas Kuhn showed how new paradigms use textbooks and other disciplinary devices to consign early studies to oblivion or pre-history. Modern disciplines seldom take their predecessors seriously as sciences or disciplines. Present disciplines seldom regard the earlier ones as anticipations, let alone as alternatives. To emerge as a thoroughly modern discipline is to stand alone in a newly defined field . . . time and again.

Not counting lesser reforms and revolutions along the way, this is the pattern of what we now call the social sciences. Economics, political science, and sociology each emerges first in the seventeenth and eighteenth centuries as an "ideology" in the distinctively modern sense of a "science of civilization pursued as a logic of ideas."[5] Thus the modern discipline of economics begins as capitalism, political science as liberalism, sociology as socialism. Ideologists such as Adam Smith, John Locke, Auguste Comte, Karl Marx, and company often took themselves to be scientists of society; and disciplined studies arise in their wakes. Communication, geography, and psychology show similar patterns but might be more patchwork as academic endeavors; while history includes some of these dynamics, as Hayden White showed, but its operation as a social science is more debatable.[6] Hence such social sciences emerge as modern disciplines to analyze specifically modern, secular, especially civil societies as they form to complement the continually centralizing states and increasingly open markets of modernity.[7]

These ideologies displaced classical complexes of disciplined inquiry that receded into philosophy or myth. In the study of politics, the ideology of liberalism supplanted a mythos of republicanism that early modernity had recuperated and disciplined from ancient Rome.[8] (The Romans had constructed the republican-rhetorical tradition in turn from the Greek Sophists and especially from Aristotle.) Liberal ideology did not take shape until the seventeenth century at the earliest, and it did not begin to make itself into a specifically modern discipline until the eighteenth century. (Political theorists trace these eruptions to the modernizing authoritarian treatises of Thomas Hobbes.[9]) With John Locke, Montesquieu, and the American founders, the Enlightenment discipline of political science became a science of (ideas about) institutions (as textures of ideas). For the most part, it was liberal in form—in its conception of science—yet its contents were principally republican. (This adapts the precept of Marshall McLuhan that new media make old media into their contents: the new scientific forms of modern disciplines take their contents mainly from their predecessor disciplines.[10])

This high modern discipline of political science remained only a residual presence after the American Civil War, when a network of scholars in the United States and Europe, especially in Germany, worked to invent the late modern profession of political science. From roughly the 1880s onward, these figures (re)founded a disciplined study of politics that eventually turned by the twentieth century toward a focus on individuals. Its conception of science became more democratic, and its contents more liberal. John Gunnell has emphasized how recent are the latest refoundings of the discipline, yet how fully they have effaced any significant sense of their predecessors.[11] Thus they dismiss the classical discipline of rhetoric as political manipulation, and they reject the modern discipline of institutions as armchair speculation.

The politics that inform political science move through the mythos of republicanism and the ideology of liberalism on their way to current senses of discipline, science, and profession. Consequently a first move is to rehabilitate the republican-rhetorical tradition as a serious, if pre-modern, science of politics. A second shift is to appreciate the modern, but still mostly republican, discipline of institutions. And a third step is to explain the professional science of individuals as also modern but largely liberal. All this implies a recent re-emergence of earlier topics and strategies of study, so a fourth turn is to see their relevance for politics and inquiries arising in the twenty-first century. The contrasting disciplines of political science in modern times feature different ideas of political institutions, so let us trace them to show what it means for an academic discipline to emerge more than once in modern universities.

CLASSICAL TRADITIONS AND MEDIEVAL FACULTIES

Western politics go from classical to medieval to modern, and they may well be on their way to postmodern. Classical politics get theorized, in part retrospectively by the Romans, as the politics of republics. This is not to say that the organization of the classical academy was republican, because the ancient academy located itself mythically in a grove, to put it apart from the public market or forum where the *agon* of classical politics would play out. Instead classical backgrounds of republican politics continued through medieval universities to set the stage for modern reinventions of classical traditions in Renaissance studies and Enlightenment sciences.

The university began as a medieval invention, and its initial politics of organization were neither classical nor modern but mostly feudal. Before that, though, the classical academy included authors and pupils, to use the Roman parlance. The academic office of the authors, as Cicero explained, was to teach. Thus the academy took shape as itinerant Sophists, literally and notoriously pedagogues, settled with their counterparts in other areas of learning into specific sites for thinking, talking, and writing.[12] In the classical academy, there were nothing much like modern disciplines. Instead authors and pupils ranged widely across topics, fitting Aristotle's work as a polymath.

By contrast, the medieval university constructed itself of scholars formed into faculties. Sometimes the faculties clustered into schools led by people whom we may loosely regard as directors. The faculties themselves were to be led by professors. This language survives into modern universities, but we do well to re-poeticize the terms to appreciate the organization of medieval universities.[13] Thus "faculties" were for medieval universities what they were in the medieval psychologies that also featured the word: capabilities for performances of particular kinds. Faculty psychologies regarded people's capacities for mental operations as divided into specific resources of emotion, imagination, reason, will, and more. These were conceived to be distinct ways in which people engage the world of experience and action. University faculties likewise were to be the organization's separable resources for learning about the world and tutoring students. Each faculty engaged different topics in distinctive ways.

The medieval university had faculties rather than disciplines. Politically there is a world of difference between the two modes of organization.*Disciplines* follow modern principles of politics, whether republican or liberal, whereas *faculties* work in medieval ways shaped by the politics of courts and churches. Through forgetting and elegant variation, we now treat the two as synonyms, but that can obscure the specifically modern projects of academic disciplines.

As we can tell from names that remain in modern universities, medieval faculties within universities most often formed colleges. Thus members of the university faculties were—more or less as they continue to be—colleagues. They were not principally employees, and they were not to be bossed by anybody. Rather they were the medieval university's rough equivalent for feudal nobility. They were led in colleges by deans, who were to be the best among them rather than governors or administrators in a modern sense. *Deans* (from the Greek for *one set over ten*) were to lead by example, not edict or even decision. Colleagues were to do the essential work, defining the university's principles along the way. Within faculties, the learning and any rules of study were to be articulated within the university by the *professors*, whose title denotes (from Latin) the power to *declare publicly* what the learned members of the faculties have to say. To study at the medieval university meant more or less to apprentice yourself for a time to a focal member of the faculty who would tutor you. The collateral work of the university also drew from feudal politics. Just as medieval kings would commission nobles to act for the good of the realm in restoring the peace or building a bridge, medieval deans would commission the faculty members to recruit students, regulate studies, and conduct examinations. These became the faculty committees (and later the tripartite committees of faculty, students, and staff) that do important parts of the work in modern universities. Of course, committees still ornament the operations of late modern multiversities, yet they seldom contribute much beyond the conduct of oral and written examinations for graduate students.[14]

As the name suggests, *universities* are defined by the ambition to provide the *one word*, the *unified truth* about the world—and in one place, one complex organization. These scholars, faculties, schools, and colleges appear together in universities because coming to terms with the whole universe requires many resources organized in more complicated ways than the classical world had contemplated. From their inception in the middle ages, universities have been more differentiated and encompassing than (classical) academies. Modern universities continue that tradition, even as they redefine many of the medieval components. A rough attempt to arrange the specific names of the institutions, their components, and their participants can be revealing. Below these appear in networks meant to evoke period by period the organizational complexes connected with several learned or scholarly "disciplines," in a loose sense of the word that pays some attention to the specific political takes on "disciplines" yet to come (table 13.1).

Sometimes the results have been new meanings for old names. Late modern colleges still have deans as leaders, even though these no longer are exemplary scholars so much as specialists in administering faculty members. Typically they learn the craft of academic administration as department heads or chairs, then they join the itinerant class of academic administrators who move from one university to another as they pursue the career trajectory from dean to provost to university president. Other times, the modernization has generated new concepts. The talk of academic administrators is one example, and the notion of post-doctoral fellows is another.

MODERNITY AS MULTIPLE EMERGENCE

The standard histories of modern disciplines date their inceptions to the late nineteenth century. Before that, universities organized themselves through increasingly modern versions of scholars in faculties in schools in colleges. And as their scientists began to supplant scholars, republican then liberal modes of discipline appeared in universities. Yet the standard histories of

Table 13.1 From the Academy to the Multiversity

Periods	*Classical*	*Medieval and Early Modern*		*High Modern*	*Late Modern*
Institutions	academy	university	university	university	multiversity
Divisions	none	schools	colleges	colleges	colleges
and leaders	scholars	directors	deans	deans	administrators
Subdivisions	none	faculties	faculties	departments	disciplines
and leaders	scholars	professors	professors	heads	chairs
Individuals	authors	scholars	doctors	professors	scientists
Relations	members	colleagues	staffs	ranks	standings
Teachers	pedagogues	tutors	instructors	lecturers	teachers
Learners	pupils	students	undergraduates	graduates	post-graduates
Devices	offices	commissions	committees	committees	staffs

Source: Compiled by author.

disciplines seldom pay much attention to disciplines as specifically modern organizations with distinctive political dynamics. This holds for histories of political science as a discipline.[15] Thus the usual tale of political science locates its disciplinary origins in the 1880s, when faculties from leading American universities moved toward professional associations for social sciences.

The American Political Science Association was established in 1903. Its predecessor was the American Academy of Political and Social Science, founded in 1889, and its counterparts for economics and sociology appear in 1885 and 1903. Although rooted in German studies of law, economy, and society, political science began its professional life as an American discipline. Its intellectual framework came from American liberalism, as did its sense of scholarly discipline.[16]

In consequence, disciplinary histories of political science fail to recognize that there are at least two political sources of modern disciplinarity. The late nineteenth-century template is liberal, authoritative, professional, and presentist, especially in political science.[17] It is the kind of discipline that universities recognize today. Since World War II, it has become the kind of discipline that outdoes academic departments for American multiversities in providing individual faculty members with professional identities and performative loyalties.[18] It gives political scientists their professional standings, which is why promotion through local ranks of the professoriate depends less on local evaluations in departments and more on evaluations from members of "the invisible college" of disciplinary colleagues nation- or worldwide.[19]

Yet the liberal discipline of political science had itself emerged from an earlier discipline of political science. American political scientists especially ought to recognize this, because they routinely teach that the United States was founded by men who claimed a science of politics so sophisticated that they had created "a machine that would go of itself."[20] The earlier discipline of political science was republican and practical rather than liberal and professional. A century after the founding era, however, the new political scientists were declaring their predecessors to be unscientific, undisciplined "theorists" who had no notion of trying to evidence their claims about political realities. The time had come to exchange the mongering of ideas and ideals for the systematic, scientific, realistic study of political behavior. Only then would political science be a genuine, modern discipline.

There ensued in political science a "behavioral revolution." Then another. And another. In the 1870s–1880s, the 1910s–1920s, and the 1950–1960s, each generational "revolution" became a new attempt to discipline the study of politics into a modern science. Each generation forgot that it was not the first to dedicate itself to adequately scientific, specifically behavioral studies of politics. Each ignored its predecessor's notions of what it could mean for political studies to become behavioral and realistic. So it is hardly a surprise that none of these liberal iterations of the discipline of political science preserves much sense that they were preceded by republican disciplines of politics and, eventually, political science. These come in classical, early modern, and high modern versions, with only the Enlightenment edition counting as a political science in a fully modern sense. The classical discipline gradually diminished to a something more like a technology of scholarship in the middle ages, before it was recuperated and updated by such Renaissance humanists as Guiciardini and Machiavelli.

PRE-MODERN DISCIPLINES OF POLITICS

The European meaning of science as systematic study is first satisfied for politics during the emergence of classical antiquity. In ancient Greece, the Sophists invented the discipline of rhetoric as the study and practice of speech-in-action-in-politics.[21] Relatively soon, the Romans invented the republic and constructed politics as speech-in-action-in-public. Hence we might say that political science began in classical times as the republican discipline of rhetoric.[22] Yet it was in no sense a modern discipline. It did not appear in universities, which were yet to be invented, nor was it exactly academic. In fact, the academy formed by the likes of Plato and Aristotle favored philosophy and knowledge over the insistent practicality and sophistry of rhetoric. Rhetoric was a public and practical discipline, not an academic one. (Indeed it is not clear that the academy could be said to include any "disciplines," even of a classical—which is to say, a republican—kind.) Rhetoric was pursued in the academic groves of antiquity mainly as preparation for leaving them, typically to take their learning into public arenas of practice.

Notwithstanding the academic hostility to rhetoric in the classical and medieval worlds of the West, it continued to be pursued as a practical discipline comparable to what Westerners now acknowledge as the Eastern disciplines of the martial arts. Republican disciplines often are martial too. They are exercises of mind and body to shape characters in public action. Rhetoric is no exception. Modern republicanism in the Renaissance regenerates this sense of discipline. Modern republicanism in the Enlightenment turns it into a kind of book learning that insists on relevance to public affairs but feels comfortable situating itself within modern universities. We might distinguish between the classical kind of republican discipline in politics and the modern kind of republican discipline in universities by reserving the term "discipline" for endeavors based in universities. Then we might write of "the republican-rhetorical tradition" to evoke the classical, medieval, and early modern trajectory of rhetoric as a study and practice of speech-in-action-in-public.[23] We can use this resurrected republican-rhetorical tradition as a platform for making sense of the double emergence of political science as a modern discipline.

The first heyday of republicanism, in Rome, preceded modern ideologies by more than a thousand years.[24] The second, in the Renaissance, stayed too prudential, rhetorical, and verbal to meet the ideological tests of logic and behavior.[25] The third, in the Enlightenment, spurred modern ideologies without exactly turning into one.[26] And a possible fourth, lurking on our electronic horizons, has affinities for postmodern cultures where ideologies no longer pipe the civilizational tune.[27] Even now, republicanism is far more a mythos than an ideology of politics. That is, it is more a network of stories and symbols than a platform of policies or a foundation for arguments.[28] Yet dynamics of publicity are so strong in electronic modes of communication, community, and therefore inquiry that it would not be surprising to see republican disciplines re-emerge for education in coming centuries, whether inside or outside recent multiversities.

MODERN DISCIPLINES OF POLITICAL SCIENCE

Republican politics inflected the modernization of medieval universities, informing the mutation of their faculties into academic disciplines and, later, departments. From the early notion of a republic of letters to the later template of a republic of science, modern disciplines in the social sciences take shape initially as republican institutions in the developing university.[29] But later they re-emerge as liberal governments. As an iron fist in the velvet glove of liberal freedom, these include authoritative unto authoritarian dynamics. Michel Foucault indicted them as the modern "discipline" that taps punishment to impose quasi-mechanical routines of mind and body that regiment professional conduct.[30] This displaces the earlier modern, more republican disciplines so fully that they no longer remain acknowledged as academic disciplines. Political science has done this to its earlier disciplinary self, disparaging as speculation earlier studies of institutions, arguments, and transactions.

The First Modern Discipline of Political Science

In the eighteenth and nineteenth centuries, republican institutions become liberal machines for the first modern discipline of political science. The modern republican discipline of political science arises from the classical tradition that connects republican politics and rhetoric as a concerted study of public politics. Its notion of disciplinarity is specifically republican; and it helps turn faculties of modern universities into proto-republican institutions, even as they study the institutions generated by the republican and increasingly liberal (or other ideological) politics in countries like the United States. The resulting discipline of political science is strikingly modern, and it predates the liberal discipline of political science by a century or more. Professional practitioners of the liberal discipline can be said to recognize it implicitly through their attacks on older versions of learning as armchair speculation and merely historical or documentary inquiry about institutions. Still these later disciplinarians missed the distinctive kind of discipline—which is to say, republican institution—of political science that had preceded them in the (high) modern university.

The founders of the United States participated in a practical discipline of political science that stemmed from modern republicanism. This takes itself to develop an institutional science of politics. It enjoys increasing knowledge of government branches, orders, powers, publics, and venues. It develops deliberation, founding, liberty, and revolution. It invents bicameralism, consultation, federalism, and martial law. Yet this discipline is also academic, forming itself into faculties of government or politics in the increasingly modern universities of the eighteenth and nineteenth centuries. It becomes book learning about what institutions are, how they work, how to design them, how to take part in them, and what to generate from them. As modern republics create written constitutions, this first modern discipline for the study (and practice) of politics becomes systematic inquiry into constitutional government that could prove responsive to the voices of citizens who no longer are expected merely to remain subject to the sovereign authority of the modern, centralized state.

To appreciate this republican discipline of political science, we do well to remember that republicanism predates modernity. Hence it influences modern politics less as a developed ideology than as a ramshackle set of myths, principles, and styles for forming, conducting, and (when appropriate) revolting against governments. Classical republicanism also survives as the tradition of civic rhetoric that high modern sciences at once revile in politicians yet seek to perfect in themselves. This is the inspiration for celebrations of "the republic of science," already noted to be a mythos immensely important in the institutional imagination of science fictions as well as science disciplines. Altogether the republican-rhetorical tradition provides three families of substantive conceptions available for takes on modern institutions.

For advocates of most postmodern politics, the modern imagery of republican *orders* is all too "disciplined"—in a military sense closer to the disciplines of body and character in martial-arts movies than to the professional mode of academic disciplines or the Foucauldian systems of surveillance and punishment. It also is too hierarchical. For it fits into the republican politics of tribunes and citizens or leaders and led, which direct democrats fault as dictatorial. This makes institutions into the "orders" of offices performed by the officials, the officers, of the republic. Nonetheless the notion of orders gradually becomes secondary in modern republicanism, because the offices of orders are significantly rhetorical. Hence each institution, as an order, is to include or function as something of a forum: as a small, partial, or proto-public for at least its own constituents.[31]

Modern republicans conceive institutions as the stitches in time and space that form *venues*.[32] Venues are ways to come into public visibility or audibility. This makes republican institutions into in-ventions that prevent disorder and disaster through the coming together of con-ventions.[33] Consequently republican institutions in modern times are con-ventions, pre-ventions, even inter-ventions. As modern images of vents and venues imply, this can configure them as networks of veins to circulate the lifeblood of a body among and within its vital organs. Thus republican institutions are connective, actively so. Because constitutions can come from conventions, and conventions from constitutions, modern institutions are also constitutive.[34] Venues tie better than classical orders to the republican tradition of civic rhetoric.

This is how American founders could expect to create a political culture sufficient for supporting their self-perpetuating political machine. In time, their republican institutions of government would *stitch* themselves into the citizenry. The dynamics of university disciplines in the mode of modern republicanism would be similar. They would be sewing machines to outfit the emerging gentility with the clothes of civilization. They would stitch into students the figures of learning and virtue for advancing civilization and especially their country's part in it.

Stitching in cloths includes not only the threads that join pieces of fabric into clothes but also the embroideries that color and texture the clothes into styles. Institutions embroider as well as tailor societies into civilizations and polities. Theirs are the arts of decoration (from Rome's republican decorum) that endow people in society with daily manners that reach from the everyday politics of politeness to the more sophisticated skills of informal governance and power called *politesse* by French republicans. This stylish stitching is what that postmodern republican Hannah Arendt called "doing beauty."[35] It is intrinsic to good action—rather than being "merely or perversely ornamental," as puritans or utilitarians might say. Accordingly the first modern discipline of political science was active, practical, and prudential rather than primarily contemplative or merely academic. Most republican disciplinarians addressed the issues of the day. Few could feel comfortable as antiquarians or as scholars for the sake of scholarship only. The republican discipline of political science has stressed action far more than has the liberal discipline, notwithstanding the liberal discipline's two early eras of strong interest in political reform.

In the same centuries that republicanism gives a modern disciplinarity to universities, it generates liberalism as a modern ideology for politics.[36] Ideologies treat disciplines and other institutions as machines, organizations, and mediators. The liberal image of the machine dominated the development of late modern universities, first in Germany and the United States then throughout the world. The republican portrait of institutions as stitches in time that form venues must be reconstructed from classical and early modern sources, as well as high modern disciplines, because images for institutions already featured machines by America's founding. Even as republican disciplines were forming, their tropes were changing out from under them.

The Second Modern Discipline of Political Science

Consequently the American university has continued to draw its sense of discipline mainly from liberalism. During the twentieth century, political science abstracted the liberal institution from a machine into a representation. This helped it leave behind the republican sense of discipline. Thus liberal machines turn into liberal representations for the second modern discipline of political science. Political science displaces the older discipline, without ever acknowledging it as a modern discipline. Ironically this transpired through a series of generational revolutions that enacted a republican principle for founding. Starting in the 1880s, and continuing throughout the 1900s, political science emerged repeatedly as a thoroughly liberal, more insistently modern discipline.

As the modern-republican discipline of political science moved toward the twentieth century, its accounts of politics became more and more liberal. (Politics in the United States also became more liberal, but there was an interaction between academic accounts and constructions within politics, so these are not completely independent dynamics.) Eventually political science re-emerged in the 1880s as a modern discipline in the liberal sense. The contrast between liberal and republican politics can be charted with room for imagining more politics possibly to come.

To articulate fully even the liberal concepts in table 13.2 could take books, and the same goes for the republican tropes.[37] Here the aim is just to evoke in catch-phrases a general contrast in politics between liberalism as a modern ideology and republicanism as a modern mythos.[38] The key point for the emergence of modern disciplines is that the two networks of politics projected two kinds of disciplines. After forming as a modern republican discipline in the seventeenth and eighteenth centuries, political science re-founded itself as a modern liberal discipline from the 1880s onward. Might political science arise anew, if postmodern or post-Western politics were to keep erupting in the twenty-first century? The last column is for fun![39]

Table 13.2 Different Political Sciences from Different Periods

Periods	*Early Modern*	*High Modern*	*Postmodern or Postwestern*
politics	republicanism	liberalism	existentialism or perfectionism
genres	mythos	ideology	philosophy or persuasion
styles	idealism	realism	constructivism or perspectivism
protections	survival, honor	security, prosperity	safety net, play
ambitions	stability, expansion	reform, progress	meaning, generativity
values	communal liberty	individual freedom	personal invention
laws	maxims, principles	rules, procedures	slogans, figures
compositions	institutions	processes	systems
members	citizens	individuals	intelligences
relations	imitation	representation	participation
social units	orders	groups	movements
policy places	venues	lobbies	fandoms
claims	stakes	interests	concerns
obligations	responsibilities	rights	reasons
powers	cooperation	leverage	flow
governments	commonwealth	sovereign nation-state	decentered state
regimes	republic	democracy	polyarchy
dynamics	public voice	popular opinion	uncommon (sub) cultures
modes	leadership	equality	diversity
decisions	consensus	majority	plurality or affinity
mutualities	respect	recognition	reconception
principles	independence	autonomy	charisma
oppositions	public vigilance	private criticism	public criticism
psyches	external character	internal self	decentered self

Source: Compiled by author.

In the middle of the twentieth century, Louis Hartz traced *The Liberal Tradition in America* back some two centuries to the country's founders.[40] His is a retrospective construction, and it projects liberalism onto a past American founding that had been far more republican than Hart, contemporary historians, or his successors were prepared to notice.[41] Even Lincoln's re-founding of America in the Civil War is more republican-rhetorical than liberal-democratic.[42] In fact, the relative recency of liberalism in the American disciplinary matrix of political science has become a theme in inquiries by the discipline's preeminent historian.[43] Liberalism as the political representation of interests is as old as John Locke or maybe even Thomas Hobbes in Britain's seventeenth century.[44] Yet it dominates the discipline of political science only with its re-emergence in the 1880s, the transactionalist turn to interest groups in the 1910s and 1920s, and especially the behavioralist stress on belief systems as sets of interests.[45] In this connection, the rationalist revolution means importing from economics into political science a more systematic, individualist, yet also institutionalist account of interests.[46] In becoming a fundamentally liberal discipline, political science generates more abstract, representational notions of institutions; and these transform the character and self-conception of political science as an academic discipline.

Behavioralist revolutions in political science take themselves to turn against established attention to details of institutions. This has been mere redescription of formal and informal rules for organizations. The behavioralists complain that little was being explained about why institutions operate as they do and that nothing was being learned about the many processes that occur between or beyond the institutions of modern government. Behavioralism would bring a genuinely scientific focus on human individuals, the actual atoms of political life.[47]

If modern institutions are machines, as liberals conceive them, modern explanations of their operations require comprehending what compose them and how those elements interact. So behavioralism would not abandon the republican concern with institutions but liberalize and make it scientific by coming to terms with the individuals whose interactions fundamentally are the institutions. This would configure the individuals more or less as cogs in machines, then it would abstract the machines into processes of interest re-presentation. When all goes well, the university institutions of academic disciplines would function as free markets of ideas that test putative truths and tap a community of inquirers to establish the plausibility of explanations for political phenomena.[48] Perhaps needless to say, this idea of disciplines dominates universities in the second half of the twentieth century, and not just in political science.

Actually behavioralism eclipsed institutional studies. Attention continued in America to the Presidency and the Supreme Court, and some students of the Congress stressed its folkways. Yet these inquiries increasingly came to be regarded as "historical" rather than social-scientific. As scientific surveys became immensely expensive and co-opted by campaign consultants and news organizations, technologies of behavioralism made way for inexpensive pencil-and-paper calculation of rational choices by abstracted versions of the individuals who are supposed to comprise institutions. Articulated opinions became attributed preferences. Institutional routines became individual games. For decades, even the rationalist revolution meant that institutions slipped deeper into the dark. The supposition became that just about anything can be explained, at least in principle, in terms of self-interested calculations of individuals, preferences, games, and genes. The fossilized dinosaurs of institutions became modern machines—only to be translated into processes of representation.

As progenitors of rational-choice work in political science demonstrated decades ago, the catch is that the representational algorithms of rational choice do not yield determinant solutions for most situations in politics.[49] Only when special, delimiting assumptions are made does it become even vaguely plausible for political scientists to re-present political situations as (solvable) problems for economic decision by self-interest individuals. Political institutions are seldom markets, and politics of most institutions keep them from good approximations of free markets.[50] Without those, we lack the interpersonal comparisons of utilities crucial to collective efficiency in choice. But if not as markets, how else might most social and political situations be institutionalized? Enter "the new institutionalism," which has treated institutions as sets of rules.

The Postmodern Disciplines of Political Science

In institutional terms, this might still be the discipline of political science that we know of late. Yet it keeps changing (and markedly). *Methodenstreiten* have fulfilled Thomas Jefferson's generational (and republican) pattern of constitutional revolutions (as "revolvings") through behavioral rededications of the liberal, realist discipline in the 1870s–1880s, 1910s–1920s, and 1950–1960s.[51] The rationalist revolution of the 1990s–2000s continues to treat calculations of expected utility and experiments in political cognition as focusing clearly on individual behavior. But then these liberal representations become kinds of cultural studies in the twenty-first century (table 13.3).

"The" behavioral revolution of the 1950s and 1960s pursues the political strategy of contrasting itself to an older approach of "institutionalism." This is evident in the work of Robert Dahl at Yale and Heinz Eulau at Stanford.[52] It is also apparent in criticisms lodged from "traditional institutionalists" to "post-behavioralists."[53] By sparing, ignoring, or allying with remaining transactionalists,[54] these behavioralists produce a particularly concerted shift of the modern, liberal discipline. This helps account for the two disciplinary regimes of political reform and political report, a separation first constructed by behavioralists and later embraced by rationalists. Again the table could be articulated, but it mainly collects familiar labels into recognizable groups in order to evoke the liberal discipline's overall patterns of inquiry.

Political science has moved from a classical discipline to a modern one. It has emerged and re-emerged as a modern discipline. It has revolved around behavioral reinventions nearly every generation. It seems unlikely to stop evolving. Many additional "approaches" have been ventured. (The amorphous idea of an "approach" is a recurrent, virtually defining trope of the modern liberal discipline of political science.[55]) The others have caught on, if at all, only in one or two subfields at a time. Cybernetics, political

Table 13.3 Generational Revolutions in Late Modern Political Science

Disciplines	*Political Science as Reform*		*Political Science as Report*	
Revolutions	*1870s–1880s*	*1910s–1920s*	*1950s–1960s*	*1990s–2000s*
inquiry methods	institutionalism	transactionalism	behavioralism	rationalism
ideas of polity	states	governments	systems	markets
units of analysis	institutions	groups	individuals	choices
kinds of data	documents	interests	beliefs	utilities
sources of data	archives	case studies	surveys	experiments
sorts of statistics	kinds	counts	correlations	regressions
measurements	nominal	ordinal	interval	interval

Source: Compiled by author.

psychology, political socialization, and political geography are examples. None of these has disappeared from the modern liberal discipline of political science; and some have formed subfields of their own, usually for a fairly short time. Yet none has come close to permeating the modern disciplines of political science as their liberal institutionalism, transactionalism, behavioralism, and rationalism have done.

Yet comparative political inquiries and some branches of international studies entered the current century turning toward "thick" encounters with cultural institutions by contrast with the "thin" generalizations available from statistical analysis of most national and international data. Arguably this development appropriates questions as well as methods from the "thick description" of cultures pursued for more than a generation by some anthropologists.[56] Two of the innovations now most likely to reconfigure political science as a discipline are informatics and cultural studies (in non-Marxian forms). The discipline's late twentieth-century interest in democratization and its rediscovery of civil society combine with renewed interest in political cognition and communication to lead from liberal representations to cultural representations. Some contributions in this vein even show how culture is a republican-rhetorical category by finding republican politics in liberal institutions.[57] Might political science reinvent a republican discipline as an institutional course that inquiries can run? Stay tuned.

NOTES

1. See Nelson (1998, 150–79).
2. See Kuhn (1970). Frederic J. Fleron is the first political scientist to make me aware of the historical development of political science as a discipline—by including me in his explorations of attempts to study Russian politics in times of Soviet secrecy and American behavioralism: what a privilege, and what a treat!
3. On history of science, see Porter (1986); Latour (1987); Shapin (2010). On sociology of scientific knowledge, see Mulkay (1979); Collins (1982); Gilbert and Mulkay (1984); Ashmore (1989); and Barnes, Bloor, and Henry (1996). On rhetoric of inquiry, see Nelson, Megill, and McCloskey (1987); Bazerman (1988); Simons (1989); and McCloskey (1998).
4. See Nelson (1998, 34–46).
5. See Nelson (1980a).
6. See White (1973) and White (1978). See also Nelson (1975) and Nelson (1980b).
7. A case can be made for treating each of these modern disciplines as the emergence of a significantly political science. See Nelson (1998, 72–98).
8. See Pocock (1975); Skinner (1990); Skinner (1995); and Pettit (1997).
9. See Skinner (1996); Miller (2011); and Tuck (2015).

10. See McLuhan (1964, 7–21).

11. See Gunnell (1998) and Gunnell (2004). Also see Nelson (1986a).

12. See Nelson (1983b).

13. This republican move traces to Giambattista Vico. See Nelson (1998, 117–204).

14. On the late modern multiversity, see Nelson (1986b, 18 n. 3)

15. Somit and Tanenhaus (1967) and Seidman and Harpham (1985).

16. See Crick (1959) and Crick (1962).

17. See Nelson (1998, 34–46).

18. See Kerr (1963).

19. See Crane (1972).

20. See Kammen (1986).

21. See Nelson (1983b).

22. See Nelson (1993).

23. See Nelson (2003).

24. See McGee and Nelson (1985).

25. See Struever (1970) and Struever (1992).

26. See Nelson (1983b).

27. See Nelson (1998, 205–30).

28. See Robertson (1980).

29. See Michael Polanyi (1962). A powerful argument for modern scientific inquiry as inherently republican is made in story form by Kim Stanley Robinson in his Mars trilogy: *Red Mars* (1993), *Green Mars* (1994, esp. 182–83), and *Blue Mars* (1996).

30. See Foucault (1977).

31. These days, we can look back on the Order of Cincinnatus in the early years of the United States. Or we can see how J. K. Rowling uses this republican device in *Harry Potter and the Order of the Phoenix* (2003). Also see Nelson (2021, 201–208).

32. On policy venues in the latest French republic, see Baumgartner (1989).

33. See Cavell (1979).

34. See Nelson (1980b) and Nelson (1998).

35. See Arendt (1971); Gray (1977). Also see Nelson (2013, 87–90); Nelson (2015, 179–81); and Nelson (2018, 22–25).

36. See Rosenblum (1987) and Terchek (1997).

37. See Unger (1975); Wood (1972); and Nelson (1998, 135–49).

38. On the possibilities of post-Western politics, see Nelson (2018, 3–10).

39. See Roelofs (1976).

40. See Hartz (1948) and Hartz (1955).

41. See Bailyn (1960) and Bailyn (1967a, 1967b). Also see Wood (1969).

42. See Wills (1992).

43. See Gunnell (1990) and Gunnell (2001).

44. See Birch (1971); Pitkin (1967); Mack (1984); and Ankersmit (2002).

45. See Nelson (1977).

46. See Nelson (1987); McCloskey and Nelson (1990).

47. See Eulau (1963); Eulau (1969). Also see Nelson (1983c); Graham and Carey (1972).

48. See Wills (1969).

49. See Arrow (1963); Riker (1982); Riker (1983); Green (1994); and Hauptmann (1996).

50. See Lindblom (1977).

51. See Arendt (1963).

52. See Dahl (1956); Dahl (1961); Dahl (1970); and Dahl (1971).

53. See McCoy and Playford (1967); and Ricci (1984).

54. See Bentley (1908) and Truman (1951). Also see Kress (1970).

55. See Haas (1970).

56. See Geertz (1973); Geertz (1983); Clifford (1986); Clifford (1988).

57. See Norton (1993); Dolan and Dumm (1993); Bennett and Segerberg (2013); and Hart (2020).

REFERENCES

Ankersmit, F. R. 2002. *Political Representation*. Stanford, CA: Stanford University Press.

Arendt, Hannah. 1963. *On Revolution*. New York: Viking Press.

———. 1971. "Thinking and Moral Considerations." *Social Research* 38, no. 3 (Autumn): 417–46.

Arrow, Kenneth J. 1963. *Social Choice and Individual Values*. 2nd ed. New Haven, CT: Yale University Press.

Ashmore, Malcolm. 1989. *The Reflexive Thesis*. Chicago: University of Chicago Press.

Bailyn, Bernard. 1960. *Education in the Forming of American Society*. Chapel Hill: University of North Carolina Press.

———. 1967a. *The Ideological Origins of the American Revolution*. Cambridge, MA: Harvard University Press.

———. 1967b. *The Origins of American Politics*. New York: Random House.

Barnes, Barry, David Bloor, and John Henry. 1996. *Scientific Knowledge*.Chicago: University of Chicago Press.

Baumgartner, Frank R. 1989. *Conflict and Rhetoric in French Policymaking*. Pittsburgh, PA: University of Pittsburgh Press.

Bazerman, Charles. 1988. *Shaping Written Knowledge*. Madison, WI: University of Wisconsin Press.

Bennett, W. Lance, and Alexandra Segerberg. 2013. *The Logic of Connective Action*. New York: Cambridge University Press.

Bentley, Arthur F. 1908. *The Process of Government*. Chicago: University of Chicago Press.

Birch, Anthony H. 1971. *Representation*. New York: Praeger.

Cavell, Stanley. 1979. *The Claim of Reason*. New York: Oxford University Press.

Clifford, James. 1986. *Writing Culture*. Berkeley, CA: University of California Press.
———. 1988. *The Predicament of Culture*. Cambridge, MA: Harvard University Press.
Collins, Harry M. 1982. *Frames of Meaning*. London: Routledge and Kegan Paul.
Crane, Diana. 1972. *Invisible Colleges*. Chicago: University of Chicago Press.
Crick, Bernard R. 1959. *The American Science of Politics*. Berkeley, CA: University of California Press.
———. 1962. *In Defense of Politics*. Chicago: University of Chicago Press.
Dahl, Robert A. 1956. *A Preface to Democratic Theory*. Chicago: University of Chicago Press.
———. 1961. "The Behavioral Approach in Political Science." *American Political Science Review* 55, no. 4 (December): 763–72.
———. 1970. *After the Revolution?* New Haven, CT: Yale University Press.
———. 1971. *Polyarchy*. New Haven, CT: Yale University Press.
Dolan, Frederick M., and Thomas L. Dumm, eds. 1993. *Rhetorical Republic*. Amherst, MA: University of Massachusetts Press.
Eulau, Heinz. 1963. *The Behavioral Persuasion in Politics*. Stanford, CA: Stanford University Press.
———. 1969. *Behavioralism in Political Science*. New York: Atherton Press.
Foucault, Michel. 1977. *Discipline and Punish*, trans. Alan Sheridan. New York: Random House.
Geertz, Clifford. 1973. *The Interpretation of Cultures*. New York: Basic Books.
———. 1983. *Local Knowledge*. New York: Basic Books.
Gilbert, G. Nigel, and Michael Mulkay. 1984. *Opening Pandora's Box*. Cambridge: Cambridge University Press.
Graham Jr., George J., and George W. Carey, eds. 1972. *The Post-Behavioral Era*. New York: David McKay.
Gray, J. Glenn. 1977. "The Winds of Thought." *Social Research* 44, no. 1 (Spring): 44–62.
Green, Donald P. 1994. *Pathologies of Rational Choice Theory*. New Haven, CT: Yale University Press.
Gunnell, John G. 1990. "In Search of the State." In *Discourses on Society, Volume XV*, edited by P. Wagner, B. Wittrock, and R. Whitley, 123–61. Amsterdam: Kluwer.
———. 1998. *The Orders of Discourse*. Lanham, MD: Rowman and Littlefield.
———. 2001. "Archaeology of American Liberalism." *Journal of Political Ideologies* 6, no. 2 (June): 125–45.
———. 2004. *Imagining the American Polity*. University Park, TX: Penn State University Press.
Haas, Michael. 1970. *Approaches to the Study of Political Science*. Scranton, PA: Chandler.
Hart, Roderick P. 2020. *Trump and Us*. New York: Cambridge University Press.
Hartz, Louis. 1948. *Economic Policy and Democratic Thought*. Chicago: Quadrangle Books.

———. 1955. *The Liberal Tradition in America*. New York: Harcourt, Brace and World.
Hauptman, Emily I. 1996. *Putting Choice Before Democracy*. Albany, NY: State University of New York Press.
Kammen, Michael. 1986. *A Machine That Would Go of Itself*. New York: Random House.
Kerr, Clark. 1963. *The Uses of the University*. New York: Harper and Row.
Kress, Paul F. 1970. *Social Science and the Idea of Process*. Urbana, IL: University of Illinois Press.
Kuhn, Thomas S. 1970. *The Structure of Scientific Revolutions*. Chicago: University of Chicago Press.
Latour, Bruno. 1987. *Science in Action*. Cambridge, MA: Harvard University Press.
Lindblom, Charles. 1977. *Politics and Markets*. New York: Basic Books.
Mack, Arien, ed. 1984. Special Issue on "Representation." *Social Research* 51, no. 4 (Winter): 839–1097.
McCloskey, D. N. 1998. *The Rhetoric of Economics*. 2nd ed. Madison, WI: University of Wisconsin Press.
McCloskey, D. N., and John S. Nelson. 1990. "The Rhetoric of Political Economy." In *From Political Economy to Economics . . . And Back?*, edited by James H. Nichols Jr. and Colin Wright, 155–74. San Francisco, CA: Institute for Contemporary Studies Press.
McCoy, Charles A., and John Playford, eds. 1967. *Apolitical Politics*. New York: Thomas Y. Crowell.
McGee, Michael Calvin, and John S. Nelson. 1985. "Narrative Reason in Public Argument." *Journal of Communication* 35, no. 4 (Autumn): 139–55.
McLuhan, Marshall. 1964. *Understanding Media: The Extensions of Man*. New York: McGraw-Hill.
Miller, Ted H. 2011. *Mortal Gods*. University Park, PA: Penn State University Press.
Mulkay, Michael. 1979. *Science and the Sociology of Knowledge*. London: George Allen and Unwin.
Nelson, Anna Lorien, and John S. Nelson. 1998. "Institutions in Feminist and Republican Science Fiction." *Legal Studies Forum* 22, no. 4: 641–53.
Nelson, John S. 1975. "Review Essay [on *Metahistory*]." *History and Theory* 14, no 1: 74–91.
———. 1977. "The Ideological Connection, Parts I-II." *Theory and Society* 4, nos. 3–4 (Fall-Winter): 421–48 and 573–90.
———. 1980a. "Ashcraft's Problem of Ideology." *Journal of Politics* 42, no. 3 (August). 709–15.
———. 1980b. "Tropal History and the Social Sciences." *History and Theory* 19, no. 4: 80–101.
———, ed. 1983a. *What Should Political Theory Be Now?* Albany, NY: State University of New York Press.

———. 1983b. "Political Theory as Political Rhetoric." In *What Should Political Theory Be Now?*, edited by John S. Nelson, 169–240. Albany, NY: State University of New York Press.

———. 1983c. "Education for Politics," In *What Should Political Theory Be Now?*, edited by John S. Nelson, 413–78. Albany, NY: State University of New York Press.

———, ed. 1986a. *Tradition, Interpretation, and Science*. Albany, NY: State University of New York Press.

———. 1986b. "Irony and Autonomy." In *Tradition, Interpretation, and Science*, edited by John S. Nelson, 1–20. Albany, NY: State University of New York Press.

———. 1987. "Stories of Science and Politics." In *The Rhetoric of the Human Sciences*, edited by John S. Nelson, Allan Megill, and D. N. McCloskey, 198–220. Madison, WI: University of Wisconsin Press.

———. 1993. "Commerce Among the Archipelagos." In *The Core and the Canon*, edited by L. Robert Stevens, G. L. Seligmann, and Julian Long, 78–100. Denton, TX: University of North Texas Press.

———. 1998. *Tropes of Politics*. Madison, WI: University of Wisconsin Press.

———. 2003. "Prudence as Republican Politics in American Popular Culture." In *Prudence*, edited by Robert Hariman, 229–57. University Park, PA: Penn State University Press.

———. 2013. *Popular Cinema as Political Theory*. New York: Palgrave Macmillan.

———. 2015. *Politics in Popular Movies*. Boulder: Paradigm.

———. 2018. *Cowboy Politics*. Lanham, MD: Lexington Books.

———. 2021. *Defenses Against the Dark Arts*. Lanham, MD: Lexington Books.

Nelson, John S., Allan Megill, and D. N. McCloskey, eds. 1987. *The Rhetoric of the Human Sciences*. Madison, WI: University of Wisconsin Press.

Norton, Anne. 1993. *Republic of Signs*. Chicago: University of Chicago Press.

Petit, Philip. 1997. *Republicanism*. Oxford: Oxford University Press.

Pitkin, Hanna Fenichel. 1967. *The Concept of Political Representation*. Berkeley, CA: University of California Press.

Pocock, J. G. A. 1975. *The Machiavellian Moment*. Princeton, NJ: Princeton University Press.

Polanyi, Michael. 1962. "The Republic of Science." *Minerva* 1, no. 1 (Autumn): 54–73.

Porter, Theodore M. 1986. *The Rise of Statistical Thinking, 1820-1900*. Princeton, NJ: Princeton University Press.

Ricci, David. 1984. *The Tragedy of Political Science*. New Haven, CT: Yale University Press.

Riker, William H. 1982. *The Art of Political Manipulation*. New Haven, CT: Yale University Press.

———. 1983. "Political Theory and the Art of Heresthetics." In *Political Science*, edited by Ada W. Finifter, 47–67. Washington, DC: American Political Science Association.

Robertson, James Oliver. 1980. *American Myth, American Reality*. New York: Hill and Wang.

Robinson, Kim Stanley. 1993. *Red Mars*. New York: Bantam Books.

———. 1994. *Green Mars*. New York: Bantam Books.

———. 1996. *Blue Mars*. New York: Bantam Books.

Roelofs, H. Mark. 1976. *Ideology and Myth in American Politics*. Boston, MA: Little, Brown.

Rosenblum, Nancy L. 1987. *Another Liberalism*. Cambridge, MA: Harvard University Press.

Rowling, J. K. 2003. *Harry Potter and the Order of the Phoenix*. New York: Scholastic Press.

Seidman, Raymond, with Edward J. Harpham. 1985. *Disenchanted Realists*. Albany, NY: State University of New York Press.

Shapin, Steven. 2010. *Never Pure*. Baltimore, MD: Johns Hopkins University Press.

Simons, Herbert W., ed. 1989. *Rhetoric in the Human Sciences*. Newbury Park, CA: Sage.

Skinner, Quentin. 1990. *Machiavelli and Republicanism*. Cambridge: Cambridge University Press.

———. 1995. *Milton and Republicanism*. Cambridge: Cambridge University Press.

———. 1996. *Reason and Rhetoric in the Philosophy of Hobbes*. Cambridge: Cambridge University Press.

Somit, Albert Somit, and Joseph Tanenhaus. 1967. *The Development of Political Science*. Boston, MA: Allyn and Bacon.

Struever, Nancy S. 1970. *The Language of History in the Renaissance*. Princeton, NJ: Princeton University Press.

———. 1992. *Theory as Practice*. Chicago: University of Chicago Press.

Terchek, Ronald J. 1997. *Republican Paradoxes and Liberal Anxieties*. Lanham, MD: Rowman and Littlefield.

Truman, David B. 1951. *The Governmental Process*. New York: Knopf.

Tuck, Richard. 2015. *The Sleeping Sovereign*. Cambridge: Cambridge University Press.

Unger, Roberto Mangabeira. 1975. *Knowledge and Politics*. New York: Free Press.

White, Hayden. 1973. *Metahistory*. Baltimore, MD: Johns Hopkins University Press.

———. 1978. *Tropics of Discourse*. Baltimore, MD: Johns Hopkins University Press.

Wills, Garry. 1969. *Nixon Agonistes*. Boston, MA: Houghton Mifflin.

———. 1992. *Lincoln at Gettysburg*. New York: Simon and Schuster.

Wood, Ellen Meiksins. 1972. *Mind and Politics*. Berkeley, CA: University of California Press.

Wood, Gordon. 1969. *The Creation of the American Republic, 1776-1787*. Chapel Hill, NC: University of North Carolina Press.

Chapter 14

Political Polarization, Electoral Support for the AKP, and the Challenge of Democratization in Turkey, 2002–2021

Munroe Eagles and Seymen Atasoy

In this chapter we take up a central theme in the work of Frederic Fleron, namely the identification of preconditions for stable democratization. We do this in the context of an exploration of the contemporary challenges facing the democratization of Turkey, a strategic geopolitical partner in NATO and an emergent economic and regional power in the Middle East. Our analysis focuses on changes and continuities in the electoral support base of the AKP, the party founded by Recep Tayyip Erdoğan that has governed Turkey since 2002. Specifically, we use the three most recent Turkish waves of the World Values Survey (fielded in 2007, 2012, and 2017) to explore the social and value foundations of AKP voting in the three phases of the party's evolution—the golden age between 2002 and 2007, a transitional phase between 2007 and 2011, and a declining phase since June 2011. We show that the party's Islamist and right-wing appeal are relatively constant across the decade studied, but that other sources of the party's electoral success are more variable. We also discuss the challenge that increased polarization in the Turkish electorate presents for the prospects of future democratic consolidation in the country.

INTRODUCTION

One of the many research themes that arise in the wide-ranging writings of Fred Fleron is his concern with the social and cultural preconditions for democracy and democratization. This question arises in a number of

Professor Fleron's writings, particularly as it concerned the process of democratization in post-Soviet Russia (see in particular his coauthored book with Harry Eckstein, Erik Hoffmann, and William Reisinger [1998]). In this chapter, we take up this research topic in an exploration of the contemporary challenges facing the democratization of Turkey, a strategic geopolitical partner in NATO and an emergent economic and regional power in the Middle East.[1] With only a couple brief interludes, since the establishment of free and competitive elections in 1950, Turkey appeared to be on its way to becoming the first stable and institutionalized liberal democracy in an Islamic society. However, the Turkish experience over the last 20 years gives evidence of many of the concerning trends associated with the rise of "authoritarian populism" in other democratic and democratizing countries (Norris and Inglehart, 2019).

We inquire about the prospects for democracy in Turkey by examining sentiments evident in the country's electorate since 2002, a period that has been dominated by former Prime Minister and now President Recep Tayyip Erdoğan and his Justice and Development (AK) Party. Specifically, our chapter employs three Turkish waves of the World Values Survey (fielded in 2007, 2012, and 2017) to look at the sources of voter support for this party over a period in which its commitment to democratic practices appears to wane. Fortunately, these surveys were fielded during each of what Ziya Öniş (2016, 142) has described as the three phases in the development of the AKP. As a result, we are in a position to assess the extent to which these phases were characterized by different relationships between the AKP and its voters. The first period, which he refers to as the golden years (2002–2007), was marked by economic recovery and growth, democratizing reforms, and foreign policy advances centered on the drive for Turkish membership in the European Union. The second "transitional" period (2007–2011) saw the consolidation of AKP power with the continued marginalization of the armed forces and the judiciary, key defenders of the Kemalist secular order, and a slowing of economic and political reforms. The third phase in the development of the AKP began after the June 2011 election and was essentially characterized by a reversal of the developments of the earlier "golden age." These setbacks prominently included an erosion of judicial independence that signaled a retreat in terms of the rule of law. Police crack-downs on protestors, allegations of high-level corruption, and proposals for constitutional reform that would replace Turkey's parliamentary system with a presidential alternative that concentrated power in the hands of the chief executive, all marked a retreat from democratization.

After a brief review of political developments in Turkey since 2002 that focus on the importance of political polarization in the electorate, we develop a multivariate model incorporating a variety of perspectives on potential sources of AKP support, including theories of social capital that have been advanced to explain the success of democracy, religious convictions, government performance evaluations, and measures of political values. Using the WVS data we look for changes in the social and political foundations of AKP support over the period that might account for the party's continued dominance despite the degradation of democratic values and practices. Through this investigation we seek to evaluate the social underpinnings of the AKP's weakening of Turkey's democratic state institutions and practices. In conclusion, we turn to a consideration of the prospects for a resumption of democratization in the country.

POLITICAL POLARIZATION IN CONTEMPORARY TURKEY

Particularly troubling for the institutionalization of democracy in the post-2002 Turkish experience has been a growing polarization in the electorate. The roots of this extend deeply into Turkish history. The polarization between modernizing elites and religious conservatives dating back to eighteenth-century Ottoman Empire re-emerged in twenty-first-century Turkey between the supporters and the opponents of President Erdoğan. When the mainstream political parties lost control during the economic crisis of the early 2000s, Erdoğan came to power riding the historic resentment wave of Islamists and traditional masses toward the modernist establishment. His constant angry verbal attacks on opponents articulated the feelings of these aggrieved masses and endeared Erdoğan to them. Having thus become an identification object for the indignant conservatives, he politically thrived on conflict. Scheduling the stages toward his grandiose vision for the "new Turkey" for 2023, 2053, and 2071, he is drawing a parallelism to the turning points of Turkish history: establishment of the Republic in 1923, the conquest of Istanbul in 1453, and the Battle of Manzikert in 1071 (Erdoğan in 2017, 2013). Setting bygone victories as a standard for future greatness, he attempts to march forward to the past with cheerful followers sharing his nostalgia for power (Yavuz, 2020), wasting the opportunity to lead Islamists and conservative Muslims in Turkey and beyond toward democracy.

There is no longer a single overarching socio-political-cultural reality in Turkey. Traumatic identity politics during the last two decades has split the national psyche into two associated groupings of proponents and dissidents that have socially constructed their competing consensus realities. The mental world of those pleased with Erdoğan and his "new Turkey" is largely shaped by pro-government media and the AKP propaganda apparatus. In it, a visionary leadership is generating unprecedented successes in economic development, foreign policy, and cultural enrichment, while existing problems are temporary and caused by the machinations of external and internal enemies. In the contrasting interpretation of reality by the opposition, an alliance of reactionary forces under the leadership of Erdoğan is looting the country and squandering its economic resources in trying to hold on to power through populist perception-management, in the process, destroying Turkey's aspiration to become a modern democracy. Subsumed under the opposition reality, there is a separate Kurdish reality. This dissociation complicates cooperation within the opposition block and forms its soft underbelly.

Founded in 2001, Erdoğan's AKP (also referred to as Ak Party—Justice and Development Party) originally presented itself as a conservative democratic party and was legitimately elected into office in 2002. However, it has gradually shed many of its democratic qualities in favor of an authoritarian synthesis of Islamism with nationalism during the 2010s. As Erdoğan sought to pragmatically adapt to changing circumstances in order to remain in power, a new Islamo-nationalist political elite consisting of believers and opportunists took shape and consolidated itself around him. Although economic decline has been reducing electoral support for this regime in recent years, as of 2021 it is still attempting to consolidate its rule with its increasingly centralized political power. Claiming to construct a stronger "new Turkey," Erdoğan is weakening the fundamental institutions of the modern state such as, the rule of law, separation of powers, transparent accountability, free media, and a pluralistic civil society.

According to a comprehensive 2019 report by Konda (2019), a reputable public opinion research company in Turkey, polarization over values determines politics in the country: the values of a more educated, younger, urbanized, secular, and modern middle/upper class are clashing with the values defended by those from middle/lower socioeconomic classes with roots in rural areas and small towns, having traditional life-styles and less education. A more recent study by Turkuazlab (2020) of the dimensions of polarization in Turkey in 2020 confirms that Turkey remains on a path of increasing division that is strongly related to political partisanship. The survey stresses the overlap of political party preferences with corresponding collective identities in Turkey turning partisanship into a "supra-identity" and determines that supporters of AKP identified more with religious people and conservatives, supporters of MHP (Nationalist Movement Party) identified more with nationalists and ultranationalists, supporters of İyi Parti (the Good Party) identified more with educated and modern people, supporters of CHP identified more with Kemalists, secularists and Alawites, and supporters of HDP (Peoples' Democratic Party) identified more with Kurds (Turkuazlab, 2020).

These developments are reflected in the declining freedom scores assigned to Turkey by Freedom House (see figure 14.1). As one recent analysis argued:

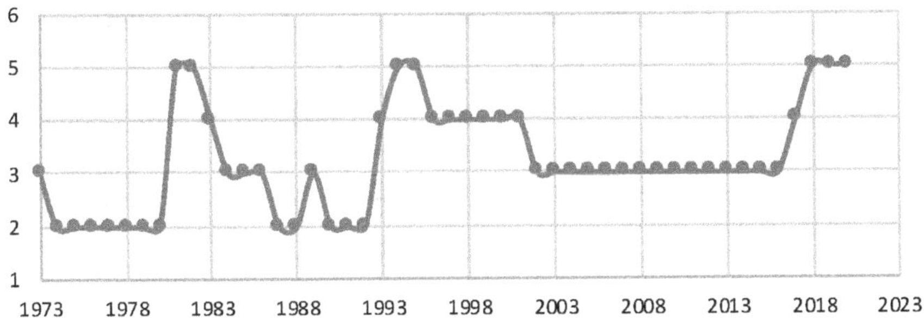

Figure 14.1 Freedom House Political Rights Score, Turkey. *Source*: Compiled by authors from data by Freedomhouse.org. The scale ranges from a minimum of 1 (most free) to a maximum of 7 (least free).

> The Justice and Development Party and President Recep Tayyip Erdoğan have been implementing highly comprehensive, multiple and innovative strategies so as to suppress the emergence of any democratic alternatives and consolidate this newly rising political regime, which is organized around the supreme power of the President, erosion of checks and balances and separation of powers. (Yilmaz and Turner 2019, 691)

THE PUBLIC OPINION CONTEXT

To what extent does the AKP's retreat from democratic freedoms and norms reflect an underlying shift in the public's support for these achievements? Have Turks become disillusioned with democracy? Have they lost confidence in the key institutional pillars of democratic governance? Alternatively, have Erdogan and other political leaders been able to consolidate their personal hold on power despite significant grassroots support for democracy and its institutional requisites? To begin answering these questions we turn to the evidence concerning the attitudes and orientations of the Turkish people as they have been revealed in the six waves of the World Values Survey for this country since 1990.

One of the sets of questions bearing most directly on these questions concerns taps the preferences of Turks with respect to their political regime. Figure 14.2 presents the percentages of respondents preferring the following alternatives: a democratic political system; a system in which strong leaders are relatively unconstrained by parties or parliament; a technocratic system in which experts and not elected officials decide issues; and rule by the armed forces. Despite the armed forces' traditional view of itself as the custodians of Turkish democracy, support for rule by the armed forces is concentrated in a minority of Turkish respondents and declines only slightly over the almost

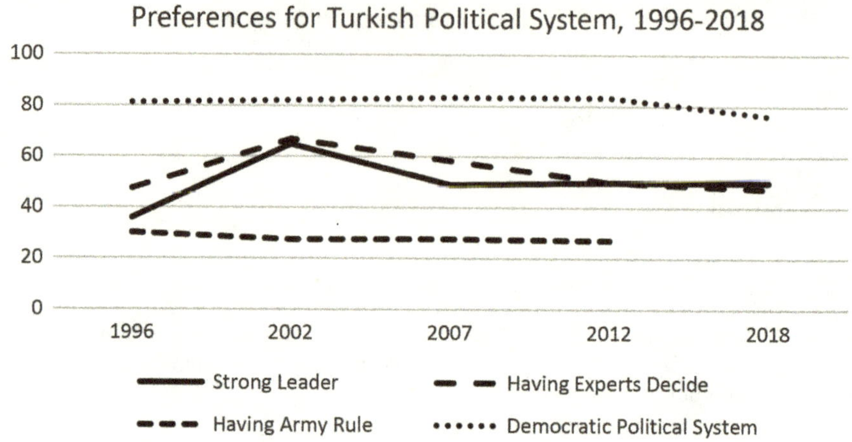

Figure 14.2 Preferences for Turkish Political System, 1996–2018. *Source*: Compiled by authors from data by World Values Survey, Turkish waves.

three decades covered by the surveys. Support for technocratic administration rose in the first two surveys but has declined rather sharply since the 2002 survey. It is the democratic option that attracts the support of a large and relatively stable majority of Turkish respondents. Perhaps ominously, there is a slight decline in the preference for democracy between the 2012 and 2017 surveys (and a smaller growth in support for the "strong leader" option over that period).

It seems unlikely, then, that the setbacks in the path toward democracy that Turkey has experienced in recent years has resulted from any sudden collapse in public support for democratic norms and practices, nor from a groundswell of popular demands for a strong-man or authoritarian style of leadership. Rather, the picture appears to be one of relatively stable preferences for democratic rule since 1996 (when this battery of questions was first included in the WVS). However, it might be troubling to note that the strong leader and technocratic alternatives both retain robust and relatively stable followings that hover around the 50% mark, as shown in figure 14.2.

Another way of examining the public opinion context pertaining to democracy is to look at the relative levels of confidence that respondents express toward the major institutional powers in Turkish society (figure 14.3). Despite the relatively low level of preference for rule by the armed forces, this institution retains the highest level of confidence of any in the country. In fact, it is striking that the three institutions enjoying the highest levels of public confidence are those of the "repressive apparatus" of the state—the

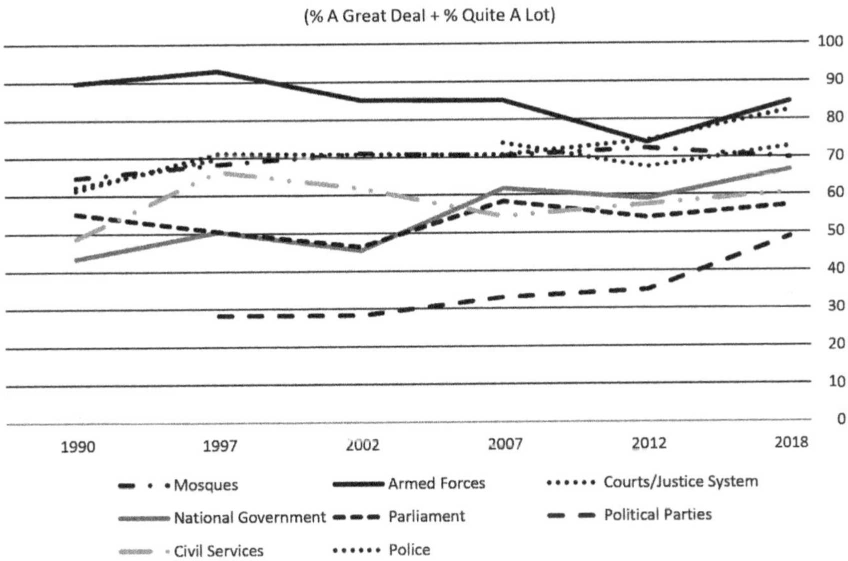

Figure 14.3 Confidence in Turkish Institutions, 1990–2018. *Source*: Compiled by authors from data by Turkish Waves of the World Values Survey, 1990–2018.

armed forces, the police, and the judiciary. Only confidence in mosques rivals these institutions. By contrast, confidence in the national government and parliament both declined between 1990 and 2002, when less than half of respondents expressed confidence in these critically important institutions. However, these numbers have improved over the 2002–2017 period and by the end of that period two-thirds of respondents had confidence in the national government and roughly 57% trusted parliament.

The data presented in figure 14.3 also reveals that public confidence in political parties and the press is the lowest of all institutions. Despite being critical to successful democratic functioning, these two institutions only have the confidence of minorities of Turkish respondents. This likely reflects the negative impact of the polarizing Turkish electorate on these critically important sectors. Clearly, although there is some evidence of the consolidation of democratic institutions since 1990 to be found in the trends reported in figure 14.3, there remains ample indication that the institutional configurations most important for democratic governance remain challenged by other foci of power in the Turkish state and in Turkish society. Arguably, this ambiguity in the public's embrace of democratic institutions has provided Erdoğan and his supporters in the AKP with an opportunity to consolidate their hold on power and to undermine some of the key institutional supports for Turkish democracy. Could it be that AKP supporters are decidedly lukewarm concerning democracy and its associated institutions when compared with other Turkish citizens?

To address this question, we need to look at the bases of support for Erdoğan and the AKP in recent elections. Do AKP voters embrace distinctively anti-democratic values when compared to supporters of other parties or non-voters? Or are AKP voters motivated by factors such as the approval of the government's performance, ideology, for example, when they express support for the AKP? Do these relationships change as the AKP moved during the decade from a democratizing force to one championing repressive and increasingly authoritarian positions? Is there evidence of political polarization in the electorate that potentially threatens the progress of democratic consolidation? Answering these questions necessitates a multivariate analysis to identify the independent explanatory power of each measure when the influence of other variables in the model is statistically controlled. We turn to this in the next section in an examination of whether AKP voters' attitudes and orientations to democracy contribute in a significant way to explaining electoral support for the AKP when compared to other citizens, after the potential impact of other potential influences have been statistically controlled.

Multivariate Models of the Electoral Support for the AKP, 2007–2017

In this section we utilize the items included in the three most recent Turkish waves of the World Values Survey (2007, 2012, and 2017) that coincide with the period after Erdoğan's AKP came to power to attempt to capture the likely social, cultural, and political sources of support for the AKP. Our dependent variable in these analyses is whether respondents indicated that they would vote for the AKP if a national election were to be held tomorrow (scored 1 if they would vote for the AKP; otherwise the variable is scored 0). Our focus on vote intentions rather than reported voting choices at a particular election helps us avoid the potentially distorting effects of campaign-related events or issues. In order to appreciate whether AKP supporters are distinctive from non-supporters in their valuation of democracy and its associated institutions, and that these factors contribute to their propensity to support the party, it is important to simultaneously take into account other plausible rationales that might be advanced for AKP voting. There are three broad and distinctive rationales for being willing to cast a ballot for the AKP; those relating to social capital endowments; the religiosity of respondents (virtually all respondents to the three survey waves are Muslim); the evaluations of the performance of AKP governments; and the political values and attitudes of respondents. We discuss each of these factors in turn.

Social Capital

Our first consideration is the role of indicators of social capital in accounting for AKP electoral support. Previous research, notably by Robert Putnam and his colleagues (1994), has found that societies that are rich in social capital endowments are more likely to be economically successful and democratically governed. In this research social capital represents a syndrome of cultural properties, most notably high levels of social and political trust and tolerance and strong social networks based on mutual respect and a sense of mutual responsibility and obligation. Societies rich in social capital are characterized—and supported—by robust patterns of informal sociability and vigorous associational life, and when this occurs collective action and democratic self-government is most successful. Individuals in societies characterized by weak social capital, by contrast, lack the cultural infrastructure that would enable them to work successfully together for economic development or to cooperate in effective democratic self-governance. When considered in terms of the AKP's evolution over the 2007–2017 period, we might hypothesize that social capital attributes might be positively related to voter support for the party in the earliest phase but declining in the subsequent periods as the party drifted away from its democratizing role.

Research into social capital in the Turkish context is not highly developed, but it appears from what has been done that Turkey presents a unique setting in terms of its endowments in this area. First, comparative research suggests that Turkey stands out in terms of the low levels of interpersonal trust found among its citizens (Kalaycıoğlu 2012, 175). In fact, only approximately 5% of respondents to the 2007 WVS agreed that "most people can be trusted." The number agreeing with this statement increased to 14.4% in 2017, and most people are inclined to trust members of their family and neighborhood more than strangers. By comparative standards, however, Turkish people are remarkably distrustful of one another. This is likely associated with the relatively low levels of associational group activity in the country. In 2007, for example, fully 85% of respondents reported that they did not belong to any voluntary association. While this figure dropped to 69% by 2017, it is possible that much of this growth in associational vitality could be associated with anti- Erdoğan protestors in civil society during this period.

Another key feature of social capital is toleration and respect for social and political difference. Distinguishing between trends in social and political trust over the 2001–2011 period, Erişen found that levels of social tolerance (measured by a battery of questions about whether members of a diverse array of social groups, such as homosexuals, drug addicts, among others would be acceptable as neighbors) had increased over the decade while measures of political tolerance (where racial groups, people of different religions, and those speaking another language) had increased (Erişen, 2016). However, our WVS survey data suggests that as recently as 2017 three-quarters of respondents regarded Islam as "the only acceptable religion." This might suggest widespread intolerance of religious minorities but because of the overwhelming preponderance of Islam in the country (and the relatively small number of non-Muslims) there is limited opportunity for this value to produce social or interpersonal conflict. The 2017 survey also contained a question about the likely impact of immigration on social conflict, a frequent trope among authoritarian populists around the world. With almost 60% of respondents agreeing that immigrants contributed to social conflict, once again Turkish society seems relatively intolerant. We incorporate this measure in the 2017 model.

We hypothesize that individuals who exhibit attributes associated with social capital will be less willing to support the AKP over time, especially in 2017 when Erdogan's use of repression in the face of domestic unrest accelerated (i.e., an increasingly negative relationship in the 2007–2017 period between social capital and AKP support). To capture the effect of social capital on support for the AKP, we include several measures of social capital in our multivariate model. For all three surveys, questions tapping the feeling that most people can be trusted and the engagement of individuals in voluntary associations (from which we created an additive index of membership and activity in approximately 10 different types of associations) were available. We were able to add the question of whether respondents agreed that theirs was the only acceptable religion as a measure of religious tolerance, and in the 2017 survey we were able to add the item on immigration and social conflict as well.

Islam and Politics

As noted above, Turkey is an overwhelmingly Islamic country and the relationship between Islam and democracy has been one of the most significant questions in contemporary Turkish politics. Comparative research suggests that such societies generally provide hostile environments for democracy. Indeed, Turkey has been the only Islamic country that has been able to sustain the transition from authoritarian to democratic government over an extended period of time (Esmer 2008, 289; also Esmer, 2013). Many scholars attribute this success to the commitment of Mustafa Kemal and his successors to secularism in Turkish public life, creating a situation in which secular civil codes that regulate public life are paralleled by Islamic codes responsible for regulating private life (Toros, 2010: 256).

Despite the centrality of questions of the proper role of Islam in Turkish affairs, and of the possibly inherent tension between Islam and democracy, empirical researchers have demonstrated that support for democracy among Turkish Muslims is relative strong. For example, Esmer's research, using the WVS Turkish waves of 1990 to 2001, found no relationship between religiosity and interpersonal trust or support for democracy. Similarly, Toros (2010, 265) explored survey data for Turkey and concluded that democratic and religious values coexist in Turkey, and further that the two have limited and contingent connections with one another. However, after distancing his party from Islam in the early years of his administration, more recently Erdoğan has radically accelerated the politicization of Islam and eroded the secular foundations of the Turkish state. At various times his governments have supported a restoration of religious symbols in Turkish society and it is therefore to be expected that religious Muslims will be increasingly attracted to the AKP over the time period covered in our surveys.

The WVS Turkish waves contain a number of questions related to the religiosity of respondents but one is particularly helpful in capturing their personal identification as a Muslim—whether the respondent considers her/himself to be a "religious person." We employ this measure (coded 1 when respondents agreed and 0 when they indicated either that they were not a religious person or that they were an atheist). Substantial majorities of respondents (80% in the 2017 survey) classified themselves as religious, while only a small handful indicated that they were atheists. Given that the AKP has eroded the separation between Islam and the Turkish state, despite the limited variation in this measure we expect that this variable will be positively associated with the propensity to vote for the party in our analyses.

Political System and Government Performance

Of course, Turkish citizens who think that the political system and the government are performing well should be more likely than others to express their satisfaction by voting for the governing party, in this case the AKP. Erdoğan came to power following the financial crises that beset Turkey in 2001. During this time economic growth plummeted, the debt burden spiraled, poverty fell below 1994 thresholds, and the Turkish lira was devalued by half. The majority victory for the then-new AKP was widely credited to be its promise to introduce neoliberal economic reforms that were favored by the IMF while simultaneously reducing economic inequalities and fostering the economic growth beyond the Western and Europeanized regions of the country into central Anatolia and from urban to rural Turkey more generally (Patton, 2006). Initially, at least, the government's economic liberalization policies have resulted in an enviable record of economic growth, such that Turkey is now a member of the G20. According to the World Bank's recent (2020) report on the Turkish economy:

> Turkey's economic and social development performance since 2000 has been impressive, leading to increased employment and incomes and making Turkey an upper-middle-income country. However, in the past few years, growing economic vulnerabilities and a more challenging external environment have threatened to undermine those achievements. . . . For most of the period since 2000, Turkey maintained a long-term focus on implementing ambitious reforms in many areas, and government programs have targeted vulnerable groups and disadvantaged regions. Poverty incidence more than halved over 2002–15, and extreme poverty fell even faster. (Worldbank, 2020)

Previous researchers have linked voting behavior to evaluations of economic performance in Turkey (see summary in Çarkoğlu 2012, 164-167). While not everyone has benefited equally from the country's upward economic trajectory, it seems reasonable to expect that individuals who have done well would wish to reward the AKP with their votes. To capture this potential influence we include a measure of the respondent's satisfaction with their household financial situation in each of the three models we estimate below. Similarly, those who believe that the political system has been functioning well under Erdoğan and the AKP would similarly be inclined to see a continuation of this performance by voting for the AKP. Accordingly, we include a measure representing satisfaction with the performance of the political system in the 2017 model (a comparable question was not asked in the earlier waves of the WVS). However, the earlier two surveys did ask respondents to evaluate how "democratically" the country was being governed (a 1–10 scale where 10 represents "completely democratic") and we use this as a rough proxy for evaluations of the political system's performance, where high scores suggest positive evaluations. Finally, we use a dummy variable indicating that a respondent felt that economic growth (or stability) was the country's highest priority as a measure of the salience of economic evaluations generally.

Political Attitudes and Values

While the measures of social capital and religiosity we have discussed above reflect particular dimensions of the values of Turkish respondents, there are other aspects of their values and attitudes that could plausibly be related to the propensity to support the AKP (Toros, 2014: 1014-1015). Among these is the respondent's ideological self-placement on the traditional left-right scale something earlier research has established as a differentiating factor in studies of party support in Turkey (Çarkoğlu 2012, 163). Erdoğan's embrace of neoliberal economic principles, together with his, appeals to Turkish nationalism, we expect will strengthen his appeal both with those on the right of the political spectrum and among those expressing pride in being Turkish (which we take as a proxy for Turkish nationalism). If anything, we would expect the intensity and robustness of these particular value foundations of AKP support to intensify across the life cycle of the party during the 2007–2017 period. To measure these relationships we use responses to a conventional 10-point left-right self-placement scale (with higher scores representing more right-wing placements) and a measure of pride (those indicating they were "very" or "quite" proud of their country) in each of the three models.

We also expect that a propensity to vote for the AKP would reflect a respondent's overall level of confidence in political and economic institutions. Specifically, respondents who express high levels of confidence in the government and parliament would be most likely to vote for the AKP. Similarly, in light of the strong links between the AKP and the business sector in Turkey, we anticipate that AKP support would be higher among those who have confidence in those sectors.

The same positive relationship with AKP support is unlikely to apply when confidence in political parties is considered, however. The rising levels of political polarization noted earlier is likely to be reflected in supporters of one party fearing and distrusting the other parties (Aydın-Düzgit and Balta, 2019; Laebens and Oztürk, 2021).

Finally, as the data presented earlier in figure 14.2 suggests, many Turks embrace democracy while simultaneously holding attitudes that appear at least on the surface to be inherently anti-democratic. We saw that support for democratic rule appears to be exceptionally strong (approximately 80% of respondents in the three waves endorsing it), the same time significant majorities also agree that having "strong leaders who do not have to be bothered by parliament or political parties" and that "having experts and not government making decisions according to what they think is best for the country" are a "very" or a "quite" good thing. In order to capture the complexity of attitudes toward "good governance" in the determination of electoral support for the AKP, we included measures of the support for democracy, strong leaders, and expert rule in all three of our analyses.

The 2017 survey also included a question tapping respondents' views about the proper role of Islam in Turkish politics. Specifically, the questionnaire for that wave of the WVS included a question on the desirability of a "system governed by religious law in which there are no political parties or elections"—just under a third or respondents thought that this option was very or quite good. If AKP supporters are responding to the party's embrace of Islam in public life we would expect that the coefficients for this variable would be positive and significant in the 2007 analysis.

Socioeconomic Control Variables

While our principal interest in this chapter is exploring the relationship among measures of social capital, religion, and democracy on AKP support, it is important to control for potential effects coming from the social and economic group memberships of respondents. Prior research into voting choice in Turkcy has identified a variety of such relationships in terms of the support base of Turkish parties. Among the key socioeconomic factors for the understanding of AKP support is age (where older Turks are expected to be more positively disposed toward the AKP than younger voters) (see Toros 2014, 1021). Education has also been a factor that previous research has been shown to be related to party support (Çarkoğlu 2012; Toros 2014, 1020). We include a dummy variable for those with high school completion or greater in the analyses that follow to capture these influences. To control for any potential impact of household income on AKP support we include a scale measure (scored low to high from 1 to 10). Similarly, Toros (2014, 1020) presents 2009 evidence of a modest (approximately 10%) gender gap in which males are more likely than females to support the AKP. We include a dummy variable for sex (male = 1) to control for this potential relationship.

EMPIRICAL ANALYSIS AND DISCUSSION

With a dichotomous dependent variable (1 = AKP vote now; 0 = other), binary logistic regression is employed to estimate the parameters of our model. Since the underlying relationships are non-linear, logit coefficients lack the easy interpretability of those resulting from an ordinary least squares (OLS) regression. Rather, logit coefficients are literally interpreted as the change in the natural log of the odds ratio resulting from a one-unit change in the independent variable. Our current purposes are served satisfactorily by looking at the direction of impact (positive or negative changes in the likelihood of a respondent voting for the AKP) and the statistical reliability or significance of the coefficients. The results of our analysis of the three surveys are presented in table 14.1. While there is no direct analog in logit analysis for the "proportion of variance" explained (R^2) by the entire model, the Nagelkerke R^2 is an approximation that also varies between 0 and 1, with higher numbers representing generally higher explanatory power for the models being estimated. Ranging from .285 (2012) to .564 (2017), these overall tests suggest that the models as a whole are successful in accounting for differences in the probability of voting for the AKP. It is interesting to note that the models are particularly successful in 2007, during the golden age of the party as discussed above, and in the 2017 analysis of the party in decline. The "transitional" period in terms of the party's evolution marked the model's

Table 14.1 Sources of AKP Support, 2007–2017 (Logit Coefficients and Significance*)

		2007		2012		2017	
		AKP	*Sig*	*AKP*	*Sig*	*AKP*	*Sig*
Social Capital	Trust people	.511	.280	.141	.523	**-.448**	.040
	Additive index of voluntary association membership/ activity (0–20)	**-.378**	.001	.036	.499	-.058	.131
	Immigration leads to social conflict	n/a		n/a		-.258	.131
Religion	Mine is only acceptable religion	n/a		.222	.299	.158	.458
	Consider myself a religious person	**1.522**	.000	19.484	.999	**1.408**	.000
Performance	Satisfied with household financial situation (1–10)	-.036	.484	.010	.804	**-.276**	.000
	Satisfied with political system performance (1–10)	n/a		n/a		**.365**	.000
	Turkey is being governed democratically (1–10)	.013	.762	.039	.269	**.347**	.000
	Top priority economic growth	.066	.350	-.159	.314	**-.451**	.006
Political values	Left-Right (0–10) self-placement	**.253**	.000	**.289**	.000	**.292**	.000
	Proud to be Turkish	.096	.886	-.240	.403	-.329	.069
	Free Elections Important	n/a		n/a		-.154	.627
	Confident in Government	**1.740**	.000	**.688**	.000	**.787**	.000
	Confident in Political Parties	-.099	.679	**-.490**	.006	-.208	.320
	Confident in Parliament	**.557**	.032	**.443**	.021	-.073	.739
	Confident in Major Corporations	-.290	.195	.171	.331	-.006	.977
	Confident in Banks	n/a		.038	.826	-.217	.252
	Strong Leadership good	**-.605**	.008	.014	.940	**.388**	.025
	Rule by experts and not government good	-.026	.917	-.306	.087	-.340	.055
	Religious laws important	n/a		n/a		**.628**	.000
	Good to have a democratic system	**-.834**	.033	-.376	.124	.295	.187
Controls	Sex (Male = 1)	-.132	.529	.194	.202	-.165	.270
	Age (years)	.001	.866	.001	.897	.003	.647
	At least high school education	**-.496**	.038	**-.473**	.006	.081	.633
	Income scale (1–10)	.002	.971	.016	.724	-.075	.127
	Nagelkerke R^2	**.481**		**.285**		**.564**	
	N	680		1001		1191	

Coefficients in bold are statistically significant at the .05 level or better.
*Unless otherwise noted, all variables are scored 1 or 0 (i.e., are dummy variables).
Source: Compiled by authors.

poorest explanatory performance, as might be expected for a party in flux. We will discuss the results under the five categories introduced above—social capital influences, religious influences, performance evaluations, political values, and socioeconomic controls.

In the preceding section we hypothesized that support for the AKP might be related to the social capital endowments of respondents. Specifically, we expect that supporters of the AKP might be less trustful and tolerant of their fellow citizens and less likely to be engaged in voluntary associational organizations, because of the party's overtly Islamic orientation and its championing of the incorporation of Islam more fully in Turkey's public life. This relationship might appear weak in 2007. However, because social capital is widely believed to contribute to healthy and stable democratic governance, we further expected that the negative relationships between measures of social capital and AKP support might become stronger over the period covered by the 2012 and 2017 surveys as the Erdoğan governments cracked down on protest and suspended civil liberties.

The results in the top panel of table 14.1 offer some, but not universal, support for these expectations. Our measure of interpersonal trust did not return the expected significant negative coefficients in 2007 or 2012, but it was significantly negative as hypothesized in 2017. This trend is generally in keeping with our hypotheses about the changing nature of AKP policies and support over the decade. By contrast, the additive index of voluntary association membership and activity was negatively associated with AKP voting as hypothesized, but only in the analysis of the 2007 WVS (although at .013, the negative coefficient in the 2017 analysis was close to the conventional .05 threshold of statistical significance level). The measures of tolerance ("mine is the only acceptable religion" and the belief that immigration contributes to social conflict), however, showed no consistent or significant impact on the probability of an AKP vote. In sum, then, there is some weak evidence to suggest that individuals possessing some of the characteristics we tend to associate with social capital, namely trust and civic engagement, are generally less likely to vote AKP than others, but the expected intensification of these negative relationships over the time covered by our analysis was not strongly or consistently supported.

A great deal of attention has been given to the AKP's championing of a more public role for Islam in Turkish political life. Accordingly, we expected respondents who consider themselves to be a religious person to be more likely than others to support the AKP. The results in table 14.1 reveal that the expected strongly positive relationship with AKP voting is found both in 2007 and again in 2017. Surprisingly, in light of the robustness of these relationships, religiosity does not appear to be a factor in AKP support in the analysis of the 2012 WVS data.

Much has been made, in the early years of AKP governments at least, of the regime's successes in nurturing the economic development and commitment to democratization of Turkey and it should be expected that the electorate would reward the incumbent AKP with support out of satisfaction with its performance in the economy and governing. The results in the third panel of table 14.1 bear this expectation out but only in the analysis of the 2017 WVS data. Despite the relatively strong performance of the AKP government in the immediate post-2002 years, the results of the analysis of the 2007 survey suggest that neither satisfaction with personal finances or with the democratic nature of government contributed to a propensity to support the AKP. This relationship carried over to the 2012 survey, fielded during immediately after the AKP's transitional phase, though arguably the government's economic performance at that time looked less promising. By 2017, those most concerned about the economy as being the nation's top priority, and those most satisfied with their household financial situation, were less likely than others to express support for the AKP. This suggests that confidence in the AKP's economic management was waning during this period and supporters were drawn to the party for other reasons. In the face of the recent unrest in Taksim Square beginning in 2013, and the failed coup attempt in 2016, those who were still satisfied with the performance of the political system and who felt that Turkey was being governed democratically in 2017 were perhaps not surprisingly more likely than others to be AKP supporters. Otherwise, AKP voting does not appear to be strongly rooted in performance evaluations of the AKP governments. If these judgments are unable to account for AKP voting, might the political values of respondents offer a better explanation?

The fourth panel of table 14.1 gives some evidence that the values of WVS survey respondents are in fact relatively strongly and consistently linked with support for the AKP. Clearly, one of the most important and consistent sources of AKP support comes from those who locate themselves on the right side of the ideological spectrum. Together with its grounding in the Islamic community, the party's right-wing ideological appeal is apparent in all three surveys across the decade 2007–2017. Somewhat surprisingly, in light of Erdoğan's populist appeal to Turks and of the experience of authoritarian populist leaders elsewhere, the measure of feeling pride in being Turkish does not appear to have contributed to voter support for the AKP, net of other influences. Nor does a belief in free elections contribute to AKP voting in 2017 and this might reflect the increasingly obvious authoritarianism of Erdoğan's appeals. Interestingly, though, those approving of having a democratic system were less likely to support the AKP than others in 2007, ostensibly the golden age of the party's democratizing reform program. Clearly AKP supporters have a tenuous relationship when it comes to supporting democracy in Turkey.

The battery of questions tapping respondents' level of confidence in different political and economic institutions holds some interesting clues as to the nature of AKP supporters. Clearly, the significant and robustly positive coefficients for the measure of confidence in the government is positively related to AKP support, as would be expected. It is possible, of course, that these responses are more plausibly conceived as an evaluative assessment of AKP governmental performance than a deeper commitment to a strong and effective public sector.

Reflecting the growing polarization of Turkish politics over the decade, the measure of confidence in political parties in general was negatively associated with AKP support in all three surveys, though the relationship was statistically robust only in the analysis of the 2012 WVS data. Respondents who were confident in Parliament were more likely than others to support the AKP in the 2007 and 2012 analyses, though not in 2017. This could reflect either growing support for more authoritarian governance, or it might simply be the result of the critiques of parliamentarianism and the championing of presidentialism that accompanied the debates over constitutional reform during that time.

Surprisingly, despite the AKP's appeal to the right wing of the political spectrum, its supporters were not distinctive in terms of their confidence in the private sector. Both confidence in major corporations or banks did not emerge as a determinant of AKP support in any of the models. Initially (in the 2007 WVS), AKP supporters appear more likely to believe that having a democratic system was not important but they were also unsupportive of a strong political leader who would be relatively unencumbered by political parties or parliament. By the time of the 2017 survey, though, the perceived importance of having a democratic system had slipped among AKP supporters (the positive coefficient was no longer statistically significant—though perhaps this reflects the positive impact incorporated in the model for that year of the perception that Turkey was in fact being democratically governed at that time) and instead the feeling that it was good to have a strong leader had become a significant determinant of electoral support for the party. Though the attractiveness of a technocratic alternative to electoral democracy was never significantly related to AKP's electoral support across the three surveys, in 2017 the negative coefficient narrowly missed the conventional .05 level of significance. This suggests that the rejection of technocracy had intensified somewhat over the period under scrutiny. Finally, though available only in the 2017 WVS, the item measuring support for religious laws playing an important role in government was robustly positive for that model, suggesting that there exists an important reservoir of support for the AKP among devout Turkish Muslims. Further, it is clear that AKP supporters are not enthusiastic democrats. In 2007 AKP support was negatively related to support for a democratic system and in the two subsequent models the relationship dropped beyond the range of statistical significance.

Turning to the socioeconomic control variables, the results in the bottommost panel of table 14.1 suggest that AKP support is not tightly grounded in the country's demographic groups. Respondents' income nor gender is never significantly related to AKP voting in any of the three models/years. Only in the 2007 and 2012 analyses does the possession of high school or higher educational credentials appear to be significantly and negatively related to the propensity to support the AKP.

From our analysis it seems clear that electoral support for the AKP over the decade 2007–2017 underwent some changes that may be associated with the party's evolution from its golden age (2002–2007), transitional phase (2008–2011), and its subsequent retreat from democratizing policies (post–2012). Most importantly, the association of Islam with AKP voting appears especially strong in the 2007 and the 2017 surveys, when those who considered themselves to be religious were especially likely to say they would vote for the AKP. Similarly, in 2017 those who were in favor of religiously inspired laws was also strongly positive. Clearly, the party's appeal to Muslims—and in particular those who feel that Islam should have an important role in public life—provides a strong foundation for the party's electoral fortunes that seems to remain intact over the three phases of the AKP's development during the decade.

Second, there was relatively sparse evidence in our analyses to support the notion that Erdoğan's and the AKP's supporters were drawn to vote for the party as a means of rewarding the government's economic or political performance. Those most satisfied with their family's financial situation, and those feeling that Turkey's top priority should be the economy, were less likely than others to register support for the AKP in 2017 although the relationships in earlier elections were not statistically significant. Taken as a whole, and despite the early economic successes of AKP governments, positive economic evaluations were not a significant source of AKP support. Rather, as the AKP evolved over the period, it appears that economic reforms and policies may have been displaced in the public's mind, leading to support for other parties among those most concerned about these issues.

Third, the character of the AKP as a right-wing party also is apparent across the three phases of its development. Along with those expressing confidence in AKP governments, this was the most consistent value associated with AKP voting across all three phases in the party's evolution. The initial association of AKP vote with confidence in parliament apparent in the analyses of the 2007 and 2012 surveys had dissipated by 2017, when AKP supporters appeared to be more likely than others to embrace the role of a strong and relatively unencumbered political leader—a reversal of the impact of this factor from the results of the analysis of the 2007 WVS. By 2017, also, the party's accommodation with Turkey's secular past was weakened and party supporters were more positive than others concerning the importance of religious laws in the country's public life. The transformation of the AKP in an authoritarian populist direction is clearly apparent in this third phase in the party's evolution.

LOOKING AHEAD—THE PROSPECTS FOR A RESUMPTION OF DEMOCRATIZATION

As the Turkish electorate continues to evolve in the post-2017 period, support for Erdoğan and the AKP (the AKP-MHP electoral alliance since February 2018) has primarily been based on: i) the religious and nationalistic values of the electorate, ii) the clientelistic economic networks sustaining voter loyalty, and iii) a popular foreign policy posture aspiring to great power status. However, this equation is currently under major pressure on the economic and foreign policy fronts. During the recent years, Turkey's economic downturn, the loss by AKP in the 2019 local elections of most big city mayorships and associated clientelistic mechanisms, and the Covid-19 pandemic have significantly eroded the economic basis of political support for Erdoğan. Despite massive media manipulation, it is also becoming harder to hide major foreign policy failures, let alone present them as successes. In response, Erdoğan is becoming more authoritarian and is increasing repression of political dissent using his control of the judiciary and the law enforcement system. In their turn, these measures are scaring off domestic and foreign investors, triggering Western sanctions, and further accelerating economic decline.

Hence, the competitive authoritarian regime of Turkey has gradually maneuvered itself into a bind between economic collapse and democratic removal from office. Erdoğan and his collaborators seem to be more averse to the latter eventuality that will likely have them stand trial in impartial courts for accusations of corruption and constitutional violations. Instead, Erdoğan's so-called palace regime may well continue its illiberal course trying to rule into the future an impoverished Turkey mostly cut off from the West. Given Turkey's economic and political development, however, this option's sustainability in the absence of electoral support and democratic legitimacy is rather low. Risks associated with this dilemma range from chaos and new coup attempts to civil war.

The next presidential and parliamentary elections in Turkey are scheduled to take place in 2023 although deteriorating economic and political circumstances will likely force a rescheduling to an earlier date. In 2019 and 2020, two former AKP politicians who served at top level positions at earlier

Erdoğan governments formed two new political parties and joined opposition ranks. They have significant potential to appeal to disgruntled AKP voters. The common election promise of the opposition parties is the termination of the hyper-presidential system in force since 2018 in favor of a "strengthened parliamentary system" with a nonpartisan and symbolic president, strict separation of powers, a strong and independent judiciary, a parliament that can effectively supervise and check the government, and an executive cabinet composed of elected parliamentarians.

The responsibility for deciding the fate of the country at this critical juncture lies with an electorate divided by intense polarization that reduces social trust and cooperation. Erdoğan's rule generally improved the conditions of conservatives, at least until recent years, but more modern segments of the citizenry increasingly felt victimized. The growing resentment of opponents gradually trapped Erdoğan's supporters in a new dilemma: even if they realize that the regime no longer serves their interests, they feel obliged to support it lest the opposition comes to power and takes revenge on them. Born of polarization, Erdoğan still inflames polarization to remain in power. His demonization of the opposition frightens his supporters and compels them to close ranks.

During the 2019 local elections, the main opposition party CHP (Republican Peoples Party) overcame this hurdle by adopting an original campaign strategy called Radical Love. Wuthrich and Ingleby have summarized this new approach in two main principles: "First, opponents should defuse polarization by ignoring the populist while loving his supporters; and, second, they should demonstrate their responsiveness to voters by avoiding debates about high politics and focusing instead on voters' felt needs and concerns" (Wuthrich and Ingleby, 2020). The strategy allowed CHP to defeat AKP in most of the big cities of Turkey despite an uneven playing field. Whether these victories can be repeated at national elections including voters from small towns and rural areas remains to be seen. In any case, effective alliances between opposition parties and obtaining the support of Kurdish voters remain to be necessary conditions for a change of government at the national level.

The precondition for Turkey's return to democratization is the relaxation of the hostile polarization that sustains the current regime. The government can hardly survive in a more democratic environment, but without democratization economic recovery is unlikely. Central Bank reserves have already been depleted and foreign borrowing opportunities dwindled at a time when export and tourism revenues crashed. Unlike oil-rich rentier states, Turkey needs its people to be creative and generate income. It cannot afford to continue suppressing and alienating the majority of its population. There is already an exodus of Turkish citizens with capital and knowledge to foreign countries, especially to Western democracies. Repeated surveys indicate that large percentages youth, even AKP and MHP supporters, prefer to live abroad if they get a chance.

Continuation of the present trend will in the longer term lead to a lose-lose outcome for the overwhelming majorities of both camps, and both of them need to change to free themselves from this vicious cycle. As the WVS data suggest, the two opposing poles share many historically inculcated anti-democratic values regarding civil and political rights. For the resolution of the current identity conflict, the supporters of the current regime need to develop more peaceable interpretations of Islam and nationalism, while opposition factions have to adopt and internalize stronger liberal democratic values. The consolidation of a genuine democracy in Turkey requires that the two antagonistic blocks have to expand the range of what they can accept and try to communicate with each other at a higher level of democratic consciousness.

If and when an effective democracy alliance emerges and is elected into office in Turkey, it will face the daunting task of reviving and reconstructing fundamental institutions of democracy. It will have to build social, political, economic, and legal safeguards into a renewed democratic system to prevent a relapse to authoritarian populism. The experiences of the last decade suggest critical guidelines to this end. Laicism remains to be a key precondition for the survival of democracy in Turkey. Unlike in the past, however, it needs to be institutionalized properly whereby the state remains equidistant to all religions and sects rather than trying to control and impose upon society its own interpretation of Sunni Islam alone.

NOTE

1. The authors are grateful to the World Values Survey project for making the results of the six Turkish waves of surveys (1990; 1997; 2001; 2007; 2012; 2017) available to the scholarly community for analysis. See Inglehart, R., Haerpfer, C., Moreno, A., Welzel, C., Kizilova, K., Diez-Medrano J., M. Lagos, P. Norris, E. Ponarin, B. Puranen et al. (eds.). 2020. *World Values Survey: All Rounds–Country-Pooled Datafile*. Madrid, Spain & Vienna, Austria: JD Systems Institute & WVSA Secretariat [Version: http://www.worldvaluessurvey.org/WVSDocumentationWVL.jsp].

REFERENCES

Atasoy, Seymen. 2011. "The Turkish Example: A Model for Change in the Middle East?" *Middle East Policy* XVIII, No. 3 (Fall): 1–15.

Aydın-Düzgit, Senem and Evren Balta. 2019. "When Elites Polarize Over Polarization: Framing the Polarization Debate in Turkey." *New Perspectives on Turkey* 60, no. 1 (May): 153–176.

Çarkoğlu, Ali. 2012. "Voting Behavior." In *The Routledge Handbook of Modern Turkey*, edited by Metin Heper and Sabri Sayarı, 160–170. London: Taylor and Francis.

Eckstein, Harry, Frederic J. Fleron, Jr., Erik P. Hoffman, and William Reisinger eds. 1998. *Can Democracy Take Root in Post-Soviet Russia? Explorations in State-Society Relations*, Lanham, MD: Rowan and Littlefield.

Ekici, Tufan, and Selda Koydemir. 2014. "Social Capital, Government and Democracy Satisfaction, and Happiness in Turkey: A Comparison of Surveys in 1999 and 2008." *Social Indicators Research* 118, no. 3 (September): 1031–1053.

"Erdoğan'ın 2071'den önce yeni hedefi!" ["The new goal of Erdoğan before 2071!] 2013. *Yeni Şafak*, May 07). https://www.yenisafak.com/ politika/erdoganin-2071den-once-yeni-hedefi!-518641

Erişen, Cengiz. 2016. "Tolerance and Democratization in Turkey." In *Democratic Consolidation in Turkey: Micro and Macro Challenges*, edited by Cengiz Erişen and Paul Kubicek, Ch. 3. London: Taylor and Francis.

Esmer, Yılmaz. 2008. "Islam, Gender, Democracy and Values: The Case of Turkey, 1990-2001." In *Changing Values, Persisting Cultures: Case Studies in Value Change*, edited by Thorleif Pettersson and Yılmaz Esmer, 275–301. London: Brill Academic Publishers.

Esmer, Yılmaz. 2013. "Democracy, Civil Society, and Islam." In *Religion and Civil Society in Europe*, edited by Joep de Hart, Paul Dekker, and Loek Halman, 267–284. Dordrecht: Springer Publications.

Kalaycıoğlu, Ersin. 2012. "Political Culture." In *The Routledge Handbook of Modern Turkey*, edited by Metin Heper and Sabri Sayarı, 171–181. London: Taylor & Francis.

Konda Barometresi. 2019. *Temalar: Türkiye'de Kutupl*aşma, (Ocak). Konda Barometer. Themes: *Polarization in Turkey,* January. https://konda.com.tr/wp-content/uploads/2020/08/ TR1901_Barometre94_TurkiyedeKutuplasma.pdf

Laebens, Melis, and Aykut Öztürk. 2021. "Partisanship and Autocratization: Polarization, Power Asymmetry, and Partisan Social Identities in Turkey." *Comparative Political Studies* 54, no. 2 (February): 245–279.

Norris, Pippa, and Ronald Inglehart. 2019. *Cultural Backlash: Trump, Brexit, and Authoritarian Populism.* Cambridge: Cambridge University Press

Öniş, Ziya. 2016. "Turkey's Two Elections: The AKP Comes Back." *Journal of Democracy* 27, no. 2 (April): 141–154.

Patton, Marcie J. 2006. "The Economic Policies of Turkey's AKP Government: Rabbits from a Hat?" *Middle Eastern Journal* 60, no. 3 (Summer): 513–536.

Putnam, Robert D., Robert Leonardi, and Raffaella Nanetti. 1994. *Making Democracy Work: Civic Traditions in Modern Italy*. Princeton: Princeton University Press.

Taş, Hakkı. 2015. "Turkey- From Tutelary to Delegative Democracy." *Third World Quarterly* 36, no. 4: 776–791.

Toros, Emre. 2010. "The Relationship Between Islam and Democracy in Turkey: Employing Political Culture as an Indicator." *Social Indicators Research* 95, no. 2 (January): 253–265.

Toros, Emre. 2014. "Social indicators and Voting: The Turkish Case." *Social Indicators Research* 115, no. 3 (February): 1011–1029.

Turkuazlab. 2020. "Dimensions of Polarization in Turkey - 2020 Survey". https://www.turkuazlab.org/wp-content/uploads/2020/12/Survey_Key_Findings.pdf

World Bank 2020. "Turkey Overview." https://www.worldbank.org/en/country/turkey/overview

Wuthrich, F. Michael, and Melvyn Ingleby. 2020. "The Pushback Against Populism: Running on 'Radical Love' in Turkey." *Journal of Democracy* 31, no. 2 (April): 24–40.

Yavuz, Hakan. 2020. *Nostalgia for the Empire: The Politics of Neo-Ottamanism.* Oxford: Oxford University Press.

Yılmaz, Zafer, and Bryan S. Turner. 2019. "Turkey's Deepening Authoritarianism and the Fall of Electoral Democracy." *British Journal of Middle Eastern Studies* 46, no. 5: 691–698.

Chapter 15

Perfect Deterrence Theory

Frank C. Zagare

Perfect deterrence theory and classical deterrence theory are two theoretical frameworks that have divergent empirical implications and dissimilar policy recommendations.[1] In perfect deterrence theory, threat credibility plays a central role in the operation of both direct and extended deterrence relationships. But credible threats are neither necessary nor sufficient for deterrence to prevail and, under certain conditions, the presence of a credible threat may actually precipitate a deterrence failure. In perfect deterrence theory the cost of conflict and status quo evaluations are also important strategic variables in so far as their values determine the characteristics of the players' threats. Classical deterrence theorists tend to fixate on the former and ignore the latter. This theoretical oversight precludes a nuanced understanding of the dynamics of deterrence.

INTRODUCTION

In the aftermath of World War II a large, oftentimes contradictory, but nonetheless influential, literature emerged in the field of security studies that is commonly referred to as (classical) deterrence theory.[2] Although its roots can be traced to the contentious debate between realists and liberals during the interwar period about the causes of great power wars in general, and of World War I in particular (Carr 1939), it is generally understood that Bernard Brodie's (1946, 1959) work is seminal. Shortly after atomic bombs were dropped, first on Hiroshima and then on Nagasaki, Brodie realized that war prevention would become the primary goal of the American security apparatus in what was sure to become a world of nuclear plenty. How and under what conditions that goal might be achieved is the principal question addressed in this vast literature.

It is quite understandable that the earliest attempts to answer this question relied heavily on extant realist theory. Since the conventional wisdom at the time was that a power asymmetry was an all-but sufficient condition for major power conflicts, it followed that the key to peace was a carefully calibrated strategic balance. Balance of power theory, however, did not hold up to intense logical and empirical scrutiny. As evidence began to accumulate that both world wars were actually contested under parity conditions (Organski 1958: Ch. 11; Organski and Kugler 1980), a new variable was added to explain away the glaring discrepancy between fact and theory: the cost of war. What eventually emerged was a part of the literature I have elsewhere referred to as *structural deterrence theory* (Zagare 1996a). Structural deterrence theorists, of whom Kenneth Waltz (1964, 1979, 1981) is the exemplar, focus on the interplay of strategic structure and the cost of conflict to explain the absence of a superpower conflict during the Cold War period. In their view, parity, when coupled with sufficiently high war costs, all but guarantees peace (Intriligator and Brito 1984). By contrast, structural deterrence theorists contend that peace may break down—even under parity—when the costs of conflict are, or are believed to be, low. For Waltz (1993: 77), the breakdown of the international system in 1914 occurred precisely because decision-makers in Berlin, Vienna, St. Petersburg, Paris, and London thought that a war could be waged on the cheap.[3]

While Waltz and other structural theorists (e.g., Mearsheimer 1990) explored the systemic conditions that they believed explained the "long peace" (Gaddis 1986) of the Cold War period, a second group of strategic thinkers approached the question from a choice theoretic perspective. Pitched at the micro level of analysis, this strand of the literature, which I label *decision theoretic deterrence theory*, includes the work of psychological choice, expected utility, and game theorists. The exemplar of this part of the deterrence landscape is Thomas Schelling (1960, 1966), who dabbled in all three genres. Zakaria (2001) credits Schelling as the "inventor" of modern deterrence theory. Others, however, point to William Kaufmann (1966).

These two strands in the strategic studies literature, which together constitute the dominant paradigmatic (i.e., realist) articulation of deterrence theory, have much in common. For example, structural deterrence theorists conclude that bilateral nuclear relations are exceeding stable. In fact, they argue, that as the costs of conflict rise, the probability of a war between nuclear rivals "approaches zero" (Waltz, 1990: 740; see also Intriligator and Brito 1981: 256). Since rational conflicts are believed to be unlikely, the gravest threat to peace in the nuclear era is seen to be accidental war.

Decision-theoretic deterrence theorists take these conclusions as axiomatic. Indeed, they are built into the very structure of the game they use as the underlying metaphor of a bilateral nuclear relationship: Chicken (Jervis 1979: 291). In Chicken—see figure 15.1—the outcome labeled *Conflict* is a mutually worst outcome. In consequence, rational conflict is precluded. In a strict 2 x 2 ordinal game like Chicken, a mutually worst outcome can never be part of a Nash equilibrium, which is the accepted standard of rational play in a normal-form game. Thus, *Conflict* can only occur when rational players miscalculate, that is, when an accident occurs.

Structural deterrence theory and decision-theoretic deterrence theory share many of the same logical and empirical flaws.[4] For example, structural deterrence theorists are unable to explain the absence of a superpower conflict during the periods of American nuclear superiority without making an ad hoc adjustment to the theory, as Waltz himself points out (1993: 47). Even when the motivation exists, states generally do not jump through "windows of opportunity" (Lebow 1984; Jervis 1985: 6). The abstract version of the theory clearly implies that the United States should have exploited the obvious strategic advantage it enjoyed throughout the 1950s and the early 1960s, not only against the Soviet Union but against lesser powers as well. As Jervis (1988: 342) notes, structural deterrence theorists are unable to "explain the fact that the United States did not conquer Canada sometime in the past hundred years." Or as Gaddis (1997: 88) more tactfully puts it, "the actions the United States took [during the early Cold War years] failed to fit traditional patterns of great power behavior."

For their part decision-theoretic deterrence theorists are also hard put to explain the absence of a superpower conflict during the most intense periods of the Cold War period without logical contradiction. And it is easy to

		State B	
		Cooperate (C)	Defect (D)
State A	Cooperate (C)	*Status Quo* (3,3)	*B Wins* (2,4)*
	Defect (D)	*A Wins* (4,2)*	*Conflict* (1,1)

Key: (x,y) = payoff to State A, payoff to State B
4 = best; 3 = next-best; 2 = next-worst; 1 = worst
* = Nash equilibrium

Figure 15.1 Chicken. *Source*: Compiled by author.

understand why. *Conflict* is not the only outcome in Chicken that is inconsistent with rational play. The outcome labeled *Status Quo*, which results when both states cooperate and neither attacks the other, is also not a Nash equilibrium. As a result, the long peace can only be explained within the confines of decision-theoretic deterrence theory by assuming, simultaneously, that the players are rational—when they are being deterred—and irrational when they are deterring and threatening mutual destruction.[5] All of which helps to explain why Achen (1987: 92) has observed that "far from leaning too heavily on rational choice postulates, 'rational deterrence theory' necessarily assumes that nations are not always self-interestedly rational."[6]

PERFECT DETERRENCE THEORY

Perfect deterrence theory was developed to overcome the empirical and logical problems that plague classical deterrence theory. As developed by Zagare and Kilgour (2000), this theoretical structure is composed of a number of interrelated game models that are analyzed under a common set of preference assumptions. The assumptions are both intuitively obvious and, for the most part, innocuous. In these models the players are assumed to prefer winning to losing and to do so at the lowest possible cost. Most other preference relationships are taken as strategic variables. For example, some players might prefer *Conflict* to losing. Players with such a preference are assumed to have *credible* threats, that is, threats that are rational to execute. Other players, with the opposite preference, have threats that lack credibility. The players also may or may not prefer the *Status Quo* to *Conflict*. A player whose opponent prefers the *Status Quo* to *Conflict* is said to have a capable threat, that is, a threat that hurts (Schelling 1966: 7). Threats that do not hurt are considered incapable. Finally, in perfect deterrence theory the players are not necessarily undifferentiated as they are in classical deterrence theory (Legro and Moravcsik 1999: 13). Specifically, in perfect deterrence theory some players, called *Defenders*, prefer the *Status Quo* to all other outcomes; by contrast, *Challengers* are those who are motivated to upset it. A bilateral relationship wherein both players are Challengers are said to constitute a *Mutual Deterrence Game*. *Unilateral Deterrence Games* are those in which a satisfied Defender and a dissatisfied Challenger are involved.[7] Perfect deterrence theory examines the strategic impact of various configurations of credible and capable threats under conditions of complete and incomplete information in each of its four constituent games.[8]

The variable nature of these critical preference relationships is, perhaps, the most important way that perfect deterrence theory is distinguished from decision-theoretic deterrence theory (Quackenbush 2011: 747). In either the formal or informal studies that take as their starting point the game of Chicken, all preferences are necessarily fixed. But another important difference between these two theoretically distinct variants of deterrence theory is perfect deterrence theory's strict adherence to Selten's perfectness criterion which requires players who make rational choices at every decision point in a game, including those that they might never face.[9] As is well known, some Nash equilibria are supported by threats that are not rational (or credible) to execute. Selten's perfectness criteria eliminates these equilibria as rational strategic possibilities and, not incidentally, the logical inconsistency that is associated with them.

In a dynamic (or extensive-form) game of complete information, Selten's rationality postulate is associated with the concept of a *subgame perfect equilibrium*; in a game of incomplete information, with the concept of a *perfect Bayesian equilibrium* (Harsanyi 1967–1968). Perfect deterrence theory's name stems from its reliance on these two accepted measures of rational strategic behavior. Adherence to the perfectness criterion assures logical consistency which is, arguably, perfect deterrence theory's most important characteristic. Walt (1999) notwithstanding, logical inconsistencies are clearly fatal to the health and well-being of any theory. As is well-known, logically inconsistent theories are incapable of being falsified. By contrast, because it has clear empirical implications, perfect deterrence theory can, and has, been rigorously tested (Quackenbush 2010a, 2011). Many of its theoretical propositions are also consistent with the empirical record, as I discuss below.

STRATEGIC VARIABLES

Perfect deterrence theory is a general theory of conflict initiation and resolution. Unlike classical deterrence theory, perfect deterrence theory makes no particular assumption about the cost of conflict. It is, therefore, applicable to a much wider range of strategic relationships. Perfect deterrence theory is simply not a divergent theory of nuclear war avoidance. Rather, it is a universal theory, applicable to both nuclear and to non-nuclear interactions. As such, it can be used to help explain why crises occur, why some conflicts escalate and others do not, and when and why limited and all-out wars are waged. Perfect deterrence theory's empirical domain is not even restricted to interstate interactions. As a general theory of strategic interaction, it is potentially applicable to inter-group or inter-personal conflict of interest situations whenever and wherever they may occur.

In perfect deterrence theory the cost of conflict is, nonetheless, a critical strategic variable. Its value relative to other variables determines both the *capability* and the *credibility* of a deterrent threat. As noted, capable threats are threats that hurt. Threats that hurt are those that leave a player worse off than if the prohibited action was not taken. Operationally, this means that one player's deterrent threat is capable only if the other player, the threatened player, prefers the status quo to the outcome that would result if the threat were executed. Conversely, a deterrent threat will lack capability whenever the threatened player prefers to act even if the threat is carried out (Zagare 1987: 34).

The threat of nuclear retaliation is clearly a capable threat. Classical deterrence theorists contend that capability constitutes a *sufficient* condition for deterrence success, which is why they believe that the mere possession of nuclear weapons all-but guarantees a lasting peace (e.g., Waltz 1993: 53–54; Bundy 1983; Levy 1988: 489–90). In perfect deterrence theory, by contrast, deterrence may fail even when all threats are capable. For instance, by definition, both players have a capable threat in the game of Chicken—see figure 15.1. Yet the status quo does not survive rational play in this game.

On the other hand, within the theoretical confines of perfect deterrence theory, a capable threat constitutes a *necessary* condition for deterrence success, that is, deterrence will always fail whenever a deterrent threat lacks capability (Zagare and Kilgour 2000: 81–84). To illustrate, consider for now the Unilateral Deterrence Game given by figure 15.2. This game, which is one of perfect deterrence theory's four constituent games, depicts a one-sided (or asymmetric) deterrence relationship in which a Defender seeks to deter a Challenger, but not the other way around.

In the Unilateral Deterrence Game Challenger begins play (at decision node 1) by deciding whether to contest the existing order. If no demand is made, the *Status Quo* prevails. But if a demand is made, Defender must decide (at node 2) whether to resist it or concede the issue. Concession results in the outcome *Defender Concedes*. Resistance brings about a subsequent choice for Challenger at node 3: if Challenger backs down, the outcome labeled *Challenger Defeated* results. If Challenger holds firm, there is *Conflict*. The four outcomes in this game correspond, roughly, to the four outcomes in Chicken.

As before, the ordered pair beneath each outcome represents the ordinal payoff to the players, from best (i.e., 4) to worst (i.e., 1). The first entry represents Challenger's evaluation, the second, Defender's. For example, in this variant of the Unilateral Deterrence Game *Conflict* is Challenger's next-best outcome (i.e., 3) and Defender's next-worst (i.e., 2). Since the present assumption is that Challenger prefers *Conflict* to the *Status Quo*, Defender's threat to resist at node 2 lacks capability, by definition.

The version of the Unilateral Deterrence game given by figure 15.2 is an extensive-form game with complete information. In such a game rational play is determined by applying backward induction, starting with Challenger's

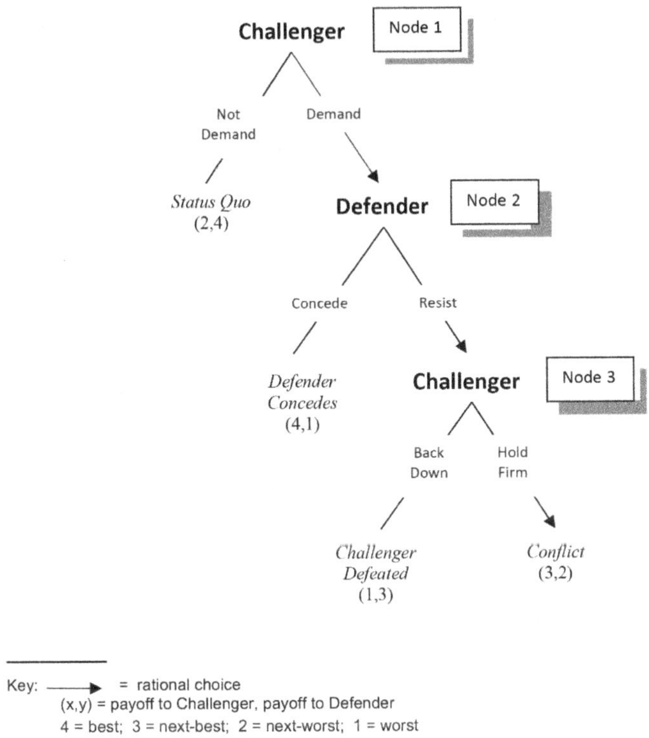

Figure 15.2 Unilateral Deterrence Game: Defender's Threat Is Credible but Not Capable. *Source*: Compiled by author.

choice at node 3, and working backward up the game tree. The outcome that survives the backward induction process in a game of complete information will be a subgame perfect equilibrium.

As the arrows indicate, a rational Challenger will hold firm at node 3 in order to avoid its worst outcome, *Challenger Defeated.* Since concession results in Defender's worst outcome, it will rationally resist should it face a choice at node 2. Anticipating both these choices, Challenger will rationally issue a demand at node 1. After all, by assumption, Challenger prefers *Conflict*, the unique subgame perfect equilibrium in this game and the outcome that is implied by the backward induction process, to the *Status Quo*. In consequence, deterrence fails—as it always will—whenever a Defender's threat lacks capability.

Notice that in this example that Defender's threat is credible, that is, it prefers *Conflict* to *Defender Concedes*. Yet deterrence does not succeed. Freedman (1989: 96) claims that credibility is the "magic ingredient" of deterrence. While there is a modicum truth to his claim, a credible threat does not constitute a sufficient condition for deterrence success, as the game given by figure 15.2 demonstrates.

Nor is credibility a necessary condition. (Table 15.1 summarizes perfect deterrence theory's conclusions about the causal conditions of deterrent threats.) To see this consider now the version of the Unilateral Deterrence game depicted in figure 15.3. In this example, neither player's threat is credible. Since *Conflict* is a mutually worst outcome, Challenger rationally backs down at node 3. But because it expects a rational Challenger to accept defeat

Table 15.1 Causal Characteristics of Deterrent Threats

	Necessary Condition	*Sufficient Condition*
Capable threats	Yes	No
Credible threats	No	No
Credible and capable threats	No	No

Source: Compiled by author.

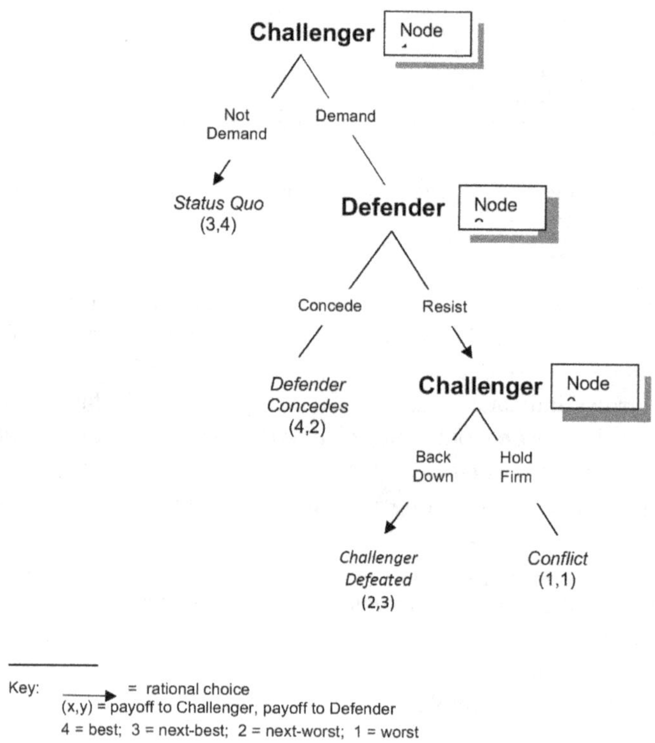

Figure 15.3 Unilateral Deterrence Game When Neither Player Has a Credible Threat.
Source: Compiled by author.

at node 3, Defender intends to resist (because it prefers *Challenger Defeated* to *Defender Concedes*) if and when it is faced with a choice at node 2. Node 2 is never reached in rational play, however, because Challenger, preferring to avoid certain humiliation (i.e., *Challenger Defeated*), will suddenly find the *Status Quo* acceptable.

In this case, then, deterrence succeeds even though Defender's threat lacks credibility. All of which illustrates that it may be the characteristics of Challenger's threat, and not of Defender's, that ultimately determines rational play in a game. This is not a trivial point. For the most part, classical deterrence theorists have fixated on a defender's threat in order to understand the conditions under which deterrence breaks down.[10] In so doing they fail to recognize the interactive impact that deterrent threats have. Empirical studies that focus attention on the characteristics of a defender's threat also miss this important dimension of not only direct but of extended deterrence relationships as well and, in the process, introduce case selection bias into their studies.[11] In a multilevel extended deterrence game where a challenger's strategic level (or end-game) threat lacks credibility, deterrence should prevail regardless of the configuration of a defender's tactical and strategic level threats (Zagare and Kilgour 2000: Ch. 9).

By now it should be clear that the relationship between credibility and the operation of deterrence is anything but straightforward. More specifically, deterrence may fail even when all threats are credible; and it may succeed even when all threats lack credibility. But this is not the end of the story. Conditions also exist under which one player's possession of a credible threat will actually undermine the stability of the status quo. The game given in figure 15.4 is a case in point.

There is only one difference, and a relatively minor one at that, between the games given in figures 15.3 and 15.4. In the former case, Challenger's threat lacks credibility, yet deterrence succeeds. In the game of figure 15.4, by contrast, Challenger's threat is indeed credible, but as the arrows indicate, deterrence rationally fails. So once again, a credible threat (or the lack thereof) is central to the operation of deterrence game, but not in the way one might suspect. In the game of figure 15.4, one player's (i.e., Challenger's) possession of a threat that is rational to execute actually incentivizes a breakdown of deterrence.

As noted earlier, classical deterrence theorists tend to focus on the defender's threat characteristics rather than the challenger's. One possible explanation is their mania for explaining deterrence failures and their comparative lack of interest in explaining deterrence success. Their focus on deterrence breakdowns also helps to explain why they are similarly prone to overlook the role played by another important strategic variable, the value of the status quo. This is clearly a significant oversight. The extent to which a player is

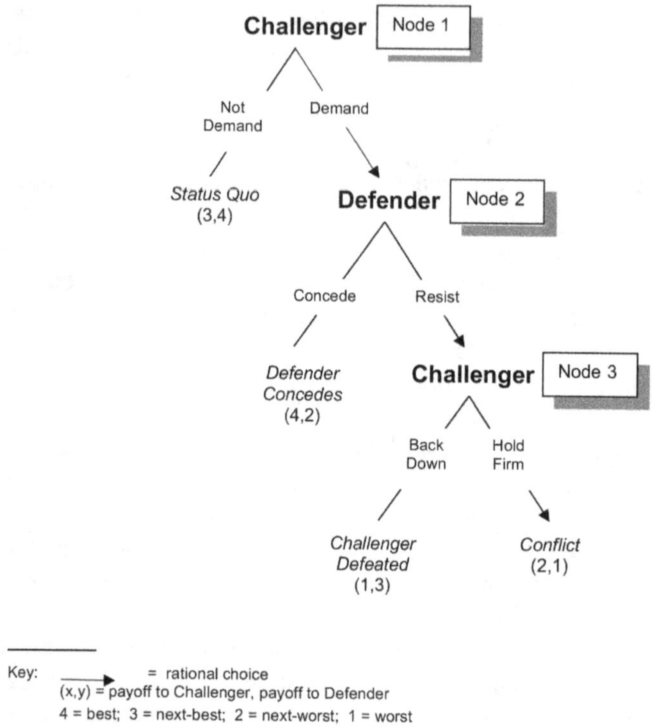

Figure 15.4 Unilateral Deterrence Game When Only Challenger's Threat Is Credible.
Source: Compiled by author.

satisfied (or dissatisfied) with the existing order is not only a critical determinant of a threat's capability; it is also the only standard that can be used to establish a player's incentive (or willingness) to overturn it (Most and Starr 1989). The failure to explore the consequences of this critical benchmark variable is yet another source of case selection bias that plagues almost every empirical examination of classical deterrence theory's central propositions.[12]

PERFECT DETERRENCE THEORY: RELATIONSHIP PREDICTIONS

In some ways the theoretical characteristics of classical deterrence theory and perfect deterrence theory are similar. For example, both frameworks assume egotistical or self-interested actors who make rational choices. But there are also some significant differences. As noted, perfect deterrence theory makes consistent use of the rationality postulate, whereas classical deterrence theory does not. In contrast to the standard version of deterrence theory, perfect deterrence theory does not treat all actors as similarly motivated (i.e., as undifferentiated); nor does it take status quo evaluations and threat credibility to be fixed and constant. In perfect deterrence theory, these entities are important strategic variables. In consequence the empirical expectations of these two competing specifications of deterrence theory are significantly at odds.

To be sure, it is not easy to summarize classical deterrence theory's core propositions. Since its sporadic application of the rationality postulate inevitably leads to logical inconsistencies, anything and its opposite can be deduced from its axiomatic base (Martin 1999: 83). Nonetheless, although there are some exceptions, there also appears to be a general consensus among mainstream strategists. Table 15.2 summarizes both this confluence of opinion and the competing relationship propositions of perfect deterrence theory. Several of these differences have already been discussed.

One that has not concerns the overall nature of contentious deterrence relationships. As previously indicated, classical deterrence theorists see strategic (i.e., nuclear) deterrence relationships as more than robust, that is, as exceedingly stable. In their view rational nuclear conflicts are extremely unlikely. Perfect deterrence theory, however, reaches a different conclusion. In the four incomplete information game models that collectively delineate the theory, a deterrence equilibrium under which no player contests the status quo always exists. But these equilibria are hardly ever unique, that is, more often than not they coexist with other equilibria some of which admit the possibility of a complete deterrence breakdown. In others words, the conditions that are most conducive to peace and stability are also consistent with the possibility of war. Depending on leadership preferences and policy choices, either denouement is possible, that is, deterrence failures, limited conflicts, and all-out conflicts can

Table 15.2 Classical Deterrence Theory and Perfect Deterrence Theory: Empirical Propositions

Propositions:	*Classical Deterrence Theory*	*Perfect Deterrence Theory*
Status Quo	unimportant/ignored	significant
Strategic deterrence	robust/all but certain	fragile/contingent
Relationship between conflict costs and deterrence success	strictly positive and monotonic	non-monotonic
Asymmetric power relationships	Unstable	potentially very stable
Parity relationships	very stable	potentially unstable
Capability	sufficient for deterrence success	necessary, but not sufficient, for deterrence success
Limited conflicts and escalation spirals	unexplained	placed in theoretical context

Source: Compiled by author.

almost never be ruled out as a rational strategic possibility. In perfect deterrence theory, then, deterrence success is highly contingent and anything but robust.

A related difference concerns the strategic characteristics of parity conditions. Classical deterrence theorists see them as generally stable and view asymmetric power relationships as potentially unstable. Once again, perfect deterrence theory reaches a different conclusion. In both theory and principal it is much easier to stabilize the status quo when only one player is a defender than it is when both play that role. Since the former category of games are more likely to exist when power is asymmetrically distributed, parity or balance of power conditions are judged, *ceteris paribus*, to be less stable than one-sided deterrence relationships, but especially those in which a dominant and highly satisfied great power clearly controls the agenda of the international system.

Finally, classical deterrence theorists see a monotonic and strictly positive relationship between the cost of conflict and the probability of deterrence success. Specifically, the higher war costs, the less likely a deterrence breakdown, and conversely (e.g., Mearsheimer 1990: 19). In perfect deterrence theory, by contrast, the relationship is neither. To be sure, there is a minimum cost threshold below which deterrence success is not possible. This is the point at which a non-capable threat becomes a threat that hurts. But there is also a maximum threshold beyond which additional increases in the cost of conflict are unrelated to the probability of successful deterrence. Moreover, in perfect deterrence theory, extended deterrence relationships are actually more likely to unravel, *ceteris paribus*, as war costs increase.

PERFECT DETERRENCE THEORY: EMPIRICAL SUPPORT

There is considerable empirical support for both the relationship and, as will be seen, for the equilibrium predictions of perfect deterrence theory (Morton 1999). Perfect deterrence theory is, in other words, a more plausible theory of strategic interaction than is classical deterrence theory. In part, this advantage stems from classical deterrence theory's loose formulation and its inconsistent use of the rationality postulate. By contrast, perfect deterrence theory's straightforward empirical expectations are the result of an analytic framework that respects the requirements of strict logic.

Take, for instance, the empirics that support the stabilizing effect of satisfaction with the status quo.[13] For the most part, classical deterrence theorists have ignored this literature precisely because their conceptual lens has blinded them to its importance. This wide and largely straightforward literature, however, is more than consistent with the gestalt of perfect deterrence theory. It should be patently obvious that highly satisfied states are, *ceteris paribus*, less prone to contest the governing structure of either a regional or a systemic structure. Classical deterrence theorists, however, seem not to have noticed.

Much the same can be said about perfect deterrence theory's claim that a capable threat is a necessary (though not a sufficient) condition for deterrence success. Harvey's (1998: 691) empirical study "indirectly support [perfect deterrence theory's] claim about the crucial role of capabilities" in deterrence relationships. But so does Bueno de Mesquita's (1981: 154–56) finding that conflict initiators, in general, tend to be more capable then those they attack, regardless of the belligerents' alignment status or the level of initiated conflict.

There is also impressive empirical support for perfect deterrence theory's claim about the central role that credible threats play in deterrence relationships. For instance, in an important study of extended deterrence, Danilovic (2002) finds that a state's inherent credibility—as reflected in large part by its regional interests—is a far more important predictor of deterrence outcomes than are the coercive bargaining tactics recommended by decision-theoretic deterrence theorists. Huth's (1999) earlier review of the literature reaches a similar conclusion and, at the same time, undermines the empirical foundation of many of Schelling's most well-known policy prescriptions. More recently Johnson, Leeds, and Wu's (2015: 309) comprehensive study of strategic alliances clearly shows that "defense pacts with more capability and more credibility reduce the probability that a member state will be the target of a militarized dispute." Their results reinforce both Danilovic's conclusions and perfect deterrence theory's propositions about the pacifying role played by both these variables in extended deterrence relationships. In this context it should also be mentioned that the vast literatures supporting action-reaction models, reciprocity and tit-for-tat behavior[14] are also consistent with perfect deterrence theory's key finding that conditionally cooperative strategies (or policies) are associated with deterrence success, and that unconditionally hard line policies are generally prone to fail.

In another significant examination of the dynamics of deterrence, Senese and Quackenbush (2003) studied the long-term consequences of different types of conflict settlements on recurring conflicts. Their hypothesis that imposed settlements, which they contend create one-sided (or unilateral) deterrence relationships, should last longer than negotiated agreements, which they associate with bilateral (or mutual) deterrence situations, was independently deduced from perfect deterrence theory's axiomatic base. In an exhaustive analysis of 2,536 interstate conflict settlements between 1816 and 1992, this now clear implication of perfect deterrence theory was "strongly supported." Senese and Quackenbush's result held even when they controlled for regime type, relative capability, contiguity, decisive outcomes, power shifts, and war, leading them to observe that in their test of one of perfect deterrence theory's relationship predictions, the theory performed "quite well." Follow-up studies by Quackenbush and Venteicher (2006) and Quackenbush (2010b) reach the same conclusion.

Space and other considerations preclude a full discussion of empirical studies that support the relationship predictions of perfect deterrence theory.[15] But mention should be made of one study that attempted to test perfect deterrence theory's equilibrium predictions and also of those analytic narratives that have been constructed to illustrate the "theory in action."

In the literature of deterrence, attempts to test equilibrium predictions of a game theoretic model are virtually nonexistent, in large part because of the numerous methodological hurdles that stand in their way. Quackenbush (2011) is the rare exception in more than one way. Not only is it a direct test of a game model's equilibrium predictions, but it is also one of the few attempts to test a theory of general deterrence. The empirical literature of deterrence is dominated by tests of extended immediate deterrence (Morgan 1977) in which general deterrence has already failed. Huth (1988) and Danilovic (2002) are representative of best of this literature.

In order to test perfect deterrence theory's equilibrium predictions and, not coincidentally, minimize case selection bias, Quackenbush had to construct a relevant data set. For this he first developed a category of relationships he termed "politically active" (Quackenbush 2006). He also had to develop measures that reflected the players' utility functions, perhaps the most daunting precondition for a meaningful test of any rational choice theory. Finally, using binary and multinomial logit methods to examine the predictions of various game outcomes, he found that the predictions of perfect deterrence theory were "generally supported by the empirical record." He also found that his results provide much stronger support for perfect deterrence theory than the support that Bennett and Stam (2000) found for Bueno de Mesquita and Lalman's (1992) international interaction game.

Because it is a direct test, Quackenbush's study is the most persuasive evidence to date that perfect deterrence theory stands on firm empirical grounds. Less systematic, but significant nonetheless, is the accumulated collection of case studies that have been constructed using the constituent models of perfect deterrence theory as an organizing mechanism. For instance, Zagare (2016) uses the *Asymmetric Escalation Game* (see figure 15.5) to explain the strategic decisions of the Soviet Union and the United States during the 1962 Cuban Missile Crisis. He also uses it, along with *Tripartite Crisis Game* to examine four critical decisions that he claims account, collectively, for the initiation, escalation, and expansion of World War I.

In the Asymmetric Escalation Game limited conflicts are most likely to occur under a *Constrained Limited-Response equilibrium*; escalation spirals

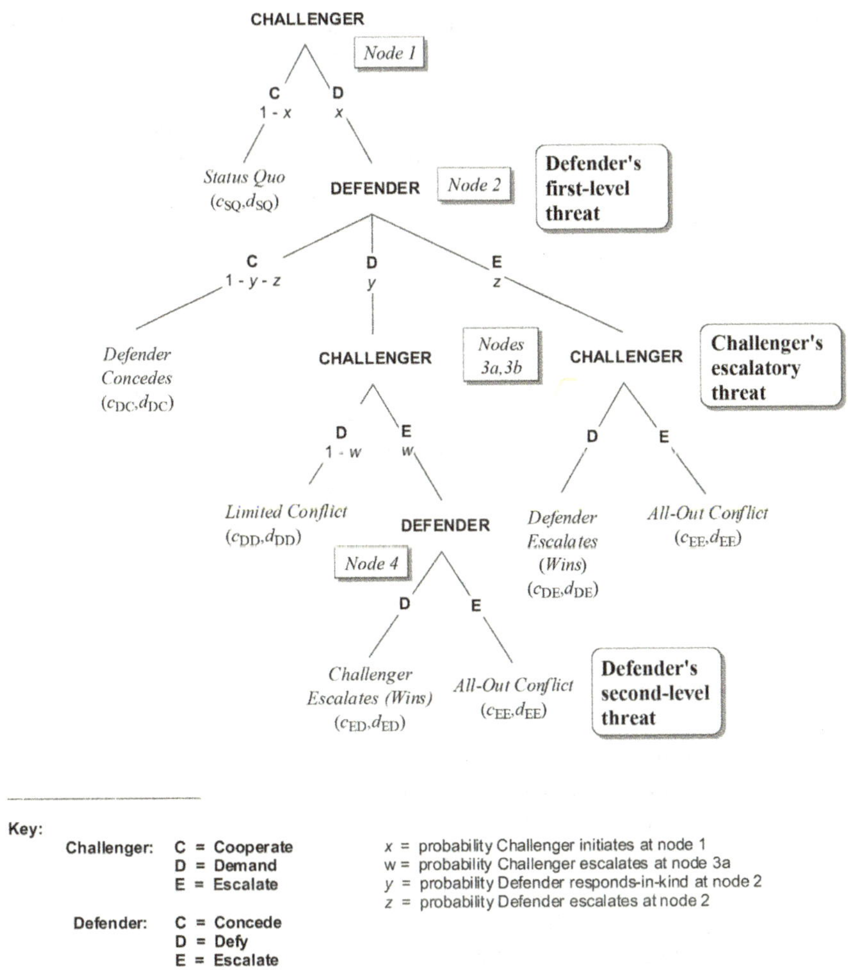

Figure 15.5 Asymmetric Escalation Game. *Source*: Compiled by author.

and all-out conflicts under an *Escalatory Limited-Response equilibrium.*[16] Under either of these equilibria, a Challenger will initiate a crisis but only when it judges it very likely that Defender will capitulate and that the outcome will be *Defender Concedes*. In either case, if Defender in fact responds, it will come as a complete surprise to Challenger. What distinguishes the two equilibrium forms from one another, however, is the inference that Challenger draws after observing Defender's response. Under a Constrained Limited-Response equilibrium, Challenger believes that Defender will counter-escalate if it further intensifies the conflict. Hence it backs off and a limited conflict ensues. Zagare (2016) argues that a political compromise was reached, and the Cuban crisis resolved, precisely because the Soviet leadership (i.e., Premier

Khrushchev) came to believe, even before the blockade was announced, that the United States was prepared to remove the missiles by force, if necessary. By contrast, under an Escalatory Limited-Response equilibrium, Challenger simply believes that escalation will likely force Defender to capitulate. All out conflicts like World War I occur when that belief is mistaken.

In one sense the explanations Zagare develops for these and other real-world conflicts can also be considered a test of perfect deterrence theory's equilibrium predictions. Specifically, the perfect Bayesian equilibria of the incomplete information models he applies make specific predictions about not only the likelihood of certain events but also about the conditions (i.e., specific beliefs) that are necessary and sufficient to bring them about. Explanations are developed when a plausible connection between these conditions and a real-world outcome is established (Riker 1990: 175). But the explanation can also be considered as additional, albeit limited, evidence of perfect deterrence theory's empirical robustness.

PERFECT DETERRENCE THEORY: POLICY IMPLICATIONS

Classical deterrence theory and perfect deterrence theory stand in sharp opposition to one another. The classical formulation is plagued by logical inconsistencies and empirical anomalies. By contrast, perfect deterrence theory respects the laws of logic and is not contradicted by the empirical record. As well, it has performed quite well when tested directly, better in fact than other theories, formal or not. The distinctions, axiomatic, theoretical, and empirical, are simply not arcane academic nitpicks. The policy implications of these two competing formulations of deterrence theory are also widely divergent, as table 15.3 shows. In other words, there are significant real-world consequences for which variant is used, not only to understand how interstate relationships operate but also how best to navigate through them.

One important difference can be traced to the conclusions the two theoretical frameworks reach about the implications of manipulating the cost of conflict. As already noted, classical deterrence theorists, but especially decision-theoretic deterrence theorists, assume fixed preferences. Specifically, players are assumed to always prefer an advantage to the status quo, and to always prefer backing off rather than enduring the costs associated with conflict. In consequence, any change in the cost of conflict will have the same impact relative to these other outcomes. Since they assume that the probability of successful deterrence increases monotonically as these costs rise, they see no obvious limit to the pacifying impact that expanded expenditures for weapons systems that are capable of imposing pain and suffering

Table 15.3 Classical Deterrence Theory and Perfect Deterrence Theory: Policy Prescriptions

Policies:	*Classical Deterrence Theory*	*Perfect Deterrence Theory*
Overkill capability	supports	opposes
Minimum deterrence	opposes	supports
"Significant" arms reductions	opposes	supports
Proliferation	supports	opposes
Negotiating stances	coercive, based on increasing war costs and inflexible bargaining tactics	conditionally cooperative, based on reciprocity

Source: Compiled by author.

on an opponent can have. For this reason, most classical deterrence theorists favor an "overkill capability," opposed "significant" arms control agreements, and stand in opposition to minimum deterrence policies.

In perfect deterrence theory, however, the cost of conflict relative to other variables is not fixed. Rather it is gauged against two other important strategic variables. The first, of course, is the value of the status quo. The second reference point is the value of concession. In perfect deterrence theory, the players may, or may not, prefer to concede rather than execute a deterrent threat. In consequence, there are two strategically significant cost thresholds, one minimum and the other maximum. The minimum cost threshold is the point below which deterrence cannot succeed. This is the point separating threats that are capable from those that are not. The two theoretical frameworks are not at odds over the strategic impact of increasing conflict costs beyond this minimum cost threshold. Both agree that deterrence success can only be achieved once this threshold is crossed.

In perfect deterrence theory, however, the maximum cost threshold is also strategically significant. Once this point is reached, further increases in the cost of conflict do not contribute to the probability of deterrence success. Rather than an overkill capability, then, the logic of perfect deterrence theory is consistent with a policy of minimum deterrence, which rests on a threat that is costly enough to deter an opponent, but that is not so costly that the threat itself is rendered incredible.

An equally important difference stems from the fact that in perfect deterrence theory there is no simple monotonic relationship between the cost of conflict and the stability of the status quo, as there is in classical deterrence theory. Since extended deterrence becomes more and more difficult to maintain as conflict costs rise, an increased military capability may actually have a destabilizing implications. In other words, in perfect deterrence theory, increased conflict costs can, under some circumstances, be stabilizing but, under others, may have the opposite consequence. For this and other reasons, perfect deterrence theory stands in opposition to unconstrained armaments programs and an overkill capability, and supports defense postures that are sufficiently capable but not unnecessarily redundant.

Perhaps the most significant policy difference between classical and perfect deterrence theories concerns proliferation policies. Those classical deterrence theorists who fully understand the logical implications of their paradigm favor them. In the past Mearsheimer (1990, 1993), Posen (1993), Van Evera (1990/1991), and Waltz (1981), *inter alia*, have argued that nuclear weapons can help stabilize contentious interstate rivalries and that, therefore, nuclear weapons should be disseminated selectively. More recently, Waltz (2012) made the case that if Iran acquired nuclear weapons the possibility of an all-out conflict between Iran and Israel would be all-but eliminated.[17]

Of course, those deterrence theorists who favor proliferation argue that nuclear technology should not be distributed indiscriminately. An exception, they assert, should be made for so-called rogue states that operate on the fringes of the interstate system and whose behavior is borderline "rational." Of course, there is no such category in realism, classical or neo, or in the standard formulations of deterrence theory where all states are taken as like-units (Waltz 1979; Mearsheimer 1990). Nonetheless, this qualifier is frequently called upon to help those classical deterrence theorists who favor proliferation avoid a conclusion they wish to avoid. But the very fact that this anomalous category of states exist is further evidence that realism in general, and classical deterrence theory in particular, is a degenerative research program (Vasquez 1997).

The proliferation of nuclear and other weapons of mass destruction is not a policy prescription that can be derived from the axioms of perfect deterrence theory. To be sure, the increased costs of conflict that are associated with these weapons imply, *ceteris paribus*, an increased probability of deterrence success. But all things are hardly ever equal in interstate relations. For one thing, the minimum cost threshold that renders a threat capable can also be achieved with more conventional weapons. For another, the increased probability of success that nuclear weapons imply must be balanced against the risks associated with the possibility of a massive breakdown of deterrence. Since in perfect deterrence theory these risks are seen as considerable, it opposes proliferation policies, selective or otherwise.

There is one additional significant policy dispute between classical deterrence theory and perfect deterrence theory that remains to be discussed: how best to manage a crisis, how best to negotiate or bargain with an opponent. This is a question that has received considerable attention from decision-theoretic deterrence theorist from Schelling (1960, 1966) on down. In general, decision-theoretic deterrence theorists favor coercive bargaining tactics that involve either increasing the cost of conflict or making an irrevocably commitment to a hard line policy so that the opponent is forced to make the difficult choice between war and peace. The standard example involves a player forfeiting control in a game of Chicken by pulling the steering wheel off the steering column. Snyder (1972) provides a useful summary of less colorful but equally counterintuitive tacit negotiating tactics.

Empirically speaking, the stratagems that decision-theoretic deterrence theorists recommend have no basis in fact (Huth 1999: 74; Danilovic 2002; Snyder and Diesing 1977: 489–90; Betts 1987: 30). And for good reason. As Jervis (1979: 292) notes, many of Schelling's policy prescriptions are "contrary to common sense." Rapoport (1992: 482) found the tacit bargaining tactics conjured up by decision-theoretic deterrence theorist to be just plain "bizarre," while Morgenstern (1961: 105) concluded that they would be "dangerous should they have an influence on policy."

By way of contrast, perfect deterrence theory recommends conditionally cooperative bargaining stances rooted in reciprocity. The large majority of the deterrence equilibria in its constituent models are supported by strategies that offer to cooperate if the other player cooperates, but threatens not to cooperate if the other player does not reciprocate. Hard line (unconditionally non-cooperative) and soft line (unconditionally cooperative) bargaining stances generally do not lead to either stable relationships or political compromises.

It is noteworthy that the efficacy of conditionally cooperative negotiating stances is well-established not only in (perfect deterrence) theory, but also in standard diplomatic practice. For example, in a large-*n* statistical analysis of extended deterrence relationships, Huth (1988) found that firm-but-flexible negotiating styles and tit-for-tat deployments are highly correlated with extended deterrence success. Each of these more or less standard diplomatic or military postures involves reciprocity, a behavioral norm that is pervasive in interstate relationships, contentious or not (Cashman 1993: ch. 6). It is also a norm that decision-theoretic deterrence theorists have a hard time explaining. It is, in a word, inconsistent with their underlying conceptual framework (Zagare 2011: 55).

CODA

In this chapter I have drawn a sharp contrast between classical deterrence theory and perfect deterrence theory. Perfect deterrence theory is a completely general theory of conflict initiation, escalation, and resolution. It is applicable across time and space. Indeed, its empirical domain is not restricted to contentious nuclear relationships. Rather, its analytic framework can be used to understand the full range of situations wherein at least one actor's goal is to preserve the existing distribution of value, which is Arnold Wolters's (1951) neologism for the status quo. Unlike classical deterrence theory, perfect deterrence theory is logically consistent and in accord with the empirical record. In a direct test, perfect deterrence theory even outperformed what is, according to Bennett and Stam (2000: 451), "one of the most important theories of international conflict." Observing all this, Quackenbush (2011: 74) recommends that the academic and policy communities "take note."

In perfect deterrence theory, a capable threat is a necessary condition for deterrence success. But it is not sufficient, as it is in classical deterrence theory. Threat credibility plays an important role in the operation of both direct and extended deterrence relationships, but it is neither necessary nor sufficient for deterrence to prevail; under certain conditions, the presence of a credible threat may actually precipitate a deterrence failure. In perfect deterrence theory the cost of conflict and status quo evaluations are also important strategic variables in so far as their values determine the characteristics of the players' threats.

Significantly different policy recommendations also distinguish perfect deterrence theory from its classical rival. Perfect deterrence theory is consistent with a policy of minimum deterrence, it recommends a conditionally cooperative diplomatic approach to resolve disputes, opposes even the selective proliferation of nuclear and other weapons of mass destruction, and supports arms control agreements and other limitations on redundant military expenditures.

NOTES

1. This chapter was published as Frank C. Zagare, "Perfect Deterrence Theory," in William R. Thompson (ed.), *Oxford Encyclopedia of Empirical International Relations Theory*. New York: Oxford University Press, 2018, Vol. 3, pp. 34–52. Reproduced with permission of the Licensor through PLSclear.

2. Classical deterrence theory is also sometimes referred to as rational deterrence theory. However, there are other theories of deterrence based on rational choice, and would therefore seem to fall under the umbrella of rational deterrence theory.

3. The empirical basis for this claim is weak. See, for example, Förster (1999).

4. For a full discussion, see Zagare (1996a).

5. For a discussion of several unsuccessful attempts to eliminate this logical inconsistency see Zagare and Kilgour (2000: ch. 2).

6. For specific examples of this theoretical pirouette, see Schelling (1966: 37) or Brodie (1959: 293).

7. The assumption of differentiated actors is not ad hoc in perfect deterrence theory, as it is in most manifestations of classical deterrence theory. Perfect deterrence theory is connected, theoretically, with power transition theory (Organski and Kugler, 1980), which sees the international system as hierarchical rather than anarchistic. In a hierarchical system, the dominant state and its allies are generally content with the status quo. For a discussion of the linkage between power transition theory and perfect deterrence theory, see Zagare (1996b, 2007).

8. The *Asymmetric Escalation Game* and the *Tripartite Crisis Game* (Zagare and Kilgour, 2003) are also component parts of the theory.

9. Powell (1990), whose work is in the tradition of Schelling and other decision-theoretic deterrence theorists, is an exception to the rule. His analysis of nuclear deterrence is consistent with Selten's criterion. But there are other problems with his explanation of the long peace. For a discussion see Zagare and Kilgour (2000: 54–57).

10. Lebow's (1981: 85) conclusion is typical. For Lebow and most strategic analysts "four conditions emerge as crucial to successful deterrence. Nations must (1) define their commitment clearly, (2) communicate its existence to possible adversaries, (3) develop the means to defend it, or to punish adversaries who challenge it, and (4) demonstrate their resolve to carry out the actions this entails."

11. Not surprisingly, Lebow (1981) is a case in point.

12. See, for example, Mearsheimer (1983).

13. For a detailed overview, see Geller and Singer (1998).

14. For overviews, see Cashman (1993: ch. 6) and Sullivan (2002: ch. 9). On reciprocity, see Crescenzi, Best, and Kwon (2010).

15. For a detailed discussion, see Zagare (2011: 184–86) or Zagare and Kilgour (2000: ch. 10).

16. Both games are examined under incomplete information. Hence, these are perfect Bayesian equilibria.

17. For a trenchant rebuttal, see Kugler (2012).

REFERENCES

Achen, Christopher H. 1987. "A Darwinian View of Deterrence." In *Exploring the Stability of Deterrence*, edited by Jacek Kugler and Frank C. Zagare. Denver: Lynne Rienner.

Bennett, D. Scott, and Alan C. Stam. 2000. "A Universal Test of an Expected Utility Theory of War." *International Studies Quarterly* 43: 451–80.

Brodie, Bernard, ed. 1946. *The Absolute Weapon: Atomic Power and World Order*. New York: Harcourt Brace.

Brodie, Bernard. 1959. "The Anatomy of Deterrence." *World Politics* 11: 173–79.

Bueno de Mesquita, Bruce. 1981. *The War Trap*. New Haven: Yale University Press.

Bueno de Mesquita, Bruce and David Lalman. 1992. *War and Reason: A Confrontation Between Domestic and International Imperatives*. New Haven: Yale University Press.

Bundy, McGeorge. 1983. "The Bishops and the Bomb." *New York Review of Books* (June 16) 40: 3–8.

Cashman, Greg 1993. *What Causes War? An Introduction to Theories of International Conflict*. New York: Lexington Books.

Crescenzi, Mark J. C., Rebecca H. Best, and Bo Ram Kwon (2010). "Reciprocity in International Studies." In *The International Studies Encyclopedia*, edited by Robert A. Denemark et al. Oxford: Wiley-Blackwell.

Danilovic, Vesna. 2002. *When the Stakes Are High: Deterrence and Conflict among Major Powers*. Ann Arbor: University of Michigan Press.

Förster, Stig. 1999. "Dreams and Nightmares: German Military Leadership and the Images of Future Warfare, 1871–1914." In *Anticipating Total War: The German and American Experiences, 1871–1914*, edited by Manfred F. Boemeke, Roger Chickering, and Stig Förster. Washington, DC: German Historical Institute.

Freedman, Lawrence. 1989. *The Evolution of Nuclear Strategy*. 2nd ed. New York: St. Martin's.

Gaddis, John Lewis. 1987. *The Long Peace: Inquiries into the History of the Cold War*. New York: Oxford University Press.

Gaddis, John Lewis. 1997. *We Now Know: Rethinking Cold War History*. New York: Oxford University Press.

Geller, Daniel S. and J. David Singer. 1998. *Nations at War: A Scientific Study of International Conflict*. Cambridge: Cambridge University Press.

Harsanyi, John C. 1967–1968. "Games with Incomplete Information Played by 'Bayesian' Players." 3 pts. *Management Science* 14 (Series A): 159–82, 320–34, 486–502.

Huth, Paul K. 1988. *Extended Deterrence and the Prevention of War*. New Haven: Yale University Press.

Huth, Paul K. 1999. "Deterrence and International Conflict: Empirical Findings and Theoretical Debates." *Annual Review of Political Science* 2: 61–84.

Intriligator, Michael D. and Dagobert L. Brito. 1984. "Can Arms Races Lead to the Outbreak of War?" *Journal of Conflict Resolution* 28: 63–84.

Jervis, Robert. 1979. "Deterrence Theory Revisited." *World Politics* 31: 289–324.

Jervis, Robert. 1985. "Introduction." In *Psychology and Deterrence*, edited by Robert Jervis, Richard Ned Lebow, and Janice Gross Stein. Baltimore: The Johns Hopkins University Press.

Jervis, Robert. 1988. "Realism, Game Theory, and Cooperation." *World Politics* 40: 317–49.

Johnson, Jesse C, Brett Ashley Leeds, and Ahra Wu. 2015. "Capability, Credibility, and Extended Deterrence." *International Interactions* 41: 309–36.

Kaufmann, William. 1956. "The Requirements of Deterrence." In *Military Policy and National Security*, edited by William Kaufmann. Princeton: Princeton University Press.

Kugler, Jacek. 2012. "A World beyond Waltz: Neither Iran nor Israel Should Have the Bomb." http://www.pbs.org/wgbh/pages/frontline/tehranbureau/2012/09/opinion-a-world-beyond-waltz-neither-iran-nor-israel-should-have-the-bomb.html#ixzz28ItL7mq1

Lebow, Richard Ned. 1981. *Between Peace and War: The Nature of International Crisis*. Baltimore: The Johns Hopkins University Press.

Lebow, Richard Ned. 1984. "Windows of Opportunity: Do States Jump Through Them?" *International Security* 9: 147–86.

Legro, Jeffrey W. and Andrew Moravcsik. 1999. "Is Anybody Still a Realist?" *International Security* 24: 5–55.

Martin, Lisa. 1999. "The Contributions of Rational Choice: A Defense of Pluralism." *International Security* 24: 74–83.

Mearsheimer, John J. 1983. *Conventional Deterrence*. Ithaca, NY: Cornell University Press.

Mearsheimer, John J. 1990. "Back to the Future: Instability in Europe After the Cold War." *International Security* 15: 5–56.

Mearsheimer, John J. 1993. "The Case for a Ukrainian Nuclear Deterrent." *Foreign Affairs* 72: 50–66.
Morgan, Patrick M. 1977. *Deterrence: A Conceptual Analysis*. Beverly Hills, CA: Sage.
Morgenstern, Oskar. 1961. "Review of The Strategy of Conflict." *Southern Economic Journal* 28: 105.
Morton, Rebecca B. 1999. *Methods and Models: A Guide to the Empirical Analysis of Formal Models in Political Science*. Cambridge: Cambridge University Press.
Most, Benjamin A. and Harvey Starr. 1989. *Inquiry, Logic and International Politics*. Columbia: University of South Carolina Press.
Organski, A.F.K. 1958. *World Politics*. New York: Knopf.
Organski, A.F.K. and Jacek Kugler. 1980. *The War Ledger*. Chicago: University of Chicago Press.
Posen, Barry R. 1993. "The Security Dilemma and Ethnic Conflict." *Survival* 35: 27–47.
Powell, Robert. 1990. *Nuclear Deterrence Theory: The Search for Credibility*. New York: Cambridge University Press.
Quackenbush, Stephen L. 2010a. "General Deterrence and International Conflict: Testing Perfect Deterrence Theory." *International Interactions* 36: 60–85.
Quackenbush, Stephen L. 2010b. "Territorial Issues and Recurrent Conflict." *Conflict Management and Peace Science* 27: 239–52.
Quackenbush, Stephen L. 2011. *Understanding General Deterrence: Theory and Application*. New York: Palgrave Macmillan.
Quackenbush, Stephen L. and Jerome F. Venteicher II. 2008. "Settlements, Outcomes, and the Recurrence of Conflict," *Journal of Peace Research* 45: 723–42.
Rapoport, Anatol. 1992. "Comments on 'Rationality and Misperceptions in Deterrence Theory.'" *Journal of Theoretical Politics* 4: 479–84.
Riker, William H. 1990. "Political Science and Rational Choice." In *Perspectives on Positive Political Economy*, edited by James E. Alt and Kenneth A. Shepsle. Cambridge: Cambridge University Press.
Schelling, Thomas C. 1960. *The Strategy of Conflict*. Cambridge, MA: Harvard University Press.
Schelling, Thomas C. 1966. *Arms and Influence*. New Haven: Yale University Press.
Selten, Reinhard. 1975. "A Re-examination of the Perfectness Concept for Equilibrium Points in Extensive Games." *International Journal of Game Theory* 4: 25–55.
Senese, Paul D. and Stephen L. Quackenbush. 2003. "Sowing the Seeds of Conflict: The Effect of Dispute Settlements on Durations of Peace." *Journal of Politics* 65: 696–717.
Snyder, Glenn H. 1972. "Crisis Bargaining." In *International Crises: Insights from Behavioral Research*, edited by Charles F. Hermann. New York: Free Press.
Snyder, Glenn H. and Paul Diesing. 1977. *Conflict Among Nations: Bargaining, Decision Making and System Structure in International Crises*. Princeton: Princeton University Press.
Sullivan, Michael P. 2002. *Theories of International Relations: Transition vs. Persistence*. New York: Palgrave MacMillan.

Van Evera, Stephen. 1990/1991. "Primed for Peace: Europe After the Cold War." *International Security* 15, no. 3: 7–57.

Vasquez, John A. 1997. "The Realist Paradigm and Degenerative versus Progressive Research Programs: An Appraisal of Neotraditional Research on Waltz's Balancing Proposition." *American Political Science Review* 91 (December 1997): 899–912.

Walt, Stephen M. 1999. "Rigor or Rigor Mortis? Rational Choice and Security Studies." *International Security* 23: 5–48.

Waltz, Kenneth N. 1964. "The Stability of the Bipolar World." *Daedalus* 93: 881–909.

Waltz, Kenneth N. 1979. *Theory of International Politics*. Reading, MA: Addison-Wesley.

Waltz, Kenneth N. 1981. "The Spread of Nuclear Weapons: More May Be Better." Adelphi Paper No. 171. London: International Institute for Strategic Studies.

Waltz, Kenneth N. 1990. "Nuclear Myths and Political Realities." *The American Political Science Review* 84: 731–45.

Waltz, Kenneth N. 1993. "The Emerging World Structure of International Politics." *International Security* 18: 44–79.

Waltz, Kenneth N. 2012. "Why Iran Should Get the Bomb: Nuclear Balancing Would Mean Stability." *Foreign Affairs* 91, no. 4: 2–5.

Wolfers, Arnold. 1951. "The Pole of Power and the Pole of Indifference." *World Politics* 4: 39–63.

Zagare, Frank C. 1987. *The Dynamics of Deterrence*. Chicago: University of Chicago Press.

Zagare, Frank C. 1996a. "Classical Deterrence Theory: A Critical Assessment," *International Interactions,* 21: 365–87.

Zagare, Frank C. 1996b. "The Rites of Passage: Parity, Nuclear Deterrence and Power Transitions." In *Parity and War: Evaluations and Extensions of "The War Ledger,"* edited by Jacek Kugler and Douglas Lemke. Ann Arbor: University of Michigan Press.

Zagare, Frank C. 2007. "Toward a Unified Theory of Interstate Conflict." *International Interactions* 33: 305–27.

Zagare, Frank C. 2011. *The Games of July: Explaining the Great War*. Ann Arbor: University of Michigan Press.

Zagare, Frank C. 2016. "A General Explanation of the Cuban Missile Crisis." *International Journal of Peace Economics and Peace Science* 1, no. 1: 91–115.

Zagare, Frank C. and D. Marc Kilgour. 2000. *Perfect Deterrence*. Cambridge: Cambridge University Press.

Zagare, Frank C. and D. Marc Kilgour. 2003. "Alignment Patterns, Crisis Bargaining, and Extended Deterrence: A Game-Theoretic Analysis." *International Studies Quarterly* 47: 587–615.

Zakaria, Fareed. 2001. "Don't Oversell Missile Defense: The Old Theory of Nuclear Deterrence Still Makes Sense. Just Ask the Man Who Invented it." *Newsweek* (May 14).

Chapter 16

Uncovering the Causal Mechanism in a Crucial Case Study

The Crimean War

Vesna Danilovic

The increasing recognition of the multitude of benefits from the so-called mixed research design, combining qualitative and quantitative methods, has swept all subfields in political science. Although commonplace today, the disciplinary acceptance of combining methodological approaches as scientifically legitimate has not been smooth, with the divisions probably most acutely expressed between the proponents of "area studies" and "quantitative behaviorism" in the concluding decades of the last century. These fault lines have been nearly eradicated by now as evident in an almost universal adoption of King, Keohane, and Verba's *Designing Social Inquiry* (1994) as a standard methodological textbook in political science graduate programs. While influential, it was not the first major attempt of the kind, but rather a culmination of a process slowly moving in this direction in several subfields. Probably the most dramatic in a scientific sense occurred in the late 1960s and early 1970s, when a group of American scholars shifted "Kremlinology" into the scientific "Sovietology." The turning point came over 50 years ago with the landmark study, edited by Frederic J. Fleron, *Communist Studies and the Social Sciences: Essays on Methodology and Empirical Theory* (1969). The challenges were manifold, ranging from resistance to the idea that the Soviet Union, at the height of the Cold War, could be studied within the comparative framework rather than as a unique case due to the lack of access to reliable data.

The advancements were not just methodological, but also theoretical, carving the path for what Laitin termed "triangulation" with its scientific promise eloquently encapsulated in the recent reflections of one of the leading scholars at the frontiers of the new Sovietology.

> We should be impressed by the power of triangulation to bring quantitative-statistical, historical, and theoretical analyses to bear on the solution of a particular research problem . . . [Besides] the positive effect of bringing more history back into our research [. . .], it would have the added benefit of protecting us from the temptation to view our subject unique. (Fleron 2017, 57)

In this chapter, I will analogously attempt to "triangulate" theoretical, qualitative-historical, and quantitative analysis but in a different subfield, where the research puzzle of war takes the central place. By crossing the divide between diplomatic history and international relations theory, while also subjecting it to the quantitative test of generalizability, it exposes the practice and theory of crisis bargaining behavior that *inadvertently* leads to war. The question is not why states want to fight, the answers to which are myriad, but rather the prima facie paradox of why they fight wars they preferred to avoid and did *not* want to fight in the first place.

RESEARCH PUZZLE AND THEORETICAL PRELIMINARIES

In his influential "Rationalist Explanations for War," Fearon (1995) raised the question that has given rise to several strands of research in an attempt to address it: Why do states fight wars even though the ex ante bargaining range allows them to reach an agreement short of the costliness of wars? Fearon's main argument is that private information about each state's true preferences, as well as an incentive to misrepresent it, obscures each side's recognition that the agreement acceptable to all could have been reached short of war. We may pursue this argument further, and in a way challenge Fearon's premise on his own logic, that if this indeed makes it difficult to ascertain the actual presence and limits of a pre-war bargaining range for states, then it should equally apply to analysts as well. Moreover, we may be reasonably skeptical about the universality of such cases, that is, whether there is indeed a bargaining range acceptable to all sides short of war as history provides ample evidence that at least one of the principal parties may see in war an effective bargaining leverage to make greater gains over its opponents. In other words, states do willfully choose war as an option for a range of reasons rather than simply because of the miscalculations about each side's preferences under uncertainty.

One of the rare, and to the best of this author's knowledge, only major cases over which scholars have uncommonly reached a consensus that there is no evidence, nor was there a strong rationale, for any of the principal powers to want to fight concerns the Crimean War of 1853–1856 (see, among others, Temperley 1936; Henderson 1947; Taylor 1954; Gooch 1956; Anderson 1966; Albrecht-Carrie 1968; Wetzel 1985). By taking a closer look at the bargaining process as well as the contextual factors in such a crucial case (Lijphart 1971; Eckstein 1992), we can evaluate the validity of the most influential arguments about bargaining and war and, moreover, move toward theory-building by uncovering new or modified causal mechanisms.[1] It is of a "least-likely" type as the payoff structure of all involved powers formed a strong disincentive for war, making it a highly improbable event, and yet it occurred. Schelling's canonical works on deterrence in the early 1960s has directed the focus on several strategies for averting war while ensuring one's own payoff maximization. Of these strategies, two have especially received wider attention—costly signaling and ambiguous commitments—as effective manipulative methods that increase the risks for an adversary by projecting greater resolve while also keeping one's true preferences private. My main contention is that these are precisely the causal pathways to war as will be shown in the focused analysis of Crimean case.

Briefly to preface the case study with a few conceptual clarifications and theoretical preliminaries. It is traditional to separate two types of bargaining "costs"—as "sunk costs" and "tying-hands"—with the premise that each works out differently in the bargaining process. The former is primarily seen as "productive waste" that might increase threat credibility, but without changing the player's payoff structure, while the latter transforms it by raising the reputational costs of reneging on threats (Fearon 1997). In other words, the premise about the effects of the sunk-cost strategy is that the payoffs remain immutable which differentiates it from the tying-hands tactics. The argument advanced in this study is that these two strategies are both analytically and empirically inseparable, and the higher the sunk costs during the bargaining process the higher the probability that the players' payoffs will change by increasing their costs for backing down and thus reducing their reservation points for war. That is, while the coercive strategies based on high sunk costs are intended to increase a player's credibility, they also change the payoff structure, transforming the original contest over the issue at stake into a contest of resolve. Consequently, although initially each side's preferences could have been for peace over war, the employment of such publicly costly strategies has the resulting transformation of their payoff structures that drastically reduce or even entirely eliminates the original bargaining range.

The logic of presumed efficacy of another strategy, the ambiguity of commitments, is somewhat different from the costly signaling tactics. Instead of reducing or eliminating the players' bargaining range, it can mislead about its scope and value for either player. However, as critics point out, instead of gaining the bargaining leverage by keeping the opponent "guessing," it can raise the risk of war through miscalculations. While also taking a critical angle on the ambiguous commitments, the additional insight offered here is that they can be employed for a number of reasons other than the intention to mislead the opponent.[2]

Moreover, the emphasis has been primarily placed on the bargaining strategy that raises the opponent's critical risks for war through coercion, whereas an alternative strategy of decreasing his value for war through accommodation without "losing face," has not been sufficiently integrated into the current strategic studies. While there are a number of tactics for the latter, I will particularly explore how the issue-linkage strategy might resolve the problem of credibility, leading to a peaceful resolution without the "self-entrapment" perils. Instead of diminishing the bargaining range through sunk-cost moves or inadvertently misleading about it due to the ambiguity of commitments, I argue that there are indeed alternative strategies that actually increase the bargaining range and thus the prospects for peaceful resolution. The key is to reduce the opponent's level of humiliation (e.g., reputational costs) for backing down on the original issue, such as through the exchange of concessions with the issue linkage. Such a strategy is clearly premised on the willingness for preference-revelation, rather than obfuscation, indeed as a perfectly rationalist approach to conflict resolution.

I start with a case study of the Crimean War, describing in greater detail how these factors contribute to escalations toward unintended war. As already suggested, the case of the Crimean War is truly exceptional since there is a near consensus among modern scholars that it was completely unwanted by the principal powers, and the puzzle remains why indeed it occurred despite the participants' intentions to avoid it (Temperley 1936; Henderson 1947; Taylor 1954; Gooch 1956; Anderson 1966; Albrecht-Carrie 1968; Wetzel 1985). It might thus fit the criteria for a "crucial case" (Lijphart 1971), and more specifically "the least likely" case (Eckstein 1992), due to the thoroughly documented evidence about the principal actor's firm preferences for peace, which, in turn, explains a rarely found consensus in the historiography of any war. The larger theoretical question, of course, concerns the factors that trigger inadvertent wars. The case study is thus followed by a detailed theoretical discussion of sunk-cost and ambiguous commitments as triggering factors for war, and the potentials of alternative strategies—issue-linkage in particular here—for avoiding the perils of misplaced bargaining. A quantitative analysis follows the theoretical discussion to supplement the case study with a more robust test.

A "LEAST-LIKELY" CASE: THE CRIMEAN WAR

It is commonly believed that the Crimean War was a rare example of an unintended war, for "none of the three [powers] had conscious plans of aggression" (Taylor 1954, 60–61) and "essentially, all the principal powers wanted peace" (Gooch 1956, 58; also, see Henderson 1947, 99; Albrecht-Carrie 1968, 159). "None of them had the slightest desire for war, but all were now using their armies and navies for essentially diplomatic purposes without any real understanding of the dangers this involved" (Anderson 1966, 125). Only Turkey had an incentive to identify "Ottoman independence with European safety" (Gooch 1956, 33) and *probably* preferred war (Henderson 1947, 99).

The dispute between France, Russia, and Turkey over the Holy Places, starting in May 1850, was an immediate precursor to the Crimean War. The dispute concerned the privileges of the Roman Catholic and Christian Orthodox churches in the Ottoman Empire. Napoleon III demanded greater rights for the former and Russian Tsar Nicholas I predictably responded as a "protector" for the latter, with the Ottomans eventually conceding to Napoleon's pressures in December 1852. In reality, neither side had intrinsic religious stakes in the dispute as their official courts publicly claimed (Florinsky 1953, 864). The Catholic population of Jerusalem was less than 6% by1850, which seemed to give greater validity to Russian claims as over one-third of the Ottoman population comprised Orthodox Christians. That the Russian "protectorate" claims were hardly genuine was soon revealed in their letter to the Porte in May 1853. It implied that the issue of Holy Places was "a secondary matter and could be easily abandoned" (Florinsky 1953, 864), and instead suggested an entente between Russia and Turkey in order to contain France (Temperley 1936, 307). Even in the Tsar's memorandum issued to London earlier in the year, "nothing is said about the religious issue. It therefore becomes obvious that the Tsar's harping on that question in his public and diplomatic declarations is a pure masquerade" (Baumgart 2020, 20). The religious issue itself was thus "quite trifling" (Albrecht-Carrie 1968, 153), "trivial" (Gooch 1956, 35), and a "minor and readily divisible issue" (Wohlforth 2009, 44), but tactfully used by all sides as the pretext for raising the more profound problems of European diplomacy (e.g., Anderson 1966; Curtiss 1979; Rich 1985; Goldfrank 1994), influence in the Near East (Puryear 1931; Saab 1977; Baumgart 2020) or even the general status issue of global power rankings (Wohlforth 2009).[3] *Neither principal power, however, wanted to settle the problems of the European and Near Eastern order through war.*

As to how they got entangled in this "unnecessary" costly war, the Crimean War historiography brims with a wide range of "war blame" pointing in all directions. Schroeder (1972), for example, faults the outright hostility and rigid biases of the British cabinet members, most prominently Clarendon and then Palmerston, against Russia. Goldfrank (1994), on the other hand, puts blame squarely on the mistakes and escalating behavior by Tsar Nicholas I, whereas Rich (1985) places greater responsibility on the provocative behavior by Napoleon III. Another thesis, quite frequently resonating in a number of other "war guilt" situations, finds all parties responsible but still drawing fine shades in the degree of "guilt." To illustrate, Curtiss (1979, 236) concludes that "the primary blame for it rests first of all with Britain and also with France, and to a lesser degree with Russia."

All the same, all acknowledge that neither power had "rational reasons" for war (Goldfrank 1994, 77). Instead of settling the issue of who is more to blame for the Crimean War, therefore, the more productive approach is to find a common thread in all these analyses, which, on the whole, leads to a singular general conclusion that it was "the outcome of a series of misjudgments, misunderstandings and blunders, of stupidity, pride and obstinacy rather than of ill will. More than any great war of modern times, it took place by accident" (Anderson 1966, 132). The plausibility of this general historical impression will indeed become evident in the careful reconstruction of the crisis bargaining behavior of all principal sides in the Crimea. At the same time, by adding both theoretical and empirical rigor to the historical case analysis, this study renders a greater validity to generalizable inferences from a single "crucial" case such as the Crimean War. These will indeed be tested against a larger dataset of cases in the concluding part of the present study. As such, it combines qualitative and quantitative methodological paths. As will become clearer in this case study, several factors are particularly critical for understanding the processes precipitating this "unwanted" war: (1) the French and Russian initial pursuits of a sunk-cost strategy, by which each put itself in the position of choosing between humiliation or escalation;[4] (2) the ambiguity of British foreign policy resulting from its deeply divided Cabinet;[5] (3) the misplaced issue-linkage between Russia and England, mostly due to Russian miscalculation of Britain's actual stakes.

Coercive Diplomacy of "Sunk-Cost" Threats

One of the factors that propelled escalation was the French and Russian use of a sunk-cost strategy in the initial stages of crisis. Later, similar British approaches at raising the hostility level through sunk-cost moves further contributed to the escalation to war. Perhaps war would not have been the only possible outcome, but this strategy raised the reputational costs of backing down for all sides. In reaction to the Sultan's decision to accept Napoleon's demands (December 1852), Nicholas felt his prestige was challenged by France and immediately ordered the mobilization of two army corps and sent a flotilla to the Black Sea. Even more provocative was the Mission of Prince Alexander Menshikov to Constantinople in the spring of 1853, confronting the Sultan with a virtual ultimatum to guarantee the Russian protectorate over all Orthodox Christians (not just the Church) in the Empire. The mission quickly failed: as will be shown below, Nicholas was quite reluctant to go to war. Neither was the British cabinet willing to respond to the Turkish plea for protection and they declined to join the French Fleet dispatched to Salamis off the Greek coast.

The Menshikov Mission turned out to be a bluff, but the crisis soon escalated to a higher level, ending with the Russian occupation of the Danubian principalities. The problem was that the Tsar tied his own hands by opting for the strategy of intimidation, including partial mobilization and naval movements into the Black Sea to accompany the Menshikov Mission, all done under the assumption that the tactical moves of military preparedness and other "costly signals" would make Russian threats credible and compel the Ottomans into an agreement. If anything, however, this strategy only pushed Russia further toward conflict with both England and France that it wanted to avoid in the first place. At the time when the Russian fleet was dispatched to the Black Sea, the Tsar confided his motivations to the French Ambassador Castelbajac: "I wished to avoid war, in the East as in the West and, so as not to be obliged to undergo it, . . . I felt the necessity of speaking to these wretched Turks with firmness" (Temperley 1936, 303–304). The danger of such a bluffing attempt to achieve peace through a dramatic show of force is that "a power which threatens force may be driven to use it" (Temperley 1936, 305).

In addition, the Tsar's conversations with Castelbajac were counterproductive in another sense—Napoleon, informed of Russia's genuine intentions to avoid war, felt encouraged to undertake firmer action, for the Tsar's admitted bluff appeared to remove any danger of escalation. Like Nicholas, Napoleon initially launched a resolute campaign regarding the Holy Places dispute, though more to impress the domestic clerics than irritate the Russians. By adopting such an approach in the early stages of the crisis, however, he precommitted himself to a policy of firmness throughout the crisis, for then, even "a minor Russian success might appear as a defeat for France and himself" (Gooch 1956, 48). Consequently, assured the Russians were intent to avoid war, he ordered the French Fleet to Salamis in March 1953. Contrary to Napoleon's expectations, this show of force only hastened the escalation to war. Although not Napoleon's objective, the Tsar's bluff was de facto called, and he was forced to act.

At the risk of losing face if it backed down, Russia now proceeded with the ultimatum laid out in Nesselrode's letter to the Sultan of May 31, threatening that Russian troops would occupy the Danubian principalities if Menshikov's demands were not accepted. In response to the Sultan's refusal, the occupation took place in July 1853, setting the stage for the Crimean War. "For all the misguided good intentions of the Tsar, Russian troops in the principalities had more to do with the outbreak of war than any other single incident" (Gooch 1956, 42). By March 1854, the three powers were drawn into the "most unnecessary war," for all it achieved could have been accomplished by peaceful means (Albrecht-Carrie 1973, 85; Rich 1985).

As shall be seen in the following section, a combination of high sunk costs and ambiguous signals on the British side finalized the self-entrapment process into the war for all three sides.

Ambiguous Commitments

Besides the escalatory effects of sunk-cost strategies pursued by both France and Russia, the ambivalence in British allegiance to either side additionally aggravated the path to war through a series of miscalculations. In this case, the British domestic context and Anglo-Russian regime differences were at the root of the dynamic of miscalculations through British ambiguous signals and Tsar Nicholas's reactions to them. The British Cabinet was deeply divided over Franco-Russian frictions regarding the Holy Places (Temperley 1936; Henderson 1947). Both Prime Minister Aberdeen and his Foreign Secretary Clarendon were reluctant to antagonize the Russians. On the other hand, Palmerston was reputed for his anti-Russian and pro-French positions (Schroeder 1972; Rich 1985). Though for the moment he occupied a relatively minor post in the coalition cabinet of 1852, his faction was particularly influential in the cabinet debates over the Crimean crisis. As a result, throughout the pre-war crisis, British diplomacy lacked "a clear and strong direction" (Albrecht-Carrier 1968, 158). At best, it appeared to suggest a policy of neutrality. Only a few days before the ill-fated Menshikov Mission, for instance, Aberdeen told Brunow, Russian ambassador to London: "Whether right or wrong we advise the Turks to yield" (Taylor 1954, 53). At almost exactly the same time (February 1853), Foreign Secretary Clarendon and Walewski, Napoleon's ambassador to London, agreed that Britain would stay neutral (Gooch 1956, 37). Based on these and similar statements, both the French and the Russians counted on British neutrality. Yet both also attempted to use the dispute to draw Britain closer to their side while preventing the other from succeeding in the same aspiration.

Related to the internal cabinet divisions in London, the additional contributing factor to the Russo-British ambivalent commitment concerns the differences between the Russian and British institutions and, even more important, the Tsar's failure to see the critical implications of these regime differences for their conduct of foreign policy. Unlike Aberdeen, Nicholas I had continually governed since he ascended the throne in 1825. Moreover, Nesselrode served as Chancellor and Foreign Minister from 1814 until the aftermath of Crimea, and Brunow provided a continual linkage between St.

Petersburg and London as the Russian ambassador to England for 15 years (1839–1854). It was, in a sense, an unfortunate coincidence that Aberdeen was Foreign Secretary in 1844, when he had conducted talks with Nesselrode over the partition of Turkey, only to become the Prime Minister on the eve of the Crimean War (1852). The Tsar was keenly aware of Aberdeen's favorable inclinations toward Russia, but he made a most serious mistake in assuming that this would ensure continuity in British foreign policy between 1844 and 1853.

Prime Minister Peel verbally approved the 1844 "agreement" between Nesselrode and Aberdeen, but it was not submitted for adoption to the cabinet or parliament and was, therefore, simply considered as a "mutual expression of opinions." That is, Aberdeen and Peel "may have bound themselves, but they had not bound their own cabinet, so they certainly could not bind that of their successors in office" (Temperley 1936, 256). It was not difficult for Nicholas, a monarch of absolute power, to misunderstand the implications of such an agreement for two very different political systems. According to the scholarly consensus, he genuinely continued to believe that the British were still interested in the partition of the Ottoman Empire, even renewing such offers to the British ambassador Seymour in January 1853. In fact, since the Napoleonic Wars, the Ottoman Empire had served as a protective buffer for British strategic and commercial interests in the region. This then "made the independence of Turkey a vital element of British policy" (Wetzel 1985, 15; also Taylor 1954; Albrecht-Carrie 1973; Rich 1985), which was quite inconsistent with the Tsar's interpretation of the British objectives.

Miscalculated Stakes and the Issue-Linkage Problem

Either high sunk costs or ambiguous commitments carry the peril of preventing conflict resolution through peaceful means. As shown above, costly signals are likely to result in raising the costs of compromise or backing down, thus changing the payoff structure that decreases the reservation point for fighting. The ambiguity of commitments does not necessarily change the payoffs, but is likely to mislead about the other side's values and payoff structure. Both strategies thus impede preference revelation as a war-avoidance mechanism.[6] The question then is how to locate the negotiated peaceful outcome by avoiding the problem of preference misrepresentation and/or preference transformation that raises the stakes for war, while at the same time minimizing losses and maximizing gains for both sides. One of the rarely explored bargaining strategies with such a possible effect is to link the original issue to another one through an exchange of concessions. Thus, instead of being reduced, eliminated, or misplaced, the bargaining range could be expected to expand through alternative bargaining tactics such as the issue-linkage policy. Its clear advantage is that it reduces the reputational (domestic and/or international) costs for backing down or compromising on one issue and, also, requires a sufficient level of preference revelation, which in turn clarifies, rather than confuses, the extent of involved stakes on the original disputed issue. The main impediment to its effectiveness, however, is if the parties employ it concurrently with sunk-cost and ambiguous strategies. If one or all sides have already engaged public ex ante costs and/or ambiguous commitments, it severely impedes the requirement of complete or nearly complete information about states' preferences for the issue-linkage policy to work. This was exactly the case in Crimea.

This brings us to the next important factor, which probably played the most critical role in the outbreak of war. It concerns misplaced issue-linkage that resulted primarily from Tsar Nicholas's failure to recognize the real stakes for Britain and France. By repeatedly raising the issue of Turkish partition, Nicholas erroneously assumed that there was a convergence in British and Russian interests in the Near East, and only further aggravated their actual *conflict* of interests regarding the fate of the Ottoman Empire. As shown above, the ambiguity of British diplomacy was perhaps the key factor leading to the Tsar's miscalculation of British stakes. Britain did not flatly reject the Tsar's proposals for Turkish partition in the crucial "Seymour conversations," although neither did it accept these proposals (Albrecht-Carrie 1973, 87). Cabinet divisions over British policy toward Russia made it difficult to give a clear response, which had the unintended consequence of misleading Nicholas about the nature of British interests. Ironically, Nicholas was more concerned with a free exit from the Black Sea than with making drastic changes through Turkish partition (Henderson 1947, 153; Taylor 1954, 49; Albrecht-Carrie 1968, 100).

On the other hand, while fearing Anglo-French rapprochement, the Tsar failed to take an active role in preventing their eventual alliance. He correctly perceived the British concern with possible French designs on Belgium, but instead of pursuing a "Bismarckian" issue-linkage diplomacy, the only conclusion he drew from this observation was that an alliance between France and Britain was very unlikely. He was correct to a point, but failed to see that what could draw these two states together was their fear of Russian hegemony in central Europe. Prussia and Austria suppressed the revolutions of 1848 only after Russia aided them with substantial army support. From the English angle, especially that of Palmerston's faction, this meant that the Concert of Europe was slipping into Russian hegemony through its Holly Alliance with Prussia and Austria. Britain's chief objective was, therefore, to restore the balance of power in continental Europe. The French and British interests coincided on this singular goal of destroying the Holly Alliance. For France, it was an ideal opportunity to finally upset the European status quo established through the anti-French settlements of 1814 at the Congress of Vienna. As Drouyn de Lhuys, Napoleon's Foreign Minister, later candidly admitted, "All this Eastern Question which provoked so much noise was nothing more for the imperial government than a means of dislocating the continental alliance which had tended to paralyze France for almost half a century" (Rich 1985, 20–21). Napoleon saw in an Anglo-French alliance a principal means for destroying the anti-French basis of the European order since the Congress of Vienna.

As much as the Holly Alliance was a joint target for both Britain and France, the British goal was very different from Napoleon's objectives. Instead of eliminating the Congress of Vienna order, Britain wished to restore it. Russia was, therefore, still seen as a viable partner. After all, Russia did not have any intrinsic interests in Central Europe on the same scale that it had in the Balkans and the Near East. But the revolutions of 1848 had warned Nicholas of the possibility of revolutionary waves reaching St. Petersburg, and the Holly Alliance was seen as the key factor in protecting European conservatism, necessary for the preservation of his imperial power in Russia. Napoleon's policy of active support for revolutions, particularly the Italian struggle for unification, was motivated by the objective of establishing a new European order, with a restored France at its center; hence, the anti-French theme in both Russian and Austrian foreign policy. In this sense, Nicholas must have seen the Central European issue as linked to the Near East in a way that made it difficult to offer any bargains to Britain: "If her Black Sea flank was open, the revolution might triumph in Germany and Italy." Similarly, for Britain and France, "The real stake in the Crimean War was not Turkey. It was central Europe; that is to say, Germany and Italy" (Taylor 1954, 50, 61; also, see Gooch 1956, 52).

The contending nature of both issues (Central European and Near Eastern) between Russia and Britain made it difficult to use linkage policy across these issues as a means of abating the Crimean crisis. For Russia, the Holly Alliance was the guardian of conservatism in Central Europe and its own domestic imperial order. For Britain, the alliance was an aberration from the system established through the Congress of Vienna system, replacing the balance of power with, as the British saw it, Russian hegemony. For France, it was a final obstacle toward eliminating the last residuals of the Congress of Vienna system. Neither power wanted this issue to be resolved through war (e.g., Taylor 1954; Gooch 1956; Albrecht-Carrie 1968), but their behavior fundamentally reduced the bargaining space in the Crimean crisis. Put simply, if there had been another issue with a different salience for the parties, the linkage policy could have been attempted and perhaps would even have succeeded in diffusing the crisis. Instead, Nicholas narrowed his bargaining range with England to the issue of Turkish partition, which was actually undermining the British goal of preserving the Ottoman Empire as a buffer for their interests. On their part, the British failed to see the critical link between Central European and Near Eastern issues for the Tsar and his regime. His stakes in Central Europe were domestically motivated for the fear of revolutionary spillover into Russian lands. Whereas the British saw the ambition for Russian hegemony on the Continent, Nicholas feared the political downfall of his imperial rule. The nature of his stakes was quite different from those assumed by British statesmen and Palmerston particularly.

Finally, note that the behavior of Turkey as the British (and French) protégé only exacerbated the crisis, often acting against the wishes of London. Turkey was the only party to refuse the last chance of peace offered in the Vienna Note, agreed upon by all four powers (Russia, Britain, France, and Austria). It also hastened to declare war on Russia on October 4, 1853, despite British and French advice not to militarily resist the Russians.[7] Nevertheless, it is questionable whether the Crimean crisis would have taken a different course even if the Sultan had opted for a more conciliatory approach and had not acted independently from Britain on certain occasions. It seems that the examined factors moving the powers toward war were too strong, regardless of the Turkish actions, and had already set up the crisis management process for failure.

THEORETICAL DISCUSSION

I will turn now to a theoretical discussion of the main implications of this brief case study of Crimean diplomacy as it pertains to how different bargaining strategies can be critical to the outbreak of war, despite each side's ex ante preferences for peace. It is worth repeating that it is by no means my claim that the employment of such commonly accepted strategies is the only war-triggering factor—indeed, factors such as the balance of power and interests are found as critical causes for war in a number of studies. The main point here is to focus on the issue of how the choice of particular bargaining tactics can lead rational actors to war despite their ex ante preferences for peace. The main theoretical challenge I raise is that the coercive bargaining that manipulates the levels of risk through sunk-cost signaling—still the most influential bargaining approach since Schelling's (1960, 1966) original formulation—as well as the ambiguity of commitments arising from several possible sources, solve neither of the two rationalist explanations discussed in Fearon's (1995) seminal article. It also challenges the common view about the immutable payoffs if only a sunk-cost strategy is employed. It indeed has the most likely effect to change the payoff structure in the direction of diminishing, rather than preserving, let alone expanding, the bargaining range.

Sunk-Cost Signaling

Deterrence studies have been shaped by the traditional concerns over costly signals and other methods of enhancing threat credibility. Since superpower nuclear threats are premised on the possibility of mutual assured destruction, their credibility is assumed to be weak. For this reason, research on costly signals, which typically presumes weak credibility, has continued to grow. Schelling (1960, 1966), probably the most influential scholars in deterrence studies, outlined a new paradigm for strategic bargaining studies when he proposed to solve the problem of nuclear threat credibility through the refinements of signaling techniques that manipulate the levels of risk. Other deterrence theorists subscribing to the signaling approach generally examine and refine a number of ideas that resulted from Schelling's works on "the art of manipulation" (e.g., Jervis 1970; Fearon 1997). The main idea remains, however, that threats need to be costly for the deterrer in order to be an effective deterrent.

Fearon (1997) adds further refinements to this approach by distinguishing between the "tying-hands" and "sunk-cost" strategies. He generally finds that signaling states do better by tying their hands, that is, by creating costs that would be paid ex post if they fail to honor their commitments, rather than by using a sunk-cost strategy (Fearon 1997, 82). "Leaders might . . . sink costs by taking actions such as mobilizing troops or stationing large number of them abroad that are financially costly *ex ante*" (Fearon 1997, 82). The most important aspect of his distinction for the analysis here is that "sunk-cost" signals are presumed not to change a player's payoffs, whereas the "tying-hand" signals do, which actually then make them more effective. This approach is commonly accepted in other studies as well that routinely assume sunk costs as potentially "productive waste" without having a direct bearing on a player's payoffs for backing down. Among the rare exceptions to this received knowledge is, for example, Slantchev (2011). Unlike my argument here, however, his is based on the idea that sunk-cost strategies such as the movement of troops and mobilization increase war-preparedness and provide for a war-fighting advantage. While this may certainly be the case, my focus is more on how high sunk costs can actually diminish the prospects for an ex ante negotiable peaceful outcome leading to the actor's "self-entrapment" in an unintended war. In other words, my interest is more on the effect of this strategy on preference transformation that eventually can eliminate the bargaining range by raising the reservation points for both sides.

The case of the Crimean War does not seem to support the premise of the deterrent effects of sunk-cost strategies. In fact, the pursuit of these strategies had two detrimental effects on crisis stability. First, each side was communicating a signal of higher resolve than it actually held. Their bluffs were called, transforming the crisis into the game of reputation and prestige in which initial preferences over the issues at stake had become secondary. Moreover, costly signaling behavior pushed all sides into actions counter to their own preferences. Second, each side's costly signals only further confused the opponent about the nature of their stakes in the additional issue (Central Europe), one that could have been linked to the settlement of the Near Eastern crisis. Their miscalculations of the other side's real stakes in the initial and linked issues resulted, at least in part, from their use of sunk-cost strategies, which signaled a higher resolve on the initial issue than each actually had, and prevented de-escalation through some sort of issue-linkage diplomacy.

What occurred was that the high level of sunk costs locked each side into the game of high stakes, which now added the reputational value (r) for backing down to the initial value (v) for prevailing over the issue at stake. In other words, their preferences had not remained immutable but rather transformed. If either side backed down, the losses would not be simply a reflection of the ex ante costs for committal acts during the crisis (sunk costs s) but also r and v. Thus, the payoff for backing down would equal the sum of v, r, and s, whereas r might be a function of the level of the domestic audience's ability to penalize their leaders, but can also involve international audiences (allies and enemies alike) as well. Its size is also a function of the scope of s—the higher the ex ante sunk costs (s), the higher the concern for ex post reputational losses (r). Consider a leader issuing a verbal threat of intervention if the other side does not comply to his demands (cheap talk) or even involving a small degree of costly moves such as putting a limited number of troops on alert (sunk costs). Now consider the same leader issuing a threat by moving 500,000 troops into the area of dispute. Would the costs for backing down, that is taking off the alert and withdrawing such a large contingent of troops, have the same effects on his value for reneging on the threat? It is hard to believe so. The costs can be either domestic or international in a reputational sense—in either case, the size of s clearly affects the size of r, thus inevitably having the potential to change the payoff structure.

The third-wave deterrence theorists were perhaps much more aware of the perils of costly bargaining regarding preference change than Schelling, whose second-wave paradigm still seems to dominate the current bargaining studies. The main emphasis is on the fact that costly committing moves engage "prestige, honor, and future bargaining reputation" (Snyder and Diesing 1977, 199) which increases the credibility of one's firmness by changing one's payoffs. The above argument about the effect of increased readiness of capabilities is also listed as a bargaining tactic that increases one's credibility, not in a sense of changing one's valuation of the stakes, but, as Slantchev (2011) argues, by reducing one's net cost of war. Ellsberg (1968) similarly argues that the deterrer's costly signals have the effect to "reduce his own payoff incentive to break the pledge" and "change his payoffs," and then primarily refers to reputational reasons for such a change. Both cited studies refer to honor, prestige, and reputation for honesty or resolve, and Ellsberg (1968, 27) directly refers to such effects of costly behavior "as subtraction from his [deterrer's] previously-determined payoff to choosing Accept when the victim chooses Resist" (i.e., the payoff for choosing not to fight).

In short, sunk costs have the effect of tying one's hands, rather than being paid only ex ante without changing the payoffs, for international and/or reputational reasons. In this sense, my argument strongly departs from Fearon's study on the separating dynamics of these two bargaining strategies (1997). Second, the costlier the bargaining tactics in terms of the involved sunk costs, the narrower the bargaining range due to increased costs for compromise or backing down.

The Ambiguity of Commitments

It has also been suggested, again in the tradition of Schelling's "second-wave" paradigm, that sometimes, rather making irrevocable or costly commitments, the deterrer could have greater success by keeping "the other side guessing," that is, through the ambiguity of commitments. As seen from the Crimean case, the effects of ambiguous signals and/or situations actually can also have detrimental effects for locating a negotiated settlement. The British in particular were often taking an ambiguous stance regarding their value for the Turkish question. Recall, for instance, that French and Russian ambassadors to London were each simultaneously communicated very different positions by the British representatives (February 1853)—the former was informed about British neutrality, the latter about the intention to pressure Turkey into accommodation to Russian demands. As discussed, the principal reasons for such ambiguity stemmed from the divisions in the Aberdeen's government over the Crimean policy. The divisions within Aberdeen's Cabinet further contributed to the ambiguity of his diplomacy. The difference between the Russian and British political regimes was, in turn, one of the main sources of Russian miscalculations concerning British interests.

Another factor that allowed for such an ambiguous stance during the stage of three-way secret diplomacy was the absence of alliance commitments toward Turkey. In fact, there was a tacit agreement between Britain and Russia in 1840 about the Turkish partition which Tzar Nicholas believed—as it later turned out to be incorrectly—was still a guiding principle for British policy vis-à-vis Russia concerning the Turkish question (note that this agreement has generally been considered as an entente by historians, and as such also coded in the COW alliance dataset). At the same time, until the onset of open violence in 1853, there was no alliance between either England or France and Turkey. In the absence of alliance ties, previous studies on extended deterrence have shown that the defender rarely upholds his threats to defend the Protégé (e.g., Huth 1988; Danilovic 2002). If this is the case, then the presence of alliance ties should have a deterring effect and, more relevant for the argument here, work toward the clarity, rather than ambiguity, of the intentions to use force in defense of the protégé.

Regime differences, wherein the internal divisions in democracies can have the misleading policy effects of an ambiguous and shifting stance that can be contrasted to the opaqueness (though not to be confused with a lack of political divisions) in autocratic regimes, could lead the latter to miscalculate the intentions of the former. The lack of alliance ties between a potential defender and protégé further allows for the ambiguity of commitment, which, similar to regime differences, results in misplaced beliefs about the scope and value of the bargaining range over the issue at hand for one or both sides. There is then the key question of how to avoid the perils of both sunk-cost signaling and the ambiguity of commitments. That is, there is the issue of how to avoid minimizing the bargaining range (as the consequence of the sunk-cost signaling) or misinterpreting its scope (as a consequence of commitment ambiguity) while at the same time having both sides make sufficient gains to avoid the costs of compromise or backing down. Here, I particularly examine the issue linkage policy as an alternative bargaining tactic, which may or may not be effective, depending on whether the antagonists have already engaged large sunk costs, and thus their reputation, or taken an ambiguous stance about their commitments.

Issue Linkage

A theory of issue linkages is largely underdeveloped (Morgan 1990) and empirical studies have been anecdotal or strictly qualitative (Haas 1980). In contrast to the scarcity of empirical work, the issue-linkage problem has been relatively solidly addressed through the use of formal modeling techniques, such as spatial models of crisis bargaining (Morgan 1990), microeconomic theory of exchange (Tollison and Willett 1979; Sebenius 1983), limited information games (Morrow 1992), and simple 2 X 2 single-shot or repeated games (Stein 1980; McGinnis 1986). Almost all authors concur that linkage is likely to fail if it would mean the entry of third parties with strong stakes in the linkage issue (Tollison and Willett 1979, 446; Sebenius 1983, 303; Morgan 1990, 320). For the most part, however, the results of their formal analyses are not uniform nor are they always mutually consistent. For example, Stein (1980, 80–81) finds it critical for negotiation success that an actor using the linkage strategy knows both actors' preferences and also clearly communicates its own interest to the other party. Yet, Morrow (1990) does not find uncertainty about each other's preferences and resolve to always be detrimental.

The factor most extensively analyzed in each study is related to the so-called issue salience ratio. In this respect, the impact of the intensity of each actor's preferences in the initial and linked issues on negotiation success has been interpreted quite differently. If the issues are differentially valued so that one party benefits more on the initial issue and the other party gains more from the linked issue, the prospect for conflict avoidance through linkage success increases (Tollison and Willett 1979; Sebenius 1983; McGinnis 1986). Morgan (1990) qualifies this *quid pro quo* approach across issues with the power configuration requirement. His model predicts that success increases only if the linkage issue favors the weaker party, but it is more salient for the stronger state, while the initial issue is more salient for the weaker party. Morgan further introduces the role of "appendant costs" incurred by the very act of linking issues that might impede the linkage success. In general, "as these costs increase for a given amount of additional direct benefit, the likelihood of linkage success decreases" (326). For instance, a state can reject the linkage settlement if it would lead to domestic political or reputational costs.

Morrow's game-theoretic analysis raises different implications, generally at odds with the *quid pro quo* requirement for peaceful settlements. "Linkage becomes more likely to be successful as each side's beliefs that the other side is not interested in linkage increase" (1992, 166). Morrow's argument follows from his premise that the linkage strategy might be interpreted as a signal of weak resolve—a premise that has yet to be empirically validated—thus logically expecting that the linkage strategy is more likely to be perceived as a credible signal if the actor is less interested in the linked issue.

The Crimean case study lends stronger support to the *quid pro quo* approach to issue linkages. If there had been a trade-off in saliences between the Central European and Near Eastern problems for either power, the prospects for successful linkage bargaining would have increased. The study also validates the argument that the clarity of each side's interests in the initial and additional issues is vital for achieving a peaceful settlement. Both Britain and Russia miscalculated each other's stakes since each misunderstood the opponent's source of concerns. For example, instead of clearly communicating their interests, the British pursued an ambiguous policy that was easily misinterpreted as a policy of low stakes or neutrality in the initial issue regarding the Ottomans.

In order to robustly test the arguments concerning issue linkage and other factors, such as costly signals and policy ambiguity (due to regime differences and the lack of alliance ties), the Crimean case study, while strongly theory-informing as a "least likely" type of the "crucial case" for testing arguments about unintended wars, will be briefly supplemented with the quantitative analysis.

EMPIRICAL MEASURES AND STATISTICAL MODEL

Dependent Variable and Immediate Deterrence Dataset

In extended deterrence, one major power (Defender) attempts to deter another power (Challenger) from starting, or continuing, a conflict involving a third party (Protégé). It is interesting to note that, historically, almost all cases of wars between major powers have resulted from the failure of extended deterrence as did the analyzed case of the Crimean War.[8] For this analysis, I use a data set of all cases of major power deterrence, both extended and direct, for the 1895–1985 period (Danilovic 2002).

Deterrence Cases

The cases of general deterrence failure include all instances in which at least one major power (Challenger) upsets the *status quo* by becoming involved in a conflict with a third state (Protégé). Since general deterrence failure is a necessary but not sufficient condition for immediate deterrence to occur, cases of immediate deterrence are identified *only if* the Defender demands that the Challenger pull out from the conflict with the Protégé. As deterrent threats can be manifested both verbally and behaviorally, the range of these moves includes: (1) the threat of force; (2) the display of force; or (3) the use of force.[9] Based on these operational rules, and after consulting a number of historical sources, a data set of all cases of major power deterrence was compiled. During the period from 1895 to 1985, there were 105 cases of general deterrence failures between major powers that did not escalate into immediate deterrence crises, that is, no other major power reacted as the third party's Defender against the Challenger. On the other hand, a total of 44 cases of general deterrence failures escalated into extended-immediate deterrence (EID). Some of the EID cases had more than one Challenger, Defender, or Protégé, which resulted in a total of 70 cases of EID dyads.

Deterrence Outcomes

Once general deterrence between major powers fails, that is, conflict breaks out between at least one major power (Challenger) and a third nation (Protégé), it can either escalate into immediate deterrence between the Challenger and another major power (Defender), or not. If there is at least one other major power that would aid the Protégé as its Defender, then the analysis differentiates four possible outcomes of immediate deterrence between the Defender and the Challenger, two of which indicate deterrence failure: (1) *EID Failure* occurs either through peace (Defender acquiesces without fighting) or war; (2) *Challenger's acquiescence* to the Defender's demands to pull out from the conflict against the Protégé (AcqCh); (3) *compromise* between the Challenger and the Defender in which each side achieves some goals while also making certain concessions without any use of force (compromise).[10]

Model

Since the outcomes of international deterrent crises represent a categorical variable that can take more than two discrete values—*AcqCh, Compromise, and EID Failure (AcqDef or War)*—multinomial logit (MNL) would then be the method of choice for such a polychotomous nominal variable (Amemiya 1981, 1517; also, see Greene 1997; Maddala 1983).[11] The coefficients indicate the predicted marginal effects of each explanatory variable (x_i) on the log-odds ratio between two outcomes in each possible pair of deterrence outcomes. It is specific for the MNL model to estimate the effects of the independent variables on the likelihood of having one outcome (e.g., compromise) versus another outcome (e.g., war), requiring separate estimates for each pair of outcomes.

Explanatory Variables

To reflect the discussion of the factors in the Crimean case analysis and the main theoretical concern with the bargaining strategy choices, the quantitative test consequently estimates whether both the bargaining behavior concerning the costliness of signals and issue-linkage attempts as well as the exogenous factors to the bargaining process affect the outcomes of major powers crises. For the latter, I examine two standard *realpolitik* variables, that is, relative power and interests at stake.

Issue Linkage

The issue linkage variable is fairly easy to operationalize: if there was an attempt made to link the settlement of the original dispute to the resolution of additional issues—whether originating within or outside the region of primary dispute—the variable was coded 1. It was coded 0 if no such attempt was made by either party.

Costly Signals

I select a straightforward indicator for measuring the Defender's threats as costly signals. If the highest hostility level for the Defender's behavior in a crisis stage, that is, before the potential outbreak of war, incurred sunk costs in delivering the threat, such as troop mobilization or a display of force, the variable was coded 1 ("a costly signal"). If the Defender's threat was a verbal statement without any costly movement of troops or display of force, the variable was coded 0 ("cheap talk").

Alliance Commitments

The situation of ambiguous commitments is difficult to quantify directly—it can exist even without ambiguous acts. It is a matter of our belief of what conditions facilitate the rise of ambiguity or one's belief about the opponent's ambiguous commitments. As I argue above, it is plausible to consider the absence of alliance ties (specifically, in case of extended deterrence, it refers to the absence of an alliance between the Defender and the Protégé) as a source for the ambiguity of commitments. The strength of a Defender's ties with its Protégé is generally considered an important indicator of its commitment to protect the Protégé against another major power. Data on alliances were taken from Small and Singer (1969) for the period until 1965, and from Oren (1990) for the 1965–1980 update.[12] I use a simple dichotomous measure of alliances, indicating their absence (coded 0) or presence (coded 1) of an alliance between the defender and protégé.

Balance of Power

As a standard realpolitik contextual variable, I calculate power parity or disparity according to the following formula (see Danilovic 2002):

$$Power\ Parity = -abs\left|\left(DefCAP - ChCAP\right)/\left(DefCAP + ChCAP\right)\right|$$

Where DefCAP = Defender's capability, and ChCAP = Challenger's capability.

The resulting value ranges from -1 (absolute imbalance to one side's advantage) to 0 (exact parity), with lower values indicating a larger distance from parity and higher values indicating a greater proximity in relative power. Data on power capabilities were obtained from the Correlates of War (COW) National Capabilities Data Set.

Balance of Interests

In addition to the balance of power, I also control for the balance of interests as an obvious element of the value (payoff) structure. I assume that the main indicator of major powers' interests extending beyond their borders is reflected by the intensity of their linkages with different regions around the world. For this measure, I use my previously developed dataset on the ties between major powers and world regions (Danilovic 2002). This "index" of major powers' regional ties includes a varying number of indicators such as alliances, trade, colonies, and diplomatic exchange. Given the varying significance of these different forms of linkages over the period 1895 to 1985, I develop the index of regional ties by including alliances for the entire time span (1895–1985), while adding colonial possessions and diplomatic exchanges to the alliance bonds only for the period 1895–1939. They are replaced by the level of foreign trade for the period from 1945 to 1985. Foreign trade is also included for the 1920–1941 period. Since the composite score of regional ties or stakes is an additive index, it is constructed as a sum of the components and then averaged out by dividing the sum by the number of included components (for more details, see Danilovic 2002). After obtaining the values of this variable indicating a major power's interests vis-à-vis each region on an annual basis, I use the same computational method for estimating the balance of interests between major powers with respect to the region of conflict that is used for estimating the power parity variable. The resulting value ranges from -1 (absolute disparity of involved stakes) to 0 (exactly the same intensity of regional interests).

RESULTS

Since multinomial logit is not restricted to binary choices, it is an appropriate model for the variety of possible deterrence outcomes examined here. In table 16.1, the parameter estimates indicate the predicted marginal effects of the explanatory variables on the log-odds ratio between deterrence failure (either violent—war, or peaceful—Defender's acquiescence) and two forms of what we can proximately label deterrence "success" (see the caveat in fn. 10): either complete—AcqCh, or partial—compromise.

The obvious pattern in table 16.1 is the variation in statistical significance across explanatory variables depending on whether the alternative to deterrence failure is compromise or Challenger's acquiescence. The balance of interests and costly signals are significant predictors of the choice between the Challenger's acquiescence and deterrence failure (the Defender's acquiescence or war). In accounting for the probability of compromise versus failure, however, besides the balance of interests, alliance commitments and the issue linkage strategy become the significant variables. The findings therefore indicate that different forms of deterrence success are not equally affected by the same set of factors. While the parameter estimates in a multinomial logit (or probit) analysis are convenient for establishing the statistical significance

Table 16.1 EID Failure (War or AcqDef), Multinomial Logic Coefficients

Variable	*AcqCh vs. EID Failure*	*Compromise vs. EID Failure*
Balance of Power	-.800 (1.552)	1.380 (2.506)
Balance of Interests	-2.943*** (1.181)	-5.830*** (1.852)
Defender-Protege Alliance	.557 (.765)	2.399*** (1.167)
Defender's Costly Signal	1.138** (.683)	-.691 (1.073)
Issue Linkage	.445 (.852)	2.633*** (1.091)
Constant	-1.932*** (.947)	-4.758*** (1.593)

Model Chi-Square (df) = 42.80*** (14).
Log Likelihood Function = −47.807.
N = 68 (missing data for 2 EID dyads).
NOTE: Numbers in parentheses are standard errors.
**p* <. 10, ***p* < .05, ****p* < .01 (one-tailed *t*-tests).

of independent variables and the direction of their effects on deterrence outcomes, they do not allow a direct assessment the magnitude of those effects. To estimate the substantive impact of the statistically significant independent variables, predicted probabilities of deterrence outcomes were computed from the multinomial logit coefficients in table 16.1 and are presented in table 16.2.[13]

The values in table 16.2 can be interpreted as the net effects of a change in the independent variable (x_i), from its minimum to maximum value, on the percentage change in the probability of deterrence outcomes (y), while holding all other independent variables at their mean or modal values. Equal and high intensity of stakes in the issue of dispute (balance of interests) has the strongest effect on deterrence failure while their asymmetry has the highest impact on the Challenger's willingness to peacefully back down from its initial demands. This willingness is also impacted by the degree to which

Table 16.2 Marginal Change in the Probability of Deterrence Outcomes (%)

Variable Change	*AcqCh* Δ	*Compr.* Δ	*EID Failure* Δ
Change in the Balance of Power: From min (imbalance) to max (balance)	-11.85	+2.11	+9.73
Change in the Balance of Interests: From min (imbalance) to max (balance)	-45.28	-7.79	+53.06
Change in Defender-Protege Alliance Ties: From min (0) to max (1)	+1.58	+9.55	-11.12
Change in the Defender's Costly Behavior: From min (threat) to max (display of force)	+28.42	-4.83	-2.36
Change in Issue Linkage: From min (0) to max (1)	-2.91	+13.25	-10.33

Note: The marginal effect of each explanatory variable is calculated by changing its value while holding the other variables at their mean or modal value. Change in power parity is not calculated as this variable was not statistically significant for most pairs of outcomes.

the defender is using costly signals as a bargaining tactic. While this pattern at least partly supports the rival hypothesis, if peaceful and violent forms of deterrence failure are separated in the model, then the estimates show that it also carries a much higher risk of failure through war than peace.[14] The most critical for theoretical purposes here are the results concerning the probability of compromise, that is, reaching a peaceful solution within each side's bargaining range rather than resolving it through war. As expected, the issue-linkage bargaining attempts and, to lesser but still significant effect, the clarity of commitments (as in those through alliance ties), are the only variables positively associated with compromise, with the highest substantive impact on the chances of reaching it.

On the whole, the conclusions from the Crimean case study are largely supported by the quantitative analysis. Strong and equal stakes in the same region of conflict are conducive for war (see also Danilovic 2002), whereas issue linkage is the strongest variable, besides the Defender-Protégé alliance, in raising the likelihood of compromise. Since issue linkage also decreases the probability of war, the findings presented here do not support skeptical views about the peaceful impact of this variable. In addition, the Crimean case study showed that the failure to use an issue-linkage policy was one of the critical factors contributing to the outbreak of war. The need for linkages across issues becomes essential when the contestants have equal stakes in a region, as Russia and Britain did in the Near East. As the empirical results here indicate, the probability for war substantially increases and the chances for compromise diminish under such conditions. By diffusing the problem of conflictual interests regarding one issue (region) and linking it to the settlement of another issue (region) over which the interests are not as contentious, then a peaceful solution in the form of a compromise might arise.

As an illustration, if the Russians had addressed British concerns regarding the Holly Alliance in Central Europe, the acuteness of the Crimean Crisis would perhaps have been diffused. Instead, issue-linkage of this type was ignored by the Tsar, giving Napoleon an opportunity to create an alliance with the reluctant Aberdeen. Certainly, other factors were at play too, such as the French and Russian pursuit of sunk-cost strategies in the very early stages of crisis, thus raising the reputational costs of backing down. Such bargaining behavior of costly signals made it, in turn, difficult for either side to back down despite both sides' preference for peace over war.

CONCLUSION

Overall, the evidence from the "least-likely" crucial case study is supported in the quantitative analysis about the disadvantages of pursuing a sunk-cost strategy to induce a favorable outcome. Regarding the sources of ambiguous commitments—indicated by alliance ties—the results are confirming as well. Alliance ties especially have a deterring effect, and it could be argued, as is done here, that its effectiveness can be explained by considering alliance bonds as a factor that reinforces the clarity of commitments as opposed to their ambiguity. As an alternative strategy, issue-linkage is conducive to compromise, while costly signaling moves the process away from it as the state pursuing this strategy is less likely to back down or make concessions. Given the finding that, out of all contextual factors, equal stakes in the disputed issue are most likely to create a volatile situation, to diffuse the problem of escalation over the contentious issue the linkage policy, rather than a costly signaling strategy, should be the road to peace. It is perhaps a suboptimal peace, as it requires an exchange of concessions across issues through compromise, but, if neither side prefers war, as was the case in the Crimea, then it is certainly a more rational (i.e., Pareto optimal) solution.

NOTES

1. Thanks to the methodological advances in qualitative research designs (e.g., George and Bennett 2005), there has been a resurgence in the case-study method approach to crisis bargaining. Zagare (2019), for example, uses game-theoretic models to organize analytic narratives in his comparative case study analysis, that is, formal theory is used to explain the strategic dynamic in historical cases. While also theoretically informed, a crucial case-study approach, on the other hand, also aims to specify the causal path through the analysis of a crucial empirical case for the theory at hand.

2. In an empirical sense, I later discuss in greater detail two principal sources of ambiguity with potentially misleading effects about the player's bargaining range, that is, the lack of firm alliance commitments, and regime differences between the principal players.

3. Although the Crimean War continues to attract scholarly attention in diplomatic history, it has received hardly any treatments in the international studies literature. Two recent studies that include it, albeit briefly, among the qualitative case studies, lead to similar conclusions. The initial quarrel over the Holy Places was hardly a real issue for war, but rather resulting from the Anglo-Russian competition for their overall balance of influence although neither preferred to resolve it through war (Wohlforth 2009, 44–47) or, at least, not initially (Weisiger 2017, 141–47).

4. The term "sunk-cost" strategy refers to those threats that generate the ex ante costs for a deterrer, such as troop mobilizations, displays of force, and similar costly moves (see Fearon 1997).

5. As shall be seen, the root for such a policy lied in the absence of any alliance commitments toward Turkey. Moreover, the detrimental effects of British ambiguity were also due to its changing policy toward Turkey that the Russians miscalculated. Specifically, the difference in political systems between Russia and Britain was

critical in this respect, with Russia's autocracy providing greater continuity that the British democracy could not understandably sustain, and the Tsar's failure to recognize this. This, in turn, led to the Tsar's miscalculation about the shifted British preferences over the issue at stake from those in 1840 (see more details in the case narrative).

6. This point is not inconsistent with Fearon's (1995) argument. It should be expected that the common interest for rational actors should be to avoid wars as an alternative to a negotiated bargain that can be reached without the risks and costs of war. He argues that there are only two plausible rationalist accounts for why states are unable to locate a negotiated settlement: (1) private information about preferences and the incentive to misrepresent them and (2) commitment problems.

7. As Rich (1985, 86) points out, it is often erroneously assumed that the dispatch of the British and French fleets to the Dardanelles on September 23 decisively influenced the Turkish decision to declare war on October 4. The fact is that "news of this order arrived after the crucial decisions of the Turkish government had already been made." The influence of the Turkish war faction on the Porte's escalating decisions has been documented in Saab's detailed analysis (1977). For the role of a protégé in extended deterrence, see especially Zagare and Kilgour (2003).

8. Notable exceptions include those that led to the U.S. and Soviet entries into World War II.

9. This typology is based on the coding rules of the Militarized Interstate Disputes (MID) data project (see Gochman and Maoz 1984). For operational coding and case summaries, see Danilovic (2002). Major powers are identified following the standard COW list (Small and Singer 1982).

10. Note that neither outcome is measured as a "success" because of the problematic nature of identifying cases of "successful" deterrence. Challenger might have met the deterrer's demands for reasons other than the threatened punitive actions.

11. To address the concerns regarding potential selection bias in estimating immediate deterrence cases, that is, those in which general deterrence already failed, I estimate both the onset and outcomes of crises using Heckman's probit model with sample selection (i.e., censored probit). The correlation for the error terms is statistically insignificant, that is, firmly showing the absence of selection bias. In other words, we can proceed with the standard approach of assessing both stages (onset and outcomes) as statistically independent events.

12. The alliance dataset was additionally augmented with semi-colonial ties. If a country was considered officially independent at the time of a conflict, but nevertheless had a semi-colonial relationship with at least one of the major power, this semi-colonial aspect of their relations was added as the fourth category to the other three types of ties (ententes, neutrality pacts, and defense pacts). Townsend's (1941) comprehensive survey and *Encyclopaedia Britannica* were the primary sources of information on semi-colonial ties.

13. See Greene (1997, 915) for the algorithm.

14. To conserve space, the results from multinomial logit analysis of all four distinct outcomes are not presented here, but indeed available upon request.

REFERENCES

Albrecht-Carrie, Rene, ed. 1968. *The Concert of Europe.* Documentary History in Western Civilization Series. New York: Walker.

———. 1973. *A Diplomatic History of Europe Since the Congress of Vienna.* Rev. ed. New York: Harper & Row.

Amemiya, Takeshi. 1981. "Qualitative Response Models: A Survey." *The Journal of Economic Literature* 19, no. 4: 1483–56.

Anderson, Matthew S. 1966. *The Eastern Question, 1774–1923: A Study in International Relations.* London: Macmillan.

Baumgart, Winifried. 2020. *The Crimean War, 1853-1856.* 2nd ed. London: Bloomsbury Academic.

Bennett, Andrew, and Alexander George. 2005. *Case Studies and Theory Development in the Social Sciences.* Cambridge, MA: MIT Press.

Curtiss, John Shelton. 1979. *Russia's Crimean War.* Durham, NC: Duke University Press.

Danilovic, Vesna. 2002. *When the Stakes Are High: Deterrence and Conflict among Major Powers.* Ann Arbor: University of Michigan Press.

Eckstein, Harry. 1992. "Case Study and Theory in Political Science." In *Regarding Politics: Essays on Political Theory, Stability, and Change,* edited by Harry Eckstein, 117–76. Berkeley: University of California Press.

Ellsberg, Daniel. 1968. "The Theory and Practice of Blackmail." RAND transcript P-3883.

Fearon, James D. 1995. "Rationalist Explanations for War." *International Organization* 49, no. 3: 379–414.

———. 1997. "Signaling Foreign Policy Interests: Tying Hands versus Sinking Costs." *Journal of Conflict Resolution* 41, no. 1: 68–90.

Fleron, Frederic J., Jr., ed. 1969. *Communist Studies and the Social Sciences: Essays on Methodology and Empirical Theory.* Chicago: Rand McNally.

———. 2017. *Russian Studies and Comparative Politics: Views from Metatheory and Middle-Range Theory.* Lanham, MD: Lexington Books.

Florinsky, Michael T. 1953. *Russia: A History and an Interpretation.* Vol. 2. New York: Macmillan.

Gochman, Charles S., and Zeev Maoz. 1984. "Militarized Interstate Disputes, 1816-1976: Procedures, Patterns, and Insights." *Journal of Conflict Resolution* 28, no. 4: 585–616.

Goldfrank, David. 1994. *The Origins of the Crimean War.* London: Longman.

Gooch, Brison D. 1956. "A Century of Historiography on the Origins of the Crimean War." *American Historical Review* 62, no. 1: 33–58.

Greene, William H. 1997. *Econometric Analysis.* 3rd ed. Upper Saddle River, NJ: Prentice Hall.

Haas, Ernst B. 1980. "Why Collaborate? Issue-Linkage and International Regimes." *World Politics* 32, no. 3: 357–405.

Henderson, Gavin Burns. 1947. *Crimean War Diplomacy and Other Historical Essays.* New York: Russell & Russell.

Huth, Paul. 1988. *Extended Deterrence and the Prevention of War.* New Haven: Yale University Press.

Jervis, Robert. 1970. *The Logic of Images in International Relations.* Princeton: Princeton University Press.

King, Gary, Keohane, Robert O., and Sidney Verba. 1994. *Designing Social Inquiry: Scientific Inference in Qualitative Research.* Princeton: Princeton University Press.

Lijphart, Arend. 1971. "Comparative Politics and the Comparative Method." *American Political Science Review* 65, no. 3: 682–93.

Maddala, G. S. 1983. *Limited-dependent and Qualitative Variables in Econometrics.* Cambridge, UK: Cambridge University Press.

McGinnis, Michael D. 1986. "Issue Linkage and the Evolution of International Cooperation." *Journal of Conflict Resolution* 30, no. 1: 141–70.

Morgan, T. Clifton. 1990. "Issue Linkages in International Crisis Bargaining." *American Journal of Political Science* 34, no. 2: 311–33.

Morrow, James D. 1992. "Signaling Difficulties with Linkage in Crisis Bargaining." *International Studies Quarterly* 36, no. 2: 153–72.

Oren, Ido. 1990. "The War Proneness of Alliances." *Journal of Conflict Resolution* 34, no. 2: 208–33.

Puryear, Vernon John. 1931. *England, Russia, and the Straits Question, 1844-1856* [University of California Publications in History, vol. 20.] Berkeley: University of California Press.

Rich, Norman. 1985. *Why the Crimean War? A Cautionary Tale.* Hanover, NH: Brown University & University Press of New England.

Saab, Ann Pottinger. 1977. *The Origins of the Crimean Alliance.* Charlottesville: The University Press of Virginia.

Schelling, Thomas C. 1960. *The Strategy of Conflict.* Cambridge: Harvard University Press.

———. 1966. *Arms and Influence.* New Haven: Yale University Press.

Schroeder, Paul W. 1972. *Austria, Great Britain, and the Crimean War: The Destruction of the European Concert.* Ithaca, NY: Cornell University Press.

Sebenius, James K. 1983. "Negotiation Arithmetic: Adding and Subtracting Issues and Parties." *International Organization* 37 no. 2: 281–316.

Slantchev, Branislav. 2011. *Military Threats: The Costs of Coercion and the Price of Peace.* New York: Cambridge University Press.

Small, Melvin, and J. David Singer. 1969. "Formal Alliances, 1816-1965: An Extension of the Basic Data." *Journal of Peace Research* 6, no. 3: 257–82.

———. 1982. *Resort to Arms: International and Civil Wars, 1816-1980.* Beverly Hills: Sage.

Snyder, Glenn H., and Paul Diesing. 1977. *Conflict among Nations: Bargaining, Decision Making, and System Structure in International Crises.* Princeton: Princeton University Press.

Stein, Arthur A. 1980. "The Politics of Linkage." *World Politics* 33, no. 1: 62–81.

Taylor, A. J. P. 1954. *The Struggle for Mastery in Europe, 1848-1918.* Oxford: Clarendon Press.

Temperley, Harold. 1936. *England and the Near East: The Crimea.* London: Longmans, Green.

Tollison, Robert D., and Thomas D. Willett. 1979. "An Economic Theory of Mutually Advantageous Issue Linkages in International Negotiations." *International Organization* 33, no. 4: 425–49.

Townsend, Mary Evelyn. 1941. *European Colonial Expansion since 1871.* Chicago: J.B. Lippincott.

Weisiger, Alex. 2013. *Logics of War: Explanations for Limited and Unlimited Conflicts.* Ithaca: Cornell University Press.

Wetzel, David. 1985. *The Crimean War: A Diplomatic History.* Boulder, CO: East European Monograph No. 193, distributed by Columbia University Press, New York.

Wohlforth, William C. 2009. "Unipolarity, Status Competition, and Great Power War." *World Politics* 61, no. 1: 28–57.

Zagare, Frank C. 2019. *Game Theory, Diplomatic History and Security Studies.* Oxford: Oxford University Press.

Zagare, Frank C., and D. Marc Kilgour. 2003. "Alignment Patterns, Crisis Bargaining, and Extended Deterrence: A Game-Theoretic Analysis." *International Studies Quarterly* 47, no. 4: 587–615.

Chapter 17

Women Heads of State and Government

Facilitating Conditions and Empowering Effects

Farida Jalalzai

INTRODUCTION

This chapter focuses on actors that have received relatively scant attention in the gender and politics scholarship—women heads of states and government. Offering an overview of the state of the literature, the chapter also highlights opportunities that abound in linking women heads of state and government to the empowerment of women within society writ large.

While cases of women executives have noticeably increased globally, academic focus primarily assesses women in parliaments (Alexander, Bolzendahl, and Jalalzai, 2016; Franceschet, Krook, and Piscopo, 2012). Work examining women executives more often engages cabinet ministers than presidents and prime ministers (Barnes and Taylor-Robinson, 2018; Escobar-Lemmon and Taylor-Robinson, 2009; Annesley, Franceschet, and Beckwith, 2019; Franceschet and Thomas, 2015). Though women's incorporation in parliaments and cabinets is important, examining women's attainment of additional political posts, including presidencies and prime ministerships, paints a more comprehensive picture of women's empowerment through formal office holding.

Literature on women prime ministers and presidents is growing. Country-level studies, regional analyses and global studies all offer increasingly methodical and rigorous research. Quantitative models coexist with rich qualitative investigations (and increasingly a combination of both approaches) and consequently we now better understand factors hastening women's rise to power and authorities exercised in their capacities of presidents and prime ministers. More research, however, should be pursued to evaluate the myriad effects women at the helm of power exert on societies, particularly in terms of women's political empowerment. Globally, women still face obstacles to achieving political empowerment, defined here as "the enhancement of assets, capabilities, and achievements of women to gain equality to men in influencing and exercising political authority worldwide" (Alexander, Bolzendahl and Jalalzai, 2016). Women heads of state and government (also referred to here as women presidents and prime ministers and women executives) may be better positioned than legislators or cabinet ministers to empower women in societies at large given their more powerful and visible roles.

With this in mind, this chapter first focuses on the current state of the gender and politics literature, particularly scholarship on women presidents and prime ministers. An assessment of the potential benefits women executives offer women as a group follows. Advancing a model of women's political empowerment emanating from executive roles, I argue that women executives may advance women's political empowerment within the society, through their roles as policy makers, selectors, and symbols.

EXISTING LITERATURE

As stated, most scholarship focusing on women in politics assesses women parliamentarians (Alexander, 2012, 2015; Celis and Childs, 2020; Franceschet, Krook, and Piscopo, 2012; Ellerby, 2017; Kittilson and Schwindt-Bayer, 2012; Hinojosa and Kittilson, 2020). When scholars consider women in executive positions, most often this is as cabinet ministers rather than as heads of state and government (Annesley, 2015; Annesley, Franceschet, and Beckwith, 2019; Barnes and O'Brien, 2018; Escobar-Lemmon and Taylor-Robinson, 2009; Franceschet and Thomas, 2015).

The relative inattention to women heads of state and government is likely due to their small sample size. The number of cases of women presidents and prime ministers, however, has more than tripled in size since 1960, the first year a woman prime minister ascended to power (Jalalzai, 2019). Still, the levels of women executives throughout history and at any single point in time never approach that of their male counterparts, reinforcing the masculine nature of this institution (Baturo and Gray, 2018).

Research on women prime ministers and presidents is growing. Some of the earliest works were more descriptive analyses of women leaders documenting background details like women's career preparation or political inspirations (Opfell, 1993; Jensen, 2008; Liswood, 2007). Biographical details regarding educational and career paths are critical to knowing the pipelines from which women leaders are drawn. Family background also provides insight into political socialization and networks related to career paths. Moreover, interviews with women further shed light on the personal influences on women's political trajectories and lessons learned once in office (Liswood, 2007). The multitude of conditions shaping political opportunity structures including structural and institutional factors within and across countries, however, tended not to be emphasized in this literature. Moreover, the role of gender as a social construct influencing women's paths and power was also routinely ignored.

In contrast to research above, more current scholarship on this topic provides an array of methodical, rigorous, and systematic examinations. Time spans engaged leverage periods when more women leaders have achieved executive office but also better illuminate the historical context in which women's executive leadership transpires. Gendered constructs in relation to prevailing paths and powers of women executives also stand at the center of analysis. Increasingly, the literature offers an array of rich qualitative investigations, quantitative analysis, or a combination of techniques. I will now engage key findings within the growing literature on women executives including global (Jalalzai, 2013; Thames and Williams, 2013; Barturo and Gray, 2018; Wiltse and Hager, 2021) as well as regional and case studies (Adams, 2017; Hinojosa, 2012; Lee, 2017; Saint-Germain, 2013; King, 2002; Shair-Rosenfield and Stoyan, 2018; Clemens, 2006; Franceschet, 2016; Hendersen, 2013; dos Santos and Jalalzai, 2015, 2021; Peña, Aguayo, and Orellana, 2012; Stevenson, 2012; Thompson 2019; Waylen, 2016). Before discussing women's behavior once in office, I first outline conditions facilitating their ascensions.

Women's Rise—Facilitating Conditions

Political institutions are key to explaining women's executive presence. Women tend to govern more often within dual executive systems, which have both presidents and prime ministers. Women, compared to their male colleagues, often hold the weaker position (Jalalzai, 2013). Women disproportionately arise within parliamentary systems (Thames and Williams, 2013). While a larger segment of women prime ministers holds dominant authority, vulnerabilities faced, include the possibility of untimely removal. Powers tend to also be dispersed, with the expectation that governance transpires more collaboratively. A major liability facing nearly all weak prime ministers is that they may be removed by both parliament *and* the president. Though exceptions now exist, few women presidents that hold the preponderance of executive power in a system were elected to office by a popular vote without also having family ties to power, a point discussed later in this chapter.

Gendered ideologies, such as notions of masculinity and femininity, directly connect to executive offices and systems. Parliamentary systems fuse executive and legislative authorities and prime ministers share power with their cabinet ministers. Requisite traits that seem particularly relevant for prime ministers include being deliberative and collaborative, stereotypically viewed as more feminine. Presidents that are powerful and especially the most dominant actors (rather than being essentially symbolic) are afforded more autonomy from the legislature; corresponding traits include decisive and rapid decision-making, more often linked to conceptions of masculinity. This may culminate in greater acceptance of women as collaborators and deliberators, explaining their greater tendency to ascend as prime ministers versus presidents. Prime ministers also obtain their positions through appointment while presidential ascension (particularly for posts that are powerful or dominant) depend at least in part on popular election. While party gatekeepers' sexism may still lead to barriers for women in parliamentary system, direct popular vote proves more difficult for women to navigate. Presidential primaries in particular present hurdles for women given their hesitancy to self-nominate and run for office in the first place (Hinojosa, 2012). Self-nomination also strengthens the influence of local power monopolies and clientelism which typically works against women's incorporation. More centralized and selective executive processes alleviate the problems of self-nomination and limited access to local networks (Hinojosa, 2012).

Parties also matter for women's ascensions. Women executives tend to have left, center-left, or centrist affiliations (Jalalzai, 2019; Gray and Barturo, 2018). Leftist parties are thought to hold more progressive values regarding gender (Kittilson, 2006). Regional differences regarding party ideologies, however, surface. Women's leftist affiliations tend to be confirmed in Latin America and Sub-Saharan Africa while in Asia and Europe, particularly in formerly Eastern bloc countries, women have routinely ascended from centrist, center-right, or right parties (Skard, 2015; Rashkova and Zankina, 2019; Wiliarty, 2010).[1] Transitions to both democracy and market economies at the same time in post-communist countries in Central and Eastern Europe, often triggered different patterns regarding social spending and party ideology than one might expect. Parties on the right often spent more on social programs, while leftist parties, typically arising from the former communist party, faced different incentives that pushed them to adopt austerity measures (Tavits and Letki, 2009). As a result, parties on the right in this region may be more prone to recruit women and even support spending on women-friendly policy (Rashkova and Zankina, 2019). Finally, symbolic presidents (which include several women leaders) often do not represent a party while in office (Jalalzai, 2019).

Structural conditions, though not entirely separable from institutional factors, yield mixed findings. Executive aspirants navigate a plethora of official and unofficial qualifications such as having political experience. Legislative office is a typical training ground for future presidents or prime ministers (and most parliamentary systems require the prime minister to hold a parliamentary seat). Cabinet ministers can also leverage their political experience to become heads of state and government. More generally, women's presence across political institutions can indicate how open a system is to women's participation. While the percentage of women legislators is positively associated with a country having a woman president or prime minister, women have governed numerous countries where the overall percentage of women in the legislature is quite low (Jalalzai, 2013; Thames and Williams, 2013). Women's educational and professional rates within the country have also often lagged behind men's where women have governed (Jalalzai, 2008; Thames and Williams, 2013). Women presidents and prime ministers are as educated and politically experienced as their male counterparts (Murray, 2010; Genovese and Steckenrider, 2013; Thompson, 2020; Baturo and Gray, 2018). In fact, women often amass additional qualifications such as being political activists before also gaining foothold within formal political institutions (Jalalzai, 2013). Still, women's credentials may be more scrutinized and often times dismissed out of hand (Murray, 2010; Genovese and Steckenrider, 2013; Thompson, 2019; Baturo and Gray, 2018).

Political instability surfaces among narratives of several women leaders (Montecinos, 2017; Raicheva-Stover and Ibroscheva, 2014; Jalalzai, 2013). Military dictatorships dominated many regions including Asia, Africa, and Latin America between the 1960s and early 1990s as leaders clung to power. Women actively participated in opposition activities at the country, regional, and international levels (Bauer, 2011; Montecinos, 2017). Women demanded and seized myriad opportunities before, during, and after transition (Montecinos, 2017). Political change more broadly can help explain women's rise. For example, major electoral defeats or corruption scandals can create opportunities for women (Campus, 2013). Exclusion from the inner realms of male networks shelters even politically senior women from scandals embroiling their male counterparts, occasionally providing women entry (Beckwith, 2015).

Women executives tend to be from higher income family backgrounds compared to their male colleagues (Baturo and Gray, 2018). Women have also utilized family ties to gain power (Derichs, Fleschenberg, and Hüstebeck, 2006; Jalalzai, 2013; Thompson, 2019). While political dynasties in executive politics is largely on the decline in most democratic countries, it is still quite a common path in less democratic systems (Besley and Reynal-Querol, 2017; Smith, 2018). Men, of course, have long taken advantage of benefits offered by family connections. Women executives, as a group, however, disproportionately possess family connections compared to their male counterparts (Jalalzai and Rincker, 2019; Baturo and Gray, 2018). Women's reliance on this pathway may lessen once democracy takes route and women's political engagement is normalized (Baturo and Gray, 2018). Women in some regions including Asia and Latin America repeatedly stood at the forefront of democratic regime change—first toppling dictators—then holding formal political office. These were not just anyone; they were daughters and wives of charismatic male leaders (Genovese and Steckenrider, 2013; Thompson, 2002, 2019). Two-thirds of women executives in Asia through 2019 belong to political families (Jalalzai and Rincker, 2019). Even though usually highly credentialed, they are often portrayed as political novices or lightweights.

Strategically using gender stereotypes such as women being less corrupt, compromising, and virtuous presents a potential avenue for women leaders, but can also create their undoing. Downfalls transpire in myriad ways such as assassination, attempted/successful coups, impeachment, or (less dramatically) simply not securing a subsequent term (Thompson, 2019). While their entry to office is, in part, credited to the perceived transfer of political skill from male relatives, the public and political elite can rapidly withdraw support if women fail to provide charismatic leadership they were expecting (Khondker, 2017; Thompson, 2019). Therefore, family ties, though often considered a benefit, poses significant burdens on women's leadership.

Women are less prone to run for office in the first place, particularly in presidential systems (Jalalzai, 2013). Their losses cannot easily be explained by candidate quality; relatively inexperienced male challengers running as "populists" routinely outperform them (Coolidge and Bell, 2017). Most research, however, fails to support claims that women candidates do not prove victorious because of sexism (Dolan, 2014, Teele, Kalla, and Rosenbluth, 2018; Horiuchi, Smith, and Yamamuto, 2020). Still, women gain the greatest electoral benefits if they fit traditional feminine roles such as being wives and mothers (Teele, Kalla, and Rosenbluth, 2018). Given the difficulty of navigating the double bind, these same backgrounds voters prefer keep political careers out of women's reach (Teele, Kalla and Rosenbluth, 2018).

Overall, factors facilitating women's rise to power and authorities exercised in their capacities as presidents and prime ministers are now well-understood. Much more research, however, must be conducted to evaluate the myriad effects women executives have in terms of women's political empowerment. The next section engages this topic more fully.

WOMEN PRESIDENTS AND PRIME MINISTERS: EMPOWERING WOMEN?

Scholarship focusing on women executives increasingly examines the circumstances under which women's governance improves women's status writ large. The evidence is much less straightforward regarding the positive effects linked to women executives' governance than regarding their powers and paths. This chapter proposes a model directly linked to women's political empowerment emanating from the executive.

When scholars consider the potential benefits of women executives by their inclusion in these positions of power, they often rely on Pitkin's seminal work, *The Concept of Representation* (1967). Representation theory primarily references the role of legislators (Pitkin, 1967; see also Runciman and Brito Vieira 2008) *not* executives. To move this research on women executives forward, this chapter emphasizes the benefits women executives offer for women's political empowerment in three main roles: policy makers, selectors, and symbols.

Empowerment as Policy Makers

Women leaders' abilities to propose or implement policies related to women's equality can empower women in the very societies they govern. While several additional factors such as partisanship, legislative party/coalition dynamics, as well as executive authorities to propose and advance legislation must be considered, women executives may be particularly poised to facilitate women's empowerment through policy making. Their shared status as women can hasten a greater awareness of gender inequality. As a result, women executives could be more likely to promote policies advancing women's equality, addressing women's special needs, or issues central to women's traditional roles as caregivers.

Limited research assessing the potential of women executives to promote policies exists and usually take the form of case studies of individual women leaders (Khondker, 2017; Stevenson, 2012; Wolchik, 2017). Several examinations confirm that women leaders promote policies empowering women (Hendersen, 2013; Wiliarty, 2010; Ferree, 2006; Steckenrider, 2013; Peña, Aguayo, and Orellana, 2012; Stevenson, 2012; Thomas, 2016; Waylen, 2016; dos Santos and Jalalzai, 2021). I will offer just a few examples here. Norwegian Prime Minister Gro Harlem Brundtland's government implemented several measures facilitating work/life balance including the adoption of substantial paid family leaves for both men and women with added flexibility in how parents could use this time (Hendersen, 2013). German Chancellor Angela Merkel, who hailed from a party on the right, supported funding for kindergartens and led an effort for new legislation regarding women's equal rights (Wiliarty, 2010). Merkel's leadership regarding is generally regarded less explicitly feminist in tone but essentially feminist in effect (Ferree, 2006; Steckenrider, 2013). Chilean President Bachelet empowered women through policy making as well, particularly to the areas of legislative quotas, expanded reproductive rights, and pay equity (Peña, Aguayo, and Orellana, 2012; Stevenson, 2012; Waylen, 2016). President Dilma Rousseff expanded and reframed existing social programs targeting the poor to more explicitly promoting women in Brazil but failed to address reforms including abortion, placing her at odds with feminist groups (dos Santos and Jalalzai, 2021).

Several conditions, however, limit progress of even the most ardent supporters of women's political empowerment (Adams, 2017; dos Santos and Jalalzai, 2021). Primary among these include the types of positions women hold; women's policy influence may be curtailed if the post is more ceremonial or focuses on a limited array of issues (particularly ones that are considered less prestigious, discussed later in this chapter). Other critical factors include party and ideology. For example, if women hail from parties more resistant to women's political empowerment, they may be less inclined to promote these measures, even if as individual (critical) actors, they support them. Even when affiliates of parties more receptive to women's empowerment, their parties may not be particularly well-positioned to introduce or advocate relevant policies. Matters are further complicated given the prevalence of coalition governments resulting in widely disparate party ideologies governing together. It is also important to consider the strength and diversity of women's and feminist movements and related organizations demanding policy action (Fallon et al., 2018).

More research should explore whether women executives empower women as policy makers. Of particular significance would be studies that compare the advantages prime ministers or presidents have in leading policy change within specific institutional settings. Prime ministers may benefit in policy implementation given the fusion of executive and legislative powers in parliamentary systems. Yet, presidents exercise significant legislative authorities in some regions, including Latin America and Africa. More research could analyze women's use of specific powers including public declarations (Jalalzai and dos Santos, 2021), executive orders or decrees (Shair-Rosenfield and Stoyan, 2016). Scholars can also examine different influences related to policy design including legislative, cabinet, party, coalition, and constituency demands in relation to executive policy making. Opportunities abound in similarly scrutinizing men holding executive power in terms of whether they empower women through policy making (Chhabria, 2016).

Empowerment as Selectors

Formal and informal selection processes prove pivotal to women's cabinet inclusion and help explain why particular individuals are selected as ministers

(Annesley, Beckwith, and Franceschet, 2019). Cabinet selectors increasingly are expected to create more gender-balanced cabinets. While systems with institutionalized rules prioritizing diversity as a selection criterion may help reduce gender gaps, informal rules also create opportunities for women's inclusion. This may be the case, for example, if cabinet selectors are committed to diversity and enjoy the flexibility of including close friends and political allies from underrepresented groups (Annesley, 2015; Annesley, Beckwith, and Franceschet, 2019).

Women executives appear especially positioned to select *other* women to power compared to their female legislative and ministerial counterparts. While their male colleagues may also empower women through the power of selection, women may be more cognizant of women's exclusion from the political realm and tend to operate within the same networks as other women (Franceschet, 2016; Krook and O'Brien, 2012; Reyes-Housholder, 2016).

Even if seemingly committed to diversifying their cabinets, myriad factors shape an executive's ability to follow through on this goal once in power. Formal rules guide cabinet selection, affecting both the supply and demand for women. Some executives select nominees while other actors or institutions formally accept or reject these candidates. Countries may also formally constrict the eligibility pool. In parliamentary systems, the pool of eligibles often consists of current legislators (Annesley, 2015). Women within the legislative pipeline shape the supply of women considered for cabinet appointments. Smaller numbers of women legislators are statistically associated with fewer women ministerial appointments (Krook and O'Brien, 2012; Reyes-Housholder, 2016). If governing within legislative coalitions, partners are allocated a certain number of portfolios, which may have negative consequences for women's inclusion; unified cabinets tend to feature fewer women cabinet ministers (Krook and O'Brien, 2012).

Globally based studies fail to find that women executives promote more women to cabinet positions (Krook and O'Brien, 2012; O'Brien et al., 2015). Beyond numbers, women also do not necessarily appoint women to more stereotypically masculine and higher prestige portfolios (Barnes and O'Brien, 2018). Regionally examinations, however, partially confirm that women presidents appoint more women to their cabinets compared to their male counterparts in Latin America (Jalalzai, 2016; Reyes-Housholder, 2016). Again, however, we see that they do not necessarily appoint women to more prestigious positions (Jalalzai, 2016). Women may still be relegated to holding "feminine" portfolios (Reyes-Housholder, 2016).

The complexity of selecting women to power is evident in the case of President Dilma Rousseff of Brazil. During her first term, Rousseff appointed more women to her cabinet than her male predecessors. Moreover, many women held key ministerial posts. Rousseff's second term posed usual institutional constraints such as coalition governance requiring her to manage diverse ideological demands and additional ones including a political crisis (dos Santos and Jalalzai, 2021). Women's presence in the cabinet declined and women tended to hold less prestigious positions. Removed from her office prematurely following impeachment proceedings, Rousseff's replacement, Michel Temer, failed to appoint any women to his cabinet when he first assumed the presidency (dos Santos and Jalalzai, 2021). Women's complete lack of presence sent shock waves around the world. The concept of the "concrete floor" in part posits that the number of women cabinet ministers tends not to dip below previous levels cabinets, even when other parties or newly elected governments take power (Franceschet, Annesley, and Beckwith, 2019). That neither of Rousseff's male successors (first Temer and then Bolsonaro) prioritized women's inclusion signaled the importance of having women at the helm particularly as it concerns promoting women to the cabinet (dos Santos and Jalalzai, 2021).

Empowerment as Symbols

As symbols, women holding the highest political offices can heighten women's political agency in society writ large as they see members of previously excluded groups holding power (Mansbridge, 1999; Lombardo and Meier, 2014; Simien, 2015). Women executives also are well positioned to advance women's political empowerment through their symbolic significance. The visibility offered positions analyzed here, presidencies and prime ministerships, may give way to potentially larger impacts than those available to other actors operating within larger bodies such as parliaments or cabinets. Perceptions of presidents and prime ministers as synonymous with men may be challenged as women make gains into executive office. Seeing women at the top of the most "masculine" of domains sends important messages about women belonging in the political sphere.

Arguably, the more influential the country is and the more powerful position held, the greater the potential symbolic benefits women executives offer. Additionally, women's selections of other women to high offices such as cabinet minister can further provide important symbols to the public (Franceschet, Annesley, and Beckwith, 2019), who may also advance policies empowering women within the ministries they head. Confirming symbolic empowerment emanating from women's leadership, however, proves daunting. Common techniques employed include tracking changes in public opinion measures including but not limited to levels of political engagement, participation, political efficacy, and perceptions related to democracy, women, or gender equality.

Expectations that women executives empower women as symbols derive from the larger gender in politics literature. Among findings, women positively affect societal views regarding democracy and political engagement (Atkeson, 2003; Burns, Schlozman, and Verba, 2001; Norris and Krook, 2009; Norris, Lovenduski, and Campbell, 2004). Women may increasingly consider themselves capable of political leadership when they see women at the helm (Norris, Lovenduski, and Campbell, 2004; Wolbrecht and Campbell, 2007). Other research, however, does not find these same positive effects (Dolan, 2006; Kittilson and Schwindt-Bayer, 2012; Lawless 2004; Morgan and Buice, 2013).

Literature focusing on the symbolic empowerment offered by women prime ministers and presidents include country case studies, regional examinations and, increasingly, global analyses. For example, in Germany, women sharing partisanship with Chancellor Angela Merkel registered greater levels of political interest though the effect was limited to only one year after she first assumed office (Espírito-Santo 2011, 146). In Latin America, the presence of women presidents is positively associated with women's intentions to vote, their involvement in political campaigns, and participation in local meetings (Reyes-Housholder and Schwindt-Bayer, 2016). Public support for women's political role is also greater (Reyes-Housholder and Schwindt-Bayer, 2016, 105) where women govern. Women presidents in Chile, Brazil, Argentina, and Costa Rica, however, offered mixed findings regarding how women presidents in shape views and participation among the general public with the first two countries demonstrating positive effects and the latter more negative ones (Jalalzai, 2016).

Even highly visible women executive candidates do not necessarily offer symbolic empowerment to women. Specifically, races with more competitive and salient women candidates around the world appear unconnected to increased political engagement among women (Carreras, 2017, 174). This might be related to more successful women candidates asserting a more masculine style and distancing themselves from women constituencies and issues. Moreover, more visible women executive candidates often tend to be associated with political families or their male political predecessors, possibly curtailing their positive influence. Women and men are, however, more supportive of women leaders in countries with women heads of state or government (Alexander and Jalalzai, 2020). This cannot be explained by the public already being more supportive of women leaders and thus prone to elect or appoint women presidents and prime ministers respectively; as mentioned, women leaders regularly ascend where public support for women in power is relatively low. Women's presence in these positions also correlates positively with higher levels of political interest for both men and women and especially with women's greater likelihood to vote in national and local elections (Alexander and Jalalzai, 2020).

Much more research should investigate women executives' tendencies to empower women symbolically, particularly on a global scale. Increased data collection can be used to test whether women's executive leadership elicits positive changes in attitudes and behaviors among the public. Global public opinion data rarely exists before and after women executives came to power. Large-scale global surveys do not offer panel data, which could best unpack possible effects generated by women leaders (see Alexander and Jalalzai, 2020). Experimental designs, particularly those that are more global in scope, may also prove valuable in assessing symbolic empowerment through executive office holding.

CONCLUSION

Focusing on presidencies and prime ministerships paints a more comprehensive picture of empowerment through formal office holding than limiting analysis to women in parliaments and cabinets. This relative inattention to women executives is glaring as they can wield substantial political influence. While there is widespread agreement that institutions greatly shape women's chances of gaining power, consensus breaks down when evaluating the differences women make once in office. Scholars face difficulties empirically demonstrating clear connections between women executives and tendencies to promote women through their governance.

Scholars need to engage in more debate regarding application of Pitkin's (1967) model of representation to executives and develop theories specific to prime ministers and presidents. This chapter's emphasis on women's ability to empower women through their roles as policy makers, selectors, and symbols, offers an alternative but complementary way to assess the effects of women executives. By better connecting paths, powers, and impacts, scholars can move this burgeoning area of research forward and leverage the much larger number of women executives to analyze a greater array of data on impacts, employing a wide spectrum of quantitative and qualitative techniques which are best used in combination.

NOTE

1. Rashkova and Zankina (2019) analyze women in cabinet positions but also reference women prime ministers since they may technically be considered cabinet ministers.

REFERENCES

Adams, Melinda. 2017. "Assessing Ellen Johnson Sirleaf's Presidency: Effects on Substantive Representation in Liberia." In *Women Presidents and Prime Ministers in Post-Transition Democracies*, edited by Veronica Montecinos, 183–204. London: Palgrave MacMillan.

Alexander, Amy C. 2012. "Change in Women's Descriptive Representation and the Belief in Women's Ability to Govern: A Virtuous Cycle." *Politics and Gender* 8, no. 4: 437–64.

Alexander, Amy C. 2015. "Big Jumps in Women's Presence in Parliaments: Are These Sufficient for Improving Beliefs in Women's Ability to Govern?" *Advancing Women in Leadership Journal* 35: 82–97. doi: 10.18738/awl.v35i0.122

Alexander, Amy C. Catherine Bolzendahl, and Farida Jalalzai. 2016. "Defining Women's Global Political Empowerment: Theories and Evidence." *Sociology Compass* 10, no. 6: 432–41.

Alexander, Amy C. and Farida Jalalzai.2020. "Symbolic Empowerment and Female Heads of State and Government: A Global, Multilevel Analysis." *Politics, Groups, and Identities* 8, no. 1: 24–43. doi: 10.1080/21565503.2018.1441034

Annesley Claire. 2015. "Rules of Ministerial Recruitment." *Politics & Gender* 11, no. 4: 618–42.

Annesley,Claire, Karen Beckwith, and Susan Franceschet. 2019. *Cabinets, Ministers, and Gender*. New York: Oxford University Press.

Barnes, Tiffany D. and Diana Z. O'Brien. 2018. "Defending the Realm: The Appointment of Female Defense Ministers Worldwide." *American Journal of Political Science* 62, no. 2: 355–68.

Barnes, Tiffany. D. and Michelle Taylor Robinson. 2018. "Women Cabinet Ministers in Highly Visible Posts and Women's Empowerment: Are the Two related?" In *Measuring Women's Political Empowerment around the Globe: Strategies, Challenges and Future Research*, edited by Amy C. Alexander, Catherine Bolzendahl and Farida Jalalzai, 229–55. London, U.K.: Palgrave.

Baturo, Alexander and Julia Gray. 2018. "When Do Family Ties Matter? The Duration of Female Suffrage and Women's Path to High Political Office." *Political Research Quarterly* 71, no. 3: 695–709.

Bauer, Gretchen and Manon Tremblay, M. eds. 2011. *Women in Executive Power*. London: Routledge.

Beckwith, Karen. 2015. "Before Prime Minister: Margaret Thatcher, Angela Merkel, and Gendered Leadership Contests." *Politics & Gender* 11, no.4: 718–45.

Besley, Timothy and Marta Reynal-Querol. 2017. "The Logic of Hereditary Rule: Theory and Evidence." *Journal of Economic Growth* 22: 123–44. doi: 10.1007/s10887-017-9140-4

Campus, Donatella. 2013. *Women Political Leaders and the Media*. London, UK: Palgrave Macmillan.

Carreras, Miguel. 2017. "High-Profile Female Executive Candidates and the Political Engagement of Women: A Multilevel Analysis." *Political Research Quarterly* 70, no. 1:172–83. doi: 10.1177/1065912916680034

Celis, Karen and Sarah Childs. 2020. *Feminist Democratic Representation*. New York: Oxford University Press.

Chhabria, S. 2016. "India's Prime minister: Narendra Modi, Gender and Governance." In *The Gendered Executive: A Comparative Analysis of Presidents, Prime Ministers, and Chief Executives*, edited by Janet M. Martin and MaryAnne. Borrelli, 64–80. Philadelphia: Temple University Press.

Clemens, Clay. 2006. "From the Outside In: Angela Merkel as Opposition Leader, 2002–2005." *German Politics & Society* 24, 3: 41–81.

Coolidge, Kelsey and Curtis Bell. 2017. "The Number of Countries with Female Political Leaders has Plummeted." *The Monkey Cage*. January 9, 2017. https://www.washingtonpost.com/news/monkey-cage/wp/2017/01/09/this-is-whats-behind-the-stunning-decline-in-female-political-leaders/?utm_term=.72a10108e274

Derichs, Claudia, Andrea Fleschenberg, and Momoyo Hüstebeck. 2006. "Gendering Moral Capital: Morality as a Political Asset and Strategy of Top Female Politicians in Asia." *Critical Asian Studies* 38, no. 3: 245–70. doi: 10.1080/14672710600869665

Dolan, Kathleen. 2014. *When Does Gender Matter? Women Candidates and Gender Stereotypes in American Elections*. New York: Oxford University Press.

Ellerby, Kara. 2017. *No Shortcut to Change: An Unlikely Path to a More Gender Equitable World*. New York: NYU Press.

Escobar-Lemmon, Maria and Michelle M. Taylor-Robinson. 2009. "Women Ministers in Latin American Government: When, Where, and Why?" *American Journal of Political Science* 49, no. 4: 829–44.

Espírito-Santo, Ana. 2011. "The Symbolic Value of Descriptive Representation: The Case of Female Representation." Ph.D. Thesis. European University Institute.

Everett, Jana. 2013. "Indira Gandhi and the Exercise of Power." In *Women as National Leaders: Studies in Gender and Governing,* edited by Michael A. Genovese and Janie S., Steckenrider, 103–34. New York: Routledge.

Fallon et al. 2018. "Social Movements as Women's Political Empowerment: The Case for Measurement." In *Measuring Women's Political Empowerment around the Globe: Strategies, Challenges and Future Research*, edited by Amy C. Alexander, Catherine Bolzendahl and Farida Jalalzai, 97–116. London, U.K.: Palgrave.

Ferree, Myra Marx. 2006. "Angela Merkel: What Does It Mean to Run as a Woman?" *German Politics and Society* 24, no.1: 93–107.

Franceschet, Susan. 2016. "Disrupting Informal Institutions? Cabinet Formation in Chile in 2006 and 2014." In *Gender, Institutions, and Change in Bachelet's Chile,* edited by Georgina Waylen, 67–94. New York: Palgrave Macmillan.

Franceschet, Susan, Mona Lena Krook, Jennifer M. Piscopo. 2012. "Conceptualizing the Impact of Gender Quotas." *The Impact of Gender Quotas,* Susan Franceschet, Mona Lena Krook, Jennifer M. Piscopo, 3–26. New York: Oxford University Press.

Franceschet, Susan and Gwynn Thomas. 2015. "Resisting Parity: Gender and Cabinet Appointments in Chile and Spain." *Politics & Gender* 11, no. 4: 643–64.

Genovese, Michael., A. 2013. "Margaret Thatcher and the Politics of Conviction Leadership." In *Women as National Leaders: Studies in Gender and Governing,* edited by Michael A. Genovese and Janie S., Steckenrider, 270–305: New York: Routledge.

Hendersen, Sarah. 2013. "Gro Harlem Brundtland of Norway." In *Women as National Leaders: Studies in Gender and Governing*, edited by Michael A. Genovese and Janie S., Steckenrider, 43–79. New York: Routledge.

Hinojosa, Magda. 2012. *Selecting Women, Electing Women: Political Representation and Candidate Selection in Latin America*. Philadelphia: Temple University Press.

Hinojosa, Magda and Miki Caul Kittilson. 2020. *Seeing Women, Strengthening Democracy*. New York: Oxford University Press.

Horiuchi, Yusaku, Daniel M. Smith and Teppei Yamamoto. 2020. "Identifying Voter Preferences for Politicians' Personal Attributes: A Conjoint Experiment in Japan." *Political Science Research and Methods* 8, no. 1: 75–91. doi: 10.1017/psrm.2018.26

Khondker, Habibul Haque. 2017. "Sheikh Hasina of Bangladesh: Politics, Personality and Policies." In *Women Presidents and Prime Ministers in Post-Transition Democracies*, edited by Veronica Montecinos, 221–37. London: Palgrave MacMillan.

Jalalzai, Farida. 2013. *Shattered, Cracked, or Firmly intact: Women and the Executive Glass Ceiling Worldwide*. New York: Oxford University Press.

Jalalzai, Farida. 2016. *Women Presidents of Latin America: Beyond Family Ties?* New York: Routledge.

Jalalzai, Farida. 2019. "Women Leaders in National Politics." *Oxford Research Encyclopedia, International Studies*. doi: 10.1093/acrefore/9780190846626.013.506

Jalalzai, Farida and Pedro G. dos Santos. 2015. The Dilma Effect? Women's Representation Under Dilma Rousseff's Presidency. *Politics & Gender* 11, no. 1: 117–45.

Jalalzai, Farida and Pedro G. dos Santos. 2021. *Women's Empowerment and Disempowerment in Brazil: The Rise and Fall of President Dilma Rousseff.* Philadelphia: Temple University Press.

Jalalzai, Farida and Meg Rincker. 2018. "Blood is Thicker Than Water: Family ties to Political Power Worldwide." *Historical Social Research* 43, no. 4: 54–72.

Jensen, Jane S. 2008. *Women Political Leaders: Breaking the Highest Glass Ceiling*. New York: Palgrave Macmillan.

King, Anthony. 2002. "The Outsider as Political Leader: The Case of Margaret Thatcher." The *British Journal of Political Science* 32, no. 3: 435–54.

Kittilson, Miki Caul and Leslie Schwindt-Bayer. 2012. *The Gendered Effects of Electoral Institutions*: New York: Oxford University Press.

Krook, Mona Lena Diana Z. O'Brien, D.Z. 2012. "All the President's Men? The Appointment of Female Cabinet Ministers Worldwide." *Journal of Politics* 74, no. 3: 840–55.

Lee, Young-Im. 2017. "From First Daughter to First Lady to First Woman President: Park Geun-Hye's Path to the South Korean Presidency." *Feminist Media Studies* 17, no. 3: 377–91.

Liswood, Laura A. 2007. *Women World Leaders: Great Politicians Tell Their Stories.* 2nd ed. Washington, DC: The Council Press.

Mansbridge, Jane. 1999. "Should Blacks Represent Blacks and Women Represent Women?"*Journal of Politics* 61, no. 3: 628–57.

Montecinos, Veronica. 2017. "Introduction." In *Women Presidents and Prime Ministers in Post-Transition Democracies*, edited by Veronica Montecinos, 1–36. London: Palgrave MacMillan.

Murray, Rainbow, ed. 2010. *Cracking the Highest Glass ceiling: A Global Comparison of Women's Campaigns for Executive Office.* Santa Barbara, CA: Praeger.

O'Brien, Diana Z., Matthew Mendez, Jordan Carr Peterson and Jihyun Shin. 2015. "Letting Down the Ladder or Shutting the Door: Female Prime Ministers, Party Leaders, and Cabinet Members." *Politics & Gende*r 11, no. 4: 689–717.

Opfell, Olga S. 1993. *Women Prime Ministers and Presidents.* Jefferson, NC: McFarland.

Peña, Brito Alejandra, Beatriz E. Cid Aguayo and Carla Donoso Orellana. 2012. "Ruling the Womb: The Sexual and Reproductive Struggle During the Bachelet Administration." *Latin American Perspectives* 39, no.4: 145–62.

Pitkin, Hanna. 1967. The *Concept of Representation.* Berkley. University of California Press.

Raicheva-Stover, Maria and Elza Ibroscheva, eds. 2014. *Women in Politics and Media: Perspectives from Nations in Transition.* New York: Bloomsbury.

Rashokva, Ekaterina R. and Emilia Zankina. 2019. "Ministerial Politics in Southeastern Europe: Appointment and Portfolio Allocation to Female Ministers." *Politics & Gender* 15, no. 2: 211–39. doi:10.1017/S1743923X18001071

Reyes-Housholder, Catherine. 2016. "Presidentas Rise: Consequences for Women in Cabinets?" *Latin American Politics & Society* 58, no. 3: 1–23.

Reyes-Housholder, Catherine and Leslie A. Schwindt-Bayer, L.A. 2016. "The Impact of *Presidentas* on Political Activity." In *The Gendered Executive: A Comparative Analysis of Presidents, Prime Ministers, and Chief Executives*, edited by Janet M. Martin and MaryAnne. Borrelli, 103–22. Philadelphia: Temple University Press.

Runciman, David., Monica Brito Vieira. 2008. *Representation.* Boston: Polity Press.

Saint-Germain, Michelle A. 2013. "Women in Power in Nicaragua: Myth and Reality." In *Women as National Leaders: Studies in Gender and Governing*, edited by Michael A. Genovese and Janie S., Steckenrider, 110–43: New York: Routledge.

Shair-Rosenfield, Sarah and Ali T. Stoyan A.T. 2018. "When Women Run the Show: Female Executive Authority and Agenda Setting in Latin America." *Political Research Quarterly* 71, no. 3: 586–99.

Simien, Evelyn. M. 2015. *Historic Firsts: How Symbolic Empowerment Changes U.S. Politics.*New York: Oxford University Press.

Skard, Torild. 2015. *Women of Power: Half a Century of Female Presidents and Prime Ministers Worldwide.* Bristol: Policy Press.

Smith, Daniel M. 2018. *Dynasties and Democracy: The Inherited Incumbency Advantage in Japan.* Stanford, CA: Stanford University Press.

Stevenson, Linda. 2012. "The Bachelet Effect on Gender-Equity Policies." *Latin American Perspectives* 39, no. 4: 129–44.

Tavits, Margit and Natalia Letki. 2009. "When Left Is Right: Party Ideology and Policy in Post-Communist Europe." *The American Political Science Review* 103, no. 4: 555–69.

Teele, Dawn, Joshua Kalla and Frances Rosenbluth. 2018. "The Ties that Double Bind." *American Political Science Review* 112, no.3: 525–41.

Thames, Frank.C.,and Margaret S. Williams. 2013. *Contagious Representation: Women's Political Representation in Democracies around the World.* New York: New York University Press.

Thompson, Mark P. 2002. "Female Leadership of Democratic Transitions in Asia." *Pacific Affairs* 75, no. 4: 535–55.

Thompson, Mark P. 2019. "The Rise and Downfall of Dynastic Female Leaders in Asia." In *Asian Women Leadership,* edited by Chin-Chung. Chao and Luisa Ha, 49–62. London: Routledge.

Thompson, Mark P, and Ludmilla Lennartz. 2006. "The Making of Chancellor Merkel." *German Politics,* 15 no. 1: 99–110.

Waylen, Georgina, ed. 2016. *Gender, Institutions, and Change in Bachelet's Chile.* New York:

Palgrave Macmillan.

Wiliarty, Sarah. 2010. *The CDU and the Politics of Gender in Germany.* New York: Cambridge University Press.

Wiltse, Evren Celik and Lisa Hager. 2021. *Women's Paths to Power: Female Presidents and Prime Ministers, 1960–2020.* Boulder: Lynne Reinner.

Wolchik, S. L. Iveta Radičová: 2017. "The First Female Prime Minister of Slovakia." In *Women Presidents and Prime Ministers in Post-Transition Democracies*, edited by Veronica Montecinos, 239–58. London: Palgrave MacMillan.

Chapter 18

Methodological Pluralism and Analytical Eclecticism in Political Science

The Logic of Political Inquiry

Lisa K. Parshall and Frederic J. Fleron, Jr

One of the several book projects on which Frederic Fleron was working right up until the time of his death was the *Logic of Political Inquiry*, a work we coauthored and which built upon Fleron's many years teaching graduate courses on the philosophy of science. The manuscript is about meta-methodology, that is, the logic of inquiry or methodology in political science. It was designed with five complementary goals in mind. The first was to serve as an introduction to political inquiry—a primer on the logic of inquiry in political science. As such, it distinguished the logic of inquiry from research methods and techniques, focusing on the former—methodology and the logic of inquiry—and not the latter. Second, it was intended as an introduction to leading schools in the philosophy of science and their relevance to political inquiry. Third, it was designed to help readers in developing a sensitivity to and appreciation for the diverse forms of knowledge collected under the rubric political science. Fourth, in that process, it was also designed to enable readers to develop both analytic and critical skills regarding those various forms of knowledge. And, fifth, the ultimate goal of this book was to explore the possibilities for commensurability of logical positivist/empiricist (LP/E) and post-LP/E approaches to the philosophy of science with the hope of developing a new epistemic community based on methodological pluralism and analytic eclecticism that transcends the competing paradigms. The central message of this work is not only that competing philosophical approaches to social science inquiry exist but also that the paradigm or approach employed both frames and limits the types of questions which can be asked and answered.

The vehicle for this reflection and integration is the examination of two seemingly straightforward questions: What do we know? How do we know it? That is, what kinds of things do we know—know not only as individuals, but as societies (or civilizations) and as a species? These are "big" questions indeed, and Fleron encouraged us all to be able to think "big." Although unfinished, *The Logic of Political Inquiry* reflects issues at the very heart of Frederic Fleron's academic career as an educator, a philosopher, and a scholar. It is not possible to do justice to a lifetime of knowledge that is reflected in Fleron's tour de force chapters on concept formation, explanation, prediction, causality, and so on, or to distill a 300-page manuscript into a book chapter. Rather, I offer here a glimpse into a work in progress by addressing the importance of familiarizing political scientists with the philosophy of science, and including an excerpt of our discussions on the production of knowledge and commensurability—the great and unresolved questions that most intrigued and motivated Fleron in the quest for analytical pluralism.

WHY SHOULD WE STUDY THE PHILOSOPHY OF SCIENCE?

Mark Bevir (2009, 48) has suggested that "the meta-methodology of political science is the philosophy of social science." It is, he says,

> the deliberate attempt to reflect theoretically about what methods are appropriate to the study of what aspects of politics and on what occasions. It was the attempt to clarify what kind of knowledge and what kind of explanations fit the kinds of objects that are the concerns of political science.

Within the field of political science there is a long-standing schism between LP/E and post-LP/E approaches to inquiry with respect to these questions. The *Logic of Political Inquiry* set about offering a synopsis of different strands of inquiry and epistemological distinctions of approaches within these broad labels. We recognized that there are limitations and issues with our division of approaches into these broad LP/E and post-LP/E traditions (particularly given our plea against paradigmatic-bound thinking). But rather than a binary characterization, we view LP/E and post-LP/E as antipodes. This ontological distinction reflects what Baldwin (2008) sees as the heart of the modern "science wars" in which adherents and defenders of the view that there is an absolute truth stand at one pole and those who insist on absolute relativism on the other. It captures what Lamont (2015) has described as the "enduring rivalry" within international relations—the "underlying methodological contestations between those who embed their research within an empiricist natural science tradition and those who embed their research within a reflexive interpretive tradition" (15).

Other scholars have certainly offered finer distinctions, greater detail, and alternate categories or labels of division which are differentiated with more or less magnification within certain subfields. The relevant point, as we saw it, was not to precisely demarcate all the possible divisions but to acknowledge that there are there are separate sects (or "tables") within the discipline, and that the fundamental differences between the LP/E and post-LP/E traditions have led many researchers to definitively choose on which side of the cafeteria to sit (Almond 1990). Those who are oblivious to the choices, whether due to a lack of exposure to the philosophies of science or because they have been constrained in their training or exposure to alternatives, may nevertheless find themselves professionally assigned (labeled) by others or else aimlessly adrift.

Some may argue that our initial privileging of ontological questions (is there a real world?) over epistemology ones (how do we know it?) is in itself reflective of a LP/E point of view. To be clear: we engage ontological distinctions as central to distinguishing LP/E and post-LP/E approaches, and thus as the basis for the bifurcation and presentation of our intended discussion of each school. While we will engage some ontological questions, the focus of many chapters of the book were to be primarily dedicated to epistemological issues and secondarily some ethical questions, both in the sense of normative ethics (the making of value judgments) and especially meta-ethics (the nature of value statements). It is important to recognize that answers to certain ontological questions will influence (if not outright determine) the answers to some central epistemological questions. But political science *qua* science is considered solely with epistemological questions, and those epistemological questions were at the heart of this project.

The lingering divide between LP/E or post-LP/E logics of inquiry misses the point that there is no such thing as a single, holistic approach to social inquiry that would allow an answer to every worthy inquiry. The research approach taken, whether LP/E or post-LP/E in its orientation, will limit the kinds of questions to be asked and how, or whether, one can answer them. Without some knowledge of the basic issues and controversies in contemporary philosophy of science, that myopia will be perpetuated by each successive generation of political scientists.

Yet, there is an arguable lack of metatheoretical awareness regarding the ontological and epistemological assumptions underlying political science research. We agree that "as the field of political science has become, over the past decade, increasingly methodologically self-aware, it is high time for the field to become philosophically self-aware" (Gerring and Yesnowitz 2006, 133). This necessary foundation is too frequently missing from political science graduate curricula or is only implicitly present in methods-oriented courses, particularly of the quantitative variety. In undergraduate political science programs, exposure to philosophy of science concerns and basic scientific literacy also widely vary, with studies confirming generally "low level requirements for research methods" (Parker 2010, 124). This dearth of training in the philosophy of science is part of what some scholars lament is a broader deficiency in teaching basic scientific literacy.

> Political science is falling behind a broad movement in the United States that seeks to reform the teaching of scientific literacy in undergraduate education. Indeed, political science is far behind that movement because the discipline does not have a collective commitment to science education at the undergraduate level. (Hill and Meyers 2014, 835)

Exposure to the philosophy of science early on in one's graduate career will better prepare student for training in research methods and provide the tools to engage with rigorous political inquiry in graduate coursework and to embark on a lifetime of good research.

As a community of scholars, both our pre-understanding and professional understanding of what constitutes "good research" *shape and are shaped by* the research tradition in which we operate. Eclectic analysts and methodological pluralists similarly have different answers to the degree to which knowledge produced through seemingly incommensurable approaches can be combined, recombined, and/or cumulatively evaluated. In our last two chapters, we explore the possibilities of utilizing analytic eclecticism and methodological pluralism to build a new epistemic community in political science—one that transcends the constraints and strictures of both positivist and post-positivist assumptions, perspectives, and applications to develop truly cumulative knowledge in the discipline of political science.

Fleron particularly emphasized the notion of pre-understanding as central to inter- and intra-disciplinary divides. One of the problems with the development of academic disciplines is that each community of scholars has developed a set of terms and a language that has arisen from the pursuit of its own interests. Each discipline can be viewed as a separate text that can be understood only by members of that scholarly community. Consider, for example, walking into a university departmental faculty meeting as a new member of the faculty. The subject of the meeting is a major curricular reform or a discussion concerning which of two recently interviewed candidates should be appointed to fill an opening on the faculty. You may have met the two candidates, examined their curriculum vitae, and read their published works as have your colleagues who have been together in the department for more than 10 years. Should you choose to participate in the ensuing discussion, however, you would soon find that you were either out in the cold or substantially off the mark. You would find it very difficult to relate to the discussion. Why? Because you, unlike your colleagues, come to the meeting with a different *pre-understanding* of the issue or issues. Since their discussion derives from a common shared history (even though they may sharply disagree with one another, or at least break down into two or more factions), you are the odd one out. There is at least one hidden agenda, and that hidden agenda derives from the history of shared experiences. Those experiences impart meanings to certain words and issues that completely escape the uninitiated, as was the case for our dinner guest (see Brunner 1986, 66, for pre-understanding in a social context). Practicing political scientists are often not conscious of the paradigm or philosophical approach in which they are working. Just as scholars must be trained to defend their research methods, so too should they be prepared to defend their philosophical choices and approaches. Doing so not only allows scholars to situate their own research within the existing constellation of scholarship, but it also allows them to be conversant with scholars working and researching in other approaches in order to better respond to critics and to more productively dialogue with scholarship across different approaches.

The failure to fully grasp the philosophical schisms and potential fault lines within the discipline can have practical consequences in how one's scholarship is received, in how well one can respond to academic critique, how attractive one might be on the job market, and how readily one fits in with or adapts to the dominant culture of their academic department. While some scholars are quite comfortable working within one paradigm or school or may be adamant regarding the perceived superiority of their own preferred approach, other scholars may be far less comfortable with what they perceive as the strictures of labeling.

Thus, we sought not to preach any particular gospel, positivist or post-positivist, or to advocate for one kind of logic of inquiry over another. Rather, what we championed is the systematic study and explication of the beliefs of various schools in the philosophy of social science that they may be instructive to political scientists in becoming self-aware of what they do when they do political science. Political science, we think, is enriched when scholars are conversant beyond one philosophical approach. Scholars may prefer to work within one epistemological approach, but they need to be quite familiar (even conversant) with other approaches—not just different research designs (be they qualitative or quantitative), theoretical approaches, or research methods, but basic ontological and epistemological positions.

Because the logic of inquiry and the approach which one uses not only shapes the questions that we can ask, but also determines the evidence to be considered and the answers that are likely to emerge, we believe that it is only through understanding the logic of inquiry from different perspectives and paradigms can we ask appropriate research questions. Only then can we hope to achieve a pragmatic approach in which the cumulative knowledge acquired by these different research traditions can help to better understand and explain political phenomena (not merely accumulated knowledge, but cumulative knowledge).

THE PRODUCTION AND PROGRESS OF KNOWLEDGE

Among the key questions of debate between the positivist and post-positivist traditions are what constitutes the proper form of political inquiry and what constitutes valid knowledge? These questions were central to Fleron's way of thinking. How are competing knowledge claims to be addressed within a specific paradigm/approach, and how may knowledge produced by ontologically and epistemologically different approaches to be compared or evaluated? Competing arguments exist between those who emphasize incommensurability (holding that differently produced knowledge is not commensurable and therefore cannot be cumulative) and those who seek consilience (seeking the convergence or concordance of knowledge resulting from separate realms of inquiry and divergent approaches).

To better understand these central questions, *The Logic of Political Inquiry* explores issues related to the production, verification, and evaluation of knowledge, or the question: "How does social science produce knowledge?" (Diesing 1991, 303). We examined two quite different modes of knowing in political science, indeed in all the social sciences: the paradigmatic or logico-scientific (positivist) mode and the narrative (post-positivist) mode (Brunner 1986). We saw within the ensuing discussion the relevance of the philosophy of science for political science and for the "enduring rivalry" between positivists, "those who embed their research within an empiricist natural science tradition," and post-positivists, "those who embed their research a more reflexive interpretive tradition" (Lamont 2015, 15). These alternate modes of knowing are relevant not just in the evaluation of knowledge produced by individual researchers but, and more importantly to our purposes, in assessing the validity of knowledge cumulatively produced by those operating within a particular research approach. Because, as Brunner (1986) argues, they "convince" of different things, both their functions and structures are quite different. Their systems of signification differ as do the criteria for evaluating the validity of the knowledge produced: how they regard fact-value distinctions and the role of theory in the development of knowledge.

The narrative mode of knowledge rejects the epistemic hegemony of science as the only unique form of logic capable of valid knowledge production. What constitutes truth (even in the hard sciences) is theory-driven and value-laden. Language, historical context, subjectivity, and the human as both researcher and object of social inquiry shape the method and the meaning, rendering all forms of inquiry, even those conducted in the logico-scientific mode as interpretative to some degree. Because post-positivists are generally mind-world monists, they reject the idea of a Cartesian duality in which researchers are capable of mapping external reality with absolute objectivity or certainty. This shift in the natural sciences, for example, between classical physics and quantum theory, led scientists to "abandon physical ontology, and construe mathematical formulas to be directly about the knowledge of human observers, rather than about external reality itself" (Strap 2011, 13). How then are knowledge claims to be evaluated without sliding into absolute relativism (the belief that there is no "truth" and all claims to knowledge are equally valid, or invalid)?

Post-positivist approaches, while rejecting absolute truths, nevertheless have shared and established criteria for the evaluation of knowledge claims (Marsh and Stoker 2002). Many post-positivists recognize the interdependence between theory and observation yet still tend to test theories and explanations against empirical observations (Marsh and Stoker, 25–26). While "much less assertive that there is only one way of doing social science," post-LP/E still largely "emphasizes explanation, rather than understanding, and the primacy of direct observation" (Marsh and Stoker, 26). The challenge for the various strands of post-LP/E is establishing how knowledge is to be comparatively evaluated without the warrant provided by science. King (1989, 4) wrote: "if progress is to be made in substantive research, we must work toward some uniform, discipline-wide methodological standards. Pluralism and diversity in methods are welcome features; however, diversity in standards to evaluate the merits of these different methods is equivalent to the absence of standards."

It is important to draw a fundamental distinction between methodology (or the logic of inquiry) and research techniques: the methods by which we collect and analyze "data." In Fleron's view—and following Sartori's (1970) dictum—there is no methodology without some very serious "thinking about thinking." Many advocates for a more pragmatic, pluralistic political science maintain that research should "not be evaluated chiefly by whether its methods most closely approximate the best method in other scientific endeavor. They ask instead whether its methods have been honestly pursued and presented and whether they really enable us to make better-founded statements about politically important matters than we could otherwise do" (Smith 2002, 199–200). Rather than being evaluated against an *a priori* epistemological commitment, or adherence to scientific method, research must be judged by its own internal validity or verisimilitude. "While pragmatists and positivists share a broad commitment to uncovering 'truth' . . . pragmatists reject the application of standardized methods and techniques for the purpose of definitively verifying or falsifying truth claims" (Katzenstein and Sil 2008, 115). Such claims, in their view, are only partial and tentative.

Pragmatists argue that LP/E's privileging of scientism and quantification in the name of classic objectivity has purged the discipline of its normative, evaluative foundations, and has impoverished lines of inquiry. "A considerable quantity of contemporary work in political science simply does not seem to matter very much. These studies might be methodologically sophisticated, their claims might be true (at standard probability levels), and they may have meaning within the rubric of some theoretical framework or some established empirical question in the discipline. But they do not have any obvious bearing on public policy or on the sorts of things that ordinary citizens might care about" (Gerring and Yesnowitz 2006, 104). Moreover, some questions are undertheorized or researched because they may be less amendable to empirical or quantitative inquiry (105). "Good social science must integrate both elements; it must be empirically grounded, and it must be relevant to human concerns" (Gerring and Yesnowitz 2006, 133).

Schweller (2003) offers an alternative yardstick to "good research" focused not on adherence to method but on the *utility* of the knowledge gained by the endeavor: As Vincent Tarascio (1975) argued, in order to "take advantage of the full range of approaches . . . all one should demand of his colleagues is that their work conform to prescribed standards of research which have been established in various approaches—theoretical, statistical, historiographical, etc." (54). Jackson (2010) sounded a similar note in rejecting rigid adherence to scientific method or practice as the dominant criterion of good research while still employing a foundation in systematic and empirically-grounded inquiry: "The basic point here is that even someone who rejects our values should be able to acknowledge the validity of our empirical results within the context of our perspective . . . [and] the decisive issue is internal validity: whether, given our assumptions, our conclusions follow rigorously from the evidence and logical argumentation that we provide" (Jackson 2010, 22).

Marsh and Stoker (2002) similarly address the importance of methodological awareness to the production of knowledge and on the assessment of disciplinary progress:

> First, knowing about ontology and epistemology is important, not only because it helps us be aware of the biases and limitations of our own chosen research

> strategies, but also because, by being aware of where different theories are coming from we can better appreciate what constitutes better and worse work in the field as a whole. Second, by examining how the concepts of institutions and ideas have been used by different bodies of theory, we can better understand not only the payoffs from different approaches, but also whether such conceptual shifts and borrowings are theoretically productive or not. Third, an awareness of these former two aspects taken together allows us to understand how the field progresses as a whole. (307–308)

Standards for the accumulation of disciplinary knowledge are heavily influenced by LP/E. "A positivist image of scientific progress generally suggests some common notion of objective reality that can be approximated with increasingly greater accuracy through the application of increasingly more sophisticated techniques in conjunction with theories that explain a larger slice of reality than their predecessors did. . . . The implication is that the accumulation of knowledge is desirable, possible, and indeed, inevitable" (Katzenstein and Sil 2008, 112).

It is a positivistic adherence to ideals of science that drives a progressive theory of disciplinary progress: "Scientific progress, on this account, is the result of collecting more and more truths over time" (Roth 1987, 118). Progress is the product of cumulative inquiry, a linear progression in which new theories successfully explain and subsume old ones. This conception was challenged by the adoption of Kuhn's theory of scientific revolutions. Kuhn, who was writing on the history of science (natural science), "emphasized the discontinuities, the *absence*, of a single, unbroken skein of scientific truths connecting disparate theories. . . . The process of scientific change is not one of gradual accumulation; it is better understood as one of destruction and recreation" (Roth 1987, 120) (emphasis in original). For Kuhn—in history and practice—logical verification and empirical falsification are not the primary driver of revolutions, or paradigm shifts. Kuhn's challenge to the notion of linear, progressive accumulation of knowledge shook LP/E's faith in a unified method through its introduction of non-rational scientific revolutions and paradigms ("a divergent set of beliefs about the nature of reality, the problems it poses, and the proper way to investigate those problems") (Ricci 1984, 191).

Although the social sciences were preparadigmatic (or prescientific) in Kuhn's view, his *Structure of Scientific Revolutions* nevertheless served to reinforce paradigmatic thinking in the social sciences. The notion of paradigms (Kuhn) or research programs (Lakatos) is predicated upon incommensurability. That is, "collections of specific theories constitute a paradigm when they share common content that renders them incommensurable vis-a-vis other paradigms" (Jackson and Nexon 2009, 908). This incommensurability may be conceptual, observational, or methodological (Kuhn 1982). But among the various "isms" of the discipline lie multiple fault lines between traditionalistic and scientific approaches, between the type of knowledge produced (logico-scientific versus narrative), and in the adoption of problem-solving or a critical approach (Jackson and Nexon 2009).

For some, the establishment of such schisms (or paradigms) became the hallmark of a mature science. The existence of competing research approaches reinforced the idea of a mainstream, in which a preponderance of literature fit comfortably within a dominant theory or methodological approach, as akin to a period of "normal science." An element of linearity remained in that paradigmatic shifts were thought to involve the displacement of one reigning paradigm (or theory) with another. In such a way, "science destroys its past" (Kuhn 1969, 407).

Roth (1987) argues that Friedrichs (1970) "inaugurated a second tradition in the social scientific view of paradigms"—the notion of multiple, competing paradigms vying for hegemonic status (Roth 1987, 124). In this view, "supporters of one paradigm are constantly questioning the basic assumptions of those who accept other paradigms" (Roth 1987, quoting Ritzer 1975, 12). In the Lakatosian model of scientific change, progress advances through the competition of multiple, scientific research programs. Research programs comprise a "hard core" of fundamental premises which cannot be abridged and a "protective belt" of auxiliary hypotheses subject to contestation and revision. Multiple programs can exist as progressive (capable of predicting novel facts) or degenerative. In such a view, scientific progress is based on rational criteria. In Laudian terms (1977, 1996) "there are three kinds of problems in science: unsolved (no theory solves them), solved (a theory solves them), and anomalies (one theory solves them while another does not). Progress occurs when the first and third problems are transformed into the second by solving either an empirical or a conceptual problem. Scientists choose between theories by evaluating the number and the importance of empirical problems solved minus the number of anomalies and conceptual problems the theory generates" (Walker 2003, 270).

Walker (2010) points out that neither Kuhn nor Lakatos felt their theories were well-suited to the social sciences, but nevertheless they had a remarkable impact on social science.

> The emergence of paradigm mentalities, as depicted by Kuhn and Lakatos, leads to narrow, rigid, highly specialized, and conservative research approaches that suppress alternatives. For Kuhn, evidence that falls outside the dominant framework is considered "incommensurate" and can be "ignored." For Lakatos, such evidence can be "shoved aside" if the research program is held to be progressing. When political scientists are guided by paradigm mentalities they hold tightly to both their theory and their method while seeking to insulate

themselves from opposing theory and method. They also engage in hostile, zero-sum turf wars when challenged by alternatives. Paradigm mentalities prompt scholars to break into narrow, highly-specialized, esoteric research communities. (Walker 2010, 434)

Walker argues "that this misappropriation of the models of science of Kuhn and Lakatos, especially their principle of incommensurability, encourages hyper-specialized tribalism within subfields and furthers the Balkanization of political science as a discipline" (2010, 434). Adherence to these standards as the measure of cumulative knowledge, in other words, has hindered progress in the social sciences. He connects the calls for pluralism to the production of more relevant knowledge of practical utility as a means of ending what he calls the paradigm mentality and the corresponding efforts of one particular approach to "legislate appropriate and exclusive methods of inquiry" (2010, 446). He finds that a Popperian model of scientific progress (as an ongoing process of corroborating or falsifying theory) is more amenable to the evaluation and advancement of knowledge in the social sciences. Dryzek (1988) agrees that because of its methodological diversity "unlike natural science, political science cannot 'destroy its past' and 'global' progress, at least in the commonly understood terms of linear succession of increasingly successful research traditions, cannot occur in political science" (1250).

One might ask why social scientists should not reject the authority claim of philosophers of science and merely follow their own logic-in-use. If philosophy of science developed as nothing more than a description of what natural scientists do when they do natural science, why is it not the case that the philosophy of social science is nothing more than a description of what social scientists do when they do social science? Why extrapolate a "scientific method" from natural science and impose it on social science as a set of "prescriptive maxims"?

One of the interesting points of Gunnell's (1986) analysis is that while "the philosophy of science originally evolved out of the practice of natural science, the social sciences in large measure evolved out of philosophy" (1986, 49). This fact, in his view, has resulted in several distortions in the social sciences as they have, in large measure, been subservient "to philosophical authority." One of these distortions, according to Gunnell, is that, "in the work of someone like Hempel, the concept of scientific explanation is explicitly a very different thing from explanations in science" (1986, 51).

Such distortions in the social sciences come about from the fact that philosophy of science proclaims itself as an exercise in the reconstruction of science from scientific practice. The problem in this presentation is that there are disagreements about the nature of that reconstruction.

- Whose reconstruction of scientific practice are we social scientists to take as the true or appropriate one?
- By what criteria are we to decide?
- Which reconstruction of scientific practice is most useful for the social sciences?

To the last question we must introduce the caveat "useful for what purposes"? The answer to that question depends upon what you think the social sciences should be about in the first place.

Another important question considered by Gunnell is that "philosophical theories of theory are logically distinction from, and only contingently related to, the practice of science"; hence, "it would be as bizarre to think of such philosophical claims as guides to scientific practice as it would be to think of the philosophy of religion as the basis for religious practice" (1986, 51).

Even among positivists then "there is no agreement on what matters most for generating and measuring intellectual progress in a given field of research" (Katzenstein and Sil 2008, 112).

> If philosophers of science as a group do not agree on what science is, what intellectual warrant do we [as social scientists] have to pluck out one or another position on science from within their discussions and place it as a standard in front of our particular campaign to alter the field? (Jackson 2010, 24)

Post-positivists challenge such positivist theories on the progress of knowledge and whether disciplinary progress should be evaluated only as a science or whether such criteria might be assigned in terms of its practical relevancy—inside and outside of the discipline (Stoker, Pierre, and Peters 2015). Writing specifically about the field of international relations, Reuss-Smit and Snidal similarly redefine progress as "the extent to which we have expanded our understanding of the subject matter—viewed broadly to include explanatory, interpretive, normative, and other approaches to understanding—and whether this has improved our ability to act effectively in international affairs" (2008, 25). The authors detail alternative measures of progress, including whether a research program has resulted in more conceptual rigor and greater understanding of foundational concepts, challenges to existing theories, strenuous and constructive scholarly debate, improved and innovative methodologies or techniques, important insights, development of new lines of inquiry, application of understanding to new problems, critique of dominant or mainstream knowledge, "borrowing" and application of knowledge from other theories or approaches, or significant contestations between competing research programs and paradigms.

The recognition that researchers are explicitly (or implicitly) confined (and constrained) within a particular approach or research tradition has led to calls for greater methodological (meta-theoretical) awareness and a more eclectic, pluralistic approach to conducting political inquiry. Post-LP/E thus brought with it the call for methodological pluralism, not as an end in itself, but as a *critical* endeavor meant to "reveal embedded power and authority structures, provoke critical scrutiny of dominant discourses, empower marginalized populations and perspectives, and provide a basis for alternative conceptualizations" (Biersteker 1989, 264).

Goodin (2009), for example, rejected adoption of an "either or" approach within political science that would preclude researchers from developing synergies of collaboration and learning across disciplinary divides, even those with disparate ontological and epistemological assumptions (9–12). Succinctly stated: it is not just that "different questions demand different methods," but rather that the variety and scope of the different objects of interest require multiple paths of inquiry (Smit and Snidal, 2008, 9).

Peter Katzenstein and Rudra Sil (2008, 2010) are particularly notable for advocating "analytical eclecticism" in the study of international relations which moves us beyond mere tolerance toward a meaningful dialogue. Theirs is not an argument for a unified or synthesized theoretical approach nor license for individuals to recklessly "mix and match" research approaches without regard for ontological or epistemological inconsistencies. Rather it is a pragmatic, problem-based call for a "bridged pluralism."

Sil and Katzenstein (2010, 19) summarize the key features of the approach as

- "The articulation of problems that reflect, rather than simplify, the complexity and multidimensionality of social phenomenon of interest to both scholars and practitioners"
- "Middle-range causal account incorporating complex interactions among multiple mechanisms and logics drawn from more than one paradigm"
- "Findings and arguments that pragmatically engage both academic debates and the practical dilemmas of policymakers/practitioners."

This brand of eclecticism thus favors the attempt to "extricate, translate, and selectively integrate analytical elements—concepts, logics, mechanisms and interpretations—of theories or narratives that have been developed within separate paradigms but that address related aspects of substantive problems that have both scholarly and practical significance" (Sil and Katzenstein 2010, 10). Theirs is a

> problem-driven approach featuring the extraction, adaptation, and integration (but not synthesis) of discrete concepts, mechanisms, logical principles, and interpretive moves normally embedded in emergent research traditions, each identified with distinct styles of research reflecting distinct combinations of ontological and epistemological principles. (Sil 2009, 649)

In so doing, they argue that the approach encourages the type of competition which drives disciplinary progress "as scholars seek to defend their substantive theories against criticisms and challenges by refining their arguments and generating more sophisticated analyses" (Sil 2009, 649).

Within the field of international relations, Sil and Katzenstein view eclecticism as a point of connection between the three dominant paradigms of realism, liberalism, and constructivism, at the intersection of the material/ideational and agency/structural divides, capable of producing middle range theories that are "neither universal theories or idiographic narratives" (2008, 21). In this way, analytical eclecticism is as a complement to, rather than a displacement of paradigm-bound research (23). It is a form of "self-conscious 'trespassing,'" allowing researchers to move "beyond recurrent meta-theoretical debates" (2008, 111).

In short, analytical eclecticism calls for the suspension of *a priori* methodological commitments and the kinds of questions that can be asked (Sil and Katzenstein 2010, 9) to a new "commitment to addressing substantive questions using the conceptual and methodological resources most appropriate to answer those questions" (Schwartz-Shea 2003, 384). In breaking scholars away from paradigmatic dogmatism, analytical eclecticism thus broadens the potential for theoretical and empirical insight on questions of interest. Such approaches thus

> embrace some common understandings about the nature, limits, and uses of social inquiry. These understandings suggest a different conception of progress from what is assumed in positivist research traditions, one that stresses the quality and scope of dialogue among social scientists and the proximity of this dialogue to socially important normative and policy issues. (Katzenstein and Sil, 2008 113)

In essence, they "bypass" metaphysical disputes which value the certainty of knowledge in exchange for problem-oriented, "practically relevant knowledge" (Katzenstein and Sil 2008, 113).

Most advocates of methodological pluralism do not suggest that eclecticism displace separate or distinct research approaches but rather argue that researchers must be well versed in ontological and epistemological distinctions and limitations as "rival and exclusive ontologies are both unavoidable and desirable" (Blyth 2002, 310). Jackson and Nexon (2009), for example, argue that the "isms" reflect the major debates within and surrounding the questions we collectively study—questions that "are amenable to many different tools of social science inquiry" (921). Nor do most pluralists advocate the approach of "anything goes," or the omission or blurring of ontological assumptions or epistemological positions. "By expanding the repertoire of assumptions, analytic tools, theoretical concepts, methodological devices, and empirical data" available to researchers, the supporters of eclecticism argue that "analytic eclecticism allows for the development of complex explanations that reveal how different kinds of causal mechanisms and processes might relate to one another" (Sil and Katzenstein, 2008, 118).

Lake (2011) supports Sil and Katzenstein's brand of analytical eclecticism, advocating for the discipline to be less focused upon what he terms the "academic relations" of the "isms" and reframed around problems. He identifies damaging "pathologies" associated with rigid adherence to a particular research tradition, including the reification and academic socialization which constricts the literature used to frame one's research and the types of questions which a researcher seeks to answer. The confusion of research traditions with theory, he argues, has led to the proliferation of finer epistemological distinctions within approaches which confines the range of knowledge produced and increases problems of incommensurability. As importantly, Lake notes that researchers in these traditions seek a claim "to be *the* scientific paradigm" (471) (emphasis in original). The meta-methodological debate thus overtakes valuation of the knowledge produced. In his view,

> We should focus on what we have in common, not what makes us distinct. This will be difficult, no doubt, because of the professional pathologies I have outlined earlier, but it is the only way forward and the only basis on which we can really conceive of ourselves as a single discipline. Above all, we should recognize our duty as scholars is to promote not ourselves but understanding and social progress. (Lake 2011, 474)

He joins others in calling for modesty: "First, recognize the legitimacy of alternative forms of explanation and respect the approach used by colleagues. . . . Second, judge each approach on its terms. . . . Third, accept that each approach is likely to apply more or less well to differ questions" (Lake 2011, 477).

This approach represents, in some ways, a middle ground between positivist and post-positivist entrenchment—an avenue for the combination or recombination of knowledge produced by incommensurable (or seemingly incommensurable) research approaches and a shift toward external criteria for the evaluation, cumulation, or comparison of the knowledge claims which they produce. Although it is one that does not lend itself to "paradigmatic thinking," pragmatism is itself another "ism" (Hellmann et al. 2009, 648). Its critics maintain that pragmatism reflects "enmity towards the view that there are firm, unchangeable foundations to knowledge" (Baert 2005, 147). It "dispenses" with questions of ontology and epistemology (Hellmann et al. 2009, 638).

But Jackson (2008) finds the ontological foundation of pragmatism lies in the grounding of knowledge in both experience and a mind-world monism rejection of Cartesian theories of knowledge (657). Instead, he adopts a Weberian approach "which is less about a presumptive effort to grasp an externally existing world, and more about a disciplined effort to envision what the world would look like if explained and understood according to some ideal-typically elaborated set of value-commitments" (658). In his view, no one approach can legitimately claim the ability to have produced all knowledge of the world as it really exists.

Topper (2005) also supports abandoning "the foundationalist 'quest for certainty,' and substituting in its place historical and contextualist standards of assessment" (191). He warns that there is a tendency to oversimplify and dichotomize the methodological debates within social science inquiry, when there is in actuality a significant amount of complexity in the range of viewpoints and epistemic positions. The voices for pluralism, he notes, are not "quarantined in a single field of political inquiry or on one side or the other of the standard methodological and ideological cleavages," but rather are "scattered orthogonally across them" (Topper 2005, 216). This thus gives hope for a "revitalization" of political inquiry that does not insist upon a hegemonic status or search for universal standards of knowledge. Pragmatism is in many ways "a confrontation with analytic philosophy" and its dominant methodological perspective (Sil 2009, 648).

Jorg Friedrichs (2009) argues both discursive practice and a practical device for producing knowledge (Friedrichs 2009, 648). In practice, Markus Kornprobst (2009) maintains that both positivists and post-positivists already frequently engage in "rhetorical pragmatism," relying on "modes of reasoning . . . much broader and less rigorous than usually acknowledged" (653). The adjudication (in the interaction of scholarly dialogue) as to what constitutes accepted knowledge is, he argues, also dependent on creative rhetoric: "What counts as fruitful knowledge is, in practice, the product of persuading peers rather than upon self-evident objectivity" (653). In the dissemination and defense of research too, he finds the tendency to "overstretch" the "truth-claims" of one's findings (653). Rhetorical pragmatism—or "argumentatively generating intersubjective working truth"—thus not only embraces what "comes naturally," but amplifies discourse between those working within different approaches, enriching scholarly debate and problem-solving.

THE PROBLEM OF INCOMMENSURABILITY

The purpose of the *Logic of Political Inquiry* was to examine the various methodologies of the social sciences, especially political science, and their logics of inquiry to understand the extent to which the conclusions of these various approaches are commensurable or incommensurable. For Fleron this was the central problématique of this book: whether or not the assumptions, methodology, and logic of inquiry of positivism and post-positivism are commensurable or incommensurable, whether their ontologies and epistemologies could be transcended or at least reconciled. Eschewing both ontology and epistemology, pragmatism, in his view, has not solved the question of commensurability but merely sidesteps it.

While calls for greater dialogue between the positivist and post-positivist approaches are not uncommon, this quest for "synthesis is more contentious due to the positivist connotation that it involves unifying what are possibly incompatible theories or bodies of knowledge" (Hellmann et al. 2003, 123). Yet, for some like Amed and Sil (2012), this problem of incommensurability can be "overstated." As they note, "foundational assumptions can get reified to the point where they obscure connections between substantive findings and block off communication across research communities dealing with aspects of the same problems" (2012, 939). Such assumptions can sometimes be "relaxed," or dealt with through an analytically eclectic approach "which aims to develop flexible, middle-range frameworks to tackle substantive problems while linking together analytic constructs originally formulated within research traditions thought to be incommensurable" (2012, 939). But they acknowledge that "not all foundational assumptions can be relaxed easily, particularly those cast at the level of ontology and directly relevant to the execution of specific methods" (939). This is true because while "in principle, ontology may be distinct from epistemology and methodology . . . ontological assumptions can place significant constraints on one's range of epistemic commitments and methodological choices" (939). Ontological assumptions, in other words set

> certain boundary conditions for the investigation of particular questions, assign priority to certain types of observations and certain aspects of social reality, specify certain understandings of whether and when some set of observations constitute causation, and suggest certain strategies for presenting and assessing research products. (939)

Their point is that where incommensurability can be legitimately reduced (or relaxed), the deployment of mixed methods or methodological pluralism has much greater utility in producing and validating knowledge claims. But these attempts at methodological pluralism must be "genuine," involving neither the needless proliferation of mixed methods nor mindless "hodge-podgery." Pluralism, in other words, must be motivated by one's best efforts to engage in "good research."

There may indeed be more common ground between positivist and post-positivist approaches via *methods* than adherents to the different schools acknowledge (something which our chapters outlining the two broad approaches of LP/E and post-LP/E explored). If they share some common methods, does this open the door for pluralism in research design and the progress of knowledge, but not at the pre-level of methodology and the logic of inquiry? Perhaps so, but is that knowledge cumulative if (1) they define their concepts differently, use nomological networks, and/or (2) violate basic positivist rules and requirements for proper concepts formation, explanation, and theory construction and testing? Common research methods and techniques may produce incommensurable outcomes if the meta-methodological rules and precepts are violated or superficially compromised in the name of "analytic eclecticism" or "engaged pluralism."

The overall quest for greater methodological pluralism parallels in a way what happened with the qualitative/quantitative divide and the push for multimethod research designs. King, Keohane, and Verba's (1994) call for diversity was a major development, but it was soon critiqued for being essentially positivist in orientation. Brady and Collier's (2010) work was an effort to identify the common ground between quantitative and qualitative research—they are diverse tools, but they share standards. We followed that arc beyond data methods and trying to lay the foundation for a shared tool (logic of inquiry) that applies similarly in both positivist and post-positivist approaches and that those commonalities make these incommensurable approaches equally necessary to address different questions about objects of common interest.

Marsh and Stoker (2002) liken one's ontological and epistemological positions to a skin not a sweater—arguing that one cannot simply pull it on or off. "Researchers cannot adopt one position for one project and other on another occasion for a different project. These positions are not interchangeable because they reflect fundamentally different approaches to what social science is and how we do it" (21). In other words, without commensurable ontological and epistemological assumptions, there can be no "shared criteria" for the evaluation of theories or the progress of cumulative knowledge. In this view, shared by Thomas Kuhn (1969), research can be advanced and progress of a field measured, only within a shared paradigm or approach. "If a particular individual adopts one philosophical stance toward one problem and another toward another problem, they are showing themselves to be generously pluralistic but rather intellectually confused" (Bevir 2009, 49)

And as a result, of course, they have in no way contributed to cumulative knowledge.

Critics of eclectic or methodological pluralism thus dispute its value to the production of knowledge because positivist and post-positivist approaches rest upon fundamentally irreconcilable ontological and epistemological assumptions. They argue that "it is one thing to believe one's colleagues should be allowed their own views, and it is quite another to believe that any individual political scientist can hold incompatible philosophical ideas" (Bevir 2008, 49). Topper (2005) is similarly cautious, warning that without the necessary attention to methodological commitments, the "appeals for greater pluralism and diversity amount to little more than an invitation to abandon all epistemic and political distinctions in favor of a laissez-faire approach to questions of methodology" (186–87). Such a development, he maintains is a cure that would be worse than even the "the most oppressive form of monism or hegemony" (186–87). In his 2005 book, *The Disorder of Political Inquiry*, Topper argues for "critical pluralism" and also seeks to develop "a more general and systematic view of political inquiry, reconceiving as complimentary traditions of inquiry that are often deemed to be in conflict with one another" (Topper et al. 2006, 742). Topper's "approach requires not just philosophical engagement but a sustained narrative and critical assessment of the history of forms of inquiry in political science" (Topper, et al., 2006, 735–36).

Yanow (2003) too views positivist and post-positivist (interpretive) approaches as essentially "incompatible." She suggests that when many researchers claim to be employing both, they are actually addressing distinct research questions:

> When shifting from one approach to another, the research question itself is reformulated, although the two formulations are both engaging the same general topic. In that sense, then, both approaches can be useful in informing knowledge on the topic of concern, but the research itself proceeds differently in both cases, starting from the character of the knowledge that the researcher is interested in accessing. (2003, 12)

Sil and Katzenstein (2010) recognize the barriers of incommensurability and agree that there can be no "shared objective criteria" for evaluating theories produced by different paradigms. They call upon researchers to recognize that there is a trade-off—what is good in terms of allowing

> adherents of a research tradition to proclaim progress become *disadvantages* in terms of exploring real-world puzzles that force scholars to confront the questions of the empirical accuracy and the practical and normative relevance of

> their work rather than justify their work primarily on methodological or epistemological grounds. (2008, 117)

Jackson (2010) sounds a similar note in rejecting rigid adherence to scientific method or practice as the sole criterion of good research or good research programs that still employs a foundation in systematic empiricism:

> The basic point here is that even someone who rejects our values should be able to acknowledge the validity of our empirical results within the context of our perspective. . . . The decisive issue is internal validity: whether, given our assumptions, our conclusions follow rigorously from the evidence and logical argumentation that we provide. (Jackson 2010, 22)

Such approaches thus "embrace some common understandings about the nature, limits, and uses of social inquiry, suggesting a "different conception of progress from what is assumed in positivist research traditions, one that stresses the quality and scope of dialogue among social scientists and the proximity of this dialogue to socially important normative and policy issues" (Katzenstein and Sil, 2008, 113). In essence, they "bypass" metaphysical disputes which value the certain of knowledge in exchange for problem-oriented, "practically relevant knowledge" (113).

Indeed, most advocates of methodological pluralism do not advocate for a unification of the approaches or a synthesized singular mode of knowing, but rather for an improved dialogue and enhanced opportunities for building bridges between seemingly incommensurable methodologies and approaches. "It is undeniable that communication between those endorsing positivist research and those endorsing interpretive research is and will be difficult not only because their standards differ but because they often have different visions of the purposes of social science" (Schwartz-Shea 2003, 384).

For Gerring (2001), however, there simply "is no profit in 'incommensurability'" (6). He argues that when researchers "employ idiosyncratic or field-specific frameworks, we become islands in a boatless archipelago. Knowledge will not cumulate; progress—define it however you will—will not occur" (6). Gerring proposed a unified criterial framework for the evaluation of social science research (its concepts, propositions, and research design) by which the knowledge produced can be relatively judged in terms of its methodological rigor and validity. Gerring includes himself within the pragmatic approach—refocusing criterion for evaluation not by *a prior* commitment to prescribed methodology or method, but to the unique purpose of a *social* science (as distinct from natural science or humanistic approaches to social inquiry). In other words, he proposes criteria against which "good" social science can be evaluated. He wants to find common standards by which to evaluate research dedicated to the shared goal of "provid[ing] useful answers to useful questions" (247).

Dowding (2016) too refutes the notion that differing ontological and epistemological commitments cannot be empirically examined or compared: "one can examine the logic, the coherence and honesty" of those commitments in the evaluation of the knowledge produced. But he writes, "I am skeptical about the claims of different epistemologies because often their approaches are not contrary. They are simply asking different questions and can be critiqued in terms of their own evidence. What matters is what counts as justified belief and if something counts as justified belief is part and parcel of our epistemology" (161). Dowding draws an analogy to mixed methods approaches—"different methods can be employed to grapple with different aspects of the same political enquiry to give a more rounded and complete story" (2016, 162).

As Dowding (2016) argues, "pluralism in research does not imply that we all have to be pluralists, but simply to accept that other researchers approach the topic with different aims and use appropriately different methods to try to answer their questions" (162). Nor does all research require the employment of mixed (or multiple) methods (Ahmed and Sil 2012, Dowding 2016). In Dowding's view,

> The most important elements for any political science approach are that the evidence is marshalled in support of the conclusions drawn, which are then replicable by others. If others do not draw the same conclusions from the same evidence, then that evidence is not conclusive but rather speculative. Some areas of research have produced cumulative results, with later work building on earlier work. Others tend to revolve in circles. Where work is non-cumulative, we can be assured that the conclusions draw from the evidence re non-conclusive. That is the most effective way of judging the best methods. (Dowding 2016, 188)

Dowding describes analytical eclecticism *a la* Sil and Katzenstein as a "strong swing" away from the tendency of scholars to constrict themselves to a particular research approach, and he refers to himself as a "ismitic pluralist" embracing multiple approaches and methods (2016, 4–5). The design of his book is thus not framed around the approaches, or isms, but on the examination of philosophical issues in how political scientists approach logical inquiry. In his view, the labeling of a particular research is frequently an attempt to minimize or pigeonhole its contributions—that it is essentially a form of *ad hominin* attack in which the product of that research is quickly dismissed through association "with the ism you have criticized, without having to do the hard work of proper analysis or contextualization" (2016, 4). It was an approach not to Dr. Fleron's liking and one he could not condone as rather too "anything goes."

Nevertheless, whether through self-identification or labeling, a complex array of approaches can be distinguished—although Dowding's slicing of them varies significantly from ours. Where we agree is in our shared recognition that these various approaches are differently suitable to asking different questions or to addressing different aspects of an object of political inquiry. Equally or perhaps more importantly, as Dowding (2016, 5) states it, is the accompanying recognition that there also exist clear "constraints upon what each method can explain." As we read Dowding, he seems to be in favor of an eclectic or pluralistic approach, although he is not specific as to the contours or limits of such pluralism. As one reviewer puts it, "There is a danger of hodge-podgeism here, however. How can we embrace eclecticism while remaining theoretically/methodologically coherent? At times, the reader is thirsty for better guidance on that question" (von Stein 2017). Dowding too seems to have bypassed the meta-methodological debate by viewing the philosophical debates "through the lens of political science methodology" and focusing on the "how to" approach to conducting political science (2016, 1). Dowding is akin to Jackson (2010) in altering the criteria of what constitutes "good research." For Dowding it is not fidelity to a particular approach or *a priori* commitment to certain ontological or epistemological assumptions, but rather a fitting of the approach and method to the questions to be asked or answered with recognition of the assumptions being adopted and the corresponding limits of that approach.

Political science arguably demands some form of analytical eclecticism if for no other reason than the fact that we are a methodologically diverse and eclectic discipline. In the variety of research approaches, and the often-confusing proliferation of labels, not all that is presumed incommensurable is incomparable or uncomplimentary. That is, there may be conceptual, observational, and methodological commonalities between the diverse approaches. Kuhn identified three dimensions regarding the incommensurability of paradigms as identified by Kitcher (2020):

- "paradigms are conceptually incommensurable in that the languages in which they describe nature cannot readily be translated into one another."
- "paradigms are observationally incommensurable in that workers in different paradigms will respond in different ways to the same stimuli . . . ; they will see different things when looking in the same places."
- "paradigms are methodologically incommensurable in that they have different criteria for success, attributing different values to questions and to proposed ways of answering them."

To Kuhn's list, we should add at least two other possible levels of incommensurability that a more fundamental: the ontological and epistemological levels. These precede in importance Kuhn's three dimensions of incommensurability both logically and procedurally, for if there is incommensurability at these two levels, it renders Kuhn's three dimensions moot.

The question for Jackson (2010, 191–92) is how to "simultaneously acknowledge the diversity of philosophical assumptions *and* make it possible for concrete work stemming from those assumptions to occupy a conceptual space in which they might be meaningfully contrasted with one another." Jackson (2010, 189) proposes a broader definition of science rather than a "unitary mode of knowledge-production." There are, in his view, three components to a scientific knowledge claim:

> It must be *systematically* related to its presuppositions; it must be capable of public criticism within the scientific community—and in particular, *public criticism* designed to improve the knowledge being claimed; and it must be intended to produce *worldly knowledge*, whatever one takes "the world" to include (emphasis in original). These three necessary components, jointly sufficient, form the broad parameters of the proposed definition of science. (2010, 193)

Jackson's intention is not to introduce additional disciplining criteria or to establish a strict demarcation between scientific and unscientific methods, but rather to articulate a shared criterion against which "good research" reflecting the "amazing diversity" of approaches of political inquiry can be evaluated (2010, 195). In so "putting the science question to rest," Jackson does not argue that different methodologies (he reconstructs four: neo-LP/E, analyticism, critical realism, and reflexivity) conform to the same notions of what constitutes a valid knowledge claim, how research designs are structured, or to the same understanding of causation or explanation. "Methodologically different arguments have different bases in philosophical ontology, and are therefore strictly speaking *incompatible* with one another in the sense that what one regards as decisive another sees as irrelevant" (2010, 208). Therefore, directly comparative evaluation is not possible, and the quality of the knowledge produced must be based on internal validity—an intellectually honest adherence to the commitments, assumptions, and methodology and methods appropriate to the approach in which the research has been conducted. "Standing on the ground of any given methodology, it is reasonably easy to propose and propound a way of conceptualizing scientific research in general that results in the assimilation of alternative methodologies to one's own" (2010, 209). This in Jackson's view, a sound basis for methodological *pluralism* though not *relativism.* "Methodological pluralism envisions a situation in which different scientific methodologies generate different bodies of knowledge, each of which is internally justified in distinctive ways, but one of which commands unqualified universal assent. Knowledge remains inextricably bound to the methodology that warrants it, but this does not present a problem so long as each particular claim enjoys the kind of validity conferred by its own methodology: then all claims are valid, albeit in different ways" (Jackson 2010, 210).

The critical task of any pluralist is in the translation—of making "claims comprehensible to speakers of other methodological languages" (210). For Jackson then, "progress" is made through the division and dialogue between methodological commitments and debate. His too is a problem-centric view as stated in his concluding arguments:

> The issues we study and the problems with which we grapple are too important for us to countenance the categorical dismissal of alien ways of producing knowledge simply because they do not "world" in the way that we are used to worlding, are not systematic in the way that we are used to being systematic, and do not engage in the kind of public criticism with which we are comfortable. (2010, 212)

Regarding the various calls for pluralism in relation to the questions of whether or not eclectic approaches can or do allow for the progress of cumulative knowledge within the field, there are at least six different approaches to answering these questions: (1) those who call primarily for tolerance and discourse between approaches (Marsh and Stoker 2002, 2010); (2) those who argue there can be some integration of knowledge produced by different approaches (Katzenstein and Sil's analytical eclecticism 2008, 2010); (3) those who challenge the criteria of what constitute the standards (challenging science as the standard, by calling for a broader definition of science such as Jackson's (2010) "engaged pluralism"; (4) those who call for a shift of criteria entirely, reframing good research as that which is valid according to its own internal methodology/standards (Jackson 2010); (5) those willing to adhere to that approach most relevant to a specific problem or question (the pragmatic approach) (Mead 1964; Baldwin 2008); or (6) those who see relevance insofar as the adopted approach produces knowledge that is utilized by political actors in the real world (Stoker, Pierre, and Peters 2015). Peregrine Schwartz-Shea (2003) warns that any "genuine grappling, in contrast to claims of *a priori* methodological superiority, will require a professorate minimally conscious of itself as a discipline and of the varieties of approaches to social problems" (384). Our book, we hoped, would contribute to that long-overdue and discipline-strengthening development.

CONCLUDING THOUGHTS

In Fleron's view, while scholarship advocating for multimethod research has provided mechanisms for at least a *modus vivendi* between quantitative and qualitative research methods and techniques, the more difficult and prior question that remains to be solved regarding the conflict between positivist and post-positivist approaches at the level of methodology and the logic of inquiry: whether research techniques based on positivist ontology and epistemology can be reconciled with research agendas and techniques based on post-positivist ontologies and epistemologies. Arguing for it and demonstrating *how* it could be done were, in his view, two very different things. To his way of thinking, this question has significant consequences for the construction of cumulative knowledge in the social sciences generally and the commensurability/incommensurability of research findings gleaned through theories constructed from the utilization of similar research techniques and methods yet based on quite dissimilar logics of inquiry. Why? Because the competing paradigms "lack a common measure" as "they use different concepts and methods to address the same [or even similar] problems, limiting communication across the revolutionary divide" (Oberheim and Hoyningen-Huene 2016). Hence, no commensurability and, therefore, no cumulative knowledge.

Whether inquiry is positivist or post-positive in approach, empirically or interpretive-normatively oriented, intellectual progress in the pursuit of knowledge requires the continued seeking of answers. Progress ceases within the field only when the conclusion is drawn that there is nothing more to know on the subject, no new questions yet to be asked, or no new ways to ask them. Political science research, we agree, should be permeated but not unduly restricted by a healthy understanding of the various paths of inquiry. We believe that positivist and post-post-LP/E approaches, although often deemed incommensurable, can coexist and add value to political science as they are the two sides of the same coin. While the paradigms represent different philosophies at the levels of ontology, epistemology, and the logic of inquiry in political inquiry, they can frequently work together to answer different parts of the same puzzle. In sum, despite the differences between the logic of inquiry in these two approaches, each excels at asking different kinds of questions, and in answering them in different but complementary ways.

REFERENCES

Ahmed, Amel, and Rudra Sil. 2012. "When Multi-Method Research Subverts Methodological Pluralism—or, Why We Still Need Single-Method Research." *Perspectives on Politics* 10, no. 4: 935–53.

Almond, Gabriel A. 1990. *A Discipline Divided: Schools and Sects in Political Science*. Newbury Park, CA: Sage Publications.

Baert, Patrick. 2005. *Philosophy of Social Science: Towards Pragmatism*. Cambridge: Polity Press.

Baldwin, John D. 2008. *Ending the Science Wars*. Boulder, CO: Paradigm Publishers.

Biersteker, Thomas J. 1989. "Critical Reflections on Post-Positivism in International Relations." *International Studies Quarterly* 33, no. 3: 263–67.

Blyth, Mark. 2002. *Great Transformations: Economic Ideas and Political Change in the Twentieth Century*. Cambridge: Cambridge University Press.

Bevir, Mark. 2009. "Meta-methodology: Clearing the Underbrush." In *Oxford Handbook of Political Methodology*, edited by Janet M. Box-Steffensmeier, Henry E. Brady, and David Collier, 48–70. Oxford: Oxford University Press.

Brady, Henry E., and David Collier, eds. 2010. *Rethinking Social Inquiry: Diverse Tools, Shared Standards*, 2nd ed. Lanham, MD: Rowman & Littlefield.

Bruner, Jerome. 1986. *Actual Minds, Possible Worlds*. Cambridge, MA: Harvard University Press.

Diesing, Paul. 1991. *How Does Social Science Work?: Reflections on Practice*. Pittsburgh: University of Pittsburgh Press.

Dowding, Keith. 2016. *The Philosophy and Methods of Political Science*. London: Palgrave.

Dryzek, John S. 1988. "History and Discipline in Political Science." *The American Political Science Review* 82, no. 4: 1245–60.

Friedrichs, Jorg. 2009. "From Positivist Pretense to Pragmatic Practice Varieties of Pragmatic Methodology in IR Scholarship." In Forum: "Pragmatism and International Relations." *International Studies Review* 11, no. 3: 645–48.

Friedrichs, Robert W. 1970. *A Sociology of Sociology*. New York: Free Press.

Gerring, John. 2001. *Social Science Methodology: A Critical Framework*. 2nd ed. Cambridge: Cambridge University Press.

Gerring, John, and Joshua Yesnowitz. 2006. "A Normative Turn in Political Science?" *Polity* 38, no. 1: 101–33.

Goodin, Robert E. 2009. The State of the Discipline, the Discipline of the State. In *Oxford Handbook of Political Science*, edited by Robert E. Goodin, 3–57. Oxford, UK: Oxford University Press.

Gunnell, John. G. 1986. *Between Philosophy and Politics: The Alienation of Political Theory*. Amherst, MA: The University of Massachusetts Press.

Hellmann, Gunther, Friedrich Kratochwil, Yosef Lapid, Andrew Moravcsik, Iver B. Neumann, Steve Smith, Frank Harvey, and Joel Cobb Source. 2003. "Are Dialogue and Synthesis Possible in International Relations?" *International Studies Review* 5, no. 1: 123–53.

Hellmann, Gunther, Helena Rytovuori-Apunen, Jorg Friedrichs, Rudra Sil, Markus Kornprobst, and Patrick Thaddeus Jackson. 2009. In Forum: "Pragmatism and International Relations." *International Studies Review* 11, no. 3: 638–62.

Hill, Kim Quaile and Rebecca Myers. 2014. "Scientific Literacy in Undergraduate Political Science Education: The Current State of Affairs, an Agenda for Action, and Proposed Fundamental Benchmarks." *PS, Political Science and Politics* 47, no. 3: 835–39.

Jackson, Patrick Thaddeus. 2008. "Situated Creativity, or the Cash Value of a Pragmatist Wager for IR. In Forum: Pragmatism and International Relations." *International Studies Review* 11, no. 3: 656–59.

———. 2010. *The Conduct of Inquiry in International Relations: Philosophy of Science and Its Implications for the Study of World Politics*. 1st ed. New York: Routledge.

Jackson, Patrick Thaddeus, and Daniel H. Nexon. 2009. "Paradigmatic Faults in International-Relations Theory." *International Studies Quarterly* 53, no. 4: 907–30.

Katzenstein, Peter, and Rudra Sil. 2008. Eclectic Theorizing in the Study and Practice of International Relations. In *The Oxford Handbook of International Relations*, edited by Christian Rues-Smit and Duncan Snidal, 109–30. Oxford: Oxford University Press.

King, Gary. 1989. *Unifying Political Methodology: The Likelihood Theory of Statistical Inference*. New York: Cambridge University Press.

King, Gary, Robert O. Keohane, and Sidney Verba. 1994. *Designing Social Inquiry: Scientific Inference in Qualitative Research*. Princeton, NJ: Princeton University Press.

Kitcher, Philip S. 2020. Philosophy of Science. *Encyclopedia Britannica*. http://www.britannica.com/topic/philosophy-of-science (accessed on March 3, 2022).

Kornprobst, Markus. 2009. "Doing What Comes Naturally Without Being Oblivious to It: Rhetorical Pragmatism and International Relations." In Forum: "Pragmatism and International Relations." *International Studies Review* 11, no. 3: 652–55.

Kuhn, Thomas S. 1962. *The Structure of Scientific Revolutions*. Chicago: The University of Chicago Press.

———. 1982. "Commensurability, Comparability, Communicability." *PSA: Proceedings of the Biennial Meeting of the Philosophy of Science Association* 2: 669–88.

Lakatos, Imre, and Paul Feyerabend. 1999. *For and Against Method*. Chicago: University of Chicago Press.

Lakatos, Imre, and Alan Musgrave. 1970. *Criticism and the Growth of Knowledge*. Cambridge, UK: Cambridge University Press.

Lake, David. 2011. "Why 'isms' Are Evil: Theory, Epistemology, and Academic Sects as Impediments to Understanding and Progress." *International Studies Quarterly* 55, no. 2: 465–80.

Lamont, Christopher. 2015. *Research Methods in International Relations*. Los Angeles: Sage.

Laudan, Larry. 1977. *Progress and Its Problems: Towards a Theory of Scientific Growth.* Berkeley, CA: University of California Press.

———. 1996. *Beyond Positive and Relativism: Theory, Method, and Evidence.* Boulder: Westview Press.

Marsh, David, and Gerry Stoker, eds. 2002. *Theory and Methods in Political Science.* 2nd ed. London: Palgrave Macmillan.

———. 2010. *Theory and Methods in Political Science.* 3rd ed. London: Palgrave Macmillan.

Mead, George Herbert. 1964. *Selected Writings.* Chicago: The University of Chicago Press.

Oberheim, Eric and Paul Hoyningen-Huene. 2016. "The Incommensurability of Scientific Theories." In *The Stanford Encyclopedia of Philosophy* (Winter 2016 Edition), edited by Edward N. Zalta. https://plato.stanford.edu/entries/incommensurability/ (accessed on March 4, 2022)

Parker, Jonathan. 2010. "Undergraduate Research-Methods Training in Political Science: A Comparative Perspective." *PS: Political Science and Politics* 43, no. 1: 121–25.

Popper, Karl. 1952. *The Open Society and Its Enemies.* London: Routledge & Kegan Paul.

———. 1959. *The Logic of Scientific Discovery.* London: Hutchinson.

Ricci, David M. 1984. *The Tragedy of Political Science.* New Haven, CT: Yale University Press.

Roth, Paul A. 1987. *Meanings and Method in the Social Sciences.* Ithaca, NY: Cornell University Press.

Rues-Smit, Christian and Duncan Sidel. 2008. *The Oxford Handbook of International Relations.* Oxford: Oxford University Press.

Sartori, Giovanni. 1970. "Concept Misformation in Comparative Politics." *American Political Science Review* 64, no. 4, 1033–53.

Schwartz-Shea, Peregrine. 2003. "Is This the Curriculum We Want? Doctoral Requirements and Offerings in Methods." *PS: Political Science and Politics* 36, no. 3: 379–86.

Schweller, Randall L. 2003. The Progressiveness of Neoclassical Realism. In *Progress in International Relations Theory: Metrics and Measures of Scientific Change,* edited by Colin Elman and Miriam Fendius, 311–47. Cambridge, MA: MIT Press.

Sil, Rudra. 2009. "Simplifying Pragmatism: From Social Theory to Problem-driven Eclecticism. In Forum: Pragmatism and International Relations." *International Studies Review* 11, no. 3: 648–52.

Sil, Rudra, and Peter J. Katzenstein. 2010. *Beyond Paradigms: Analytic Eclecticism in the Study of World Politics.* London: Palgrave Macmillan.

Smith, Rogers M. 2002. "Should We Make Political Science More of a Science or More about Politics?" *Political Science & Politics* 35, no. 2: 199–201.

Stoker, Gerry, Jon Pierre, and B. Guy Peters. 2015. *The Relevance of Political Science.* New York: Palgrave Macmillan.

Strap, Henry P. 2011. *Mindful Universe: Quantum Mechanics and the Participating Observer.* London: Springer.

Tarascio, Vincent J. 1975. "Intellectual History and the Social Sciences: The Problem of Methodological Pluralism." *Social Science Quarterly* 56, no. 1: 37–54.

Topper, Keith. 2005. *The Disorder of Political Inquiry*. Cambridge: Harvard University Press.

Topper, Keith, Stephen K. White, J. Donald Moon, James Farr, and Lynn M. Sanders. 2006. "Book Symposium on Political Methodologies The Disorder of Political Inquiry." *The Journal of Politics* 68, no. 3: 733–43.

von Stein, Jana. 2017. "Not Just Another Book on the Philosophy and Methods of Political Science." *Australian Journal of Political Science* 52, no. 1, 149–53.

Walker, Stephen G. 2003. "Operational Code Analysis as a Scientific Research Program." In *Progress in International Relations Theory: Metrics and Measures of Scientific Change*, edited by Colin Elman and Miriam Fendius, 245–76. Cambridge, MA: MIT Press.

Walker, Thomas C. 2010. "The Perils of Paradigm Mentalities: Revisiting Kuhn, Lakatos, and Popper." *Perspectives on Politics* 8, no. 2: 433–51.

Yanow, Dvora. 2003. "Interpretive Empirical Political Science: What Makes This Not a Subfield of Qualitative Methods." *Qualitative Methods* (Fall): 9–13.

Chapter 19

The Compleat Academic

Fred Fleron's Academic Troika

Claude E. Welch

Members of the professoriate traditionally carry out three types of academic endeavor. In this chapter, I contend that Professor Fred Fleron excelled in all three. I shall first identify these three types, then discuss each in detail, and conclude with other facets of his contributions to the University at Buffalo.

First, historically and basically, comes teaching. Consider the sketch provided by Geoffrey Chaucer:

A clerk ther was of Oxenford also,/
that unto logyk hadde longe ygo/
For hym was levere have at his beddes heed/
Twenty books, clad in blak or reed,/
Of Aristotle and his philosophie . . .
Sownynge in moral vertu was his speche,/
And gladly wolde he lerne, and gladly teche.[1]

The poetry dates from the late fourteenth century, but the sentiment dates from centuries earlier. Transmission of learning, wisdom, judgment and—in the liberal arts perspective Fred Fleron embraced—a sense of historical context and of comparison among civilizations—stands at the core of any professor's duties. We were, are, and shall remain, *teachers*.

At the same time, however, faculty members undertake to "lerne." *Research*, to enrich their teaching and to enlighten others through publication, provides the second part of the academic troika. Whether via books, chapters, papers, or posters at professional conferences, faculty members disseminate what they have discovered. Just as continual dialogue between students and teachers forms a critical part of the "academic troika," so too does interchange between scholars, members of their profession, and, in many instances, the general public.

Third, and less known, faculty members contribute to their institutions via *service*. They serve on committees with highly varied responsibilities. Most fundamental, they maintain and update the curriculum. Hence, not only do they teach content: they carry out research to keep their classes *au courant*, but they also shape what is taught through serving their individual units (usually their departments) and their colleges or universities. Members of the professoriate also may become involved in selecting their future colleagues and, especially at the graduate level, their new students.

My contention in this chapter is that Fred Fleron excelled in all three of these broad responsibilities. He became respected for the quality of his *instruction*, whether in high enrollment undergraduate classes, small graduate seminars, or guided independent study with individual students. He published widely and extensively, sharing the fruits of his *research* with others. Confronting drastic changes in "Sovietology" and recognizing the significance of technological advances on political systems, Fred expanded the purview of his publications and teaching. Finally, Fred[2] gave generously of his time, during his 33 years at the University at Buffalo. His extensive *service* touched hundreds, most notably via the Undergraduate College, discussed below.

BACKGROUND: THE UNIVERSITY AT BUFFALO, 1970 TO THE EARLY TWENTY-FIRST CENTURY

Fred joined UB's Department of Political Science at its numerical crest. The Department had been created in 1963, shortly after the formerly private University *of* Buffalo merged into the State University of New York. The merger led to a massive infusion of funds, enabling dramatic expansion in enrollment, staff size, and construction. When Fred arrived, the Department had already outgrown its former home in once-private houses on the perimeter of the Main Street campus. It occupied an unattractive concrete block and metal-sided temporary building, "Annex B," from 1965 to 1967. Poorly insulated and located far from classrooms and lecture halls, the Department shared Annex B with the Department of English. Political Science then relocated to an exceptionally remote location on Ridge Lea Road. As I wrote in the Department history, "The next relocation took faculty members of Political Science to what then seemed like the swamplands of Siberia. Ridge Lea Road had a typical Buffalo misnomer, since it ran through flat, wet territory barely suitable for major construction." We profited from our "own" seminar room, while the Department's isolation reinforced its sense of unity.

In 1975, five years after Fred's arrival, the Department moved again, this time to unoccupied, brand-new student housing on the still-abuilding North Campus, on the floodplain of Amherst, New York.

Political Science started small in 1963, with a mere four professors. It more than doubled in size the following year, growing to nine. The Department grew to 13 in 1965, to 26 by 1967 (!), and to 30 in 1970, the year Fred arrived as a tenured associate professor.[3] Faculty members fell into five rough categories. Some taught American Politics; others, such as Fred, focused on Comparative Politics. Empirical Political Science and Political Philosophy constituted fields unto themselves. Finally, several professors taught "IR," International Relations. Students took classes in all areas. For example, large enrollment introductory classes and "core" seminars existed for each subdivision. When Fred retired in 2003, the Department had eliminated two subfields as areas of specialization, and the faculty had shrunk to 14.

At every point in its history, professors in Political Science took pride in their teaching and research, while many also participated in Departmental and University service. Fred's accomplishments as a teacher constitute the next section of this chapter.

FRED FLERON AS A TEACHER

Probably none of Fred's colleagues matched his instructional range. Quoting from an autobiographical statement he kindly shared with me in 2012,

> Although I was hired as a specialist on Soviet politics and foreign policy (annually teaching undergraduates courses and occasionally graduate courses on those subjects), I soon began teaching courses on Comparative Communist Political Systems and East European Politics. In addition, I introduced both undergraduate and graduate courses on Politics & Technology—a new area of research interest for me soon after I joined the faculty—and regularly taught courses on that subject. All told, I taught more than two dozen different undergraduate and graduate courses during my 33 year tenure at UB.

What is more, Fred willingly taught at all levels, from first year undergraduates to advanced graduate/doctoral level students. Irrespective of the students' backgrounds and prior knowledge, Fred taught with warmth and insight. His special qualities shine forth in the chapters of this *Festschrift* written by his former students. Yes, he expected a great deal in his courses, especially graduate seminars.[4]

The same held true for his colleagues. Fred brought his range of learning to the Political Science Department as a whole, not only to students. Talking with him, whether one-on-one or collectively in committees or Department meetings,[5] became an intellectual adventure. His questions opened potential new vistas, encouraging others to go beyond their standard paradigms of thought.

FRED FLERON AS A SCHOLAR

Other chapters in this *Festschrift* chronicle his multifaceted contributions to academic learning. I cannot add significantly to their insights. Suffice it to say that, over our decades as colleagues, we shared multiple discussions on Russian history, trends within the former USSR, and the rapidly changing Russia, or the multiple impacts of artificial intelligence, advances in computer capacity and the purposes, sometime nefarious, to which they could be put. These conversations invariably enhanced my understanding of interesting, important matters.

FRED FLERON AS A DEPARTMENT AND UNIVERSITY CITIZEN

The least recognized, but in many ways most significant, part of the academic troika comes with service. At research universities such as UB, publications in leading disciplinary journals or with first-rate academic presses rank as most important. They constitute the ticket to promotion, salary increases, and, if appropriate, appointment with more favorable aspects—including potential moves to other institutions.

Effective instruction ranks second in this hierarchy. Even the most mediocre teacher will command top dollar and gain the most prestigious position globally, should he or she win a Nobel Prize. Adequate performance in the classroom and in guiding individual students, coupled with a sufficient number of publications[6] and possibly a modicum of service, would normally result in tenure and potentially a full professorship.

Bluntly, the reward system at UB was weighted overwhelmingly toward research, with teaching secondary. Service was "good to carry out," "desirable," in effect "okay if you are willing to spend some time there."

Fred Fleron stood out among individual faculty members willing to carry out significant amounts of service. More important, he did so at many levels of the University. Most significant, his service invariably proved innovative, exciting and well adapted to issues undergraduates in particular would confront in their own careers.

Let's see how Fred displayed these qualities at the Departmental, College[7] and University levels.

Within the Political Science Department

As noted earlier, Fred arrived at the University at Buffalo at the end of its period of maximum growth. The Department grew to 31 in 1970. When he retired in 2003, Political Science had diminished to 14. Two of its previous five subfields had been dropped. The mood among faculty members and students oscillated, reaching a nadir in the early 1980s.

Three factors accounted for this shrinkage. First, despite its best efforts, the Department ranked low among decanal priorities. Putting the matter bluntly, Fred wrote as follows:

> The Dean's low ranking of the department resulted in the immediate loss of three junior faculty members from our public policy program. They saw the hand-writing on the wall and bailed out. One became a faculty member at the University of Delaware, a second became a dean at the University of Missouri, and the third became president of the University of New Hampshire. All soon became established scholars with national reputations.[8]

Fred aptly described the second, intra-Departmental cause thus:

> a small group of faculty continuously engaged in gallows humor that included put-downs of their own colleagues. When added to the division created by the Gang of Four, this did little to set a tone of collegiality in the department.[9]

Third, UB as a whole experienced significant financial distress, starting shortly after Fred's appointment. The near-bankruptcy of New York City in the mid-1970s rippled through the State's finances as a whole. Direct budgetary support to SUNY dropped precipitously. Tuition and fees started to climb. OTPS funds—"other than personal services" dollars used for travel, supplies, and the like—similarly shrank.[10] The air whistled forth from the balloon of punctured expectations.

In the College of Arts and Sciences

Compared with many of his colleagues in the Department of Political Science during his years at Buffalo, Fred Fleron compiled an exceptional record of University service, initially to the Faculty of Social Sciences and, starting in the early 1990s, to the College of Arts and Sciences. His most significant contributions came with the "Undergraduate College," a grassroots faculty initiative to rethink baccalaureate curricula.

Fred described his pleasure in fundamentally changing the requirements all BA candidates had to meet.[11]

> Helping to design the GenEd requirements for future generations of UB undergraduates was one of the most stimulating and rewarding experiences of my pedagogical lifetime—from the development of Freshman Seminars (one of which I taught on an experimental basis) to the World Civilization sequence (the pilot program for which I administered and brokered for two years, although never taught) to an effort with Ed Strainchamps (Music) and Ed Dudley (Modern Languages and Literatures).

Fred's high level of commitment can be seen in the significant UGC Committees on which he served: its Executive Committee, 1988–1990; the Governance Committee, 1986–1988; the Resources Committee, 1986–1987; and the Innovations in Undergraduate Science Education Committee, 1986–1988. He went further and, with colleagues from English and the Law School, presented and defended the new GenEd curriculum to the Faculty Senate Executive Committee, and then the Faculty Senate. That's not all! In addition, Fred designed the Freshman Seminar component of the new GenEd curriculum; served on its Subcommittee on Arts and Letters/ Social Sciences Core, chaired its Subcommittee on World Civilizations;[12] and chaired the Subcommittee on Senior Integrative Courses! Truly extraordinary contributions, leading to the establishment and effective operation of the new Undergraduate College.

On Behalf of the University as a Whole

The previous sections of this chapter amply illustrate Fred Fleron's contributions to the University at Buffalo as a whole. His exceptional teaching, research, and academic service helped not only the Department of Political Science, and the Faculty of Social Science/ College of Arts and Sciences, but UB generally. His many fine graduate students, some of whom have contributed to this volume, testify to what the "compleat academic" seeks to accomplish: *to apply their learning to the improvement of their environment by sharing knowledge with others, thereby enhancing the performance of all.*

Fred, on this happy occasion, на здоровье!

NOTES

1. Geoffrey Chaucer, *The Canterbury Tales*, "The Clerk's Tale," published ca. 1400 as one of 24 stories, left unfinished.

2. As his colleague for Fred's entire career at UB, I shall refer to him in the first person. Our offices shared a common wall, on which we would occasionally pound. For several years, we shared a telephone line, and the "jungle telegraph" served us

well. For details about the Department's history, check https://arts-sciences.buffalo.edu/political-science/about/political-science-ub/our-history.html. I am grateful to Fred for his perceptive comments on it.

3. Fred's prior extensive experience and his growing publication record made appointment at this level appropriate. He had previously served as Teaching Associate and Lecturer, Department of Political Science, Indiana University, 1964–1965; Instructor, Department of Political Science, University of Kentucky, 1965–68; Visiting Professor, Department of Political Science, Indiana University, Summer 1967; and Assistant Professor, Department of Political Science, University of Kentucky, January 1969–June 1970.

4. I recall one student, for whom English was his third or fourth language, concerned about an assignment in a seminar. Its members had to read hundreds of pages in Barrington Moore's magisterial study, *Social Origins of Dictatorship and Democracy*, in a single week! Fred's lists of required and recommended reading ranked among the longest in the Department, whether for individual courses or for doctoral comprehensive qualifying exams. The range of these lists testified to Fred's erudition and own extensive research.

5. These meetings included job talks, when prospective candidates for faculty appointment spoke about their research. Fred always came up with probing, apposite questions, especially about the range and potential interdisciplinary significance of their analyses.

6. Criteria differ markedly by discipline and by professional area. At UB, and indubitably at practically all colleges and universities, each academic unit utilizes written criteria as guides to promotion and tenure. The possibility of litigation has made written standards near universal, especially in public institutions. Having spent nine years on UB's President's Review Board on Appointments, Promotions and Tenure, three of them as its chair, I received and learned how to apply scores of different sets of such criteria.

7. From Fred's initial appointment until the early 1990s, the Department of Political Science formed part of the Faculty of Social Sciences. It then joined the Faculty of Arts and Letters, and the Faculty of Natural Sciences and Mathematics, to create the College of Arts and Sciences. For readers' ease, I have used "College" through most of this chapter, rather than "Faculty of Social Science."

8. Fred Fleron, "History of Our Political Science Department—The University at Buffalo, State University of New York," unpublished manuscript. I am most grateful to Fred for allowing me to quote from it.

9. Ibid. Also see my history of UB's Political Science Department, especially the chapter "Reforming the Reforms": https://arts-sciences.buffalo.edu/political-science/about/political-science-ub/our-history.html

10. More details appear in my history of the Department, available at https://arts-sciences.buffalo.edu/political-science/about/political-science-ub/our-history.html.

11. These requirements also covered some quasi-professional undergraduate degrees, such as the BFA or the baccalaureate degree in audiology.

12. In this respect, Fred designed, implemented, and administered the World Civilizations component of the UGC curriculum.

Index

About the Contributors

Seymen Atasoy completed his PhD studies in the Department of Political Science at the University of Buffalo and is currently an independent researcher based in North Cyprus. He has previously taught at the Bilkent University, Ankara, Turkey and the Eastern Mediterranean University, North Cyprus. He has published articles in *Brown Journal of World Affairs*, *Middle East Policy*, and *Perceptions: Journal of International Affairs.*

Christofer Berglund is senior lecturer in the Department of Global Political Studies at Malmö University, Sweden. He specializes in the region of post-Soviet Eurasia and has published numerous articles on ethnic politics, state-building, and strategic studies. His most recent work has appeared in *Nationalism and Ethnic Politics*, *Europe-Asia Studies*, *Dynamics of Asymmetric Conflict*, and *Nations and Nationalism.* He currently serves as principal investigator for two projects, "Planning for Integration: Landscapes of Power in Borderland Governance" and "Conscription as Political Socialization in Divided Societies? Evidence from post-Soviet Estonia and post-independence Finland."

Timothy K. Blauvelt is professor of Soviet and Post-Soviet Studies at Ilia State University in Tbilisi, Georgia, and is also regional director for the South Caucasus for American Councils for International Education. He defended his PhD dissertation at the University of Buffalo in 2001 under the supervision of Frederic J. Fleron Jr. He has published several dozen peer-reviewed articles and book chapters. His co-edited volume *Georgia after Stalin: Nationalism and Soviet Power*, with Jeremy Smith, was published by Routledge in 2016, and his co-edited volume *The Transcaucasian Democratic Federative Republic of 1918: Federal Aspirations, Geopolitics and National Projects*, with Adrian Brisku, was published by Routledge in 2021. His monograph *Clientelism and Nationality in an Early Soviet Fiefdom: The Trials of Nestor Lakoba* was also published by Routledge in 2021.

Russell Bova is professor of Political Science and the J. William Stuart & Helen D. Stuart '32 Chair in International Studies at Dickinson College. He is the editor of *Russia and Western Civilization: Cultural and Historical Encounters*, and the third edition of his international relations text, *How the World Works*, was published in 2016. His work on Russian politics and comparative democratization has appeared in *World Politics*, *Journal of Democracy*, and in numerous other scholarly journals and edited volumes.

Vesna Danilovic is an associate professor of Political Science in the Department of Political Science at the University at Buffalo. She is the author of *When the Stakes Are High: Deterrence and Conflict among Major Powers*. Her research in the area of international conflict and peace has also been published in the *American Journal of Political Science*, *Journal of Conflict Resolution*, *Political Research Quarterly*, *Journal of Theoretical Politics*, *Conflict Management and Peace Science*, *International Interactions*, and edited books. She has served as a member of the editorial boards of the *Journal of Politics* and *International Interactions*.

Jesse Driscoll is an associate professor of Political Science at the University of California, San Diego and serves as chair of the Global Leadership Institute at the School of Global Policy and Strategy. He is an area specialist in Central Asia, the Caucasus, and the Russian-speaking world. His first book, *Warlord and Coalition Politics in the Post-Soviet States*, was published in the Cambridge Studies on Comparative Politics series of Cambridge University Press in 2015. His second book *Doing Global Fieldwork: A Social Scientist's Guide to Mixed-Methods Research Far From Home* was published by Columbia University Press in 2021.

Joanna Drzewieniecki is a translator and editor of academic articles based in Lima, Peru. She translates the peer-reviewed journal of the Universidad del Pacífico, *Apuntes*, with her colleague, Kenneth Hermse. She recently worked closely with Jarsosław Piekałkiewicz on his book *Dance with Death* (2020). During the course of her career she has worked as a librarian, human rights activist, consultant, and college professor. She holds a PhD in Political Science from the University at Buffalo. She has authored articles on the history of the Peruvian human rights movement and the administration of justice in indigenous communities in Peru, published in Mexico and Colombia. She regularly collaborates with the Peruvian Section of Amnesty International and the Afro-Peruvian NGO, CEDET, a Latin American leader in promotion of research on Afro-Latin Americans.

William N. Dunn is professor emeritus at the Graduate School of Public and International Affairs at the University of Pittsburgh. He is a Russian and East European Studies specialist with some 40 years working in Central and Eastern Europe, with an emphasis on the former Yugoslavia. His teaching and research interests include public policy analysis, philosophy and sociology of science, research design for mixed-methods research, and the use and abuse of scientific evidence by policy makers. He has published on comparative and international policy, organization theory and behavior, and methods of policy analysis and evaluation. His most recent publicatgions are *Pragmatism and the Origins of the Policy Sciences: Rediscovering Lasswell and the Chuicvago School* (2019) and *Public Policy Analysis: An Integrated Approach*, 6th ed (2017), which is the most widely cited book on the subject with translations into eight languages including Ukrainian, Romanian, Macedonian, and Chinese.

Munroe Eagles is a professor and chair in the Department of Political Science at the University at Buffalo and former associate dean for graduate studies in the College of Arts and Sciences. He has served as president of the Association for Canadian Studies in the United States (ACSUS) and the International Council for Canadian Studies (ICCS), and has been a member of a number of editorial boards and on the Board of Directors of the Canadian Political Science Association. His coauthored book, *Politics Is Local: National Politics at the Grassroots* (with Ken Carty of the University of British Columbia), was published by Oxford University Press, and was shortlisted for the CPSA's "Donald Smiley Prize" for the best book published on Canadian politics.

Andrew Feenberg is Canada research chair in Philosophy of Technology in the School of Communication, Simon Fraser University. He is the author of *Lukacs, Marx and the Sources of Critical Theory* (1981; 1986), *Critical Theory of Technology* (1991), *Alternative Modernity* (1995), and *Questioning Technology* (1999). A second edition of *Critical Theory of Technology* appeared with Oxford in 2002 under the title *Transforming Technology*. *Heidegger and Marcuse: The Catastrophe and Redemption of History* appeared in 2005 with Routledge. *Between Reason and Experience: Essays in Technology and Modernity* appeared with MIT Press in 2010. *The Philosophy of Praxis: Marx, Lukacs and the Frankfurt School* was published by Verso Press in 2014. His *Technosystem: The Social Life of Reason*, appeared with Harvard University Press in 2017. Dr. Feenberg is also co-editor of

Marcuse: Critical Theory and the Promise of Utopia (1987), *Technology and the Politics of Knowledge* (1995), *Modernity and Technology* (2003), *Community in the Digital Age* (2004) and *(Re)inventing the Internet* (2012). His coauthored book on the French May Events of 1968 appeared in 2001 with SUNY Press under the title *When Poetry Ruled the Streets.* A book on Feenberg's philosophy of technology entitled *Democratizing Technology* appeared in 2006. A second book appeared in 2017 entitled *Critical Theory and the Thought of Andrew Feenberg.*

Frederic J. Fleron, Jr. is university research scholar and emeritus professor of Political Science at the State University of New York at Buffalo. He received his PhD in political science from Indiana University, Bloomington, and holds AB and AM degrees from Brown University. His publications include *Communist Studies and the Social Sciences: Essays on Methodology and Empirical Theory* (1969), *The Conduct of Soviet Foreign Policy* (1971, 1980), *Comparative Communist Political Leadership* (1973), *Technology and Communist Culture: The Socio Cultural Impact of Technology Transfer under Socialism* (1977), *Soviet Foreign Policy: Classic and Contemporary Issues* (1991), *Post-Communist Studies and Political Science: Methodology and Empirical Theory in Sovietology* (1993), *Can Democracy Take Root in Post-Soviet Russia? Explorations in State-Society Relations* (1998), *Russian Studies & Comparative Politics: Views from Metatheory & Middle-Range Theory* (2017). His research has been supported by the National Endowment for the Humanities, The Ford Foundation, The Carnegie Corporation, and The Rockefeller Foundation. His articles have appeared in *The American Political Science Review*, *Comparative Politics*, *Polity*, *Soviet Studies*, *Europe-Asia Studies*, *Communist and Post-Communist Studies*, and *Journal of Communist Studies and Transition Politics.*

David Foley retired in 2020 as an associate professor and program director of Political Science at Salem College. He received his PhD in Comparative and International Politics from the State University of New York at Buffalo in 2004. He presented a series of research papers in the fields of Comparative Politics, Political Change and Political Geography to include *Crisis, Instability and Democratic Breakdown* presented at the spring 2006 Midwest Political Science Association Conference, *Transition and Integration in Central and Eastern European Democracies* at the spring of 2006 Midwest Political Science Association Conference, *The Political Geography of International Development Policy* at the 2010 Southeast Political Science association meeting in Atlanta, Georgia, *The Navigation of the Single System Structure and the Multiplicity of National Development Demands* in the context of west African democratization at the 2010 Southeast Political

Science Association meeting in Atlanta, Georgia, *A Failure of Federalism: The Legacy of Asymmetry in the Russian Federation* at the 2012 NCPSA Conference at Duke University, and his essay *An Ethno-federal Disguise: Russia's failed pursuit of geo-political unity through hybrid democracy* at the 2017 MPSA Conference in Chicago Illinois. He is the author of *The Legacy Structure of Russia's One Hundred Year Transformation* (2018).

Farida Jalalzai is associate dean for Global Initiatives and Engagement in the College of Liberal Arts and Human Sciences and Professor of Political Science at Virginia Tech. She received her PhD in Political Science from SUNY Buffalo in 2004. Her research analyzes the role of gender in the political arena including women national leaders. Her books include: *Shattered, Cracked and Firmly Intact: Women and the Executive Glass Ceiling Worldwide* (2013), which offers a comprehensive analysis of women, gender, and national leadership positions; *Women Presidents of Latin America: Beyond Family Ties?* (2016), a comparative analysis of women presidents in Latin America; and *Senhora Presidenta: Women's Empowerment and Disempowerment in Brazil: The Rise and Fall of President Dilma Rousseff*, which examines the first female president of Brazil (coauthored with Pedro dos Santos, Temple University Press, 2021). She is also coeditor of the volume, *Measuring Women's Political Empowerment Worldwide* (with Amy C. Alexander and Catherine Bolzendahl; Palgrave 2018). She has authored dozens of articles and book chapters related to women in politics around the world. Her work has appeared in leading journals including *International Political Science Review*, *Politics & Gender*, *Politics, Groups & Identities*, *Politics & Religion*, and *Women, Politics & Policy*. Her research has been funded by the Thyssen Foundation and she is a recipient of the Fulbright Commission Global Scholar Award. She is frequently quoted and featured as an expert in high-profile media outlets including *The Atlantic*, *The Washington Post*, *The New York Times*, *the PBS Newshour*, *The Guardian*, *The Christian Science Monitor*, *VOX*, *Politico*, *Vanity Fair*, and *NPR*.

William Leiss is a fellow and past president (1999–2001) of the Royal Society of Canada and an Officer in the Order of Canada. He is currently scientist and associate director for Risk Communication, McLaughlin Centre for Population Health Risk Assessment, University of Ottawa. He was professor, School of Policy Studies, Queen's University (1994–2005), where he held the Eco-Research Chair in Environmental Policy; from 1999 to 2005 he was seconded to the Haskayne School of Business, University of Calgary, for the NSERC/SSHRC/Industry Research Chair in Risk Communication and Public Policy. He is author or senior coauthor of *In the Chamber of Risks: Understanding Risk Controversies* (2001), *Mad Cows* *and Mother's Milk: The Perils of Poor Risk Communication* (1997, 2004), *Risk and Responsibility* (1994), *The Domination of Nature* (1972), *The Limits to Satisfaction* (1976), *Under Technology's Thumb* (1990), and *C. B. Macpherson* (1988, 2009), all from McGill-Queen's University Press; also *Social Communication in Advertising* (1986, 1990, 2005) and *The Doom Loop in the Financial Sector, and Other Black Holes of Risk* (2010), from the University of Ottawa Press, and the fourth edition of *Social Communication in Advertising* (2018).

Guoli Liu is professor of Political Science at the College of Charleston. He is the author of *China Rising: Chinese Foreign Policy in a Changing World*; *States and Markets: Comparing Japan and Russia*; *Politics and Government in China*; and editor of *Chinese Foreign Policy in Transition*, (with Lowell Dittmer) *China's Deep Reform: Domestic Politics in Transition*, and (with Quansheng Zhao) *Managing the China Challenge: Global Perspectives*. He received his BA and MA in International Politics from Peking University, and PhD in Political Science, from the State University of New York at Buffalo.

Carl Mitcham is professor emeritus of Humanities, Arts, and Social Sciences at the Colorado School of Mines and visiting professor of Philosophy at Renmin University of China. His disciplinary background is in philosophy with an emphasis on the philosophy and ethics of science, technology, and engineering. His scholarly publications, however, have been as much interdisciplinary as disciplinary, especially insofar as he worked to bring philosophy of technology into the interdisciplinary field of Science, Technology, and Society (STS) studies. Recent work has influenced a focus on science policy and philosophy of engineering. His publications include *Thinking through Technology: The Path between Engineering and Philosophy* and *Steps toward a Philosophy of Engineering: Historico-Philosophical and Critical Essays*.

Alexander J. Motyl is professor of Political Science at Rutgers University-Newark. A specialist on Ukraine, Russia, and the USSR, and on nationalism, revolutions, empires, and theory, he is the author of seven books of non-fiction, including *Pidsumky imperii* (2009); *Puti imperii* (2004); *Imperial Ends: The Decay, Collapse, and Revival of Empires* (2001); *Revolutions, Nations, Empires: Conceptual Limits and Theoretical Possibilities* (1999); *Dilemmas of Independence: Ukraine after Totalitarianism* (1993); and *The Turn to the Right: The Ideological Origins and Development of Ukrainian Nationalism, 1919–1929* (1980); the editor of 15 volumes, including *The Encyclopedia of Nationalism* (2000) and *The Holodomor Reader* (2012); and a contributor of dozens of articles to academic and policy journals, newspaper op-ed pages, and magazines.

John S. Nelson teaches political theory and communication at the University of Iowa. He's written *Video Rhetorics* (1997), *Tropes of Politics* (1998), *Popular Cinema as Political Theory* (2013), *Politics in Popular Movies* (2015), *Cowboy Politics* (2018), plus *Defenses Against the Dark Arts* (2021). And he's edited three books on political theory and epistemology; *Poroi*, an ejournal on rhetoric in culture, inquiry, and politics; as well as book series on New Practices of Inquiry and Rhetoric of the Human Sciences.

Lisa K. Parshall is a professor of Political Science at Daemen College in Amherst, NY. She is the author or coauthor of several books, including *Reforming the Presidential Nominating Process: Front-Loading's Consequences and the National Primary Solution* (2018), and the *Icelandic Federalist Papers*, David Carrillo, et. al. (2018); and *Directing the Whirlwind: The Trump Presidency and the Deconstruction of the Administrative State* (2020), as well as the author of several law review articles and policy briefs. Dr. Parshall is the immediate past president of the Northeastern Political Science Association and is a public policy fellow at the Nelson A. Rockefeller Institute of Government in Albany, NY.

Jarosław Piekałkiewicz is professor emeritus of Political Science and Russian and East European Studies at the University of Kansas, and former Lecturer at the U.S. Army Command and Staff College. He is the author or coauthor of five books and co-editor of two, including *Politics of Ideocracy* with Alfred W. Penn and *Dance with Death: A Holistic View of Saving Polish Jews during the Holocaust*. He fought in the Polish Underground Army as a teenager and participated in the 1944 Warsaw Underground Uprising. He was awarded the Polish military Cross of Valor for his bravery. He and his best friend, Holocaust survivor Lou Frydman, are the subject of the book *The Needle in the Bone: How a Holocaust Survivor and a Polish Resistance Fighter Beat the Odds and Found Each Other* by Caryn Mirriam-Goldberg (former Kansas Poet Laureate).

William M. Reisinger is professor of Political Science at the University of Iowa. He received his PhD from the University of Michigan, and his research concerns authoritarianism and democracy in the former communist states, especially Russia. He has written or edited eight books, including *The Regional Roots of Russia's Political Regime*, coauthored with Bryon J. Moraski (2017), as well as numerous articles and book chapters. His research has been supported by a Fulbright Hays Fellowship and grants from the National Science Foundation, the U.S. Army Research Office, and the Minerva Initiative.

Nathaniel I. Richmond is professor emeritus of Political Science at Utica University. He has published in *Slavic Review*, *Slavic and East European Journal*, *Journal of Communist Studies*, and *Nationalities Papers* among others and he was a long-time member of the *Editorial Advisory Board for Annual Editions: Comparative Politics* and *Annual Editions: American Foreign Policy*. He has presented at many national and international conferences, mostly on the topic of Russia (or the USSR). Dr. Richmond has appeared in approximately 150 media interviews locally, nationally, and internationally, mostly on some aspect of international relations. Besides teaching at UU he has taught (as a visiting professor) at Colgate University (2008–2009), Hamilton College (2010), Union College (2013), and the American University of Paris, France (2007–2008–2009). Before coming to UU he taught at the University of Northern Iowa (1985–1988). Dr. Richmond regularly taught courses on European politics, Russian politics, political risk analysis, political corruption, international political economy, international relations, American foreign policy, and political philosophy. In 2005 he received Utica University's Crisafulli Distinguished Teaching Award. He received his BA, Political Science, from State University of New York at Buffalo, and MA and PhD, Political Science from the George Washington University.

Blair A. Ruble is distinguished fellow at Wilson Center, where he formerly served as vice president for Programs and director of the Kennan Institute for Advanced Russian Studies. His a half-dozen monographs examine Russian and Ukrainian subjects as well as the performing arts in cities (including *Second Metropolis: Pragmatic Pluralism in Gilded Age Chicago, Silver Age Moscow, and Meiji Osaka*; *Washington's U Street: A Biography*; and, *Leningrad: Shaping a Soviet City*). Reading Frederic Fleron's works while studying at the University of North Carolina and the University of Toronto shaped his research ever since.

Claude E. Welch holds the ranks of SUNY distinguished service professor and is a retired professor of the Department of Political Science at the University at Buffalo. His academic specializations include African politics, the roles of armed forces in politics, and human rights. Professor Welch has published widely on these subjects, with 14 books and close to 40 chapters and articles in academic journals. In 2006, he received the first-ever Lifetime Achievement Award given by TIAA-CREF and the SUNY Research Foundation. In 2015, he received a Lifetime Achievement Award in Human Rights, given by the International Studies Association. In 2014, the American Political Science Association gave Welch an Award for Distinguished Contributions to Human Rights, for his "exceptional contribution to the field through research, teaching and mentorship." The New York African Studies Association (NYASA) honored him in 2017 with its Distinguished Africanist Award. Welch's major books include *Protecting Human Rights in Africa: Strategies and Roles of Non-Governmental Organizations*; *NGOs and Human Rights: Promise and Performance*; *Economic and Social Rights in Canada and the United States* (with Rhoda Howard-Hassmann); *Civilian Control of the Military: Theory and Cases from Developing Countries*; *Soldier and State in Africa: A Comparative Analysis of Military Intervention and Political Change*; and *Dream of Unity: Pan-Africanism and Political Unification in West Africa.*

Frank C. Zagare is UB Distinguished Professor of Political Science. A former Vice President of the International Studies Association, Dr. Zagare has served on the Advisory Panel of the National Science Foundation, on the editorial boards of *International Studies Quarterly*, *International Interactions*, and Oxford Bibliographies Online in International Relations, as a panelist for the National Academies of Sciences, Engineering, and Medicine, as a member of the Presidential Nominating Committee and the Professional Rights and Responsibilities Committee of the International Studies Association, as a councillor for the Peace Science Society (International), as a council member of the Conflict Processes Section of the American Political Science Association, and on the Academic Advisory Board of the United Arab Emirates University. His research has been supported by grants from the National Science Foundation, the International Studies Association, and the U.S. Institute of Peace. In 2005 he received the Susan Strange Award from the International Studies Association. Professor Zagare is the author, coauthor, or editor of seven books including *Perfect Deterrence* (with D. Marc Kilgour), *The Dynamics of Deterrence*, Game Theory: Concepts and Applications, and *The Games of July: Explaining the Great War*. His most recent book is *Game Theory, Diplomatic History, and Security Studies*. He is also curator of The Deterrence Project.

Marina Zaloznaya is associate professor in the Departments of Sociology and Criminology and Political Science at the University of Iowa. Professor Zaloznaya received an MA from the University of Wisconsin, Madison and a PhD from Northwestern University. She is the author of *The Politics of Bureaucratic Corruption in Post-Transitional Eastern Europe* (2017). Her research explores public sector corruption, political behavior, and gender in nondemocratic regimes from a range of methodological perspectives, including ethnography, survey methods, comparative-historical, and network analysis. Her work has appeared in a range of top sociology, political science, and area studies journals, such as *Social Forces*, *Electoral Studies*, and *Post-Soviet Affairs*.

CPSIA information can be obtained
at www.ICGtesting.com
Printed in the USA
LVHW112322220422
716976LV00003B/37

9 781666 906356